# THE
# MORMON
# DELUSION

Volume 4

## The Mormon Missionary Lessons – A Conspiracy to Deceive

Jim Whitefield

# The Mormon Delusion. Volume 4.
The Mormon Missionary Lessons
– A Conspiracy to Deceive

Hardback Edition

First published in January 2011 by
Lulu Press Inc. Raleigh, North Carolina, USA.

First Edition – January 2011

Copyright © Jim Whitefield 2011

ISBN 10: 1446688399
ISBN 13: 978-1-4466-8839-7

British Library Catalogue System Number: 015497834

Lulu ID: 9744495

All rights reserved. No part of this publication may
be reproduced, stored in a retrieval system, or
transmitted in any form or by any means,
electronic, mechanical photocopying, recording,
or otherwise, without the prior permission
of the author.

One download version may be stored on computer
for the sole use of the purchaser.
All other restrictions apply.

themormondelusion.com

Email the author: jim@themormondelusion.com

# Dedication

This work is written for those
investigating Mormonism
who want the underlying facts
regarding each aspect the
Mormon missionaries teach them.

Mormons considering a mission
will also benefit if they have the courage
to read this work prior to spending two years
teaching provable falsehoods contained
in the missionary manual.

Concerned members may want to re-run
things that missionaries or parents
once convinced them were true
which have now come into question.

This is dedicated to those who have
a brush with Mormonism and
are sensible enough to
question every aspect
thus discovering the truth
before entering the delusion.

Also, to those called to serve missions
who had the courage to discover the truth
before entering the mission field
and wasting two years in
teaching provable fiction.

You now have a life free from delusion.
May you enjoy that freedom.

*Jim Whitefield 2011*

Also by this author

**The Mormon Delusion. Volume 1.**
The Truth Behind Polygamy
and Secret Polyandry

First Edition – Feb 2009
Second Edition – Aug 2009
Third Edition – Sept 2010

**The Mormon Delusion. Volume 2.**
The Secret Truth Withheld
From 13 Million Mormons

First Edition – May 2009
Second Edition – Sept 2010

**The Mormon Delusion. Volume 3.**
Discarded Doctrines and
Nonsense Revelations

First Edition – July 2009
Second Edition – Sept 2010

Available in hardcover, paperback, as downloads and PDF e-Books.
Visit themormondelusion.com and link to TMD Lulu Bookstore.

**I spent 43 years believing in a false religion.
Now I want my 43 years as an atheist.
God owes me that.**
*Jim Whitefield*

**What other authors have had to say about Volume 4.**

Whitefield's four volumes are a rich compendium of little-known facts about Mormonism and the Mormons. Even with my own 25 years as a Mormon and my 50 years of subsequent study, I learned many new things from this author. He has done a monumental job of researching and studying. An ultimate reference tool!

Richard Packham.
Founder, The Exmormon Foundation.

\*\*\*\*\*\*\*\*\*\*

Notwithstanding Whitefield's extensive exposure of the truth behind all things Mormon in his first three books, in Volume 4, as he journeys through the Mormon missionary lessons, he somehow manages to include a whole raft of further devastating information presented in ways not previously seen. This remarkable work is essential for anyone seeking the truth behind everything the Mormon Church has its unsuspecting missionaries teach investigators. No stone remains unturned and no question unanswered. The lies and deceptions of Mormonism are laid bare, page after page and stage by stage, in line with the missionary lessons, from beginning to end, until there is nothing left for the impartial investigator to consider. The hoax is systematically analysed, the fraudulent claims fully revealed, and the entire Mormon conspiracy to deceive is completely exposed – once and for all.

Arza Evans
Author of 'The Keystone of Mormonism'.

\*\*\*\*\*\*\*\*\*\*

If you are investigating the LDS church you owe it to yourself to learn the full story of Mormonism. Any church claiming to be the only true church on the earth deserves, and should withstand, the closest of scrutiny. In his characteristically detailed, comprehensive and upfront style, Jim Whitefield tells the side of the Mormon story the missionaries cannot tell because they have never heard it themselves.

Simon G. Southerton Ph.D.
Author of 'Losing a Lost Tribe; Native Americans, DNA, and the Mormon Church.'

\*\*\*\*\*\*\*\*\*\*

In this raw and real exposé of the Mormon Delusion, Whitefield thoroughly dismantles the key claims of Mormonism, in the order they are presented to an investigator. His logic is irresistible, the facts indisputable, and the research impeccable. Jim will have life-long members thinking about things that never occurred to them – a big one for me it was the ludicrous Nephite system of currency and coinage. Having served a two-year mission overseas myself, I was struck by the extent of the contradictions and falsehoods I unwittingly spread. With a flair for detail and a knowledge of relevant little-known facts associated with church history, Whitefield illustrates how the LDS church fails miserably to uphold the very standards of ethics and honesty it expects of its membership. In the bright light of day, when all the evidence is brought to bear on the so-called pillars of LDS doctrines taught in the missionary lessons, each pillar falters and collapses in turn. Truly Whitefield illustrates how truth does indeed 'cut its own way'.

Lyndon Lamborn.
Author of 'Standing for Something More'.

**********

In The Mormon Delusion series, Jim Whitefield takes on the multi-billion dollar public relations machine that is the Mormon Church. In this, his fourth volume, he exposes the church's missionary program for what it is: a cadre of well-trained, brain-washed salespeople. With meticulous research, irrefutable evidence, and microscopic attention to detail, Whitefield tackles the programming of impressionable young men and women to illustrate the half-truths and lies they are taught to regurgitate to the unsuspecting masses that are impressed by their clean-cut appearance and air of confidence.

Whitefield dissects the lessons, precepts and scriptural teachings of the missionaries and empirically proves the falsehoods of the gospel they so earnestly preach. In the end, his passion for truth and desire to live a principled life wins the day. With humor, intelligence and impeccable scholarship, Whitefield refutes and rejects the teachings of what he proves to be nothing more than one of the world's largest corporations intent on recruiting tithe-paying stockholders. A must read.

Pamela McCreary.
Author of 'Dancing on the Head of a Pin'.

**********

## Comments from around the world on Jim Whitefield's earlier books, articles and 2010 Exmormon Foundation Conference live presentation.

I again commend Jim Whitefield's books. …put off buying a number of lesser volumes … For my money, they are on a par … with *Mormonism - Shadow or Reality*. The Tanners' topics are more numerous; Jim Whitefield's, much more detailed. (A).

He does do his homework very, very thoroughly and presents the data as a detached impartial historian would be expected to do… (T).

I would like to thank you for your books … I appreciate your integrity and I do believe your books will make a difference. (MD).

…the style and pace was excellent. I found it content rich and very well written. (BB).

I… can't tell you how much I appreciate the great work that you are doing… (MA).

You thoroughly covered a lot of material. I don't see how anyone could still believe after reading your 3 books where you call a spade a spade… (DO).

Jim's article is the best study on the First Vision that I have read so far. (De).

I used a link on RfM to get to your site, hadn't been to it before and found it intelligent and enlightening. (DA).

…thank you so much for letting people know the truth about Mormonism. (NH).

I saw your lecture. The documented timeline of Joseph's monotheism evolving into polytheism was positively breathtaking. Very solid work. (CZ).

I purchased your three books and can never thank you enough for taking the time to write them. I do not think I can explain in words what you have done for me in helping me piece together the truth. (C).

I am so amazed by your courage and the depth and amount of research that you have done. (AE).

I hope you help the many who will come seeking with open hearts and curious minds. (TM).

Thank you for the awesome presentation. Now my testimony of Joseph's Myth is buried 12' in the earth, instead of only 6'. (K).

I loved your presentation. …Thank you for your insightful research and ability to synthesize all this for the rest of us. (Du).

What a pleasure it was to meet you and hear your amazing presentation. (E).

The presentation was awesome and you are fun to listen to. (NR).

…within the first minute of your presentation, I knew it was going to be good and I was so very excited for all of us who would be listening to you speak, and for you who had come all that way to deliver such a riveting presentation. (S).

I enjoyed your presentation! … Thank you so much! I thought about it for days and days. I thought, "No wonder I was always so confused in Mormonism!" (F).

I want to thank you for your work to expose the truths of the LDS faith. (RG).

…very well researched and well presented. (DM).

My biggest regret is that I can't meet you in person to express my thanks for what you are doing. (CN).

Thanks -- love your work! (TC).

I am not at all surprised that people have been picking up on the fruits of your massive achievement. Everything good that has happened has been thoroughly well-deserved and I congratulate you most heartily for it. (DP).

The data Jim revealed checked out 100%. (VM).

I found your "testimony" on ExmormonScholarsTestify and wanted to say how much I enjoyed reading it… (BF).

Your books are very well researched and thought out. I want to thank you for your efforts and time. (GJ).

I can never repay the debt I owe you; your work is saving my family. (PG).

Please accept my heart-felt thanks for these incredible sources of valuable information. They are a treasure of information… Your irrefutable logic, laying out plainly and simply, the lies and contradictions of J.S. and those who followed – even to today, is unmatched in any other work I've read on this topic. (DJ).

**Author's note:** After submitting evidence to a Mormon apostle regarding the Church's conspiracy to deceive, I wrote up material which later became a book – and ultimately three books which I hoped my active Mormon children may one day find the courage to read. I had no idea they would help so many other people along the way. Now I have found myself asked to publicly speak about these issues and have met many fellow exMormons who are in various stages of recovery. No one other than such exMormons could ever begin to imagine the intense pain and suffering someone endures on such a devastating journey. My writing, and now speaking aloud about the evidence, has been my therapy. This fourth volume is written in the hope that it will assist investigators and perhaps even some doubting missionaries to discover the truth before it is too late.

# Acknowledgements

My thanks once again go to my wife, Catriona, for freely allowing me the time and space to write this further volume in which she has no personal interest at all. Once again, I have effectively interrupted our intended retirement in order to complete yet another project. Her continued unconditional support allowed me to spend each day working on this volume uninterrupted. We retired when I turned sixty in February of 2006. My journey began the following month when I accidentally discovered Mormon polyandry. I will be sixty-five in February of 2011, the month following publication of this fourth volume. I owe Catriona a huge debt of gratitude for allowing me five years of research and writing with no word of complaint. I hope I can somehow repay her tolerance and support.

I am also very grateful once again to my good friend, Jean Bodie, for her proof reading and editing suggestions. Her tireless efforts on my behalf always help to hone things into a format which sits far better than the original final draft – even after my own numerous rewrites. For this volume, I have also been lucky in having the assistance of another friend, John Bleazard, who has reviewed the manuscript and suggested a number of corrections and alterations to grammar and text. The combined efforts of these good friends will undoubtedly make the journey through this work more flowing and enjoyable than would otherwise have been the case. I am deeply grateful to them both for their help and advice.

My grateful thanks also go to my friends and fellow authors, Arza Evans and Simon Southerton, for reviewing the final draft of volume four and once again kindly endorsing my work. Their own exceptional books, along with their continued encouragement, have been an inspiration to me. My thanks on this occasion also go to Pamela McCreary, author of 'Dancing on the Head of a Pin'; Lyndon Lamborn, author of 'Standing For Something More'; and Richard Packham, founder of The Exmormon Foundation and well known author of many articles on Mormonism. Richard is renowned for his generous assistance to those in recovery though his lectures and his web site which can be found here: http://home.teleport.com/~packham/ All of the above kindly reviewed and enthusiastically endorsed this volume. I am most grateful to them all.

To date, I have still not received the promised response from Mormon Church leaders concerning my research and questions regarding polyandry and other issues that I submitted in 2006. As mentioned in volumes 1-3, published in 2009 and updated in 2010:

I can only assume that the Church *(still)* has no answers…

# Guidance Notes

The Mormon Church spent several decades trying to remove what they seemed to consider a 'stigma' regarding the nicknames 'Mormon' and 'Mormonism' which had followed the Church from the beginning. The following paragraph appeared in earlier volumes of this work for that very reason:

"This work is an exposé regarding the Church of Jesus Christ of Latter Day Saints. Today, the Church prefers the nickname 'LDS' (Latter Day Saints) rather than 'Mormon' which was previously the case, both inside and outside the religion. As the term 'Mormon' is actually still more widely recognised, particularly in the United Kingdom, that is the term I have used throughout this work."

Now, it transpires the Church has changed its view and has once again decided to embrace terms which it once found offensive. Church related web sites are now replete with references to Mormons and Mormonism. It seems that my comment that 'the only thing consistent about Mormonism is its inconsistency' applies to even more aspects than I imagined. Perhaps the lacklustre growth in recent years has made Church public relations advisers clutch at straws in order to try and make Mormonism more familiar to the general public; who knows?

Where quotes are included, original spellings and grammar have been retained. Unless otherwise stated, any emphasis was in original quotes.

The word 'Church', with a capital 'C', is used throughout this book. Where it occurs without further explanation, it always refers to the Mormon Church. The expression 'the Church' *specifically* refers to the controlling leaders of the organisation or to the organisation itself. The context in each case should be self-evident. In other contexts, 'church' in the lower case is used as normal.

Internet addresses are notorious for changing or even disappearing altogether. Nevertheless, I have included a number, as so much information is now available on the internet, allowing readers access to further research with relative ease. If sources cannot be located, just use a search engine, referencing the topic or related words, to locate the required information.

Many and some rare, historical books are now available to read or research online. Some such works that I recommend are listed in the bibliography. In addition to those listed, *Google Book Search* is building an online collection very quickly. Before purchasing a book, it is always worth first checking to see if it is available to read or download free online at: http://books.google.com/

As there are numerous scriptures, and many Mormon *so-called* scriptures, included in my work, I have adopted what I believe will be a clearer system of referencing them in this volume. Particularly, as some verses are separated by my comments, sources appear at the *start* of each reference rather than at the end as is traditionally the case. I hope this will help the reader keep track of where we are at each stage.

Due to some of the aspects that are covered in this volume, such as laws of obedience and prayer, it has been quite difficult *not* to include a more atheistic viewpoint when reviewing them than I have previously allowed myself. I hope readers will understand the reasoning behind this and accept that it is difficult for me to accommodate the idea of God within some aspects being considered. Indeed, I have found more and more, that for me, the very notion that any God could be involved in such things as us and this planet to be absurd. This is based on evidence and science compared to many continuing religious notions, Mormon and otherwise. However, I do try hard to limit my thoughts to "If there is a God – could, or would, He be involved in such things as these" as much as I can in respect to the fact that some readers do remain Christian. I accept the fact that the existence of a God still cannot be proven either way.

In light of that, I have tried, amid any such observations, to restrict comments as much as possible and leave the reader to decide what they may or may not choose to believe. Before accepting anything that anyone *says* is true, study the evidence and also any related science. My underlying theme has been that if the reader wishes to believe in a God, at least find one that is plausibly *real*. That will certainly *not* be the Mormon version of course.

A copy of the Mormon missionary manual: *A Guide to Missionary Service – Preach My Gospel* can currently be located in PDF format which I recommend downloading from:
http://www.lds.org/languages/additionalmanuals/preachgospel/PreachMyGospel__00_00_Complete__36617_eng_000.pdf

If the link doesn't work, Google: 'Mormon missionary lessons full manual text' and it should be the first item on the page.

Online copies of all of the Mormon Scriptures – *Book of Mormon, Doctrine and Covenants, Pearl of Great Price* – are available to research and review along with the *King James Version* of the Bible. All these are made available online by the Mormon Church and their web site is useful for researching anything you may need to review or compare. This is the current link:
http://scriptures.lds.org/

This site was recently updated when yet again the Mormon Church made some changes. The introduction to the *Book of Mormon* incorporates the 'Doubleday' 2006 edition change from the original claim still found *in older copies of the book*, "...they are the *principal* ancestors of the American Indians" to read "...*among* the ancestors of the American Indians" watering down something that all Mormons accepted as a known *fact* until irrefutable DNA evidence proved otherwise. The Church would never accept the idea that Joseph Smith could be *entirely* wrong, so whilst being effectively forced to accept conclusive evidence that he was absolutely *not correct*, it has to settle on suggesting that residual Lamanites must be out there – *somewhere*.

With these online tools to hand, the serious student of Mormon missionary teachings is ready to read *TMD Volume 4* and fully compare the truth with the fiction Mormon missionaries are trained so well to teach their investigators. To assist in locating material referenced from the lesson manual the *(page number)* is always shown with extracts.

The reader will *not* need the lesson manual or the scriptures in order to enjoy simply reading through this work. I have however, constructed each chapter in a fashion where the more serious student can easily locate the relevant lesson manual pages and references for further study. Whatever each reader decides, my hope is that the resulting journey will be easy to understand, logical in sequence and presentation, and a worthwhile undertaking.

As we meander through the lesson manual, sometimes taking time along the way to review adjacent material to that which is directly referenced, at the end, it will be discovered there is nothing left that missionaries teach which could remotely be considered to be true. Whatever your route, you will find the historical facts and modern-day evidence provided to be *conclusive* regarding the truth behind Joseph Smith's original hoax and the continued conspiracy to deceive members, missionaries and investigators today.

Whilst not as many 'Mormon' terms appear in this work compared with earlier volumes, I have once again included a note in the following pages of some abbreviations and a glossary of terms for general information.

# Abbreviations & Glossary of Terms

Some abbreviations are used in the text. Not all the following terms appear in this work. Some are included as a guide to a few words and phrases used within Mormonism, as an aid to understanding the religion and to help the reader's perspective. There are many more terms in use which are not referenced here.

AARONIC PRIESTHOOD — Consists of Deacons, Teachers and Priests. The office of Bishop is also technically an Aaronic Priesthood office, although only High Priests hold this office. Whilst in the early church only adult men held these offices, it has gradually changed and today Deacons are called at age twelve, Teachers at fourteen and Priests at sixteen. Although they have various responsibilities, the best known are that Deacons pass the sacrament to members, Teachers prepare it, and Priests bless it. Boys over fourteen are often junior companions to Home Teachers, visiting members each month in their homes.

AF — Ancestral File. See *FS*.

AoF — Articles of Faith. Thirteen statements of some basic beliefs held by the Mormon (LDS) Church.

Apx — Appendix. Sometimes used in abbreviated referencing for works cited within the text.

APOSTLE — Member of the Quorum of Twelve Apostles. Seated at number twelve when called (for life), they move up in position when someone dies. Traditionally, the longest serving apostle becomes the next prophet. This is termed 'The Law of Apostolic Succession'. Although theologically it is not established as automatic, most members accept that it is, as the tradition has always eventually been followed. Today, it is unlikely that a young person would be called as an apostle. Brigham Young ordained young teenage sons as apostles, even though they were never called to the Quorum of Twelve.

BCE — Before Common Era. Non-religious alternative to the use of B.C. (Before Christ).

BISHOP — Head of a Ward, which is the equivalent of a Parish.

BISHOPRIC — Consists of a Bishop and two counsellors who administer a Ward.

BOA — *Book of Abraham.* Supposedly written by Abraham and translated by Joseph Smith.

BOC — *Book of Commandments* - 1833. Original title of what became the *Doctrine and Covenants* (1835).

BOM — *Book of Mormon.* Supposed history of Native Americans, accepted by Mormons as scripture translated from gold plates by Joseph Smith.

BRANCH — Equivalent to a Parish in a smaller, not fully developed Mormon demographic area.
BRANCH PRESIDENCY — Consists of a President and two counsellors who administer a Branch.
BRANCH PRESIDENT — Head of a Branch of the Mormon Church.
BY — Brigham Young.
BYU — Brigham Young University.
c: — citing, or: c. in: — cited in. Referencing from works cited in the text.
CE — Common Era. Non-religious alternative to A.D. (Anno Domini - The Year of Our Lord).
CELESTIAL KINGDOM — Highest of three degrees of glory available to Mormons. It contains three further degrees of glory, the highest of which is 'exaltation' where people become Gods and create worlds.
CES — Church Educational System. Includes Seminary and Institute Courses.
DIALOGUE — *Dialogue, A Journal of Mormon Thought.* An ongoing series of articles concerning the Church, available: www.dialoguejournal.com
D&C — *Doctrine and Covenants.* One of the Mormon 'standard works' of scripture, containing revelations of Joseph Smith. First published 1835.
DISTRICT — Equivalent to a Diocese in smaller, not fully developed Mormon (LDS) demographic area.
ELDER — An office in the Melchizedek Priesthood, also the official title of a missionary.
E.M. — *Encyclopaedia of Mormonism.*
ENDOWMENT — Mormon temple ceremony during which members make covenants with God and learn rituals which they believe will enable them to enter the Mormon 'Celestial Kingdom'.
FAIR — Foundation for Apologetic Information and Research. (Mormon Apologetics). Available at: www.fairlds.org/
FARMS — Foundation for Ancient Research and Mormon Studies. (Mormon Apologetics). Available at: http://farms.byu.edu/ (Now renamed: The Neal A. Maxwell Institute for Religious Scholarship).
FS — Family Search. Online genealogical research facility provided by the Mormon Church. This incorporates Ancestral File (AF), Census records, International Genealogical Index (IGI), Pedigree files and the U.S. Social Security Death Index. See: www.familysearch.org
GA — General Authority (First Presidency, Quorum of Twelve Apostles and the Quorums of Seventy).
HC — *History of the Church.* Seven volume official (but falsified) History of the Church.
HELL — See *Spirit World* and also *Sons of Perdition.*

HOME TEACHING — A system of visiting members in their homes once a month on behalf of the Bishop, checking welfare, giving a spiritual message and praying with them.
IGI — International Genealogical Index. See *FS*.
IMPROVEMENT ERA — Church magazine, published from 1897-1970.
INSTITUTE — Institute of Religion. A four year, weekly course of religious study for nineteen to twenty-nine-year-old young single adults.
IR — Inspired Revision. Also known as JST. (Joseph Smith's Translation). Smith's Inspired Revision of the King James Version of the Bible.
ISL — *In Sacred Loneliness: The Plural Wives of Joseph Smith* by Todd Compton.
JD — *Journal of Discourses.* 26 volume set containing sermons of early Mormon Church leaders.
JST — See IR.
KJV — *King James Version* of the Bible.
LDS or LDS CHURCH — The Church of Jesus Christ of Latter Day Saints. LDS stands for 'Latter-Day Saints', a nickname the Church now prefers, rather than 'Mormon' which was used by members and non-members alike until recent years. This work uses 'Mormon' rather than 'LDS' as it is the name generally known by non-members in the U.K.
MELCHIZEDEK PRIESTHOOD — Name used by the Church because the true name 'The Holy Priesthood after the order of the Son of God' is too holy to use. Consists of Elders, Seventies, High Priests, Patriarchs, Apostles and Prophets. Anyone over 18 can technically be called to any office. Once ordained, no matter what else someone is called to, the Priesthood office remains with them forever. Previously there were Seventies Quorums in every Ward. These days there are a just a handful of such quorums which consist of full time representatives of the Church, assigned from Salt Lake City.
MILLENNIAL STAR — Church magazine, published in England, 1840-1970.
MORMON — Name of a character from the *Book of Mormon*. Also used to identify a member of The Church of Jesus Christ of latter Day Saints – more commonly called 'The LDS Church' in the United States today.
MORMONISM — Nickname for the theology of the Mormon (LDS) sect.
MORMONITES — Early 1800s nickname to identify members of the Mormon sect.
MORMONS — Nickname for the collective, a group or the entire membership.
n. — note. Referencing notes from works cited in the text.
OCCAM'S RAZOR — This medieval philosophy can best be restated in modern terms as: All other things being equal, the simplest and most obvious solution is usually the best.
PARADISE — See *Spirit World*.

PoGP — *Pearl of Great Price*. A Mormon book of canonised scripture, including the supposed *Book of Abraham* which Smith claimed to translate from papyrus, which has now been fully exposed as a fraud. However, despite the RLDS Church disclaiming it, the LDS Church ignores the evidence and says nothing. It also includes Smith's version of *Matthew*, an expanded version of *Genesis (Moses)*, and some of Smith's own history as well as the *Articles of Faith*.

PRIESTHOOD — See *Aaronic Priesthood* and *Melchizedek Priesthood*.

PRIMARY — A Sunday programme for children from nursery age up to age eleven. In years gone by, this was a midweek programme.

PROPHET — The President of the Mormon Church. However, the three men in the Presidency as well as the quorum of twelve are all sustained as 'prophets, seers and revelators'.

PROXY — Someone being sealed for eternity to a deceased person has a living person stand as *proxy* for the deceased. In the early Church, a woman was automatically also sealed for *time* only, to the proxy husband, usually as a plural wife. Any future children they had would belong to the deceased husband in the eternities. The practice is still used today but a proxy is just a *stand in* for the ceremony and could be anyone who is available 'for and in behalf of' the dead, with *no* marriage for time being entered into by the proxy spouse.

RLDS or RLDS Church — The Reorganised Church of Jesus Christ of Latter Day Saints, now known as the 'Community of Christ'. One of several schisms formed following the death of Joseph Smith when Brigham Young and the twelve apostles took over the main body of the Church.

RS — RELIEF SOCIETY. Women's organisation first headed by Smith's wife Emma. Women do not have the Priesthood or any authority within the Church, nor do they hold positions which have any. The Relief Society is directed and supervised by the Priesthood.

SA — Single Adult programme for singles over the age of twenty-nine.

SACRAMENT — Bread, anything will do, but white bread is preferred by some Bishops, and ordinary water, taken from small individual paper or plastic cups are used to represent the body and blood of Christ.

SACRAMENT MEETING — The main Sunday worship service, where the prime purpose is partaking of the sacrament.

SAINT or SAINTS — A member, or group of members of the Mormon Church. A generic term not meant to imply any saintly attributes, simply an acknowledgement and designation of church membership.

SEMINARY — A four year weekday course of religious study for fourteen to eighteen year olds.

SHIELDS — Scholarly & Historical Information Exchange for Latter-Day Saints. See: www.shields-research.org

[sic] — Latin, 'thus' signifying a spelling mistake, grammatical error, or use of a wrong word.

SLC — Salt Lake City, Utah, USA.

SPIRIT WORLD — A place where spirits go, between death and the resurrection. It consists of two separate places (or conditions, or states of mind) which are commonly believed to be *Paradise* and the *Spirit Prison.* Theologically, in days gone by (including when I was young) the Spirit World *was* the *Spirit Prison*, as no one can leave there in the way we leave earth through death. The two aspects which described the *condition* of people there were then known as *Paradise* and *Hell.* This concept appears to have been toned down somewhat in latter years.

SONS OF PERDITION — Those very few who will go to *Outer Darkness* with Satan. These are people who have known the truth and had a sure witness of it and then deliberately turned their backs on the Saviour and followed Satan.

STAKE — Equivalent to a Diocese, fully organised with a large multi-purpose meeting house.

STAKE HIGH COUNCIL — Twelve men who assist in administering a Stake under the direction of the Stake Presidency. When a new High Counsellor is called, he sits in the number twelve position at High Council meetings. As someone is released and called to a different Church role, he moves up one place until eventually (unless released earlier) he will sit at number one. Sometimes referred to as the 'Senior High Counsellor' or 'Number 1', this is more of a colloquialism than an official position.

STAKE PRESIDENCY — Consists of a President and two counsellors who administer a Stake.

STAKE PRESIDENT — Head of a Stake which consists of several Wards.

STAND — Pulpit.

TBM — True Blue Mormon (A devout, faithful, unquestioning disciple of the Church).

TELESTIAL KINGDOM — Lowest of three degrees of glory. A place described as *better* than Earth. It is where evil people, whom other faiths and religions may consider deserving of Hell (murderers, adulterers and liars etc) will end up in the hereafter.

TERRESTRIAL KINGDOM — Second of three degrees of glory. A place in the hereafter for good people who did not accept the Mormon Church.

THE BRETHREN — Terminology (colloquialism) used to represent the top fifteen leaders of the Church (known as the 'Big 15' in the ex-Mormon community) comprising the First Presidency and Quorum of Twelve Apostles, all of whom are set apart as prophets, seers and revelators.

TMD — The Mormon Delusion.

UTLM — Utah Lighthouse Ministry. Anti-Mormon Christian ministry which was founded in 1959 by Jerald and Sandra Tanner.
v. — reference to a verse or verses of scripture.
V. — reference to a Volume, followed by the volume number.
WARD — Unit of the Church equivalent to a Parish, fully organised, usually with a multi purpose Chapel. In areas of dense Mormon population, two or more Wards may utilise one building.
WoW — Word of Wisdom. Mormon 'health code'. Members are required to live this principle among others in order to hold positions in the Church or attend the Mormon temple.
YLT — *Young's Literal Translation* of the Bible.
YM — Young Men Organisation for boys aged twelve to eighteen.
YSA — Young Single Adult Programme for eighteen to twenty-nine year old singles.
YW — Young Women Organisation for girls aged twelve to eighteen.
ZION'S CAMP — A band of some 200 men plus some women and children made an ill-fated two month trek which resulted in many of the participants getting cholera. The attempt at a negotiated return failed and Smith disbanded the group rather than try to use force. Smith claimed he had a revelation to raise a militia in Kirtland (Ohio) which would march to Jackson (Missouri) and redeem Zion from where they had been chased by the old settlers.

# Contents

| Chapter | | Page |
|---|---|---|
| Endorsements | | vi |
| Comments from around the world | | viii |
| Acknowledgements | | xi |
| Guidance Notes | | xii |
| Abbreviations and Glossary of Terms | | xv |
| Preface | | 1 |
| | | |
| The Basis of Expectation – Honesty and Integrity | | 11 |
| | | |
| 1. A Guide to Missionary Service. Preach my Gospel | | 19 |
| 2. Programming the Missionaries Continues | | 29 |
| 3. Continuous Self-Induced Missionary Brainwashing | | 57 |

### Lesson 1. The Restoration of the Gospel of Jesus Christ

| | | |
|---|---|---|
| 4. | Part A. Missionary Preparation | 63 |
| | God loves us; Christ Atoned for us | 65 |
| | The Great Apostasy | 76 |
| 5. | Part B. The Joseph Smith Story | 83 |
| | Joseph Smith's First Vision | 91 |
| 6. | Part C. The Book of Mormon | 123 |

### Lesson 2. The Plan of Salvation

| | | |
|---|---|---|
| 7. | Part A. The Plan of Salvation | 141 |
| | Pre-Earth Life | 143 |
| | The Creation | 146 |
| | Agency and the Fall of Adam & Eve | 151 |
| 8. | Part B. In the Garden | 155 |
| | The Fall | 164 |
| | Our Life on Earth | 167 |
| 9. | Part C. The Atonement | 171 |
| | Resurrection | 173 |
| | Atonement | 176 |
| | The Gospel – The Way | 179 |
| 10. | Part D. The Spirit World | 185 |
| | Gospel Preached to the Dead | 192 |

| | | | |
|---|---|---|---|
| 11. | | Part E. Resurrection, Judgment & Immortality | 209 |
| | | Resurrection and Restoration | 210 |
| | | Judgment | 211 |
| | | Kingdoms of Glory | 212 |
| | | Eternal Life | 218 |
| 12. | **Lesson 3. The Gospel of Jesus Christ** | | 225 |
| 13. | **Lesson 4. The Commandments – Part A** | | 259 |
| 14. | **Lesson 4. The Commandments – Part B** | | 299 |
| 15. | **Lesson 5. Laws and Ordinances** | | 351 |
| 16. | **Post Lesson Material** | | 387 |
| 17. | **What Is the Role of the Book of Mormon?** | | 405 |

| | |
|---|---|
| Conclusion: | 461 |
| Appendix A: Apologists Dispute the Existence of Nephite Coins | 463 |
| Appendix B: Mosiah 12 & 13 | 487 |
| Appendix C: 3 Nephi 24 compared to The Tanakh – Malachi 3 | 493 |
| Appendix D: The Charles Anthon Fable | 497 |
| Appendix E: The Beatitudes | 509 |
| Appendix F: Hinckley denies knowing God was once a man | 517 |
| Appendix G: Adam God and Blood Atonement | 519 |
| Bibliography and Recommended Books | 531 |
| Index | 541 |

# Preface

I have mentioned previously, when writing about the Mormon Church, that it really should be illegal for a Church to be able to portray so many lies as the truth in order to gain followers who commit, not just their time but also ten percent of their gross income to the Church for *life*. It has recently occurred to me that although my wish is for the truth to be made publicly known *prior* to people being enticed into joining the Mormon Church that of course remains wishful thinking.

Then I came across the latest Mormon 'missionary lesson manual' online and just skimming those pages, it occurred to me that the manual is full of provable lies and misleading statements. The intention is to first more fully convince and 'train' new and unsuspecting missionaries and then subsequently their 'investigators' that the things they teach are actually true. The least I could do would be to publish an account of those lies myself, since the Church is unwilling to do so. Then at least, should anyone wish to compare what they are taught with evidence of the truth behind the hoax, they can do so in an organised and sequential manner.

In a manual spanning over two-hundred-and-twenty pages, the fact that only a *quarter* of it relates to actual material designed to teach those who investigate the Mormon Church, indicates the sheer magnitude of ongoing psychological brainwashing that Church leaders consider necessary to keep missionaries in their continually deluded state.

Years ago, certainly in the United Kingdom, serving a mission was something that was not expected but was gently encouraged. There was no stigma attached to anyone who felt unable to serve a mission for whatever reason. Indeed, particularly in England where I live, when I first joined the Mormon Church it was rare for young English men to serve missions at all as they could ill afford to do so. Most families struggled to pay tithing let alone support a missionary. Not many members could even afford a car. The Branch we attended (Wards and Stakes were only just starting to be established at that time in England) was quite large compared to many, with over a hundred attending and yet there were only three or four cars in the car park. Everyone caught busses to get to Church.

In more recent years, as the UK has started to become more affluent and the concept that every young man should serve a mission has evolved to become the expected norm, it has become more and more awkward for anyone who really does not care to serve a mission. The stigma of not going eventually disappears but young men in their mid-twenties who are called to serve in Bishoprics or other more senior callings are invariably 'returned missionaries' as they are considered to be strongest in their faith. There are of course always exceptions to the rule but that is generally the case in my experience.

Young women can choose to serve a mission if they wish to, but there is no pressure to do so and there is certainly no stigma if they don't. It is much less common for young women to serve missions although some do so. One of my own daughters chose to go on a mission. They serve for eighteen months and have to be over twenty-one years of age, whereas the young men serve for two years, starting anytime from age nineteen until age twenty-five.

Some young men who have never been away from home do not survive the first few days or weeks of a mission and return home due to being homesick. Others leave the mission field later on, when they just don't want to continue, while a few are sent home once it is discovered that they are not 'worthy' to be there. There are sometimes sexual transgressions during missions. One young man I knew very well was sent home for sleeping with his landlady. When questioned about it, he responded that he was only human. That is probably the most honest and open response I have ever heard. Many young men quite naturally have sexual experiences before they are of mission age. Some then lie about it in their 'worthiness interviews' before attending a Mormon temple to receive their 'endowment' which they all do prior to going off on their mission.

The alternative is to have everyone know why they did not go when they came of age; they would then usually have to wait a year until they had 'repented' of their sexual transgressions. Some experience feelings of guilt later during their mission and then confess prior sexual transgressions. They also usually get sent home, not just for their transgressions but also for lying about them in interviews.

All Mormon Church leaders are supposedly endowed with the 'spirit of discernment' but in my experience, from local leaders through to the Prophet, they can discern little of anything at all. I reveal some instances of the inability of the prophet and apostles to discern what was going on in the Church and within their own quorum in earlier volumes. One twentieth-century *apostle* lived an adulterous life for eighteen years and no one noticed. A Church

# PREFACE

*patriarch* was homosexual, where again no one noticed. So much for Mormon (so-called) power of discernment. *(See: TMD Vol.1:213-14 re: Apostle Lyman & Vol. 2:261-63 re: Patriarch Joseph F. Smith).*

Statistically, between six and nine percent of missionaries are of course bound to be homosexual (in my work, that refers to both male and female) – depending on which national statistics you reference. That is about the normal distribution of homosexual men and women in society in general and Mormons are *not* excluded from such a statistic in their own community merely because they believe their God doesn't approve of it. Some young missionaries discover they are homosexual while they are actually on their mission, when they find themselves becoming attracted to a particular companion and the realisation sets in. Being with a same gender companion twenty-four hours a day and sleeping in the same room is not a problem, unless two missionaries find themselves attracted to each other.

Clearly, since science has now firmly established that sexual orientation in humans, as well as some other species, is hard-wired into the brain and *not* just a curable illness or a 'reversible disposition' as the Mormon Church proclaims, this orientation can be extremely difficult for a young person on a mission. It is a quite natural disposition for them but the Church teaches that it is *not* natural.

Occasionally, two homosexual missionaries find themselves together as companions. As stated above, this is not a problem, unless they find themselves attracted to each other. Occasionally, a couple who are attracted to each other will act on their mutual emotions; some get caught and some do not. If you are a young single heterosexual, imagine spending twenty-four hours a day with the most adorable member of the opposite sex who you are falling in love with and you may begin to understand such a situation more readily.

Unfortunately, such is the (mis)treatment of homosexuals by the Mormon Church and also many devout Mormon families, to which they may belong, that the incidence of suicide and also of homeless homosexual youngsters, particularly in Salt Lake City, is exceptionally high. The Mormon Church has a lot to answer for – but that is another topic for another day.

Missionaries who are sent home are disgraced missionaries; they do not 'return with honour' as expected of them. They are invariably excommunicated for their 'sins' and have to work their way back into the Church. That usually takes a couple of years or so. By comparison, someone excommunicated when I was young would expect to take five or six years to return to full fellowship. Times change, and so does the Mormon Church. Whilst disciplinary councils which handle such matters are entirely confidential, it is hard to keep reasons for an early return secret and invariably Church members soon become aware of what happened.

There is an interesting story, resulting from a friend's request for copies of disciplinary council minutes following his excommunication when he was 'sent home' from his mission. He no longer believes the Church to be true and will not be returning to membership. As part of the European Union, the United Kingdom is required to comply with European data privacy laws and created the Data Protection Act 1998 (DPA) for this purpose. Under this Act an individual is entitled to copies of *any* and *all* of their personal information held by a company or an organisation. Mormon Church leaders seem to consider the Church to be above some laws and they try to bamboozle anyone who asks for something they do not want to accommodate and *never* provide such minutes.

Throughout the last year or two, following my friend's complaint to the Information Commissioner's Office (ICO), the Church has continually claimed that either they do not have to provide the disciplinary report, that they can't find it – and even that the Act does not protect personal information transferred outside of the United Kingdom. Personal information transferred outside of the United Kingdom *is* protected by the contractual European Union Model Clauses that protect individuals' rights, including the right of access to information held about them. The Mormon Church claimed the information requested was *not* subject to the DPA and was now under European Clauses but they still refused to provide copies of the disciplinary records.

Luckily, my friend is intelligent and immediately realised they did not understand the law regarding the issue at all. The Church had been sending him letters via their lawyers in England. Recently my friend located an Internet video of a talk given by an in-house Church lawyer at the *J. Reuben Clark Law Society Conference* on 13th February 2010. This is a transcript of part of it. Ellipses indicate pauses and hesitations in speech rather than missing words.

> In the last month in the UK alone I think we've spent... err, well, for two individuals... two former members of the church who don't want to leave the church alone but want to be aggravants to us... have filed complaints with the regulatory authorities in the UK and I've spent close to eighty-thousand dollars in legal fees to respond to these. They're demanding copies of their membership records, of course they were disciplined so now they're demanding copies of their disciplinary courts... proceedings... so... councils. That's a problem we're facing... and that's just in one little... it's not a little country but it's two individuals and look at the cost and the aggravation it's caused us. So we're going to see more in the data privacy area... that's why I mention more disclosure in the confidential information.
>
> The First Presidency feels that that [disciplinary record] is very privileged... and we cannot disclose that unless we get First Presidency approval. That's how sensitive this type of information is with respect to the Brethren, so this is a big deal for us as we go around the world. *(Addressing Issues for Good Around the World - William F. Atkin).*
> http://www.law2.byu.edu/news/item.php?num=676

# PREFACE

So, the Church spent close to $80,000 of tithing money in just *one month* on legal advice which my friend already provided in copies of the legislation he obtained directly from the ICO. All they had to do was send him copies of the information requested and spend *no* money at all. They *will* comply because the law demands it and they cannot do otherwise. It may also cost them a lot more money if they prevaricate. Mormon leaders represent the Mormon God, honesty and integrity, and supposedly have the power of discernment, yet their lawyers appear to have a problem in getting them to obey the laws of the land.

As I write this added paragraph (January 2011), the ongoing investigation into Mormon Church non-compliance in respect of the DPA by the ICO on my friend's behalf is now starting to bite. The ICO does *not* pursue cases that they do not consider a *breach* of law. The ICO has confirmed that Church leaders are being asked to explain themselves to the ICO; to provide my friend with the information he requested and to address his request as a matter of priority. The letter that my friend just received from the ICO indicated that if the Church in England really does have no control over the data asked for, then their breach is even more serious, considering the EU contractual clauses they entered into. The Church has been *instructed* to comply with U.K. law.

The other of the 'two' people mentioned above may well be another friend who has also been requesting documents. If not, then he is a third person to add to the list of those demanding their rights be observed and honoured. If the Church obeyed the law instead of ignoring it, they could save a fortune and do some good with the money instead of wasting it by having lawyers send letters to excommunicated missionaries who ask for disciplinary council minutes.

In addition to the minority of missionaries who do not make it through the first days or weeks of their mission or later get sent home for one reason or another, most do survive the two years and return home 'with honour' and have 'marvellous' faith promoting stories to tell. Even then, it is estimated that up to a third of returned missionaries become what is termed 'less active' in the Church over the next three or four years as they mature and start to question or simply become less interested in Church activity. Nevertheless, that still leaves most of them to run the Church at various levels in future years.

The Church 'prepares' young men for their missions from birth. They are programmed to prepare to serve a mission by loving parents, Church leaders and friends. It is what everyone does and there is no question about what is expected of every young man.

In earlier days, many missionaries were called 'from the stand' (pulpit) at conference in Salt Lake City and that was the first thing they knew about it. They didn't volunteer; they were just called to go. In my younger day, we were taught that the names of potential missionaries were submitted for prayerful consideration by the First Presidency in the Holy of Holies room in the temple and their destination a matter of inspiration. The First Presidency personally signed every missionary call letter. Now, missionaries are assigned to their area by computer and First Presidency signatures added to call letters by a machine.

The First Presidency generally has no idea at all of who goes where, unless a prominent member requests a specific destination for his son, for example to the same area where he served. This is sometimes accommodated. It depends on the position they hold and how well placed they are in the Church. I won't cite specific examples but I am aware it has happened from first hand claims by missionary sons of senior Church leaders I met over the years. I have known similar requests from local members to be refused. The Mormon God works in very modern, as well as extremely mysterious ways in the twenty-first century.

There are currently over fifty-thousand Mormon missionaries at any one time, walking the streets and knocking on doors around the world, seeking to teach people about Mormonism. (51,736 as of December 2009). This currently results in the conversion of about a quarter of a million people each year.

Statistically, at least when I was a member, a good third of these 'converts' leave the Church within about the first three months or so following baptism. Another third will stop attending within the next one to three years. About one third remain faithful; meaning they pay tithes and offerings, attend the temple and accept callings to serve, often in leadership positions.

Most members who do leave the fold usually just stop attending; their names are *not* removed from Church records and they are still 'counted' as members. Such people generally have no idea that they have to request name removal in order not to be associated with the Mormon Church. Most do not really care and just drift away. Some go on to join other religions and no longer consider themselves to be Mormons at all. Nonetheless, they remain members as far as the Mormon Church is concerned. This is one reason why, although the Church may boast it is heading towards fourteen million members (2010), the true *active* membership actually attending and considering themselves real members is more like five million at best. The Mormon Church is not as 'big' as many members seem to believe it is.

Whilst overall membership still nominally increases each year, membership numbers, conversion figures, and actual retention, have all been declining (in percentage growth terms per annum) over the past few years. The Church still claims overall that it is 'growing' by about a quarter of a million people year on year. This figure is artificially increased by keeping those who do not attend (and may have relocated and cannot be found), on record until they are one-hundred-and-ten years old, when only then is it assumed they must have died and their names removed. Thus Mormon Church membership statistics include many thousands of dead people who may not have even considered themselves 'real' Mormons when they were alive. The number of 'members' is also now bolstered by including member *births* which once were not included in the

## PREFACE

statistics at all. Births account for close to one-hundred-thousand new *members* each year. You can hardly consider a baby an actual member of anything other than its own family and most other denominations do not include babies in membership statistics. The Mormon Church began to include them some years ago when the statistics started slipping away from optimistic projection figures.

This 'bolstering' of the figures is largely to compensate for the increasing number of members who, after discovering the truth behind the hoax, leave the fold and do in fact resign membership. Until recent decades, there was only one way out of the Mormon Church and that was through excommunication. I can remember, as a 'Home Teacher', visiting people who were technically Mormon but who had no memory of ever joining the Church. Their membership records dated back to the early nineteen-sixties when they were baptised as children during what was termed the 'baseball baptism' era. Missionaries would round up young teenagers to play baseball and tell them they had to be 'members' to play in their league. They were often baptised without parental consent. Many never even attended Church.

This actually happened to my first wife's younger brother in 1961 when she had no idea that he had been baptised until after the event. He has never attended Church other than for weddings and funerals. For people to have their names removed, we used to have to get them to sign an affidavit stating "I no longer have a testimony of Jesus Christ and wish my name removed from the records of The Church of Jesus Christ of Latter Day saints." Some people did not wish to state that and only wanted to be disassociated with Mormonism, but that was the *only* acceptable method and statement at that time. I remember 'culling' membership records that way and several times I was obliged to write out the statement and have it signed and two of us as Melchizedek Priesthood Home Teachers would have to sign as witnesses to the statement. They would then be (voluntarily) 'excommunicated' for apostasy in a disciplinary council.

No one could just 'leave' Mormonism, until one day legal action against the Church succeeded when a member demanded that he should be able to simply 'resign'. The success of the case introduced a new era enabling any member to legally resign Church membership by writing a letter of resignation and having his or her name removed from Mormon Church records without any ecclesiastical 'action'. That is what I did in 2003. Many ex-Mormons still say they have great difficulty in getting confirmation of the Church's acceptance of their resignation and that they have to be persistent.

Since the advent of the internet and so much information now being readily available for study, the number of people resigning each year appears to be steadily rising. I am given to understand from ex-Mormons in Salt Lake City, who know people who are involved, that a whole Church department now deals with such resignations. This has not been substantiated but it would not be at all surprising. The pressure is constantly on missionaries to find new converts and on members to provide more 'referrals' for missionaries.

Despite all this pressure, having spent some time analysing the overall trend, I confidently predict that the Church will continue to lose ground and have smaller and smaller overall growth figures each year (if they are honest about them that is), and within two or three decades, the overall membership numbers will begin to fall, just as has been the case with other religions which became less popular for one reason or another. Currently, those steadily *losing* membership each year include the Methodists and Presbyterians. *(See TMD Vol. 2:351-52)*. The pattern their membership statistics followed in the years *prior* to their ultimate, and now steady decline, mirrors the Mormon Church today. Statistically, the decline and fall of the Mormon Church is therefore just a matter of time rather than opinion.

The fact of the matter is that whilst previously the Church grew well in the western world, today that growth is notional. The only real growth now comes from areas where people are unlikely to have easy access to the internet and are therefore less likely to discover the truth before it is too late. Of the twenty countries providing the highest growth for the Mormon Church in 2009, ten were in Africa and five were in the Caribbean. The Mormon Church, in terms of overall claimable membership numbers, is slowly grinding to a halt. Then it will begin its inevitable decline. Nevertheless, many Mormons still believe the myth that their Church is the fastest growing Church in the world and to date, whilst to the best of my knowledge the Church itself has never actually claimed this, it has also done little to correct the *perception* and many missionaries still seem inclined to teach their investigators that it is.

This book is written in order to provide established historical facts and evidence, directly related, and in sequence, to the claims made by the Mormon Church in its 'missionary lessons' to the unsuspecting public. It also includes some things that missionaries do not teach at all. In reviewing what *is* said, I also mention some things that are *not* said but which perhaps should be said. In addition, as scripture references are provided to missionaries for personal use and also to share with their investigators, many invariably cover additional aspects that are not part of the subjects being taught. In such cases, where important issues are right there in black and white, I have allowed myself to digress and write about those too. Some of the aspects that appear in references contradict modern Church teachings and investigators deserve the details and background. This I provide.

Sometimes, I may even appear to have become distracted from the subject matter that the manual is covering – but this is not the case. The point in each instance where this may appear to happen, is to take the opportunity to expose what is in adjacent 'reference' material that is *not* covered, as well as what is intended. The information is provided in the hope that investigators may use it

# PREFACE

to compare the truth with what they are taught (and also *not* taught) by the missionaries before they are taken in by Mormon Church claims. Perhaps even some Mormon missionaries who have begun to question, may somehow come across this book and read it before wasting two years of their lives unwittingly perpetuating lies represented by their Church as truth.

Missionaries mean well; they have no more idea of the truth than their investigators do, and they are not to blame. Having faith to believe in God is one thing (which I generally try to leave alone), but to have faith in provable *fiction* is quite another; it is neither sensible nor is it healthy. It is simply not honourable to teach provable fiction as if it is the truth. This situation requires *someone* to at least stand up and defend truth and integrity by saying NO; this is *not* right. That is all I have ever tried to do; it has been my personal therapy.

This work contains the truth behind the Joseph Smith hoax as it relates to what Mormon missionaries teach investigators. The modern Mormon Church continues in a conspiracy to deceive people today through selective, fictional and fanciful story telling. Modern Mormon leaders undoubtedly believe Joseph Smith did see God and Jesus and that he translated the *Book of Mormon*. But, they also *know* at least some of the underlying truth surrounding those and other things which make them, and also Smith's credentials, more than suspect.

In my personal experience, Mormon apostles claiming to be prophets, seers and revelators, do not readily face and answer questions themselves; instead, they refer members to apologetic web sites. Yet they will be *fully* aware of the many lies and falsifications. Because their predecessors falsified Mormon history, changed Mormon scripture and created a raft of Mormon mythology in the stead of original facts, they must feel their hands are tied by such history, as they continue to conspire to hide the truth from their members, missionaries and their investigators alike. They do absolutely *nothing* to correct matters that could be corrected if only they had the integrity to do so. 'Lying for the Lord' and leaving things as they are 'for the greater good' seem to still be the order of the day for modern Mormon leaders. Nothing changes. What is presented in the missionary lesson manual is **not** the truth by any stretch of the imagination.

I had not intended to write any more about the Mormon Church following volume three. I even called it a 'trilogy' on the original hardcover jacket of the third volume. But I had always considered something was 'missing' from my work. One morning, when I woke up, the title of this volume was in my head. I just knew it had to be written as a support vehicle for anyone being introduced to the Church via missionary lessons, or for questioning members who wanted to 're-run' all the things the missionaries, or their parents, had once convinced them were true and felt God had confirmed. If I were still a Mormon, I would have considered the experience of waking up with such a thing in my head to have been 'inspiration' or even personal 'revelation'. The reality is that such things work for *everyone*, religious or otherwise, simply by the subconscious mind working while we are asleep, pondering things for us. It has absolutely nothing to do with God or religion. It is the science behind the human brain.

I had a clear picture of what I needed to research and write. I wanted people to be able to fully comprehend that if the sequence of tactics used to convert them had resulted in *provable fiction* being taken to the Lord in prayer, then the perceived answer *must* have been wishful thinking, as no God could provide a positive response to lies and deception. *That* is the bottom line of the matter.

In writing about some aspects, memories were jogged and I was reminded of personal experiences relating to things I had long forgotten. I have included one or two stories and anecdotes along the way which I hope will add interest to the journey. They are few and they are short, and I hope, relevant.

Through this book, the investigator will become armed with the underlying truth at each stage of the missionary lesson material. At certain stages there will be specific questions that should be asked; little projects or 'tests' to do, and observations regarding the 'fullness of the Gospel' supposedly being in the *Book of Mormon*. Investigators will ultimately arrive at a point where they can (should they still wish to do so) take what is left intact and viable, to the Lord for verification. Invariably, there will be nothing left for the Lord to consider. There will be no more to say or do. Common sense and reason will be more than enough to determine the matter. God will not need to be disturbed. In the (supposed) immortal words of the Lord to Joseph Smith:

> **D&C 5:29.** And if this be the case, I command you, my servant Joseph, that you shall say unto him, that he shall do no more, nor trouble me any more concerning this matter.

Finally, if it was not already clear enough in my earlier books, or on my web site, *none* of my work is directed at faithful Mormons. I have *no* intention of trying to convince the faithful that they are wrong. My work is intended *solely* for those *questioning* Mormonism, for whatever reason; for those who demand answers and the honest and evidenced truth; be they investigators, Ex-Mormons, interested bystanders, members or missionaries who *are* questioning and have had an epiphany or a 'what if' moment; for *anyone* who is starting to have serious concerns and is now ready to seek and find the ultimate truth.

If you *do* happen to be a faithful Mormon who has *no* wish to discover the truth behind Mormonism, then may I urge you now to take the following scriptures to heart and go, along with your testimony, safely on your way.

> **Job 38:11.** Hitherto shalt thou come, but no further…

> **2 Timothy 3:9.** But they shall proceed no further: for their folly shall be manifest unto all men, as theirs also was.

Jim Whitefield. January 2011.

# Prelude – The Basis of Expectation

## Honesty and Integrity

In my work, I often accuse the Mormon Church of lies, deception and a conspiracy to deceive through countless additions, deletions, interpolations and suppression regarding their historical documentation and so-called scriptures. I do so only when and where the evidence is conclusive and it is proven to be the case. I offer no personal opinions on aspects that are questioned. I provide only evidentiary proof of the underlying truth of each matter and compare that with what the Church erroneously claims to be the case.

The fact of the matter is that the Church has always promoted an internal concept at the highest levels that 'lying for the Lord' as it is termed, is somehow justified for some supposed 'greater good'. I cannot personally conceive of any greater good than honesty and integrity. If there is a God, it is generally accepted that He is not even capable of lies or deception, representing only truth, integrity and everything that *is good*. Any other perception would render Him evil and incapable of *being* God. I do not expect a church or its leaders who claim to represent Almighty God and Jesus Christ as 'ordained' prophets and apostles to be anything other than what they publicly *proclaim*.

I hold the Mormon Church and its leaders (as well as their God) to the same standards they themselves advertise as being expected of themselves and their members – no more, and certainly no *less*. Yet the fundamental claims of the Mormon Church are worse than suspicious, they can be proven to contain carefully concealed falsehoods and many outright lies. There are so many that it is impossible to even begin to count them. Some even appear to be endorsed by their own version of God. Nothing that the Mormon Church publishes or teaches is untainted. Some provable deceptions, such as the publication of *D&C 101* which proclaimed monogamy the *only* approved form of Mormon marriage, are *admitted* as lies, considered unfortunate but necessary at the time, to protect Church leaders and the secret practice of polygamy.

That it was directed at *members* rather than non-members in order to hide polygamy from many of the faithful is reprehensible. Many known lies are still hidden from members today in a continued conspiracy to deceive them about the past, supposedly as "some things that are true, are not helpful". *(Do not spread disease germs! Boyd K. Packer. BYU Studies, Summer 1981:259, 262-271).* The fact is that Mormon origins, as proclaimed to investigators in the missionary lessons, are entirely *fraudulent*. People are first deceived and then deluded. They then pay for their mistake by devoting their lives to Mormonism and donating their money to further the lies. If this sounds harsh, it is meant to as deception regarding faith in fiction is one of the worst crimes imaginable. The evidence is conclusive and needs to be fully exposed.

**The Mormon Articles of Faith**

The first eleven 'articles' are short statements of basic Mormon belief. *(See: Pearl of Great Price; or* History of the Church *Vol. 4. pp.535-541).* The last two articles are declarations of the expected *behaviour* of all Church members.

It is not unreasonable to hold claimed prophets and apostles to their own declared standards for their followers. For them to expect anything less would in fact nullify their claim to such status. They *must* stand and be counted. The final two Mormon 'Articles of Faith' are:

> **12.** We believe in being subject to kings, presidents, rulers, and magistrates, in ***obeying, honoring***, and ***sustaining*** the law.
>
> **13.** We believe in being ***honest, true, chaste, benevolent, virtuous***, and in ***doing good to all men***; indeed, we may say that we follow the admonition of Paul - We believe all things, we hope all things, we have endured many things, and hope to be able to endure all things. If there is anything virtuous, lovely, or of good report or praiseworthy, we seek after these things. (Emphasis added).

Most Mormons have no idea that Smith was not the originator of these articles. They were derived from some earlier statements, which were actually penned and published by Orson Pratt in 1840, in his pamphlet; *An Interesting Account of Several Remarkable Visions*. Smith, as usual in his writings, simply

## PRELUDE – THE BASIS OF EXPECTATION

plagiarised them, altering them to suit his own requirements. He first published them as *his* in *Times and Seasons,* Vol. 3, 15 March 1842:709-710. *(See: The Changing Articles of Faith by Sandra Tanner, online resource available at* www.utlm.org; *also: Tanner 1991:27-28).*

Oliver Cowdery wrote a version in the *Latter Day Saints Messenger and Advocate* in October 1834 and later, Joseph Young, brother of Brigham Young, had a go at writing some articles while proselyting in Boston in 1836. Orson Hyde later wrote some that were similar to Orson Pratt's version when he was in Frankfurt, Germany, in 1842 in his German language pamphlet '*A Cry From the Wilderness'.* It was the same year in which Smith wrote what has famously become known as the 'Wentworth Letter'.

Smith included the thirteen articles in a letter he wrote to 'Long' John Wentworth when explaining Mormonism to him. Hence the average Mormon believes Joseph Smith invented the articles himself. As ever, the Church makes no real effort to ensure members are remotely aware of the truth.

Regarding the above two 'Articles of Faith', note the Mormon Church claims they not only 'obey' the laws of the land, but that they also 'honour' and 'sustain' those laws. This means actively upholding and supporting the law. It does not by any stretch of the imagination mean ignoring or disregarding the law and then lying about doing so. The Church actually claims that at times God has *told* them to do so. *(See: TMD Vols. 1-3 for several examples).*

The Articles were first published in the 1840s when polygamy was being secretly practiced by an inner circle of Mormon leaders. Polygamy was always completely *illegal*. In 1890, the prophet Wilford Woodruff issued a Manifesto which is now held as canonised scripture in the *D&C*, known as 'Official Declaration 1'. They claim it was from *God*. It forbade any further polygamy and the Church agreed with the government that they would not allow any further plural marriages and also that they would each only cohabit with *one* wife following an amnesty in 1891.

As an example of the Mormon leaders' attitudes to Articles of Faith 12 and 13, the following three questions (out of many that could be asked) should be addressed by the current leaders – that is, if they want to continue to claim that *Official Declaration 1* is in fact a canon from their God. Otherwise, integrity *demands* they accept the truth, remove it from the *D&C* and then discard it completely. Rank and file Mormons deserve to know the *truth*. They should be free to decide what they make of it for themselves rather than have leaders conceal the truth just because they consider it not helpful. The fact is that it is not just 'not helpful'; the overall truth confirms Mormonism *not* of God at all.

**Question No. 1.** Why did the prophet, Wilford Woodruff, marry his sixth wife, Lydia Mountford, on 19 August 1897 (when he was ninety and she was thirty-nine years old; fifty-one years his junior), seven years *after* he himself had issued the Manifesto and declared that God told him to stop the practice for good? Either Woodruff lied (history shows he *did* – see *TMD Vol. 1* for full details), or he not only disobeyed the laws of the land, having entered a legal agreement not to continue polygamy, but he also directly disobeyed his *God*. Either way, Woodruff could not possibly therefore qualify as a true prophet. 'By their fruits ye shall know them.'

**Question No. 2.** Why did the following happen? In 1904, the *prophet,* Joseph Fielding Smith, published an official declaration confirming and upholding Wilford Woodruff's 'Manifesto'. Then, in 1906, Smith was arrested, convicted and fined $300 for cohabiting with *four* women. In today's money that would be well over $7,000. Another *prophet* thus lied and deceived the government and his own Church members alike. Ergo; he also could *not* have been a true prophet.

**Question No. 3.** Why was I able to locate and document *(See: TMD Vol. 1 for full list of names and dates)* well over one-hundred babies *conceived* and *born* to polygamous (not first) wives of general authorities during the *two decades following* the 1890 Manifesto. The fact is that the Mormon prophets and apostles publicly proclaimed one thing to their Church and to the world at large via a proclaimed revelation from God, whilst they themselves completely *ignored* it. You can try to hide the truth but you can't hide all the babies.

The 1890 Manifesto was originally conceived by a committee; worded by lawyers, and reworked by Woodruff who issued it, fait accompli, while most apostles were out of town. Had they all been there to vote, it would have been rejected out of hand as with previous attempts to introduce such an idea. Most apostles were obliged to approve it retrospectively and ultimately did so only very grudgingly. That hardly constituted a unanimous quorum vote or humble acceptance that God was declaring His divine will for the Church. *(See: TMD Vol 1. Ch.14 for full details).* When the Manifesto was voted on at Conference, many members and a number of apostles abstained from voting.

The 'Manifesto' was the only way to get the United States government to release seized Church assets in order for the Church to survive. The obviously fraudulent 'revelation', now known as *D&C Official Declaration 1*, became canonised, despite the fact that all the apostles (with the notable exception of Lorenzo Snow) *completely* ignored it. Had any of them remotely considered it to actually be God's will, clearly they would have obeyed it. Modern Mormon Church leaders know perfectly well that the document was a manufactured *lie*. It could not possibly have constituted revelation from God; everyone knew it then – and Mormon leaders know it now. They *ignore* truth. Is that **honest**?

# PRELUDE – THE BASIS OF EXPECTATION

It is however a *convenient* document, used in order to explain away the supposed end of the polygamy story. The recent prophet, Gordon B. Hinckley, responded to the press "It's behind us". Hinckley never wanted to face and deal with such things. So, *Official Declaration 1* stays, even though it is known to be as much of a lie as *D&C 101* was in its day. The honourable thing to do would be to acknowledge that it was *not* received from God and remove it from the *D&C*, explaining that circumstances, rather than God, dictated that it originally be published. Not to do so constitutes a major contribution to the continuing conspiracy to deceive rank and file Mormons, missionaries, and investigators today. Modern leaders *know* the truth and do *nothing* about it.

And that is just one example of the many *provably* fraudulent Mormon claims. In my forty-three years as a Mormon, I had no idea that such lies and conspiracy existed. They are that well hidden. If I had been apprised of any of this before contemplating Mormonism I would never have considered the possibility that God was involved and most certainly would never have joined the Church. The fact that no one else would either is clearly understood by Mormon Church leaders and that is why they continue in their conspiracy to deceive everyone rather than come clean and publish the truth.

The following statement encapsulates *official* Church policy on *honesty* and *integrity:*

> Honest people love truth and justice.
> They are honest in their words and actions.
> Lying is intentionally deceiving others.
> We can also intentionally deceive others
> by a gesture or a look, by silence,
> or by telling only part of the truth.
> Whenever we lead people in any way
> to believe something that is not true,
> we are not being honest.

*(Mormon Lesson Manual, 'Gospel Principles' 1979. Chapter 31. Honesty).*

Historically, many Mormon Church leaders can be proven to have told outright lies. Modern leaders can do nothing other than admit this was the case, (but even then, they only do so when there is no alternative) and try to excuse them as being for some 'greater good'. On many occasions, modern leaders violate their own more detailed requirement for all members included above. Many may indeed have lied by a gesture or a look. They most certainly have often lied by *silence* or by telling only *part* of the truth. They have become extremely adept at using words in statements which at first glance appear to be the truth and yet at the same time are *full* of hidden lies. I relate details of some good examples of that in my earlier volumes. One I will summarise here is from *TMD Volume 1* where I write about the Church having the following statement on its web site regarding Zina Diantha Huntington, an early Mormon Relief Society President. This will more than illustrate the point. At the end of her short biography, Zina's marriages are explained thus:

> Widowed by her first husband, she raised two sons from that marriage, one daughter from her later marriage to Brigham Young... *(Zina D. H. Young Biographical Sketch. Available at:* www.lds.org *under the heading of 'Relief Society').*

Each statement is actually true. Zina *did* outlive her first husband. They *did* have two children. She *did* later marry Brigham Young. She *did* have a daughter by Young. However, within the true statements are a number of very carefully hidden lies. The *inferences* are clear but the real underlying story is *entirely* different. These are the established historical facts and Zina's marriage sequence which the Church accepts but would rather people did not discover.

As happened with several other young 'housemaids', Joseph Smith tried to get Zina to marry him when she was a teenager living in his home. She was too frightened to accommodate him and she twice refused his illicit advances.

This was the subsequent real sequence of events:

Zina married Henry Bailey Jacobs on 7 March 1841 aged 20.

Joseph Smith later sent Zina's brother to tell her that an angel with a drawn sword had threatened to kill Smith if she did not marry him.

Zina subsequently entered a polyandrous marriage with Joseph Smith on 27 October 1841. She was almost seven months pregnant with her first son, Zebulon, at the time.

Joseph Smith died in June of 1844.

Zina entered a second polyandrous marriage with Brigham Young in September of 1844, aged 23.

Zina's marriage to Brigham Young was confirmed in the Nauvoo Temple on 2 February 1846. She was over seven months pregnant with her second son, Henry, at that time.

Zina was simultaneously sealed to Joseph Smith for eternity and Brigham Young stood proxy.

Zina had a baby by Young (Zina Presendia) on 3 April 1850 within their polyandrous marriage.

Brigham Young died on 29 August 1877 aged 76.

Henry B. Jacobs died some nine years later, on 1 August 1886, aged 69.

When Henry died, Zina's two sons were actually forty-four & forty years old respectively.

Zina & Henry were never divorced.

# PRELUDE – THE BASIS OF EXPECTATION

The above are historically verified facts which are accepted by Mormon Church apologists and historians. No one can theologically explain or justify the polyandrous relationships.

Compare the historical facts with the Church statement that Zina was:

> Widowed by her first husband, she raised two sons from that marriage, one daughter from her later marriage to Brigham Young…

The reason this is carefully hidden is that polyandry is officially confirmed by the Mormon Church as "contrary to doctrine" and "those who participated would have to account for it". Compare the truth of the matter and the Church statement about it with Church published 'standards' on honesty and integrity. Joseph Smith had no integrity whatsoever and today there is very little integrity to be found among the ranks of senior Mormon Church leadership.

I complained directly to a current Mormon apostle about some of the lies – including this one. Whilst Zina's biography remains in place on the Mormon Church web site, the above statement has subsequently been removed. She is now the only Relief Society President with no marriage details. She is however referred to throughout as 'Sister Young'. If removal of the detail was an act of contrition regarding honesty and integrity then it is at least a step forward. It is a start. However, overall, I fear that it is too little, too late.

I have started this work with the above notes to establish both the standard that should be expected of Mormon Church (or any church) leaders compared with the *actual* behaviour of Mormon leaders through the ages. In the chapters that follow, everything taught by the Church is held to these same standards. It will soon be discovered that Mormon leaders rarely if ever abide by their own mandates. Mormon leaders most certainly do *not* practice what they preach. They pretend to represent a Church established (restored) by divine mandate and yet what they claim to be from God is peppered with lies and deception to the extent that if God exists, He could and would never have been involved with such things. They are *not* of God.

The Mormon Church disciplines its own historians if they publish history which is considered 'not helpful' when nevertheless it is actually true. If the leaders could only understand, when the ultimate truth is revealed, **none** of it is helpful to the Church. The leaders deliberately lie and deceive members by obfuscating the truth, sometimes even when there appears no real reason to do so. The *truth* undermines every aspect that the Church *pretends* is truth until it leaves *nothing* for anyone to take to the Lord in prayer for an ethereal response in which they may perceive it is true. This work will prove that to be the case *conclusively* as we look, step by step, at what the Church portrays as truth to investigators and compare it to the historical facts.

This will be a very bumpy ride.

# THE MORMON DELUSION

# Chapter 1

## A Guide to Missionary Service – Preach My Gospel

### Missionary programming begins here…..

The 'Mormon Missionary Manual' commences with a message from their First Presidency. Urging the new missionary to "rise to a new sense of commitment to assist our Father in Heaven in His glorious work" the message then includes the following statement:

> Every missionary has an important role in helping "to bring to pass the immortality and eternal life of man" (Moses 1:39). *(Page v).*

    No; they don't. Evidence in this book will conclusively show that although the Mormon Church pretends to *offer* this, it actually *provides* no such thing. It has neither *truth* nor *integrity* within it. The Mormon Church cannot bring anything to pass at all, other than a lifetime of subservience to fictional claims, financial contributions of ten percent of gross income (and more), plus constant personal commitment of time and energy. It is not just a matter of *opinion* that the Mormon Church is not the true Church of a real God; the facts stand alone in evidence of the truth of the matter.

# THE MORMON DELUSION

The Mormon First Presidency makes promises to missionaries:

> The Lord will reward and richly bless you as you humbly and prayerfully serve Him. More happiness awaits you than you have ever experienced as you labor among His children. *(Page v)*.

Once again, no, He *won't* and no, they *won't* experience more happiness than they have ever experienced before. That is an illusion. The truth is that it may elicit an initial euphoria but the psychological effects are temporary and delusional. It will then settle into a long hard struggle to remain 'worthy' and to be 'good enough' in so many areas that are individually logged each day and reported, that no one could ever achieve all they feel they should. Some missionaries can't cope financially. Many missionaries suffer from ill health; some get very depressed and some just muddle along and get by. Some try to shine and do well but still never seem to get startling results. At the end of the day it's numbers (baptisms) that count. It is the *only* statistic that *really* matters to Mormon Church leaders, regardless of what they may tell their missionaries.

Many people who are converted suffer from anxiety and constantly feel unable to achieve all they should once they become members and begin to realise what is expected of them. The novelty of being treated gently and lovingly as new converts soon wears off and they are expected to take on callings; they must learn to 'perform' well. In return they will be assigned to nurture other new converts. I noted as a member, how good we were at nurturing people along and 'loving' them into the Church and then almost immediately put more and more pressure on them until we drove them away again. Then we would start on a 'reactivation' process to get them back – entering the very same cycle over and over again. I used to call it a 'Mormon syndrome'. Love people back by expecting nothing of them and then drive them away by expecting everything of them. I have seen some people leave and return several times over the years through this repetitive cycle of treatment.

Men run the Church and many women and children are neglected for the sake of 'callings'. Couple this pressure with more meetings than are healthy for a family to endure and you have Mormonism in a nutshell. Happiness that is experienced is tempered with a reality which is very hard to sustain along with a job and a family. As a family, we didn't do too badly with expected family prayer morning and evening, family and personal scripture study every day, Family Home Evening each Monday, complete with a prepared lesson and activity, journal writing, family history, Sunday lesson preparation, talks to present… Still, my wife and I felt inadequate, as though we could never do enough to keep the children active in the Church, prepare our sons to go on missions, and accomplish all that was expected of us.

But then, it is only years later that many people realise and understand that they can *never* do enough, if ever they do realise it at all. A good percentage of missionaries and new members won't doubt the promise of happiness, but many converts find out pretty quickly that they have been had – and vote with their feet.

The daily missionary schedule is exhausting and all encompassing, leaving no time to think. A proper study of all the facts behind the teachings before entering the mission field will help any potential missionary reach the only real and logical conclusion about their Church and the truth, prior to devoting two years to teaching fiction to the general public, most of whom will immediately see through what it is for themselves and won't even begin to listen.

Making missionaries feel important, having specific 'power and authority' to act on behalf of the Saviour is reinforced by spaced repetition throughout the manual. It is not just mentioned once at the start so they know the Lord is with them. It is repeated many times. From page vii:

> All of the chapters in *Preach My Gospel* will help prepare you to fulfill your purpose as a missionary. However, as you begin to study chapter 3, you may sense a difference in approach. Most of the chapters are addressed to you. Chapter 3 is addressed to a more general audience. You learn the doctrines in chapter 3 (a) to strengthen your own gospel knowledge and testimony and (b) to teach others and prepare them to make and keep commitments and covenants. The doctrines in some of the other chapters may also help you teach investigators and new members. For example, chapter 4, "How Do I Recognize and Understand the Spirit?" may help you teach some investigators about how to gain a testimony by the power of the Holy Ghost. Chapter 5, "What Is the Role of the Book of Mormon?" may help you resolve an investigator's concerns about reading the Book of Mormon. Ideas from chapter 2, "How Do I Study Effectively and Prepare to Teach?" may help new converts gain more from their study of the Book of Mormon.

The concept is for the missionary to more fully determine Church claimed 'facts' and obtain a stronger 'testimony' of each aspect that he or she is to then teach investigators. Thus the missionary becomes more 'prepared' to teach with 'power and authority'. In reality, he or she becomes more 'convinced' (or deluded). Page vii also informs the missionary that:

> *Preach My Gospel* focuses on the fundamentals of missionary work. It does not answer every question or situation you will encounter.

That's very true. For example, there is absolutely no instruction whatsoever on how to deal with enquiries regarding the age old questions that always arise regarding polygamy. Many people seem to believe that Mormon men still have several wives each and the question is often raised by the uninformed.

# THE MORMON DELUSION

Unfortunately, new missionaries are equally uninformed and cannot answer such questions adequately. The recent Mormon Prophet, Gordon B. Hinckley, decided to skip over the question when he was asked about it by saying "It's behind us" but this will not satisfy an enquiring investigator who asks for details concerning the practice.

The early 'saints' would have turned over in their graves hearing President Gordon B. Hinckley asserting on national television that polygamy was restricted, limited, and that only a few practiced it. He claimed, "It is behind us" as if it were an embarrassment and something of which to be ashamed and best forgotten.

By 1882, polygamy had become such a core fundamental doctrine that was an absolute *requirement* which if not followed required local leaders to resign their positions. If it had been legal to practice polygamy in the United States then it would most certainly still be practiced today. There is no question about that. Doctrinally, it will be a requirement in the eternities for those who reach the Mormon 'Celestial kingdom'. Multiple wives are *required* in order for a man (who can become a God) to populate his own world. Monogamy will *not* be part of Celestial life. That is, despite the fact that if you ask many Mormon women about it they will say that that is fine for other women, but their own husband will only have *one* wife. They clearly do not understand the 'Law of Sarah' as explained in *D&C 132*. (See: *TMD Vol. 1:26-32*).

If that doctrine *is* part of the heaven that awaits faithful Mormons, why do missionaries *not* teach it to their investigators? The Church answer would undoubtedly be 'milk before meat'. However, they will never find any explicit details about future polygamy in current Church manuals, as they are very conspicuously absent – as far as I can ascertain. Many converts in recent years still have no idea about that doctrine. The Church generally just ignores it these days, but it won't go away. It is still fundamental core Mormon doctrine even if currently the practice is banned by law. This is how Hinckley responded:

| | |
|---|---|
| Larry King: | First tell me about the Church and polygamy. When it started it allowed it? |
| Pres. Hinckley: | **When our people came west they permitted it on a restricted scale.** |
| Larry King: | You could have a certain amount of… |
| Pres. Hinckley: | The figures I have are from - **between two percent and five percent** of our people were involved in it. It was a **very limited** practice; carefully safeguarded. **In 1890, that practice was discontinued**. The President of the Church, the man who occupied the position which I occupy today, went before the people; said he had, oh, prayed about it, worked on it, and had received from the Lord a revelation that it was time |

## PREACH MY GOSPEL

to stop, to discontinue it then. That's 118 years ago. ***It's behind us.*** *(Larry King Live. Aired 8 Sep 1998).* (Emphasis added).

Likewise, there is no mention in the missionary lesson manual of how to deal with questions on 'blood atonement' or 'Adam-God'; not that these topics will generally arise very often these days. If asked, missionaries will scarcely know what they are being asked about and can only reply that the Saviour suffered for all our sins and that the concept refers only to His atonement. They will not know any different. They will know nothing of the Adam-God doctrine which was held as correct throughout the time of several successive prophets. *(See: Appendix G for summary of Adam-God and Blood Atonement doctrines).*

If they are even aware of the concept, they will have been informed it was just a discarded theory or even a myth rather than reality. However, they would be entirely, and as ever, *provably* wrong. See *TMD Volume 3* for coverage of the reality of blood atonement in practice during the mid-late 1800s and of Adam-God being a core *doctrine* within Mormonism. Today, despite the abundant evidence, Mormon leaders *pretend* these doctrines did not even exist.

Mormon missionaries are highly disciplined in their daily endeavours.

> **Missionary Daily Schedule.**
> 6:30 a.m. Arise, pray, exercise (30 minutes), and prepare for the day.
> 7:30 a.m. Breakfast.
> 8:00 a.m. Personal study: the Book of Mormon, other scriptures, doctrines of the missionary lessons, other chapters from *Preach My Gospel,* the *Missionary Handbook,* and the *Missionary Health Guide.*
> 9:00 a.m. Companion study: share what you have learned during personal study, prepare to teach, practice teaching, study chapters from *Preach My Gospel,* confirm plans for the day.
> 10:00 a.m. Begin proselyting. Missionaries learning a language study that language for an additional 30 to 60 minutes, including planning language learning activities to use during the day. Missionaries may take an hour for lunch and additional study, and an hour for dinner at times during the day that fit best with their proselyting. Normally dinner should be finished no later than 6:00 p.m.
> 9:00 p.m. Return to living quarters (unless teaching a lesson; then return by 9:30) and plan the next day's activities (30 minutes). Write in journal, prepare for bed, pray.
> 10:30 p.m. Retire to bed. *(Page viii).*

Under the heading of 'Personal Study' missionaries are advised that they should study the 'Standard Works' and the 'approved' missionary library only.

The Standard Works comprise the *King James Bible*; the *Book of Mormon*; the *Doctrine and Covenants* and the *Pearl of Great Price*. The Approved

Missionary Library consists of just four books; *Jesus the Christ*; *Our Heritage*; *Our Search for Happiness*; and *True to the Faith*. Limiting study controls what the mind absorbs. Missionaries are encouraged to keep a 'study journal' as a source of future spiritual help.

'Information boxes' are introduced which are to assist the missionaries as they study the manual. There are five kinds of box.

**Box Type 1.** 'Consider this' boxes are provided at the start of most chapters urging missionaries to focus on key points by asking questions of themselves which are posed in the boxes. The psychology applied is very powerful and assists in keeping missionaries in a constantly deluded state.

For example, the very first page (1) of the very first chapter asks them to 'consider this':

1. What is my purpose as a missionary?
2. What is the gospel?
3. Why do we preach the gospel?
4. Why must I teach with power and authority?
5. What is the message of the Restoration? Why is it so important?
6. What is my responsibility in helping others become converted?
7. How will I know whether I am a successful missionary?

I have numbered the questions, and the reason for that will soon become apparent. Every Mormon already *knows* the 'appropriate' answers to those questions but constant self-induced brainwashing is enabled by reconsidering them over and over again. Spaced repetition does its job very effectively.

**Box Type 2.** 'Remember this' boxes usually appear at the end of each chapter, reinforcing points that have been made, carefully structured to confirm to the missionary answers to the very questions asked at the start of the chapter in the 'consider this' box. Again, for example, at the end of Chapter 1:

1. Your purpose is to invite others to come unto Christ by helping them receive…
2. …the restored gospel through faith in Jesus Christ and His Atonement, repentance, baptism, receiving the Holy Ghost, and enduring to the end.
3. The restored gospel of Jesus Christ is the only way by which we can find eternal happiness.
4. Your calling gives you authority; keeping your covenants gives you power.

5. The fulness of the gospel of Jesus Christ was restored through the Prophet Joseph Smith. The Book of Mormon is evidence that Joseph Smith was a prophet.

6. You help people live the gospel by inviting them to make and keep commitments.

You show your love for the Lord and gratitude for His Atonement by bringing souls unto Him.

7. You are successful when you are obedient, live righteously, and do your best in helping others live the gospel.

Once again, I have numbered these and I am sure the reader can now see why. Each of the seven questions asked at the beginning of the chapter is answered at the end, along with an admonition to remember them. No mention is made of the correlation and missionaries are left to discover the fact that the (supposedly correct) answers to the questions are right there at the end of the chapter. I am tempted to respond to the statement "The Book of Mormon is evidence that Joseph Smith was a prophet". In reality, it actually contains more conclusive evidence than you could ever *imagine*, that he was anything *but* a prophet; but that must wait until later.

The manual gives missionaries questions to consider, spells out the 'lesson' to them, and then reinforces it by telling them to remember points which are in fact answers to the questions first asked. The psychology is thorough and complete – and it is repeated over and over throughout the manual. Some of the 'training' compares with sales training to a large degree. A good salesman always uses his own product so he can believe in it and talk effectively about it; so do missionaries. The manual repeats the same things over and over again, constantly bombarding the missionary with ideas that must be internalised to facilitate teaching with the power and authority claimed by *Book of Mormon* characters, Alma and Amulek. For a salesman, it is important to believe in your product; for the missionary, that 'product' is Joseph Smith and the *Book of Mormon*. Belief in them must be absolute to dynamically 'testify' of them.

**Box Type 3. 'Scripture study'** boxes contain recommended scriptures which back up what is being taught, first to the missionaries and subsequently to investigators. "These boxes direct you to references that can build your understanding and testimony" explains the manual. Again, this is just applied psychology. Keep reading the source material, which is deemed 'from God', and *belief* in it will increase. It doesn't have to be true or false; like a sponge, the brain absorbs and eventually accepts *anything* that is put into it.

If one thinks positively enough about something and repeats it often enough, it will *become* true. Then the supposed 'knowledge' is reinforced by constantly telling others that one *knows* it is true, thus adding further self-input to one's own deep seated delusional state.

A person cannot possibly *know* something to be true when there is *zero* evidence, regardless of faith, and yet that is how the programming of Mormons and the missionaries works. I cannot count the times when I stood and affirmed that "I know the Church is true" when somewhere deep inside a voice was saying "Really; and how can that possibly be? Surely you mean you 'believe' it with all your heart, because you want it to be so – but *know* it is true? I don't think so." But I wanted to stand as tall as others with my testimony. If someone in the Mormon Church stands up and declares "I *believe* the Church is true", it is not only an extreme rarity, they will be considered to have a very low level of faith and still have a long way to go with their testimony.

These 'boxes' appear regularly throughout the manual. It is interesting to note that of all the scriptures recommended and used to convince missionaries and investigators alike at each stage, very few of them stem from the Bible.

Most are from Mormon so-called scripture. In terms of the many hundreds of 'scripture study' references recommended, seventy-five percent are Mormon based 'scripture' and only twenty-five percent are biblical. The rest of the 'scriptures' referenced in the manual are used for joint study or for teaching investigators. Of those, the ratio is a massive eighty-five percent Mormon based scripture with only fifteen percent being biblical. This is because Mormons pay little attention to the Bible, using it in the main only to back up their own theology when it is needful.

**Box Type 4. 'Activity'** boxes also appear regularly, suggesting joint study activities, where missionaries can enhance their teaching skills and knowledge together during joint study time. It is pretty much the same idea as the 'Scripture study' boxes but experienced jointly rather than alone. The daily missionary schedule included above *(page 23)* allows for two hours study time. The first hour is for personal study and the second hour for joint study. The 'Activity' boxes give missionaries something to do during the second hour. Everything they do and experience is designed to keep them 'close to the spirit'. This means giving them no time to think or reason; just study and do. Their days are filled from the moment they wake up until the moment they fall asleep.

**Box Type 5. 'Red boxes'** are scattered throughout the manual and "have important information and suggestions for many teaching and proselyting situations". Most are to do with information regarding what is expected of investigators prior to their baptism and questions to ask them along the way, to ensure they fully understand and accept each Mormon doctrine and teaching. For example, on page 32 of the manual a 'red box' suggests reading from *Alma 18:24-40* and *22:4-23*, then asking investigators: "What did these missionaries teach about the *nature of God*?" *(See Ch.4, pp.66-68 for further discussion).*

# PREACH MY GOSPEL

I find this an incredulous choice of Mormon 'scripture' to use. The Church today teaches that God and Jesus are two separate and distinct personages who each have bodies of flesh and bone. They claim Joseph Smith saw God and Jesus *with bodies* in an early 1820 vision. We will return in a later chapter to the fact that Smith himself said no such thing. But it is impossible to derive that idea from the *Book of Mormon* no matter what passage is chosen. In fact, the one and *only* place that concept is ever mentioned *anywhere* in supposed scripture is *D&C 130:22* which Smith wrote on 2 April 1843. *Nothing* he wrote prior to that date confirmed a *physical* God. Even then, it does not say "Thus saith the Lord"; it is buried at the end of some "items of instruction given by Joseph Smith". I will be reviewing the sequence of Smith's evolving theology further in the proper sequence of the manual. *(See Chapter 5).*

Meanwhile, the question remains, prior to Joseph Smith's 1843 declaration in *D&C 130:22* that "The Father has a body of flesh and bones as tangible as man's; the Son also;" – when did God *ever* declare that He was anything other than an omnipresent *spirit*? The answer to that question is *never*. Not once in six-thousand years had God ever declared any such thing.

In one single phrase, taken from one single sentence at the end of some "items of instruction", Joseph Smith would have us believe that he captured the very essence of the character of God in a manner that God Himself had been entirely incapable of conveying during the previous six-thousand years.

God had previously declared *explicitly* that He is a spirit, even in Smith's *Book of Mormon. (See below).* Not *once* does God mention he has a body in the *Old Testament*; not once in the *New Testament*; not in the *Book of Mormon*; not in any earlier *D&C* revelations; not in the *Book of Moses* or the rest of Smith's *Inspired Revision* of the Bible or in the *Book of Abraham*; not *anywhere* did God *ever* previously declare Himself to have a body – until Smith's late change in theology which then completely contradicted *everything* he (and everyone else) had previously written.

When Smith wrote the *Book of Mormon*, he was still entirely monotheistic in his outlook. He believed God was an omnipresent spirit and that Jesus *was* God manifest in the flesh, just as most Christians believe. The *Lectures of Faith* in particular affirmed that concept and the lectures were later canonised as the 'Doctrine' part of the *Doctrine and Covenants* in 1835. Some years later, Smith changed his theology and then altered some *Book of Mormon* passages to accommodate his changed thinking, separating God from Jesus *(See Ch. 5. pp. 97-99)* but he still did *not* indicate that God had a body and he did *not* change the book of Alma in the *Book of Mormon*. Throughout the story, God does *not* have a body, Lamoni is *not* corrected and God is determined as a being a *spirit*.

That does not fit with modern Mormon theology at all and yet it is used in the missionary lesson manual.

# THE MORMON DELUSION

From the suggested verses, the ones that speak of God read as follows.

> **Alma 18:26.** And then Ammon said: ***Believest thou that there is a Great Spirit?***
> 27. And he said, Yea.
> 28. And Ammon said: ***This is God.*** And Ammon said unto him again: Believest thou that ***this Great Spirit, who is God,*** created all things which are in heaven and in the earth?

> **Alma 22:8.** And now when Aaron heard this, his heart began to rejoice, and he said: Behold, assuredly as thou livest, ***O king, there is a God.***
> 9. And the king said: ***Is God that Great Spirit*** that brought our fathers out of the land of Jerusalem?
> 10. And Aaron said unto him: ***Yea, he is that Great Spirit***, and he created all things both in heaven and in earth. Believest thou this?
> 11. And he said: Yea, I believe that ***the Great Spirit*** created all things, and I desire that ye should tell me concerning all these things, and I will believe thy words. (Emphasis added).

So, if the Mormon missionaries have their heads screwed on properly, when reviewing the 'red box' question "What did these missionaries teach about the *nature of God*?" they *should* conclude that they taught He was a personage of *spirit* with no body mentioned whatsoever. It is beyond me how the Church expects missionaries to conclude that God has a body from that (or any other) *Book of Mormon* passage. Not *once* was Lamoni corrected regarding his perception that God is a spirit. It is the same story elsewhere in the *Book of Mormon*. God has *no* body. We will review this more thoroughly later on. *(See Ch. 4. pp.65-72).*

# Chapter 2

## Programming the missionaries continues…

### Preach My Gospel – Chapter 1

### My Purpose as a Missionary

As already mentioned, in the manual, missionaries are taught to 'take control' and their 'power and authority' to do so is mentioned regularly. Having already mentioned it several times before even getting to Chapter 1 it then immediately features on page 1. It appears again on page 2. A whole section includes the concept on page 4 in which it is mentioned twice more. It appears again on page 8 but even then that is not the last of it. The 'power and authority' of missionaries is repeated at least ten separate times. Teaching with spiritual 'power' is mentioned well over two dozen times in addition to many instances where the 'power of the Holy Ghost' or the 'power of the spirit' will help them. 'Priesthood authority' is referred to dozens of times in one context or another, solidifying the missionaries' perception that they have and can use such power and authority. Spaced repetition is carefully used to firmly instil in the minds of missionaries the concept that they represent Jesus Christ and have his power and his authority to teach the gospel.

Missionaries are to call people to repentance; even the ones already living a good 'Christian' life. *Everyone* is a sinner or there would be no need for God. Create sinners and then they need a God to forgive them. In order to create sinners, you first have to create sins. Every religion is good at determining what God considers to be sinful. Mormonism provides a raft of things that are deemed sinful. No one can escape feeling guilty or that they constantly need to repent. Making even some *thoughts* a sin ensures control over people who are drawn to believe in the idea.

There is quite naturally a concept of 'right and wrong' in people's minds and different societies make their own rules and laws regarding what that entails for them. In different parts of the world it can mean different things – sometimes even *opposite* views prevail regarding what is 'right'. Society also evolves; points of view are constantly subject to *change*. Public opinion plus scientific knowledge and understanding develop with intelligent consideration.

For example – once upon a time, women were essentially considered secondary to men (only by men I might add) and now they are treated more readily as equals, although not in all societies. Even in the supposedly most advanced cultures, women still do not feature as prominently as men and it is taking time for the evolution towards real equality to complete itself. Once, women were not allowed (again by men) to vote or to hold political office. In recent years, Margaret Thatcher was Prime Minister of Great Britain and there are now many female politicians. Years ago, women would never have been considered suitable as Christian ministers within *any* denomination and yet (although notably, not yet within Mormonism) they now quite rightly hold prominent positions in many different religious settings.

Likewise, people of African descent were treated as sub-human and used as slaves for thousands of years. In retrospect, as modern thinkers, we recognise how wrong this was, yet it was the custom and practice for thousands of years. When Joseph Smith started his Church, slavery was still commonly accepted and thus the so-called 'Negro and the priesthood' doctrine came into being and they could not hold the priesthood. It was *God's* decision and God revealed His theological reasoning through Smith. In 1978, God was obliged to change His mind, due to the tide of popular public opinion having turned violently in favour of equality for all people. Racism was becoming a major stumbling block for the Church, just as polygamy had previously; and once again God had to cave to popular opinion and change yet another fundamental *doctrine*. Prior to that, Mormon doctrine stated explicitly that *no one* of African descent could or would *ever* be given the priesthood until *after all* the sons of Abel had received the opportunity – and that meant not until the *millennium*. Every Mormon knew and accepted that.

In the nineteenth century, Mormonism declared that God dictated a black man could not be involved in Church leadership *or* politics. They, like women, were certainly not allowed to vote, let alone be considered for the office of President of the United States as we see today. It was *unthinkable*. Times change and therefore God is also obliged to – particularly the Mormon version. Yet God is supposed to be the same yesterday, today and forever. In Mormon terms He is constantly changing – both His mind *and* His opinion.

# PROGRAMMING THE MISSIONARIES CONTINUES

To the non-believer, there is no such thing as *sin*. Sin is as much a man made concept as is a God who doesn't like it when we don't do what He wants us to do; or rather, when someone else *tells* us what He supposedly wants us to do. Likewise, a devil is there to 'tempt' us only when people believe it. It is only when one believes in God that Satan and sin are also considered to exist.

God's wishes vary from religion to religion and also *change* from era to era as our understanding evolves. What God once expected of people thousands of years ago would not go down very well today, but in every case, in religion – especially Mormonism, natural acts and choices are transformed into sins because they say it is so. This causes many to feel inferior, never able to live up to what they could and should be. The concept of sin requires belief in a God. Non-believers think there isn't much wrong with most people and if religions (and their Gods) left people alone, they would fare far better than they do by being made to constantly feel they are not 'worthy' of the respect of their God.

Original sin was never biblical *(O.T.)* in the first place. Mentioned almost in passing by Paul, in *Romans 5:12*, the whole concept of original sin and sin *entering* the world was the late invention of St. Augustine in the fourth century CE. How did 'sin' get into the world? Augustine 'decided' that sex and death came via Eve. He was working with a Latin mistranslation of Paul's Epistle to the Romans and understood Paul to say that Adam's sin was hereditary. The Mormon Church at least somewhat gets away from this, declaring that "man will be punished for his own sins and not Adam's transgression" but retains the concept that everyone is a 'sinner'. Religion *defines* sin and then *makes* sinners of us. That means *control.* Take away the *concept* of sin and you lose control.

Much of *Genesis* as we now read it stems from no earlier than 600 BCE. It was written when the Jews were in exile. The *concepts* stem from even earlier mythologies emanating from a variety of cultures. We tend to forget that the *Old Testament* is Jewish Scripture hijacked by Christians and made to fit new Christian theology that was invented many years after Jesus supposedly lived.

The Jews never did and still do not believe in the devil – or heaven or hell in the Christian sense for that matter. Judaism is an entirely different concept to Christianity in every way. Do not confuse the Jewish 'HaSaTan' with the devil. That character sits on God's council as an adversary working on behalf of God – and he is *not* evil.

People who believe that sin is a man made concept, inserted into religion to control people, also find the need for God disappears, in which case Satan also becomes obsolete. To such people, no God, no Satan and no sin, leaves them free to choose what society alone decides is right and wrong, legal and illegal, moral and immoral. Conscience works very well without the need for God or religion. If you have faith to believe in a God, at least try to believe in one who doesn't think almost everything is sin, so you can live happily. Some religions appear quite sensible and very liberal, allowing for a fairly 'guilt free' ride.

Back to the indoctrination of Mormon missionaries:

> Repent, all ye ends of the earth, and come unto me and be baptized in my name, that ye may be sanctified by the reception of the Holy Ghost" (3 Nephi 27:20). *(Manual cover).*

> To preach my gospel by the Spirit, even the Comforter which was sent forth to teach the truth. (D&C 50:14). *(Manual cover reference).*

> Invite others to come unto Christ by helping them receive the restored gospel through faith in Jesus Christ and His Atonement, repentance, baptism, receiving the gift of the Holy Ghost, and enduring to the end. *(Page 1).*

Missionaries are instructed regarding the people they meet every day:

> They want "peace in this world, and eternal life in the world to come" (D&C 59:23), but they are "kept from the truth because they know not where to find it" (D&C 123:12). *(Page 1).*

The concept taught to Mormon missionaries is that people *want* eternal life but they don't know where to find it. Mormonism has the answer. Note that the 'scriptures' used are exclusively from the *Doctrine and Covenants* created by Joseph Smith, and purportedly revealed by the Lord. *D&C 59* is claimed as revelation and *Section 123* is part of a letter *(D&C 121-123)*, supposedly including some revelations, from Smith to the saints while he was in Liberty Jail awaiting trial in March 1839, following 'The Mormon War' of 1838.

> **D&C 59:23.** ...he who doeth the works of righteousness shall receive his reward, even peace in this world, and eternal life in the world to come.

> **D&C 123:12.** For there are many yet on the earth among all sects, parties, and denominations, who are blinded by the *subtle craftiness of men*, whereby they lie in wait to deceive, and who are only kept from the truth because they know not where to find it— (Emphasis added).

The irony is that there never was a man more 'subtle' or 'crafty' than Joseph Smith, as revealed in *TMD Vols 1-3*. A few lines before this 'missionary encouraging' verse, Smith is bemoaning his lot and wants revenge against his oppressors. Verses four and five see Smith wanting a committee to get the names and details of those whom he wants chased down, driven out or killed.

# PROGRAMMING THE MISSIONARIES CONTINUES

> ...perhaps a committee can be appointed to find out these things ... and present the whole concatenation of diabolical rascality and nefarious and murderous impositions that have been practised upon this people—

Smith uses a list of long words to describe claimed unwarranted atrocities against the Mormons. But he, and also the Church today, fails to admit to all the Mormon looting, burning and murders. Apologists concentrate instead on aspects such as the 'Haun's Mill' murders which constituted an expected and avoidable reprisal to earlier Mormon looting, burning and murders. Those who were killed at Haun's Mill had actually been advised by Church leaders to leave the mill long before the attack happened. However, all that is yet another story for yet another day.

The manual encourages missionaries that:

> The gospel of Jesus Christ as restored through the Prophet Joseph Smith will bless their families, meet their spiritual needs, and help them fulfill their deepest desires. Although they may not know why, ***they need relief from feelings of guilt*** that come ***from mistakes and sins.*** They need to experience the joy of redemption by ***receiving forgiveness of their sins*** and enjoying the gift of the Holy Ghost. (Emphasis added). *(pp. 1-2)*.

As mentioned previously, in the manual, missionaries are repeatedly told "You can teach people with power and authority". The concept described above is that people may not know why, but they need relief of *guilt* which is created by *sin* and they must obtain *forgiveness* from God.

Whilst this may very well be the case for those who already believe in God, the thing is that prior to Mormon missionaries introducing the idea to them, some people who had not believed in God previously, may not have considered themselves 'sinful' at all. They may have experienced no guilt whatsoever relating to things only considered sin within religion, and may not have felt any need whatsoever to 'repent' of anything or to seek forgiveness from anyone. They may have been perfectly happy just as they were. The *concepts* of God and sin are first *created* in the minds of such investigators, and then the Mormon *solution* can be proffered.

It is at this point that if investigators fall for the con, they may end up becoming Mormons. Even for believers, much more sin is created in the mind, and then it *becomes* a burden which previously it may not have been, for which suddenly, they must 'repent' and obtain 'forgiveness' from the Mormon God. Sin is *created* in a new believer's mind and *added to* in a believer's mind. It is the sale of the century. First create *guilt* and then offer the solution.

# THE MORMON DELUSION

Next the missionaries are reminded that:

> "...redemption cometh in and through the Holy Messiah," and that no one "can dwell in the presence of God, save it be through the merits, and mercy, and grace of the Holy Messiah" *(Page 2)*.

But this concept is not taken from the Bible. It is once again taken from Mormon so-called scripture; this time, the *Book of Mormon*. Written in 1828-9 and published in 1830 by Joseph Smith, he pretended it was a real history of Native Americans who traversed the ocean from Israel to America hundreds of years BCE. The above quote is taken from *2 Nephi 2:6, 8*.

The message to the missionary is that he must study and pray for hours each day in order to bring himself to a point where he is filled with a desire to teach the gospel to others. Constant self-induced brainwashing creates the perfect ambassador. The psychology is powerful. However, the 'message' is not.

> As your understanding of the Atonement of Jesus Christ grows, your desire to share the gospel will increase. You will feel, as Lehi did, the "great . . . importance to make these things known unto the inhabitants of the earth" (2 Nephi 2:8). *(Page 2)*.

So, psyched up to teach what they learn, missionaries stop people in the street and knock on doors, unsolicited, and try to engage people in conversation that, once in thousands of attempts, may result in a conversion.

The concept that "only the gospel will save the world" and that "only the gospel will bring joy, happiness, and salvation…" is provided for missionaries from a more recent Mormon Prophet.

> President Ezra Taft Benson taught: "We are commanded by God to take this gospel to all the world. That is the cause that must unite us today. Only the gospel will save the world from the calamity of its own self-destruction. Only **the gospel will unite men of all races** and nationalities in peace. **Only the gospel will bring joy, happiness, and salvation to the human family**" (*The Teachings of Ezra Taft Benson* [1988], 167). (Emphasis added).

Only the Mormon version of the gospel will save the world. It wasn't that long ago that at least one race was not permitted to hold the priesthood or participate in Mormon temple rites. An early Mormon doctrine declared that those of 'negro' ancestry would only gain entrance into the Celestial kingdom as *servants* or *slaves* and would not be 'saved' until the millennium. To intermarry meant "death on the spot" according to Brigham Young, who added "This will always be so". A *prophet* declares eternal *truth*. Now, *everyone* can be saved. In the eyes of Mormons, God is 'marvellous' for capitulating.

# PROGRAMMING THE MISSIONARIES CONTINUES

> Shall I tell you the law of God in regard to the African race? If the white man who belongs to the chosen seed mixes his blood with the seed of Cain, **the penalty, under the law of God**, is **death on the spot. This will always be so.** *(Brigham Young. JD. V. 10:110. The Tabernacle. 8 Mar 1863).* (Emphasis added).

Although the overall concept appears to be that people can only be saved through Christ, so far, there has been no mention of him or of accepted biblical scripture at all. Everything discussed is of Mormon origin. Thus far, it is to convince the missionary that he is engaged in the Lord's work rather than to teach others of Christ.

The manual includes a picture representing the 'Tree of Life' story. This is a well known dream supposedly experienced by Lehi and later by his son, Nephi, around 600 BCE.

Missionaries are advised to:

> Examine the picture of the tree of life on this page as you study the vision of the tree of life found in 1 Nephi 8 and 11. In this vision, the tree of life symbolizes the love of God (see 1 Nephi 11:21–22). *(Page 2).*

Then the missionaries are asked:

> What did Lehi desire after he had eaten the fruit? (See 1 Nephi 8:10–18.)
>
> In the vision, what did the people need to do to be able to partake of the fruit? What do we need to do to receive all the blessings of the Atonement? In what ways do commitments and covenants help us partake of these blessings?
>
> As a missionary, what is your duty in helping others find and partake of the fruits of the gospel? *(Page 2).*

In simple terms, the Church is applying the psychology that Lehi's dream holds the key the missionaries need to explain to investigators how and why they should come to find the true path to earthly happiness and then eternal life.

There is only one problem with the whole idea. It is provably a fairy-tale and the dream was not one sent from God to Lehi who was just a fictional character in an equally fictional book.

As space is too limited to include the whole saga here – and the reader can review the entire story online at http://scriptures.lds.org/ – evidence of the true origin of Lehi's dream can best be evaluated by a summary analysis of the content. In the *Book of Mormon, 1 Nephi, Chapter 8*, the following sequence encapsulates the detail we require. Nephi declares that his father had a dream or a vision, around 600 BCE. These are the point by point details that Joseph Smith claims Nephi recorded concerning what Lehi apparently saw in his dream:

> A dark and dreary wilderness.
> A man in a white robe stands before Lehi and asks Lehi to follow him.
> Lehi follows the man and finds himself in a "dark and dreary waste".
> Travelling many hours in darkness, Lehi prays to the Lord for mercy.
> Having prayed, Lehi sees a large and spacious field.
> He sees a tree, the fruit of which will make people happy.
> He eats the fruit, which is pure white; it is sweet and makes him happy.
> He is full of joy.
> He wants his family to taste the fruit as it is so desirable.
> Looking around for his family, Lehi sees a river of water near the tree.
> He sees his wife Sariah and sons Sam and Nephi.
> They do not know where to go.
> Lehi calls to them, beckons them to him to eat the fruit. This they do.
> He looks for and sees his sons, Laman and Lemuel.
> They will not go and eat the fruit.
> A rod of iron extends along the bank of the river, and leads to the tree.
> A strait, narrow path, runs by the rod of iron, to the tree.
> It also runs, at the head of the "fountain" to a spacious field.
> It is as if the field was a "world".
> Numerous people are there, many trying to get on the path to the tree.
> Some people get on the path but then lose their way.
> They get lost in a mist of darkness.
> More people get on the path and hold on to the rod of iron.
> They get to the tree and eat.
> After eating they are ashamed.
> Across the river is a "great and spacious building" high in the air.
> The building is full of people.
> The people, in fine clothes, are mocking those who have eaten the fruit.
> Due to the mocking, those who ate, fall away, lost in "forbidden paths".
> More people come, holding to the rod of iron.
> They arrive, fall down and eat the fruit.
> Others "feel" their way to the great and spacious building.
> Many drown in the river or are lost, wandering in strange roads.

In *1 Nephi 11*, Nephi explains the meaning of his father Lehi's dream. During the explanation, he also sees the "Son of God" preaching among men and many of them worshiping him. He sees the "Redeemer" and the prophet who will come before the "Lamb of God" who is baptised of him. He sees the "Holy Ghost" come down in the form of a dove after his baptism. He sees him preaching and sees the "twelve apostles of the Lamb." He sees him performing

## PROGRAMMING THE MISSIONARIES CONTINUES

all sorts of healings and miracles in addition to being taken, judged and crucified "for the sins of the world". All this, again remember, is around 600 BCE, when none of the above events had happened nor were such descriptions invented to recount them. From *1 Nephi 11* plus other locations shown below, Smith provides Nephi's interpretation of Lehi's dream:

> The tree of life and fountain of living waters represent the love of God.
> The rod of iron is the word of God.
> The building is the pride and wisdom of the world.
> Those in the building are the people of the earth.
> An awful gulf divides wicked from the Tree of Life and saints of God. *(1 Nephi 15:28)*.
> In Nephi's vision, the building fell and "great was the fall thereof."
> The river of water is filthiness. *(1 Nephi 15:27)*.
> The fruit is greatest of all gifts, taken to be eternal life. *(1 Nephi 15:36 & D&C 14:7)*.
> The mists of darkness are the temptations of the devil. *(1 Nephi 12:17)*.

Here we have a quite clever vision idea, together with a convincing and plausible interpretation. Mormon missionaries thus know they are responsible for leading people to the tree of life which is the love of God by providing them a rod of iron to hold to by teaching them the true gospel. If such a character as Lehi really lived and experienced this around 600 BCE, and if Nephi was also real and obtained the interpretation and recorded it as written, including details of the Saviour, centuries before he was born – it is one of the most profound records of divine revelation and particularly of prophecy and its subsequent fulfilment, in all recorded history. There is nothing like it anywhere in the Bible that includes such detailed and accurate prophecy of the Saviour.

However, it is *so* good, the expression 'too good to be true' immediately springs to mind. Was it *recorded* 600 years BCE or *invented* in 1828-9? Is there reliable evidence that Smith may have plagiarised the idea of Lehi's dream in some way and then included details that everyone now knows about the Saviour to make it all sound convincing? Writing prophecy in 1828-9 and backdating it to 600 BCE and having it fulfilled two-thousand years ago is not exactly a difficult task. I can 'prophesy' last week's lottery numbers today and pretend someone wrote them down last month. What Smith really did regarding plagiarism in his writing is usually quite easily discovered once we look for the evidence – and this is no exception. Lehi's dream was anything *but* original.

As it happens, Smith's own mother, Lucy, had a dream with several similar details which she recorded. However, that dwindles into insignificance when we consider dreams that Smith's father had and which Lucy also recorded. Smith likely heard these dreams recounted many times from his youngest years. Smith's father's first recorded dream has some similarities but it is his second dream which was dutifully recorded by Lucy that is summarised below.

> Smith Sr. dreamed he was again travelling in an open barren field.
> He stopped and thought he should reflect on what he was doing before going further.
> The same guide that was with him before, says it is the desolate world and to travel on.
> The road is broad and barren so he thinks to himself:
> "Broad is the road, and wide is the gate that leads to death, and many there be that walk therein; but narrow is the way, and straight is the gate that leads to everlasting life, and few there be that go in thereat."
> Travelling a short distance on, he comes to a narrow path.
> Walking along the narrow path he sees a beautiful stream.
> The stream runs east to west.
> There is a rope running along the bank.
> The rope is placed such that one would have to reach up to grasp it.
> He could not see the beginning or the end of the stream or the rope.
> Beyond him is a low, pleasant valley in which stands a beautiful tree.
> The tree bore fruit, like a chestnut bur, white as snow or even whiter.
> The burs open, revealing dazzling white fruit. He eats; it is delicious.
> He feels he must bring his wife and children to eat the fruit.
> He goes to get them.
> He, his wife and seven children eat and praise God for this blessing.
> They are exceedingly happy, such that their joy cannot be expressed.
> He sees, opposite the valley, a spacious building which reaches the sky.
> It is full of doors and windows, with people who are finely dressed.
> The people see him and his family, point their fingers and scorn them.
> Asks guide the meaning of the fruit and is told it is pure love of God.
> He is told to bring the rest of his children. Explains he has no more.
> He is told to look, as he has two more.
> He looks and sees two more small children.
> He goes to them, brings them to the tree and they eat the fruit.
> They all rejoice together.
> The more they eat, the more they want.
> They get on their knees, eating by double handfuls.
> He asks the guide the meaning of the spacious building.
> He is told that it is Babylon and it must fall.
> People in it are inhabitants who scorn and despise the Saints of God.
> Then he soon awoke, clapping his hands together with joy.
> *(Smith, Lucy, 1853:58-59; Anderson. L, 2001:296-298).*

This account is *entirely* Lehi's dream. Apart from making the rope into a rod and the stream filthy instead of clean, this is the same story in almost *every* detail. Joseph Smith Jr's fertile imagination needed very little stretching on this occasion; he simply recounted his own father's dream as if it were Lehi's.

# PROGRAMMING THE MISSIONARIES CONTINUES

Mormon missionaries, unless they are of a mind to research, which few ever do, would have no idea that not just the basis, but in effect, the very same story Smith attributes to Lehi 600 years BCE, was nothing more than a plagiarised dream his own father likely related to him many times as a child. *(See: TMD. Vol.2, Ch.13 for an expanded and more detailed discussion of this area).*

Armed with the concept that they are to save people, the missionaries move on in their manual to learn:

> The message of the Restoration of the gospel of Jesus Christ blesses families.
>
> The divine plan of happiness enables family relationships to be perpetuated beyond the grave. Sacred ordinances and covenants available in holy temples make it possible for individuals to return to the presence of God and for families to be united eternally. (The Family: A Proclamation to the World, Ensign, Nov. 1995, 102). *(Page 3).*

Mormon missionaries are 'programmed' with all the information they are expected to relay to their 'investigators'. Someone becomes an investigator the moment they accept an offer from the missionaries to enter their home and share a message with them. After expounding on the 'Tree of Life' story, the missionary manual makes this statement:

> Satan is attacking the family on many fronts, and too many families are being destroyed by his efforts. *(Page 3).*

Missionaries accept this core Mormon concept, along with the idea that being baptised into the Mormon Church and receiving the Holy Ghost, which is only available on an ongoing basis to Mormons, is the only real way to overcome Satan's power.

The big problem with this concept goes way beyond Mormonism but it is first worth mentioning the fact that Mormons really believe that only they have the Holy Ghost as a constant companion. Other people may feel his influence long enough to confirm the Mormon Church is the one true Church, but other than that, everyone outside Mormonism apparently only has access to the 'Spirit of Christ' which is an entirely different concept within Mormonism.

Introducing Satan and his influence, accompanied by the concept that people can be 'saved' in Mormonism, is designed to help people feel they may need to investigate Mormonism further. However, what missionaries generally do not know and most 'investigators' have never learned is that Satan does not exist. He is a mythological being who was created in the fourth century by Augustine, who also invented the concept of the 'fall' and the mainstream

Christian concept of 'original sin'. The controlling influences of fear and guilt introduced by these concepts have manacled believers ever since.

Christians in general just do not realise that the Old Testament or Tanakh do not include such a character as Satan. As previously mentioned, the Jews never did and still do not believe in such a creature and references to 'HaSaTan' in the Bible refer to an adversarial being who sits on God's council and who cannot act without God's permission. He is *not* evil. Likewise, 'Lucifer' is misinterpreted in the Old Testament by Mormons and also by many other Christians who do not understand the meaning, nor the fact that Christ effectively referred to *himself* as 'Lucifer' in the New Testament.

The Hebrew text in Isaiah was translated to the Latin word 'Lucifer' which actually meant Venus as a morning star. Isaiah was using this metaphor for a bright light, referring to the power of the Babylonian king which had faded. It was never anything other than that. It is now a serious problem for the Mormon Church which refers to 'Lucifer' as a *character*, particularly in the temple endowment ceremony. Some Mormon writers have tried to accommodate the error by claiming the text may have had a double meaning but it could not have done as the very concept of the *character* 'Lucifer' is non-Jewish.

This may seem a digression but it is an important historical point, as when investigators become members and ultimately attend the endowment in a Mormon temple, they will encounter a being (Satan) who is always referred to as 'Lucifer' because of the ongoing misperception.

Smith, and subsequently his Church, fell foul of the same inaccuracies that many other Christian denominations have been deceived by in the past. The Old Testament (as non-Jews call it) has been hijacked from the Jews by the Christian community at large. The Tanakh, which is in part a little different to what is now the Old Testament, is *Hebrew* scripture and in reality has little to do with Christianity. The Jews never have believed and still do not believe in Satan – period. The Tanakh includes no mention of such a creature, despite what Christians (and especially Mormons) now *claim* to be the case.

Mormons freely use the name of 'Lucifer' to describe Satan, particularly in their temples where he appears as a real character in role play regarding the Garden of Eden. 'Lucifer' is a biblical *(O.T.)* anachronism. The term 'Lucifer' appeared three times in some early biblical texts and all referred to the same thing – and it was *not* a character otherwise known as Satan. The word now appears once and *only* once, in the entire Bible *(KJV)*. The reference is *Isaiah 14:12*.

> **Isaiah 14:12.** How art thou fallen from heaven, O Lucifer, son of the morning! How art thou cut down to the ground, which didst weaken the nations!

# PROGRAMMING THE MISSIONARIES CONTINUES

It appears that early Christian scribes first deliberately created in the third century, and then perpetuated, the myth of 'Lucifer' through the interpolation of the word Lucifer to represent Satan or the Devil, in Jerome's Vulgate in the fifth century. It was not the use of the *word* that was wrong; rather, it was the associated teaching that it was a *name* for Satan instead of the metaphoric description of the Babylonian king to whom the original Hebrew phrase "heleyl ben shachar" (which literally means 'shining one, son of the dawn') referred. This could be reasonably translated into Latin as 'lucifer' which really should be looked at more closely by the Mormon Church and admitted as a major error. As the *Old Testament* was written by Jews who do not and never did believe in the much later Christian concept of the Devil, it is therefore completely *impossible* that this verse referred to a 'personage' that Christians, and in particular Mormons, now term 'Satan'.

Did the word Lucifer always exist? No, it most certainly did not. In the Hebrew language, the word Lucifer is derived from the Hebrew word לליה (Hêlēl). The term 'Lucifer' did not exist in biblical times. Lucifer is a Latin word. (L. lux, lucis = light/fire; Ferre = to bear/to bring). The Old Testament was written primarily in Hebrew, so the word Lucifer could *not* have been in their language.

In CE 382, Pope Damasus I, commissioned St. Jerome to write a revision of the Latin translation of the Bible. This task was completed sometime during the 5th century CE, and eventually it was considered the official and definitive Latin version of the Bible according to the Roman Catholic Church. By the 13th century it was considered the *versio vulgate* – the common translation.

It was St. Jerome who placed the word Lucifer into the Bible, and not just once as we now see it in the King James Version, but three times. *Isaiah 14:12*; *Job 11:17* and *2 Peter 1:19*. This is how they appear in the *Vulgate* translation:

> **Isaiah 14:12.** Et habemus firmiorem propheticum sermonem : cui benefacitis attendentes quasi lucernæ lucenti in caliginoso donec dies elucescat, et **lucifer** oriatur in cordibus vestries

> **Job 11:17.** Et quasi meridianus fulgor consurget tibi ad vesperam; et cum te consumptum putaveris, orieris ut **lucifer**.

> **2 Peter 1:19.** Et habemus firmiorem propheticum sermonem : cui benefacitis attendentes quasi lucernæ lucenti in caliginoso donec dies elucescat, et (**lucifer**) oriatur in cordibus vestries

This is how these verses now read in the *King James Version*:

> **Isaiah 14:12.** How art thou fallen from heaven, O **Lucifer**, son of the morning! how art thou cut down to the ground, which didst weaken the nations!

> **Job 11:17.** And thine age shall be clearer than the noonday: thou shalt **shine forth**, thou shalt be as the **morning**.
>
> **2 Peter 1:19.** We have also a more sure word of prophecy; whereunto ye do well that ye take heed, as unto a light that shineth in a dark place, until the day dawn, and the **day star** arise in your hearts:

The *New International Version* translates the same scriptures thus:

> **Isaiah 14:12.** How you have fallen from heaven, O **morning star**, son of the dawn! You have been cast down to the earth, you who once laid low the nations!
>
> **Job 11:17.** Life will be brighter than noonday, and darkness will become like **morning**.
>
> **2 Peter 1:19.** And we have the word of the prophets made more certain, and you will do well to pay attention to it, as to a light shining in a dark place, until the day dawns and the **morning star** rises in your hearts. (Bold added in the above nine references).

Note that the term 'morning star' is used throughout the New Testament and is in reference to Jesus the Christ. In the Vulgate, *2 Peter 1:19*, Lucifer (correctly in the true original context) *is* Jesus Christ. I think that should be enough information for anyone to understand the truth behind the 'Satan' and 'Lucifer' misconceptions. *(See: TMD Vol 2. Ch. 16 for more details).*

Whilst Mormons have developed a concept that 'man will be punished for his own sins and not for Adam's transgression', they still accept the idea of a 'fall' and need for 'redemption' through the 'atonement' of Christ.

They add to that the idea of the early Common Era Church falling into apostasy and the need for a full restoration of the original Gospel – enter Joseph Smith and his clever con – a prophet of the new age, circa 1820.

The manual proclaims:

> Happiness in family life is most likely to be achieved when founded upon the teachings of the Lord Jesus Christ. Successful marriages and families are established and maintained on principles of faith, prayer, repentance, forgiveness, respect, love, compassion, work, and wholesome recreational activities. *(Page 3).*

# PROGRAMMING THE MISSIONARIES CONTINUES

Missionaries are instructed:

> ...to find and teach families—a father, mother, and children—who can support one another in living the gospel and eventually be sealed as a family unit by restored priesthood authority. *(Page 3).*

This is the priority, rather than find and teach singles or couples living together outside of marriage, and of course they are to particularly *avoid* gays. Heterosexual couples living together as partners, who are not married, are not to be baptised any more than are practicing gays. Only celibate single people and faithful married couples can be baptised into the Mormon Church.

The following statistics indicate a growing problem for the Mormon Church regarding who can actually join it. The majority of Americans simply don't qualify – unless they are willing to change.

> Since 2005, the majority of US households have not been headed by married couples. The number of non-married-couple households continues to grow. (ACS 2005-2007).
>
> There are more than 51 million households headed by unmarried Americans, representing roughly 44% of all households and the majority of households in 23 states, plus the District of Columbia. (CPS 2007).
>
> There are more than 31 million one-person households in the U.S., representing roughly 27% of all households. (CPS 2007).
>
> The number of cohabiting unmarried partners increased by 88% between 1990 and 2007. (CPS 2007).
>
> The majority of couples marrying today cohabited first. (Larry Bumpass and Hsien-Hen Lu, 2000).
>
> 39.7% of all births are to unmarried women (CDC 2007).
>
> Nearly 40% of opposite-sex, unmarried American households include children. (CPS 2007).
>
> In a 1995 Harris poll, 90% of people believed society "should value all types of families". (Stephanie Coontz, 1997).
>
> 55% of Americans approve of men and women living together without being married. (Gallup, 2007).
>
> The majority of Americans aged 18-64 consider living in unmarried households as having either no effect or a positive effect on children. (Gallup, 2008).

# THE MORMON DELUSION

> Only one-quarter of American households consist of what most people think of as a "traditional family," i.e. a married couple and their children. (National Opinion Research Center (University of Chicago), 1999).
>
> *(Above statistics collated by 'Alternatives to Marriage Project' at:* http://www.unmarried.org/).

Thus the Mormon Church is aiming at just a quarter of, at least American, society in real terms. Many cohabiting couples have been faced with a demand they marry or separate before joining the Mormon Church. In my experience, a few do but most just don't bother to join the Church and then the problem goes away. Mormonism creates a strict set of requirements which may well once have been considered noble and 'proper' but in terms of modern society are more and more considered to be unduly restrictive and seriously outdated.

The world moves on but Mormonism is very slow to follow.

God *requires* marriage. Good or bad, 'marriage' is still a man made idea and has absolutely nothing to do with any God whatsoever. The fact that God is considered real and that marriage has become the norm in 'society', at least as a *legal* definition, and therefore acceptable norm in religion, has been extended by various religions to the view that marriage was 'ordained' of God. In point of fact, marriage, or early tribal 'pairing', predates recorded human history and of course pairing is also evident in some other classes of animals that remain essentially monogamous. Concepts of 'gods' then 'one God' came much *later.*

Human 'marriage' was certainly around long before the Jewish or Christian God came on the scene. It was therefore hardly 'ordained' of Him. It is simply part of human culture which is accepted in Christianity and therefore their God approves, endorses, even requires, or ordains it. It is yet another controlling influence a church can be involved with. To believe marriage was 'ordained' of God and that it was introduced with Adam and Eve, means you have to be a creationist, and as science has long proven how things really evolved, that is a very silly notion indeed.

That doesn't mean that it makes any *difference* whether a couple marry or not. It is just the way society has evolved, and religion has opted for another *control* using the concept of marriage. As with blacks and the priesthood, for Mormons, and women and the priesthood and gays and the priesthood for all Christian denominations, many churches have already changed their attitudes, as marriage is now becoming less popular as an institution. One day, in the dim and distant future, no doubt the Mormon Church will have to review its attitude to *couples* in order to survive. Some churches already have and they accept couples without requiring marriage. Society in general accepts couples; be they married or partners, male and female, or of the same sex. Some religions, especially Mormonism, are very slow to move with the times. Only when public opinion becomes strong and means they will lose members if they don't capitulate, does the Mormon Church cave on issues and invoke their God to change his unchangeable mind. We live in a more enlightened and liberated world than we once did and Mormonism will one day catch up. What was once considered impossible will become the norm. It has before and it will again. It just takes time. A few decades, or a century or two, will make all the difference and the impossible will become the inevitable. Don't rule *anything* out. If two people choose to live together rather than marry, it is a much healthier thing than living in a world dictated by religious 'virtues' where they *must* marry whether they want to or not. Such dictatorial religious 'rules' do far more harm than good. The point here is that if missionaries come across a couple who are cohabiting, who have elected *not* to actually marry and are quite happy as they are, *why* should Mormonism dictate that they *must* marry to become members?

Religion argues that marriage was instituted by God. However, that claim is just as questionable as the existence of such a being. As with everything else, *man* instituted various concepts of marriage, and what we have locally depends very much on the society in which we live. Marriages vary from the western concept where couples are supposedly equal, to arranged marriages where they have no choice in a partner. From marriages where the woman is inferior and must walk behind her man and never publicly show her face, to tribal plural marriages where four wives are required to tend the livestock, clean and cook, and repair the home. There are some arrangements where there is a more liberal understanding between people which the western world would not recognise as marriage at all. Which of these did God decide on and when? Mormons of course were once polygamous – and still would be if they could get away with it. As their polygamous 'marriages' were all actually *illegal*, they really don't have much to shout about, and all they really practiced in law was *bigamy*. But of course, they do not talk about that and keep very quiet about their own past.

The Mormon Church finally capitulated over its perceived racial prejudice against those of black African descent in 1978, following years of disagreement within the Quorum of Twelve Apostles, and one day no doubt it will have to once again capitulate regarding such things as women and the priesthood. It is all just a matter of time and circumstance – coupled of course with the ever changing tide of popular opinion. Marriage is a different issue and I would not expect any change in attitude about that any time soon. However, the issue of gays will continue to rear its head as long as the Church continues to interfere in proposed national and local government legislation. The active, and some would suggest, illegal, considering the Church was fined $5,000, Mormon Church involvement in California's 'Proposition 8' is evidence of interference in matters of State which are supposed to be kept separate from religion. The popularity of the Mormon Church, as well as those in public office associated with it, is declining fast as it continues to be perceived as out of touch with reality and more and more non-Mormon people are coming to understand and accept homosexuality as a perfectly normal and natural part of society.

The problem for the Mormon Church, as well as several other religious organisations, is that since scientific evidence has shown sexual orientation is hard wired into the brain, rather than it just being a curable 'illness' or personal 'weakness' to be overcome, society is fast moving on from its general prior bigotry. This leaves the Church to consider where it stands – which will soon be on its own, just as it was with what Mormons termed 'blacks and the priesthood', once considered unchangeable doctrine, much like the idea of practicing gays and Church membership is today.

The missionaries are preferably to find 'families' to teach. The concept that 'families can be together forever' is a compelling idea that certainly hooked me as a young teenager. The manual affirms that:

> On earth, family associations can be the source of some of our greatest joy. ***Satan is attacking the family on many fronts, and too many families are being destroyed by his efforts.*** The message of the restored gospel of Jesus Christ makes it possible for families to be united now and in eternity. *(Page 3)*. (Emphasis added).

To the unbeliever, Satan is a mythical creature who has nothing to do with anything. People are quite capable of their own mistakes without outside help. Mormons have just as many marital and family problems as anyone else. The Church pretends they don't, and references to lower divorce rates stem from a single and narrow source which is entirely inaccurate overall. The Mormon divorce rate is often declared to be considerably lower than average by Church members who repeat what leaders tell them. Whenever I heard talk of statistics on marriage, it was generally said the national average was that around 45% of marriages fail and temple marriage failure was below 10%. This was certainly in at least one published work which quoted what was a narrow local survey that led to decades of worldwide Church belief in yet another fraudulent claim.

> In a Salt Lake County survey only one in ten temple marriages ended in divorce, far better than the one in two to one in three national average. *(Marriage and Divorce, Spencer W. Kimball. 1976:3)*.

Whatever that referred to, it certainly wasn't the whole of Utah let alone the world. Kimball claimed the local divorce rate for temple marriage to be ten percent against the national average of "one in two or one in three" which was just a wild and speculative guess at a national statistic by someone who wanted to promote how wonderful marriage was in the Mormon Church. The reality is somewhat different. From the *same year* as Spencer Kimball's publication, the following statistic appeared in the local paper:

# PROGRAMMING THE MISSIONARIES CONTINUES

> Utah continues to outstrip the rest of the nation in divorces... 5.1 per 1,000 population were filed, compared with an average of 4.8 per 1,000 nationally." *(The Salt Lake Tribune. 22 February 1976).*

Considering the fact that in that year Utah was still well over 70% Mormon, the statistic was clearly highly influenced by Church membership. As late as 1990, Utah was still 71.76% Mormon. See:
http://www.adherents.com/largecom/com_lds.html

But by 2008, it was down to 60.4% and it continues to fall. See:
http://www.mormontimes.com/article/11371/Utahs-Mormon-population-percentage-shrinks)

Kimball's local 'statistic' appears to have been wishful thinking more than anything. Many temple marriages that do not appear to fail are nevertheless extremely unhappy and I know of couples who stay together as there seems little choice for them – and there are always the children to consider. This is not overstated; it is the same whether people are Mormon or not. It is obvious when you consider many non-Mormons are equally faithful to other religions with similar standards. Good and bad marriages are not unique to religious or non-religious unions. People and their relationships remain influenced by the same problems which religion doesn't solve. In fact, in many instances religion effectively exacerbates problems, as people feel unable to walk away from their marriage and start again. To many people, it would be sinful and they must try to resolve problems within their marriage. There are many unhappy marriages held together by religion, Mormon and otherwise, and that is not a good thing.

The fear factor of not being good enough and failing to achieve Celestial glory can be all consuming and to some it is completely overwhelming. The results of this often cause family and marital problems. Although the divorce rate in Utah is currently 4.4 per 1000 (Lowest State 2.3 and highest 6.8 – Mean/Median 4.0), it is still above the national average when one would expect it to be much lower. *(See:* www.divorcereform.org/StateRateChart.html*).*

Certainly, in the past, Utah has claimed a much higher than average divorce rate in the United States.

> Utahans have a higher divorce rate than the national average, marry younger, and bear more children. *(The Deseret News. 16 May 1979).*

The idealism of Celestial marriage does not seem to save a higher than average number of marriages in *this* life, never mind the next one.

The Church has now evolved into a mainstream family religion with many Christian ideals. Mormon leaders like it to be considered as such. However, some things are still traditionally 'Mormon' concepts. Women who know their place should have as many children as possible, staying at home to raise them, while unquestioningly supporting their husbands in their callings, no matter how busy that keeps them. Women in Mormonism are forbidden from holding the priesthood and therefore they have no say in the running of the Church or in making any of its laws or rules. Their role is to raise the next generation to stay true to the faith. Fear of failure to achieve that keeps most of them vigilant and at the same time, somewhat unwittingly, subservient.

I have gay friends in the Church who were taught that homosexuality is a *curable* disposition. They were encouraged to marry a member of the opposite sex and to try to *overcome* it. Fear of rejection by the Lord prompts some to try and change. Others simply cannot and are disciplined. There are many young gay homeless people in Salt Lake City who have been cast off by their Mormon families and the suicide rate of gay Mormons is exceptionally high as many cannot cope with Church and family ridicule and some simply cannot shake the guilt they are made to feel for their supposed sinful behaviour. If He is real, the Mormon God has a lot to answer for, as it was He who hard wired their brains that way. Practicing gays are immediately excommunicated if they will not 'repent' and investigators who are discovered to be gay must reform or they can never join the Mormon Church.

The requirements, standards and expectations of the religion are for many, very demanding and for some they are utterly impossible. For a person born into Mormonism, they can actually be extremely damaging and yet, as a so-called 'normal' member, you just do not see it that way at all. At least I didn't.

Fear of failure to please the Lord or his chosen leaders and be a worthy member is a constant companion. The way to be certain you are in a position to receive Celestial glory is to be worthy of and hold a 'temple recommend', only available to interviewed and worthy tithe paying and commandment living members. A temple recommend is like a season ticket to the Mormon concept of heaven. No self respecting true-blue Mormon leaves home without one.

Religion or not, problems still exist within Mormon marriages and in many instances they are magnified due to the perceptions held within the religion. Mormonism *creates* many problems so the Church can then solve them, thus justifying the religion. The answers to everything for an investigator are of course bound up in joining the Mormon Church. The 'family forever' *reward* is based on following rules that are set by the Mormon God – or at least His representatives in the Mormon Church. Do what they say and pay what they say and you will be rewarded – *after* you die.

So called 'blessings' are often promised in this life too, but after all my years in the Church, I have seen more problems and more trials caused to faithful members than I have ever seen worthwhile quantifiable *blessings*, even after people have paid and slaved at being good Mormons until they drop. That is, no better or enjoyable a life than would have been the case without the

# PROGRAMMING THE MISSIONARIES CONTINUES

Church. Indeed, without the pressures and expectations, many lives would have been a lot simpler and much happier. One thing is for certain, they would have had far more *time* to be together as a family and much more *money* in order to enjoy life more. Many people will be familiar with the term 'Bishop's widow' which refers to the wife of a busy Bishop who rarely sees his wife and family in the way normal husbands would. Of course most Mormons would disagree with that as it is only when you know the truth that it all becomes clear and obvious. However, ex-Mormons will, I am sure, readily agree and understand the point. Prospective Mormons should consider that *very* carefully.

The 'blessing' of being a Mormon can seem almost tangible at times but in the cold light of day it is purely an ecstatic religious delusional state based on false information and an erroneous belief that God confirmed to us that it was true. Proven lies *cannot* be confirmed as truth from God. Only our own wishful thinking can do that, although of course we have no idea that we are taking lies to the Lord in prayer at the time we make our supplication. That really is the end of the matter regarding Mormonism. It is strange that everything will be okay after we die rather than before. As with everything that can't be answered or explained, we may have to await the hereafter to understand. Meanwhile – don't worry about it as it won't affect our salvation.

The missionaries are told that:

> The gospel of Jesus Christ defines both your message and your purpose; that is, it provides both the "what" and the "why" of missionary work. *(Page 5).*

They are to teach investigators that through Christ's atonement they can be forgiven of their sins. Of course, the missionaries will teach them all about new concepts which only *become* sins once they accept Mormonism. Before that, most people would not have had any idea such things could even be considered sins – tea and coffee, etc. The carrot is not without the stick however, should an investigator think they don't need Mormonism.

> Those who do not endure in faithfulness to the end will be "cast into the fire . . . because of the justice of the Father." (See 3 Nephi 27:13–22…) *(Page 5).*

Whether or not casting people into the fire is in any way 'justice' for people not being considered strong enough to follow many of the Mormon dictates I will leave the reader to contemplate. It certainly doesn't seem like justice to me and in any event that is a *Book of Mormon* quote, written when Smith was in monotheistic mode and heaven and hell were still *real*. Hence the 'fire' quote.

> The purpose of the gospel is to cleanse people of their sins so they can receive the Savior's mercy at the day of judgment. *(Page 6)*.

Teach the Gospel. People will receive a 'remission' of their 'sins' through baptism and thereafter have the gift of the Holy Ghost to guide them through so they can 'endure to the end'.

> These are not just steps that they experience once in their lives; rather, when repeated throughout life these principles become an increasingly rewarding pattern of living. In fact, *it is the only way of living that will bring peace of conscience* and enable Heavenly Father's children to return to live in His presence. *(Page 6)*. (Emphasis added).

The fact is that Mormon missionaries effectively create an acute whole new 'conscience' within a believing investigator who, prior to this programming, was quite capable of normal discernment between right and wrong without help. Now life becomes inundated with ideas of things that are not acceptable to the Mormon God which no one outside Mormonism could care less about.

As previously stated, the Church *creates* sin for people to overcome. Think of now having to *avoid* smoking, drinking alcohol, tea, coffee, more than one set of earrings for women, tattoos, swearing, gambling, a myriad of now *bad* thoughts and suchlike; and *doing* daily prayer, study, family home evening, missions, meetings, talks, lessons, callings, family history, temple attendance; and *paying* tithes and many other offerings, paying for children's missions and so forth – none of which were part of a persons life previously and now God commands attention to in finite and constant never ending detail.

Salvation in the next life is offered in return for total subservience to Mormonism in this life. In Mormonism, it is not the accumulation of your lifetime of effort at being a good person that rewards you – it is where you end up. Thus you cannot be a good Mormon all your life and then go 'apostate' near the end and expect to be saved. However, you can be a reprobate all your life and then hear and accept the gospel near the end and all will be well.

Unlike some Christian denominations, there is no set of scales on which to balance the good against the supposed evil in your life. In the real world, most people are in fact basically good, yet once the concept of sin is introduced to them, they merely 'become' bad as applied to those concepts. By inventing lots of 'sins of omission;' as well as 'sins of commission', the mine-field is far wider for the guilt complex to be instilled and then thrive in a Mormon mind.

Missionaries are taught that no matter where they serve or who they teach, they must centre their efforts on teaching the restoration of the gospel. They are admonished that no matter what else they teach, they must ensure investigators understand the following:

# PROGRAMMING THE MISSIONARIES CONTINUES

> ***God is our literal Father*** in Heaven. He loves us. Every person on earth is a child of God and a member of God's family. Jesus Christ, the Son of God, is our Savior and Redeemer.
>
> Our loving Father in Heaven reached out to His children throughout biblical history by revealing His gospel to prophets. Sadly, many people rejected that gospel; even some of those who accepted it **changed gospel doctrines and ordinances and fell into unbelief and apostasy.**
>
> Our Father in Heaven sent His Beloved Son, Jesus Christ, to earth. He performed miracles and taught His gospel. He accomplished ***the Atonement*** and was resurrected.
>
> Beginning with the ***First Vision***, God has again reached out in love to His children. He **restored the gospel** of Jesus Christ and His **priesthood authority** and organized His Church on the earth **through the Prophet Joseph Smith. The Book of Mormon is convincing evidence of this Restoration.** *(Page 7).* (Emphasis added).

This sequence will be familiar to many people. Starting with the concept that God is *not* a spirit but is our literal father, He has a body of flesh and bone. The missionaries will not mention the core Joseph Smith doctrine that God was once a man – which we will return to in a later chapter; they will cover the concept of Christ's atonement and that there was a subsequent apostasy from the truth which required a 'restoration of all things'. They will explain how Joseph Smith was called by God to achieve this, including the idea that the *Book of Mormon* is compelling evidence of it.

On the same page *(p.7)* of the manual, there is a typical Mormon Church picture of the young Joseph Smith seated at a table poring over the gold plates, presumably translating them, while a 'scribe' is seated opposite him, writing down the translation. Adjacent to the picture is the statement:

> The Book of Mormon: Another Testament of Jesus Christ is convincing evidence that Joseph Smith was a prophet and that the gospel of Jesus Christ has been restored. It is the keystone of our religion, the most powerful resource for teaching this message. *(Page 7).*

They say a picture is worth a thousand words. In this case it is worth a complete lie without a single word of truth as Joseph Smith is admitted as never having translated the *Book of Mormon* in such fashion. Most Mormons believe that he did, due simply to the Mormon pictorial depictions, all of which show Smith looking *at* the plates. In reality, Smith did not look at the supposed plates and he used his old money-digging seer stone in his hat in order to 'translate' them while the plates were either tied up in a linen cloth or sometimes even buried somewhere else entirely while he 'translated' them. What would an investigator think if they were told that? Most Mormons have no idea that this was the case and that he didn't actually *look* at the plates, but it is accepted by the Church and an Ensign article once even referred to it.

> Joseph Smith would put the seer stone into a hat, and put his face in the hat, drawing it closely around his face to exclude the light; and in the darkness the spiritual light would shine. A piece of something resembling parchment would appear, and on that appeared the writing. One character at a time would appear, and under it was the interpretation in English. Brother Joseph would read off the English to Oliver Cowdery, who was his principal scribe, and when it was written down and repeated to Brother Joseph to see if it was correct, then it would disappear, and another character with the interpretation would appear. Thus the *Book of Mormon* was translated by the gift and power of God, and not by any power of man. *(A Treasured Testament, Russell M. Nelson, Ensign, July 1993, p.61).*

It seems strange that God would go to all the trouble of having gold plates engraved and buried, only to have Joseph Smith translate them without actually *looking* at them. It is even stranger that the 'translators' provided with the plates were taken away by an angel, leaving Smith to translate using his old seer stone which he had used as a con artist when claiming he could locate buried treasure. Of course neither the missionaries nor their investigators are apprised of any of these historical details. Morally, of course they should be.

The missionaries who taught me and my mother in 1960 explained that Smith translated the *Book of Mormon* using the Urim and Thummim, two seer stones which were provided with the plates. However, they did *not* tell us that after the first one-hundred-and-sixteen pages of the translated book were lost, the Urim and Thummim were confiscated by an angel. Nor did they explain that Smith did not retranslate what had been lost but instead created another slightly different version of the same events within the *Book of Mormon* which also included a revelation that the loss was anticipated by God who prepared an alternative source for the very same information. It seems to me that once we become deluded we really do just believe anything, regardless of how silly it is.

Unfortunately for Smith, he couldn't remember many of the (particularly female) names that he had used, so they are conspicuous by their absence in the first two books of Nephi. There is a very good reason why no one is told about all that, especially before they join the Church. It is so absurd, that no one would ever believe it without gaining a firm 'testimony' beforehand; that is to say, without becoming completely deluded first. The concept of 'milk before

# PROGRAMMING THE MISSIONARIES CONTINUES

meat' really means teach the plausible and get people into the delusion *before* they learn the things that are so silly that no one in their right mind would even begin to contemplate them being true. Only a deluded mind will accept some of the Mormon 'meat'.

Mormon apostle Jeff Holland is quoted as saying:

> The first thing you will do when an investigator tells you he or she had not read and prayed about the Book of Mormon is be devastated! . . .

In my own experience as a missionary, it was a very uncommon thing indeed if someone actually *had* read anything we had asked them to read when we returned to see them. Holland tells the missionaries to:

> ...take control of this situation. Teach with power and authority *(Page 8)*.

As previously mentioned, missionaries are reminded to do this over and over again. They are to 'declare repentance' *(D&C 15:6)* and are reminded that:

> Repentance requires a sincere and lasting change of thoughts, desires, habits, and actions. It is a positive experience that brings joy and peace. Be bold and loving in helping people understand what they must do to repent. By inviting people to make commitments, you can effectively raise a voice of both warning and hope. *(Page 8)*.

So, missionaries will teach people about all the sinful things they are doing and then encourage them to repent and change their lives forever. The Mormon God will forgive them if they repent.

In speaking of the need for repentance, baptism, and confirmation, the manual refers to this statement by Dallin H. Oaks:

> We do not preach and teach in order to 'bring people into the Church' or to increase the membership of the Church. We do not preach and teach just to persuade people to live better lives. . . . We invite all to come unto Christ by repentance and baptism and confirmation in order to open the doors of the celestial kingdom to the sons and daughters of God. *No one else can do this.* (The Purpose of Missionary Work. Elder Dallin H. Oaks. Missionary satellite broadcast, Apr. 1995). *(Page 9)*. (Emphasis added).

The Mormon Church concept of 'heaven' is somewhat different to that of mainstream Christianity. We will look more closely at it later but for the moment, the 'Celestial' kingdom is the highest 'degree' of heaven within the

# THE MORMON DELUSION

Mormon mindset. The goal is to become 'exalted' which means reaching the highest 'degree' within that kingdom. Only then can you, if you are a *male*, become a God yourself and go on to create and populate your own worlds. It is a compelling proposition and one that at age fourteen I fell for completely.

Missionaries are next advised that they must help investigators 'qualify' for baptism. This is the set requirements if someone wishes to join the Mormon Church. They must:

> Humble themselves before God.
> Desire to be baptized.
> Come forth with broken hearts and contrite spirits.
> Repent of all their sins.
> Are willing to take upon themselves the name of Jesus Christ.
> Have a determination to serve Christ to the end.
> Manifest by their works that they have received the Spirit of Christ unto the remission of their sins. *(Page 9)*.

Obviously, some missionaries are better at the job than others; some get lucky and some don't; some work hard and others are just lazy. Inevitably, as with any sales team, eighty percent of the success comes from twenty percent of the sales force. There is nothing new about statistics. The Church wants to encourage even the less successful missionaries. Nevertheless, it's their fault.

> Your success as a missionary is measured primarily by your commitment to find, teach, baptize, and confirm people and to help them become faithful members of the Church who enjoy the presence of the Holy Ghost. *(Page 10)*.

Note the psychology in the next statement. Whatever you do, don't get depressed about it.

> ***Avoid comparing yourself*** to other missionaries and measuring the outward results of your efforts against theirs. Remember that *people have agency* to choose whether to accept your message. ***Your responsibility is to teach*** clearly and powerfully so they can make a correct choice. ***Some may not accept your message even when they have received a spiritual witness that it is true.*** You will be saddened because you love them and desire their salvation. You should not, however, become discouraged; ***discouragement will weaken your faith.*** If you lower your expectations, your effectiveness will decrease, your desire will weaken, and ***you will have greater difficulty following the Spirit.*** *(Page 10)*. (Emphasis added).

The concept that some people may not accept the Church even if they have received a witness that it is true, is a very strange one but it is meant to make

## PROGRAMMING THE MISSIONARIES CONTINUES

missionaries feel better – they did their best – they led the horses to water (who could even see that it *was* water) – but they could not *make* them drink. The discouragement spoken of, which may weaken their faith and cause difficulty following the spirit, is one way of thinking. The other is that if almost everyone rejects the message out of hand, perhaps they have a point and the whole thing deserves to be reconsidered by the missionary. Naturally, most never do that.

Getting people into the water reaffirms to the missionary that his 'message' is true, simply because someone else *believed* it. As I state elsewhere, you can eventually find someone who will believe almost anything if you look hard enough.

The missionaries' mental state is bolstered through positive affirmation. The manual suggests to them that: "**You can know you have been a successful missionary when you**":

> Feel the Spirit testify to people through you.
> Love people and desire their salvation.
> Obey with exactness.
> Live so that you can receive and know how to follow the Spirit, who will show you where to go, what to do, and what to say.
> Develop Christlike attributes.
> Work effectively every day, do your very best to bring souls to Christ, and seek earnestly to learn and improve.
> Help build up the Church (the ward) wherever you are assigned to work.
> Warn people of the consequences of sin. Invite them to make and keep commitments.
> Teach and serve other missionaries.
> Go about doing good and serving people at every opportunity, whether or not they accept your message.
> When you have done your very best, ***you may still experience disappointments, but you will not be disappointed in yourself.*** You can feel certain that the Lord is pleased when you feel the Spirit working through you. *(Pages 10-11)*. (Emphasis added).

They will of course suffer disappointments but should not get discouraged or disappointed in themselves. Many a missionary gets to a stage where he or she really has had enough and just wants to go home. Most never do though as that admits to *"discouragement will weaken your faith"* and having *"difficulty following the Spirit"* mentioned above. *(p.54)*. Lots of encouraging statements from past and present Mormon Church leaders are included in this lesson for missionaries to cling to as they strive to be good at their job.

The above 'lesson' material is directed at the missionary so he or she can better appreciate what to say and do to convince an 'investigator' of each aspect covered. He or she is not to become discouraged which almost all will at some stage of their mission. As the missionary studies this and subsequent chapters, he or she becomes ready to 'teach' the five lessons. There is more of what is effectively further 'sales training' for the missionary to study before getting to the meat of the five missionary lessons though.

# Chapter 3

## Continuous Self-Induced Brainwashing

### Preach My Gospel – Chapter 2
### How Do I Study Effectively and Prepare to Teach?

In order for missionaries to teach effectively, as with any successful salesman, they must 'know' their product. This is encouraged by having them:

> Seek not to declare my word, but first seek to obtain my word, and then shall your tongue be loosed; then, if you desire, you shall have my Spirit and my word, yea, the power of God unto the convincing of men" (D&C 11:21). *(page 17)*.

The message is the same for missionaries as it is for investigators.

> Getting good results from your study depends on having a strong desire to learn, *studying with "real intent"* (Moroni 10:4) "hunger[ing] and thirst[ing] after righteousness" (Matthew 5:6), and *searching for answers to your investigators' questions and concerns. (Page 17)*. (Emphasis added).

They can *only* study 'recommended' material (the manual and scriptures plus four additional books; *Jesus the Christ*; *Our Heritage*; *Our Search for Happiness*; and *True to the Faith*) which actually contain *no* answers to any serious questions. As long as investigators don't know more about the Church than the missionaries do, then everything should be okay. Problems will arise if an investigator asks questions to which missionaries are themselves given no answers. The manual is bereft of information that a truly informed investigator may ask for concerning many aspects. A few that spring to mind are:

When did Joseph Smith first *record* his 1820 First Vision story?
How many different and conflicting vision stories did Smith record?
When did he first *record* details of what Moroni *said* in the 1823 vision?
How many wives did Joseph Smith actually have?
How many 'Smith wives' were already married when he married them?
Was polygamy legal when it was introduced – or indeed, *ever*?
Did polygamy cease *in* 1890 when the Church published the Manifesto?
Why was *D&C 101* used as scripture when it was a complete lie?
Why does the modern Church lie about the Adam–God doctrine?
Didn't Young declare blood atonement was sometimes a *requirement*?
Wasn't the prophet John Taylor on the run from the law when he died?

Or to pose just one of many 'modern' questions:

Why did recent Mormon prophet, Gordon B. Hinckley, publicly declare he knew little of anything about God once being a man and didn't know they taught it, when Smith declared it was "plain beyond disputation?" *(See Apx F).*

The list could be endless. No one usually asks such things of missionaries, but if they do, there is no mention of any of these or dozens of other very awkward questions in any material provided to missionaries. They simply do not know anything about such things at all. They may have a guess at the number of Joseph Smith's wives but that's about it really. The Church keeps very quiet about anything and everything concerning its past. I managed to survive as a Mormon for forty-three years without having a clue about any of the above at all. I wouldn't have even thought of such questions to ever ask.

In my case, I *assumed* Smith wrote down the visions almost immediately after receiving them. I was taught that polygamy was perfectly legal when introduced and thought Smith had about a dozen wives, who were naturally all single when he married them. I assumed polygamy *did* stop in 1890 because the Manifesto is canonised. I wouldn't have even known that *D&C 101* ever existed. To me, Adam-God was a discarded theory, blood atonement meant only the Saviour's atonement, and of course John Taylor was a prophet and would never have disobeyed the law. I had no idea he had a price on his head and would have argued vehemently against the notion, without having a clue that I was entirely wrong. I had of course effectively been lied to throughout my life through endless *misinformation*. Mormon Church leaders equally keep

# CONTINUOUS SELF-INDUCED BRAINWASHING

its members and missionaries, and therefore investigators, completely in the dark concerning the truth behind the Church.

Under the subheading of 'Learning by the Holy Ghost', missionaries are encouraged to pray and study.

> Your gospel study is most effective when you are taught by the Holy Ghost. Always begin your gospel study by *praying for the Holy Ghost to help you learn*. He will bring knowledge and conviction that will bless your life and allow you to bless the lives of others. Your faith in Jesus Christ will increase. *Your desire to repent and improve will grow.* This kind of study prepares you for service, offers solace, resolves problems, and gives you the strength to endure to the end. Successful gospel study requires desire and action. *(Page 18)*. (Emphasis added).

Note that amid the energetic admonition to study and pray for the Holy Ghost to teach them – faith will increase; but along with the carrot, the usual stick is thrown in. To assert that a "desire to repent and improve will grow" means that a deeper sense of guilt and feeling the need to do so must first be implanted. It is actually a retrograde step used to keep people feeling unworthy no matter how well they do. What do obedient missionaries need to repent of or improve in, other than unnecessarily feeling unworthy or ineffective when people won't listen to them?

The manual explains how they are to learn.

> Learning the gospel is also a process of receiving revelation (see Jacob 4:8). To Oliver Cowdery the Lord said: "Behold, you have not understood; you have supposed that I would give it unto you, when you took no thought save it was to ask me. But, behold, I say unto you, that **you must study it out in your mind; then you must ask me if it be right, and if it is right I will cause that your bosom shall burn within you**; therefore, you shall feel that it is right" (D&C 9:7–8). As you study, **pay careful attention to ideas that come to your mind and feelings that come to your heart**, particularly regarding the people you are teaching. *(Page 18)*. (Emphasis added).

As an example of the idea that the missionaries must study things out which the Holy Ghost will then confirm, the manual refers to *D&C 9:7-8* but completely neglects the surrounding verses and also what they refer to. This is a very telling point.

> **D&C 9:2.** And then, behold, *other records have I, that I will give unto you power that you may assist to translate.*
> **3.** Be patient, my son, for it is wisdom in me, and *it is not expedient that you should translate at this present time.*

**4.** Behold, the work which you are called to do is to write for my servant Joseph.

**5.** And, behold, it is because that *you did not continue as you commenced, when you began to translate, that I have taken away this privilege* from you.

**6.** Do not murmur, my son, for it is wisdom in me that I have dealt with you after this manner.

**7.** Behold, you have not understood; *you have supposed that I would give it unto you, when you took no thought save it was to ask me.*

**8.** But, behold, I say unto you, that *you must study it out in your mind; then you must ask me if it be right, and if it is right I will cause that your bosom shall burn within you; therefore, you shall feel that it is right.*

**9.** But *if it be not right you shall have no such feelings*, but you shall have a stupor of thought that shall cause you to forget the thing which is wrong; therefore, you cannot write that which is sacred save it be given you from me.

**10.** Now, *if you had known this you could have translated*; nevertheless, it is not expedient that you should translate now.

**11.** Behold, *it was expedient* when you commenced; but you feared, and the time is past, and *it is not expedient now*; (Emphasis added).

The referenced verses *(7-8)* explain that you can't just ask for answers, you have to study things out in your mind, reach your *own conclusions*, and then ask the Lord if you got it right. When you feel good about them that is the Lord confirming things are correct.

What the manual does *not* explain is that this section of the *D&C* was directed to Oliver Cowdery who was supposed to be actually translating part of the *Book of Mormon* for Joseph Smith. He failed to do so and so the Lord tells him that He will give him further things to translate later, but for now it is no longer what he is to do. Clearly Smith did not want Cowdery muddling up his storyline so he invented this revelation to get him away from trying to write it.

The interesting point here is that this is not just directed at everyone in the way the missionary manual suggests. It was originally a revelation specifically for Cowdery and it directly related to the *method* of translation of the *Book of Mormon*. Here, the Lord is telling Cowdery that the translation will not just come to him – he has to make it up himself in his own head – and if it feels right, then it is true. If it is not right, then he will forget what he was thinking. The Church doesn't see it that way today but that is what the 'revelation' ***says***.

Indeed, that is exactly what Smith himself did. He buried his head in a hat which contained his old money-digging seer stone and 'translated' the book while the gold plates were not even in view. Thus he just made it up as he went along (other than the transposed *KJV* chapters of Isaiah etc.,) and if it felt right – then it ***was*** right. It was as simple as that. Cowdery hadn't figured that out.

# CONTINUOUS SELF-INDUCED BRAINWASHING

Additionally, the whole idea that God would let Cowdery translate other things fell by the wayside when he was excommunicated in 1838. The Lord obviously didn't see that coming. Cowdery actually resigned membership in protest at Smith's devious and illegal manipulation of people and property (among other things) but he was excommunicated anyway despite his formal resignation. Years later, Cowdery returned to membership but the reasons are sketchy at best. He died a couple of years after that. He never did personally translate anything for the Lord.

The missionaries are taught to 'live what they learn' and not to memorise exactly what to say. This is a complete departure from the lessons given years ago when we had to learn and teach them parrot fashion. The dialogue was exact and even the name of a fictional investigator, Mr. Brown – which quickly became 'Brother Brown' in conversation – appeared in the text. In those days the manual instructed missionaries in every single detail, manipulating almost every word they said, including:

> In all discussions except the first, the contact should probably be called "Brother Brown" rather than "Mr. Brown." This is never offensive, and it makes the contact feel much closer to being a member of the church, since he knows that the members refer to each other in this way. People enjoy being called "brother" and "sister."

Note the psychology of trying to make a person feel "closer to being a member of the church". In the 'old days', if you said the right things, you could predict almost exactly what an investigator would say next and be ready with the most appropriate answer – which was provided in the manual. Things have changed.

> The Lord said, "Neither take ye thought beforehand what ye shall say; but treasure up in your minds continually the words of life, and it shall be given you in the very hour that portion that shall be meted unto every man" (D&C 84:85). *(Page 19).*

It is somewhat surprising that the Church quotes *D&C 84:85* today in order to justify the current teaching method, when years ago there were set lessons spoken word for word. Yet *D&C 84* was penned in 1832. It seems to have taken the Mormon God a very long time to get around to the 'correct' method of teaching the gospel. The quoted text means, study well and know your stuff and then it will be easy to talk about it when the time comes. It is not that the Holy Ghost will really prompt them or bring things to memory when needed; it is just the result of good preparation such as any salesperson or speaker can achieve. I have had those experiences all my life, both in the Church and in sales seminars and secular meetings, both while I was a Mormon and also as a non-Mormon. It makes absolutely no difference at all – unless you are a Mormon in a delusional state of mind and choose to believe that it does.

Exactly the same experience is claimed by any number of people from any number of religions – and also by many people in any number of non-religious settings.

Missionaries are then trained how to learn the lesson material and teach it in their own words. They will of course be able to teach with 'spiritual power' (yet again). Instructions include the admonition to bear frequent testimony of the things they are teaching. This reinforces the belief and commitment of the missionary. They are taught how to learn, focus, organise and prepare what they will teach. Page after page assists them to be ready for every supposed eventuality.

After every single teaching situation, missionaries must evaluate how well they did. I doubt many just sit down and say "we were fantastic – we were just brilliant. We sucked up every question and delivered our pitch perfectly. We had them right where we wanted them". Even if investigators were 'receptive', this kind of evaluation is highly unlikely. It is far more probable missionaries will focus on what was missed or where they went wrong and how they could improve next time. They must repent and study and pray more and be more prepared – or at least conclude that they should. It is the way the training is structured. They can never be good enough. This is ensured by the kind of evaluation questions they are to consider:

> Did you focus on the doctrine?
> Did you invite investigators to repent and to make and keep commitments?
> Did you work to prepare them for baptism and confirmation?
> Did you use effective questions?
> Did you share your testimony?
> Did you ask for referrals?
> *Adjust your lesson plans as you improve.* (Emphasis added).

The assumption is that there is *always* a need to *improve*. The missionaries must "Actively work to teach with greater power". There is always greater 'power' required. What it really means is that if they learn well, they will have more *confidence*, that's all. The chapter continues, page after page after page, with requirements for effective missionary lifestyle and study techniques so they can be ready for anything. The only problem is that the manual contains absolutely nothing of the truth behind the Church or answers to any serious questions that a truly informed investigator would ask if only they knew the right questions.

# Chapter 4

## Lesson 1

### The Message of the Restoration of the Gospel of Jesus Christ

### Part A

### Missionary Preparation

The first 'lesson' is probably considered the most important and most powerful as it contains the foundation of Mormonism which sets the Mormon Church apart from all other denominations. It is also the one, after which, most people ask the missionaries *not* to return. Most investigators do not move on to a second 'lesson'. One is more than enough for them.

Instructions to the missionaries prior to giving this lesson start with their goals:

> As you teach, prepare your investigators to meet the qualifications for baptism taught in Doctrine and Covenants 20:37 and in the baptismal interview questions. *(Page 31)*.

> **D&C 20:37:** *And again, by way of commandment to the church concerning the manner of baptism*—All those who humble themselves before God, and desire to be baptized, and come forth with broken hearts and contrite spirits, and witness before the church that they have truly repented of all their sins, and are willing to take upon them the name of Jesus Christ, having a determination to serve him to the end, and truly manifest by their works that they have received of the Spirit of Christ unto the remission of their sins, shall be received by baptism into his church. *(Italics in original).*

As this is to prepare missionaries rather than convince investigators, it is neither here nor there that it comes from Mormon so-called scripture. However, it is worthy of note that just a few verses *before* the above reference, the following statements are also made, which are *not* referenced:

> **D&C 20:26.** Not only those who believed after he came in the meridian of time, in the flesh, but ***all those from the beginning, even as many as were before he came, who believed in the words of the holy prophets, who spake as they were inspired by the gift of the Holy Ghost,*** who truly testified of him in all things, should have eternal life,
> 27. As well as those who should come after, who should believe in the gifts and callings of God by the Holy Ghost, which **beareth** record of the Father and of the Son;
> 28. ***Which Father, Son, and Holy Ghost are one God***, infinite and eternal, without end. Amen. **(Emphasis added).**

These are two aspects which will rear their heads again later but for now suffice it to say that the Holy Ghost is a Common Era concept which had no place in the Old Testament or any Jewish theology at all. What Christians refer to as the 'Old Testament' was of course from the Tanakh and hijacked by the Christians and included in their Bible. It is *Hebrew* scripture. Jews do not believe in the concept of the Holy Ghost, or that Jesus Christ was the Messiah, or of course Trinitarianism, let alone the Mormon idea that the Holy Ghost is a 'personage' of spirit. To the Jews, who wrote this stuff, the 'spirit of God' referred to in the Bible is the 'mind of God' and alludes to His *energy* – and that is all. Perhaps we should take note of that. After all, He is *their* God and the Old Testament is a supposed record of His dealings with His chosen race –which was the Jews. Their prophets should know what He was like and what He meant when He communicated with them.

Note also that v.28 clearly states that the Father, Son and Holy Ghost are *one* God. Everyone in the Mormon Church including Joseph Smith was entirely Monotheistic in their views in 1830 when this section was penned.

# MISSIONARY PREPARATION

If, as the Mormon Church now teaches, Joseph Smith saw God and Jesus as two separate and distinct beings, both with tangible bodies, in 1820, then surely this 1830 set of beliefs and instructions, written at the time of the inauguration of the Church, would have been an ideal place for that concept to appear. Better yet, it would be the perfect place to include an *account* of the First Vision story. Yet it does not appear. There is a very good reason why it does not and we will come back to that more fully later on.

Missionaries are then instructed that:

> This is best accomplished by inviting your investigators to make and keep the commitments listed below.
>
> **Baptismal Interview Questions**
>
> Do you believe that God is our Eternal Father?
> Do you believe that Jesus Christ is the Son of God, the Savior and Redeemer of the world?
> Do you believe that the Church and the gospel of Jesus Christ have been restored through the Prophet Joseph Smith?
> Do you believe that [current Church President] is a prophet of God? What does this mean to you?
>
> **Commitments**
>
> Will you read and pray to know that the Book of Mormon is the word of God?
> Will you pray to know that Joseph Smith was a prophet?
> Will you attend church with us this Sunday?
> May we set a time for our next visit?
> Other commandments from lesson 4 that you choose to include.
> *(Page 31).*

So, those are the objectives set for the missionaries to achieve in the first lesson. It is quite a task to accomplish in a one hour meeting really, which is probably why most people ask the missionaries not to return.

## God Loves Us – Christ Atoned For Us

The lesson starts off by establishing a perception of the existence of God and a need for atonement through Jesus Christ in the mind of the investigator. At some stage, the missionaries must establish the idea that God has a body. That concept will be something entirely new to anyone outside the Mormon Church. Interestingly, in my own missionary experience, a number of people accepted that concept far more readily than the idea that Smith 'restored' the true gospel. Many people warm to the idea of a personal God who can be visualised rather than a spirit that is omnipresent. What missionaries *don't* teach people is *why* God has a body. The concept that God was once a man who lived on an 'Earth' and progressed to *become* a God is carefully withheld. The closest the manual gets to the idea is this:

> God is our Heavenly Father. We are His children. He has a body of flesh and bone that is glorified and perfected. *(Page 31).*

> God has a perfect, glorified, immortal body of flesh and bones. *(Page 50).*

Despite the fact that 'As man is, God once was; as God is, man may become' has always been a core fundamental teaching of the Mormon Church, firmly established by Joseph Smith and clearly defined in the Mormon temple ceremony today, the recent prophet, Gordon B. Hinckley, dismissed the whole idea when questioned by the press. *(See Ch.5, p.103 and Appendix F).*

The manual explains to missionaries that they must teach these concepts:

> God is our Heavenly Father. We are His children. He has a body of flesh and bone that is glorified and perfected. Central to our Father's plan is Jesus Christ's Atonement. Through the Atonement we can be freed from the burden of our sins and develop faith and strength to face our trials. *(Page 31).*

The following statements in the manual are designed to help missionaries along. *(See also Chapter 7. p.153).*

> Determine what each person you are teaching understands regarding Christian beliefs about God.

> Many people in today's world either have no concept of God or a very different perception of Deity.

> Two Book of Mormon missionaries, Ammon and Aaron, taught people who did not have a Christian background. They taught simple truths and invited their investigators to pray. Lamoni and his father were converted. Read Alma 18:24–40 and 22:4–23, and answer the questions below:

> What did these missionaries teach about the nature of God?

> How can you follow their examples? *(Page 32).*

# MISSIONARY PREPARATION

The outcome of this initial foray into the *Book of Mormon* is designed to have missionaries conclude Lamoni was converted by the powerful testimonies of Ammon and Aaron – whom they must become like. However, should the missionaries actually bother to carefully study the words, the conclusion they would arrive at, but clearly most do not, is something entirely different. I doubt they would ever share this so-called 'scripture' with investigators. Intelligent questions that would subsequently arise could not possibly be answered.

Missionaries and members alike are taught to look for the faith promoting aspects of their scriptures. When anything remotely appears less than plausible or out of sync with reality, the brainwashed mind simply passes over it as if it doesn't matter and has no bearing on the truth they are seeking. It is not 'seen' by the faithful. Perhaps that is why missionaries do not 'see' what is in Alma.

Let's take a look at the recommended reading in Alma and pause at times to consider what is actually being claimed. We briefly looked at the concept of a 'great spirit' in Chapter 1 *(pp. 26-28)*. It appears to have been a Joseph Smith idea, possibly derived from the notion that some Native North Americans in his day believed in such a thing, so he included it in his *Book of Mormon*. The chapter 'header' for Alma 18 states:

> *King Lamoni supposes that Ammon is the Great Spirit—Ammon teaches the king of the creation, of God's dealings with men, and of the redemption that comes through Christ—Lamoni believes and falls to the earth as if dead. About 90 B.C.* (Italics in Original).

> **Alma 18:24.** And Ammon began to speak unto him with boldness, and said unto him: Believest thou that there is a God?
> **25.** And he answered, and said unto him: I do not know what that meaneth.
> **26.** And then Ammon said: **Believest thou that there is a Great Spirit**?
> **27.** And he said, Yea.
> **28.** And Ammon said: **This is God**. (Emphasis added).

Did Ammon take occasion here to clarify the Mormon concept that God is actually *not* just a spirit but that in fact He has a tangible body? No, he did not. And, why? Because the entire *Book of Mormon* always was and (mainly) still is monotheistic throughout, in line with Smith's theological concepts at the time the *Book of Mormon* was written around 1828-9. We will come back to evidence of this and of Smith's falsifications to the *Book of Mormon* which he later made when his theology evolved, at the point missionaries teach God has a body.

> And Ammon said unto him again: Believest thou that this ***Great Spirit***, who is God, created all things which are in heaven and in the earth?

> **Alma 18:29.** And he said: Yea, I believe that he created all things which are in the earth; but I do not know the heavens.
> **30.** And Ammon said unto him: The **heavens is a place where God dwells** and all his holy angels.
> 31. And king Lamoni said: Is it above the earth?
> **32.** And Ammon said: Yea, and he looketh down upon all the children of men; and he knows all the thoughts and intents of the heart; for by his hand were they all created from the beginning.
> **33.** And king Lamoni said: I believe all these things which thou hast spoken. Art thou sent from God?
> **34.** Ammon said unto him: I am a man; and **man in the beginning was created after the image of God**, and **I am called by his Holy Spirit** to teach these things unto this people, that they may be brought to a knowledge of that which is just and true;
> **35.** And a portion of that Spirit dwelleth in me, which giveth me knowledge, and also power according to my faith and desires which are in God.

Verse 30 confirms that God lives in "the heavens" rather than the Celestial kingdom – which appears absolutely *nowhere* in the *Book of Mormon*; v.26 and v.28 confirm that God is a *spirit* and v.34 confirms man was created after the 'spirit' image of God, in line with mainstream Christianity.

The modern Christian concept of the Holy Spirit *(v.34)* was not developed until *after* Christ. This particular passage from the *Book of Mormon* was supposedly written in about 90 BCE, before the term was ever invented. It should be remembered that the Old Testament, or Tanakh, when referring to the Holy Spirit, alludes *only* to God's 'energy' in line with Judaism. The concept referred to in the *Book of Mormon* could not have been known or understood nearly a century BCE on a different continent. Supposed ancestors of the claimed writer had lived for several hundreds of years in the Americas. This fact is completely ignored regarding this reference and also many other passages throughout the *Book of Mormon*.

> **Alma 18:36.** Now when Ammon had said these words, he began at the creation of the world, and also the creation of Adam, and told him all the things concerning the fall of man, and rehearsed **and laid before him the records and the holy scriptures of the people, which had been spoken by the prophets, even down to the time that their father, Lehi, left Jerusalem.** (Emphasis added).

Assuming someone is inclined to believe Lehi was real and obtained 'brass plates' containing Hebrew Scriptures when he left Jerusalem around 600 BCE, then the writings and stories within them should be far closer to original ideas and more accurate and informative than the modern day *King James Version* which was written *after* 600 BCE while the Jews were in exile. Yet for some reason, the brass plates were not buried with or even copied to the supposed gold plates and do not form part of Smith's initial work. That is despite the fact that Nephi claimed he wrote things *from* the brass plates onto the gold plates, including Isaiah which reads identically to the *KJV* rather than an original text.

> **2 Nephi 4:15**. And *upon these I write the things of my soul, and many of the scriptures which are engraven upon the plates of brass*. For my soul delighteth in the scriptures, and my heart pondereth them, and writeth them for the learning and the profit of my children. (Emphasis added).

Not only did Nephi claim to write things from the brass plates onto the gold plates, he also claimed they would not perish and would be seen by all nations, kindreds, tongues and people *(see below)*. Yet no one has ever heard of them or claimed to have seen them at all.

> **1 Nephi 5:18.** That *these plates of brass should go forth unto all nations, kindreds, tongues, and people* who were of his seed.
> **19.** Wherefore, he said that *these plates of brass should never perish; neither should they be dimmed any more by time*. And he prophesied many things concerning his seed. (Emphasis added).

The awkward historical fact of the matter for the Mormon Church is Jewish theologians and historians accept that the versions of many early biblical events which appear in the Old Testament were not actually written the way they now appear until the Jews were in exile around 550-400 BCE, long *after* Lehi supposedly left the area. Nineteenth-century dating of the final form of Genesis and the Pentateuch to c.500–450 BCE continues to be widely accepted, irrespective of the model adopted, although a minority of scholars known as 'biblical minimalists' argue for a date largely or entirely within the last *two* centuries BCE. Whatever the case, Lehi could not possibly have had access to early details as they *now* appear in the *Book of Mormon*. When Lehi left Jerusalem, they had not yet been written that way. Smith relied on the *KJV* in his *Book of Mormon*, constantly muddling Old and New Testament concepts.

That is without even getting into the fact that much of Isaiah was included in the *Book of Mormon* almost word for word as it appears in the *KJV*, including a number of the known *KJV* translation errors. Mormon Church apologists offer a pathetic excuse; they surmise that perhaps Joseph Smith noticed the similarity and copied the *KJV* instead of bothering to actually translate that part of the book. Considering the fact that had he done so, it would have provided a far more accurate and original work, this is just an excuse *not* to accept the only alternative, and obvious fact – Joseph Smith just made it all up. God was supposedly *dictating* the translation directly into Smith's hat, so why would Smith *stop* that process and *copy* material from his modern day Bible instead? It makes absolutely *no* sense; that is, until the truth dawns on you...

> **Alma:18:37.** And he also rehearsed unto them (for it was unto the king and to his servants) all the journeyings of their fathers in the wilderness, and all their sufferings with hunger and thirst, and their travail, ***and so forth***. [See p.72].
> **38.** And he also rehearsed unto them concerning the rebellions of Laman and Lemuel, and the sons of Ishmael, yea, all their rebellions did he relate unto them; and he expounded unto them all the records and scriptures from the time that Lehi left Jerusalem down to the present time.
> **39.** But this is not all; for he expounded unto them the plan of redemption, which was prepared from the foundation of the world; and he also made known unto them concerning the coming of **Christ**, and all the works of the Lord did he make known unto them.
> **40.** And it came to pass that after he had said all these things, and expounded them to the king, that the king believed all his words. (Emphasis added).

Once again, something that will escape missionaries is the fact that the title 'Christ' was a CE English creation long after the Saviour allegedly lived. This conversation supposedly transpired around 90 BCE. There was no BCE *word* for 'Christ' and it is not one that Ammon could or would have known or used in *any* language. The concept of a 'Messiah' is one thing, but 'Christ' entirely another. Lehi and his family were supposedly Jews and Jews were, and remain, singularly monotheistic, believing in neither the Christian idea of Satan or of Jesus as the Christ. The *concepts* did not *exist* in Judaism.

Alma 22. Header:

> *Aaron teaches Lamoni's father about the creation, the fall of Adam, and the plan of redemption through* **Christ**—*The king and all his household are converted—How the land was divided between the Nephites and the Lamanites. Between 90 and 77 B.C.* (Italics in original, bold added).

> **Alma 22:4.** And Aaron said unto the king: Behold, the Spirit of the Lord has called him another way; he has gone to the land of Ishmael, to teach the people of Lamoni.
> **5.** Now the king said unto them: What is this that ye have said concerning the Spirit of the Lord? Behold, this is the thing which doth trouble me.

# MISSIONARY PREPARATION

> 6. And also, what is this that Ammon said—If ye will repent ye shall be saved, and if ye will not repent, ye shall be cast off at the last day?
> 7. And Aaron answered him and said unto him: Believest thou that there is a God? And the king said: I know that the Amalekites say that there is a God, and I have granted unto them that they should build sanctuaries, that they may assemble themselves together to worship him. And if now thou sayest there is a God, behold I will believe.
> 8. And now when Aaron heard this, his heart began to rejoice, and he said: Behold, assuredly as thou livest, O king, there is a God.

Recommending this for missionaries to read is clearly an attempt to show them that if they are faithful and preach with 'power and authority', some people, perhaps even kings, will listen and believe. The fact that teaching *anything*, no matter how bizarre, will eventually be believed by *someone* also helps the missionaries. On a British TV show, some years back, half a dozen followers in a little cult claimed they would never die. Convinced by their leader that he had discovered the secret to eternal life, which was simply that you must *believe* you will *not* grow old and die, they duly believed that they wouldn't. Everyone dies because they *expect* to. They won't die because they have faith to believe they won't. They actually believed, because of their new-found faith that they would not grow any older and would never die.

I never heard what happened to them but I expect they came to their senses as they grew older, and of course they will die – if some of them haven't already. The point is that some people will believe absolutely *anything*. People seem to want to believe they have truth and direction in their lives and the warm, fuzzy feeling this provides is most compelling, often *preventing* people from considering reasons why they may be *wrong*. The alternative is far too painful to even consider once someone has 'found' their personal truth. The fact that there are over thirty-four-thousand different Christian denominations alone, with about ten new ones emerging every week, should be a clue to that psychological need.

Including the concept that God is a *spirit* rather than a physical being, the following is the 'faith promoting' story that missionaries review so they feel empowered to teach with authority and able to convert investigators.

Remember, this is supposedly around 90 BCE in America using 'scriptures' brought from the Holy Land several hundreds of years earlier by their Jewish ancestors. I have emphasised the 'great sprit' references once again and also some of the aspects which are quite impossible. They were of Jewish stock and yet we have the "plan of redemption … through Christ" as well as the King's fanciful response and conversion.

Note that the King has no idea what Aaron is going to say but says he will believe *anything* he is told. This is intended to make him sound faithful rather than gullible. Question: why would a king, who has already let the Amalekites establish places of worship *(v.7)*, yet not converted to their ways, suddenly be willing to believe *anything* he is now told? It makes no sense whatsoever. Kings would hardly behave that way. It is a fanciful storyline and that is all it is. Missionaries however will want to emulate Aaron, the hero of the story.

> **9.** And the king said: Is God that **Great Spirit** that brought our fathers out of the land of Jerusalem?
> **10.** And Aaron said unto him: Yea, he is that **Great Spirit**, and he created all things both in heaven and in earth. Believest thou this?
> **11.** And he said: Yea, I believe that the **Great Spirit** created all things, and I desire that ye should ***tell me*** concerning all these things, ***and I will believe thy words***.
> **12.** And it came to pass that when Aaron saw that the king would believe his words, ***he began from the creation of Adam, reading the scriptures unto the king***—how God created man after his own image, and that God gave him commandments, and that because of transgression, man had fallen.
> **13.** And Aaron did expound unto him the scriptures from the creation of Adam, laying the fall of man before him, and their carnal state and also ***the plan of redemption, which was prepared from the foundation of the world, through Christ, for all whosoever would believe on his name.***
> **14.** And since man had fallen he could not merit anything of himself; but the sufferings and ***death of Christ atone for their sins***, through faith and repentance, ***and so forth;*** and that he breaketh the bands of death, that the grave shall have no victory, and that the sting of death should be swallowed up in the hopes of glory; and Aaron did expound all these things unto the king.

Let me just mention here that Smith uses the phrase, "and so forth" *(v.14)* as he did in *Alma 18:37 (see p.70)*, which is the equivalent of saying 'etcetera' (as if the reader will already know the sorts of things that could follow) and which is not exactly something expected in ancient scripture. It is interesting that although Smith originally used the term '&c' at the end of his *Articles of Faith 6 & 7*, they were later altered to exactly the same phrase "and so forth", giving a huge clue as to whether the phraseology used in the *Book of Mormon* was from 90 BCE or more typical of language of the 1800s. It was *not* an expression that found its way into the *KJV*.

> **AoF 6.** We believe in the same organization that existed in the Primitive Church, namely, apostles, prophets, pastors, teachers, evangelists, ***and so forth.***
> **AoF 7.** We believe in the gift of tongues, prophecy, revelation, visions, healing, interpretation of tongues, ***and so forth.*** (Emphasis added).

# MISSIONARY PREPARATION

The story in Alma 22 continues:

> **15.** And it came to pass that after Aaron had expounded these things unto him, the king said: ***What shall I do that I may have this eternal life*** of which thou hast spoken? Yea, ***what shall I do*** that I may be born of God, ***having this wicked spirit rooted out*** of my breast, and ***receive his Spirit, that I may be filled with joy, that I may not be cast off*** at the last day? Behold, said he, ***I will give up all that I possess, yea, I will forsake my kingdom, that I may receive this great joy.***
> **16.** But Aaron said unto him: If thou desirest this thing, if thou wilt bow down before God, yea, if thou wilt ***repent of all thy sins***, and will bow down before God, and call on his name in faith, believing that ye shall receive, ***then shalt thou receive the hope*** which thou desirest.

This is every missionary's dream story, and its inclusion is clearly intended to inspire them to great achievements, which few, if any of them ever realise. The story gets even more dramatic, and to the rational mind, unbelievable:

> **17.** And it came to pass that when Aaron had said these words, the king did bow down before the Lord, upon his knees; yea, even he did prostrate himself upon the earth, and cried mightily, saying:
> **18.** O God, Aaron hath told me that there is a God; and if there is a God, and if thou art God, wilt thou make thyself known unto me, and I will give away all my sins to know thee, and that I may be raised from the dead, and be saved at the last day. And now when the king had said these words, he was struck as if he were dead.
> **19.** And it came to pass that his servants ran and told the queen all that had happened unto the king. And she came in unto the king; and when she saw him lay as if he were dead, and also Aaron and his brethren standing as though they had been the cause of his fall, she was angry with them, and ***commanded that her servants, or the servants of the king,*** should take them and slay them.
> **20.** Now the servants had seen the cause of the king's fall, therefore they durst not lay their hands on Aaron and his brethren; and they pled with the queen saying: Why commandest thou that we should slay these men, when behold one of them is mightier than us all? Therefore we shall fall before them.
> **21.** Now when the queen saw the fear of the servants she also began to fear exceedingly, lest there should some evil come upon her. And she commanded her servants that they should go and call the people, that they might slay Aaron and his brethren.
> **22.** Now when Aaron saw the determination of the queen, he, also knowing the hardness of the hearts of the people, feared lest that a multitude should assemble themselves together, and there should be a great contention and a disturbance among them; therefore he put forth

his hand and raised the king from the earth, and said unto him: Stand. And he stood upon his feet, receiving his strength.

**23.** Now this was done in the presence of the queen and many of the servants. And when they saw it they greatly marveled, and began to fear. And the king stood forth, and began to minister unto them. And he did minister unto them, insomuch that his whole household were converted unto the Lord. (Emphasis added).

Before we continue, note once again that Smith *corrects* himself, or he has Alma (or possibly the Queen) correct himself *(v.19)*, just as someone might in speech, but certainly *not* when writing, especially when using hieroglyphs.

So, Smith's ability to tell fanciful stories finds its way into the *Book of Mormon*. All ends well and Lamoni and all his household are converted by Aaron.

Once again we have the impossible mention of *Christ* and also that it was *known* from the *beginning* that redemption can come through believing in him.

Yet the Jews never did – and they still don't. Remember, they wrote the original scriptures. It was *their* religion. Early Christians hijacked what became the *Old Testament* and Joseph Smith went a step further and altered the very basis of early Judaic theology to suit his own purpose and here he impossibly backdated it via Lehi into the Old Testament era. If it was always 'known' then *where* is the *real* historical *evidence* in Judaism?

Smith claims that Aaron 'read' from the scriptures *(v.12. See p.72 above)* which Lehi had taken with him when he left Jerusalem. Thus it is claimed the 'brass plates' physically existed and were used. What happened to them?

Considering these people had been in the Americas for many hundreds of years and supposedly wrote in 'reformed Egyptian' on the gold plates as they went along, the question is who still spoke and wrote in Hebrew which would have been the language of the brass plates? No civilisation anywhere in the Americas has ever been discovered where the root of their language compares with Hebrew.

The unanswerable questions which investigators should ask are absolutely endless – but they *should* be asked. Also, if that record had been preserved onto their 'gold plates', we would now have the oldest and therefore most accurate account in the world rather than just a copy of parts of Isaiah extracted directly from the *KJV* into the *Book of Mormon*, including the many translation errors, concerning everything before 600 BCE. Clearly, this did not happen, so we are deprived of such earlier, more accurate accounts. These factors combine to once again expose not just the *story* as just fanciful on Smith's part, it bearing no resemblance to reality whatsoever, but the rest of the *Book of Mormon* as well.

# MISSIONARY PREPARATION

The monotheistic theology of Smith at the time the *Book of Mormon* was written comes though in these chapters as much as anywhere. The Great Spirit *is* God in Smith's mind. God does *not* have a body and this is confirmed over and over again in the *Book of Mormon*. Had Smith already developed his *later* concept that God has a physical body, the *Book of Mormon* would be replete with such references, yet all of them confirm just the opposite. The *Book of Mormon* is actually a powerful witness *against* Smith in every way imaginable. Mormon leaders claim *faith* has to be stronger than *reason* but whatever they may claim, it is a fundamental fact that *truth* (evidence) trumps *faith* in *fiction*.

Time after time, in Alma 18 & 22, God is confirmed as being a 'Great Spirit' and *not once* is there a reference to physical attributes there or anywhere else in the *Book of Mormon*. Why does Alma read 'Great Spirit' instead of explaining that God has a physical body? Smith was entirely monotheistic until at least 1835 which is why the *Book of Mormon* is completely monotheistic throughout. It is compelling evidence that Smith did *not* have a vision in 1820 and that his whole 'plurality of Gods' concept was a mid to late eighteen-thirties idea which he backdated to 1820 for dramatic effect. The fact that absolutely *everything* surrounding the first vision is demonstrably *not* true should be a clue to the facts. We will be looking closely at each aspect of that in Chapter 5.

The term 'Christ' could not have been used *anywhere* in the pre-Christian era. *Christ* is the *English* term for the Greek Χριστός (*Khristós*) meaning "the anointed one". It is a translation of the Hebrew חישמ (*Māšîah*) which is usually transliterated into English as *Messiah*. The pronunciation 'Christ' began in the 14th century CE. Prior to that it was usually spelt 'Crist' – and pronounced that way (as in Christmas).

The term *Christ* (or similar) appears in English and also in most European languages, due to the Greek usage of *Christós* transcribed in Latin as *Christus* in the New Testament as a description for Jesus. In the Septuagint version of the Hebrew Bible, it was used to translate into Greek the Hebrew *mashiach* (messiah), meaning 'anointed'. *Khristós* in classical Greek usage could mean *covered in oil*, and is thus a literal translation of messiah. *(See also pp.338-9)*.

If the *Book of Mormon* were truly an original historical work, translated from gold plates, then this supposed first century BCE account taken from 'scripture', written down *prior* to 600 BCE, when Lehi and his family left Jerusalem, would have been written in and read from original *Hebrew* which would have translated to 'Messiah' and *not Christ* in modern day English. Even if we were to accept the claim that Smith's fictional 'reformed Egyptian' was used somewhere or other, that, or *any* language of the day, real or imagined, could not possibly have translated into a word that did not *exist*. The word 'Christ' had not been invented in *any* language. This point, which can be made about many other aspects of the *Book of Mormon*, may not seem important to some, but it is just one of hundreds of similarly impossible aspects which point to the conclusively fraudulent claim of Joseph Smith that the book was a true record of a real people.

> Only after the Resurrection did the title gradually pass into a proper name, and the expression *Jesus Christ* or *Christ Jesus* became only one designation. But at this stage the Greeks and Romans understood little or nothing about the import of the word *anointed*; to them it did not convey any sacred conception. Hence they substituted *Chrestus*, or "excellent", for Christus or "anointed", and *Chrestians* instead of "Christians." There may be an allusion to this practice in 1 Peter 2:3; *hoti chrestos ho kyrios*, which is rendered "that the Lord is sweet." Justin Martyr (*First Apology* 4), Clement of Alexandria (*Stromata* II.4.18), Tertullian (*To the Nations* II), and Lactantius (*Divine Institutes* IV.7), as well as St. Jerome (In Gal., V, 22), are acquainted with the pagan substitution of Chrestes for Christus, and are careful to explain the new term in a favourable sense. The pagans made little or no effort to learn anything accurate about Christ and the Christians; Suetonius, for instance, ascribes the expulsion of the Jews from Rome under Claudius to the constant instigation of sedition by Chrestus, whom he conceives as acting in Rome the part of a leader of insurgents.
>
> The use of the definite article before the word *Christ* and its gradual development into a proper name show the Christians identified the bearer with the promised Messias of the Jews. He combined in His person the offices of prophet (John 6:14; Matthew 13:57; Luke 13:33; 24:19) of king (Luke 23:2; Acts 17:7; 1 Corinthians 15:24; Apocalypse 15:3), and of priest (Hebrews 2:17; etc.); he fulfilled all the Messianic predictions in a fuller and a higher sense than had been given them by the teachers of the Synagogue. *(Catholic Encyclopaedia: Origin of the name of Jesus Christ).*

Whilst it has been clearly identified that the use of Christ's *modern* title in the pre-Christian era was simply *impossible*, Mormon apologists will no doubt continue to conjure up implausible and unconvincing reasons why it could have been included in Smith's 'translation' of the *Book of Mormon*. Considering Smith's method of translation was having his face buried in a hat, nothing that came out of it should really surprise us.

## MISSIONARY PREPARATION
### The Great Apostasy

> After the death of Jesus Christ, wicked people persecuted the Apostles and Church members and killed many of them. With the death of the Apostles, priesthood keys and the presiding priesthood authority were taken from the earth. The Apostles had kept the doctrines of the gospel pure and ***maintained the order and standard of worthiness for Church members***. Without the Apostles, over time the doctrines were corrupted and unauthorized changes were made in Church organization and priesthood ordinances, such as baptism and conferring the gift of the Holy Ghost. *(Page 35).* (Emphasis added).

There was no real long term "order and standard of worthiness" in the so-called 'early church' either during or just after Christ's life. Initially, there was no 'formal' church, as Christ did not organise one. He required nothing to be written down at the time he spoke it – and nothing ever was according to biblical scholars and backed up by history. During his short ministry, Jesus just called twelve disciples and was an itinerant preacher; if he even lived as an individual entity at all; an aspect that is actively disputed by many historians. There was no formal 'organisation' during his ministry. People were baptised and just got on with their new-found belief system.

The church later 'created' by the Romans, was an entirely different concept in many ways and did not remotely represent the free ideas that Jesus Christ originally taught. If Christ was supposed to have brought a formal church organisation into the world which was capable of surviving intact when he died, he (and God) did not do a very good job of it. Note that the above quote from Mormon leaders to their missionaries speaks of the idea that the disciples kept the doctrines pure and maintained the order and 'standard of worthiness' for church members. There is actually no recorded requirement to any *standard* at all – just the admonition to 'believe'.

Likewise, the Mormon Church offers criticism that unauthorised changes were made to ordinances – such a baptism. This is a very clear reference to the idea that the early Christian church substituted total immersion with what is now termed 'sprinkling' as an accepted form of baptism. It is fine to make such a comment if you are personally consistent in your own affairs. Unfortunately for Mormon leaders, their own Church falls foul of exactly the same kinds of unauthorised change to its own procedures and they are therefore in no position to criticise.

When the Mormon 'endowment' was originally (re)introduced and the 'washing and anointing' instituted, it was supposedly *exactly* as had been practiced from the time of Adam and certainly claimed to be as it was at the time of Solomon – according to Mormon theology. Joseph Smith stated that it must *never* be altered and was to remain the same forever.

# THE MORMON DELUSION

> The Prophet Joseph Smith taught: '***Ordinances instituted in the heavens*** before the foundation of the world, in the Priesthood, for the salvation of men, ***are not to be altered or changed.***' *(Ensign. Aug. 2001:22. Published BYU fireside address 27 Oct 2000. Dennis B. Neuenschwander (Presidency of the Seventy) c: Teachings of the Prophet Joseph Smith, sel. Joseph Fielding Smith. 1976:308).* (Emphasis added).

> ...He set the ***temple ordinances to be the same forever and ever*** and set Adam to watch over them, to reveal them from heaven to man, or to send angels to reveal them. *(H.C. Vol.4:208).* (Emphasis added). *(There are many other quotes available. A good selection can be found at:* www.mormoncurtain.com/topic_templechanges.html*).*

Yet, despite original 'initiatory' work requiring complete washing, where initiates lay naked in bathtubs, with enough virgin olive oil used to saturate someone's hair for days, this ritual has gradually changed and evolved until it is no longer even remotely recognisable. Evidence of the use of bathtubs was confirmed by Heber Kimball 'borrowing' one from the temple to use for the rebaptism of Windsor Lyon when there was no other facility available. They are mentioned (www.ldsendowment.org) in early records of Mormon temple ceremonies. Twelve of the largest bathtubs ever manufactured, were ordered for the Salt Lake Temple. *(Beurger 2002: Apx. 2).*

When I was young, the 'ordinance' was already far more symbolic than jumping into a bath naked, but it was still performed by the officiator touching various parts of the body through an open 'shield' with wet fingertips. The washing was then 'sealed' by a second officiator while both laid hands on the head of the 'patron'.

The patron moved to another cubicle, where these actions were all *exactly* repeated, using virgin olive oil for the 'anointing' stage of the ordinance, when each part of the body mentioned was anointed with oil from the fingertips of the officiator whilst he (or she for women) spoke the same words, substituting 'anoint' in place of 'wash'. The patron, still naked under the open sided 'shield, would move the shield to accommodate each part of the washing and the anointing, whilst at the same time trying to retain a modicum of modesty.

> I anoint your head, that your brain and your intellect may be clear and active [oil across forehead]; your ears, that you may hear the word of the Lord [the tops of both ears]; your eyes, that you may see clearly and discern between truth and error [above both eyebrows]; your nose, that you may smell [finger drawn along length of nose]; your lips, that you may never speak guile; [above and below lips] your neck, that it may bear up your head properly [across neck]; your shoulders, that they may bear the burdens that shall be placed thereon [across top of

## MISSIONARY PREPARATION

shoulders]; your back, that there may be marrow in the bones and in the spine [from top to base of the spine]; your breast, that it may be the receptacle of pure and virtuous principles [above both breasts]; your vitals and bowels, that they may be healthy and strong and perform their proper functions [stomach]; your arms and hands, that they may be strong and **wield the sword of justice in defence of truth and virtue** [from top of both arms down to fingers]; your loins, that you may be fruitful and multiply and replenish the earth, that you might have joy in your posterity [a point slightly in from the right hip]; your legs and feet, that you might run and not be weary, and walk and not faint [from a few inches below the top of each leg in turn, down to the toes]. *(For a complete review of this area along with the rest of the Mormon Temple ceremonies as originally performed, see TMD Vol. 3. Section 3).* (Emphasis added).

The above was the way things were for men, but I understand women did not get anointed to wield swords or such; they just got to 'work' – or something similar. It would clearly not do in Mormonism to have women running around wielding swords for any reason apparently. Perhaps one day, in an age of more equality, Mormon women will be permitted to do so.

I always wondered why the only thing that was said about the *nose* was that it was anointed so you may 'smell'. Everything else has an aspect of religious virtue attaching but the nose has no purpose other than to smell. I guess they couldn't think of anything special for the nose but didn't want to leave it out. Early versions didn't even mention the nose. Following the anointing, another officiator would enter the cubicle and seal the anointing, just as before for the washing. The patron would move to a final cubicle where the officiator then somehow managed to place the one piece 'garment' on the patron by the patron stepping into the legs, the officiator pulling up the garment to the shoulders and the patron placing his arms through the sleeves whilst the shield was adjusted to accommodate the placing of the garment. Modesty was extremely difficult at this stage but it was always performed with as much dignity as possible. The patron could then, and only then, touch the garment by being allowed to tie the strings at the lower part of the front while the officiator tied the upper strings which held it together. Later, the garment had a zipper which the patron pulled all the way up. Whilst placing the garment on the patron, the officiator would say that the garment is:

> ...to be worn throughout your life. It represents the Garment given to Adam when he was found naked in the Garden of Eden, and is called the Garment of the Holy Priesthood. Inasmuch as you do not defile it, but are true and faithful to your covenants, it will be a shield and a protection to you against the power of the destroyer until you have finished your work on the earth.

Something I had not considered is the idea that women can perform these initiatory ordinances for other women. Clearly, it would not do to have men touching the various body parts of women through open-sided 'shields', so women must do it. However, the Melchizedek Priesthood is the required level of Priesthood to perform such ordinances (for other men) and women do *not* hold that Priesthood. So, where does the appropriate 'authority' for women to perform these ordinances stem from in Mormon theology? It is a mystery. But then, if (or should I say, 'when') the Church one day caves and allows women the Priesthood, perhaps they will point to the fact they always held it by virtue of the men; anyway, they have always performed such ordinances in temples. They will rationalise the inevitable change in any way they can when the time comes and they become more or less obliged to do so.

A Church survey among selected members found that many considered the initiatory work to be awkward and embarrassing, unpleasant, even a distasteful experience, overshadowing the concept of it being fulfilling and spiritual. This resulted in it being modified yet again in January of 2005. The ritual is now the equivalent of a Catholic baptism; members no longer have *any* body parts below the neck touched, washed or anointed. Remember, Smith proclaimed that it was the *same* as at the time of Adam and Solomon and that it should *never* be changed.

The initiatory ritual has therefore *evolved,* from immersion in a bathtub and then oil being poured on the head which ran down the body, to symbolic actions where the initiate is already clothed in the garment which they have put on themselves. Only the head is symbolically washed and anointed with a drop or two of water and then oil. The wording remains the same, but the *act* is now purely *symbolic*. Mormonism, in this respect, has ultimately followed on the heels of Catholic 'sprinkling' for baptism. The only difference is, in the case of Mormonism, their God is on record as stating *His* ordinance of washing and anointing should *never* change, whereas the Catholic Church has no recorded mandate forbidding their method of baptism.

This ritual, once performed with patrons laid naked in a bath perfumed with whisky and rolled from side to side as their various parts were 'washed', has ultimately become another ghost of the past, simply to avoid embarrassment to members, now that we live in a more evolved and completely different world of concepts and ideals. The Mormon God apparently seems to have had some difficulty in remaining the same yesterday, today and forever, within the small-minded modern world of humankind that He created. It seems we now know better than God and that He is obliged to comply with what humans are willing to accept as currently appropriate regarding His once *unchangeable* ordinances.

The Mormon God is obliged to keep up with the times. It is not the only 'unchangeable' ordinance or doctrine that *has* subsequently *been* changed.

# MISSIONARY PREPARATION

You would have thought that a God would have designed his 'washing and anointing' ceremonies in a manner suitable for every age in the first place, keeping them simple but consistent if they were *never* to be altered. Either that, or say that they *may* be modified and adapted to suit future cultural changes instead of declaring that they must always remain the same. Despite Smith's claim that it must remain unchanged, the endowment, from initiatory through to passing through the veil, has been an ever changing feast and it is now almost unrecognisable from the original ceremony, introduced less than two hundred years ago. It is in fact markedly different from the version that was used when I first attended in 1964. The unchangeable ritual, which apparently remained that way for *thousands* of years, was to virtually disappear in next to no time at all. Yet theologically the Mormon God *never* changes. *(See: TMD. Vol. 3, Section 3)*.

I wonder how they could ever explain the new structure of the initiatory ordinances *without* conceding that other religions *equally* have every right to 'symbolically' baptise. The initiatory process now includes a new quote which is taken from *Exodus 40:12-13*:

> And thou shalt bring Aaron and his sons unto the door of the tabernacle of the congregation, and wash them with water. And thou shalt put upon Aaron the holy garments, and anoint him, and sanctify him...

Following the above newly introduced quote, patrons are told that *in our day* they are washed and anointed *only symbolically*. Now, 'symbolic' washing and anointing consists of only a touch to the forehead – don't Catholics baptise that way? Today the temple patron dons the garment and the fully enclosed shield *before* entering the washing and anointing cubicles and the garment is '*authorised*' for the person's use.

Joseph Smith may have used the fact that baptism appeared to have been changed, to his advantage, but he no more reintroduced the original doctrines of Christ than the Romans maintained them before him. Each just made up what would be to his own best advantage. History now shows what happened in the early years of Christianity and equally it shows what nonsense Joseph Smith came up with in his time. All that is required in each case is a little research into the original history to discover the truth.

The missionary manual claims:

> The Savior's **Apostles foretold this universal apostasy**. They also foretold that the gospel of Jesus Christ and His Church would be restored once more upon the earth. *(Page 35)*. (Emphasis added).

# THE MORMON DELUSION

The first quote regarding the claimed apostasy is from the *Book of Mormon* and it concerns the establishment of a 'Great and Abominable' Church.

> **1 Nephi 13:6.** And it came to pass that I beheld this great and abominable church; and I saw the devil that he was the founder of it.

When I was young, we all 'knew' that this definitely referred to the Roman Catholic Church, although the idea was already starting to be played down as it was far from 'politically correct', a term yet to be invented. Ultimately, in light of it being an extremely controversial and inflammatory statement which started to cause much embarrassment for the Church, it was watered down to mean 'Babylon' – or the world at large. Thus it encompassed anything and everything *not* Mormon.

Several references are provided for missionaries to study and choose from. This is just one of them:

> **Galatians 1:6.** I marvel that ye are so soon removed from him that called you into the grace of Christ unto another gospel:
> **7.** Which is not another; but there be some that trouble you, and would pervert the gospel of Christ.
> **8.** *But though we, or an angel from heaven, preach any other gospel unto you than that which we have preached unto you, let him be accursed.*
> **9.** As we said before, so say I now again, *If any man preach any other gospel unto you than that ye have received, let him be accursed.* (Emphasis added).

Galatians says if anyone preaches a gospel other than the one they teach – let them be accursed. Based on the evidence, that preacher would be Joseph Smith as much as anyone else in recorded history.

# Chapter 5

# Lesson 1

### The Message of the Restoration of the Gospel of Jesus Christ

### Part B

#### The Joseph Smith Story

Following the header "The Restoration of the Gospel of Jesus Christ through Joseph Smith", the Joseph Smith story is expounded. It is interesting to note the way this is portrayed in the manual. Missionaries will of course tell the story in their own way and no doubt feel they are being directed by the spirit as they do so. The manual starts this section by declaring that:

> ***When the circumstances were right***, Heavenly Father once again reached out to His children in love. He called a young man named Joseph Smith as a prophet. Through him the fulness of the gospel of Jesus Christ was restored to the earth. *(Page 36)*. (Emphasis added).

I remember well being taught in church that it was only following the reformation, when people began to more openly question the religions of the day, that the time finally became 'right' for the Lord to be *able* to re-establish His gospel. For some reason, prior to that it would have been impossible.

In reality, if that actually had been necessary, He could have *created* the right circumstances to facilitate it hundreds, if not thousands, of years earlier to save so many people from being born, not just in ignorance of the truth, but in eras where the only religion available to them was (according to Mormonism) entirely false. In that case, God has deliberately 'allowed' billions of people to follow entirely the *wrong* path. What was the theological thinking in that? In that case, other than his 'atoning sacrifice', which could have been performed at any time, what was the point of the Saviour coming to Earth when he did?

Surely a different time and place would have better served the human race? I know the Mormon Church claims it had to fulfil prophecy and happen in the 'meridian of time' and the Jews were the only ones who would have killed him; but, in the cold light of day, doesn't that idea seem somewhat ridiculous?

Mormonism exists on the basis that God and Jesus got it all wrong enough that the early church quickly fell into apostasy. Most of the rest of Christianity accepts that it did *not*, despite the many different denominations now existing.

The lesson opening statement above *(p.83)* then sets the scene for a claimed restoration of the true gospel. Investigators should perhaps question why, if God sent his Son to earth two thousand years or so ago, He didn't make a better job of ensuring it all went right the first time. What kind of God sets his stall out in such a being as Jesus Christ who never personally organised a church or a formal religion of any kind, never had anything written down to record the actual first hand facts, and just spent his short life as an itinerant preacher?

God's future desires never were established in an organised fashion and He did not leave a properly organised overall formal structure for the future of an actual church. If Mormonism is accepted as true, then it also has to be accepted that having botched His first attempt at establishing the true church on Earth, God left His children with an entirely false religion for two thousand years of confusion, mayhem and murder, manipulated by men who Mormonism claims were *not* men of God. Why is that not entirely God's own fault? This *failed* God finally called upon a teenage con artist to redress things. His latter-day protégé ultimately fared no better, leaving behind a lacklustre religion in which growth is already slowing fast. This first stage of decline of a minor religion confirms a phrase I coined a year or two ago, which I posted on my web site: "If God does exist, He is not very good at religion."

The whole thing was doomed to failure from the start as there was never any real basis for continuity, let alone a firm understanding of what Jesus really said, did or expected. Many Christians today believe and accept on faith that the Apostles really did write the gospels, despite the fact history shows that they almost certainly did not. They were written long after Christ died; they are third or fourth hand hearsay at best and in one case, a mythical reconstruction.

# THE JOSEPH SMITH STORY

Many historians and theologians consider the accounts of Christ to be a conglomerate of several supposed 'saviours' of the period. The gospels were written by people who never even met or knew the man Jesus and the 'gospels' were ascribed to people who did not write them and who had nothing to do with the content. The *Gospel of Matthew* is dependent on the *Gospel of Mark* and the *Gospel of John* was written as a fanciful account by the Romans to describe the character they would have liked the Saviour to have been. *(See p.516; also summary at:* http://www.earlychristianwritings.com/matthew.html). The Gospels are, in reality, no more than fictional writing, without any first hand or ratified genuine accounts within them whatsoever.

The New Testament is, in effect, no more than a book of Chinese whispers; that is, with the notable exception of the book of Revelation – considered by many theologians to have been written by a lunatic. *(See: Ch. 17, pp.434-5).*

Why did this God allow it all to fizzle out and let the Romans rekindle (for their own convenience and control) what later became Christianity, which was effectively formed by pagans to control the masses, with doctrines *created* by Christian committees? Still, that's not the question of the moment for today.

The manual continues:

> Joseph Smith lived in the United States, which was perhaps the only country to enjoy religious freedom at the time. *(Page 36).*

I won't dwell on that point long, but it is perfectly clear that whilst it is true many people had been immigrating to the United States, from places such as Germany, so they could enjoy religious freedom, it was by far *not* the only country which actually had such freedom. It was certainly a good (and possibly the best) choice, but the Church likes to solidify its position that the United States is the chosen (or promised) land, as claimed over and over again in the *Book of Mormon. (See: 1 Ne.18:8,22-23,25 & 2 Ne.1:3,5,9-10,24 for example).*

When you consider that just a few years later, Joseph Smith introduced the practice of polygamy into his 'restored' Church and that it was completely *illegal* in the United States, we should seriously question why their God didn't select a religiously free country where polygamy was perfectly legal and then it could and would have been openly practiced from the start – and invariably would still be practiced in Mormonism today. That is yet another good question for investigators to ask missionaries. That is a significant question that Mormon leaders *cannot* answer. Why *would* a God command an *illegal* practice when it would have been so easy for it to have been instituted (and continued) quite legally somewhere else? The very idea of a God even making such a command is entirely inconsistent with every known attribute of every known concept of any deity whatsoever. It simply could and would not happen.

# THE MORMON DELUSION

Incidentally, the question of polygamy is not addressed or even mentioned *once* in the missionary manual. The Church remains quiet about it and unless an investigator is aware of its existence in the early Mormon Church they could be baptised knowing *nothing* about polygamy at all. Considering the fact that in Mormon theology it is an essential eternal principle, I consider this entirely dishonest, dishonourable and reprehensible, as although not practiced today, it still remains a core eternal *doctrine* and will be expected of Mormons in their Celestial kingdom in the eternities. It is in fact the *only* method by which new worlds can be populated according to Mormon theology. There is no getting away from that. *(See: TMD Vol. 1, for coverage of illegal polygamy and also polyandry within Mormonism).*

> It was at a time of great religious excitement in the eastern United States. His family members were deeply religious and constantly sought for truth. But many ministers claimed to have the true gospel. Joseph desired "to know which of all the sects was right," (Joseph Smith—History 1:18). The Bible taught there was "one Lord, one faith, one baptism" (Ephesians 4:5). Joseph attended different churches, but he remained confused about which church he should join. He later wrote: "So great were the confusions and strife among the different denominations, that it was impossible for a person young as I was ... to come to any certain conclusion who was right and who was wrong. ...In the midst of this war of words and tumult of opinions, *Investigators must understand that a universal apostasy occurred following the death of Jesus Christ and His Apostles. If there had been no apostasy, there would have been no need of a Restoration.* As a diamond displayed on black velvet appears more brilliant, so the Restoration stands in striking contrast to the dark background of the Great Apostasy. *(Page 36).* (Emphasis added).

With this scant information, Mormon missionaries endeavour to explain the concept that the early church fell into apostasy and therefore not one modern denomination has the truth.

> As guided by the Spirit, teach investigators about the Great Apostasy at a level of detail appropriate to their needs and circumstances. Your purpose is to help them understand the need for the Restoration of the gospel of Jesus Christ.
>
> **Key Points:**
>
> The Church of Jesus Christ is built on the foundation of apostles and prophets (see Ephesians 2:19–20; 4:11–14). These leaders have divine priesthood authority. Through revelation they direct the affairs of the

# THE JOSEPH SMITH STORY

> Church. They maintain doctrinal purity, authorize the administration of ordinances, and call and confer upon others the priesthood authority. *(Page 36)*.

The 'church' that Christ 'built' contained no more than a group of twelve apostles and contained *no* prophets among them. Christ was an itinerant preacher who did not organise a church as such during his short three year ministry. All the prophets recorded in the Bible, lived prior to Christ and they were Jews, not Christians. Christ did not personally build a *church* at all. If we are to believe the gospels, then he just taught some good principles. The manual is really setting out the stall of the Mormon Church today, claiming it has been 'restored' just as it was shortly after the time of Jesus, using the names of church officers found in the New Testament, most of which were invented *after* the time of Jesus.

> People rejected and killed Jesus Christ and the Apostles (see Matthew 24:9; 1 Nephi 11:32–34; 2 Nephi 27:5). With the death of the Apostles, the presiding priesthood authority was absent from the Church. Consequently, there was no longer authority to confer the Holy Ghost or perform other saving ordinances. Revelation ceased, and doctrine became corrupted. *(Page 36)*.

This Mormon claim assumes no one else was ever 'ordained' by any of the apostles to lead the church that they more formally established after the death of Christ. The manual quotes *Matthew 24* where Jesus tells the apostles they will be killed. It does *not* mention the following verses regarding future false prophets who will deceive many. Mormons assume that refers to every claimed prophet – except their own.

Matthew 24:9 (plus v.10-11 which are *not* referenced in the manual):

> **9.** Then shall they deliver you up to be afflicted, and shall kill you: and ye shall be hated of all nations for my name's sake.
> **10.** And then shall many be offended, and shall betray one another, and shall hate one another.
> **11.** And many false prophets shall rise, and shall deceive many.

The other 'scriptures' referenced are from the *Book of Mormon*; claimed to have been written around six hundred years before Jesus Christ was even born. To use these as 'evidence' of a *later* apostasy is absolutely ridiculous.

1 Nephi 11:32-34:

> **32.** And it came to pass that the angel spake unto me again, saying: Look! And I looked and beheld the Lamb of God, that he was taken by

> the people; yea, ***the Son of the everlasting God*** was judged of the world; and I saw and bear record.
> 33. And I, Nephi, saw that he was lifted up upon the cross and slain for the sins of the world.
> 34. And after he was slain I saw the multitudes of the earth, that they were gathered together to fight against the apostles of the Lamb; for thus were the twelve called by the angel of the Lord. (Emphasis added).

Apart from the absolute nonsense idea that such things could or would ever have been originally recorded several hundred years *prior* to the time of Christ, there is another real problem for the Mormon Church in verse 32. The original *Book of Mormon* was written (1828-9) when Joseph Smith was still entirely monotheistic in his outlook. His theology concerning plural gods was to surface much later, in the mid-late 1830s. Verse 32 above *originally* stated that it was: "…the Lamb of God, that he was taken by the people; yea, *the Everlasting God*, was judged of the world..." *(1830 Edition: p.26 lines 8-10).*

So, Smith not only wrote *in* his *Book of Mormon* that Jesus was in fact *God* appearing in the flesh, aligning his ideas with traditional monotheism, but he pretended that it was recorded centuries before it would have made any sense to anyone. When Smith later changed his *own* theology, he then interpolated the words "the son of", thus instantly also *changing* the already firmly established supposed theology of the Nephites, thus thoroughly exposing his *Book of Mormon* as an entirely fraudulent and fictional work.

'Revelation' and 'prophecy' are things that have to be taken on faith, and that is one thing, but the absurd notion that these things were *revealed* in this way are quite another. We will review other similar falsifications to the *Book of Mormon* later in this chapter. *(See: pp. 97-99).* Remember that a voice from heaven supposedly declared the *Book of Mormon* 'correct' when it was written.

Astute investigators should ask why it is that subsequent to the first edition, there have been *thousands* of corrections, alterations, deletions, additions and interpolations to the original text. It is still not correct. Much of the text and grammar in the *Book of Mormon* remains absolutely awful even today. There are useful notes available on Richard Packham's web site addressing linguistic problems. (http://home.teleport.com/~packham/ or http://packham.n4m.org/).

The manual continues:

> Even before the death of the Apostles, many conflicts concerning doctrine arose. The Roman Empire, which at first had persecuted the Christians, later adopted Christianity. Important religious questions were settled by councils. The simple doctrines and ordinances taught by the Savior were debated and changed to conform to worldly philosophies (see Isaiah 24:5). ***They physically changed the scriptures,***

*removing plain and precious doctrines from them* (1 Nephi 13:26–40). They created creeds, or statements of belief, based on false and changed doctrine (see Joseph Smith—History 1:19). Because of pride, some aspired to positions of influence (see 3 John 1:9–10). People accepted these false ideas and gave honor to false teachers who taught pleasing doctrines rather than divine truth (see 2 Timothy 4:3–4). (Emphasis added).

Of course, there is a great deal of truth in the above statement concerning Rome adopting Christianity as a concept and committees or councils deciding what the actual doctrines should be. All they had to go on was (at best) third or fourth hand versions of events that were recorded by people who never met or knew Jesus.

However, for the Mormon Church the above claims incorporate yet another major problem which they cannot wriggle out of, although no doubt they will try. If the *original* 'scriptures' *were* changed (see bold text above) remember, Joseph Smith effectively *rewrote* the Bible, creating an *'Inspired Revision'* so any and all *changed* text which removed any 'plain and precious doctrines from them' should now appear there and thus resolve this supposedly terrible problem. Equally, the Romans did not alter Hebrew Scriptures available today.

The fact of the matter is that Smith changed little of anything in the Bible relatively speaking and he never finished his revision anyway, but he added a lot of nonsense which is anything but 'plain and precious' and contains no substantive missing 'doctrine' at all. On occasion however, where he did make changes, he got things entirely *wrong* or later even *ignored* what he had revised when preaching new and outrageous doctrines, such as in his use of *Revelation 1:6* concerning plural gods during his 'King Follett' sermon. *(See p.103)*.

So, the questions are, if Smith wrote an *Inspired Revision* of the Bible which had lost so much plain and precious doctrine:

**1.** Where *is* all Smith's *restored* plain and precious doctrine in his rewritten work?

– And even more importantly:

**2.** Why doesn't the Mormon Church ever use or promote Smith's *Inspired Revision* in its entirety today?

Why do they *only* use the standard *King James Version,* relegating what the Church finds to be a few useful segments from Smith's *Inspired Revision* to footnotes in the Seminary edition? If you read it and compare it to the *KJV*, the answer is painfully obvious. It contains absolutely *nothing* of any merit. Also, the copyright rests with the Reorganised Church (Community of Christ), so it is not actually owned by the Mormon Church, although Deseret Book does sell it as 'Joseph Smith's New Translation of the Bible' which includes other material.

The other thing is, if Lehi had Nephi obtain Laban's brass plates when his family left Jerusalem, the scriptures they contained would have predated 600

BCE. The version that we now have, including the five 'books of Moses', was definitely written in the form we now know it, *later* than that, when the Jews were in exile. So, the question is why did they not get buried with or copied into the gold plates? And, regarding the parts that supposedly did, from Isaiah, why did Smith dictate so many chapters of Isaiah, directly and almost exactly from the *King James Version*, including all the translation errors? Why didn't God continue dictating from what was purported to be better quality original text on the gold plates? The origin of *that* text supposedly predated 600 BCE.

> Throughout history, many **people have sincerely believed false creeds and doctrines.** They have worshiped according to the light they possessed and have received answers to their prayers. Yet they are **"kept from the truth because they know not where to find it"** *(D&C 123:12).* (Emphasis added). *(Page 36).*

This supposition is only supported by modern Mormon so-called scripture, penned by Joseph Smith, so missionaries must simply ignore the fact that they are qualifying one supposition with yet another. Sometimes the trick may work on people but it is not exactly convincing. This is extracted from a letter Joseph Smith wrote while he was in prison and has nothing to do with revelation from God, although the Church canonised it and claims it does contain revelation. The letter comprises *D&C 121-123* which Smith penned after several months of being in jail.

> Therefore, a restoration, not a reformation, was required. Priesthood authority did not continue in an unbroken line of succession from the Apostle Peter. To reform is to change what already exists; to restore is to bring back something in its original form. Thus, restoration of priesthood authority through divine messengers was the only possible way to overcome the Great Apostasy. *(Page 36).*

From what missionaries are instructed to tell their investigators, I am not quite sure how someone investigating the Church can conclude that Mormonism definitely has the answer to the claimed apostasy, but I suppose those who ultimately join the Mormon Church must be willing to believe it. The supporting 'evidence' is no more than a record of someone *claiming* to have the truth with absolutely no supporting evidence that they actually *do* have it, but then, the fact is that I myself am evidence that people do accept these things as true, because I certainly did. However, I can only remember the First Vision story and being asked to pray about Joseph Smith and the *Book of Mormon* from those early lessons as a young teenager. The rest seemed unimportant once the vision and the book were accepted.

# THE JOSEPH SMITH STORY

The concept of an apostasy is firmed up by Smith's own record as presented by the Church. The following is how the 'restoration' idea, which to Mormons now essentially means the 'First Vision' story, is portrayed and explained in the missionary manual; although it didn't when the Church was first organised, as no one even knew of such a thing. We will of course come back to that.

Quoting Joseph Smith's own story:

> I often said to myself: What is to be done? Who of all these parties are right; or, are they all wrong together? If any one of them be right, which is it, and how shall I know it?" (Joseph Smith—History 1:8, 10).

> As Joseph sought truth among the different faiths, he turned to the Bible for guidance. He read, "If any of you lack wisdom, let him ask of God, that giveth to all men liberally, and upbraideth not; and it shall be given him" (James 1:5). Because of this passage, Joseph decided to ask God what he should do. In the spring of 1820 he went to a nearby grove of trees and knelt in prayer. He described his experience: "I saw a pillar of light exactly over my head, above the brightness of the sun, which descended gradually until it fell upon me. . . . When the light rested upon me I saw two Personages, whose brightness and glory defy all description, standing above me in the air. One of them spake unto me, calling me by name and said, pointing to the other—*This is My Beloved Son. Hear Him!*" (Joseph Smith—History 1:16–17).

> *In this vision God the Father and His Son, Jesus Christ, appeared to Joseph Smith.* The Savior told Joseph not to join any of the churches, for they "were all wrong" and "all their creeds were an abomination." He stated, "They draw near to me with their lips, but their hearts are far from me, they teach for doctrines the commandments of men, having a form of godliness, but they deny the power thereof" (Joseph Smith—History 1:19). Even though many good people believed in Christ and tried to understand and teach His gospel, they did not have the fulness of truth or the priesthood authority to baptize and perform other saving ordinances. They had inherited a state of apostasy as each generation was influenced by what the previous one passed on, including changes in the doctrines and in ordinances such as baptism. As God had done with Adam, Noah, Abraham, Moses, and other prophets, He called Joseph Smith to be a prophet through whom the fulness of the gospel was restored to the earth. (Emphasis added).

I will deal with the First Vision in its entirety, including the above, from Smith's own full account, just as he had it recorded in *Joseph Smith – History*, as there is much that missionaries are *not* taught to teach. The underlying truth is as equally withheld from the missionaries, and thus their investigators, as it is from the rest of the Mormon Church membership.

## Joseph Smith's 'First Vision'

Investigators of the Mormon Church are taught that in the spring of 1820, Joseph Smith had a glorious vision of God and Jesus Christ. Members believe that Smith was persecuted from the start for telling all and sundry of his visionary experience. It is assumed that he immediately told his family about it; that the version we read in 'Joseph Smith – History' is in fact the first and *only* version of claimed events, and that he recorded it shortly after his experience.

People take that concept to the Lord in prayer and consider their subsequent 'testimony' that it really happened, to have come to their minds in an answer to prayer from the Lord himself. After that, they rely on their faith to sustain them regarding any awkward questions that may arise. After all, if Smith had that vision and later translated the *Book of Mormon*, a 'testimony' of which is also obtained through the same ethereal means, then verification of the rest hardly seems necessary.

However, suppose Joseph Smith lied. How would we ever determine that? The fact of the matter is that if Smith did lie, then the 'witness' received could *not* have come from God and it would have just been wishful thinking on our part. No matter how wonderful or real the 'response' seemed, it must have been a self-induced experience.

So... what really did happen and what evidence is there to prove the real sequence of events which led to Smith's claim? Only that will determine the truth. The following evidence should more than answer that question.

The first thing to understand is that almost everything Joseph Smith claimed happened – provably did *not*. Also, much of what actually *did* happen is conveniently left out of the fanciful story related to investigators by missionaries. It is not their fault. They simply have no more idea about the truth themselves than their investigators do. They cannot answer questions truthfully as they just don't know the truth themselves. Thus the deception is unwittingly perpetuated by unsuspecting Mormon missionaries.

For example, it would be most unusual for a missionary to be aware of the fact that although the official version of the First Vision is claimed to have *occurred* in the spring of 1820, Joseph Smith did not actually *record* that 'official' version of events which is now used, until the year 1838 and it wasn't published until 1842, twenty-two years *after* the claimed event. That was twelve years *after* the Church was organised in 1830. Until 1842, the 'First Vision' was an *unknown* concept to almost all rank and file Mormons. This was a complete surprise to me, as Smith claimed that he told anyone and everyone

## THE JOSEPH SMITH STORY

who would listen all about it immediately following the experience. However, it will be discovered that this was *not* the case by any means.

Regarding Smith's original *concept* of a 'First Vision', he first considered the idea in 1832. Smith's record, dated to 1832, appears within his work, *A History of the life of Joseph Smith*, partly written by his then scribe, Frederick G. Williams, and partly (including this version of events) in Smith's *own* handwriting. In it, Smith declares that between the ages of twelve and fifteen he became "exceedingly" distressed concerning the situation of the world and of his own sins, and concluded that mankind had "apostatised [sic] from the true and living faith and there was *no* society or denomination that built upon the gospel of Jesus Christ". This is an astonishing conclusion for Smith to have written down in his own hand in 1832 as it completely contradicts the official version (written in 1838 and published in 1842) wherein Smith claims that he went to the grove "to know which of the sects was right" and that "at this time it had never entered into my heart that all were wrong". We know this was *not* the case from Smith's own earlier handwritten claim of 1832. If the event he described in 1838 was a *true* account of something that actually happened in 1820, then why did he write an entirely *conflicting* account of the same event in 1832?

Smith's 1832 account goes on to state that he was in his *sixteenth* year of age. In the later official version, Smith was only *fourteen* years old. Within the pillar of light (originally written as 'fire' which Smith crossed through) 'the Lord', *assumed* to be Jesus Christ, appeared *alone* and addressed Smith as his son. It is interesting to note that this account is very similar to the reported experiences of several other youngsters of the time who, seeking forgiveness of sins – also claimed to have seen the Lord. Several accounts were published in the press, to which Smith had ready access. Notably, Smith's account was *not*.

Smith's own claim to a vision didn't appear anywhere in the press at the supposed time (1820) or subsequent years, despite his claims about constantly telling everyone and getting severely persecuted for so doing. The location, later to become a grove of trees, does not get mentioned at all and there is no mention of any revival. In this account, Smith is not tormented by an evil force; he is filled with the 'spirit of God' and has his sins forgiven, consistent with the published stories of other youngsters of the day who claimed similar ethereal experiences.

In 1835, within the same week, Smith attempted two further 'First Vision' accounts. In the first, Smith relates what he told "Joshua the Jewish Minister", an alias for 'Matthias' who was actually from another cult. One personage appeared in a pillar of "flame"; then a second personage appeared who forgave Smith's sins and testified that "Jesus Christ is the son of God", thus clearly identifying the fact that neither visitor *was* actually the Saviour, as he is spoken of in the third person. Neither 'personage' is specifically identified, but Smith confirms that he saw "many angels" during the vision and that is all. Smith states that he was about fourteen years old "when I received this first communication."

Smith continues his diary, relating that he told Joshua of "another vision of angels" when he was seventeen, thus confirming the 'First Vision' was deemed by Smith, in 1835, to be one of *angels* rather than deity. We would expect this record of Smiths to be included in Church history alongside others appearing in *History of the Church, Vol.2* but the account is conspicuous by its absence. The Church has simply ignored it, along with Smith's visitor, and it has been left out of 'Joseph Smith–History' altogether. Presumably this is because it is inconsistent with the 1838 official version which is preferred. Nevertheless, it was recorded in Smith's personal journal in 1835 and it *contradicts* what he claimed three years later in his 1838 version of events.

Erastus Holmes visited Joseph Smith the following Saturday afternoon, on 14 November 1835, enquiring about the Church and asking to be instructed. Smith recorded what he said to Holmes, in his diary. Relating the experience of his 'First Vision', Smith states that he was about fourteen years old when "I received the first *visitation of Angels*", thus *confirming* his intended meaning when he had spoken to 'Joshua' just a few days earlier. Smith also writes that he told Holmes of later visitations concerning the *Book of Mormon*. Clearly, in late 1835, Smith was still sticking with the idea, in two separate accounts in his own journal, that it was an angel (or angels) rather than deity that first visited him in an 1820 First Vision experience at age fourteen.

The exact wording of this version of the First Vision from Smith's diary was later faithfully published word for word in the Church newspaper. *(Deseret News, Vol. 2. No. 15, Saturday, 29 May 1852)*. This *published* 'First Vision' account by Joseph Smith included Smith's *own original* words:

### "I received the first visitation of Angels"

However, when the account was entered into the *History of the Church (V2:312)*, Smith's own wording was deliberately *altered*. Rather than tell the truth about what Smith claimed at the time he wrote of the experience, the account was *falsified* by the Church. It was *changed* from:

### "first visitation of **angels**" to read "**first vision**".

This **lie** was in order to make the account *appear* consistent with the *later*, more dynamic idea that the First Vision ultimately became, which was not to be one of angels as Smith had earlier claimed, but one of actual deity. As noted above, the 9th November account related to Joshua does not even appear where it should appear in *History of the Church* at all. *(HC V2:312)*. This method of *falsifying* the truth went on to become a regular habit within the Church.

# THE JOSEPH SMITH STORY

Changing the *truth* about something a supposed *prophet* wrote, replacing it with known *lies*, does nothing to support the idea that God was ever involved. We cannot have confidence in such people and no God could or would have had anything to do with such things – *period*. Mormon Church leaders disagree however and they accept that sometimes lying becomes *essential*. I cite several examples in my earlier work. They actually have a name for it. They call it 'lying for the Lord' – and it still continues to this day. This change was *not* just a matter of 'clarification'. Joseph Smith created a complete *contradiction* and rather than question Smith's integrity, or at least leave what he wrote alone, allowing readers to make up their own minds about it, the Church 'covered up' Smith's crime by falsifying the account to make it appear consistent with his *later* claim. People pray for and obtain a 'testimony' of what is here evidenced as an entirely *fraudulent* claim. Ergo; God could *not* confirm it to be true.

The fact that Joseph Smith's own record was *changed* and *falsified* to suit later thinking clearly shows that the idea of a vision of deity had *evolved* over time from one of angels, rather than it being a first time, first hand, true account of something that actually transpired *in* 1820. It also evidences the contempt that Church leaders have for historical accuracy and truth – to say nothing of *integrity* – of which there was and is demonstrably absolutely *none*. I have copies of all of Smith's verified dated journal accounts. The above details are entirely accurate, as recorded by Smith and his scribes.

When questioned, the Church claims that each account gradually reveals what happened in the vision, yet the reality is they contradict each other. Smith was clearly making things up as he went along. Unless pressed, of course the Church rarely mentions the fact that there were several conflicting accounts of the vision, or that the official version did not get written until eighteen years after the claimed 1820 event, in 1838, or published until twenty-two years after it in 1842.

If you carefully read JS–History, you will find the following claims (in sequence) made by Joseph Smith himself in the 'Official Account' of his First Vision. It should however be noted that Smith did not write this account; it was penned by his scribe; so, no one knows for certain if all the ideas contained in it were Smiths or whether some were provided by other people. However, he certainly published it as his own work. At the start of it all, you will note a statement in *HC Vol. 1.* that "…a history more correct in its details than this was never published". Well, we shall see…

> **1.** My father, Joseph Smith, Senior: left… Vermont, and moved to Palmyra… when I was in my tenth year, or thereabouts. [1814]. …about four years after… he moved with his family into Manchester [1818]. [The claimed 'First Vision' occurred] …in the second year after our removal to Manchester… [1820].

**2.** There was a religious revival in the district [in 1820].

**3.** Great multitudes joined various religious parties.

**4.** Four of Smith's family joined the Presbyterians.

**5.** Smith personally came across and pondered on James 1:5.

**6.** He went to a grove to ask God "which of all the sects was right, that I might know which to join."

**7.** Smith was told to join with none of them as they were all wrong.

**8.** "A few days later…" the persecution started.

Once you verify the fact that those are Smith's own surrounding statements, you are ready to proceed with a comparison of the verified historical evidence. Regarding each of the above eight claims Smith made, the following is the true historical position:

**1.** The Smiths' early moves may well be correct. However, the family did *not* move to Manchester from Palmyra in 1818, two years *before* the supposed vision. They actually moved there no earlier than July of 1822, over *two years afterwards*. Smith's youngest sister, Lucy, is also recorded as having been born in Palmyra in 1821. The fact of the matter is that the Smith family didn't even live in the claimed area of Manchester at the time of the supposed vision. They lived several miles away in an entirely different location.

**2.** There was *no* religious revival in the area in 1820. There was minor one a couple of years earlier, in 1818, and there was certainly one there in 1824 (possibly spanning from late 1823-1825 overall).

**3.** 'Great multitudes' did not join anything in 1820. Half a dozen *fewer* Methodists and a notional increase in Baptists and Presbyterians – the main players of the period – were recorded that year. By comparison, during the 1824 revival, there were recorded increases of 99 Presbyterians, 94 Baptists and 208 Methodists. *(Dialogue - A Journal of Mormon Thought, Spring 1969. Reverend Wesley P. Walters (1967) p66 & n35. Quoting Geneva Presbytery records, Geneva Synod records and Minutes of the Ontario Baptist Association).*

**4.** Four of the Smith family did *not* join the Presbyterians prior to an 1820 vision. How do we know? Joseph Smith *and* his own mother, Lucy, recorded elsewhere that she and three of Smith's siblings joined the Presbyterians in *1824*, following the death of Smith's brother Alvin, in late 1823.

## THE JOSEPH SMITH STORY

**5.** Smith may well have claimed (in 1838) to have found James 1:5 all by himself in 1820, but considering the fact that he didn't live in the area where he claimed to have a vision – where there was no revival that year – when no multitudes joined any various sects – it is not surprising that he also failed to credit his source of the idea "What church shall I join" and James 1:5. Smith doesn't mention the fact that he and all his family attended a sermon given by a Methodist minister, Elder George Lane, who preached on the very subject of 'What Church Shall I Join', where interestingly, his text was James 1:5, which he recommended to his listeners. The problem with this for Smith is that Lane didn't arrive in the area until July of 1824 – which is when the entire Smith family attended and heard the sermon. Smith later took the idea and backdated it to 1820 – as his own.

**6.** Smith's claim to have gone into a grove of trees in order to ask God which church was right is a complete contradiction to his earlier personally handwritten statement of 1832 in which he confirmed he had already concluded that they were *all wrong*.

**7.** Smith claimed in this account that God *twice* told him that he should join none of the existing churches as they were *all* wrong. Later in his narrative, Smith reminds us for a third time that he was told this. Yet in 1828, eight years *after* the supposed vision, he joined a Methodist Sunday School, only to be asked leave again as he was considered an undesirable, due to his reputation as a glass-looker (a money-digging con artist).

**8.** No persecution was ever encountered by Smith during the period in question, a fact that is now accepted by BYU historians. I will come back to this important lie later on, as it ties in with other evidence following Smith's pretended vision.

So, *everything* that Smith claimed to have surrounded the vision is *provably* fictitious. But that is just the start. What of the vision itself. Did Smith see God and Jesus as two separate beings with *bodies* in 1820 as the Church now claims? The answer lies in what Smith actually believed himself at the time which we will now review.

Bear in mind the 'official' version of the vision was first written down in 1838. Prior to that, Joseph Smith had written the *Book of Mormon* – in 1828-9; it was published (and the Church was also formed) in 1830 and his *'Inspired Revision'* of the Bible followed in 1831-1834. The *Book of Commandments* was published in 1833. The *Lectures of Faith* were written in 1834 and published within the first edition of the *Doctrine and Covenants* in 1835. A review of these 'Smith' writings should determine his perception of God and Jesus during the years *before* 1838 and his official 'First Vision' story.

Let's start with the first – The *Book of Mormon*.

# THE MORMON DELUSION

When Smith and others conspired to write the *Book of Mormon*, Smith was still entirely monotheistic in his theological outlook. He remained this way until about 1836 when his 'plurality of Gods' theology finally started to emerge.

Thus, the handwritten transcripts and first edition of the *Book of Mormon* were entirely monotheistic throughout, with *no* mention of God having a body. God was a spirit and Jesus, who was in the bosom of the Father, was God manifest in the flesh. With that information in mind, let's look firstly at what the original handwritten copies of the *Book of Mormon* actually stated. The 1830 edition did not have verses but the equivalent page numbers and lines are shown for reference. The later falsifications were exposed by the Tanners in their comprehensive work, *Mormonism – Shadow or Reality?*

---

**1830 Edition: p.25 lines 3-5.** And he said unto me, Behold, the virgin which thou seest, is the mother of God, after the manner of the flesh.

**1981 Edition: 1 Nephi 11:18.** And he said unto me, Behold, the virgin which thou seest, is the mother of **the Son of** God, after the manner of the flesh.

---

**1830 Edition: p.25 lines 10-11.** And the angel said unto me, behold the Lamb of God, yea, even the Eternal Father!...

**1981 Edition: 1 Nephi 11:21.** And the angel said unto me, behold the Lamb of God, yea, even **the Son of** the Eternal Father!...

---

**1830 Edition: p.26 lines 8-10.** ...And I looked and beheld the Lamb of God, that he was taken by the people; yea, the Everlasting God, was judged of the world...

**1981 Edition: 1 Nephi 11:32.** ...And I looked and beheld the Lamb of God, that he was taken by the people; yea, **the Son of** the Everlasting God, was judged of the world...

---

**1830 Edition: p.32 lines 9-11.** ...and shall make known to all kindreds, tongues, and people, that the Lamb of God is the Eternal Father and the Savior of the world...

**1981 Edition: 1 Nephi 13:40.** ...and shall make known to all kindreds, tongues, and people, that the Lamb of God is **the Son of** the Eternal Father and the Savior of the world...

---

(Emphasis added to above 1981 references to identify the later falsifications).

# THE JOSEPH SMITH STORY

This last 'scripture' was originally not just another definitive affirmation of Jesus Christ *being* God; it was an *instruction* to ensure that everyone knew it, so it was clearly an important aspect in Smith's theological thinking when he wrote it in 1828-9. If the original was indeed from God, then *1 Nephi 13:40* could never justifiably be *changed* and was certainly what the Nephites taught hundreds of years ago – if one accepts they were a real race of people.

It cannot be argued that Joseph Smith simply misunderstood the translation, because his face was buried in a hat when he translated and he didn't look at the gold plates. They were either tied up in a linen cloth or buried elsewhere when he supposedly translated them. The Church accepts that this *was* the case and a modern-day apostle even referred to it in an Ensign magazine article. (*A Treasured Testament. Russell M. Nelson, Ensign, July 1993:61).*

The words are claimed to have been revealed *precisely* to Smith, one at a time, in his hat, by means of the same seer stone he had previously used in his money digging glass-looking days and when he was arrested and taken to court for being a con artist just three years earlier. That the conviction occurred in 1826, long *after* the supposed vision of 1820 and also after the first claimed visitation of Moroni in 1823, says little in favour of Smith's character. Smith mostly called the visiting angel 'Nephi'. Later the Church falsified the accounts to read 'Moroni', which says just as little in favour of Church integrity. God's 'chosen' continued to be a con man, using the very same *tools* – a pebble and a hat, in his new venture – religion. After the *Book of Mormon* was finished, remember, a voice from heaven supposedly declared it to be 'correct'.

In 1964, Sidney B. Sperry, claimed in his book, *The Problems of the Book of Mormon*, that the four 'omissions' were simply printer's errors. He stated:

> Why were these changes made in the text? …the early leaders in the Church… knew that typographical errors had crept into the 1830 edition in the course of printing. So they attempted to correct those errors by comparing the original manuscripts with the 1830 text. The changes they made… are simple corrections of error in the First Edition.

However, that was not the case, as the original hand-written manuscripts confirm otherwise. Sperry either lied outright or just didn't bother to check the original documents. Luckily, Jerald and Sandra Tanner's *did* check them. Since the first edition was published, there have been several *thousands* of entirely unreferenced alterations to the grammar and text of the *Book of Mormon*. Such is the Mormon conspiracy to deceive.

We just don't notice what is still *in* the *Book of Mormon* even today. There isn't a single reference to God and Jesus as two separate and distinct beings *anywhere*, as Smith considered them at the time to be one and the same. In it,

God is a *spirit* – He does *not* have a body. Consider the following – look them all up in any modern-day copy of the *Book of Mormon*.

Here, Zeezrom is speaking with Amulek. *Alma 11:28-29, 38-39* remain even today as:

> **28.** Now Zeezrom said: Is there more than one God?
> **29.** And he answered, **No**.

And yet years later, Smith went on to claim there are many Gods.

> **38.** Now Zeezrom saith again unto him: *Is the Son of God the very Eternal Father?* (Emphasis added).

Now, here is a very good chance for Amulek to say – No, in fact, they are two separate and distinct beings – both with bodies. But what does he say?

> **39.** And Amulek said unto him: Yea, *he is the very Eternal Father* of heaven and of earth, and all things which in them are; he is the beginning and the end, the first and the last; (Emphasis added).

Amulek here confirms that 'the Son of God' *is* 'the very Eternal Father', reflecting Smith's traditional concept of monotheism at the time it was written. (That means in 1828-9, *not* in 82 BCE as Joseph Smith claimed).

**Mosiah 15:1-5** today *still* reads:

> **1.** And now Abinadi said unto them: I would that ye should understand that *God himself shall come down among the children of men, and shall redeem his people.*
> **2.** And *because he dwelleth in flesh he shall be called the Son of God*, and having subjected the flesh to the will of the Father, *being the Father and the Son—*
> **3.** The Father, because he was conceived by the power of God; and *the Son, because of the flesh; thus becoming the Father and Son—*
> **4.** And *they are one God, yea, the very Eternal Father* of heaven and of earth.
> **5.** And thus the flesh becoming subject to the Spirit, or *the Son to the Father, being one God…* (Emphasis added).

We just don't 'see' Smith's monotheistic theology in the *Book of Mormon*, as we are taught otherwise. Yet it stares us in the face when we read it with a foreknowledge of his then current theology. If members question it, they are just told that it means 'one in purpose' and they may go away accepting that idea but still feel somewhat uneasy. Now we can understand why.

# THE JOSEPH SMITH STORY

Alma chapters 18 & 22 concern traditions of belief in 'the great spirit'. What do they confirm?

> **18:5.** ...this was the tradition of Lamoni, which he had received from his father, that there was ***a Great Spirit***.
>
> **18:18.** King Lamoni ... said unto him: Who art thou? Art thou that ***Great Spirit***, who knows all things?"
>
> **18:26.** Believest thou that there is a ***Great Spirit***?
>
> **18:28.** Ammon said unto him again: Believest thou that this ***Great Spirit, who is God***, created all things...
>
> **22:9.** And the king said: Is God that ***Great Spirit*** that brought our fathers out of the land of Jerusalem?
>
> **22:10.** And Aaron said unto him: ***Yea, he is that Great Spirit***, and he created all things...
>
> **22:11.** And he said: Yea, ***I believe that the Great Spirit*** created all things... (Emphasis added).

No 'body' is mentioned regarding God *anywhere* in the *Book of Mormon*. Even the title page *still* reads:

> - And also to the convincing of the Jew and Gentile that JESUS is the CHRIST, the ETERNAL God, manifesting himself unto all nations - (Capitals in original).

The Testimony of Three Witnesses to the Book of Mormon still includes:

> "And the honor be to the Father, and to the Son, and to the Holy Ghost, ***which is one God***. Amen." (Emphasis added).

So, Jesus *is* God manifesting himself and the 'three' – *is one God* (singular; not even '*are* God', let alone 'form the Godhead'). That is what they *all* believed throughout the early years of the Church – including Joseph Smith.

Next came Smith's *Inspired Revision* of the Bible. Did Smith, in 1831-1834, take the opportunity to 'clarify' Bible teachings in any way to confirm that God and Jesus are separate and distinct beings and that God has a physical body? Well, he does make one related change to Genesis (6:8-9) which also appears as Moses 6:9 in the Pearl of Great Price.

> **6:9.** And a genealogy was kept of the children of God. And this was the book of the generations of Adam, saying, In the day that God created man, (in the likeness of God made he him,) ***in the image of his own body***, male and female created he them, and blessed them, and called their name Adam, in the day when they were created, and became living souls, in the land, upon the footstool of God. (Emphasis added).

This is several years before any other mention is made by Smith regarding an individual physical nature of God and is supposedly the writing of Moses. At the time, Smith still considered God and Jesus to be one and the same being. So, the statement does not clarify whether the reference is to the 'image' of a spiritual or a physical body. Either way, it is of no real significance as Smith's theology was ever evolving. However, it would appear that at the time Smith still believed God was a *spirit* as that is what he repeatedly claimed elsewhere *after* this was written, which we will come on to shortly.

In fact, another change that Smith made in his *IR* identifies quite clearly his monotheistic view of the time. Smith did *change* something else in his *Inspired Revision* that could possibly have been construed to mean God and Jesus *were* two separate beings and he *altered* it to more clearly read that in fact they are one and the same being.

In the *King James Version, Luke 10:22* reads:

> **Luke 10:22.** no man knoweth who the Son is, but the Father; and who the Father is, but the Son, and he to whom the Son will reveal him.

Now, that could be construed as slightly ambiguous. It could be argued (although weakly, considering what the rest of the Bible contains) that it means God and Jesus are two *separate* beings. Smith – in monotheistic mode – clearly seemed to think that it could, so he *changed* it. It becomes verse 23 in his *'Inspired Revision'*, and it reads as follows:

> **I.R. Luke 10:23.** ...no man knoweth that the Son *is* the Father, and the Father *is* the Son, but him to whom the Son will reveal it.

It couldn't be clearer than that, now could it?

The Lectures of Faith (1834) include references to God as a *spirit* alone. This is an example. Lecture Fifth of Faith...

> There are **two personages** who constitute the great, matchless, governing, and supreme power over all things ... They are the Father and the Son—*the **Father being a personage of spirit**, glory, and power, possessing all perfection and fullness, **the Son, who was in the bosom of the Father, a personage of tabernacle*** ... (Emphasis added).

# THE JOSEPH SMITH STORY

Elsewhere in the Lectures, God is referred to as an 'omnipresent spirit' which means he dwells *everywhere* at once – and that is another traditional monotheistic Christian concept. Many older people who attended the Mormon endowment ceremony when they were young may remember the days when a 'minister', complete with dog collar, appeared on the scene. There was mention of the (false) teaching that God was "so large that he filled the universe and yet so small that he could dwell in your heart". It is strange that in the early 1830s, that is *exactly* what Smith and his followers still perceived to be the case.

The 'holy spirit', by the way, is the 'mind of God' in these lectures and is *nowhere* referred to as a 'personage' of spirit at all. The lectures confirm the same theology which had remained in place within Smith's *Inspired Revision* of the Bible and before that in the *Book of Mormon*.

Talking of the *Inspired Revision* – here's an example of Smith's ever changing ideas where he completely ignores what went before. This happened over and over again, proving he was anything *but* a prophet. In his infamous King Follett sermon, at the funeral of a man who was killed by a bucket of bricks falling on his head during the construction of a well, Smith starts to talk about plural gods for the *first time* in public. This was 7 April 1844, a couple of months or so before his death. Following the disclosures in his sermon, many hundreds of Mormons reportedly left the fold as they considered what he said to be a heresy.

Smith takes as his text *Revelation 1:6*. Smith says:

> God ... is an exalted man, and sits enthroned in yonder heavens! That is the great secret.

> He was once a man like us; yea, that God himself, the Father of us all, dwelt on an earth ... and I will show it from the Bible. *(History of the Church. Volume VI, Chapter 14).*

Gordon B. Hinckley – at least *twice*, publicly stated he did not know that they taught that and that he didn't know much about it. *(See: Appendix F for transcripts)*. Hinckley's comments completely *contradict* Smith.

Joseph Smith declared "It is plain beyond disputation…"

Smith quotes *Revelation 1:6* directly from the *King James Version*:

> And hath made us kings and priests unto **God and His Father**; to him be glory and dominion forever and ever. Amen. (Emphasis added).

Note the phrase, "God *and* His Father". Smith then states "It is altogether correct in the translation". This is because he wants to introduce his *new* concept that God had a father (and therefore a body) and that there are many Gods. However, Smith either forgot, or more likely he simply ignored, the fact that when he had been 'inspired' to *correct* biblical scripture in his earlier *Inspired Revision*, he had *altered* that very verse by *removing* the word 'and' in order to clarify the fact that God of course does ***not*** have a father. Here, in 1844, he completely ignores his own earlier 'inspired' correction and claims the *KJV* is "altogether ***correct***", just to suit his newly developed thinking.

> ***Inspired Revision:*** **Rev 1:6.** ...and hath made us kings and priests unto ***God his Father***. To him be glory and dominion, forever and ever. Amen. (Emphasis added).

If Smith's claim that the *KJV* is "altogether correct" is accepted by the Church to justify his plural Gods theology, he *lied* in his *Inspired Revision*.

Either way, he is completely caught out and *cannot* be a true prophet by *any* standards.

For once though, Smith quite accidentally actually got something right, as the *IR* is closer to a literal translation than the *KJV*:

> **Young's Literal Translation:** ...and did make us kings and priests to his God and Father, to him [is] the glory and the power to the ages of the ages. Amen.

Regardless of the earlier *IR* 'correction', Smith proves himself here to be a complete *fraud*, reverting back to the *KJV* just to suit his *new* ideas.

Moving on – to ask who *knew* about the vision; if it happened, as Smith claimed, *in* 1820, when then, was the 'First Vision' *ever* mentioned in print *anywhere* before the year 1840? Answer: absolutely *nowhere*. The following publications came into print and there was no word about any kind of 'First Vision' recorded in *any* of them.

1830. The Book of Mormon. (The 'First Vision' would have made an excellent preface).
1832. Delusions: An Analysis of the Book of Mormon; Alexander Campbell – Anti-Mormon book. There is no mention of any Mormon claim to a First Vision.
1832-1834. Evening and Morning Star; Church newspaper – nothing.
1833. Book of Commandments: Early revelations; yet the first and most important is not mentioned.
1834. Mormonism Unvailed [sic]; E. D. Howe: Another Anti-Mormon book – still no mention of a claimed First Vision.

# THE JOSEPH SMITH STORY

1834-1835. Lectures of Faith. No mention of a First Vision – but they talk of God being an 'omnipresent spirit'.

1835. Doctrine & Covenants: Early revelations, and still no mention of the first, most important and glorious one.

1834-1836. Latter Day Saints Messenger and Advocate; Church newspaper – no First Vision account ever.

1837. A Voice of Warning: Parley P. Pratt; Missionary booklet with well over 200 pages – includes revelations and 'restoration' details etc., and yet no mention of any 'First Vision' whatsoever.

1839-1846. Times and Seasons: Church newspaper – no First Vision is mentioned before the 1842 publication of the 'official' version.

1840-1970. Millennial Star: UK publication – again, no mention of any First Vision prior to 1842.

1842. Mormonism in All Ages: J. B. Turner; yet another anti-Mormon book. It was published in the very same year Smith finally published his 1838 official account and still there is *no* mention of any such thing as a claim to a glorious First Vision, twenty-two years after the supposed event. The author had no more idea about it than anyone else.

So, who ever *did* know about this 'First Vision' in the early years? What did the non-Mormon newspapers have to say about Joseph Smith during those first few years? Well, absolutely nothing before 1830. For the first decade, Joseph Smith was mostly unknown to anyone outside his own small circle. In 1831, ironically, the local paper ran three articles which actually provide evidence – not that Smith made such a claim as having had a glorious First Vision in the spring of 1820 – but as it happens, quite the opposite...

> It however appears quite certain that the prophet himself never made any serious pretensions to religion until his late pretended revelation [the discovery of the Book of Mormon]. *(Palmyra Reflector. Vol. II Series 1. No. 12. 1 Feb 1831).*
>
> It will be born in mind that no divine interposition had been dreamed of at the period. *(Palmyra Reflector. Vol. II Series 1. No. 13. 14 Feb 1831).*
>
> It is well known that Joe Smith never pretended to have any communication with angels, until a long period after the *pretended* finding of his book. *(Palmyra Reflector. Vol. II Ser. 1. No. 14. 28 Feb 1831).*

So... who knew about this mysterious First Vision *in* 1820 or even shortly thereafter?

# THE MORMON DELUSION

Joseph Smith's mother, Lucy Mack, started her autobiography in 1845, the year *after* her sons were killed. Lucy's autobiography clearly states that it was the *angel* that appeared to Smith in his bedroom who told him "there is not a true Church on earth, no not one". The original text of Lucy's book does not mention a single word about any 'First Vision' whatsoever.

When it was published by Orson Pratt in Liverpool, England, in 1853, along with many other changes, Joseph Smith's own account was then *inserted* just as it had appeared in *Times and Seasons,* without Lucy's permission or her knowledge. Lucy had no idea about any such thing as a First Vision when she wrote her book – and that was *after* Joseph Smith had died.

In 1859, Martin Harris gave an interview to Tiffany's. He recounts what happened after Smith claimed to find the gold plates in late 1827.

> Joseph had before this described the manner of his finding the plates. He found them by looking in the stone found in the well of Mason Chase. The family had likewise told me the same thing. Joseph said the angel told him he must quit the company of the money-diggers. That there were wicked men among them. He must have no more to do with them. He must not lie, nor swear, nor steal. He told him to go and look in the spectacles, and he would show him the man that would assist him. That he did so, and he saw myself, Martin Harris, standing before him.

That's not the important part... it's what Harris says next that tells the tale:

> But I had the account of it from Joseph, his wife, brothers, sisters, his father and mother. I talked with them *separately* that I might get the truth of the matter. *(Tiffany's Vol. V:IV:163-170).*

The point here is that Smith was desperately trying to get Harris to sell part of his farm in order to finance the publication of the *Book of Mormon*. Had the First Vision been a 'shared' reality – surely **one** of them, if not Joseph himself, would have mentioned it to further convince Harris? Not one of **ten** members of the Smith family mentioned a single word about what is now proclaimed by the Mormon Church to be the greatest happening since Jesus Christ was born.

No one mentioned a glorious commencement to the final dispensation, the 'dispensation of the fullness of times', with God and Jesus appearing, both with tangible bodies, to Joseph Smith in a grove of trees in the spring of 1820. Why? Because at the time that Harris individually interviewed each member of the Smith family (around 1828) Smith had yet to invent the idea and no one knew the first thing about it.

The first ever published mentions of any kind of First Vision were:

# THE JOSEPH SMITH STORY

**Orson Pratt. 1840.** *An Interesting Account of Several Remarkable Visions, and of the Late Discovery of Ancient American Records.* Pratt includes a short narrative in which two 'unidentified' personages appear.

**Orson Hyde. 1842.** *A Cry from the Wilderness, a Voice from the Dust of the Earth. (Printed in German).* Hyde uses some almost identical wording to Pratt but this time it reads "two glorious personages".

In Hyde's case at least, he clearly considered the First Vision to be one of *angels* rather than deity as he later made the following statement:

> "Some one may say, 'If this work of the last days be true, why did not the Saviour come himself to communicate this intelligence to the world?' Because to the angels was committed the power of reaping the earth, and it was committed to none else." *(JD. V.6:335. Orson Hyde. 6 April 1854).*

As related above, in my own research, I found absolutely no evidence that *anyone* knew of any such thing as a First Vision, so how could Smith have suffered persecution for telling everyone that he did? The following is the take Brigham Young University (BYU) now has on the whole idea of Smith telling anyone and everyone about the vision. They refer to the Orson Pratt account mentioned above.

> Orson Pratt's 'Interesting account of Remarkable Visions' . . . ranks as one of the great Mormon books as it contains the first printed account of Joseph Smith's 1820 vision. Only three manuscript accounts antedating Remarkable Visions exist in the LDS Church Archives, ...

Those three accounts are of course the 1832 and the two 1835 Joseph Smith accounts reviewed earlier. *(See pp. 92-94).* The BYU article then continues:

> ...reflecting that Joseph Smith **discussed this transcendent vision only privately** with a few trusted friends during the Church's first decade. (Emphasis added).

The reference for that quote is: *Religious Studies Center, Brigham Young University*: http://relarchive.byu.edu/MPNC/descriptions/interesting.html

In an incredible complete turnaround to all that Mormons have ever been taught, the Church, faced with the facts I have just covered, appears to accept them as *proven* and therefore in agreement that Smith hardly told *anyone* about his vision in those early years. The problem is that they do not address the fact that in so admitting, they also make a complete **liar** out of Smith over and over again. Read on in JS–History to discover all the claims that Smith made about severe persecution which are all now admitted by the Church as never actually having occurred. They thus *admit* and *confirm* Joseph Smith was a complete and utter *liar*, making entirely *fraudulent* claims. He therefore does *not* qualify in any way to be considered a *prophet* of God. God doesn't hire liars.

Joseph Smith claimed he was "hated and persecuted for saying I had seen a vision".

The Church inserted 'header' above v.21 in JS–History categorically states "Persecution heaped upon Joseph Smith". Smith then goes on and on about how he was constantly persecuted for claiming that he had seen a vision.

> **JS-H. 20.** Why the ***opposition and persecution*** that arose against me, almost in my infancy?
>
> **21.** [Smith met a Methodist minister a few days later and] …took occasion to ***give him an account of the Vision***.
>
> **22.** …my ***telling the story had excited a great deal of prejudice*** against me among professors of religion, and was the cause of ***great persecution, which continued to increase…*** yet men of high standing would take notice sufficient to ***excite the public mind against me***, and create ***a bitter persecution***; and this was common among all the sects—***all united to persecute me.***
>
> **23.** …an obscure boy a ***little over fourteen years of age*** … attract the attention of the great ones of the most popular sects of the day, and in a manner to create in them a spirit of ***the most bitter persecution and reviling.***
>
> **25.** …they were ***persecuting me, reviling me, and speaking all manner of evil*** against me.
>
> **27.** …***severe persecution*** at the hands of all classes of men.
>
> **28.** …between the time I had the vision and the year eighteen hundred and twenty-three … ***persecuted by those who ought to have been my friends.*** (Emphasis added).

The Church, in order to accept the absolute *fact* that Smith made *no* First Vision claim in the early years, settles instead on confirming that he lied, lied, lied, lied, lied, lied, lied (in at least *seven* separate references) concerning persecution between 1820 and 1823 *(v.28)*. Smith is confirmed as having lied about *all* of the events surrounding his claimed vision and also telling repeated lies about non-existent persecution following it. So what credence can then be given to ***anything*** he ever said or wrote at all – including the supposed vision itself?

# THE JOSEPH SMITH STORY

But it doesn't end there; that was just the fictional beginning of Joseph Smith's hoax. These lies and deceptions were just the start. After 1827…

> **JS-H: 58.** Owing to my continuing to assert that I had seen a vision, ***persecution still followed*** **me**,
>
> **61.** The ***persecution***, however, ***became so intolerable*** that I was under the necessity of leaving Manchester … and the ***persecution so heavy***…

To summarise; *if* the First Vision did occur, as Smith claimed, in the spring of 1820 then it occurred:

2 years before the Smiths moved to the claimed location.
4 years before there was a revival in that area.
4 years before any significant recorded increase in the membership of local congregations of the Methodists, Baptists and Presbyterians.
4 years before four members of the Smith family joined the Presbyterians. In *JS–History 1:20*, Smith claims that when he returned home following his visionary experience, he "leaned up to the fireplace" and told his mother, "I have learned for myself that Presbyterianism is not true". Considering the fact that his mother and three of Smith's siblings didn't join the Presbyterians until four years *later*, had that really happened, the comment would have been completely meaningless to her. Smith was clearly making it up, claiming that he said that because he had also claimed they joined the Presbyterians just *before* he had his vision.

It raises the additional question that if Smith did have such a vision in 1820, and if he was told that all the churches were wrong, and if he told his mother that, why did she and three other members of the family join the Presbyterians in 1824? That was the year after Smith's claim to have had a further vision where Moroni appeared to him. Either Smith lied or his family didn't believe him and joined the Presbyterians anyway. The 'Presbyterian' part of Smith's First Vision story is completely inconsistent with recorded history and further confirms the absurdity of the entire claimed event.

4 years before Elder Lane preached on 'What Church Shall I Join' and recommended reading James 1:5.
6 years before Smith was in court for being a money-digging con artist.
7 years before the *only* so-called 'persecution' ever occurred; perpetrated by other treasure seekers. Smith was part of a syndicate where they all agreed that if anyone ever actually found anything of worth, then they would *all* share in the spoils. In September of 1827, Smith claimed to have found gold plate which was rightfully equally theirs. The money-diggers were the only people to ever chase after Joseph Smith, who, as far as they were concerned, had reneged

on their agreement, and Martin Harris may have paid them off to get rid of the threat. They were after his blood for a very different reason than him claiming to have seen a vision. They wanted their agreed share of Smith's 'find'. That's as close as it ever got to any persecution during the eighteen-twenties.

8 years before he joined the Methodist Sunday School; in the 1838 official account, the Lord told Smith *twice* not to join *any* church.

10 years before publication of the entirely monotheistic *Book of Mormon*.

11 years before his *Inspired Revision* of the Bible where he left all of the monotheistic references alone and even *changed* a slightly ambiguous text to ensure it had a monotheistic tone. Note that the *Book of Moses* has *dozens* of references to 'God' in the *singular* taking care of the creation process.*

12 years before recording he saw only Jesus in a First Vision experience.

12 years before the *Book of Commandments* was published – with no First Vision account included.

14 years before the *Lectures of Faith* stated that God is an 'omnipresent spirit' with *no* body.

15 years before Smith recorded two 'First Vision' accounts consisting specifically and *only* of angels.

15 years before *The Book of Abraham* was written – which now included *dozens* of references to 'Gods' in the *plural* – still with no mention of a body however – completely *contradicting* Smith's earlier *Book of Moses* where God (in the singular) did all the same things regarding the creation.*

15 years before the *Doctrine and Covenants* was published – still with no First Vision account included.

18 years before Smith finally concocted his whole *new* vision idea, which became the 'Official' version.

22 years before Smith finally published his 'official' version of events.

It is perfectly clear from verifiable history (including original Church records and Joseph Smith's own writings) that *no* circumstances which Smith claimed surrounded a First Vision in 1820 could possibly have been true.

Furthermore, it is equally clear that no persecution was experienced in the decade following 1820. The account of the vision idea itself was just an ever evolving concept in Smith's overactive imagination that he first conceived of in 1832, he revisited in 1835, and which culminated in an 1838 'official version' which he then backdated to the spring of 1820.

A myriad of impossible claims expose Smith's fraud over and over again. There is *nothing* verified as possibly true. That only leaves the vision itself to consider – that is, if after all the proven lies which surrounded the concept, it is even worthy of further consideration at all. Regardless of the other confirmed lies, or of when and if it actually occurred, what does Smith really *claim*?

# THE JOSEPH SMITH STORY

Even the modern concept that Smith saw God and Jesus as two separate and distinct personages with physical bodies was never formally *claimed* by Joseph Smith. The visitors remained unidentified and are assumed to be God and Jesus by inference alone, based on what one said to the other and what is said *about* the visitors by Smith. That may come as a bit of a shock to many people, due to the programming that all Mormons experience right from birth (or from conversion) that indeed he did personally claim it.

In any event, Smith would not have claimed such a thing *in* the spring of 1820 as it has been clearly demonstrated he was entirely monotheistic in his outlook until the mid 1830s. But even in his 1838 official version, Smith is more than cautious about claiming *whom* he actually saw in his vision and words that Smith did *not* speak were effectively put into his mouth by the Church when later claiming that he saw God and Jesus (with bodies).

In September of 1832, Joseph Smith wrote a revelation *(D&C 84)* which included the following concept:

> **21.** And **without the ordinances thereof, and the authority of the priesthood**, the power of godliness is not manifest unto men in the flesh;
> **22.** For without this **no man can see the face of God, even the Father, and live.** (Emphasis added).

This has become a problematic 'revelation' for the Church due to the claim that the First Vision occurred in 1820 when Smith held no such priesthood and therefore by his own admission (revelation) he would not have been capable of *seeing* God – with or without a body.

In 1832, while Smith was still a monotheist, the *D&C 84* concept fitted perfectly with his then current thinking. It was the year in which he personally wrote a version of the First Vision in which Jesus Christ appeared alone and forgave Smith his sins. It only created a problem later when the Church claimed Smith saw both God and Jesus in 1820, as Smith did *not* hold the required priesthood in order to be *able* to see God in 1820, according to Smith's own revelation. That priesthood and therefore ability to *see* God came many years later.

From the missionary lesson manual:

> After the appearance of the Father and the Son, other heavenly messengers, or angels, were sent to Joseph Smith and his associate Oliver Cowdery. John the Baptist appeared and conferred upon Joseph Smith and Oliver Cowdery the Aaronic Priesthood, which includes the authority to perform the ordinance of baptism. *(Page 37)*.

# THE MORMON DELUSION

The record of this supposed happening comes from Section 13 of the *D&C*. It is claimed as received on 15 May 1829, almost a year before Smith formally organised his Church. The header claims it records the *"Ordination of Joseph Smith and Oliver Cowdery to the Aaronic Priesthood along the bank of the Susquehanna River, near Harmony, Pennsylvania."*

The header also states that *"The ordination was done by the hands of an angel, who announced himself as John, the same that is called John the Baptist in the New Testament."*

D&C 13 contains only one verse:

> 1. UPON you my fellow servants, in the name of Messiah I confer the Priesthood of Aaron, which holds the keys of the ministering of angels, and of the gospel of repentance, and of baptism by immersion for the remission of sins; and this shall never be taken again from the earth, until the sons of Levi do offer again an offering unto the Lord in righteousness.

However, despite the claim that it was received 15 May 1829, this section did ***not*** appear in the 1833 *Book of Commandments* or in the first edition of the *Doctrine and Covenants* in 1835. It was just 'inserted' later on. So, the question that remains is if John the Baptist really did 'confer' the Aaronic Priesthood on Smith and Cowdery as claimed, why was the account not published in the *Book of Commandments* or the first edition of the *D&C*? Was it for the same reason that the First Vision was not known about for the best part of two decades following the supposed event? Was Smith yet to invent and then backdate the idea? The account stems from *Joseph Smith–History* which was written some years *after* the claimed event.

Smith recorded in his own history that he had only met Cowdery for the first time on 5 April 1829. He immediately became Smith's scribe when he started to translate the *Book of Mormon* two days later. Both apparently received the Aaronic Priesthood less than six weeks after that, according to Smith's account which he recorded several *years* later. To get a more complete picture as recorded by Smith, we must review the account from Joseph Smith–History.

> **JS-H: 68.** We still continued the work of translation, when, in the ensuing month (May, 1829), we on a certain day went into the woods to pray and inquire of the Lord respecting baptism for the remission of sins, that we found mentioned in the translation of the plates. While we were thus employed, praying and calling upon the Lord, a messenger from heaven descended in a cloud of light, and having laid his hands upon us, he ordained us, saying:

# THE JOSEPH SMITH STORY

**69.** *Upon you my fellow servants, in the name of Messiah, I confer the Priesthood of Aaron, which holds the keys of the ministering of angels, and of the gospel of repentance, and of baptism by immersion for the remission of sins; and this shall never be taken again from the earth until the sons of Levi do offer again an offering unto the Lord in righteousness.*

**70.** He said this Aaronic Priesthood had not the power of laying on hands for the gift of the Holy Ghost, but that this should be conferred on us hereafter; and he commanded us to go and be baptized, and gave us directions that I should baptize Oliver Cowdery, and that afterwards he should baptize me.

**71.** Accordingly we went and were baptized. I baptized him first, and afterwards he baptized me—after which I laid my hands upon his head and ordained him to the Aaronic Priesthood, and afterwards he laid his hands on me and ordained me to the same Priesthood—for so we were commanded.

**72.** The messenger who visited us on this occasion and conferred this Priesthood upon us, said that his name was John, the same that is called John the Baptist in the New Testament, and that he acted under the direction of Peter, James and John, who held the keys of the Priesthood of Melchizedek, which Priesthood, he said, would in due time be conferred on us, and that I should be called the first Elder of the Church, and he (Oliver Cowdery) the second. It was on the fifteenth day of May, 1829, that we were ordained under the hand of this messenger, and baptized.

**73.** Immediately on our coming up out of the water after we had been baptized, we experienced great and glorious blessings from our Heavenly Father. No sooner had I baptized Oliver Cowdery, than the Holy Ghost fell upon him, and he stood up and prophesied many things which should shortly come to pass. And again, so soon as I had been baptized by him, I also had the spirit of prophecy, when, standing up, I prophesied concerning the rise of this Church, and many other things connected with the Church, and this generation of the children of men. We were filled with the Holy Ghost, and rejoiced in the God of our salvation.

**74.** Our minds being now enlightened, we began to have the scriptures laid open to our understandings, and the true meaning and intention of their more mysterious passages revealed unto us in a manner which we never could attain to previously, nor ever before had thought of. In the meantime we were forced to keep secret the circumstances of having received the Priesthood and our having been baptized, owing to a spirit of persecution which had already manifested itself in the neighborhood.

**75.** We had been threatened with being mobbed, from time to time, and this, too, by professors of religion. And their intentions of mobbing us were only counteracted by the influence of my wife's father's family (under Divine providence), who had become very friendly to me, and who were opposed to mobs, and were willing that I should be allowed to continue the work of translation without interruption; and therefore offered and promised us protection from all unlawful proceedings, as far as in them lay. (Emphasis in original).

The bizarre sequence of events simply does not fit with Mormon theology. First Smith and Cowdery were 'ordained' and yet they had not been baptised or received the Holy Ghost which are prerequisites to receiving the priesthood. Smith and Cowdery then baptised each other. Next, they ordained each other to the Aaronic Priesthood for a *second* time. Such a process is utter nonsense and clearly not an idea from any God. It gets even worse, as each in turn has the Holy Ghost *fall* upon them and they both prophesy. Yet they had not had the laying on of hands for that gift, nor did they have the appropriate (higher) priesthood authority to do so. In v.70 we learn they were told they would have the Holy Ghost bestowed on them *later*. There is *no* record that I can locate indicating Smith and Cowdery ever did 'receive the Holy Ghost' from anyone.

It may be argued that Jesus had the Holy Ghost descend upon him in the form of a dove after he was baptised, but in his case, Mormon theology states that he was *born* a High Priest and therefore he would be entitled to that experience. Smith was not. It is clear that he was once again making things up as he went along. This whole event was backdated by several years and Smith clearly forgot to make up an account of later receiving the Holy Ghost himself.

Smith is to be the first Elder of the Church and Cowdery the second Elder. That idea didn't last long and disappeared from the Church in next to no time.

In v.75, Smith takes occasion to once again remind us they were in danger of being mobbed and from time to time they were threatened by 'professors of religion'. This was in 1829 and we have already established the fact that Smith lied completely about this area; he had never told anyone about a First Vision and there was *no* persecution before the Church was established in 1830. The Church itself now accepts that as a *fact. (See above: pp.107-8)*. The only 'mob' ever to chase after Smith, was about a year earlier (late 1827-8) when the rest of the money-diggers in his syndicate were after his blood for not sharing the spoils; gold plates, he claimed to have found. Smith reneged on the money-digging syndicate 'agreement' that if *any* of the money-diggers ever located anything of worth – they would *all* share equally in the find.

In Cowdery's account, which was written in 1834 and also noted in JS–History, the wording is somewhat *different*.

> But, dear brother, think, further think for a moment, what joy filled our hearts, and with what surprise we must have bowed, (for who would not have bowed the knee for such a blessing?) when we received under his hand the Holy Priesthood as he said, 'Upon you my fellow-servants, in the name of Messiah, I confer this Priesthood and this

## THE JOSEPH SMITH STORY

> authority, which shall remain upon earth, that the Sons of Levi may yet offer an offering unto the Lord in righteousness!'

It is clear that Oliver Cowdery wanted to believe this was real and it is also clear he wanted to convince others of the fact. Note that he says "who would not have bowed the knee for such a blessing" indicating that they went down on their knees. In such a position and with closed eyes, in a state of religious fervour, and Smith's charismatic encouragement, Cowdery could quite easily have imagined almost anything. This is what he added to his own account in which he claims to have heard the voice of the Saviour in addition to that of the angel. Smith made *no* such claim in his account.

> I shall not attempt to paint to you the feelings of this heart, nor the majestic beauty and glory which surrounded us on this occasion; but you will believe me when I say, that earth, nor men, with the eloquence of time, cannot begin to clothe language in as interesting and sublime a manner as this holy personage. No; nor has this earth power to give the joy, to bestow the peace, or comprehend the wisdom which was contained in each sentence as they were delivered by the power of the Holy Spirit! Man may deceive his fellow-men, deception may follow deception, and the children of the wicked one may have power to seduce the foolish and untaught, till naught but fiction feeds the many, and the fruit of falsehood carries in its current the giddy to the grave; but one touch with the finger of his love, yes, one ray of glory from the upper world, or one word from the mouth of the Savior, from the bosom of eternity, strikes it all into insignificance, and blots it forever from the mind. The assurance that we were in the presence of an angel, the certainty that we heard the voice of Jesus, and the truth unsullied as it flowed from a pure personage, dictated by the will of God, is to me past description, and I shall ever look upon this expression of the Savior's goodness with wonder and thanksgiving while I am permitted to tarry; and in those mansions where perfection dwells and sin never comes, I hope to adore in that day which shall never cease. *(Latter Day Saints Messenger and Advocate, Vol. 1:14-16. Oct 1834).*

Cowdery's enthusiastic endorsement and flowery description of ordination could, at first glance, be taken as a worthwhile affidavit concerning the event until we discover his real character and details of his later life. It was of course also written several years *after* the claimed experience. Cowdery was Smith's third cousin. He became 'Second Elder' of the Church when it was organised the following year and he was also one of the three 'witnesses' to the *Book of Mormon*, claiming that he was actually shown Smith's gold plates in his mind or imagination by an angel. Considering his above statement, it should be asked how and why the following could happen if indeed he had such an experience, rather than just being an enthusiastic believer in the *idea* of such and the above being no more than a state of fervour or religious ecstasy.

Cowdery got into competition with Smith over the leadership of the Church and he "disagreed with the Prophet's economic and political program and sought a personal financial independence [from the] Zion society that Joseph Smith envisioned" (*Encyclopaedia of Mormonism 1992*). In March of 1838, Smith and Rigdon moved to Far West, which had been under the presidency of David and John Whitmer who were Oliver Cowdery's brothers-in-law. Smith and Rigdon took charge of the Church in Missouri and initiated policies that Cowdery and the Whitmers believed violated separation of church and state.

In January 1838, Oliver Cowdery wrote to his brother Warren saying that he and Joseph Smith had "had some conversation in which in every instance I did not fail to affirm that which I had said was strictly true. A dirty, nasty, filthy affair of his and Fanny Alger's was talked over in which I strictly declared that I had never deserted from the truth in the matter, and as I supposed was admitted by himself." Fanny Alger was a young teenage housemaid living with the Smiths. The Church accepts she was Joseph Smith's first plural wife. There is *no* evidence of an actual marriage but there is ample evidence of Smith's affair with Fanny so the Church just *assumes* a marriage took place. Cowdery opposed the practice of polygamy and was outraged by Smith's (first known) adulterous affair with Fanny Alger.

Cowdery was summoned to attend a Church court but didn't turn up for the meeting, instead sending a letter of resignation from the Church. He was excommunicated anyway on 12 April 1838. To clarify: the man who witnessed an angel and the gold plates translated as the Book of Mormon, who apparently was a participant in the angelic restoration of the priesthood, not only resigned from the Church he helped organise, but was also excommunicated on the grounds of being a counterfeiter. He then joined the Methodists. These events are inconsistent with someone who experienced real visions and revelations.

Cowdery eventually returned to the Church later in life but his motives were suspect and it is uncertain how long he remained a member. *(Tanner 1968:28).* When asked why he rejoined and went to the temple, he said he just wanted to know what was going on in there. The Church claims none of the witnesses ever denied their testimony of the gold plates yet they only claimed to have 'imagined' them in the first place. The idea that Oliver Cowdery *did* deny his witness of the plates and the *Book of Mormon* was recorded in poetic verse. It appeared in the Church publication, *Times and Seasons (Vol. 2. p.482).*

> Or prove that Christ was not the Lord
> Because that Peter cursed and swore?
> Or Book of Mormon not his word
> Because denied, by Oliver?

# THE JOSEPH SMITH STORY

Other than that however, there is no record of him recanting his story. It is his *actions* that are evidence of the truth. If Cowdery actually did participate in being ordained in two separate glorious events including John the Baptist and then Apostles Peter, James and John, why did he resign his membership of the Lord's Church? Why did he not continue with a church of his own if he felt Smith had gone astray? Technically, he would have had priesthood authority to do so. Or, why did he not follow one of the other schisms, all of which claimed authority to continue, some long before and several after Smith's death. And, why did he join the Methodists? The answers are all too obvious. He may well have re-associated himself on a minor scale with Brigham Young's section of the Church many years later, but his credibility was long destroyed by his own actions. Simply based on his subsequent *behaviour*, the claimed events could not have been real. In any event, his version of things contradicted Smith's.

Missionary manual:

> Peter, James, and John (three of Christ's original Apostles) appeared and conferred the Melchizedek Priesthood upon Joseph Smith and Oliver Cowdery, restoring the same authority given to Christ's Apostles anciently. With this priesthood authority, Joseph Smith was directed to organize the Church of Jesus Christ again on the earth. Through him, Jesus Christ called twelve Apostles. *(Page 37).*

Doctrine and Covenants:

> **D&C 27:12.** And also with Peter, and James, and John, whom I have sent unto you, by whom I have ordained you and confirmed you to be apostles, and especial witnesses of my name, and bear the keys of your ministry and of the same things which I revealed unto them;

Cowdery mentioned only *angels* in connection with the restoration of the priesthood. For it to have been a real experience, he would have to confirm that Peter, James and John restored the Melchizedek Priesthood. Alternatively, Smith would have needed to corroborate the idea that it was just an angel. Cowdery doesn't even mention the first angel as being John the Baptist as claimed by Smith in *JS–H 68:72 (See p.113)*. He doesn't appear to know who it was. Cowdery declared:

> I was present with Joseph when ***an holy angel*** from God came down from heaven and conferred on us, or restored, the lesser or Aaronic Priesthood, and said to us, at the same time, that it should remain upon the earth while the earth stands. I was also present with Joseph when ***the higher or Melchizedek Priesthood was conferred by the holy angel from on high. This Priesthood, we then conferred on each***

*other* by the will and commandment of God. *(History of the Church, Vol. 1, p. 40 footnote)*. (Emphasis added).

Cowdery says a "holy **angel** from on high" conferred the *higher* priesthood. Smith claims Peter, James and John performed the ordinance. Was it just one unidentified angel – or three named apostles? The contradictory claims confirm just one thing; the whole episode was a complete *lie*.

It should be remembered that in Mormonism, John is supposedly still alive and not a spirit. He would have appeared in *person*. The two accounts are far too contradictory to remotely be regarded as confirmation of the truth of things, reflecting only wishful thinking of the moment. We might also ask, if the priesthood was conferred on them both, why did they then need to confer it on each other a second time? What would be the point of that? Neither Smith nor Cowdery ever recorded *when* the visit and their ordination to the higher priesthood actually happened. The Mormon God continued to move in extremely mysterious and very unusual ways. La Mar Petersen concluded that important details are missing from Church history:

> The important details that are missing from the 'full history' of 1834 are likewise missing from the Book of Commandments in 1833. The student would expect to find all the particulars of the Restoration in this first treasured set of 65 revelations, the dates of which encompassed the bestowals of the two Priesthoods, but they are conspicuously absent... The notable revelations on Priesthood in the Doctrine and Covenants before referred to, Sections 2 and 13, are missing, and Chapter 28 gives no hint of the Restoration which, if actual, had been known for four years. More than four hundred words were added to this revelation of August, 1829 in Section 27 of the Doctrine and Covenants, the additions made to include the names of heavenly visitors and two separate ordinations. The Book of Commandments gives the duties of Elders, Priests, Teachers, and Deacons and refers to Joseph's apostolic calling but there is no mention of Melchezedek Priesthood, High Priesthood, Seventies, High Priests, nor High Councilors. These words were later inserted into the revelation on Church organization and government of April, 1830, making it appear that they were known at that date, but they do not appear in the original, Chapter 24 of the Book of Commandments three years later. Similar interpolations were made in the revelations known as Sections 42 and 68. *(La Mar Petersen; Problems in Mormon Text 1957:7-8).*

La Mar Petersen was raised a Mormon and was excommunicated for publishing the truth about discrepancies in Mormon history. Born in 1910, La Mar died in 2005.

# THE JOSEPH SMITH STORY

My research concluded that when the original revelations were written and published, they did not contain all the information Smith later claimed and then inserted. D. Michael Quinn confirmed the same findings in his work.

> No mention of angelic ordinations can be found in original documents until 1834-35. Thereafter accounts of the visit of Peter, James, and John by Cowdery and Smith remained vague and contradictory. *(Quinn 1994:15).*
>
> Cowdery's 1834 history puzzles modern Mormons for two reasons. First, he says John the Baptist restored 'the Holy Priesthood,' when modern Mormons have been taught that he conferred the Aaronic priesthood not the 'Holy Priesthood' of Melchizedek. Second, Cowdery in 1834 does not refer to restoration of a second priesthood. *(Quinn 1994:281 n 73).*

Incidentally, Quinn was yet another Mormon who was excommunicated simply for publishing some truth about Church history which Mormon leaders would rather had remained hidden.

The missionaries explain to investigators that Joseph Smith received his priesthood authority from angels who restored it to the earth. John the Baptist restored the lesser, or Aaronic Priesthood and three Apostles, Peter, James and John, restored the higher, Melchizedek Priesthood. Mormon theology includes the concept that the Apostle John is still alive on the earth (as are three Nephite Apostles who had the same desire – to remain until Jesus returns).

This mistaken idea is from *D&C Section 7* which, according to Joseph Smith, John himself *wrote* on parchment and 'hid up'. Smith doesn't explain how or where he located the 'parchment' and it is assumed, as with Smith's *Book of Mormon* 'translation' technique; he pulled it out of his hat.

According to words claimed to have been actually *written* by John, he wanted to remain and bring souls to Christ – but naturally there is no record that he ever has. *(See TMD Vol. 3:287-92 for a review of D&C 7).*

One question is that if John really did write *anything* down, surely it would have been something more sensible, meaningful and worthwhile than *D&C 7?*

The reality of John's continued life on Earth would mean that for the ordination of Smith and Cowdery to have occurred as claimed, two angels (or spirits) in the form of the deceased Peter and James, accompanied by John, required John to travel to the location *in the flesh* in order to participate in the ordinance. There is no record of any such thing in Smith's writings or indeed in Cowdery's or anyone else's either. The Church description is of all three men appearing in a *vision*.

The whole idea of a restoration of the 'Aaronic' and then 'Melchizedek' Priesthood is highly questionable and details provided by Smith are sparse and late at best. There is excellent further coverage of the surrounding detail to be found at this link: http://lds-mormon.com/mph.shtml

The missionary lesson manual next states:

> The time in which we live is referred to by Bible prophets as the last days, the latter days, or the dispensation of the fulness of times. It is the period of time just before the Second Coming of Jesus Christ. ***It is the final dispensation. This is why the Church is named The Church of Jesus Christ of Latter-day Saints.*** (Emphasis added). *(Page 37).*

The truth is that Joseph Smith didn't seem able to decide what he wanted to call his new Church and his God certainly didn't tell him what to name it when it was first inaugurated in 1830. Perhaps God didn't yet have an opinion on it.

It was informally known as the 'Church of Christ' during 1829 and legally instituted with that same name on 6 April 1830. It became the 'Church of the Latter Day Saints' in 1834. Later it was to change to the 'Church of Jesus Christ' and then the 'Church of God' before God eventually got round to giving a revelation in 1838, stating that it should be called "The Church of Jesus Christ of Latter Day Saints."

Would it not have been far better for God to have given the revelation regarding his preferred name in the first instance and save all that confusion?

Smith published his *Book of Mormon* in 1830. It claims the Lord told the Nephites in 147-145 BCE they could call their Church the "Church of God" *or* the "Church of Christ" *(See pp.354-5)* and then about seven decades later, in about 74 BCE, to call it the "Church of God" *(See Alma 36;6,9,11)*, and then in 34 CE, to call the church the *"church of Christ"*. Even in the *Book of Mormon* God seems unable to make up his mind what to call the Church.

The 'Church of Christ' was exactly the name Joseph Smith first used, even before he inaugurated his own church. That was consistent enough with God's final choice in the *Book of Mormon* – but then Smith changed it. *Why?*

> **3 Nephi 26:21.** And they who were baptized in the name of Jesus were called the church of Christ.

It is strange that God told the Nephites what to call their church and yet Smith had no idea what to call his and kept changing it. The *Book of Mormon* gives further information and instructions:

> **3 Nephi 27:8.** And how be it my church save it be called in my name? For if a church be called in Moses' name then it be Moses' church; or if it be called in the name of a man then it be the church of a man; but if it be called in my name then it is my church, if it so be that they are built upon my gospel.

# THE JOSEPH SMITH STORY

Smith *changed* the name to the 'Church of the Latter Day Saints' in 1834, violating *3 Nephi 27:8*. Although in and of itself that is not *conclusive* evidence of the fraud, it is certainly a huge clue as to what the real position was. If God instructed Smith to form a new Church, providing supposed revelations included in the 1833 *Book of Commandments*, surely He would at the same time have instructed him, just as He supposedly had with the Nephites, as to what to call the Church – if He had an opinion and it was so important?

Judging by the quality and content of some of those original 'revelations', many of which were subsequently altered and significantly added to when the *Doctrine and Covenants* was published in 1835, it really isn't surprising that God did *not* tell Smith what to call his Church as it is a very hard stretch to imagine God giving some of the other revelations as Smith first recorded them.

It is difficult to imagine a God being involved with them at all when you read what was said and how God supposedly spoke in the originally recorded revelations.

> A living prophet directs the Church today. This prophet, the President of The Church of Jesus Christ of Latter-day Saints, is the authorized successor to Joseph Smith. He and the present Apostles trace their authority to Jesus Christ in an unbroken chain of ordinations through Joseph Smith. *(Page 37).*

Mormon prophets (and their counsellors and all the other apostles for that matter) are 'sustained' by Mormons as 'prophets, seers and revelators'. As a Mormon, I always understood and accepted that the current prophet walked and talked with God who gave direction for his Church and indeed for the world as a whole, if only people would listen. It was a complete shock for me to discover that the recent prophet, Gordon B. Hinckley, had unfortunately (and publicly) declared that God did *not* talk to him. In an interview with Don Lattin of the San Francisco Chronicle, when asked about revelation, Hinckley stated it comes as "just a perception in the mind" which is hardly a reliable thing and extremely worrying if you consider the man to be a true prophet.

> **Q:** And this belief in contemporary revelation and prophecy? As the prophet, tell us how that works. ***How do you receive divine revelation? What does it feel like?***
>
> **A:** Let me say first that we have a great body of revelation, the vast majority of which came from the prophet Joseph Smith. We don't need much revelation. We need to pay more attention to the revelation we've already received. Now, ***if a problem should arise on which we don't have an answer, we pray about it, we may fast about it, and it comes. Quietly.*** Usually no voice of any kind, but ***just a perception in the mind.*** I liken it to Elijah's experience. When he sought the Lord, there

was a great wind, and the Lord was not in the wind. And there was an earthquake, and the Lord was not in the earthquake. And a fire, and the Lord was not in the fire. But in **a still, small voice. Now that's the way it works.** *(San Francisco Chronicle. Don Lattin interview with Gordon B. Hinckley. 13 Mar 1997.* (Emphasis added).

What an incredible 'excuse' for not actually being able to report that God has ever properly communicated with a current supposed prophet. God doesn't do it that way any more – *"a still, small voice. Now that's the way it works."* They just get 'feelings'. He supposed that this was unique to him… well, there is news for the late Gordon B. Hinckley; everyone gets feelings and everyone can claim some form of inspiration, whether they are Mormon or not and even whether they are religious or not; such a thing is neither unique, nor a restricted phenomenon. Such thinking as reported by Hinckley was entirely *delusional*.

A prophet is *not* a prophet unless he prophesies – in the name of the Lord and those prophecies then *materialise*. A seer is *not* a seer unless he can claim to have personally *seen* God, or at least visions of *some* sort. A revelator is *not* a revelator unless he reveals God's will for us in the here and now.

Hinckley's *admission* confirms that he was *none* of the above. He believed that we don't need much of any revelation now and yet the missionaries tell investigators that the whole reason for the claimed 'restoration' is that today we need revelation more than ever before. Being 'sustained' as those things doesn't mean that someone *becomes* those things, until and unless they are confirmed through direct and *recorded* communication from God.

It is a continuing conspiracy to deceive Mormons and investigators alike to claim such things exist when there is *no* evidence that they do. Hinckley's own words confirm that he was definitely not an 'active' prophet of any God. He prophesied *nothing*; he saw *nothing*; he revealed *nothing* during his ministry.

He therefore did not *qualify* in claiming to be those things, regardless of how many people raised a hand to 'sustain' him as such. I could get some people to 'sustain' me as say, the 'prophet of the sun god', and it would be just as meaningful – and just as meaningless – unless I actually claimed to have seen and spoken with him and then revealed his words and wishes. Even then, they would need to be tested of course. Prophesies would have to be seen to all be fulfilled. A 'title' is a fat lot of good in terms of a person leading God's supposed one and only true Church. It takes a lot more than that. Missionaries should be instructed to advise their investigators God doesn't communicate with prophets the way he used to. That is actually what other churches *teach* and modern-day revelation is what once set Mormonism apart from the crowd.

Not to tell investigators, is effectively a 'sin of omission' and completely dishonest. It just adds more lies to the already mountainous conspiracy to deceive them.

# Chapter 6

## Lesson 1

### The Message of the Restoration of the Gospel of Jesus Christ

### Part C

### The Book of Mormon

Turning to the subject of the *Book of Mormon*, the manual *(page 38)* proclaims it "Another Testament of Jesus Christ" just as appears on the cover of each copy of the book. The same picture they use on page seven, with Joseph Smith sitting at a table poring over the gold plates, appears once again as a reminder of what he achieved. Yet again, the lie is hidden in plain sight with no need for any words. Smith clearly translated the book by *looking* at the symbols… that is, if you believe the pictorial depiction. No seer stone in a hat ever appears in any official Mormon Church pictures. The manual states only that "Joseph Smith translated the contents of these plates by the power of God", leaving missionaries and investigators alike entirely ignorant regarding *how* he did it.

The manual makes the bold statement that "This volume of holy scripture provides convincing evidence that Joseph Smith is a true prophet of God." Unfortunately, that is only the case for someone who decides to believe it and accept it without actually considering what such "evidence" in the book really tells us. When the book is analysed objectively, with no prior held 'faith' that it is true, and also with no prior 'bias' that it is *not* true, what does the actual "evidence" within it reveal? We will be considering that, without bias, in the cold light of day. No faith will be required in order to accept the truth of evidence found within its pages. The book will reveal itself for what it really is.

In addition to what follows, the missionary lesson manual devotes an entire chapter to 'The Role of the Book of Mormon' and the concept that it contains the 'Fullness of the Gospel'. We will review that in *Chapter 17*.

For the moment, let's look at the way missionaries are taught to 'help' investigators come to 'know' the *Book of Mormon* is true. A testimony will be gained, not by thoroughly studying the book and then comparing it with known American history, archaeology, geography, metallurgy, flora and fauna, tribal customs and legends, etc., but by simply reading selected verses and praying about the book based on them. The question is, is that fair – and is it enough?

Investigators are asked to read the last two paragraphs of the introduction. This is what they will read:

> We invite all men everywhere to read the Book of Mormon, to ponder in their hearts the message it contains, and then to ask God, the Eternal Father, in the name of Christ if the book is true. Those who pursue this course and ask in faith will gain a testimony of its truth and divinity by the power of the Holy Ghost. (See Moroni 10: 3-5.)
>
> Those who gain this divine witness from the Holy Spirit will also come to know by the same power that Jesus Christ is the Savior of the world, that Joseph Smith is his revelator and prophet in these last days, and that The Church of Jesus Christ of Latter-day Saints is the Lord's kingdom once again established on the earth, preparatory to the second coming of the Messiah. *(Introduction to the Book of Mormon).*

The reference within the *Book of Mormon (Moroni 10:3-5)* to which investigators are directed, is very familiar to all Mormons:

> **Moroni 10:3.** Behold, I would exhort you that when ye shall read these things, if it be wisdom in God that ye should read them, that ye would remember how merciful the Lord hath been unto the children of men, from the creation of Adam even down until the time that ye shall receive these things, and ponder it in your hearts.
> 4. And when ye shall receive these things, I would exhort you that ye would ask God, the Eternal Father, in the name of Christ, if these things are not true; and if ye shall ask with a sincere heart, with real intent, having faith in Christ, he will manifest the truth of it unto you, by the power of the Holy Ghost.
> 5. And by the power of the Holy Ghost ye may know the truth of all things.

# THE BOOK OF MORMON

Missionaries are asked to "share one or two passages that are personally meaningful to you or that might be meaningful to him or her" and then, regarding the introduction:

> Carefully explain the meaning of each concept in both paragraphs and invite the investigator to commit to reading portions of the Book of Mormon and applying the principles described in these two paragraphs.

Investigators are not asked to make a thorough and objective study of the book. If they are lucky, missionaries will manage to get people to read the few selected verses they recommend to them but most people read nothing and they return the book, asking missionaries not to return.

In support of the concept that Joseph Smith obtained gold plates and then translated them, missionaries are referred to *JS–History 1:27-64* which covers the visit of Moroni in detail. It is the only full account. There is not enough space here to repeat my research regarding the whole Moroni saga and I would refer the reader to *TMD Volume 2, Chapters 3-7* which cover this subject more thoroughly. But do please read *Joseph Smith–History v.36-41*, taking note of the scriptures Moroni *quotes* to Smith *(I review this in TMD Vol. 2, Ch.6)*, and then ask yourself (or, if an investigator, ask the missionaries) these questions.

**1.** How did Joseph Smith remember, word for word, *exactly* what Moroni quoted, fifteen years *after* the claimed 1823 event?

**2.** What was the point of all the meaningless changes Moroni supposedly made to the *KJV*?

**3.** If they were more 'correct' than the *KJV* text, why did Smith leave them just as they were in the *KJV* when he wrote his *Inspired Revision* of the Bible (1831-4) instead of altering them to read the same as Moroni's 1823 version?

The fact is that Smith *made up* what Moroni said in 1823, much later, in 1838, and so naturally he did not 'correct' the same scriptures when he created his *Inspired Revision* several years *earlier*, as he had not yet thought of the idea. That is the *only* explanation and yet again it reveals the truth – Smith was a complete and utter fraud.

**4.** Why did Moroni say all that nonsense and not reveal *anything* that would have actually been helpful, worthwhile or meaningful?

On page 38 of the lesson manual, missionaries are instructed that:

> In order to know that the Book of Mormon is true, a person must read, ponder, and pray about it. The honest seeker of truth will soon come to feel that the Book of Mormon is the word of God.

# THE MORMON DELUSION

That in fact is *not* the case at all. Only someone who accepts at face value what the missionaries say, and who reads the limited material suggested and then prays, *wanting* to know it is true, will do so. That was my experience; I trusted the missionaries; subsequently, I have learned *not* to trust *feelings*.

Anyone who actually does put the *Book of Mormon* 'to the test' and thoroughly researches it against known reality will reject it out of hand and not even bother to pray about it, as common sense alone will confirm the truth of the matter to them.

A more complete coverage of why the *Book of Mormon* cannot possibly be true can be found in *TMD Vol. 2, Chapters 7-9,11,12 & 15*. Let's just deal here with some simple aspects which people could easily determine for themselves if they look carefully at what is presented to them, but which invariably will *not* be suggested by the missionaries.

If there were any truth within the book which could be properly verified in *any* way, then Mormon missionaries would naturally be instructed to let people determine the truth by such *verification*. That there are *no* 'tests' suggested, other than ethereal, is a clear indication that if the *Book of Mormon* is subjected to *any* earthly or scientific test, it will utterly fail. Nevertheless, I suggest that investigators *should* be encouraged to make at *least* the tests that follow in this chapter to determine aspects which *can* be verified, one way or the other. There are more than I mention – but the point will be made.

In the following pages, look out for these headings which will regularly appear.

A question that investigators should ask.

A *Book of Mormon* test for investigators to do.

Here's one to start things off:

A *Book of Mormon* test for investigators to do.

Read the *Book of Mormon* to determine the layout of the Nephite and Lamanite lands. Map the various city locations, along with other geographical details mentioned, seas, rivers etc., as they relate to each other and as described, including possible distances apart. Try to determine where the resulting geography fits within the known American continent.

As a guide, the *Book of Mormon* once included lots of footnotes giving details of supposed geography. These have long since been removed, as extensive and detailed archaeology has shown no connection whatsoever to any *Book of Mormon* claims. The *Book of Mormon* states they had the entire land to themselves and Joseph Smith thought that meant the whole of North America.

# THE BOOK OF MORMON

The 1888 Edition of the *Book of Mormon* contained footnotes which explained that the "sea south" was the "Atlantic, south of Cape Horn". The "sea north" was identified as the "Artic, north of North America". The "sea west" was supposed to be the "Pacific", and the "sea east" was the "Atlantic". *(BOM, 1888 Ed. p.434.)* In modern editions of the *Book of Mormon* these footnotes have been *deleted. (Tanner 1987 Ch 6:121).* Today, the geography of the *Book of Mormon* is so impossible to entertain that all we have now are several *different* equally impossible suppositions and theories for something everyone once *knew* had an easy, and at the time, obvious answer.

A *Book of Mormon* test for investigators to do.

Joseph Smith considered all the Native North Americans to be descended from Lamanites. As the Church now plays down that idea and appears to suggest that we have no real idea where the Lamanites actually lived or which civilisations are their real descendants, let's *not* expect to find evidence of that anywhere *specifically*. We should widen the field of enquiry and be able to find evidence somewhere in the Americas as it is supposed they were there *somewhere*. Study the myths, legends, language and culture of *all* Native North American tribes along with *all* civilisations of Central and South America and see how, or even *if*, any *Book of Mormon* claims compare. I will give you a clue and save you some time. I have already done this and they *don't*. Not *one* has *any* myths, legends, customs, practices, religious history or even language that relates in any way to Lamanite supposed Hebrew ancestry or any other aspect contained in the *Book of Mormon*. There is no culture which compares in *any* way whatsoever to *Book of Mormon* characters *anywhere* in the Americas.

A question that investigators should ask.

Actually, these are *five* questions that investigators should ask. They are the same five questions that William Riter asked of Apostle James E. Talmage in 1921. Talmage was too busy to respond and passed them on to B. H. Roberts who was a renowned *Book of Mormon* apologist. Roberts became so disturbed by the questions that he asked for (and got) a meeting with the First Presidency and Quorum of Twelve Apostles to discuss them. The meeting lasted for two days. Roberts was disappointed and discouraged and four days after the meeting, in a letter to President Grant, he stated "I was greatly disappointed over the net results of the discussion. There was so much said that was utterly irrelevant, and so little said that was helpful". He said Apostle Richard R Lyman did not take the matter seriously and the others "merely one by one stood up and bore testimony to the truthfulness of the *Book of Mormon*. George Albert Smith – in tears – testified that his faith in the *Book of Mormon* had not been shaken by the questions". However, *no one* ventured to actually *answer* them.

Roberts had further equally unfulfilling meetings with a small committee of apostles and became more and more disillusioned with the *Book of Mormon* but he died before publishing documents recording his ultimate concerns and further devastating discoveries. Of the five questions, Roberts was most concerned about the linguistic problem. However, he also discovered new problems. He saw literary problems in the *Book of Mormon* as well as geographic problems. Of the geographic problems he asked: "Where were the Mayan cliffs and high mountain peaks in the Book of Mormon? The geography of the Book of Mormon looked suspiciously like the New England of Joseph Smith!"

These are the five questions that could not be answered by fifteen prophets, seers and revelators then, and still cannot be answered by *anyone* today. They will *remain* unanswered if investigators ask missionaries about them.

> **1.** Linguistics: Riter asked - if the American Indians were all descendants of Lehi - why there was such diversity in the language of the American Indians and why there was no indication of Hebrew in any of the Indian language?
>
> **2.** The Book of Mormon says that Lehi found horses when he arrived in America. The horse described in the Book of Mormon (as well as many other domestic animals) did not exist in the New World before the arrival of the Spanish Conquistadors.
>
> **3.** Nephi is stated to have had a "bow of steel." Jews did not know steel at that time. And there was no iron on this continent until after the Spaniard conquest.
>
> **4.** The Book of Mormon frequently mentions "swords and scimeters [scimitars]." Scimitars are unknown until the rise of the Moslem faith (after 600 A.D.).
>
> **5.** The Book of Mormon says the Nephites possessed silk. Silk did not exist in America in pre-Columbian times.

A *Book of Mormon* test for investigators to do.

If anyone chooses to do this test, it will first require some study, but it can be done. It concerns the language used in the book which, at first glance, appears similar to that of the Bible. People should immediately question why God would want to translate ancient scripture into anything other than the modern language of the day. The Bible *(KJV)* Smith had access to, appeared to him to be the way God *spoke*. Yet the reality is God was never recorded as having spoken in Jacobean English. It was simply the then *current* language used in translation, in one small country, at one specific, and relatively very short, period of time.

That language quickly moved on, but the Bible was not updated for a long time due to more modern printing processes not yet being available. If they had been available, Smith undoubtedly would have had access to something like *The New International Version* available today. If that had been the case then no doubt Smith would have had God speak in his own modern day English. That actually would have been a very good idea as his hoax is exposed over and over again simply due to the terrible grammar he attributes to God. Mormons stick to the *King James Version* for their Bible and assume the language in their *Book of Mormon* to be the same.

If God had actually used early modern English in his communication with modern man of 1828-9 when the *Book of Mormon* was penned, which itself is a real stretch for common sense and reason in the rational mind when you actually stop to think about it, surely he would at least have used the language *correctly?*

As most people these days do not really know how early modern English should be properly spoken or written, Joseph Smith's many thousands of inaccuracies generally get completely overlooked. That the Church has already amended *thousands* of items in the book once 'declared correct by a voice from heaven' also escapes missionaries and investigators alike. The fact is that if God did *speak* that way, he was *hopeless* at it. The same is true of many of the so-called revelations contained in the *Doctrine and Covenants* where God constantly makes a complete hash of the Jacobean English language. The language is incorrectly used throughout *everything* Joseph Smith ever wrote. *(See: TMD Vol 2. Ch 11).*

To think God would use and communicate in 17$^{th}$ century English, simply because of a common English version of the Bible best known to Smith out of many translations of the ancient text is just absurd. God's words were always spoken and written in the language of the day. In today's world, something like *Young's Literal Translation* gives a better rendering of what many scriptures were actually meant to convey than the *KJV* ever could in Smith's generation. Hence, so many new translations to help modern people understand them more easily. Equally, given that Smith chose this route, to then have God not even understand early modern English well enough to correctly speak it so Smith could write it down properly makes the whole idea not just less convincing, but entirely preposterous.

So, here's the test. Study early modern English sufficiently to properly understand the correct use of the language and grammar as it was used and written. Then compare, word by word and sentence by sentence, the mess Smith made of it. You don't even have to work from an original copy of the

*Book of Mormon*, although it is available online. Despite the thousands of changes *already* made to it, a modern day copy will still provide more evidence than you will ever need to convince you of the nonsense that Smith's use of the language still is, in the way it reads compared to the way it *should* read. That is of course, apart from the material Smith copied directly from the *KJV,* which is accurate and therefore provides even more evidence of the hoax that the rest of the book is. Completing such a task will leave you in no doubt whatsoever that Smith's rendering of the language came from anyone *but* God. A seventeenth century child would have made a better job of the language and grammar than Smith did. Let me offer a little example just to help things along.

Whilst it may have been an impressive approach in Smith's day, he did himself no favours for the future. Smith's terrible attempts at the use of the language render his God an imbecile, as Smith was completely ignorant of 17th century English language structure and usage. Had God actually been speaking, and had he really, for some bizarre reason, chosen to speak in such an archaic fashion, he would at least have spoken it beautifully, not to mention correctly, so as to leave us breathless by its quality and content. Instead, the grammar and phrasing are consistently and terribly wrong.

Smith would have us believe that the following are some of God's *own* words, via Smith's pebble in his hat, where the words actually appeared *exactly* this way. Smith read them out loud so they could be written down. Just one example of the original text of the *Book of Mormon* should suffice to show what a nonsense it all was. God *speaks* the following way. Please read this slowly and carefully in order to fully appreciate the many grammatical and textual problems. These are then, the *Lord's* own choice of words, which He dictated *exactly*, one at a time into Smith's hat; they are, according to Smith, *not* Smith's choice of words:

> And they were led by a man whose name was Coriantumr; and he was a descendant of Zarahemla; and he was a dissenter from among the Nephites; and he was a large and mighty man; therefore the king of the Lamanites, whose name was Tubaloth, who was the son of Ammoron. Now Tubaloth supposing that Coriantumr, he being a mighty man, could stand against the Nephites, insomuch with his strength, and also with his great wisdom, that by sending him forth, he should gain power over the Nephites; therefore he did stir them up to anger, and he did gather together his armies, and he did appoint Coriantumr to be their leader, and did cause that they should march down to the land of Zarahemla, to battle against the Nephites. And it came to pass that because of so much contention and so much difficulty in the government, that they had not kept sufficient guards in the land of Zarahemla; for they had supposed that the Lamanites durst not come into the heart of their lands to attack that great city Zarahemla. *(1830 Book of Mormon, pp.408-9 which now comprises Helaman 1:15-18).*

# THE BOOK OF MORMON

I doubt any Mormon missionary ever recommended *that* in its original form as suitable reading for an investigator. This is not only a paragraph from the original text of the *Book of Mormon*, it consists of just *three* long sentences which make absolutely *no* sense whatsoever. This is how the Mormon God apparently spoke, word for word and word *by* word, into the hat of his prophet.

In case the reader may think there must have been some errors created in copying the above text from the original work into this book, I can assure you that it is word for word, *exactly* how the original 1830 *Book of Mormon* text read. This *is* the way God spoke to Smith in his hat, that is, if we are inclined to believe Smith. This is what a voice from heaven declared 'correct', yet it is this kind of thing that has also required many thousands of subsequent corrections to the original text over the years just to make some sense out of it.

Of course, the original text has subsequently been doctored and no longer quite reads that way, although it still makes little if any sense, and naturally it is still not one of the recommended passages that investigators are invited to read and ask God about. But, if they *were* to do so, obviously the question is not whether or not it is remotely true, rather, it is why on Earth any God would ever dictate such words in that way? The very notion is completely insane.

Investigators are given selected passages to consider and then they are asked to pray about the book. The psychology is simple. Here is a big fat book of seemingly ancient scripture, translated by a young farm boy who could not have done it without God's help. Therefore, it is highly likely to be true...

> This message of the Restoration is either true or it is not. We can know that it is true by the Holy Ghost, as promised in Moroni 10:3–5. After reading and pondering the message of the Book of Mormon, any who desire to know the truth must ask in prayer to our Heavenly Father in the name of Jesus Christ if it is true. In order to do this, we address our Heavenly Father. We thank Him for our blessings and ask to know that the message of the Book of Mormon is true. No one can know of spiritual truths without prayer. *(Page 39).*

The gullible may do so and sometimes conclude God tells them it is true. Most don't get any such answer, that is, if they bother to pray about it at all. The reality is simple. God could *not* have dictated the book to Smith for any number of reasons that are clear, purely from the provably impossible *content.*

The missionary manual has several pages of suggestions regarding how to teach about the restoration of the gospel and the *Book of Mormon*. It tells missionaries that:

> The Book of Mormon **proves** that God inspires prophets in our day as He has in every dispensation. *(page 43).* (Emphasis added).

But, it does not reference evidence *from* the *Book of Mormon* itself. Instead, it refers to *D&C 20:5-12* which is a supposed Smith *revelation* confirming the veracity of the *Book of Mormon*. So, the *proof* spoken of consists only of writings *by* Smith which claim God gave him the power to translate. That is not actually proof of anything of course. Once again we just have one supposition supporting another, all from the pen of one and the same man – Joseph Smith.

The manual continues "The Book of Mormon contains the fulness [sic] of the gospel of Jesus Christ" but once again there is *no* reference to *any* evidence of that *from* the *Book of Mormon*. In this instance, there is a very good reason for that, as a thorough study of the *Book of Mormon* confirms that it contains absolutely *none* of what Mormons term the fullness of the gospel. The manual refers once again to the same *D&C* section, this time *D&C 20:8-9*. It is the same story all over again; Joseph Smith creates a revelation which states God gave him the power to translate the gold plates. He simply validates his own position and power and claims the book *does* contain the fullness of the gospel. The *last* thing that such a self-serving 'reference' is – is *evidence* of *anything*.

> **D&C 20:8.** And gave him power from on high, by the means which were before prepared, to translate the Book of Mormon;
> **9.** Which contains a record of a fallen people, and the fulness of the gospel of Jesus Christ to the Gentiles and to the Jews also;

A *Book of Mormon* test for investigators to do.

In case the reader is inclined to believe Smith's claim that the fullness of the gospel *is* contained in the *Book of Mormon*, may I challenge you to study it thoroughly and list *anything* you discover which correlates with his so-called *fullness* of the *restored* gospel. Don't confuse references to baptism, the Saviour or His atonement and such like, which are drawn from the Bible, with Smith's entirely *new* ideas, not found in the Bible, which combine to become the fullness of the gospel he *later* introduces.

Not only will you find absolutely *nothing* which supports a single aspect of what Joseph Smith 'restored', you will find many aspects that he taught later than 1828-9 which completely *contradict* what he wrote the *Book of Mormon*, as he later altered his theology and introduced many new ideas.

We have already reviewed a classic example of that regarding God having a body, when in the *Book of Mormon* He clearly does *not*. The reason there are no details of Smith's restoration *in* the *Book of Mormon* is that the Church was formed the year after the book was written and most of Smith's surrounding doctrines, or what eventually *became* 'the fullness of the gospel', started to appear long *after* the book was published. The Nephites could not believe in things Smith was yet to invent, so they do not appear in the *Book of Mormon*.

# THE BOOK OF MORMON

> "The Book of Mormon contains the fulness of the gospel of Jesus Christ."
>
> As we review details of the claimed restoration,
> I will reference anything found (or *not* found)
> in the *Book of Mormon* that relates to each aspect.
>
> Look out for my comments in boxes like this in Chapters 7, 10 and 11.

(Note: throughout all my work, in references, I retain original spellings such as 'fulness' above which appears in the missionary manual. In my own text, I use the correct English spellings; in this case 'fullness' is my preference).

A question that investigators should ask.

How can *Book of Mormon* claims regarding the Jaredites and Lehi's family be true?

It has been determined through extensive DNA evidence that no Hebrews crossed to America and populated the continent six-hundred years BCE as the *Book of Mormon* claims. The Church now skirts around this once clearly understood aspect and claims all sorts of nonsense in order to try to overcome what has become a completely insurmountable problem.

I firmly believe there should be a 'law of total disclosure' for religions to abide by – especially Mormonism. It should be a legal requirement for the Church to reveal *everything* that is known, rather than just a few selected, and many falsified, aspects which create a fanciful fairy story. Let an investigator make of it what they may and decide accordingly. Of course if that were to happen, no one would ever join the Church and many Mormons exposed to the truth *by* the Church, rather than by people like me, would immediately leave.

The missionaries are hardly likely to ever mention the modern day problem of DNA proving Lehi and his family did *not* cross from the Holy Land and go on to populate the Americas. They really should, as scientifically it *is* the case, and surely faith should be able to 'overcome' that problem, if somehow the Church can still be shown to be true in every other respect. Of course, it can't, and it is just another nail in the coffin for the Church. Missionaries should be *obliged* to review known *facts* with their investigators. But then, missionaries usually have no idea about what most of the *facts* really are.

A question that investigators should ask.

The word 'Bible' appears several times *in* the *Book of Mormon* but not *in* the Bible. It was not a *known* word. It is an invented *English* word, taken from the Greek from about the third or fourth century CE. It is not just the word that is wrong *in* the *Book of Mormon*, it is also the *context. (See: 2 Nephi 29:3-4,6,10. 559-545 BCE)*. Ask *why* the word 'Bible' appears in the *Book of Mormon* when there was no equivalent word in *any* language from which to translate it?

A question that investigators should ask.

According to the *Book of Mormon*, the people, who were Jews, continued to live the Law of Moses after leaving Jerusalem. Nevertheless, there is *no* mention of a single one of them in the book. The closest it gets, is to a few scant mentions of 'sacrifice' and 'burnt offerings'. *Why* do *no* ceremonies, *no* feast days, *no* Passover – the most significant feast, *no* circumcision and *no* cultural details appear *anywhere* in the book? Moreover, why do remnants of such things *not* appear in the culture of *any* civilisation ever discovered in the Americas?

A question that investigators should ask.

Missionaries do *not* point out to investigators, the fact that New Testament verses appear prolifically in the *Book of Mormon*. Ask *why*? They really should not appear there at all. Where Christ supposedly visited the Nephites after his death, something *similar* could possibly be excused. Even then, as the gospels were written long after Christ lived, by people who never met him or heard what he actually said, the wording should not be *exactly* the same as the 1611 *KJV* translation. What Jesus *actually* said, could not possibly be *identical* to what eventually found its way into various manuscripts used to construct early Bibles, from which the *KJV* eventually evolved. Therefore a 'first hand' *Book of Mormon* record of what Jesus Christ supposedly said in America should be somewhat *different* to what was later *reportedly* said in the Holy Land. What it should most definitely *not* be, but which it often is, is *identical* to the *KJV*.

New Testament material certainly should *not* appear BCE or be used as quotes from prophets in the CE in the *Book of Mormon* in matters unrelated to the New Testament. It was written on the other side of the ocean, hundreds of years *after* (Joseph Smith claimed) Lehi and his family left Jerusalem. Yet the *Book of Mormon* faithfully quotes the *King James Version* of the New Testament in the BCE period. That's *impossible*. The Tanners list well over a hundred quotations from the New Testament in the first two books of Nephi *alone*. These books were supposed to have been written between 600 and 545 BCE. *(Tanner 1987:74-79)*. Missionaries don't draw attention to the problem when teaching investigators. Faith may overcome this obvious anomaly if later discovered, by which time a 'testimony' could override cognitive dissonance.

Smith's fraudulent use of such scripture is exposed – once again by his own hand. He claimed that Jesus spoke the *same* words in America as he did in

# THE BOOK OF MORMON

the Holy Land, by making them almost *identical* to the *KJV* in his *Book of Mormon – including punctuation*. That was in 1828-9. It seems that a couple of years later, Smith *forgot* what he had written in the *Book of Mormon*. When he penned his *Inspired Revision* of the Bible, he *altered* some of the *very same verses* to provide a more 'correct' translation of what Jesus originally said. Of course, he never explained how the *Book of Mormon* came to have Jesus speak the exact same *errors* in America that appeared in the *KJV* or why he later 'corrected' Jesus in his 'Inspired' revision. Smith is completely caught out and his fraud is exposed – again. *(See: TMD Vol. 2:200-01)*. Naturally, the Mormon missionaries do *not* point out that Joseph Smith had Jesus Christ impossibly speak *identical* words in America as the *KJV* has him speaking in the Holy Land, any more than the fact that Smith later 'corrected' Christ's words to read *differently* when revising the *KJV,* leaving his *Book of Mormon* with original *KJV* text which could then only be *false* statements attributed to Christ. There is no escaping the obvious hoax perpetrated by Joseph Smith.

A *Book of Mormon* test for investigators to do.

Research the history of *manufactured transparent glass windows*.

Smith has a verse in the *Book of Mormon* declare "For behold, *ye cannot have windows, for they will be dashed in pieces*; neither shall ye take fire with you, for ye shall not go by the light of fire". *(Ether 2:23)*. Smith also imagines God providing light for submersible vessels by 'touching' sixteen stones. Amazingly, the brother of Jared *described* the stones being clear as *transparent glass (Ether 3:1)*, another *fatal* mistake and impossible analogy for the claimed time period. Smith had no idea that although some forms of glass were known and used as early as 3000 BCE, glass was not invented in a form that would generally be used for thin transparent windows until over *four thousand* years later. Neither the *word* nor the *material* existed at the time of the Jaredites. The missionaries no doubt remain quiet about that problem. *(Also see: TMD Vol. 2:215-19 for more on the history of manufactured transparent glass)*.

A *Book of Mormon* test for investigators to do.

Research the history of the wheel and see if it appeared anywhere in the Americas.

The *Book of Mormon* is replete with references to horses and chariots and farming implements which meant *wheels* were used, the use of steel and other refined metals. The Native American, Maya, Aztec and Inca civilisations did *not* develop the wheel for use with vehicles of *any* description for one simple, and obviously very good reason. There were *no* draught animals with which to pull them. There were *no* horses, *no* cattle and *no* oxen in the Americas. Yet they *all* exist in the *Book of Mormon*.

A *Book of Mormon* test for investigators to do.

Obtain a full list of all the animals that are known to have existed *anywhere* in the Americas during the *Book of Mormon* timeframe. Then go through the book. List and compare the ones that appear there with your real list. If they match, or even if they *almost* match, perhaps there is *some* truth to claims about them. How similar are the lists? Let me help with that.

The list of animals that Smith claimed existed, particularly domesticated animals, in the *Book of Mormon* era is absolutely astounding. Somehow against all the odds, Smith managed to *include* the major animals that did *not* exist at all, and *exclude* the ones that *did* exist. The list could hardly be more *incorrect* than it is.

The following are some, but not all, of the animals that *were* in existence in various parts of the Americas during the *Book of Mormon* era: alpaca; bear; boar; bison; coati (which resembles a raccoon); coyote; deer; duck; guinea-pig; jackrabbit; pronghorn (*Antilocapra americana*, often mistakenly termed an antelope); mountain sheep; jaguar; llama; monkey; reindeer; sloth; tapir; wild turkey and the domesticated turkey from about 3000 BCE; and the turtle.

Smith mentions *not one* of these *existing* animals in his *Book of Mormon*. He does however, make mention of several other animals which did *not* exist, as if they actually existed in the *Book of Mormon* era in the Americas. Apologists claim these animals were already in existence in the Americas or were introduced by the Jaredites. This would entail bringing them on the ocean voyage in 'tight like unto a dish' barges; apparently, flocks and herds were included in this methane loaded trip. *(See Ether 6:4).*

An overall list of non-indigenous *Book of Mormon* animals includes these: ass; bull; calf; cattle; cow; elephant; domesticated goat; flocks; herds; horse; ox; oxen; domesticated sheep; sow: swine; plus two unidentified animals called 'cureloms' and 'cumoms', one of which, apologists suggest, may have been the woolly mammoth, which of course went extinct several thousands of years *prior* to *Book of Mormon* times. Although God supposedly translated the *Book of Mormon* for Smith, there are no known meanings for *cureloms* or *cumoms*; God clearly *forgot* to translate them into modern (or even bad 17th century) English – in Smith's hat.

As evidence of the *Book of Mormon*, perhaps the missionaries ask their investigators to obtain a list of all the animals that are proven to have existed in the timeframe and compare it with all the animals appearing in the *Book of Mormon*. If they match, then it is an evidence of sorts of the possible validity of the book. If they do not, which as has been demonstrated, they absolutely do

# THE BOOK OF MORMON

*not*, then the book is immediately *proven* fraudulent. But then the missionaries probably *don't* suggest such a test. The reason is obvious.

A question that investigators should ask.

Why are butter and milk mentioned in the *Book of Mormon?*
The *Book of Mormon* mentions 'butter' (copied from Isaiah in *2 Nephi 17:15&22)* and 'milk' *(2 Nephi 9:50),* yet in reality, no animals existed to provide milk so they could not have known what butter and milk even *meant.*

A *Book of Mormon* test for investigators to do.

Obtain a list of all the crops and foodstuffs known to have existed *anywhere* in the Americas during the *Book of Mormon* era. Then go through the book. List and compare the ones that appear there with your real list. If they match, or even if they *almost* match, perhaps there is *some* truth to claims about them. How similar are the lists? Let me help with that in the same way that I did regarding animals.

Various foodstuffs were grown or were available and used during the *Book of Mormon* timeframe in different parts of America and included three main crops; corn, beans and squash. Other food (not all in the same locations) used by various peoples and cultures, included such things as: amaranth, eaten with chili peppers; chicham (like a turnip); chicozapote, a fruit; gourds; lima beans; manioc or cassava; yucca; peppers; peanuts; various plants; pineapples; potatoes; pumpkins; sunflowers; sweet potatoes and tomatoes. The Mayans grew cacao trees for chocolate, avocado trees and also papaya trees.

Against all odds of at least getting *some* of them right, Smith manages only *one*. He includes corn, but mentions *not one* of the rest of the above in his *Book of Mormon*, other than the broad statement 'all manner' of fruits. But they actually didn't have 'all manner' of fruits. They had very few that Smith would have recognized. Instead, Smith's book claims they cultivated *barley* and *wheat* which did not exist there, as the staple diet for *millions* of people, using manufactured implements including ploughs made from metal (none have been found), pulled by draught animals which equally did not exist there at the time.

> And they did make all manner of tools to till the earth, both to plow and to sow, to reap and to hoe, and also to thrash. And they did make all manner of tools with which they did work their beasts. *(Ether 10:25-26).*

Smith here combines *three* errors into proof positive fiction. Clearly, the ancients did *not* make ploughs or any other implements with which to work their beasts in order to plough, reap, sow and hoe, or thrash [thresh] as they did *not* have any domesticated *wheat* or *barley* nor any beasts of burden of *any* description with which to work such implements, for which there is equally *no* evidence. There couldn't be, as there was no *use* for them. *No* wheat, *no* barley, *no* ploughs and *no* draught animals – equals a story of pure and very obvious nineteenth century fiction. Once again, I very much doubt that missionaries will suggest my comparison test of reality against the claims in the *Book of Mormon*.

A *Book of Mormon* test for investigators to do.

A final suggested test is this. Go through the *Book of Mormon* and list all the refined metals that are listed as being produced and used. I won't bother to mention details of reality other than the fact that none were actually used in the Americas until centuries after *Book of Mormon* times.

This is the test. Make a list of all the actual base metals and all the other minerals and substances required in order to smelt and manufacture the refined metals required for implements, weapons and currency that appear in the Book of Mormon. Then, as these things do not relocate themselves over time and will today remain where they always were, research locations in the Americas where each of these items can be located and mined.

You will find several problems for the *Book of Mormon* characters. They would have had to travel hundreds, sometimes thousands, of miles in different directions to locate all the various required elements for such manufacturing. This would have required being directed to *exactly* the right places to locate everything. And, as there was no means of transport at all, despite *Book of Mormon* claims, this would have entailed *walking* everywhere. The task, as you will easily discover, would be monumentally impossible and as unlikely as their having knowledge of how to actually achieve all the claimed end results.

Included above, if you count them up, are dozens and dozens of entirely impossible *Book of Mormon* claims. That should be enough for anyone to come to the only possible conclusion, should they study the book, but there are many more examples if you care to look for them. *(Check in TMD Volume 2).*

A question that investigators should ask.

One final question I will mention stems from a discovery I recently made. Ask why apologists for the Church, rather than its detractors, are now attacking *Book of Mormon* Nephite coins? I considered the absurdity of the idea that the Nephites had a comprehensive currency system when I wrote *TMD Volume 2* and included details about it in *Chapter 12*. Despite the fact that currency as such was not invented until about a century *after* Lehi supposedly left the Holy

Land, I assumed apologists were happy enough with the idea that Nephites invented their system about the same time as some other cultures had, as it was almost simultaneously developed in more than one part of the world. I was absolutely astounded to discover apologists claim that the 'header' to a part of the *Book of Mormon* is invariably *wrong* and that the Nephites did not actually have 'coins' after all. Rather, they now claim, they just had a system of *weights*.

I was so taken aback by the claim that I wrote an article about it. It is an absurd thing for apologists to do. They are taking the side of some detractors who suggest that the Nephites could not have had coins as the concept had yet to be invented. To support their *new* supposition, the apologists decry an official Church placed 'header' in the *Book of Mormon* which suggests that the Nephites *did* have a complete currency system. They also state that the book itself claims *no such thing*. I disagree – as do some leading Mormon scholars. I think they have created a major problem which may come back to bite them.

I have included an updated and expanded version of the article I wrote about this as *Appendix A* for anyone interested in this absurd stance now taken by apologists – who have clearly run out of things to attack detractors over and instead appear to have turned on inspired leaders. I will leave readers to make of it what they will. *(See Appendix A)*.

Once investigators have asked some of the questions I have suggested and obtained comprehensive and *satisfactory* answers – and if each of the 'tests' prove *other* than I have discovered, and investigators determine that they actually confirm Smith *did* get everything right after all – only *then* is the book worthy of taking to the Lord in prayer in order to determine whether or not it is actually true. Only *then* would that be the fair and correct thing to do, and only *then* should an answer be expected – one way or the other.

Until then, praying about it is not a viable proposition. If God exists, He does not expect to answer things we can quite easily determine for ourselves. The Church claims that Joseph Smith himself confirmed this.

> **D&C 9:8.** But, behold, I say unto you, that you must study it out in your mind; then you must ask me if it be right.

So, study it out, ask the questions and do the tests in order to prove the case before bothering God about it, then you will find that you won't even need to.

# Chapter 7

## Lesson 2

### The Plan of Salvation

#### Part A

Starting with reference to *D&C 20:37*, as with *Lesson 1*, where God commands baptism, missionaries are prepared to teach the 'Plan of Salvation.'

Investigators must be able to answer the following questions – which are not very much different to some earlier questions. *(See Ch. 4. p.65)*.

> Do you believe that God is our Eternal Father?
> Do you believe that Jesus Christ is the Son of God, the Savior and Redeemer of the world?
> Are you willing to keep the Sabbath day holy, including partaking of the sacrament weekly and rendering service to fellow members?

The commitments investigators will be asked to make following this lesson include:

Will you pray to know that what we have taught is true?
Will you repent of your sins?
Will you attend church with us this Sunday?
Will you follow the example of the Savior and be baptized on (date)?
May we set a time for our next visit?
Commandments from lesson 4 that you choose to include. *(Page 47).*

As previously, missionaries are reminded they can include commandments from Lesson 4, if they want to *(See chapters 13&14).* If the investigators are progressing well, it may help to introduce commandments a little at a time, rather than reveal them all at once when it may be a lot for them to take in and accept.

One of the commitments, following this lesson, will be to repent of sins. Investigators will be taught that everyone has sins and they must commit to repent of theirs. Until 'sin' was introduced to them by the missionaries, many unsuspecting investigators may have been entirely ignorant of the idea such a thing as sin actually existed, let alone that they had been guilty of such a thing.

Sin is *created* as a concept and becomes a problem – then the solution is offered. It is a classic sales trick; create a need which never existed in the first place and then offer the solution.

Missionaries are taught that:

> One of the most effective ways to teach and testify of the Savior is to read together from the Book of Mormon. Passages from other standard works can also be helpful. *(Page 47).*

Over twenty *Book of Mormon* references are provided at this point as a basis for convincing an investigator that they need baptism, while the rest of the Standard Works, including the Bible, remain 'helpful', but no references are provided.

One of the most powerful 'persuasion' tools the Church has comprises three questions for which missionaries have the ready answers. I was certainly captivated by these in my time.

> Many people wonder, "Where did we come from? Why are we here? Where are we going?" The plan of salvation gives us the answers to these questions. *(Page 48).*

## Pre-Earth Life.

God is the Father of our spirits. We are literally His children, and He loves us. ***We lived as spirit children of our Father in Heaven before we were born on this earth.*** We were not, however, like our Heavenly Father, nor could we ever become like Him and enjoy all the blessings

## THE PLAN OF SALVATION

that He enjoys without the experience of living in mortality with a physical body. *(Page 48)*. (Emphasis added).

To confirm we are literally the spirit children of God and that we existed with Him before we were born, scriptural 'evidence' is cited. Some *D&C* references are provided to missionaries as evidence to share with investigators. Do Mormon missionaries or investigators ever notice they are self-serving and do not constitute *real* evidence? What do the Bible references prove?

> **Acts 17:29.** Forasmuch then as we are the offspring of God, we ought not to think that the Godhead is like unto gold, or silver, or stone, graven by art and man's device.
>
> **Hebrews 12:9.** Furthermore we have had fathers of our flesh which corrected us, and we gave them reverence: shall we not much rather be in subjection unto the Father of spirits, and live?

Biblical references do little to support the concept of *pre-Earth* life. They are not taken that way to my knowledge by anyone other than Mormons. In other religions, we are the offspring of God; He created us and the spirits within us – no more and no less than that. Mormonism goes a step, or giant leap, further.

---

"The Book of Mormon contains the fulness of the gospel of Jesus Christ."

There is no reference provided from the *Book of Mormon* to confirm the idea that we are literally the spirit children of God.
However, the Book of Mormon does appear to clearly teach the concept that the devil has children. See below.

---

> 1 Nephi 14:3. And that great pit, which hath been digged for them by *that great and abominable church, which was founded by the devil and his children,* that he might lead away the souls of men down to hell… (Emphasis added).

The Mormon Church teaches that a third of the host of heaven followed the devil and became consigned to roam the earth as spirits tempting humans. I doubt the Mormon Church wishes us to take too literally the idea that Satan actually has children. I am sure they prefer the concept that it is a purely figurative expression and children here means 'followers'. Nevertheless, it says **children** in the *Book of Mormon* and with much less specific so-called evidence, the Church expects investigators to accept that is the literal case regarding us. That is, that we are literally *spirit children* born of God, long before our life on Earth began.

To confirm so-called evidence of our 'pre-mortal' life, further references are provided.

> **Abraham 3:22.** Now the Lord had shown unto me, Abraham, *the intelligences that were organized before the world was*; and among all these there were many of the noble and great ones;
> **23.** And God saw *these souls that they were good*, and he stood in the midst of them, and he said: These I will make my rulers; for he *stood among those that were spirits*, and he saw that they were good; and he said unto me: Abraham, thou art one of them; thou wast chosen before thou wast born.
> **24.** And there stood one among them that was like unto God, and he said unto those who were with him: We will go down, for there is space there, and we will take of these materials, and we will make an earth whereon these may dwell;
> **25.** And we will prove them herewith, to see if they will do all things whatsoever the Lord their God shall command them;
> **26.** And they who keep their *first estate* shall be added upon; and they who keep not their first estate shall not have glory in the same kingdom with those who keep their first estate; and *they who keep their second estate shall have glory added upon their heads for ever and ever*. (Emphasis added).

In Mormon theology, people were not always 'spirits' in the pre-existence. What is not discussed anywhere in this lesson is the Mormon concept alluded to in v.22 above, in that we were all originally 'intelligences' and had *always* existed as such. We were 'created' or born in the pre-Earth world, as spirits, to God as our father and one of his many wives as mother. The 'first estate' was our pre-Earth spirit world experience and the 'second estate' refers to life on Earth.

Residents of the pre-Earth spirit world are referred to as 'souls' in v.23 and yet today in Mormon theology, the soul is comprised of the body and the spirit *combined*. A spirit alone does not constitute a 'soul'. Smith has Abraham make the erroneous statement. If we believe it to be a real translation, then it means Abraham completely misunderstood this and thought the spirit *was* the soul. The same is true of the Nephites and we will discuss that further in *Chapter 10. (see Pp.190-91)*.

Of course, the above text is derived from the *Book of Abraham*, which Smith himself wrote, pretending it came from papyri that were four thousand years old and written by Abraham himself. That has long been exposed as yet another fraudulent claim since some of the papyri were rediscovered, dated to about the time of Christ, give or take fifty years, and found to contain only

## THE PLAN OF SALVATION

common Egyptian funerary writings. It is a further self-serving text from the pen of Joseph Smith which does not constitute *evidence*. In fact, the real evidence proves it to be nothing but a hoax – from the dating of the papyri and the nonsense facsimiles – to what is actually written *in* the book. *(See: TMD Vol. 2. Ch.14 for more details).*

> **Moses 3:5.** And every plant of the field before it was in the earth, and every herb of the field before it grew. For I, the Lord God, created all things, of which I have spoken, spiritually, before they were naturally upon the face of the earth. For I, the Lord God, had not caused it to rain upon the face of the earth. And I, the Lord God, had created all the children of men; and not yet a man to till the ground; for in heaven created I them; and there was not yet flesh upon the earth, neither in the water, neither in the air;

Smith wrote this as part of an *Inspired Revision* of the *KJV* Bible in the latter part of 1830, the year *after* the *Book of Mormon* was written and new theology was being constantly introduced. A Biblical quote is provided from *Jeremiah, Chapter 1*.

> **Jer. 1:5.** Before I formed thee in the belly I knew thee; and before thou camest forth out of the womb I sanctified thee, *and* I ordained thee a prophet unto the nations.

This is the *only* biblical 'evidence' provided for missionaries to use to support the claim that people lived with God as spirits before they came to the Earth. Christian religions generally do not interpret it that way any more than the Mormon Church thinks the devil really has children, and therefore a wife – or more likely wives in Mormon theology. *The Amplified Bible* version of Jeremiah 1:5 gives us a slightly better idea of the intended meaning.

> **5.** Before I formed you in the womb I knew [and] approved of you [as My chosen instrument], and before you were born I separated and set you apart, consecrating you; [and] I appointed you as a prophet to the nations.

Outside of Mormonism this is accepted to mean that Jeremiah was *chosen* before he was born rather than that he *lived* before he was born. He was foreordained, or to some, predestined to his future role, as God chose him, or *knew* him, in that sense before he was even born. It is not taken to mean that he lived with God before he was born. If God *had* intended that to be a core doctrine of Judaism or later, even early Christianity, surely He would have made it clear. Before Joseph Smith came along, *no one* considered it to mean that everyone lived with God before they came to Earth.

> "The Book of Mormon contains the fulness of the gospel of Jesus Christ."
>
> There is no reference provided from the *Book of Mormon* to confirm the idea that we all lived with God in a pre-mortal life. Apparently, the Nephites had absolutely no idea about that and it did not form part of their own 'fullness of the gospel'.

## The Creation.

> ***Under the direction of the Father, Jesus Christ created the earth*** as a place for us to live and gain experience. In order ***to progress and become like God, each of us had to obtain a body and be tested*** during a time of probation on the earth. While on the earth we are out of God's physical presence. ***We do not remember our pre-earth life.*** We must walk by faith rather than by sight. *(Page 49).* (Emphasis added).

Here we find three core Mormon concepts for missionaries to teach their investigators:

**1.** Jesus Christ created the Earth.
**2.** We can become like God.
**3.** We lived before we came here and we have forgotten about it.

Unfortunately, the supporting references do not mention *any* of the above ideas at all.

> **1 Nephi 17:36.** Behold, the Lord hath created the earth that it should be inhabited; and he hath created his children that they should possess it.

This *Book of Mormon* statement is neither here nor there. It is something that any and every church on the Earth believes and proclaims, Christian or otherwise.

> **Alma 30:44.** But Alma said unto him: ***Thou hast had signs enough***; will ye tempt your God? Will ye say, Show unto me a sign, when ***ye have the testimony of all these thy brethren, and also all the holy prophets?*** The scriptures are laid before thee, yea, and all things denote there is a God; yea, even the earth, and all things that are upon the face of it, yea, and its motion, yea, and also all the planets which move in their regular form do witness that there is a Supreme Creator. (Emphasis added).

# THE PLAN OF SALVATION

Faced with no real scriptural evidence in favour of pre-Earth life, the lesson manual resorts to references suggesting investigators do not need a sign, or presumably evidence, for this; we have prophets to tell us these things. We should trust them and accept their 'testimony'.

A recommended so-called 'scripture' from the *D&C (88:41-47)* says virtually the same thing – Look around you; isn't it obvious there is a creator?

This is not *evidence* of anything. These verses are all about not seeking for signs; just believe what you see – or rather, in Mormonism, what you are *told*. The reason is that real evidence for God *or* pre-Earth life is in extremely short supply. In point of fact there isn't *any*. That really is something that is just a matter of faith.

In a rewrite of Genesis, Smith came up with a whole new concept about the creation. He penned what is termed the *Book of Moses* and the verse referenced here is:

> **Moses 2:1.** And it came to pass that the Lord spake unto Moses, saying: Behold, I reveal unto you concerning this heaven, and this earth; write the words which I speak. I am the Beginning and the End, the Almighty God; ***by mine Only Begotten I created these things; yea, in the beginning I created the heaven, and the earth*** upon which thou standest. (Emphasis added).

This Smith concoction is yet another self-supporting reference. In Genesis, it was originally *Chapter 1, verse 1,* and it simply read:

> **KJV. Gen 1:1.** In the beginning God created the heaven and the earth.

God obviously wasn't clear about things at all when originally speaking with Moses, according to Smith, who rewrote Genesis to accommodate new theological thinking. However, Smith was still monotheistic at the time and the verse also has God say "I created the heaven and the earth…" indicating God and Jesus are one and the same being, regardless of who created what. At the end of Moses, Chapter 1, Smith concludes by saying:

> **Moses 1:42.** (These words were spoken unto Moses in the mount, the name of which shall not be known among the children of men. And now they are spoken unto you. Show them not unto any except them that believe. ***Even so. Amen.***) (Brackets in original; Emphasis added).

It is interesting to note that God *only* speaks like this ("Even so. Amen.") when He is *speaking to Smith*, mainly in the *D&C*, where there are over two dozen instances, or in Smith's *rewrites* of other work, as above. He never speaks like that in the *Book of Mormon* which was written prior to the *D&C*

revelations, or anywhere in the Bible. Unless that is, Smith got the idea from Revelation 22:20, which is highly unlikely but is as close as it gets.

20 ...Surely I come quickly. **Amen**. **Even so**, come, Lord Jesus.

The phrase "I come quickly" was another Smith favourite, which makes half a dozen appearances in the book of Revelation but nowhere else in the rest of the Bible. Smith never used it in his earlier writings; he began using the term in the *D&C*.

It is also interesting to note Smith's God is still spoken of in the *singular* in his *Book of Moses* regarding the creation process, with dozens of references to *God*. By the time he wrote his later concoction, the *Book of Abraham*, he had decided there were *plural* 'Gods'. Using the same creative process, except this time carried out by *'the Gods'*, he included dozens of references to these *Gods* performing exactly the same acts that Moses had seemingly been told by God Himself that He had accomplished alone; or rather that He had Jesus do *for* Him, by *himself. ( Moses 2:1)*.

A Question that investigators should ask.

Why did God declare he managed everything quite well by Himself, just as the Bible indicates, in Smith's *Book of Moses* – and then declare that He had lots of help from other Gods in Smith's later *Book of Abraham* – not just once, but *dozens* of times in each book?

This contradiction occurs in two separate books that came from the pen of the same supposed prophet just a few years apart. Joseph Smith's earlier book contained *one* God and his later book contained *Gods*. If Abraham did write an account four thousand years ago including 'Gods' and Genesis as we now read it was written less than 600 BCE, then the chronology is actually reversed. Whatever the case, theology should remain *consistent*.

Most of the Old Testament was developed between 586 and 538 BCE when the Hebrew nation was in captivity and exile due to being conquered by the Babylonians. Before this time, the Hebrew religion followed a slow, gradual evolution that had its genesis in African tribalism, to a more sophisticated form, strongly influenced by Hinduism. The book of Genesis is a compilation written by various contributors between 900 BCE and 400 BCE, drawing on an oral tradition dating back to 1100 BCE or earlier. Most scholars believe the earliest any written versions of the stories date is 15th–10th centuries BCE. The version that we now know and read was written just a couple of hundred years BCE and is the result of much evolutionary story telling over many centuries.

Moses 6:63 is suggested reading, which again just claims that everything around us testifies of God. It is worth including as I have something to say about that concept.

# THE PLAN OF SALVATION

> **Moses 6:63.** And behold, all things have their likeness, and all things are created and made to bear record of me, both things which are temporal, and things which are spiritual; things which are in the heavens above, and things which are on the earth, and things which are in the earth, and things which are under the earth, both above and beneath: ***all things bear record of me.*** (Emphasis added).

As long as people imagine *pleasant* things – say, sunny skies and a warm breeze along with perhaps a picnic in a meadow, birds singing and colourful butterflies, or perhaps the beauty of the heavens when the stars are out on a clear night and the fragrance of honeysuckle hangs in the air, then they may be taken in by this nonsense. All sorts of good feelings can come from a pleasing environment of any description but they are not *evidence* of *anything*.

Stop to think a moment and the awful truth emerges. The corollary must surely be that all the nasty and horrid things which to a believer God is also indisputably responsible for, *also* "bear record of me" and how cruel and unkind He is. If we really are to accept that God is responsible for *everything* and that those things *all* bear record of Him – then I can provide many, many examples of horrible 'creations' that are obnoxious and completely pointless.

From the devastating effects of natural disasters, all of which result from things God created, to the results of diseases caused by living organisms which He also created, as they are life forms, all 'bear record' of God's cruelty and lack of care and attention to the way He created various ecosystems – according to His own word. Entire volumes could be written about such things but I will just mention two specific things that God is totally responsible for creating as examples.

Why did He 'create' a food chain wherein most of His creations kill and eat each other in order to survive? Countless millions of God's 'creations' have suffered terribly as they have been hunted down, ripped apart and eaten alive every day since the dawn of evolution. Many of His creatures spend their short lives just trying to survive long enough to procreate before they get eaten.

Why did God *create* the loa loa (eye) worm which exists only in human eyes, once in America but now mainly in children in the Sudan? What a terrible and unkind idea that was. For that matter, *why* did He create all the other *living* organisms which afflict and often prematurely kill humans? What was the purpose in that when there are enough other things to afflict humans? What kind of a *plan* is that for any God to consider using? Would you do it?

What purpose was there in any of that and what was God thinking? If you can accommodate the fact that these things *evolved*, you can remove direct responsibility from God and retain faith in Him, but if you don't accept that, then you really have a major problem because in that case God is positively and demonstrably evil. He could have very easily structured everything more benevolently for all His creations without detracting from whatever His real 'plan' was. Smith's 'scripture' quoted above claims *everything* bears record of God. The kind of God that some things bear record of is quite frankly not worth knowing, let alone following or worshiping.

*John 1:1-3* is referenced, but not from the *KJV* Bible; the Joseph Smith Translation or *Inspired Revision* is used:

> **I.R. John 1:1.** In the beginning was the gospel preached through the Son. And the gospel was the word, and the word was with the Son, and the Son was with God, and the Son was of God.
> **2.** The same was in the beginning with God.
> **3.** All things were made by him; and without him was not anything made which was made.

Verses 2-3 remain the same as the *KJV* but Smith altered v.1 considerably from the original which reads:

> **KJV John 1:1.** In the beginning was the Word, and the Word was with God, and the Word was God.

The change is to accommodate Smith's *new* idea that Jesus was the God of the Old Testament and that it was he who created the world under the direction of God the father – a concept that would be anathema to the Jews.

Also referenced is another Bible scripture:

> **2 Corinthians 5:6.** Therefore we are always confident, knowing that, whilst we are at home in the body, we are absent from the Lord:
> **7.** (For we walk by faith, not by sight:)

To the Mormon Church this implies that if we are absent from God then once we were *not* absent from God and therefore lived *with* Him. It is a huge and very imaginative stretch of common sense and reason to conclude such a thing from that verse.

## Agency and the Fall of Adam and Eve.

These are some of the things that missionaries must get across to investigators.

> God created Adam and Eve and placed them in the Garden of Eden. Adam and Eve were created in God's image, with bodies of flesh and bones. While Adam and Eve were in the garden, they were still in God's presence and could have lived forever…

# THE PLAN OF SALVATION

> God gave Adam and Eve their agency. ...commanded them not to eat the forbidden fruit, or the fruit of the tree of knowledge of good and evil. ...but they could not progress by experiencing opposition in mortality. They could not know joy because they could not experience sorrow and pain.
>
> Satan tempted Adam and Eve to eat the forbidden fruit, and they chose to do so. **This was part of God's plan.** Because of this choice, they were cast from the garden and out of God's physical presence. This event is called the Fall. **Separation from God's presence is spiritual death.** Adam and Eve became mortal—subject to physical death, or separation of the body and spirit. **They could now experience disease and all types of suffering.**
>
> They had ... the ability to choose between good and evil. This made it possible for them to learn and progress. ...to make wrong choices and to sin. In addition, they could now have children, so the rest of God's spirit children could come to earth, obtain physical bodies, and be tested. Only in this way could God's children progress and become like Him. *(Page 49).* (Emphasis added).

It seems strange to me now that being tempted by Satan and enduring the traumas of a 'fall' was part of God's 'plan'. Once someone becomes converted, everything is accepted without question, as it must be true. It clearly wasn't a very good plan and it sounds more and more like a fairy story, not dissimilar to many other even earlier fables. We should perhaps here be reminded once again that the version of the *Old Testament* we now read was only written that way less than six-hundred years BCE when the Jews were in exile and there were then a lot of other myths and legends, fairy tales and folk-lore available to draw on for ideas.

If Adam and Eve, upon becoming mortal, could experience disease and suffering, another **question for investigators to ask** is, why did this God create all the diseases in the first place? Surely there is enough to contend with without all that added in to the equation? Surely no real God would deliberately create such things as Mycobacterium leprae – the bacteria which cause leprosy.

There is no theological reason for introducing disease that is remotely worthy of consideration. It is in fact a positively *evil* idea. The other thing of course is we now know many diseases are caused by living organisms which, according to Mormon theology, were *all* created *before* man – so, where did God put all the ones that *only* survive in humans, *before* He created humans?

We actually know, through modern science, many organisms have evolved from one thing to another, even in our own lifetime, but of course that is never explained. Evolution is not directly addressed in Mormonism and the Church remains neutral in order to avoid unanswerable questions. When Steve Benson had conversations with his grandfather, Church President, Ezra Taft Benson, he said "the Church had decided to do nothing, since publishing the facts would only cause more controversy". (http://www.lds-mormon.com/benson2.shtml).

There are *trillions* of 'life forms' that exist both on and in each and every human, without which we could not exist. No mention is made of anything that was too small to be seen when these stories were invented and passed down.

Missionaries are advised not to go too deeply into the doctrine of the fall.

> When first teaching this doctrine, do not teach everything you know about it. Explain very simply that God chose two of His children, Adam and Eve, to become the first parents on earth. After their transgression they were subject to both sin and death. By themselves they could not return to live with Heavenly Father. **The Lord spoke to Adam and taught him the plan of salvation and redemption through the Lord Jesus Christ.** By following that plan, Adam and his family could have joy in this life and return to live with God (see Alma 18:36; 22:12–14). *(Page 50)*. (Emphasis added).

It is only since leaving the Mormon Church that I have been able to see the absurdity of such statements as the one I have emphasised above. There are many references, especially in the *Book of Mormon*, to the idea that Adam and Eve and those who followed were taught that *Jesus* would 'redeem' them with his 'plan of salvation' and that they prayed 'in the name of Jesus Christ', long before the name would have made any sense to anyone. In Judaism, of course no such things exist; they were not forgotten, the very *idea* is just plain silly.

> "The Book of Mormon contains the fulness of the gospel of Jesus Christ."
>
> 3 Nephi 18:19. Therefore ye must always pray to the Father in my name.
> 3 Nephi 19:18. And behold, they began to pray; and they did **pray unto Jesus, calling him their Lord and their God.**
>
> Mormon Doctrine now dictates that you do *not* pray to Jesus and that Jesus is *not* God – Jesus and God are separate beings and both have bodies.

It never occurred to me, although it certainly should have, that had prayer through Jesus Christ been the case for Adam and Eve and those who followed, it would have been clearly recorded in Hebrew scripture and Jews would accept him as their saviour. The fact that Jesus wasn't even Christ's real name and that such a name wasn't actually invented until well into the CE period doesn't seem to concern the Mormon Church any more than the fact it was supposedly inserted into a book *(The Book of Mormon)* on the other side of the world, long before the invention of the name occurred. The impossibilities stack up and no

# THE PLAN OF SALVATION

amount of faith can overcome the obvious deception – if you just stop to *think* for a moment. In the pre-Christian era, *nobody* prayed through *Jesus Christ*.

The scriptures referenced above for use to confirm that *"the Lord spoke to Adam and taught him the plan of salvation and redemption through the Lord Jesus Christ"* are once again taken from the *Book of Mormon. Alma: 18:36; 22:12–14. (Also see: Ch.4. pp.66-73).*

> **Alma 18:36.** Now when Ammon had said these words, he began at the creation of the world, and also the creation of Adam, and told him all the things concerning the fall of man, and rehearsed and laid before him the records and the holy scriptures of the people, which had been spoken by the prophets, even down to the time that their father, Lehi, left Jerusalem.
>
> **Alma 22:12.** And it came to pass that when Aaron saw that the king would believe his words, he began from the creation of Adam, reading the scriptures unto the king—how God created man after his own image, and that God gave him commandments, and that because of transgression, man had fallen.
> **13.** And Aaron did expound unto him the scriptures from the creation of Adam, laying the fall of man before him, and their carnal state and also the plan of redemption, which was prepared from the foundation of the world, through Christ, for all whosoever would believe on his name.
> **14.** And since man had fallen he could not merit anything of himself; ***but the sufferings and death of Christ atone for their sins, through faith and repentance***, and so forth; and that he breaketh the bands of death, that the grave shall have no victory, and that the sting of death should be swallowed up in the hopes of glory; and Aaron did expound all these things unto the king. (Emphasis added).

The *Book of Mormon* teaches that Adam and the prophets who followed him were *all* taught that *Christ* would atone for their sins. The fact that this was an absolute impossibility doesn't seem to dawn on Mormons any more than the fact that if for some obscure reason it were true, the Hebrews would have recorded it and lived by the idea. No Old Testament prophet recorded any such thing.

> **Jacob 4:4.** For, for this intent have we written these things, that they may know that ***we knew*** of Christ, and we ***had a hope*** of his glory many hundred years before his coming; and not only we ourselves ***had a hope*** of his glory, but also all the holy prophets which were before us. *(Between 544 and 421 BCE).* (Emphasis added).

# THE MORMON DELUSION

The chapter heading to Jacob 4 clearly states:

*All the prophets worshipped the Father in the name of Christ–*

There is no Old Testament record of such a title as *Christ* or worshiping the Father in his name and no Jewish theology comes close to embracing it. *(See Ch. 4. Pp.75-6)*.

Add to that the fact that the above verses from *Alma 18 & 22 (p.153)* were supposedly written in 90 BCE and you start to see the absurdity of the concept.

The claimed conversation in *Alma* is completely *impossible* due to three things; the *time*, the *place*, and the *content*. *(See Ch. 4. Pp.67-70)*.

Additionally, it is absurd that *Jacob 4:4* is written in the *past* tense rather than present tense about a *future* event. However, it makes perfect sense if you consider Joseph Smith was explaining it himself in 1828-9. The claim is thus exposed as fraudulent and the text fictional.

# Chapter 8

## Lesson 2

### The Plan of Salvation

### Part B

### In the Garden

Scriptures used to provide reference to the Garden of Eden include Genesis, of course, but also Moses – a Smith rendering of events in which he alters things significantly.

> **Gen 1:26.** And God said, Let us make man in our image, after our likeness: and let them have **dominion** over the fish of the sea, and over the fowl of the air, and over the cattle, and over all the earth, and over every creeping thing that creepeth upon the earth.

The following is Smith's development in which Christ becomes the creator of Earth and man. God also declares that man was made in the image of His 'Only Begotten' son.

> **Moses 2:26.** And I, God, *said unto mine Only Begotten, which was with me from the beginning:* Let us make man in our image, after our likeness; and it was so. And I, God, said: Let them have dominion over the fishes of the sea, and over the fowl of the air, and over the cattle, and over all the earth, and over every creeping thing that creepeth upon the earth. (Emphasis added).
>
> **27.** And I, God, created man in mine own image, in the *image of mine Only Begotten* created I him; male and female created I them.

There are six references suggested under the 'In the Garden' section. The *only* one that speaks of the garden itself in real terms is *Genesis 2:15-17*.

> **15.** And the Lord God took the man, and put him into the garden of Eden to dress it and to keep it.
> **16.** And the Lord God commanded the man, saying, Of every tree of the garden thou mayest freely eat:
> **17.** But of the tree of the knowledge of good and evil, thou shalt not eat of it: for in the day that thou eatest thereof thou shalt surely die.

*Moses 3:15-17* is also referenced, which is the Smith version of *Genesis 2:15-17*. It is the same except for a few pointless alterations meant to indicate Smith was indeed a prophet inspired to give a more 'accurate' rendering of the original scripture.

> **Moses 3:15.** And *I,* the Lord God, took the man, and put him into the *G*arden of Eden, to dress it, and to keep it.
> **16.** And *I,* the Lord God, commanded the man, saying: Of every tree of the garden thou mayest freely eat,
> **17.** But of the tree of the knowledge of good and evil, thou shalt not eat of it, *nevertheless, thou mayest choose for thyself, for it is given unto thee; but, remember that I forbid it,* for in the day thou eatest thereof thou shalt surely die. (Emphasis added showing Smith's pointless alterations to the original).

Smith has God speaking in the first person, which is strange, as, historically Moses was supposedly relating a handed down tradition and naturally speaking in the third person. Smith capitalises the 'g' in garden to make it into an actual name and adds a few meaningless words to the text. Other than that, even the punctuation remains identical to the *KJV*. Mormons may feel warm and fuzzy about the added words as they are repeated in an enactment of the Garden of Eden story during their temple endowment ceremony. Unfortunately, that does not make it something that God revealed to Smith in order to clarify matters.

# IN THE GARDEN; THE FALL; OUR LIFE ON EARTH

*Moses 5:11* is also referenced. It talks about Eve experiencing joy in their 'redemption'; a concept that was completely unknown in the context of Jesus Christ and the atonement. Naturally, the words 'redeem' or 'redemption' do not appear at all in Genesis.

> **Moses 5:11.** And Eve, his wife, heard all these things and was glad, saying: Were it not for our transgression we never should have had seed, and never should have known good and evil, and **the joy of our redemption**, and the eternal life which God giveth unto all the obedient. (Emphasis added).

In Genesis, Eve never actually says anything like that at all. Joseph Smith developed the idea Adam and Eve and their posterity had complete knowledge and understanding of Jesus Christ, the need for repentance and baptism, and the New Testament concept of the Holy Ghost. The whole idea is bizarre.

Mind you, even the Bible has some strange concepts; *Genesis 19* claims "In the sweat of thy face shalt thou eat *bread*..." The idea that the first two humans on earth would know what to make bread with, how to refine the constituents and how to make it the way Jews did, a few centuries BCE when they wrote this, and the *fire* needed, is just as absurd an idea as some of Smith's claims.

Stopping to think allows us to see a much clearer picture as long as our understanding is not influenced by predetermined faith-induced *conclusions*.

We do know something about how humans managed to survive without fire or bread, and when controlled fire was first used by early humans, tens to hundreds of thousands of years ago. What we *know* should not be influenced by what we are led to *believe*. The earliest humans did *not* know how to control or use fire – or make bread. If Adam actually existed, he was *not* the first human.

The missionary lesson manual does *not* reference the following so-called 'scripture'. Perhaps it would be too bizarre for investigators to accept. In it, God is speaking to Adam.

> **Moses 6:52.** And he also said unto him: If thou wilt turn unto me, and hearken unto my voice, and believe, and repent of all thy transgressions, and **be baptized, even in water**, in the name of **mine Only Begotten Son**, who is full of grace and truth, which is **Jesus Christ**, the only name which shall be given under heaven, whereby salvation shall come unto the children of men, ye shall receive **the gift of the Holy Ghost,** asking all things in his name, and whatsoever ye shall ask, it shall be given you.
> **53.** And our father Adam spake unto the Lord, and said: Why is it that men must **repent and be baptized in water?** And the Lord said unto Adam: Behold I have forgiven thee thy transgression in the Garden of Eden. (Emphasis added).

# THE MORMON DELUSION

Bear in mind that this is an alteration to Hebrew Scripture. Once again, we have the use of the full *name* of 'Jesus Christ', something unknown until well into the Common Era, long *after* the Saviour lived. An *'Inspired Revision'* or a 'restoration' of original biblical material should not include words or concepts that could not have appeared there in the first instance. The Holy Ghost is an example of those kinds of anachronisms; the Jews have no such thing in their religion so Smith could not have restored it into the Bible by inspiration. He just made things up as he went along. Remember, the 'holy spirit' spoken of in the Old Testament is the 'mind of God' or His 'energy' to the Jews. The 'Holy Ghost' is a much later Christian concept which has nothing whatsoever to do with Judaism or the Old Testament.

There is also reference to *2 Nephi 2* which includes some impossible things. This was supposedly written between **588 and 570 BCE,** which was *before* the Old Testament, as we read it today, was even written – and almost six centuries before the birth of Christ – and when the 'law of Moses' was still observed.

> **2 Nephi 2:7.** Behold, *he offereth himself a sacrifice for sin*, to answer the ends of the law, unto all those who have *a broken heart and a contrite spirit*; and unto none else can the ends of the law be answered.
>
> **8.** …there is no flesh that can dwell in the presence of God, save it be through the merits, and mercy, and grace of *the Holy Messiah, who layeth down his life according to the flesh, and taketh it again by the power of the Spirit*, that he may bring to pass *the resurrection of the dead, being the first that should rise.*
>
> **10.** And because of *the intercession for all*, all men come unto God; wherefore, they stand in the presence of him, *to be judged* of him according to the truth and holiness which is in him. Wherefore, the ends of the *law which the Holy One hath given,* unto the inflicting of *the punishment which is affixed*, which punishment that is affixed is *in opposition to that of the happiness which is affixed*, to answer the ends of the *atonement—* (Emphasis added).

There is a lot of information provided in those verses which is centuries out of the correct timeframe, purportedly written on the other side of the world by people who could have had no knowledge whatsoever of such things hundreds of years before they transpired. Mormons who encounter these words will accept everything they read as somehow being true because they already 'know' Joseph Smith was a prophet and he 'translated' this material from gold plates. If something does not 'compute' for any reason, such as the notion that Adam and Eve were aware of all this, the veracity is never objectively questioned, it is just glossed over, never to be seriously considered. Faithful Mormons accept that they don't fully understand or appreciate all that went on;

# IN THE GARDEN; THE FALL; OUR LIFE ON EARTH

these were prophets and God could have told them anything. The perception is that modern prophets, from Smith to the present day, appear to accept it all – and they know best – and can be trusted; rank and file members just don't need to worry about such things. It won't affect their eternal salvation.

Once it is discovered that certain things *are* highly questionable, they most certainly should be considered, and most definitely so by investigators *before* accepting them as valid. Mormon missionaries are encouraged to keep things simple, so they may not mention such concepts as Adam and Eve's knowledge of Jesus and the requirements of baptism, at this stage. Trusting investigators may not learn some details until long after their conversion. By then they will already be well versed in the circular argument that Joseph Smith was a prophet, based on the illogical premise that there is a *Book of Mormon* and it could not have come to us in any other way, and that therefore today's leaders are also the prophets that they claim to be. I have often heard the question from newer members in Sunday School classes "What do we believe about... fill in the blank?" A question phrased in such a manner suggests complete acceptance of whatever answer is provided by the teacher, without question, debate or any further consideration.

However, if they *are* taught any details, investigators most certainly *should* stop, and think, and ask all the questions raised in the foregoing paragraphs *before* accepting them as factual. Ask for historic and scientific *evidence* of the veracity of all the claims – especially Smith's bizarre concepts about God.

> **2 Nephi 2:12.** Wherefore, it must needs have been created for a thing of naught; wherefore there would have been no purpose in the end of its creation. Wherefore, this thing must needs destroy the wisdom of God and his eternal purposes, and also the power, and the mercy, and the justice of God.

The big question is why *should* there be a purpose to anything? The above assumes without God's law, or sin, repentance and/or punishment, atonement and redemption, there would have been no purpose in the creation – therefore it must be so – and true. The alternative doesn't bear thinking about as it destroys everything *about* God and therefore the very *need* for God – and by extension, the very *existence* of God. Well, it is something that we *should* stop and think about very seriously; that is, at least in the case of Joseph Smith's version of God.

> **2 Nephi 2:13.** And if ye shall say there is no law, ye shall also say there is no sin. If ye shall say there is no sin, ye shall also say there is no righteousness. And if there be no righteousness there be no happiness. And if there be no righteousness nor happiness there be no

punishment nor misery. And if these things are not there is no God. And if there is no God we are not, neither the earth; for there could have been no creation of things, neither to act nor to be acted upon; wherefore, all things must have vanished away.

Verse 13 is a real con trick. Let's break down the thread Smith is trying to use to trap people into needing his Church.

If we say there is no law – then we say there is no sin.
If we say there is no sin – we also say there is no righteousness.

Hold it right there. *Who* exactly is saying there is no 'law' or that there is no 'righteousness'? You don't have to believe in or accept the idea that 'sin' actually exists in the real world to know that even the most primitive societies developed fundamental laws or rules for their tribes to live by. But they did not have *sin* as a concept. An understanding of what was considered right and wrong developed in early 'tribes' based on the individual culture itself. Things that were acceptable to some were not acceptable to others. That didn't make one right and the other wrong. No god was involved. Early humans determined their own lifestyle. When gods were invented, things changed dramatically.

Things actually got much worse for people as gods had to be 'appeased' or 'served' and usually that meant sacrifice and people had to die. Rules became essential for group survival. Likewise, something like 'righteousness' or being 'good' *does* exist without needing *sin* as a concept. Sin means disobedience to the supposed laws of a god. To be *righteous* may to some mean obedience to such laws but the connotation is also basically being, or doing good, rather than bad things. Bad things do not equal sin, unless you accept that it exists. It *doesn't*. It is a man made concept used for control, as previously discussed.

Likewise, where does the notion come from that there can be *no* happiness without this righteousness spoken about? Most people are generally quite good and they are happy. The world is not such a bad place. That is unless you have a religion that considers it a terrible place full of bad people who love to 'sin'.

And if there be no righteousness there be no happiness. If there is no righteousness or happiness there is no punishment or misery.

Why should there be any 'punishment' or 'misery' concerning things that, unless you *choose* to believe them, are absolutely meaningless? Who cares if we don't pray enough or fast or study or do family history or attend pointless meetings until our families don't even remember who we are? The fact is that people are usually far happier when they are with their families and not tied down with Mormon requirements and activities filling up their time.

# IN THE GARDEN; THE FALL; OUR LIFE ON EARTH

With or without religion, happiness *exists*. Sin does *not*. In the real world, misery does *not* come through sin, it comes through *circumstance*. In religion, particularly Mormonism, misery often comes through the concept of failure to perform well enough for God. If you believe in God, once you understand that in fact He does *not* expect as much of us as the Mormon Church claims, then life can be far happier. Most religions do make people happy but some are so demanding that the result for many members is constant worry, feelings of inadequacy and guilt, often resulting in misery and even depression.

In terms of the Mormon gay community, as being a practicing gay is a sin in Mormonism – about which recent Mormon leaders have declared that it is better to be *dead* than gay *(see the movie: 8. The Mormon Proposition)*, it can, and far too often it does, also lead to suicide. A religion which creates an environment in which some of its members resort to suicide as the only way out is absolutely *unconscionable* and should be rejected out of hand as having nothing to do with God whatsoever. If God exists, he loves us, *all* of us, regardless. Nothing within a religious context should make any one of us feel so bad that we want to take our own lives. Mormonism, and its version of God, has a lot to answer for. God is supposed to make life worth *living*.

A question that investigators should ask.

If being gay is a *sin*, then why did the Mormon God hard wire the human brain in six to nine percent of humans, as well as some other species, in that way? Is it some kind of macabre test?

Not all of His creations are in His *image* after all – at least a proportion of them are wrongly *wired*. That doesn't constitute sin; it constitutes a bad design process by God. In reality, it is just the way things are. Such people are in the main not unhappy with their orientation and if they are just accepted and left alone rather than condemned for not being 'normal', they enjoy life as much as anyone else. Scientifically, if you believe in God, then He is to 'blame', if that is the right word, for sexual orientation in humans, so He should, and in many religions He does, accept people as they are – without judgment. The question is not *why* the Mormon Church abhors such people – but rather *when* the Mormon Church will capitulate on this and follow the same path it eventually had to take regarding polygamy and then later concerning their perceived racism regarding 'blacks and the priesthood'.

As with 'women and the priesthood', another 'equal right' yet to be addressed and corrected by the Mormon Church, it only takes a strong tide of popular public opinion to swell long enough and the Mormon Church, on behalf of God, who doesn't actually *say* anything any more, will inevitably change the unchangeable once again and eventually allow what would have been anathema to earlier Mormon leaders. As with polygamy, and in turn, as with priesthood, what was once *unthinkable* will one day become *unavoidable*.

It is just a matter of *time* rather than doctrine in real terms. History has already proven that to be the case *twice*, and mark my words, one day, in the dim and distant future, if the Mormon Church wants to survive, it will happen again – at least twice more; probably first for women – and one day for gays.

The Mormon Church will ultimately back off from the gay issue and leave well alone. It will one day find itself much better served *not* getting involved financially or organisationally in political debate, as it will be so unpopular to do so that it would be self-destructive. It will then address the gay 'problem' *only* directly to Mormons; something it should already be doing. Even then, it could be more gentle and understanding, but that has yet to evolve. It will – one day. Later, it will inevitably allow gay membership of some description as it will become as big an issue of discrimination as the priesthood problem once was. But I suspect that is a long way off yet. The issue is not so much that lots of gays wish to *join* the Mormon Church; it is the Church's public *attitude*.

There are two problems. One is the six to nine percent of Mormons who are gay and deserve far better treatment, understanding and acceptance. The other is the Mormon stance taken *against* gays who are not even associated with Mormonism in any way. Whilst the Church may have felt it 'got away' with a small fine ($5,000) over its illegal activity and financial involvement in 'Proposition 8' in California, that will be hard for them to do again without severe repercussions.

Likewise, women will one day hold the priesthood which is currently reserved for men. As with past issues, it will be a trade off between Mormon teachings, membership numbers and popularity. They will **only** stand by their guns as long as a bigger ship doesn't threaten their survival.

I had Jehovah's Witnesses at my door again the other day and they were talking about what a terrible place the world is – and so full of sin. I told them that whilst there is right and wrong, good and bad, there was no such thing as *sin* and I thought the world was actually quite a lovely place and I was very happy with it. I pointed out that most people were good and will stand up for others – even entire nations try – and all in all we are doing okay. I also pointed out that all the natural disasters they were prattling on about were under the direct control of their God who didn't seem to care that He had left the world He created in such a state that volcanoes and earthquakes still occur regularly. Couldn't He have designed the mechanics of the planet better or left it to cool for longer before 'creating' us? Look at the generosity of humans when asked to donate towards the relief of others when God's disasters indiscriminately strike. They just ignored my rant and started talking about something else.

God never seems to interfere with that any more than the severe weather systems that many have to endure. The millions of people who have died from natural disasters are His problem, not ours. He isn't a very nice God. Likewise,

# IN THE GARDEN; THE FALL; OUR LIFE ON EARTH

most major cases of carnage, murder and other unspeakable things that have taken place over the centuries by human beings have mainly been perpetrated in God's name, so He has a lot to answer for and we are far better off without Him. If you want to believe in a God, at least try to find one who makes you truly happy and doesn't expect subservience to a church that teaches pure fiction, such as in the case of Mormonism.

To pick up *2 Nephi 2:13* from the 'righteousness and happiness' line, it continues to inform us that:

> If there is no righteousness or happiness – there is no punishment or misery. If these things are not – then there is no God.
>
> And if there is no God – we are not, neither the earth; …there could have been no creation of things … wherefore, all things must have vanished away.

This is just meant to make people think it irrational to suppose *we* don't exist, so God must also exist and the rest is therefore true. Of course we exist and of course the world exists – that much we *do* know. But *why* does God therefore also have to *exist*? That premise must surely be *thoroughly* tested before acceptance; especially the Mormon version. Blindly following such a Being on faith alone, when proof of an underlying conspiracy to deceive may well be uncovered if we look for it, is not such a good idea.

Smith uses the same rationale elsewhere. For example:

> **Alma 42:17.** Now, how could a man repent except he should sin? How could he sin if there was no law? How could there be a law save there was a punishment?

Once again we have the classic con trick in play. Create the concept of sin, then invent laws from God, many of which people can't help but break as it is impossible to keep them all. Some are just plain silly. People feel bad anyway as many 'laws' are impossible to measure against a set standard so you can never actually feel that you are completely obedient; thus you *feel* like a sinner when you have actually done *nothing* wrong. That's part of the delusion. Keep people in a constantly subservient state where they can never entirely please their God. Many hope to make it to the Mormon heaven (Celestial kingdom), and worry themselves sick that the rest of their family will make it but they won't. In my experience, this is especially true of many Mormon women.

Men are usually far more positive and think they are doing quite well when in fact they are often far worse than women in terms of a subservient attitude and unquestioning obedience. Mormonism is a strange cult.

# THE MORMON DELUSION

Disobedience to laws requires repentance, or punishment will follow. We need a Saviour to redeem us. There was a poll undertaken in our Stake many years ago during a Stake Leadership meeting. Anonymous sheets were handed in on which one question was "Do you consider yourself currently worthy to enter the Celestial kingdom." Most of the men did and most of the women did not. Was that is a measure of humility or arrogance – or both perhaps?

Repentance will save the sinner and avoid punishment. Yet before the concept was introduced, an investigator would not necessarily have considered the existence of sin; they had no laws of any God to break; they had no need of being saved, let alone punished. They would actually have been far better off being left alone. In Mormon theology, if someone never hears about the Mormon Church, they are not *responsible* as they didn't know the truth. As long as they ultimately accept it when they do learn the truth – perhaps in the Millennium – then all will be well for them and it makes no difference whatsoever to their 'eternal salvation'.

## The Fall

Regarding the garden and the fall, missionaries are told to keep it simple:

> When first teaching this doctrine, do not teach everything you know about it. Explain very simply that God chose two of His children, Adam and Eve, to become the first parents on earth. After their transgression they were subject to both sin and death. By themselves they could not return to live with Heavenly Father. The Lord spoke to Adam and taught him the plan of salvation and redemption through the Lord Jesus Christ. By following that plan, Adam and his family could have joy in this life and return to live with God. *(Page 50).*

We reviewed the concept of the 'fall' of Adam and Eve earlier *(pp.150-1)* and here we find core teachings of transgression, sin and death, quickly followed by the need for redemption and salvation through Jesus Christ. There is a 'plan' to follow.

Following an explanation of the fall of Adam and Eve from the Garden of Eden, *2 Nephi 2* continues and repeats the very same nonsense previously mentioned:

> **25.** Adam fell that men might be; and men are, that they might have joy.

# IN THE GARDEN; THE FALL; OUR LIFE ON EARTH

This is an oft quoted Mormon 'scripture' which further deludes members into thinking that they are the only people in the world experiencing true joy and happiness. Throughout the rest of the world, members of various religions appear equally happy and in many instances perhaps more so. This can be ascertained through simple observation of both Mormon and non-Mormon families. Most people remain blissfully unaware that the hoax of Mormonism even exists.

> **2 Nephi 2:26.** And the Messiah cometh in the fulness of time, that he may redeem the children of men from the fall. And because that they are redeemed from the fall they have become free forever, knowing good from evil; to act for themselves and not to be acted upon, save it be by the punishment of the law at the great and last day, according to the commandments which God hath given.
> **27.** Wherefore, men are free according to the flesh; and all things are given them which are expedient unto man. And they are free to choose liberty and eternal life, through the great Mediator of all men, or to choose captivity and death, according to the captivity and power of the devil; for he seeketh that all men might be miserable like unto himself.
> **28.** And now, my sons, I would that ye should look to the great Mediator, and hearken unto his great commandments; and be faithful unto his words, and choose eternal life, according to the will of his Holy Spirit;
> **29.** And not choose eternal death, according to the will of the flesh and the evil which is therein, which giveth the spirit of the devil power to captivate, to bring you down to hell, that he may reign over you in his own kingdom.
> **30.** I have spoken these few words unto you all, my sons, in the last days of my probation; and I have chosen the good part, according to the words of the prophet. And I have none other object save it be the everlasting welfare of your souls. Amen.

The premise is that the gospel makes people free to choose 'liberty and eternal life' or 'captivity and death'; that is, choose between good and get rewarded, or evil and receive punishment. Who would actually ever knowingly *choose* from the devil, 'captivity and death'? This is interpreted to mean that if people join the Mormon Church they will have liberty and life but if they reject it then they are subject to captivity and death. That is clearly nonsense.

People are not 'acted upon' either. In Mormonism, there are 'things to act and things to be acted upon'. I won't go into detail as it is nonsensical religious verbiage. People were perfectly free to 'choose' before entering Mormonism and were not 'acted upon' by outside influences any more than Mormons are. The Mormon premise is that they have the Holy Ghost so they are guided. The rest of humanity muddle along without it and make mistakes, being 'acted upon'. People are actually far *less* free after joining the Mormon Church. Restrictions, controls and expectations stunt growth and restrict life more than many can imagine. They already had a pretty good idea of what was considered good and bad or legal and illegal but that isn't enough. The Church creates a whole new raft of rules for life to be lived by.

Children are effectively forced to accept everything their parents believe. Generally, the rule for teens is that as long as they live at home, they must attend Church, go to Seminary, study and pray and obey all the rules. Rebellion is quashed and the threat of not being 'worthy' to be with the family forever is firmly established as a reality.

The problem is that most Mormons cannot see the damage this can cause as they are too busy 'living' their religion and want their children to do the same so they can be 'together forever'. In the case of my children, two rejected the Church in their teens. They claim to have enjoyed their lives at home and the social aspects of church and they also say that I should not regret the way we raised them. Looking back, my wife and I most certainly did mistreat them and should have allowed them to choose for themselves without dictating rules, which at the end of the day made no difference to them whatsoever. At the time, it just added tension, argument and resentment and certainly didn't engender feelings of love, understanding or tolerance which would have served them much better in the long run. They are very generous in their recollections; I feel guilt and remorse and wish I could change the past for them.

They were good kids – it's just that for some reason they had an inbuilt ability to see through Mormon claims from the start and were never going to believe Mormonism to be true no matter what happened. They had the sense to see beyond the family and the Mormon Church into the world at large and realise that not many people believed the way we did. They questioned, not the rest of the world but our own family in relation to it. It is only once Mormons come to understand the truth behind everything that they can see things for what they really are. Before that happens, they are blind to the truth; I was. Our faith precludes the conscious mind from objectively considering the facts. Only after our own epiphany can we see what we were actually *like* as Mormons.

Some people seem to be able to detect the truth more easily than others, rejecting the Church immediately they are presented with it. With children, it appears that many are gullible enough to accept what their parents teach them, without question, and then fall into the delusion quite readily. They trust and accept. Some though, have an inbuilt ability to see through everything as soon as they are old enough to reason and question. And question they do. When answers are unsatisfactory, they reject the Church and that can happen at quite an early age. Why *should* it be true for them? Why should they *not* be allowed to choose for themselves? Why *should* they suffer our unrelenting attempts at coercion and indoctrination until they are eighteen years old and can then leave

# IN THE GARDEN; THE FALL; OUR LIFE ON EARTH

home? As Mormon parents, we were guilty of creating believers out of our children through constant brainwashing from birth. Every child should, in any family circumstance, be encouraged and allowed to learn all they can about the world, science, nature and historical concepts of religion *before* ever being indoctrinated with one specific creed, which most invariably blindly follow.

## Our Life on Earth

> Life on earth is an opportunity and a blessing. Our purpose in this life is to have joy and prepare to return to God's presence. In mortality we live in a condition where we are subject to both physical and spiritual death. God has a perfect, glorified, immortal body of flesh and bones. To become like God and return to His presence, we too must have a perfect, immortal body of flesh and bones. However, **because of the Fall of Adam and Eve, every person on earth has an imperfect, mortal body and will eventually die. If not for the Savior Jesus Christ, death would end all hope for a future existence with Heavenly Father**. Along with physical death, **sin is a major obstacle that keeps us from becoming like our Father in Heaven** and returning to His presence. In our mortal condition we often yield to temptation, break God's commandments, and sin. During our life on earth each of us makes mistakes. Although it sometimes appears otherwise, **sin always leads to unhappiness. Sin causes feelings of guilt and shame.** Because of our sins, we are unable to return to live with Heavenly Father unless we are first forgiven and cleansed. While we are in mortality, we have experiences that bring us happiness. We also have experiences that bring us pain and sorrow, some of which is caused by the sinful acts of others. These experiences provide us opportunities to learn and to grow, to distinguish good from evil, and to make choices. **God influences us to do good; Satan tempts us to commit sin.** As with physical death, **we cannot overcome the effects of sin by ourselves. We are helpless without the Atonement of Jesus Christ.** *(Page 50).* (Emphasis added).

I have emphasised the concepts that missionaries will try to explain. God sent us here. We will die. We can't get back to God without Jesus and while God influences us towards good, Satan constantly tempts us towards evil. We can't overcome the effects of sin by ourselves. Once again, we need Jesus. The whole story is that we are lost without Jesus and the Mormon Church is his 'restored' Church. It is our *only* hope.

It is interesting that yet again we have the idea *"...sin always leads to unhappiness. Sin causes feelings of guilt and shame."* We already discussed the fact that sin is a man made concept and that it is used for *control*. Clearly, sin only "causes feelings of guilt and shame" if we are inclined to believe in it as a concept. Perhaps I should counter that with the idea that "not *believing* in sin *always* leads to a *happier* life." That sounds a lot healthier to me.

A constant daily feeling of 'unworthiness' is created in the mind. Today, did I start the day with personal study and prayer? Did I bless the food? Did I hold family prayer before leaving home? Did I bear testimony at every opportunity during the day at work or at the gym? Did I waste time watching television rather than preparing a good lesson to teach in Sunday School next week, or doing work on my family history thus saving more ancestors? Did I hold a meaningful Family Home Evening on Monday? Have I fulfilled my callings well? Have I completed 100% 'Home Teaching' this month?

The list of expectations and potential sins of omission is endless. And, if you think things through and consider you haven't done badly, by the next day, something else will come to mind that needs attention. In Mormonism, there is so much that is expected, no one could ever achieve everything. There will always be something that is not attended to sufficiently enough to know you have pleased God in every area as well as you might. Some people just go under. Others rationalise their days and just don't get too hung up on what they do and do not achieve. Most try hard and feel inadequate to one degree or another, but they just keep on trying.

Missionaries are to teach investigators that we were sent to earth to gain a body and to go through a 'probation' or testing period. We will make mistakes, almost any of which will keep us out of heaven without the help of Jesus Christ. There are several scripture references listed to support the idea of our mortal 'probation', but none are biblical. In fact they almost all stem once again from the *Book of Mormon*, although one is from Smith's *Book of Abraham*.

> **BOA 3:25.** And we will prove them herewith, to see if they will do all things whatsoever the Lord their God shall command them;
> **26.** And they who keep their first estate shall be added upon; and they who keep not their first estate shall not have glory in the same kingdom with those who keep their first estate; and they who keep their second estate shall have glory added upon their heads for ever and ever.

That is designed to give the impression that we lived elsewhere in a 'first estate' which we 'kept' and thus earned the right to come to Earth. Here, if we keep our 'second estate', then with the help of Jesus, we can go back and live with God. The idea that we are on 'probation' is captured in the following reference.

## IN THE GARDEN; THE FALL; OUR LIFE ON EARTH

> **2 Nephi 9:27.** But wo unto him that has the law given, yea, that has all the commandments of God, like unto us, and that transgresseth them, and that wasteth the days of his probation, for awful is his state!

Also within a recommended reference, *Alma 42:2-10*, probation is further suggested.

> **Alma 42:4.** And thus we see, that there was a time granted unto man to repent, yea, a probationary time, a time to repent and serve God.
>
> **10**. Therefore, as they had become carnal, sensual, and devilish, by nature, this probationary state became a state for them to prepare; it became a preparatory state.

The rest of the recommended references just seem to emphasis the idea we are all terrible sinners and that if we don't 'repent' then *nothing* can save us. This is another reference and a real frightener for believers:

> **Alma 34:31.** Yea, I would that ye would come forth and harden not your hearts any longer; for behold, now is the time and the day of your salvation; and therefore, if ye will repent and harden not your hearts, immediately shall the great plan of redemption be brought about unto you.
> **32.** For behold, this life is the time for men to prepare to meet God; yea, behold the day of this life is the day for men to perform their labors.
> **33.** And now, as I said unto you before, as ye have had so many witnesses, therefore, I beseech of you that ye do not procrastinate the day of your repentance until the end; for after this day of life, which is given us to prepare for eternity, behold, if we do not improve our time while in this life, then cometh the night of darkness wherein there can be no labor performed.
> **34.** Ye cannot say, when ye are brought to that awful crisis, that I will repent, that I will return to my God. Nay, ye cannot say this; for that same spirit which doth possess your bodies at the time that ye go out of this life, that same spirit will have power to possess your body in that eternal world.
> **35.** For behold, if ye have procrastinated the day of your repentance even until death, behold, ye have become subjected to the spirit of the devil, and he doth seal you his; therefore, the Spirit of the Lord hath withdrawn from you, and hath no place in you, and the devil hath all power over you; and this is the final state of the wicked.

This is followed by a sweetener – of sorts.

> **Mosiah 3:19.** For the natural man is an enemy to God, and has been from the fall of Adam, and will be, forever and ever, unless he yields to the enticings of the Holy Spirit, and putteth off the natural man and becometh a saint through the atonement of Christ the Lord, and becometh as a child, submissive, meek, humble, patient, full of love, willing to submit to all things which the Lord seeth fit to inflict upon him, even as a child doth submit to his father.

Life on earth is a test and no matter what happens to us and no matter how good or bad things get, we are to be meek and submissive and handle it all without blaming God. We must submit our will to the Father. What this really means, especially in the case of Mormonism, is that we must submit to what the Church *tells* us is the will of the Father, no matter what it is.

Further scripture references are provided in the lesson manual dealing with 'choice', 'good and evil', 'sin' and the concept that 'the unclean cannot be with God'. *(Manual page 51).*

# Chapter 9

## Lesson 2

### The Plan of Salvation

### Part C

### The Atonement

This section has three sub-sections which follow below; the resurrection, atonement, and the gospel, but it starts with another affirmation that all the prophets since the world began have testified that Jesus Christ is our redeemer. Not according to the Old Testament, or to Jews; just according to Mormonism and the *Book of Mormon.*

> Before the world was organized, our Heavenly Father chose Jesus Christ to be our Savior and Redeemer. The atoning sacrifice of Jesus Christ made it possible for us to overcome the effects of the Fall. ***All of the prophets since the world began have testified of Jesus Christ as our Redeemer.*** *(Page 51).* (Emphasis added).

> Because of the Resurrection of Jesus Christ, *we will all be resurrected regardless* of whether we have done good or evil in this life. We will have a perfect, immortal body of flesh and bones that will never again be subject to disease, pain, or death. The resurrection makes it possible to return to God's presence to be judged but does not guarantee that we will be able to live in His presence. To receive that blessing, we must also be cleansed from sin. *(Page 51).* (Emphasis added).

Here, Mormon missionaries are taught to tell investigators they will be resurrected *regardless* of anything they do – or do not do. Resurrection is a gift to *everyone,* no matter how good or how bad, or evil in religious terms, people have been. Also, people are not responsible for the 'fall' but rather for their own sins – which by now investigators will have been taught they have in abundance.

> We are not responsible for the Fall of Adam and Eve, but we are responsible for our own sins. *(Page 51).*

Whilst many other religions teach that we are *saved* by grace, the Mormon Church teaches that we are *resurrected* by grace, but where we end up after that, as there is more than one 'degree' of Mormon heaven, will depend entirely on how we *perform.*

> Only through the Savior's grace and mercy can we become clean from sin so that we can live with God again. This is possible through exercising **faith in Jesus Christ, repenting, being baptized, receiving the gift of the Holy Ghost, and enduring to the end.**
>
> **Christ promises to forgive our sins on the condition that we accept Him by exercising faith in Him, repenting, receiving baptism by immersion, and the laying on of hands for the gift of the Holy Ghost, and striving faithfully to keep His commandments to the end of our lives.** Through **continuing repentance**, we may obtain forgiveness and be cleansed of our sins by the power of the Holy Ghost. We are **relieved of the burden of guilt and shame,** and through Jesus Christ we become worthy to return to the presence of God.
>
> As we rely on the Atonement of Jesus Christ, **He can help us endure our trials, sicknesses, and pain.** We can be filled with joy, peace, and consolation. **All that is unfair about life can be made right through the Atonement of Jesus Christ.** *(Page 51).* (Emphasis added).

There really isn't much about life which directly affects us that is actually 'unfair'. Things are just – the way they are. All that may *seem* unfair about life,

# THE ATONEMENT

if *not* just coincidental *to* life, evolution, our environment, climate and natural occurrence, or the hands of dictators or terrorists – which are *human* problems, appears to have been *created* by the very God who then wants us to work off our "burden of guilt and shame" which we didn't have until it was created for us by people who claim they represent Him.

Supporting references regarding the *resurrection*, the *atonement* and the *gospel* as being the way forward are provided to assist missionaries in getting those points across before they venture into details of the spirit world to which everyone goes following physical death to await resurrection and judgment.

## Resurrection

Missionaries will soon come to details of the three degrees of glory, and to set the scene, passages of scripture that reference the resurrection and which also incorporate Mormon ideas are presented. One is from the New Testament but the manual's choice is the Joseph Smith 'Inspired Revision'. Compare Smith's *IR* with the *KJV*.

> **IR. 1 Cor 15:40.** Also *celestial* bodies, and bodies ***terrestrial***, and bodies ***telestial***; but the glory of the celestial, one; and the terrestrial, another; ***and the telestial, another.***

> **KJV. 1 Cor 15:40.** There are also *celestial* bodies, and bodies *terrestrial*: but the glory of the celestial is one, and the glory of the terrestrial is another. (Emphasis added).

The actual meanings of the word *celestial* include "heavenly, divine, sublime; living in heaven; of or in the visible heavens". The word was invented in the late 14th century. The literal translation, used before the word 'celestial' was invented, was 'heavenly'. *Terrestrial* means "of, or existing on, the earth; earthly, worldly; living or growing on land or in the ground (especially as opposed to the sea or air); representing the earth;" *(Chambers Dictionary)*. The word *terrestrial* dates back as far as the 16th century and was used in the 1582 Rheims Bible. The original word used in Corinthians translates as 'ground' or 'earthly'. *(See: YLT)*. Note that Smith's version adds a new word and a new concept out of nowhere; *telestial*.

As we will discuss more fully later, Joseph Smith developed these words to mean something entirely different to the usual definitions when he invented his 'three degrees of glory'. The *Celestial* kingdom becomes a planet where the most righteous people go to live with God. It is the highest of three 'degrees'. Within the *Celestial* kingdom are three further degrees, the highest of which is 'exaltation' which is where men become Gods. Unlike anyone in any other degree or kingdom, they are the only ones who can then procreate. They will have multiple wives and father billions of spirit children who will go on to populate further planets over which they will be the Gods.

In Mormon theology, the Earth itself will go through a transformation and become *Celestial*, ready for those who are worthy to inherit it. Mark you, Brigham Young thought that men lived on the moon and also on the sun, so we should be used to bizarre concepts, some of which went on to become doctrine and others to be discarded. *(JD 13:271)*. Things that more recent leaders liked, they retained, and aspects they did not like so much, or which later became scientifically or doctrinally awkward, they not only threw out, but sometimes also denied they ever existed. *(See: Apx G; also TMD Vol. 3. Sections 2 & 4)*.

The *Terrestrial* 'kingdom', rather than meaning Earth, becomes a planet created in Smith's imagination, where 'good' people who rejected the gospel will go. There will be no marriage and they will not be able to have children.

The *Telestial* kingdom is another invention of Smith who created the word out of thin air. It does not actually exist or mean *anything*. It becomes his third or lowest degree or kingdom where everyone else goes. It is the equivalent of the Christian idea of hell but in Mormonism it is actually a place described as much better than this Earth. The real Mormon 'hell' is a place called 'outer darkness' to be ruled over by Cain to whom Satan will be subject as Cain will have a resurrected body and Satan of course has no body. The only people who will actually go there constitute a handful who apparently 'denied' the Holy Ghost and having known the truth beyond doubt, they subsequently *chose* to follow Satan. I have never met anyone who fits that description.

Most references provided concern the resurrection of Jesus Christ. Smith possibly developed his 'three degrees' idea from *1 Corinthians 15:41-42* as it is certainly a referenced scripture; or just copied Emanuel Swedenborg's ideas. Swedenborg created the three degrees concept, including the 'celestial' idea, long before Smith who had ready access to Swedenborg's work. *(See: Quinn 1998:217-8)*. Whatever the ultimate origin, the Mormon take on it is entirely inconsistent with the perceptions of the rest of Christianity – and the Bible.

> **1 Cor 15:41.** There is one glory of the sun, and another glory of the moon, and another glory of the stars: for one star differeth from another star in glory.
> **42.** So also is the resurrection of the dead. It is sown in corruption; it is raised in incorruption:

This is used to support Smith's 'three degrees of glory' concept. It may have paid him to have continued to read in Corinthians, as the verses following the above clarify something we have already covered.

# THE ATONEMENT

> **1 Cor 15:43.** It is sown in dishonour; it is raised in glory: it is sown in weakness; it is raised in power:
> **44.** It is sown a natural body; it is raised a spiritual body. There is a natural body, and there is a spiritual body.
> **45.** And so it is written, The first man Adam was made a living soul; the last Adam was made a quickening spirit.
> **46.** Howbeit that was not first which is spiritual, but that which is natural; and afterward that which is spiritual.
> **47.** The first man is of the earth, earthy: the second man is the Lord from heaven.
> **48.** As is the earthy, such are they also that are earthy: and as is the heavenly, such are they also that are heavenly.
> **49.** And as we have borne the image of the earthy, we shall also bear the image of the heavenly.

Mormons do not seem to see the irony in this. The Mormon Church claims their own scripture confirms we lived as spirits before we came to the earth. Yet these verses state quite clearly that *first* comes the *natural* body and then it is raised a *spiritual* body. Adam was *first* made a living soul and at the *last* a quickening spirit; not the other way around. This is qualified *twice* following the statement. First we are earthy and then we become heavenly. Nothing happened before that, except in Smith's imagination – and thus in Mormonism.

Of course, Mormon apologists would probably counter that with the idea that this is only referencing death and the resurrection; just because it doesn't speak about being spirits before life on Earth, it doesn't mean that we weren't.

As the reader will know, my personal views are essentially atheistic. In addition, I accept the view of most informed historians that these writings were not by anyone who remotely knew or met Jesus and they contain anything but the truth – whatever that may be; so the references are all actually meaningless in any event.

However, the significant point is that what the Mormon Church believes, teaches and references, does not compare at all well with supposed supporting biblical scripture and they have to rely on their own, which is *always* from words provided by Joseph Smith – in one way or another. I note Smith did not even alter the above passage to include a pre-earth life in his *Inspired Revision;* not that it would prove anything if he had.

Note that one *Book of Mormon* reference to the resurrection *(Alma 11:42-45)* informs us that we will "have a bright recollection of all our guilt". Well, we would, wouldn't we? The concept keeps Church members on the Mormon 'straight and narrow'. Smith's writings are replete with such things as God being angry and all sorts of bad things that are to be visited on people, and of course we are always the guilty ones, even though most try to do their best. The message here really is that no matter what we do, there is no way of pleasing the Mormon God; we will be racked with guilt and shame and we deserve His wrath, which He will ultimately mete out on everyone in due measure.

Many years ago, I was in a filmed debate in which I had to pose the concept that 'fear is *the* prime motivator' against a panel who took several alternate views. It was in an industrial setting regarding employee motivation. After weeks of preparation, in a debate lasting two hours, I eventually won over every single member of the twelve member panel. When it comes to religion, and in particular Mormonism, it most certainly is the case that fear *is* the prime motivator, once we fully understand what it can do to us. Once someone is captured in the delusion, such that they believe Mormonism is true, *fear* of not making it to the Celestial kingdom subconsciously overrides *everything* else.

## Atonement

We must do all we can, repent continuously, and try even harder. After we have done all we can do and repented as much as we can, and when we have endured to the end, only then will Christ pick up the baton and fully atone for us. Only through him, and unquestioning obedience to his servants, can we hope to be saved. That's the concept. Resurrection is a gift, freely given to all, from the best to the worst of humankind, regardless of what they have done. Where we end up after that is materially in our own hands. Christ will atone for our sins but ultimate rewards will vary significantly depending on what each individual has achieved and deserves. The ultimate prize is 'eternal life' which to Mormons means far more than mere resurrection which everyone gets, free gratis.

Eternal life means being together as a family forever; living in a perfect world with perfect people; becoming Gods, creating and populating our own worlds, and for men, having more wives than we could ever count. Mormon women, in my experience, completely disregard that last part which is core Mormon doctrine and effectively pretend to themselves that it won't happen to them. Theologically they are very *wrong*. Well, in reality they are actually quite right, as the whole concept was the weird and wonderful idea of Joseph Smith who developed his theology on polygamy when he had to make up an excuse for his adultery with Fanny Alger.

Everything started from there and if there is a life after this one, then I doubt that having to entertain their husband taking plural wives will be much of a concern for any woman, as clearly it is the last thing that could ever possibly be a reality. Common sense and reason alone should allow any sane woman to understand that if there is a God, He would not be so cruel. Having lots of wives, and even marriage as such, in the *hereafter*, was a Smith invention and not remotely something associated with a God who supposedly loves women

## THE ATONEMENT

equally to men. No woman would want to suffer the indignity and no God would condemn women to such a fate. It was bad enough for women when practiced in mortality, without entertaining the idea of being condemned to the same fate forever. To any wife, that must sound more like a description of hell than a proposal for heaven. It is a 'man-made' idea.

Once again, most references given stem from the *Book of Mormon* or the *D&C* but as the atonement is a traditional Christian concept, of course the Bible offers some suitable scripture which is freely used in this instance.

> **1 John 1:7.** But if we walk in the light, as he is in the light, we have fellowship one with another, and the blood of Jesus Christ his Son cleanseth us from all sin.

> **John 3:16.** For God so loved the world, that he gave his only begotten Son, that whosoever believeth in him should not perish, but have everlasting life.
> **17.** For God sent not his Son into the world to condemn the world; but that the world through him might be saved.

Whilst the New Testament teaches 'God so loved the world' and that the son came *not* to 'condemn the world' but to *save* it, in the case of Mormonism, God sounds more like the God of the Old Testament most of the time. If people do *not* repent, then all hell will let loose, to coin a phrase, and all sorts of abominations will be heaped upon them. A *Doctrine and Covenants* reference provided by the manual says this:

> **D&C 19:15.** Therefore I command you to repent—repent, lest I smite you by the rod of my mouth, and by my wrath, and by my anger, and your sufferings be sore—how sore you know not, how exquisite you know not, yea, how hard to bear you know not.
> **16.** For behold, *I, God, have suffered these things for all*, that they might not suffer if they would repent;
> **17.** But if they would not repent they must suffer even as I;

Whilst much of what is said by Mormon leaders today doesn't contain much of any threat of retribution, Joseph Smith's early Mormonism was full of it. The carrot and stick followed each other repeatedly, promising reward for obedience and retribution for disobedience. It is also interesting to note that Joseph Smith wrote this so-called revelation in 1830 when he was still entirely monotheistic and considered God and Jesus to be one and the same being. Note the rest of the reference. Here, in the *D&C*, **God** is suffering on the cross…

# THE MORMON DELUSION

> **D&C 19:18.** Which suffering *caused myself, even God, the greatest of all*, to tremble because of pain, and *to bleed at every pore, and to suffer both body and spirit*—and would that I might not drink the bitter cup, and shrink—
> **19.** Nevertheless, glory be to the Father, and I partook and finished my preparations unto the children of men. (Emphasis added to v.16 & 18).

*Book of Mormon* references are again provided. As you read this one, take into account that it was supposedly written about **74 BCE**. The title 'Christ' is mentioned almost a century before he was born, on the other side of the world, and a very long time before the term was invented in order to describe him.

Had the word 'Messiah' been used, it may have been a bit more convincing – but even then, not much.

> **Alma 34:8.** And now, behold, I will testify unto you of myself that these things are true. Behold, I say unto you, that *I do know that Christ shall come* among the children of men, to take upon him the transgressions of his people, and that he shall atone for the sins of the world; for the Lord God hath spoken it.
> **9.** For it is expedient that an atonement should be made; for according to the great plan of the Eternal God there must be an atonement made, or else all mankind must unavoidably perish; yea, all are hardened; yea, all are fallen and are lost, and must perish except it be through the atonement which it is expedient should be made.
> **10.** For it is expedient that there should be a great and last sacrifice; yea, not a sacrifice of man, neither of beast, neither of any manner of fowl; for it shall not be a human sacrifice; but it must be an infinite and eternal sacrifice. (Emphasis added).

In Mormon theology, Christ not only took upon himself the sins of the world, for some reason he also suffered all of the pain, sickness and suffering of every human being who ever lived, or who ever would live on this planet, as well as all other planets God has populated. He suffered all of their afflictions and infirmities as well as their temptations and sins. In Mormon theology, God has not just created, but has also populated, worlds without number. Apparently we are the *only* planet on which there were beings who would have crucified Jesus. It seems that we are the worst of *all* of Gods created beings. That's not much of a reputation really when you come to think about it.

> **Alma 7:11.** And he shall go forth, *suffering pains and afflictions and temptations* of every kind; and this that the word might be fulfilled which saith he will take upon him *the pains and the sicknesses of his people.*

# THE ATONEMENT

**12.** And he will take upon him death, that he may loose the bands of death which bind his people; and *he will take upon him their infirmities*, that his bowels may be filled with mercy, according to the flesh, that he may know according to the flesh how to succor his people according to their infirmities.

**13.** Now the Spirit knoweth all things; nevertheless the Son of God suffereth according to the flesh that he might *take upon him the sins of his people*, that he might blot out their transgressions according to the power of his deliverance; and now behold, this is the testimony which is in me. (Emphasis added).

## The Gospel – The Way

Having established the concepts of the resurrection and atonement, all that remains is to show investigators the way forward. That of course is the 'gospel' in the guise of Mormonism. Six references are provided and they all stem from the *Book of Mormon.* The first of these *(2 Nephi 9:1-24)* was supposedly written between 559 and 545 BCE and stunningly predicts a *restoration* of the true gospel, centuries before Christ was even born and able to establish it in the first place. Smith cleverly predicts the *restoration* through *him* by writing it himself and then backdating it thousands of years into the mouth of a fictitious character in an equally fictitious book. And Mormons accept that this is in reality God prophesying the future though an ancient prophet.

The reference is lengthy so I have just selected important and impossible parts that relate, not just to a future *restoration* but also the idea that *God in the body* will show Himself specifically at Jerusalem; this being further evidence of Smith's monotheism at the time he wrote it. We are also back to guilt and 'uncleanness' and the carrot and stick. And, there is mention of everlasting fire and a lake of fire and brimstone, which Mormons do not actually believe in.

> **2 Nephi 9:2.** That he has spoken unto the Jews, by the mouth of his holy prophets, even from the beginning down, from generation to generation, until the time comes that *they shall be restored to the true church and fold of God; when they shall be gathered home to the lands of their inheritance,* and shall be established in all their lands of promise.
>
> **5.** Yea, I know that ye know that in the body *he shall show himself unto those at Jerusalem*, from whence we came; for it is expedient that it should be among them; for it behooveth *the great Creator that he suffereth himself to become subject unto man in the flesh, and die for all men*, that all men might become subject unto him.

# THE MORMON DELUSION

> **11.** And because of the way of ***deliverance of our God, the Holy One of Israel,*** this death, of which I have spoken, which is the temporal, shall deliver up its dead; which death is the grave.
>
> **14.** Wherefore, ***we shall have a perfect knowledge of all our guilt, and our uncleanness, and our nakedness;*** and the righteous shall have a perfect knowledge of their enjoyment, and their righteousness, being clothed with purity, yea, even with the robe of righteousness.
>
> **16.** And assuredly, as the Lord liveth, for the Lord God hath spoken it, and it is his eternal word, which cannot pass away, that ***they who are righteous shall be righteous still, and they who are filthy shall be filthy still***; wherefore, they who are filthy are the devil and his angels; and ***they shall go away into everlasting fire***, prepared for them; and ***their torment is as a lake of fire and brimstone, whose flame ascendeth up forever and ever and has no end.***
>
> **19.** O the greatness of the mercy of ***our God, the Holy One of Israel!*** For he delivereth his saints from that awful monster the devil, and ***death, and hell, and that lake of fire and brimstone, which is endless torment.***
>
> **24.** And ***if they will not repent and believe*** in his name, and be baptized in his name, and endure to the end, ***they must be damned***; for the Lord God, the Holy One of Israel, has spoken it. (Emphasis added).

Other *Book of Mormon* passages supposedly written BCE predict that the Son of God will come into the world to save mankind. One such is *Alma 11:40*. It may at first glance seem innocent enough, taken out of context; apart from the fact that it was also (82) BCE.

> **Alma 11:40.** And ***he shall come into the world to redeem his people***; and he shall take upon him the transgressions of those who believe on his name; and these are they that shall have eternal life, and salvation cometh to none else. (Emphasis added).

What the missionaries are *not* given to include, are the two preceding verses which I mentioned in *Chapter 5 (See p.100)*. Once verses 38-39 are considered, in conjunction with verse 40, we learn exactly *who* it is that will come into the world to redeem people and Smith's monotheism of the day once again shines through.

> **38.** Now Zeezrom saith again unto him: ***Is the Son of God the very Eternal Father?***

# THE ATONEMENT

**39.** And Amulek said unto him: ***Yea, he is the very Eternal Father of heaven and of earth,*** and all things which in them are; he is ***the beginning and the end, the first and the last;***
**40.** And ***he shall come into the world to redeem his people***; and he shall take upon him the transgressions of those who believe on his name; and these are they that shall have eternal life, and salvation cometh to none else. (Emphasis added).

Another lengthy reference is *2 Nephi, Chapter 31*, which does highlight several aspects the missionaries need to convey. The irony is that much more convincing material is available in the Bible but the Mormon Church rarely uses the Bible when it can use its own scriptures. The problem here is that once again it was supposedly written long before Christ lived and yet it discusses things concerning him that were then in the dim and distant future. Prophecy is one thing, but this, well, even in the hemisphere where these things were yet to happen, no one then had a clue what the Saviour would later be *called* and the Holy Ghost as such was yet to even be introduced as a concept by the Saviour himself. That is, according to the gospels, which were actually written decades to centuries after Christ lived, by people who never knew or even met him, so accuracy is suspect concerning many of these things – and that is *after* the event. This is hundreds of years *before* the event, and yet investigators are fed this information whilst probably not being told *when* it was purportedly written.

The *2 Nephi 31* chapter heading tells it all really, without listing the details actually in the chapter. But we will review a few.

> *Nephi tells why Christ was baptized—Men must follow Christ, be baptized, receive the Holy Ghost, and endure to the end to be saved—Repentance and baptism are the gate to the strait and narrow path—Eternal life comes to those who keep the commandments after baptism. Between 559 and 545 B.C.*

The word 'Christ' is from the Greek and would not have been known by Lehi and his family at that time. The original text, if you are drawn to accept it actually existed, would have translated 'messias' from the Hebrew, or any other related language of the day, so we would expect to see 'Messiah' rather than 'Christ' in any reference dated BCE. In this chapter, Nephi supposedly speaks of the following things several centuries BCE in America. Moreover, he speaks about them in the *past* tense. The investigator should question *why*?

> **2 Nephi 31. Extracts:** "the doctrine of Christ..."; "that prophet which the Lord showed unto me, that should baptize the Lamb of God..."; "if the Lamb of God, he being holy, should have need to be baptized by water..."; "wherein the Lamb of God did fulfil all righteousness in

being baptized by water..."; "after he was baptized with water the Holy Ghost descended upon him in the form of a dove..."; "he said unto the children of men: Follow thou me. Wherefore, my beloved brethren, can we follow Jesus save we shall be willing..."; "the Father said: Repent ye, repent ye, and be baptized in the name of my Beloved Son." *[559-545 BCE remember]*; "the voice of the Son came unto me, saying: He that is baptized in my name, to him will the Father give the Holy Ghost, like unto me; wherefore, follow me, and do the things which ye have seen me do." *[The things they have **seen** Jesus do? BCE?]* "take upon you the name of Christ, by baptism..."; "following your Lord and your Savior down into the water..."; "then shall ye receive the Holy Ghost; yea, then cometh the baptism of fire and of the Holy Ghost; and then can ye speak with the tongue of angels, and shout praises unto the Holy One of Israel."; "the gate by which ye should enter is repentance and baptism by water; and then cometh a remission of your sins by fire and by the Holy Ghost."; "according to the commandments of the Father and the Son; and ye have received the Holy Ghost..."; "ye shall press forward, feasting upon the word of Christ..." *[Christ's 'word' was not written until hundreds of years later].* "this is the doctrine of Christ, and the only and true doctrine of the Father, and of the Son, and of the Holy Ghost, which is one God, without end. Amen." *[Note once again Smith's monotheism here].*

A question that investigators should ask.

Why does Nephi use the *name* of *Jesus,* over five centuries BCE, when that name was not recognised or used that way until the fourteenth century CE? *(See: Chapter 4, pp.75-6).*

In the middle of another reference are these verses, which seem innocuous enough until you realise where Smith got the idea from.

> **3 Nephi 11:33**. And whoso believeth in me, and is baptized, the same shall be saved; and they are they who shall inherit the kingdom of God.
> **34.** And whoso believeth not in me, and is not baptized, shall be damned.

Compare this supposed scripture, purportedly penned in the Americas many centuries ago, with the handed down New Testament scripture that ended up reading like this in 1611 in the *KJV:*

> **Mark 16:16.** He that believeth and is baptized shall be saved; but he that believeth not shall be damned.

# THE ATONEMENT

Smith used an almost identical phrase in the *D&C* in a supposed 1831 revelation two years after he wrote the *Book of Mormon*, once again pretending the Lord spoke it. He used the same type of wording later, several more times in the *D&C* and also in the *Book of Moses* which he wrote in 1830-31. The latter mentions the Holy Ghost and then has similar words to Mark 16:16. The trouble is that the *Book of Moses* relates to a time period many *thousands* of years BCE – to the time of Adam and Eve.

> **D&C 68:9.** And he that believeth and is baptized shall be saved, and he that believeth not shall be damned.
>
> **Moses 5:14.** And the Lord God called upon men by the Holy Ghost everywhere and commanded them that they should repent;
> **15.** And as many as believed in the Son, and repented of their sins, should be saved; and as many as believed not and repented not, should be damned; and the words went forth out of the mouth of God in a firm decree; wherefore they must be fulfilled.

Whilst investigators are effectively taught concepts of repentance, baptism and the Holy Ghost from some of this suggested source material, it is doubtful that the claimed *dating* of any of the material is ever mentioned or therefore questioned. It really should be.

It is also worth noting that Smith is clearly exposed in every case where he uses the idea that people will be 'damned' if they are *not* baptised. From his rewrite of Moses, when and where such a notion was *impossible* anyway, to his BCE 'Nephi' usage, to his *D&C* wording, Smith consistently uses the same phraseology as well as the word 'damned', because that is what the *KJV* contained when Smith plagiarised the idea. In point of fact, that was only the *KJV* 'interpretation' – lifted from earlier versions of the Bible which were used when the *KJV* was written. A literal translation gives us the word 'condemned', which is a far cry from total damnation. If God or Jesus really *were* speaking in Smith's records of *Moses* and the *Book of Mormon*, why didn't they use their own original word 'condemned'?

> **Young's Literal Translation. Mark 16:16.** He who hath believed, and hath been baptized, shall be saved; and he who hath not believed, shall be condemned.

Today, only the *21st Century KJV* retains the translation 'damned' in line with some versions that preceded the 1611 *KJV*; including the *Wycliffe Bible* (1395); *Tyndale New Testament* (1526); *Miles Coverdale Bible* (1535); *The Bishop's Bible* (1568); *The Geneva Bible* (1587); and *Wesley's New Testament* (1755).

If however, we return to 'Biblia Sacra Vulgata' (*The Latin Vulgate*, CE 405) we get: qui crediderit et baptizatus fuerit salvus erit qui vero non crediderit condemnabitur.

This translates in the *Douay-Rheims Bible* (Latin Vulgate) to: *He that believeth and is baptized, shall be saved: but he that believeth not shall be **condemned**.*

In point of fact, the word 'condemned' – meaning 'pronounced to be wrong and requiring punishment', is far less harsh than 'damned' – meaning 'to sentence to eternal punishment'. Perhaps that is the reason it is also translated as 'condemned' rather than 'damned' in the *Daniel Mace New Testament* (1729); *The Derby Translation* (1890); *Wycliffe New Testament; New International Version; New American Standard Bible; Amplified Bible; New Living Translation; English Standard Version; Contemporary English Version; GOD'S WORD Translation; American Standard Version; Holman Christian Standard Bible; New International Version – UK; Today's New International Version; Complete Jewish Bible; Green's Literal Translation;* and the *Peshitta–Lamsa Translation*. Even the *'New King James Version'* has been retranslated to read 'condemned'.

The *New Century* version, the *New International Reader's Version*, the *Worldwide English New Testament* and the *New Life Bible*, all translate as 'punished', an equally less dramatic term than 'damned'.

There are even more versions, but I hope the point is made. At the end of the day, it doesn't much matter what the word is really, it is just that the version Smith was familiar with is the one that appeared in all his writings that were supposedly spoken by deity and penned by other people centuries to millennia ago. Not just the word appeared, but almost full identical sentences which in reality would be *impossible*. Handed down stories, translated and reworked over centuries and finally appearing in the 1611 *KJV* would not even be close to anything real that Jesus may or may not have spoken. Joseph Smith was clearly working from his family copy of the *KJV* rather than *translating* actual words spoken by Jesus Christ. Christ obviously did not say precisely that while he was on the Earth and God clearly didn't say anything like that in the time of Adam.

# Chapter 10

## Lesson 2

### The Plan of Salvation

### Part D

### The Spirit World

> Even though Christ conquered physical death, all people must die, for death is part of the process by which we are transformed from mortality to immortality. At death our ***spirits go to the spirit world***. Death does not change our personality or our desires for good or evil. ***Those who chose to obey God in this life live in a state of happiness, peace, and rest*** from troubles and care. ***Those who chose not to obey in this life and did not repent live in a state of unhappiness***. In the spirit world the gospel is preached to ***those who did not obey the gospel or have the opportunity to hear it*** while on earth. We remain in the spirit world until we are resurrected. *(Page 52)*. (Emphasis added).

Technically, missionaries are not being entirely honest about this when they teach it, but once again it is not their fault. It is what they have grown up with in the Church or were taught by other missionaries if they themselves were converts. And of course, it is what is in the missionary lesson manual. In my own day, it was taught a little differently. The terminology was more specific and the wording more austere. I will come back to that shortly.

Additionally, missionaries then used 'flannel boards' on which were placed pictorial representations of aspects they were teaching in each lesson. Depictions of pre-Earth life, birth and life on Earth, the spirit world, the three degrees of glory and outer darkness would all be put in sequence on the flannel board as they were explained. Some of the early details of the spirit world have been watered down significantly, thus modern members have no idea what was originally taught.

The manual speaks of the 'spirit world' where those who have *obeyed* God in this life live in a state of 'happiness, peace and rest'. What the manual does not explicitly make clear is that the 'happiness' part is strictly for Mormons. Those who *chose* not to obey God and repent, live in 'unhappiness' or a state of 'misery', as do all those (everyone else) who never heard of the Mormon Church during their lives. Many *billions* of good people will consider they *did* choose to obey God and think that they did repent, believing wholeheartedly in Him. However, unless they became Mormons, they will not be in the 'happy' state. Only Mormons will be happy, and they will spend their time teaching the gospel to spirits in the 'unhappy' state. *(Manual p. 52)*.

Most people would *not* agree they fit that category just because they are *not* a Mormon. They were perfectly happy in this life, and would not expect to be miserable in the next one. But, according to Mormonism, doctrinally they will be miserable, even though they are yet to hear the gospel. The question is why would they be in a state of misery when they had never heard of Mormonism in life, and when they arrive in the spirit world, they have yet to hear of it? Would they not just be happy to 'wake up dead' and realise that life carries on in one form or another?

So, we have the *spirit world* and two 'states', *happiness* and *unhappiness* or misery. Previously, it was taught as the *spirit world* and the two 'states' were considered different 'places' which were *paradise* and the *spirit prison*. *Paradise* was a *place* of happiness reserved for Mormons; the *spirit prison* was for everyone else. To Mormons, Jesus went to Paradise, *not* the Spirit Prison.

The modern inference is that everyone is in the same *place* but in different states of mind. Spirits cannot be happy unless and until they repent and accept the Mormon gospel. Mormons go to the *spirit prison* to teach people about the Church. It is a place people cannot leave until they have the gospel preached to them, whereupon, if they accept it, they can be freed from the *spirit prison* and join those in *paradise* where they will then be happy instead of miserable.

However, as they are spirits and baptism is an earthy 'physical' ordinance, their 'work' will have to be performed by proxy here on Earth before they can 'progress' to paradise.

# THE SPIRIT WORLD

Mormon temples are used to perform baptisms for dead ancestors thus enabling their 'progression' in the spirit world. Temple work also includes 'sealing' couples who were married in Earth life and sealing their children to them for eternity. It is considered essential work which the spirits are unable to perform for themselves, having to rely on mortals. For Mormons, while they are alive, they must locate and confirm details of their ancestors and perform these 'saving ordinances' for them. Once, it was considered the case that we should complete as much family history as possible but in the modern Mormon Church, four generations are 'required' and any further work is discretionary.

That lets most second-generation members and beyond off the hook, as faithful parents and grand-parents will usually have more than completed at least that much work. Mormons *know* the work is essential and that people who die without the 'saving' ordinances cannot progress until they are performed.

The following was once official Church teaching and many of us knew and taught it this way in church and on missions. I suspect it still is really believed, but as with many other things, it is harder to teach people about so it has been modified or 'watered down' several times.

What is now termed the *spirit world* was previously defined as the *Spirit Prison*. The reason for this was quite logical. *No one* can leave it, Mormon or otherwise, so they are imprisoned there regardless of their state of mind (or place) until God sees fit to move them on via resurrection. People can and do leave Earth through death, old age, illness, accident, natural disaster, murder, war, or by choice through suicide, however, there is no way for a spirit to die, so no one ever leaves the spirit world through circumstance or choice. They must wait until they are resurrected.

Originally, within the *spirit prison* were two states, or possibly *places*, known as *paradise* and *hell*. Once again, *paradise* was for faithful Mormons and *hell* was for the rest. Hell was a state of temporary torment as they did not have the gospel. Once again, dead Mormons spent their time teaching the Gospel to those in *hell*. They could then progress to *paradise* to await their resurrection and judgment, but only once their 'work' had been done for them on Earth. During the flannel board presentation, the concept of paradise was firmed up using Luke 23:43 where Jesus says: "Verily I say unto thee, today shalt thou be with me in paradise."

Today, this reference is conspicuous by its complete *absence* from the missionary training manual. What was once a core teaching, verified from the Bible by the words of Jesus Christ himself, is now simply ignored. Not only that, but the word 'paradise' doesn't even appear *in* the manual. Likewise, the word 'hell' appears nowhere *in* the manual and – wait for it… 'spirit prison' also does not appear *in* the manual. So, Earth was and still is, *Earth,* and hasn't changed its name. But, the *spirit prison* which once contained *paradise* and *hell*, which later became the *spirit world* containing *paradise* and a *spirit prison*, is now just the *spirit world* with *happiness* and *unhappiness* in it.

Why would God change the names of a 'place' three times in just a few decades and at the same time drop a powerful reference supporting a doctrinal point *(Luke 23:43)* and paradise? *Why?*

This is not just **a question for investigators**; it is a question all Mormons should ask. Why the changes and why no *paradise* as substantiated in Luke any longer? It makes no theological sense whatsoever. Does it alter *doctrine*?

We reviewed part of *2 Nephi 9:1-24* under 'The Gospel – The Way' previously, but not v.13. Now we should.

> **2 Nephi 9:13.** O how great the plan of our God! For on the other hand, ***the paradise of God must deliver up the spirits of the righteous***, and the grave deliver up the body of the righteous; and the spirit and the body is restored to itself again, and all men become incorruptible, and immortal,... (Emphasis added).

Here we have confirmation in the *Book of Mormon* that *paradise* is where righteous spirits go to after death. There are in fact three other references in the *Book of Mormon* which also mention paradise. *(Alma 40:12,14; 4 Nephi 1:14; Moroni 10:34)*. If it was good enough for Luke in the Bible *(also see 2 Cor. 12:4)*, for *Book of Mormon* Nephites, and for Mormons when I was young – why isn't it the terminology used *now*?

God is unchangeable – He is the same yesterday, today and forever. But the Mormon God is *not* the same from one minute to the next. There have been at least *three* changes to this once clearly understood and fundamental doctrine since I joined the Church. The Church may say that it is the 'same meat with different gravy' to coin a phrase, but clearly it is not. The definitions were *specific* and they were backed by *scripture* which is no longer even used.

Either the state, or place, *is* paradise or it is *not*. Either Jesus confirmed that was where he was going or he did not. Clearly, he did, if you accept Luke, and the Church once used it to substantiate the doctrine. It can't be one way one minute and another way the next. Now, everything is diluted and simplified in order to capture people more easily. Once again we find earlier doctrine altered for the sake of convenience. Thus the current 'teaching' concerning the *spirit world* is a far cry from original teachings – and for no apparent reason.

The diagram below is taken from an old sheet provided in my 'Book of Remembrance' from the 1960s. It was printed in 1950 but has an earlier date of 1927 on it. The teachings of the time are clearly identified. Indeed, although it now appears not to be explicitly taught to investigators, it transpires that the New Testament Seminary Teacher Resource Manual, published as late as 1999, also speaks of *paradise* and the *spirit prison*. The earlier teaching that many of us understood to be the true teaching, regarding the spirit world itself

# THE SPIRIT WORLD

being termed the *spirit prison*, containing *paradise* and *hell*, appears to have been quietly discarded and ultimately forgotten. Yet it was once taught and it is supported in Alma 40 in the *Book of Mormon,* which is actually referenced in the lesson manual as discussed below.

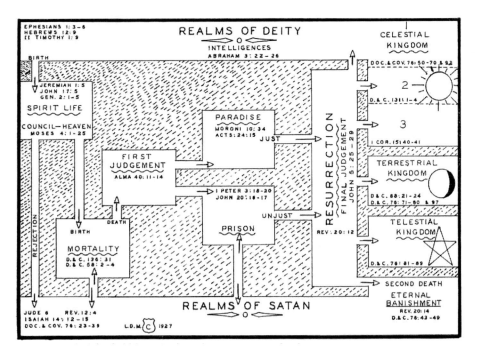

There are three scripture references provided to support the idea of the spirit world. They are Alma 34:34, Alma 40:11–14 and Ecclesiastes 12:7.

> **Alma 34:34.** Ye cannot say, when ye are brought to that awful crisis, that I will repent, that I will return to my God. Nay, ye cannot say this; for that same spirit which doth possess your bodies at the time that ye go out of this life, that same spirit will have power to possess your body in that eternal world. *(74 BCE).*

All the above passage does is confirm the idea that you can't deliberately leave repentance until the last minute and that the spirit continues to exist after life on Earth and will one day possess a resurrected body, both of which are fairly standard Christian concepts.

> **Alma 40:11.** Now, concerning the *state of the soul between death and the resurrection*—Behold, it has been made known unto me by an angel, that the spirits of all men, as soon as they are departed from this mortal body, yea, the spirits of all men, whether they be good or evil, *are taken home to that God* who gave them life.

189

12. And then shall it come to pass, that the spirits of those who are righteous are received into *a state of happiness, which is called paradise*, a state of rest, a state of peace, where they shall rest from all their troubles and from all care, and sorrow.

13. And then shall it come to pass, that the spirits of the wicked, yea, who are evil—for behold, they have no part nor portion of the Spirit of the Lord; for behold, they chose evil works rather than good; therefore the spirit of the devil did enter into them, and take possession of their house—and *these shall be cast out into outer darkness*; there shall be weeping, and wailing, and gnashing of teeth, and this because of their own iniquity, being led captive by the will of the devil.

14. Now this is the state of the souls of the wicked, yea, in darkness, and a state of awful, fearful looking for the fiery indignation of the wrath of God upon them; thus *they remain in this state, as well as the righteous in paradise, until the time of their resurrection.* (Emphasis added).

The first thing to note is that when Smith wrote the *Book of Mormon*, or at least the book of *Alma*, he considered the spirit to be the *soul* of humans – 'body and soul' – the common Christian concept. Adam was created and God put his *soul* or spirit into him. There are a number of references confirming Smith's concept of the day that the *spirit is* the *soul*. Once again, it's either that or it's what the Nephites believed – if they were real. How many references are needed before the point is satisfactorily made?

**Alma 36:15.** that I could be banished and become extinct *both soul and body*, that I might not be brought to stand…

**Alma 40:15.** this state of misery of *the soul, before the resurrection*, was a first resurrection. Yea, I admit it may be termed a resurrection, the *raising of the spirit or the soul…*

**Alma 40:18.** Behold, I say unto you, Nay; but it meaneth *the reuniting of the soul with the body*, of those from the days of Adam down to the resurrection of Christ.

**Alma 40:19.** Now, whether *the souls and the bodies of those of whom has been spoken* shall all be reunited at once, the wicked as well as the righteous, I do not say;

**Alma 40:20.** I give it as my opinion, that *the souls and the bodies are reunited*, of the righteous,…

**Amla 40:21.** there is a space between death and the resurrection of the body, and a *state of the soul in happiness or in misery* until the time

# THE SPIRIT WORLD

which is appointed of God that the dead shall come forth, and *be reunited, both soul and body*, and be brought to stand before God, and be judged according to their works.

**Alma 40:23.** The *soul shall be restored to the body, and the body to the soul;…*

**Alma 42:9.** as *the soul could never die,…*

**Alma 42:11.** as soon as *they were dead their souls were miserable,…*

> "The Book of Mormon contains the fulness of the gospel of Jesus Christ."
>
> The Mormon Church teaches that the ***body*** and the ***spirit*** combined, constitute the ***soul***.
> The *Book of Mormon* prolifically teaches in Alma that the spirit ***is*** the soul.

The spirit and body combining to constitute the soul was a later change or development in Mormon theology. In v.11 of Alma 40 above *(p.189)*, Smith discloses his then understanding – or, if you believe the Nephites to have been a real people – what they believed and understood. The verse also *confirms* the biblical concept that spirits return to *God (See Ecclesiastes below)* but in Mormon theology, God does not associate directly with the afterlife spirit world any more than He does with the Earth.

In v.12 above *(p.190),* the 'state of happiness' is determined as *paradise*, so why in the missionary lesson manual does the Church today ignore Smith's definition as recorded in his *Book of Mormon*? Those who are not in paradise go to 'outer darkness', which was otherwise known as a temporary state of *hell* in earlier Mormonism. In v.14 *(p.190)* it clearly states "they remain in this state, as well as the righteous in paradise, until the time of their resurrection." This is even more harsh than the description used when I was young, but it is at least consistent with earlier teachings. If the missionaries do mention *paradise* to investigators, the only place they will find it is in v.12 of *Alma 40 (see p.190)* in the recommended reading, as it is not mentioned once in the manual.

**Ecclesiastes 12:7.** Then shall the dust return to the earth as it was: and the spirit shall ***return unto God who gave it.*** (Emphasis added).

The above scripture is utterly pointless in context of the Mormon concept of the spirit world. It has no meaning or emphasis regarding Mormon belief. Spirits do *not* return *to* God in Mormon theology. He does not reside in the world of spirits, whatever name is used for it. It was the now discarded Luke 23:43 scripture that helped me to accept the Mormon concept of paradise, as it was Jesus Christ himself confirming the doctrine. With such powerful and supposedly first hand verification of facts from Christ, why did the Mormon Church ever discard it?

## Gospel Preached to the Dead

The missionaries are given three references regarding Jesus teaching spirits in the 'spirit world' between his death and resurrection. The missionary lesson manual does not acknowledge that in these scriptures there is reference to the *spirit prison*. The references inadvertently raise other related problematic issues which missionaries undoubtedly won't even *notice*, let alone discuss with their investigators.

> **1 Peter 3:19** By which also he went and preached unto the ***spirits in prison***;
> **20.** Which sometime were disobedient, when once the longsuffering of God waited in the days of Noah, while the ark was a preparing, wherein few, that is, eight souls were saved by water. (Emphasis added).

When the Church taught that the entire place was a *spirit prison*, the above worked well enough. However, once it becomes the *spirit world*, containing *paradise* and the *spirit prison*, it also becomes problematic because the Church teaches that Christ did *not* go to those in prison, he only went to *paradise* and organised his 'forces' there to go to those in *prison*.

Use of the above verse also seems to admit to the concept that the biblical flood and Noah's ark were a reality rather than just a fairy tale of the day. I will review that as it also appears accepted as such by the sixth Mormon prophet, Joseph F. Smith, who also referenced it as author of *D&C 138*. It is taught as factual by the Church today on the basis that the Earth needed to be 'baptised'.

> **1 Peter 4:6.** For for this cause was the gospel preached also to them that are dead, that they might be judged according to men in the flesh, but live according to God in the spirit.

Once again, this is standard Christian understanding, Mormon or otherwise. The other reference provided for missionaries to use is a canonised 'divine communication', also described as a 'vision', received by Joseph F. Smith in 1918. The entire section is referenced. I will include the heading in order to give the background and then review some of the content.

# THE SPIRIT WORLD

> **D&C 138.** *A vision, given to President Joseph F. Smith in Salt Lake City, Utah, on October 3, 1918. In his opening address at the eighty-ninth Semiannual General Conference of the Church, on October 4, 1918, President Smith declared that he had received several divine communications during the previous months. One of these, concerning the Savior's visit to the spirits of the dead while his body was in the tomb, he had received the previous day. It was written immediately following the close of the conference; on October 31, 1918, it was submitted to the counselors in the First Presidency, the Council of the Twelve, and the Patriarch, and it was unanimously accepted by them.* (Italics in original).
>
> **D&C 138:6.** I opened the Bible and read the third and fourth chapters of the first epistle of Peter, and as I read I was greatly impressed, more than I had ever been before, with the following passages:
> **7.** "For Christ also hath once suffered for sins, the just for the unjust, that he might bring us to God, being put to death in the flesh, but quickened by the Spirit:
> **8.** "By which also he went and *preached unto the spirits in prison*;
> **9.** "Which sometime were disobedient, when once the long-suffering of God waited in the *days of Noah, while the ark was a preparing, wherein few, that is, eight souls were saved by water.*" (1 Peter 3:18—20.)
> **10.** "For for this cause was the gospel preached also to them that are dead, that they might be judged according to men in the flesh, but live according to God in the spirit." (1 Peter 4:6.) (Emphasis added).

Note that the two scriptures Smith speaks of are the same two that are now recommended to missionaries, as reviewed above *(p.192)*. They include the concept of 'spirits in prison'. No such place or state is described or explained in the missionary lesson manual today.

> **138:11.** As I pondered over these things which are written, the eyes of my understanding were opened, and the Spirit of the Lord rested upon me, and I saw the hosts of the dead, both small and great.
> **12.** And there were *gathered together in one place an innumerable company of the spirits of the just, who had been faithful* in the testimony of Jesus while they lived in mortality; (Emphasis added).

Here, all the faithful – an innumerable company – are gathered in one *place* which is defined by inference to be a different *location* to those who were *not* faithful.

> **138:18.** …the Son of God appeared, declaring liberty to the captives who had been faithful;

> **19.** And there he preached to them the everlasting gospel, the doctrine of the resurrection and the redemption of mankind from the fall, and from individual sins on conditions of repentance.

Jesus visits the faithful and teaches the everlasting gospel, the resurrection, and redemption from the fall through repentance. He does not however, visit the 'wicked'. They all appear to be confined to an entirely different *place*.

> **138:20.** But *unto the wicked he did not go*, and among the ungodly and the unrepentant who had defiled themselves while in the flesh, his voice was not raised;
> **21.** Neither did the rebellious who rejected the testimonies and the warnings of the ancient prophets behold his presence, nor look upon his face.
> **22.** *Where these were, darkness reigned,* but among the righteous there was peace;

Smith's understanding, whether real or imagined, is defined by the above statements.

> **138:27.** But his ministry among those who were dead was limited to the brief time intervening between the crucifixion and his resurrection;

Mormons believe that in about thirty-six hours, between his death and resurrection, Jesus Christ established and organised an ongoing programme of teaching the gospel in the spirit world. The converted 'happy' spirits would teach all the unconverted and thus 'unhappy' spirits about the gospel and about vicarious work which could save them.

> **138:29.** And as I wondered, my eyes were opened, and my understanding quickened, and I perceived that *the Lord went not in person among the wicked* and the disobedient who had rejected the truth, to teach them;
> **30.** But behold, from among the righteous, *he organized his forces and appointed messengers,* clothed with power and authority, and commissioned them to go forth and carry the light of the gospel to them that were in darkness, even to all the spirits of men; and thus was the gospel preached to the dead.
>
> **32.** Thus was the *gospel preached to those who had died in their sins, without a knowledge of the truth, or in transgression,* having rejected the prophets.
> **33.** These were taught faith in God, repentance from sin, *vicarious baptism for the remission of sins,* the gift of the Holy Ghost by the laying on of hands, (Emphasis added).

# THE SPIRIT WORLD

In verse 28, Smith states that he wondered how Christ could have achieved all that he did in such a short space of time and the explanation comes in the verses reviewed above. Verse 28 comments on people having waited in the days of *Noah*.

> **138:28**. And I wondered at the words of Peter—wherein he said that the Son of God preached unto the spirits in prison, who sometime were disobedient, when once the **long-suffering of God waited in the days of Noah**—and how it was possible for him to preach to those spirits and perform the necessary labor among them in so short a time.

This verse, coupled with his review of verses from 1 Peter 3&4 *(in v.9-10 above on p.193)*, confirm that Smith accepted Noah really did build an ark and the Earth was indeed completely flooded for about a year. The Mormon Church today accepts and teaches that the flood *was* a reality. *(See: Old Testament Gospel Doctrine Teacher's Manual, Chapter 6; Institute of Religion 301. Old Testament Student Manual, Genesis – 2 Samuel. p.55. Available online; search 'LDS manuals').*

I remember being taught that the Earth itself needed baptism, which was another reason for the flood. This concept no longer seems to appear in Old Testament Sunday School Manuals and I found no mention of it in the *Encyclopaedia of Mormonism*, but it does appear in the *Institute of Religion* manual referenced above, including the following early Mormon quotes, used to confirm Earth-baptism is still an accepted doctrine.

> Fifteen cubits upwards did the waters prevail; and the mountains were covered.' That is, the earth was immersed. ***It was a period of baptism.***" *(John Taylor, Journal of Discourses, 26:74–75.)* (Emphasis added).

> Orson Pratt declared: "The first ordinance instituted for **the cleansing of the earth, was that of immersion in water; it was buried in the liquid element, and all things sinful upon the face of the earth were washed away.** As it came forth from the ocean floor, like the new-born child, it was innocent; it rose to newness of life. It was its second birth from the womb of mighty waters—a new world issuing from the ruins of the old, clothed with all the innocence of this first creation." *(Answers to Gospel Questions, 4:20. Joseph F. Smith, Deseret Book, 1980).* (Emphasis added).

> "The earth, in its present condition and situation, is not a fit habitation for the sanctified; but it abides the law of its creation, **has been baptized with water**, will be baptized by fire and the Holy Ghost, and by-and-by will be prepared for the faithful to dwell upon" *(Answers to Gospel Questions, 4:20 c: Brigham Young).* (Emphasis added).

# THE MORMON DELUSION

I did wonder if the absence of *Earth-baptism* in some manuals and the *EM* might actually be a precursor to modern-day common sense requiring dropping the flood idea altogether one day soon. It would not have surprised me after everything else that has been discarded by the Church over the years. Indeed, it should be dropped, as scientific evidence has long confirmed it mythological on every imaginable level.

However, the references in the Institute manual keep it in place for now. Unfortunately for Mormons, as science has proven the flood to be a complete nonsense in every respect, out goes the viability of another Mormon doctrine and in comes more conclusive proof of Smith's hoax. Clinging to the flood as a fact when it is provable fiction is as delusional as it gets, but Mormon doctrine has been written by Smith to include it and several of his successors confirmed it, so there is little choice for the Church at present but to continue to go along with it despite the absurdity. It appears that once again the Church is ignoring conclusive scientific evidence and relying instead on faith in provable fiction.

Baptism of humans was once an ordinance that could be repeated for health reasons or for personal repentance. Early Mormons could be baptised as often as they liked. Now, the *Encyclopaedia of Mormonism* simply dismisses the old idea by stating "The earlier practice of rebaptism to manifest repentance and recommitment, or for a restoration of health in time of sickness, is no longer practiced in the Church." *(EM p.94)*. In fact, the practice survived for nearly seventy years in the early Church and was only discontinued in 1897.

Investigators will never be told of this as it is 'off topic' and missionaries will not discuss it with them. **A question investigators should ask** is if it was once fine with God and it is an eternal principle, how could the *principle* ever *change*? It says elsewhere in the *EM* that some members abused the practice, but surely that is just a matter of training and control, not of changing *doctrine*. Either rebaptism *is* a correct principle or it is *not*. Such an ordinance cannot be 'revealed' as being correct during the ministry of several successive prophets and then determined as inappropriate by later prophets without someone being very *wrong*. A real God would be more consistent than that. The evidence once again points squarely to it being yet another man made nonsensical idea.

In the modern world, science has conclusively proven that no such thing as a global flood occurred four thousand years ago. The story is mythological. It was physically impossible for any number of historical, geological, ecological, archaeological, anthropological, and evolutionary – and probably many other reasons, including even floating a boat of that size made from gopher wood.

Apart from the impossibility of the world being completely covered by the available water – excused in the 'Institute' lesson manual as being added to by 'fountains of the deep' below the seas, coming up from and returning to we know not where – an ark the size of a football field, made of gopher wood and

## THE SPIRIT WORLD

pitch, is an *impossible* creation to have survived for any number of engineering reasons. And that is before a single species entered it.

Even a cursory study of all known species and their evolution immediately dispels the notion that two, or even seven of some, of every known and also *unknown* species entered an ark around 2304 BCE. Without going into detail, there are now, and there were of course then, many *millions* of species which could never have survived such a flood, so they must have been on the ark, unless you accept that some major evolution occurred, and extremely quickly at that, *following* the flood. They *all* had to be accommodated on the ark. That includes a million known species of insect that could not survive under water. It is estimated that there are a further five-million species of insect yet to be identified and catalogued. Add those – and then start on the animals.

There are some three-hundred-and-fifty species of monkey alone, so load up seven-hundred of those and then start counting – and calculating the space. That is, look at the dimensions of the ark and the number of levels and rooms there may have been. Then try to fit everything in. Never mind feeding them or considering the fact that many eat each other to survive, just assume they all hibernated for a year. You will soon understand the size of the problem when pitting fact against obvious fiction. Then of course there is the aspect of known worldwide locations of various species from before and after the flood era. So, the question must be asked, how did they live in those various places both before *and* after the flood with no evidenced gap in their evolutionary journey.

Where is the evidence of the billions of deaths of millions of species and where is the evidence that *every* known species *restarted* in exactly the same areas where they left off, from just *two* surviving examples, just 2303 years BCE? The *concept* is absolutely laughable to anyone who has even the remotest understanding of the recent history of species. And I am not talking here about *evolution* of species, just the recent – last four-thousand-odd-year history – of their *existence*.

Proof against the flood is *conclusive* in every imaginable area. Facts trump faith. The Mormon Church, along with many other denominations it should be said, chooses to ignore the facts and teach the fiction. The thing is, when will common sense ever prevail in the Mormon Church? Why not just admit that it was a fanciful 'campfire' story and be done with it? Well, if the Church did that, it would also destroy Smith's credibility concerning the *Book of Abraham* which also includes the flood. But then, the *Book of Abraham* has also been conclusively proven a fraudulent work, so perhaps they could discard that at the same time. It would at least be a good start towards common sense and reason. But then, I am sure that would be expecting far too much.

After allowing for the *millions* of species that had to be accommodated *in* the ark, you must add two of each of over ten thousand species of birds, almost all of which cannot land on water, and which would presumably have to be accommodated *on* the roof. Do you begin to see the scale of the problem? It is fine to suggest faith is required to accommodate such an idea, until you actually take time to study all the science that needs to be considered which surrounds the supposition. Understanding even a little of just *one* discipline, one immediately encounters more problems than could ever be overcome, even with the utmost and intense faith in the story. Science must *never* be discarded in favour of faith; it is more than delusional and completely absurd. When facts are firmly established, if they contradict *belief*, remember, *facts* always trump faith.

The facts, once again, outweigh the possibility of the fiction, over and over again in any number of areas in any number of scientific disciplines. Although considered by many people as real simply because it appears in the Bible, the whole notion of the flood and an ark is simply absurd. It is just a fairy story derived from earlier tales of localised flooding, some of which were extremely severe – such as the Black Sea flood some 7,600 years ago. *(See Ryan & Pitman, 2000, Noah's Flood, New York N.Y; Simon & Shulster).*

Almost none of those who believe in a literal flood would consider *fairies* to be real, although no doubt they would if they were mentioned in the Bible, and yet, although equally fictional, proof of fairies is far more probable than proof of the flood. There are even photographs of fairies which have not been proven to be fake, so who knows? Well, we do know, but you get the point. Giants are in the Bible and some people supposedly lived many hundreds of years. Those ideas are also clearly fanciful – but I more than digress.

Remember, these old legends were handed down verbally for hundreds and hundreds of years and what we now read in the Bible was only actually written that way a few hundred years BCE. Should we really expect much accuracy in tales told and retold many hundreds of times over thousands of years? 'Chinese whispers' will have more than done their work to any and every legend.

Bible chronology places the great flood at 2304 BCE which was actually during the Old Kingdom period in Egypt. World history, especially Egyptian, covers thousands of years, including lists of the Egyptian kings, right through the time of the biblically claimed flood. There is *no* gap in Egyptian history.

Evidence of human inhabitation of the Nile Valley dates to the Palaeolithic era some 2.5-2.6 million years ago and evidence of hunter-gatherers and fishers replacing a grain-grinding culture appears about 12,000 years ago. There is *no* gap in Egyptian history over the last 5,000 years which would allow for even an Egyptian, let alone global flood. The history of world population is well established. There were many millions of people already living at the supposed time of the flood and the world could never have established the current global numbers, or the evolved varieties, of modern humans from just one family over such a short period of time. That's before we even consider the many *millions* of varieties in the animal kingdom and the known evolution of species.

# THE SPIRIT WORLD

Smith's *Book of Abraham* contains equally fictitious claims regarding the flood and what transpired after the water subsided. The hoax is exposed in any number of ways in the *Book of Abraham* where it claims Egyptus 'discovered' Egypt following the flood. Her story is as ludicrous as the flood story itself.

But then, it should also be remembered that in his *Book of Abraham*, Smith has Adam name all the animals and birds, just as in Genesis. He has Abraham *impossibly* repeat, supposedly in his own handwriting, over two-thousand years BCE, the mythology that ended up worded this way in the *KJV* in 1611 CE.

> **Genesis 2:20.** And Adam gave names to all cattle, and to the fowl of the air, and to every beast of the field
>
> **Abraham 5: 21.** And Adam gave names to ***all cattle***, to the ***fowl of the air***, to ***every beast*** of the field;… (Emphasis added).

Two brief points here; there are at least 10,000 known species of birds and 1,250,000 species of animals; before getting into the undiscovered ones and to between five-million and one-hundred-million other species, catalogued or yet to be discovered. And Adam apparently named *all* of them.

Try inventing names for even a hundred species of anything. How and why then did Adam name them *all* when no one retained a list of them; in any event, how and why would one man name so many creatures? The whole idea is obviously complete nonsense. The Genesis story is mythological and Smith pretended Abraham repeated the *same* words as later appeared in the *KJV*, once again proving conclusively that the *Book of Abraham* was another hoax. That's not to even mention the fact that there were about five-million people on Earth six-thousand years ago, when Adam and Eve supposedly lived – although of course, no one could yet read or write – so there's another unresolved problem.

If such an event as a global flood took place in *any* biblical timeframe, Egypt could not have had the population that it later did and world population and human diversity as it stands today would be *impossible*. The history and movement of people on the planet has been accurately mapped by DNA and it does not allow for any possibility of a *global* flood wiping almost everyone out, at *any* biblical stage during the evolution, that is, the *development* of known physical *diversification*, colours, sizes, physical traits etc., of our species. For the flood to be a reality, *no* group of humans or animals known today would date back more than four-thousand-three-hundred years or so. The scientific evidence of that *not* being the case is *conclusive. (See TMD Vol. 2 Ch. 14 for further details).* That's not to even begin to mention problems with the survival of most flora whilst submerged in salt water for a year. About four-hundred-thousand species of *plants* need to be accounted for alone – then the rest…

The problem these days regarding such things as evolution of species, the origin, world distribution and subsequent variety within our own species, DNA mapping and so forth, is no longer just that many people accept questionable things on faith rather than evidence, but now, that they ill-advisedly accept things in *spite* of conclusive *proof* which they refuse to study or even begin to understand or accept. You don't have to *believe* in evolution, you just have to *understand* it. It is no longer a debatable theory. It is scientific fact. *Belief* in the unsubstantiated must accommodate that and somehow work alongside it.

A good link covering problems surrounding the idea of a flood is available here: http://www.talkorigins.org/faqs/faq-noahs-ark.html

Back to the rest of *D&C 138* and Joseph F. Smith's 'revelation':

People that Joseph F. Smith claimed were *in* his vision include Adam, Eve, Abel and Seth. He then mentions *(v.41)* Noah "who gave warning of the flood" which we just discussed. From that alone, we know it was not a *real* vision.

Smith goes on to say he saw Shem, Abraham, Isaac, Jacob, Moses, Isaiah, Ezekiel, Daniel, *Elias*, Malachi, and v.46 and v.47 both mention *Elijah*. The problem here, and elsewhere for Mormons, is *Elias* and *Elijah* are recognised and accepted as being names for one and the *same person*. Here Smith sees them as two *separate* people. How did Smith recognise them – or did they introduce themselves? If so, then who on earth was the 'Elias' person supposed to be? None of it fits with known reality. Therefore, it cannot have *been* a reality, but rather just a vague dream, or wishful thinking that he elaborated on.

Elijah (Elias) is biblically one and the *same* person. That absolute *fact* is accepted by *everyone* – except a few people in the Mormon Church it seems. I am at a loss as to how Joseph F. Smith would actually have recognised each individual in order to *name* them among the millions of people who would have been in such a group but I am even more at a loss as to how he could ever have possibly *identified* two different people who were actually one and the same person. "Elias: Hebrew *'Eliahu*, "Yahveh is God"; also called Elijah." *(Catholic Encyclopaedia)*. This was a huge mistake by Smith who thus exposes his fraudulent claim to have actually 'seen' these people in vision. One or the other simply did not *exist*. *Elias* is just the Greek form of the Hebrew *Elijah*. It is as simple as that – but Smith's mistake is not at all just simple – it is utterly *condemning*.

The name of *Elias* is the Latin transliteration of the Greek name Ἡλίας. It is the Hellenised form of *Elijah*. *Elias* does *not* appear in the *Old Testament* for obvious reasons. The name only appears in the *Apocrypha* and the *New Testament*. Linguistically, *Elias* is derived from *Elijah* because the Hebrew suffix *-yahu*, rendered -iah or -jah in English is replaced with *-ias* in Greek, as in other names such as Jeremiah/Jeremias and Isaiah/Esaias.

> Therefore we know *Elijah* and *Elias* are one and the same person.
> We also know *Jeremiah* and *Jeremias* are one and the same person.
> Likewise, we know *Isaiah* and *Esaias* are one and the same person.

# THE SPIRIT WORLD

And, all for the very same reason; it was simply the *translation* of a name in every instance. A true prophet, or even an amateur historian, would know this of course, but Joseph F. Smith did *not*. As it happens, neither did Joseph Smith Jnr. He seemed as confused as Joseph F. was over names of people *he* claimed to see. Both men are equally exposed as frauds by this mistake alone.

It is one thing to mistake a *name* and not realise it is someone else, but to claim to have actually *seen both* characters when they are in fact only *one* is quite another. And *both* these Smiths *did* claim they had seen *two* different characters that were in fact *one* and the same being. There can be no excuse for that; just a vivid and incorrect imagination. Mind you, Joseph Smith couldn't make up his mind who the visiting angel was that appeared in his room. Was it Nephi or Moroni? It seems he never was much good with names. Several times in the *D&C* Joseph Smith speaks of *Elijah*. On the following occasions, Smith speaks of *Elias*, as if he is a completely *different* person.

> **D&C 27:6.** And also with **Elias**, to whom I have committed the keys of bringing to pass the restoration of all things spoken by the mouth of all the holy prophets since the world began, concerning the last days;
> **7.** And also John the son of Zacharias, which Zacharias he ***(Elias)*** visited and gave promise that he should have a son, and his name should be John, and he should be filled with the spirit of ***Elias***; (Emphasis added).
>
> **D&C 77:9. Q.** What are we to understand by the angel ascending from the east, Revelation 7th chapter and 2nd verse?
>
> **A.** We are to understand that the angel ascending from the east is he to whom is given the seal of the living God over the twelve tribes of Israel; wherefore, he crieth unto the four angels having the everlasting gospel, saying: Hurt not the earth, neither the sea, nor the trees, till we have sealed the servants of our God in their foreheads. And, if you will receive it, this is **Elias** which was to come to gather together the tribes of Israel and restore all things. (Emphasis added).
>
> **D&C 110:12.** After this, ***Elias*** appeared, and committed the dispensation of the gospel of Abraham, saying that in us and our seed all generations after us should be blessed. (Emphasis added).

Furthermore, Joseph Smith continues to expose his ignorance regarding name translations by not just mentioning *Elias* again but also actually mentioning *Esaias* and *Isaiah* as two *different* people in the *same* reference. So here we have Smith referring to *Elias* and *Esaias* who both do not *exist* other than in the form of *Elijah* and *Isaiah* respectively. He had no idea what he was talking about regarding these names or the people they really represented.

> **D&C 76:100.** These are they who say they are some of one and some of another—some of Christ and some of John, and some of Moses, and some of *Elias*, and some of *Esaias*, and some of *Isaiah*, and some of Enoch;

As mentioned earlier, *Esaias* is the Greek form of *Isaiah*, constantly used in the *King James Version* of the New Testament *(Matt. 3:3; 4:14; 8:17; 12:17 etc.)*, but in the *Revised King James Version* and all other later translations I located, it is *always* "Isaiah". There is no doubt, no confusion, and no argument about the fact that *Elias/Elijah* is one and the same person and that *Esaias* and *Isaiah* also refer to one and the same person. The 'confusion' which led both Smiths to conclude they were *different* people stems from complete ignorance coupled with their clear and obvious *fraudulent* claims. It is not possible for anyone to *see* someone who positively never existed. The notion that I often pose, that they just made things up as they went along, is as clearly established and demonstrated here as anywhere else.

We are not quite done with Joseph F. Smith's vision. He claimed he also saw many of the prophets who lived among the Nephites, although he doesn't name them. He also saw Joseph and Hyrum Smith; his own father; Brigham Young; John Taylor; Wilford Woodruff and other "choice spirits" who were among the "noble and great ones" who were "chosen in the beginning to be rulers in the Church of God." *(D&C 138:55)*.

Eventually Smith concludes:

> **D&C 138:60.** Thus was the vision of the redemption of the dead revealed to me, and I bear record, and *I know that this record is true*, through the blessing of our Lord and Savior, Jesus Christ, even so. Amen.

So, there we have it, the solemn *testimony* of a Mormon prophet – that he *saw* the spirit of a man who never even *existed*. Now, that is quite clever. He was either deliberately lying or completely delusional – perhaps a little of both. Even the modern Mormon Church has figured out the error. Mormon Church Old Testament manuals make no mention of *Elias* or *Esaias* and the New Testament manuals explain, where they appear, that they refer to *Elijah* and *Isaiah* respectively. Unfortunately, a modern understanding doesn't help with past errors – it just confirms complete lies and delusional thinking – regarding *visions* no less.

Joseph Smith made the same error in a revelation in which he claims the *"Line of priesthood is given from Moses to Adam"* in *D&C* Section 84.

> **D&C 84:6.** And the sons of *Moses*, according to the Holy Priesthood which he received under the hand of his father-in-law, *Jethro*;
> 7. And Jethro received it under the hand of *Caleb*;

# THE SPIRIT WORLD

8. And Caleb received it under the hand of *Elihu*;
9. And Elihu under the hand of *Jeremy*;
10. And Jeremy under the hand of *Gad*;
11. And Gad under the hand of *Esaias*;
12. And Esaias received it under the hand of *God*.
13. ***Esaias also lived in the days of Abraham***, and was blessed of him—
14. Which ***Abraham*** received the priesthood from ***Melchizedek***, who received it through the lineage of his fathers, even till ***Noah***;
15. And from Noah till ***Enoch***, through the lineage of their fathers;
16. And from ***Enoch to Abel***, who was slain by the conspiracy of his brother, who received the priesthood by the commandments of God, by the hand of his father ***Adam***, who was the first man— (Emphasis added).

In order to identify the fact that Smith's vivid imagination was once again at work, rather than him receiving an important and informative revelation, these are the facts of the matter. Smith may at first glance appear to 'get away' with the idea that Adam gave the priesthood to Abel and then it was passed down to others, leaving out all the names he couldn't remember. That is, until we look closely at who he says received it and when. Then everything becomes unravelled and the hoax is once again exposed.

Smith works backwards in his 'revelation'. This is his claimed sequence in reverse, starting with Adam. Accepting gaps in the line, who were these people and when did they live?

Adam – Abel – Enoch – Noah – Melchizedek – Abraham. Then God – Esaias (who lived in days of Abraham) – Gad – Jeremy – Elihu – Caleb – Jethro – Moses.

According to the Bible Abel was indeed Adam's son and Enoch was the great-grandfather of Noah; so far – so good. Melchizedek was a contemporary of Abraham. After that, things go awry for Smith. He has *God* giving the priesthood to *Esaias* and v.13 *(above)* clearly states that Esaias lived in the *days of Abraham* who was born between 2100-1800 BCE. Unfortunately, as discussed, there was no such person as *Esaias*. It is the Greek transliteration of *Isaiah* and far from living in the time of Abraham, Isaiah lived from about 775-701 BCE. The alternative to accepting this as complete nonsense is for the Church to now claim that such a *person* as *Esaias* actually *existed* – and in part at least, they *don't*. Quite the contrary is stated in the New Testament student manual. *(See p.202)*. However, despite that admission, the Mormon *Bible Dictionary* **contradicts** this, making the *impossible* claim that "Esaias was also a prophet who lived in the days of Abraham" referring to *D&C 76:100* and to

# THE MORMON DELUSION

*D&C 84:11*. The Mormon Church contradicts *itself*. This of course is an utterly impossible claim. A Greek name could *not* appear in ancient Hebrew scripture.

Just to illustrate Joseph Smith's complete ignorance of the usage of *Esaias* in the New Testament, which *every* new version of the Bible now translates as 'Isaiah', here are two of his *Inspired Revision* passages with changed words.

> **I.R. Luke 3:4.** As it is written in the book of the ***prophet*** Esaias; ***and these are the words***, saying, The voice of one crying in the wilderness, Prepare ye the way of the Lord, ***and*** make his paths straight.

By comparison, the *KJV* reads:

> **KJV. Luke 3:4.** As it is written in the book of the **words of** Esaias **the prophet**, saying, The voice of one crying in the wilderness, Prepare ye the way of the Lord, make his paths straight.

Smith makes changes in the verse which destroy the English grammar and do not add any information or clarification. He leaves the name *Esaias* as it is. Then we have:

> **I.R. John 1:24.** He said, I am the voice of one crying in the wilderness, Make straight the way of the Lord, as **saith** the prophet Esaias.

Compare this with the *KJV* – in which it is v.23:

> **KJV. John 1:23.** He said, I am the voice of one crying in the wilderness, Make straight the way of the Lord, as **said** the prophet Esaias. (Emphasis added in the above four verses).

Smith once again leaves *Esaias* as is, but makes the grave error of altering the *KJV* word 'said' (past tense) to 'saith' (present tense). Presumably he thought it sounded more Jacobean. A true prophet may have had something to add that was worth hearing; he would certainly have known Esaias was *Isaiah*; and most certainly would *not* have altered the grammar, thus making himself look a complete idiot.

Smith's fictitious *Esaias* passes the priesthood on to *Gad*, but Gad was the seventh son of Jacob (Israel), and he lived in about 1700 BCE *(1690BCE [Setterfield] or 1710BCE [Ussher])*. Gad supposedly passed it on to *Jeremy* but there was *no* Jeremy in the Old Testament. There are just two references to a *Jeremy* and they are found in Matthew in the New Testament. Jeremy is widely viewed as a synonym for the prophet *Jeremiah* who was called to be a prophet at age twenty, in 627 BCE, over a thousand years *later* than in Smith's time-line. Nevertheless, Smith has a *Jeremy* receiving the priesthood from *Gad* and passing it on to *Elihu* who was a contemporary of Job, and exact dating is sketchy. However, he apparently then somehow passes it on to *Caleb* who was

# THE SPIRIT WORLD

a contemporary of Joshua. Unfortunately for Smith, whilst their lives *may* have overlapped, he lived *later* than the time when Jethro, and subsequently Moses, supposedly had the priesthood passed on to them. Smith is using names which do not fit dates that would be needed for his claimed line to be real. This is a date summary of his claimed line. The people and relative dates are all over the place with no semblance of reality, either in timescale or 'name' language.

> Abraham – probably born between 2100-1800 BCE. Lived 175 years.
> Esaias (Isaiah) – 775-701 BCE.
> Gad – 1700 BCE.
> Jeremy (Jeremiah) – 627 BCE.
> Elihu – a contemporary of Job – probably pre-Mosaic; even patriarchal, from the second millennium BCE. An *Elihu* also appears in 1 Samuel and 1 Chronicles which were written just a few hundred years BCE.
> Caleb – a contemporary of Joshua. 1450–1370 BCE.
> Jethro – Moses' father-in-law; a contemporary of Moses.
> Moses – 1557-1437 BCE.

No doubt the Mormon Church would claim that as Smith was a prophet, then additional people with those names must have existed at the appropriate times. Nevertheless, they do not appear where they should in the Bible.

They would still be hard pressed to explain away the *Greek* name variants which could *never* have appeared in Hebrew text. Trying to explain away one problem always leads to other problems in Mormonism.

Smith made up all sorts of details which cannot be ratified. Here are three prophets *no one* has ever heard of, before or since these verses appeared in the *Book of Mormon*.

> **1 Nephi 19:10.** And the ***God of our fathers***, who were led out of Egypt, out of bondage, and also were preserved in the wilderness by him, yea, **the God of Abraham, and of Isaac, and the God of Jacob, *yieldeth himself***, according to the words of the angel, ***as a man***, into the hands of wicked men, to be ***lifted up***, according to the words of ***Zenock***, and to be ***crucified***, according to the words of ***Neum***, and to be ***buried in a sepulchre***, according to the words of ***Zenos***, which he spake concerning the three days of darkness, which should be a sign given of his death unto those who should inhabit the isles of the sea, more especially given unto those who are of the house of Israel. (Emphasis added).

Look carefully at the above text. Before reviewing the fictional *characters*, what is it actually talking *about*? Once again, we have positive evidence of Joseph Smith's monotheistic views when he penned the *Book of Mormon*. The verse explains that it was *God*, the *God* of Abraham, Isaac and Jacob, who yielded *himself* as a *man* to be lifted up, crucified and buried. It is about as monotheistic – and clear as it can get, and *God* put that notion into Smith's hat.

Many Christian denominations believe that Christ was the God of the Old Testament. That is to say, they believe that God and Jesus are *one*, thus it was God Himself who came down as a man and was crucified. The Mormon Church also teaches that Jesus was the God of the Old Testament, but by contrast to mainstream Christianity, their God and Jesus are two separate and distinct beings, each with a body of flesh and bones. Christ was the God of the Old Testament under the direction of God his Father. They are one in purpose but *not* in person. The only thing is, when Smith *wrote* the *Book of Mormon* that was *not* his thinking, as is clearly established by *all* his original writing in the book. His *later change* in theological thinking is clearly evidenced by the four alterations that he made by adding "the son of", thus *falsifying* the original meanings, in 1 Nephi. *(See: Ch.5, p.98)*.

Then we have the three supposed prophets from the Old Testament era who prophesied about what would happen. They are fictional characters spoken of by Smith in his *Book of Mormon*, none of whom ever existed as real people.

Let's deal with 'Neum' before moving on to the others, as he only appears once in the *Book of Mormon* and never anywhere else in history. The word is Latin, taken from the Greek: Néov, Neon, and is the only coastal *town* in Bosnia and Herzegovina. In music, it is one of a series of notational symbols used before the 14th century. The Medieval Latin *neuma* refers to a group of notes sung on one breath, from the Greek *pneuma* – breath. It was used in the musical notation of the Middle Ages but is now employed solely in the notation of Gregorian chant in the liturgical books of the Roman Catholic Church. It is the name of a *place* or related to medieval *music*, and even if it ever was used as the name of a person, it could *not* have been a Hebrew prophet, as Greek, let alone *Latin*, could never have appeared in Hebrew text. It is clearly a Smith concoction.

Zenos and Zenock were equally fictitious.

> **1 Nephi 19:12.** And all these things must surely come, saith the prophet *Zenos*. And the rocks of the earth must rend; and because of the groanings of the earth, many of the kings of the isles of the sea shall be wrought upon by the Spirit of God, to exclaim: The God of nature suffers.
>
> **19:16.** Yea, then will he remember the isles of the sea; yea, and all the people who are of the house of Israel, will I gather in, saith the Lord, according to the words of the prophet *Zenos*, from the four quarters of the earth.
>
> **Alma 33:3.** Do ye remember to have read what *Zenos*, the prophet of old, has said concerning prayer or worship?

# THE SPIRIT WORLD

**33:13.** Behold, if ye do, ye must believe what *Zenos* said; for, behold he said: Thou hast turned away thy judgments because of thy Son.

**33:15.** For it is not written that *Zenos* alone spake of these things, but *Zenock* also spake of these things—

**Jacob 5:1.** Behold, my brethren, do ye not remember to have read the words of the prophet *Zenos*, which he spake unto the house of Israel, saying:

**Jacob 6:1.** And now, behold, my brethren, as I said unto you that I would prophesy, behold, this is my prophecy—that the things which this prophet *Zenos* spake, concerning the house of Israel, in the which he likened them unto a tame olive-tree, must surely come to pass.

**Helaman 15:11.** Yea, even if they should dwindle in unbelief the Lord shall prolong their days, until the time shall come which hath been spoken of by our fathers, and also by the prophet *Zenos*, and many other prophets, concerning the restoration of our brethren, the Lamanites, again to the knowledge of the truth—

**3 Nephi 10:16.** Yea, the prophet *Zenos* did testify of these things, and also *Zenock* spake concerning these things, because they testified particularly concerning us, who are the remnant of their seed.

**Alma 34:7.** My brother has called upon the words of *Zenos*, that redemption cometh through the Son of God, and also upon the words of *Zenock*; and also he has appealed unto Moses, to prove that these things are true.

**Helaman 8:19.** And now I would that ye should know, that even since the days of Abraham there have been many prophets that have testified these things; yea, behold, the prophet *Zenos* did testify boldly; for the which he was slain.

**8:20.** And behold, also *Zenock*, and also *Ezias*, and also Isaiah, and Jeremiah, (Jeremiah being that same prophet who testified of the destruction of Jerusalem) and now we know that Jerusalem was destroyed according to the words of Jeremiah. O then why not the Son of God come, according to his prophecy? (Names emphasized in all the above references).

According to the above, *Zenos*, an Old Testament prophet, predicted *(Helaman 15:11)* the restoration of the Lamanites to a knowledge of the truth – meaning Native Americans in Smith's day would accept the Mormon gospel.

# THE MORMON DELUSION

*Zenos* was 'slain' for 'testifying' *(Helaman 8:19)* and *Zenock* was 'stoned' as the 'people would not understand his words' *(See Alma 33:17)*. These men, of course, did not exist in real life and the notion of such a person as *Zenos* making a BCE statement like that, is utterly ridiculous.

Note that yet another fictional prophet turns up, by the name of *Ezias*, never heard of before or since the single casual mention. The name can refer to *Ozias*, an ancestor of Joseph, husband of Mary. However, Ozias was not a prophet; he was a king. Whilst Smith mentions the *name*, that's all he does – and it is completely pointless. Out of interest, these are *remote* possibilities regarding Ezias (Ozias). None qualify as a prophet for Smith to quote.

> Ozias means 'Yahweh is my strength'. It was the name of six Israelites mentioned in the Bible.
> **(1)** Ozias, King of Juda (809-759 B.C.), son and successor of Amazias. On the latter's death he was chosen king though he was only sixteen years of age (2 Kings 14:21, where, as in chapter 15 also, the name Azarias appears instead of Ozias, probably through a copyist's error; cf. 2 Chronicles 26:1). His long reign of fifty-two years is described as pleasing to God, though he incurs the reproach of having tolerated the "high places". This stricture is omitted by the chronicler, who, however, relates that Ozias was stricken with leprosy for having presumed to usurp the priestly function of burning incense in the Temple. Ozias is mentioned among the lineal ancestors of the Saviour (Matthew 1:8, 9).
> **(2)** Ozias, son of Uriel, and father of Saul of the branch of Caath (1 Chronicles 6:24).
> **(3)** Ozias, whose son Jonathan was custodian of the treasures possessed by King David outside of Jerusalem (1 Chronicles 27:25).
> **(4)** Ozias, son of Harim, one of the priests who having taken "strange wives", were forced to give them up during the reform of Esdras (Ezra 10:21).
> **(5)** Ozias, son of Misha, of the tribe of Simeon, a ruler of Bethulia (Judith 7:12).
> **(6)** Ozias, one of the ancestors of Judith, of the tribe of Ruben (Judith 8:1).
> The Book of Judith is a deuterocanonical book, included in the Septuagint, and in the Catholic and Eastern Orthodox Christian Old Testament of the Bible. *(See: Catholic Encyclopaedia)*.

The Mormon Church would try to excuse the use of *Elias* in some instances by claiming it a pseudonym for a messenger or forerunner, such as John the Baptist being referred to by Mormons as 'an Elias' but the argument does not stand up to scrutiny. Both Smiths, Joseph Jnr., and Joseph Fielding, claimed to *see* him as an individually named *person* with his own identity. He was **not**.

# Chapter 11

## Lesson 2

### The Plan of Salvation

### Part E

### The Resurrection, Judgment, and Immortality

When our bodies and spirits are reunited through the resurrection, we will be brought into God's presence to be judged. We will remember perfectly our righteousness and our guilt. If we have repented, we will receive mercy. We will be rewarded according to our works and our desires.

***Through the resurrection all people will become immortal—they will live forever.*** Immortality is a free gift to all people, whether they are righteous or wicked. ***Eternal life is not, however, the same as immortality.*** Eternal life is a gift of God ***given only to those who obey His gospel. It is the highest state that we can achieve.*** It comes to those who are freed from sin and suffering through the Atonement of Christ. ***It is exaltation, which means living with God forever in eternal families.*** It is to know God and Jesus Christ and to experience the life they enjoy. *(Page 53)*. (Emphasis added).

# THE MORMON DELUSION

## Resurrection and Restoration

The references provided for this aspect are: 2 Nephi 9:14–15; Jacob 6:8–9; Alma 42:13–15, 22–23

> **2 Nephi:14.** Wherefore, we shall have a perfect knowledge of all our guilt, and our uncleanness, and our nakedness; and the righteous shall have a perfect knowledge of their enjoyment, and their righteousness, being clothed with purity, yea, even with the robe of righteousness.
> **15.** And it shall come to pass that when all men shall have passed from this first death unto life, insomuch as ***they have become immortal***, they must appear before the judgment-seat of the Holy One of Israel; ***and then cometh the judgment***, and then must they be judged according to the holy judgment of God. (Emphasis added).

The above speaks only of guilt or righteousness and judgment following immortality through resurrection. It does not address *immortality* in relation to *eternal life.*

> **Jacob 6:8.** Behold, will ye reject these words? Will ye reject the words of the prophets; and will ye reject all the words which have been spoken concerning Christ, after so many have spoken concerning him; and deny the good word of Christ, and the power of God, and the gift of the Holy Ghost, and quench the Holy Spirit, and make a mock of the great plan of redemption, which hath been laid for you?
> **9.** Know ye not that if ye will do these things, that ***the power of the redemption and the resurrection, which is in Christ, will bring you to stand with shame and awful guilt*** before the bar of God? (Emphasis added).

Again, this is just another threat, with no further material information for investigators to consider.

> **Alma 42:13** Therefore, *according to justice*, the ***plan of redemption*** could not be brought about, only ***on conditions of repentance*** of men in this probationary state, yea, this preparatory state; for except it were for these conditions, ***mercy could not take effect except it should destroy the work of justice.*** Now the work of justice could not be destroyed; if so, God would cease to be God.
> **14.** And thus we see that ***all mankind were fallen***, and they were ***in the grasp of justice***; yea, the justice of God, which consigned them forever to be cut off from his presence.
> **15.** And now, the ***plan of mercy*** could not be brought about except ***an atonement*** should be made; ***therefore God himself atoneth for the sins***

# THE RESURRECTION, JUDGMENT, AND IMMORTALITY

*of the world*, to bring about the plan of mercy, to *appease the demands of justice*, that God might be a perfect, just God, and a merciful God also.

**22.** But there is *a law given, and a punishment affixed*, and a *repentance granted*; which repentance, *mercy claimeth*; otherwise, justice claimeth the creature and executeth the law, and the law inflicteth the punishment; if not so, the works of justice would be destroyed, and God would cease to be God.

**23.** But God ceaseth not to be God, and *mercy claimeth the penitent*, and mercy cometh *because of the atonement*; and the atonement bringeth to pass the resurrection of the dead; and *the resurrection of the dead bringeth back men into the presence of God*; and thus they are restored into his presence, to be judged according to their works, according to the law and justice. (Emphasis added).

These verses deal with 'justice' and with 'mercy', the atonement allowing for repentance to become effective and thus facilitate the resurrection of all humankind. Note in v.15, further confirmation of Joseph Smith's monotheistic thinking when the *Book of Mormon* was written. It states "therefore God himself atoneth for the sins of the world". Had the book been written later, once Smith's theology had evolved, this would undoubtedly have read that God would send Jesus Christ do to that. Smith added the words "the son of" to four similar passages *(see Ch.5, p.98)* long after the *Book of Mormon* was first published. Obviously this was one of quite a number that he missed. When the *Book of Mormon* was written, Smith still believed that Jesus *was* God manifest in the flesh; hence such a specific, and now theologically damning, statement still appearing in it.

## Judgment

All references stem from the *Book of Mormon* or the *D&C*, with the notable exception of one which confirms that Jesus has been given the responsibility for judgment.

**John 5:22.** For the Father judgeth no man, but hath committed all judgment unto the Son:

Surprisingly, one of the other references, although from the *Book of Mormon*, speaks of things which the Church does *not* literally believe in. It would no doubt now be explained away as 'metaphorical'. However, when

# THE MORMON DELUSION

Smith wrote it, he still believed in such things or it would never have appeared there in the first place.

> **2 Nephi 28:23.** Yea, they are grasped with ***death, and hell***; and ***death, and hell***, and the devil, and all that have been seized therewith must stand before the throne of God, and be judged according to their works, from whence ***they must go into the place prepared for them, even a lake of fire and brimstone, which is endless torment.*** (Emphasis added).

I am not quite sure why the words "death, and hell; and death, and hell" appear that way, but it is *not* an error. It appears that way in the original 1830 manuscript. The 'lake of fire and brimstone' is determined as a *place* prepared to endure 'endless torment'. The Church does not actually believe in such a place. It is now considered to be a 'condition' of *mental* torment. One problem regarding this in Mormon theology is that 'outer darkness', which is the *only* place *lower* than the Telestial kingdom, is reserved for the very few who 'deny the Holy Ghost', so *all* the really wicked people mentioned in such references will actually end up in the Mormon *Telestial* kingdom, which Joseph Smith once described as being a far nicer place than Earth. So, where *do* all these really evil people go, if the *Book of Mormon* "Lake of fire and brimstone, which is endless torment" is after all a non-existent place? The question is, if there is no such *place*, why then did the Mormon God dictate those words into Smith's hat, effectively lying, first to the Nephites, and then to Smith about it?

Other references identify the concept that people cannot stand before God and expect to be saved by their own works alone and the Saviour is credited with that. Everyone will have to stand in "the tribunal of God with your souls filled with guilt and remorse, having a remembrance of all your guilt…" *(Alma 5:15-21)*. It is the usual, and fast becoming tiresome, play on the idea that no matter how much we may think we have been good, that is not possible and we are positively guilty of things which prevent us from ever standing blameless before God. We will be filled with guilt and remorse. Other references speak more about damnation, condemnation and endless torment for bad people who will *never* be forgiven. People will want "rocks and the mountains to fall upon us to hide us from his presence" *(Alma 12:12-14)*. The constant message is that we are going to be judged and no matter what we have done it will *never* be good enough. Why would a loving God place his 'children' in such an invidious position where they have no clue what awaits them, or even why?

## Kingdoms of Glory

During our mortal lives we make choices regarding good and evil. God rewards us according to our works and desires. Because God rewards

# THE RESURRECTION, JUDGMENT, AND IMMORTALITY

> everyone according to deeds done in the body, *there are different kingdoms of glory* to which we may be assigned after the Judgment. *Those who have repented of their sins and received the ordinances of the gospel and kept the associated covenants* will be cleansed by the Atonement of Christ. They *will receive exaltation in the highest kingdom*, also known as the *celestial kingdom*. They will *live in God's presence, become like Him,* and receive a fulness of joy. They will live together for eternity with those of their family who qualify. In the scriptures this kingdom is compared to the glory or brightness of the sun.
>
> *People who do not accept the fulness of the gospel* of Jesus Christ but live honourable lives *will receive a place in the terrestrial kingdom*. This kingdom is compared to the glory of the moon.
>
> *Those who continued in their sins and did not repent* in this life will receive their reward in the *lowest kingdom, which is called the telestial kingdom*. This kingdom is compared to the glory of the stars. *(Page 53)*. (Emphasis added).

No one except Mormons, and even then only as long as they 'endure to the end', will receive 'exaltation' in the Celestial kingdom. Good people who, given the chance, did not accept the gospel, will go to the Terrestrial kingdom and the rest will go to the Telestial kingdom. *(The manual uses lower case for these names, but I am in the habit of capitalising them, denoting names of supposed places)*. Supporting references in the manual for these notions come from the Bible, the *Book of Mormon* and the *D&C*. As mentioned elsewhere, 'Telestial' is not a real word at all; Smith just made it up.

---

"The Book of Mormon contains the fulness of the gospel of Jesus Christ."

The Mormon Church teaches that heaven consists of three kingdoms;
Celestial; Terrestrial; and Telestial.
The highest *degree* in the Celestial kingdom is 'Exaltation'.

The *Book of Mormon* makes **no** mention of **any** such places,
but it is *replete* with references to **heaven** and **hell**.
In fact, it states (2 Nephi 12:11&17) that "the Lord **alone** shall be exalted."

---

None of the three kingdoms appear in the *Book of Mormon* because Smith made up his 'three degrees of glory' idea in 1832 with the help of Sidney Rigdon and he wrote the *Book of Mormon* in 1828-9. It is therefore not surprising that these three degrees are *not* mentioned in the *Book of Mormon*. They are not mentioned in the Old Testament either, because they are not *real*.

If the Church tries to claim that *Celestial* and *Terrestrial* could not appear in the *Book of Mormon* as those words were not invented until centuries later *(see p.173)* then ask them to explain why 'Jesus' and 'Christ' *do* appear, as those terms were also CE inventions not known in *BOM* times. *(See p.337-9).*

References to *celestial* and *terrestrial* bodies in the New Testament are in an entirely different context, yet Smith plays on the appearance of the words and in his own *Inspired Revision* he adds in the fictitious word – 'Telestial'.

The Mormon Church may 'excuse' the missing concepts from the Bible as they claim many precious truths had been removed from it. However, Nephite prophets had the ear of God and their writings remain undefiled. Jesus visited them and they wrote down what he said; although uncannily, much was word for word the same as the New Testament, which is impossible for any number of reasons as discussed elsewhere. Smith had God Himself translate the *Book of Mormon* a word at a time into his hat, so there is no excuse for either *error* or *missing* doctrine. If the Nephites were a real people, we can only assume that God did not care enough to reveal the 'fullness of the gospel' to them as claimed after all, leaving them in complete ignorance of the various available kingdoms and the one they should strive for; they had *heaven* and *hell* instead.

> **IR. 1 Cor 15:40.** Also celestial bodies, and bodies terrestrial, and bodies telestial; but the glory of the celestial, one; and the terrestrial, another; and the telestial, another.

The above is Smith's *expansion* of the *KJV* which was originally:

> **KJV. 1 Cor. 15:40.** There are also celestial bodies, and bodies terrestrial: but the glory of the celestial is one, and the glory of the terrestrial *is* another.

As it happens, most versions of the Bible don't use 'celestial' or 'terrestrial' in the translation of this verse, although the words do appear in other parts of other versions of the New Testament which were *not* translated that way in the *KJV*. This is a typical alternate translation:

> **Holman. 1 Cor. 15:40.** There are **heavenly** bodies and **earthly** bodies, but the splendour of the **heavenly** bodies is different from that of the **earthly** ones.

Use of the words 'celestial' and 'terrestrial' in the *KJV* determine exactly that same interpretation, *heavenly* and *earthly*. They are not *places*. *2 Peter 2:11* and *Jude 1:8* both speak of *celestial*, meaning heavenly, *beings* in some other translations of the Bible but the *KJV* just calls them *angels* in *2 Peter* and *dignities* in *Jude. Young's Literal Translation* says *messengers* in *2 Peter 2:11*.

# THE RESURRECTION, JUDGMENT, AND IMMORTALITY

Just to give an idea of how differently the same things can translate, just compare a few versions of *Jude 1:8*.

**KJV.** Likewise also these filthy dreamers defile the flesh, despise dominion, and speak evil of ***dignities.***

**Holman.** Nevertheless, these dreamers likewise defile their flesh, despise authority, and blaspheme ***glorious beings.***

**New International. (UK).** In the very same way, those dreamers pollute their own bodies. They don't accept authority. They speak evil things against ***heavenly beings.***

**New International.** In the very same way, these dreamers pollute their own bodies, reject authority and slander ***celestial beings.***

New American Standard. Yet in the same way these men, also by dreaming, defile the flesh, and reject authority, and revile ***angelic majesties.***

**New Living Translation.** In the same way, these people—who claim authority from their dreams—live immoral lives, defy authority, and scoff at ***supernatural beings***.

Thus we see a translation which appears as *dignities* in the *KJV*, elsewhere becomes *glorious beings, heavenly beings, celestial beings, angelic majesties* and even *supernatural beings*. It makes very little difference of course but then Joseph Smith took the words *celestial* and *terrestrial* in the *KJV* of *1 Corinthians* and *created places* in the hereafter out of them. Just as in *Jude 1:8*, other translations give entirely different wording and therefore *concepts* to the ones that Smith created entirely in his own head.

If Smith had access to such translations as are available these days, the question is, would he have perhaps made a better job of covering his back or would he have come up with even more bizarre ideas?

The next two verses are also separately suggested, to show that there are different 'degrees' of glory in the hereafter. Unfortunately, again everything is not as it seems. The Mormon Church, via Joseph Smith, takes some completely unwarranted liberties here.

**KJV. 1 Cor, 15:41.** There is one glory of the sun, and another glory of the moon, and another glory of the stars: for *one* star differeth from another star in glory.
**42.** So also is the resurrection of the dead. It is sown in corruption; it is raised in incorruption:

Once again, this is used to support Smith's 'three degrees of glory' which includes his fictional 'Telestial' kingdom, plucked out of thin air. The passage is *not* attempting to define different *kingdoms*. Paul is simply saying that the sun and the moon are different kinds of glory, adding that even the stars differ. Likewise with us, we are a lower glory when we die. It is an *analogy* showing we will be raised up to a higher glory through the resurrection and live forever.

As an example of another translation, the *New Living Translation* helps to give a much clearer picture of intended meaning. Smith took these scriptures and he simply *abused* them.

> **NLT. 1 Cor. 15:41.** The sun has one kind of glory, while the moon and stars each have another kind. And even the stars differ from each other in their glory.
> **42.** It is the same way with the resurrection of the dead. Our earthly bodies are planted in the ground when we die, but they will be raised to live forever.

I think that is just about as clear as it could be. Joseph Smith completely misunderstood it, or in any event he completely misused it, creating something out of nothing. Another reference is from *3 Nephi*. It doesn't add anything of significance regarding kingdoms; not that anything could from the *Book of Mormon*. The idea of sitting down in the Father's *kingdom* is entirely singular and there is no mention of any other kingdoms, there or anywhere else in the book. However, once again, Smith's monotheism gets inadvertently included. The *Book of Mormon* is replete with it and here we have confirmation once again that 'God' and 'Jesus' *are* one and the same being.

> **3 Nephi 28:10.** And for this cause ye shall have fulness of joy; and ye shall sit down in the kingdom of my Father; yea, your joy shall be full, even as the Father hath given me fulness of joy; and ye shall be even as I am, and I am even as the Father; and the Father and I are one;

As ever, the Mormon Church would invariably claim that this means one in purpose. However, the postulation wears thin after a while. The entire *Book of Mormon* was monotheistic when first published – and almost all of it still is.

*D&C 137* is referenced. It talks of a vision of the Celestial kingdom (1836) and we learn that people, who would have received the gospel given the opportunity, will end up there, as will young children who die before the age of eight, or accountability. Missionaries may use it to appease investigators who have lost children or who question what happens to young children who die.

The references for this section include the introduction to *D&C 76* as well as the section itself. The introduction includes this statement: *"It was after the Prophet had **translated** John 5:29 that this vision was given"*. As the reference

# THE RESURRECTION, JUDGMENT, AND IMMORTALITY

is to Smith's *Inspired Revision* of John, here is *John 5:29* from the *KJV*, followed by Smith's *Inspired Revision*, or, as the manual puts it, 'translation'.

**KJV. John 5:29.** And shall come forth; they **that** have done good, **unto** the resurrection of **life**; and they **that** have done evil, **unto** the resurrection of **damnation.** (Emphasis added).

**IR. John 5:29.** And shall come forth; they **who** have done good, **in** the resurrection of **the just**; and they **who** have done evil, **in** the resurrection of **the unjust.** (Emphasis added).

Smith's alterations to the text are absolutely meaningless, other than the fact that they then become grammatically incorrect for early modern or even modern English, whereas things were fine just as they were. Also bear in mind that John is an unhistorical document, unrelated to the apostle, created by the Romans to typify the way they would have liked the Christ to have been, rather than it remotely being a true or accurate account of an actual person. Then Smith's mind-games start to become even more apparent. If Smith had been a true prophet, he would have known that if Christ existed, nothing he said could have been remotely close to New Testament claims, as the books were written decades to centuries later by people who did not know or meet the man Jesus. They just give an *idea* of things. They cannot possibly be, word for word, the things *spoken* by Jesus. Yet *exact* wording from the Old and New Testament often appears in the *Book of Mormon* – including translation errors. Likewise, words attributed to John were not word for word things the apostle actually said. The "Gospel according to John" was 'according' to anyone *but* John.

*Section 76* covers a lot of ground and I will let the reader look that up to save space here. I will just mention the fact there are several impossibilities included, most of which are unrelated to any kingdoms of glory. For example, v.26 mentions the fictional Christian CE character of Lucifer. The Mormon Church appears to play along with the error as he appears as a real character in the temple endowment. *(See: TMD Vol.2, Ch.16 for more on Smith's 'Lucifer' mistake).*

Lucifer is also termed 'Perdition' and we learn that 'Sons of Perdition' are those who deny the Holy Spirit after having received it. For them, there is no forgiveness. The revelation is dated 1832 and the 'fire and brimstone' idea is still clearly in evidence.

**Sec 76:36.** These are they who shall go away into the *lake of fire and brimstone*, with the devil and his angels—

**37.** And the only ones on whom the *second death* shall have any power; (Emphasis added).

# THE MORMON DELUSION

Despite the fact that *Section 76* is fully referenced, the *first* and *second death* doctrine is not even mentioned in the missionary manual. This doctrine does not concern physical death. These are 'spiritual' deaths which mean separation from God rather than a spirit actually dying. Spirits cannot die. The first spiritual death has affected everyone on Earth since the fall of Adam when he, and thus humankind, became separated from the presence of God while here. The second spiritual death occurs following the resurrection, but only for those who deliberately followed Satan, having rejected Jesus after receiving a witness from the Holy Ghost. They become eternally damned and sent to 'outer darkness', never again to enter the presence of God. This condition, or second separation from God, is termed the 'second death'. *(See: EM. 833).*

Whilst I have always been aware of this – I am sure I was taught it as an investigator in 1960 – it had never occurred to me as a member that in fact the same is somewhat true in Mormon theology regarding those in the Terrestrial and Telestial kingdoms. God will reign and mix with people in the Celestial kingdom. Christ will visit and take care of the Terrestrial and only the Holy Ghost will visit the Telestial. This is all also explained in *Section 76*. In effect, that means anyone *not* in the *Celestial* kingdom, also suffers a second death of sorts as they also will never *see* God again. It is funny how we don't consider or think such things as faithful Mormons. We just accept what we are told without question. We feel no need to understand everything in order for it to be true.

Much of *Section 76* deals with who will go to each of Smith's fictional kingdoms and then for some reason he decides to put his foot in his mouth – ***twice.*** First:

> **Sec 76:98.** And the glory of the telestial is one, even as the glory of the stars is one; for as one star differs from another star in glory, even so differs one from another in glory in the telestial world;
>
> **99.** For these are they who are of **Paul**, and of **Apollos**, and of **Cephas.** (Emphasis added).

Smith mentions Paul, Apollos and Cephas. Fair enough, he had clearly been reading *1 Corinthians* to get that idea and just inserted it. Not that they relate in any way to the three glories – but Smith seems to like the concept.

> **1 Cor. 3:22.** Whether Paul, or Apollos, or Cephas, or the world, or life, or death...

But then, in *D&C 76:100*, Smith goes on to list other names, including *Elias* and *Esaias*, neither of whom were real people. We discussed this verse

# THE RESURRECTION, JUDGMENT, AND IMMORTALITY

earlier. *(See: p.201-2)*. Smith's double mistake here is to include the names of two characters that never even existed.

## Eternal Life

There are seven references relating to this concept; one from the *Book of Mormon*, two biblical and four from the *D&C*. The Mormon Church teaches that *immortality* is a gift to all, irrespective of attitude, alliance or behaviour in mortality. On the other hand, *eternal life* equates to *exaltation*. Exalted Mormons inhabit the same place as God and enjoy his company forever. This differs from the traditional Christian concept that immortality and eternal life are one and the same thing. Belief in Jesus and trying to be good and to do good, enduring to the end, is enough to earn it.

We will deal with the Bible references first as they are the only ones that are not self-serving.

> **John 3:16.** For God so loved the world, that he gave his only begotten Son, that ***whosoever believeth in him should not perish, but have everlasting life.*** (Emphasis added).

This very familiar reference confirms that *belief* in and acceptance of Jesus can provide *any* person with *everlasting* life. At this stage, the lesson manual has yet to reference *eternal life* as a separate and distinct concept to that of *immortality,* from *scripture*. So, what additional information does the other Bible reference provide?

> **John 17:3.** And this is life eternal, that they might know thee the only true God, and Jesus Christ, whom thou hast sent.

Verse 3 really needs to be read in conjunction with the preceding verses which are not referenced in the lesson manual:

> **John 17:1.** These words spake Jesus, and lifted up his eyes to heaven, and said, Father, the hour is come; glorify thy Son, that thy Son also may glorify thee:
> **2.** As thou hast given him power over all flesh, that ***he should give eternal life to as many as thou hast given him.***
> **3.** And ***this is life eternal, that they might know thee the only true God, and Jesus Christ, whom thou hast sent.*** (Emphasis added).

In mainstream Christianity, this reinforces *John 3:16*. In these verses, "life eternal" *(v.2)* and "eternal life" *(v.3)* are the *same* thing. *Eternal life* is given to "as many as thou hast given him". In context, v.3 explains knowing God and Jesus (accepting and believing) is enough to gain *eternal life*. John already explained that in 3:16. So, we are no further along with the Mormon concept that *eternal life* is a state reserved for worthy Mormons who will dwell with God. In the Bible, *eternal life* is for everyone who *accepts* Christ. Mormonism equates that to *immortality*. Eternal life has to be *earned*. However, that concept is not clear in early Mormon revelations, even the ones now provided in support of the claim. The first of the four *D&C* references provided is from the year 1829.

> **D&C 14:7.** And, if you ***keep my commandments and endure to the end you shall have eternal life,*** which gift is the greatest of all the gifts of God. (Emphasis added).

This is the same concept as seen in the Bible; believe and be good and you will gain the gift of *eternal life*. There is no mention of it having to be 'earned' nor of immortality being a *lesser* state. The next reference provided is from the following year, in 1830.

> **D&C 29:43.** And thus did I, the Lord God, appoint unto man the days of his probation —that by his natural death ***he might be raised in immortality unto eternal life, even as many as would believe;***
> **44.** And ***they that believe not unto eternal damnation***; for they cannot be redeemed from their spiritual fall, because they repent not; (Emphasis added).

This Mormon reference does no more than again confirm the traditional Christian belief that everyone who repents, believes and accepts Christ, will gain immortality – which here *is* eternal life. "…raised in immortality unto eternal life…" Here, those who do *not* believe will suffer "eternal damnation".

From 1831 we have the following.

> **D&C 45:8.** I came unto mine own, and mine own received me not; but unto as many as received me gave I power to do many miracles, and to become the sons of God; and even ***unto them that believed on my name gave I power to obtain eternal life.*** (Emphasis added).

Once again, the concept is that those who *believe* have the *power* to obtain eternal life. The fact is that Mormons already *know* what *immortality* and *eternal life* mean to them due to *modern* teachings and therefore *assume* what such passages actually mean by reading into them what they have been *taught* is the case. However, in context of when they were *written*, we must consider *only* what they explicitly *say*. Two years later, from 1833, we have the final *D&C* reference. It doesn't add much of anything new.

# THE RESURRECTION, JUDGMENT, AND IMMORTALITY

**D&C 93:19.** I give unto you these sayings that you may understand and know how to worship, and know what you worship, that you may come unto the Father in my name, and in due time receive of his fulness.

The *Book of Mormon* reference used to substantiate this doctrine is 2 Nephi 31:17-21.

> **2 Nephi 31:17.** Wherefore, do the things which I have told you I have seen that your **Lord and your Redeemer** should do; for, for this cause have they been shown unto me, that ye might know the gate by which ye should enter. For the gate by which ye should enter is *repentance and baptism by water; and then cometh a remission of your sins by fire and by the Holy Ghost.*
> **18.** And then are ye in this *strait and narrow path which leads to eternal life*; yea, ye have entered in by the gate; ye have done according to the commandments of the Father and the Son; and ye have received the **Holy Ghost**, which witnesses of the Father and the Son, unto the fulfilling of the promise which he hath made, that if ye entered in by the way ye should receive.
> **19.** And now, my beloved brethren, *after ye have gotten into this strait and narrow path, I would ask if all is done? Behold, I say unto you, Nay; for ye have not come thus far save it were by the word of Christ with unshaken faith in him, relying wholly upon the merits of him* who is mighty to save.
> **20.** Wherefore, ye must *press forward with a steadfastness in Christ*, having a perfect brightness of hope, and a love of God and of all men. Wherefore, if ye shall press forward, *feasting upon the word of Christ*, and *endure to the end*, behold, thus saith the Father: *Ye shall have eternal life.*
> **21.** And now, behold, my beloved brethren, this is the way; and *there is none other way nor name given under heaven whereby man can be saved in the kingdom of God.* And now, behold, this is the doctrine of Christ, and the only and true doctrine of the *Father, and of the Son, and of the Holy Ghost, which is one God, without end.* Amen. (Emphasis added).

Mormons will consider this to be evidence of Smith *differentiating* between *immortality* and *eternal life*. However, it really is *not*. Read it again, very carefully. It establishes once again, in line with contemporary revelations, written between 1829 and 1833, that people must *believe* on Christ, follow the commandments and endure to the end in order to receive *eternal life*. There is no mention of a *difference* between *immortality* and *eternal life* within the reference. Indeed, immortality is not mentioned at all, as it is understood to be the same thing as eternal life. If not, Smith would have had to include an explicit reference to it in order to clarify a departure from traditional Christian thinking. He did not. It is therefore no more than yet another repeat of Bible references which are *not* selected to share with investigators, such as these from Matthew and Mark.

> **Matt. 24:13.** But he that shall endure unto the end, the same shall be saved.

> **Mark 13:13.** And ye shall be hated of all *men* for my name's sake: but he that shall endure unto the end, the same shall be saved.

It should of course be remembered that *2 Nephi* was supposedly written between 559-545 BCE. Firstly, *Christ*, as well as the *Holy Ghost*, is mentioned in an anachronistic timeframe. The names and concepts, as discussed elsewhere were entirely *unknown*. Secondly, the idea that people should be steadfast in Christ, "feasting upon the word of Christ" hundreds of years before he is recorded as being born, let alone actually *saying* anything, is preposterous.

Then we have Smith's ever classic error where he once again confirms the Father, Son and Holy Ghost are *one God* in his established monotheistic state of mind at the time he wrote it (1828-9). The Church will now claim Smith meant 'enduring to the end' would bring 'eternal life', which is a different Mormon concept to that of immortality. However, when you read the above verses through in context, they are no different than the earlier teachings referenced from the Bible. That is, other than the fact the biblical references were written in the correct time and place whereas the *Book of Mormon* quote is from an entirely *impossible* time and place.

In the *Book of Mormon* 'immortality' and 'eternal life' are *synonymous*. There are almost a dozen references to immortality and close to thirty mentions of eternal life. Only four appear in the same chapter and *none* in the same verse, explaining that they are *separate* concepts as is the modern Mormon belief. Each appearance of either can be taken to mean the *same* thing but nowhere can they be identified as having entirely *different* meanings, unless you are already familiar with the *modern* Mormon concept, when that prior knowledge allows you to subconsciously determine what you *think* is meant. The irony is that originally to Smith it **was** one and the same thing. Such is the depth and the power of delusional thinking, Mormons don't even *think* about it.

> "The Book of Mormon contains the fulness of the gospel of Jesus Christ."
>
> The Mormon Church teaches *immortality* is a gift to everyone.
> *Eternal life* is different and that must be earned.

# THE RESURRECTION, JUDGMENT, AND IMMORTALITY

> The *Book of Mormon* teaches in Alma 1:4 "***all mankind*** should be saved at the last day, and that they need not fear nor tremble, but that they might lift up their heads and rejoice; for the Lord had created all men, and had also redeemed all men; and, ***in the end, all men should have eternal life***."
> (Emphasis added).

The definitive concept that Smith had in 1828-9 is encapsulated in that *Book of Mormon* reference. It doesn't get much clearer than that. "In the end, ***all men*** should have ***eternal life***." Today, in Mormonism 'all men' most certainly do not qualify for 'eternal life'; far from it. The Mormon notion of there being a theological difference between *immortality* and *eternal life* was yet to surface; therefore, it did *not* get explained in the *Book of Mormon*. The fictional Nephites could not possibly believe in something that Smith had yet to dream up. To them it was one and the same thing – assuming, once again, that you accept they were real.

Following an explanation of the 'Plan of Salvation', investigators are committed to a potential baptismal date.

> The invitation to be baptized and confirmed should be specific and direct: "Will you follow the example of Jesus Christ by being baptized by someone holding the priesthood authority of God? We will be holding a baptismal service on [date]. Will you prepare yourself to be baptized on that date?" *(Page 54).*

# THE MORMON DELUSION

# Chapter 12

## Lesson 3

### The Gospel of Jesus Christ

### Through Christ We Can Be Cleansed From Sin

As with *Lesson 2*, this one starts with a list of questions for missionaries to ask their investigators and a note of the commitments which they should be willing to make by the end of it.

> Do you believe that God is our Eternal Father?
> Do you believe that Jesus Christ is the Son of God, the Savior and Redeemer of the world?
> Do you believe the Church and the gospel of Jesus Christ have been restored through the Prophet Joseph Smith?

**Commitments**

> Will you continue to develop faith in Jesus Christ by continuing to learn about His gospel?
> Will you repent and pray for forgiveness of sins?
> Will you be baptized a member of The Church of Jesus Christ of Latter-day Saints on (date)?
> Will you be confirmed and receive the gift of the Holy Ghost?
> Will you attend church with us this Sunday?
> May we set a time for our next visit?
> Commandments from lesson 4 that you choose to include. *(Page 60).*

These questions are similar to earlier ones. Commandments from *Lesson 4* may be included if the missionaries wish to mention them. Investigators must agree once again to continue to 'repent and pray for forgiveness of sins', some of which will have been news to them.

> God sent His Beloved Son, Jesus Christ, into the world so that all of God's children would have the possibility of returning to live in His presence after they die. Only through the Savior's grace and mercy can we become clean from sin so that we can live in our Heavenly Father's presence. Becoming clean from sin is being healed spiritually (see 3 Nephi 9:13; 18:32). *(Page 60).*

So far – so good. The above is fairly consistent with most Christian religion in general. But then, one of the above questions is "Do you believe the Church and the gospel of Jesus Christ have been restored through the prophet Joseph Smith". Following on from lessons concerning an apostasy and restoration, Joseph Smith's vision and the translation of the *Book of Mormon*, investigators who accept these things as true are ready to be instructed in other aspects, many of which will at first seem familiar Christian concepts.

However, the Mormon angle on them is of course carefully constructed to guide investigators to the Mormon Church. The manual continues to explain that because of Christ's atonement and resurrection, all people will be brought back into the Lord's presence to be judged 'according to their works and desires'. References supporting this notion are all from the *Book of Mormon* and the *D&C* and thus they are all self-serving. In addition, some *Book of Mormon* references are more than quite harsh. In concert with much of the *Old Testament*, the Mormon God is always angry, unlike the more loving character depicted in *the New Testament*.

> Because of Christ's Atonement and Resurrection, all people will be brought back into the presence of the Lord to be judged according to their works and their desires (see 2 Nephi 9:10–16; Helaman 14:15–18;

# THE GOSPEL OF JESUS CHRIST

3 Nephi 27:14–22; D&C 137:9). We will be judged according to the laws of justice and mercy. *(Page 60).*

The following is just one of the above references. They are all much the same, except this one has quite detailed descriptions of what will happen to us if we do *not* obey God's will, as it is represented by Mormon missionaries.

> **2 Nephi 9:10.** O how great the goodness of our God, who prepareth a way for our escape from the grasp of ***this awful monster; yea, that monster, death and hell, which I call the death of the body, and also the death of the spirit.***
> **11.** And because of the way of ***deliverance of our God, the Holy One of Israel***, this death, of which I have spoken, which is the temporal, shall deliver up its dead; which death is the grave.
> **12.** And ***this death of which I have spoken, which is the spiritual death***, shall deliver up its dead; which ***spiritual death is hell***; wherefore, death and hell must deliver up their dead, and hell must deliver up its captive spirits, and the grave must deliver up its captive bodies, and the bodies and the spirits of men will be restored one to the other; and it is by ***the power of the resurrection of the Holy One of Israel.***
> **13.** O how great the plan of our God! For on the other hand, ***the paradise of God must deliver up the spirits of the righteous, and the grave deliver up the body of the righteous; and the spirit and the body is restored to itself again***, and all men become incorruptible, and immortal, and they are living souls, having a perfect knowledge like unto us in the flesh, save it be that our knowledge shall be perfect.
> **14.** Wherefore, ***we shall have a perfect knowledge of all our guilt, and our uncleanness, and our nakedness***; and ***the righteous shall have a perfect knowledge of their enjoyment, and their righteousness***, being clothed with purity, yea, even with the robe of righteousness.
> **15.** And it shall come to pass that when all men shall have passed from this first death unto life, insomuch as they have become immortal, they must appear before the ***judgment-seat of the Holy One of Israel***; and then cometh the judgment, and then must they be ***judged according to the holy judgment of God.***
> **16.** And assuredly, as the Lord liveth, for the Lord God hath spoken it, and it is his eternal word, which cannot pass away, that ***they who are righteous shall be righteous still,*** and ***they who are filthy shall be filthy still; wherefore, they who are filthy are the devil and his angels; and they shall go away into everlasting fire, prepared for them; and their torment is as a lake of fire and brimstone, whose flame ascendeth up forever and ever and has no end.*** (Emphasis added).

# THE MORMON DELUSION

Note that once again *God is* the Holy one of Israel *(v.11)*, which is compatible with several references from Isaiah, such as Isaiah 30:15, "For thus saith the Lord God, the Holy One of Israel…" but, it is *He* who is to deliver people "by the power of the resurrection of the Holy One of Israel" *(v.12)*. Smith's monotheism of the day shines through very regularly in his *Book of Mormon*, yet members today seldom pay any attention to such things due to conditioning of their minds to believe and think otherwise. What faithful members *read* is not what they actually *see*. The mind filters and sifts and mentally restructures what is read until it comfortably fits with their perception of what the Church *now* teaches. Thus *Book of Mormon* words are mentally adapted to suit a rank and file member's own preconceptions. Once again, it is evidence of just what a delusional mind can achieve.

Smith has v.14 declare "*we* shall have a perfect knowledge of all our guilt, and our uncleanness, and our nakedness…" and that "the righteous shall have a perfect knowledge of their enjoyment, and their righteousness…" If *'we'* will have all the guilt, who then are these righteous people spoken about? Members want to believe it is they who are 'the righteous'. Most certainly try to be, but Smith's writings constantly belittle everyday people, including his own Church members, and no one will *ever* be good 'enough'.

Everyone is going to "appear before the judgment-seat of the Holy One of Israel; and then cometh the judgment, and then must they be judged according to the holy judgment of God". We learned, in the previous chapter, from the Bible *(John 5:22)* that God is leaving all the judgment to Jesus, and here, *Jesus* is the 'Holy one of Israel', just as God is earlier. Once again, they are one and the *same* being. We also have the 'fire and brimstone' idea once again and people *will* "go away into everlasting fire, prepared for them" but, this time the situation "is *as* a lake", rather than being actual, so perhaps Smith is starting to mellow. Who knows?

The manual explains justice is the law that brings consequences for actions, blessings for obedience and penalties for disobedience. The references that are provided are once again all Mormon based. We *all* commit sin which makes us unclean – and no unclean thing can enter God's presence. As long as we repent and keep the Mormon commandments, the Saviour's sacrifice will satisfy the demands of justice. This act is the 'atonement'.

> However, Jesus did not eliminate our personal responsibility. He forgives our sins when we accept Him, repent, and obey His commandments. Through the Atonement and living the gospel we become worthy to enter the presence of our Heavenly Father permanently. We must show that we accept Christ and that we have faith in Him by keeping His commandments and obeying the first principles and ordinances of the gospel. *(Page 61)*.

# THE GOSPEL OF JESUS CHRIST

The rest of the lesson explains Mormon 'first principles'; faith, repentance, baptism and the gift of the Holy Ghost. After that, just 'endure to the end' and all will be well. It is that simple – or that difficult, depending on the way you look at it. We will look at how the manual addresses each of those five aspects, but first, let's deal with God sending His son and preparing the way for us to be *able* to utilise them.

## God Sent His Son

The concept that God sent His son is captured in a familiar Bible reference:

> **John 3:16.** For God so loved the world, that he gave his only begotten Son, that **whosoever believeth in him should not perish, but have everlasting life.**
> **17.** For God sent not his Son into the world to condemn the world; but **that the world through him might be saved.** (Emphasis added). *(Manual page 61).*

Mormon theology regarding 'everlasting life' is determined as more or less synonymous with *immortality* and not indicative of the concept of 'eternal life' which is much more.

As the words in John are not as specific as 'eternal life' perhaps we should refer to the alternative reference provided which is directly from the *Book of Mormon*. Here we find conclusive evidence that Smith, or, if you prefer, his Nephites, *erroneously*, considered *believing* in Jesus would bring 'eternal life' and in modern Mormon terms that means living with God in an *exalted* state. At the time of writing the *Book of Mormon*, Smith had yet to fully develop this area of his theology – and many others besides.

It is one thing to claim the gospel was *gradually* revealed to Smith, but quite another to excuse major theological errors in the *Book of Mormon* due to that fact. If it was *Smith* learning, why did the Nephites get things so wrong?

The idea that the Nephites didn't know many things because Smith had not yet had them revealed to *him* is of course not remotely feasible from the Mormon Church perspective and doesn't work for them at all. But what other reason could there be for Nephites having completely incorrect ideas according to some of Smith's *later* theology about such things? The alternative – that they were just a figment of Smith's imagination is of course obvious, from an abundance of such evidence – but as you would expect, that is an unacceptable explanation for the Church.

Smith's evolving theological mindset is reflected in the *Book of Mormon* over and over again. Clearly, if God was revealing what the supposed Nephite race believed, many things should be in the *Book of Mormon* which the Church claims are indeed the 'fullness of the gospel'. Yet in the main, that 'fullness' does not appear at all and where it supposedly does, it is often in direct conflict with what is believed today. Thus members need to apply all kinds of subconscious rationale in order for much of it to make any sense whatsoever. This reference is a classic example:

> **Alma 11:40.** (82 BCE). And he shall come into the world to redeem his people; and he shall ***take upon him the transgressions of those who believe on his name; and these are they that shall have eternal life***, and salvation cometh to none else. (Emphasis added).

Obviously theological evolution occurred in abundance in Smith's early Mormon Church. Naturally, because much so-called 'scripture' was written prior to newer ideas emerging, early writings, particularly in the *Book of Mormon* are often either bereft of modern Mormon theology, at best, or, as in this case, completely *contradictory* to it, at worst. Here, the *Book of Mormon* clearly states that those who "believe on His name … shall have eternal life" when today it takes far more than just *belief.* It is not what the Church now teaches, but it *is* what the *Book of Mormon* declares. We must always remember the claim is that God *dictated* this to Smith in his hat, so it should be both word perfect and doctrinally accurate. It is ***neither.***

## Christ Is Our Advocate

There is just one reference for this concept *(manual page 61)* and once again it is self-serving, from the *D&C*, in a revelation written in 1831. Smith has Christ speaking:

> **D&C 45:3.** Listen to him who is the advocate with the Father, who is pleading your cause before him—
> 4. Saying: Father, behold the sufferings and death of him who did no sin, in whom thou wast well pleased; behold the blood of thy Son which was shed, the blood of him whom thou gavest that thyself might be glorified;
> 5. Wherefore, Father, spare these my brethren that believe on my name, that they may come unto me and have everlasting life.

As this concept is fundamentally the same as any other Christian religion, there is little that needs to be said about it, other than the fact that the Mormon Church could have used more recognisable, and definitely more pleasingly structured, passages from the Bible to support it rather than the above syntactic monstrosity. These words were supposedly spoken first hand by Jesus Christ.

# THE GOSPEL OF JESUS CHRIST

In the *D&C*, Joseph Smith tends to slip into early modern English of sorts sometimes, just before or just after he has deity speaking, and sometimes back into modern day English *before* deity has finished speaking for that matter. He regularly makes a mess of his overall use of the English language of *any* era.

The Lord of course would *not*. When Smith wrote his *Inspired Revision* of the Bible, he made changes which incorporated even more such incorrect grammar, again evidencing that his alterations were anything *but* inspired.

Perhaps the Church would have been better choosing 1 John 2:1.

> **1.** My little children, these things write I unto you, that ye sin not. And if any man sin, we have an advocate with the Father, Jesus Christ the righteous:

That beautifully phrased passage outshines anything and everything Smith ever wrote and would have been far better than the nonsense selected from the *D&C*, which of course Christ would *never* have spoken in that manner. It is worth reading the whole of *Section 45* which has Christ supposedly speaking throughout. It provides no end of evidence as to who was really the author of the section. There are seventy-five verses and over forty of them start with the word 'And'. Jesus seemed to like to speak that way to Smith. The entire section is dictated by Christ and in v.44 he declares that he will come "with power and *great* glory". It is one thing for a 'pretender' of a prophet to declare such a thing, but for the Saviour to say it of *himself*? Unlikely.

> **D&C 45:44.** And then they shall look for me, and, behold, I will come; and ***they shall see me in the clouds of heaven, clothed with power and great glory***; with all the holy angels; and he that watches not for me shall be cut off. (Emphasis added).

Smith gets this from the New Testament where it appears several times, but *never* from the lips of the Saviour; it is *always* from someone else, describing what *they* think will happen, in euphoric religious terms. Luke contains this example:

> **Luke 21:27.** And then shall they ***see the Son of man coming in a cloud with power and great glory.*** (Emphasis added).

Can *you* imagine Christ *repeating exact words* attributed to Luke, which were written decades after Christ lived, by people who never met him and which provide at best, third hand hearsay? They never were words attributed *to* Christ, and whatever any original words may or may not have been, they later arrived in that final format after several retranslations, in the 1611 *KJV* and do not represent an exact or original statement from anyone.

Would you not think that Christ would choose his *own* words, and at the same time not be so dramatic and present Himself humbly? Smith puts hearsay and boastful words into the mouth of Jesus. It was Smith who publicly *boasted* that He did *more* than Jesus. It was *Smith's* style. *(See TMD 2:9; HC 6:408-9)*.

Smith has Christ speaking in the first person throughout this so-called revelation – and then towards the end, he slips into the *third* person, clearly showing that he, Smith, is starting to close the remarks and wants to emphasise the fact that Christ the Lord will return. Up to and including v.73, Christ is speaking in the *first* person and then suddenly, in the last two verses he is speaking in the third person; effectively Christ is talking about someone *else*. Well, Smith is inadvertently taking over and speaking *about* Christ and thus he gets caught in his duplicity. If Christ *was* speaking, He would say '*I*', not '*he*'.

> **D&C 45:72.** And now *I* say unto you, keep these things from going abroad unto the world until it is expedient in *me*, that ye may accomplish this work in the eyes of the people, and in the eyes of your enemies, that they may not know your works until ye have accomplished the thing which *I* have commanded you;
> 73. That when they shall know it, that they may consider these things.
> 74. For when *the Lord* shall appear *he* shall be terrible unto them, that fear may seize upon them, and they shall stand afar off and tremble.
> 75. And all nations shall be afraid because of the terror of *the Lord*, and the power of *his* might. Even so. Amen. (Emphasis added).

## Salvation through Christ

Once again, although the concept of 'salvation though Christ' *(manual page 61)* is common in Christianity, references provided are all from the *Book of Mormon* and do little to prove anything that can't readily, and more eloquently – or grammatically correctly for that matter – be referenced directly from the Bible. By now of course, the investigator has been asked "Do you believe the Church and the gospel of Jesus Christ have been restored through the Prophet Joseph Smith?" *(See beginning of chapter)*. Naturally, if an investigator has come to conclude that such is, or even *might* be the case, then 'scripture' from Mormon sources will reinforce their conclusion more readily than the Bible. That is because they will undoubtedly already accept the Bible as being true, so mainly using Mormon based references from this lesson onward makes perfect psychological sense.

The only problem with the references provided is that they are *all* set BCE when some names and terms, as well as the information used did not exist. I expect if the missionaries use these references, they don't bother to mention the *dates* when they are claimed to have been originally written.

# THE GOSPEL OF JESUS CHRIST

The Mormon faithful will readily accept the idea that Christ was 'known' from the days of Adam, it merely being one of those things you don't seriously consider when coming across the concept after having been a member for some time. It is something that creeps up on you slowly and only makes sense *within* the delusional Mormon mindset. Members will generally just accept whatever they are told is the case about anything new to them once they have received their 'testimony'. It would be very dangerous to ask a new investigator outright to accept such things as that at this stage.

> **2 Nephi 2:6.** Wherefore, redemption cometh in and through the ***Holy Messiah***; for he is full of grace and truth.
> **7.** Behold, he offereth himself a sacrifice for sin, to answer the ends of the law, unto all ***those who have a broken heart and a contrite spirit***; and unto none else can the ends of the law be answered.
> **8.** Wherefore, how great the importance to make these things known unto the inhabitants of the earth, that they may know that there is no flesh that can dwell in the presence of God, save it be through the merits, and mercy, and grace of the ***Holy Messiah***, who layeth down his life according to the flesh, and taketh it again by the power of the Spirit, that he may bring to pass the resurrection of the dead, being the first that should rise. (Emphasis added).

The above passage was supposedly written between 588-570 BCE. On its own, the Mormon Church may seem to 'get away' with this kind of revelation or prophecy, as it uses the term 'Messiah' which could indeed translate from original Hebrew, into reformed Egyptian if you must, into English. However, Smith makes the mistake of using the phrase "Holy Messiah" which is an anomaly as there could not be a Messiah who was not 'holy' and the two words are ***never*** used together. I am sure the Mormon Church would claim Smith, or rather Nephi, could use the expression if he wanted to, but nevertheless, it is incorrect. It would just be 'Messias' or 'Holy One of Israel' perhaps. The *concept* 'Messias' or 'Messiah' ***is*** holy and it needs no such additional prefix. It is like using the expression 'the Holy God' or 'the Holy Christ' when no such characterisation is required. Is there any *other* kind of God, Christ or Messiah?

Additionally, 'Messiah' only appears in *Daniel* and some translations of *Psalm 2:2*. It means 'the anointed'. **The full title 'Anointed of Jahveh' occurs in several passages of 'Psalms of Solomon' and the 'Apocalypse of Baruch', but the abbreviated form, 'Anointed' or 'the Anointed', was in common use. Smith's use of the word 'holy' is entirely superfluous.**

The expression "broken heart and contrite spirit" is drawn from Psalms 34 and 51. Smith uses the *exact* phrase again in *D&C 59:8* which was written in 1831, the year following his publication of the *Book of Mormon*. Section 59 ends with the statement "I the Lord have spoken it…" but in reality he did *not*.

Both of the biblical instances of these phrases were expressions of David, who, in the second instance, is seeking forgiveness for sleeping with Bathsheba. They are *not* the words of Christ. The original texts read:

> **Psalm 34:18.** The Lord is nigh unto them that are of a broken heart: and saveth such as be of a contrite spirit.

> **Psalm 51:17.** The sacrifices of God are a broken spirit: a broken and a contrite heart, O God, thou wilt not despise.

Smith's problem with including the phrase in his *Book of Mormon* is not the source, since it could be claimed that as Psalms is a collective, dating from about 1300-500 BCE, some could indeed have been incorporated in the brass plates Lehi supposedly took with him when he left Jerusalem around 600 BCE.

Smith's problem is that it is not *Christ's* statement and it does *not* appear in the *New Testament*. Nevertheless, Smith puts the words of David into the mouth of the Saviour. Christ could use the same words of course, but based on Smith's extensive plagiarism used throughout the book, it is highly unlikely.

> **D&C 56:18.** But blessed are the poor who are pure in heart, ***whose hearts are broken, and whose spirits are contrite***, for they shall ***see the kingdom of God coming in power and great glory*** unto their deliverance; for the fatness of the earth shall be theirs. (Emphasis added).

This is yet another 1831 revelation from Smith, in which once again it is Christ speaking. Smith uses the same concept several more times in the *D&C* and also several times in the *Book of Mormon* but Christ *never* personally used the expression in the *New Testament*.

Again, we have Smith claiming Christ used the phrase "coming in power and *great* glory" this time regarding the kingdom of God which is an unlikely and arrogant sounding first person expression for Christ to ever use in reality – and once again, is taken from the words of someone else entirely.

Smith has *Christ* speaking this way in 34 CE in his *Book of Mormon*:

> **3 Nephi 9:20.** And ye shall offer for a sacrifice unto me ***a broken heart and a contrite spirit.*** And whoso cometh unto me with ***a broken heart and a contrite spirit***, him will I baptize with fire and with the Holy Ghost, even as the Lamanites, because of their faith in me at the time of their conversion, were ***baptized with fire and with the Holy Ghost, and they knew it not.*** (Emphasis added).

"Lamanites ... baptised with fire and the Holy Ghost" – without ***knowing***?

# THE GOSPEL OF JESUS CHRIST

In my view, for what it is worth, if the missionaries relate the following passage to investigators, they should be obliged by law to add the *truth* and say something like "By the way, the fact is that although we believe this was recorded around 74 BCE it was many centuries before the English word 'Crist', (as in Christmas) was 'invented' in the fourteenth century CE – and the now common word 'Christ' appeared just after the first edition of the *KJV* and did not really become standardised until as late as the eighteenth century." Perhaps they could add "Isn't it marvellous" or something.

> **Alma 34:8.** And now, behold, I will testify unto you of myself that these things are true. Behold, I say unto you, that I do know that ***Christ shall come*** among the children of men, to take upon him the transgressions of his people, and that he shall atone for the sins of the world; for the Lord God hath spoken it.
> **9.** For it is expedient that an atonement should be made; for according to the great plan of the Eternal God there must be an atonement made, or else all mankind must unavoidably perish; yea, all are hardened; yea, all are fallen and are lost, and must perish except it be through the atonement which it is expedient should be made. (Emphasis added).

This lesson manual 'reference' is claimed to date from 74 BCE and uses the *title* of Christ which could not have been translated from any Hebrew text as the word was not invented, even as the forerunner – 'Crist', until some thirteen or fourteen-hundred years *later*. The passage should read 'messias' or similar for it to have any possible merit whatsoever. Using the term 'Christ' in the BCE period was a major Smith error which the Mormon Church ignores, or excuses, by assuming the Lord translated it directly into a modern day idiom.

Yet God did *not* do that with 'cureloms' or 'cumoms' – unknown animals, or with 'neas' or 'sheum' – unknown crops, or even with a chapter of Isaiah, when Smith faithfully transcribed into the *Book of Mormon*, *KJV* 17th century interpretations of items of apparel that would be generally recognised by the people of the day in 1611 in England but certainly *not* easily by Americans in the time of Joseph Smith in 1830. I refer here to the passage from Isaiah which contains such items as cauls, tablets, crisping pins and glasses, and reads:

> **KJV. Isaiah 3:18.** In that day the Lord will take away the bravery of their tinkling ornaments ***about their feet***, and ***their*** cauls, and ***their*** round tires like the moon,
> **19.** The chains, and the bracelets, and the mufflers,
> **20.** The bonnets, and the ornaments of the legs, and the headbands, and the tablets, and the earrings,
> **21.** The rings, and nose jewels,
> **22.** The changeable suits of apparel, and the mantles, and the wimples, and the crisping pins,

23. The glasses, and the fine linen, and the hoods, and the vails.
(Emphasis added to words *removed* for no logical reason by Smith in the *Book of Mormon* version of Isaiah 3).

**BOM. 2 Nephi 13:18.** In that day the Lord will take away the bravery of their tinkling ornaments, and cauls, and round tires like the moon;
19. The chains and the bracelets, and the mufflers;
20. The bonnets, and the ornaments of the legs, and the headbands, and the tablets, and the ear-rings;
21. The rings, and nose jewels;
22. The changeable suits of apparel, and the mantles, and the wimples, and the crisping-pins;
23. The glasses, and the fine linen, and hoods, and the veils.

Other than a few pointless and scripturally meaningless word *deletions*, Smith faithfully copied Isaiah, word for word, just as it appears in the *KJV*. Scribes in the 17th century translated the words into understandable items of apparel of their own day. Those words would *not* have been known in the time of Nephi and some may not have even existed as *items*. If Smith had been on his toes, he should have rendered the text into recognisable 19th century words for items of apparel. Today, we can much more readily understand this passage written like this:

> **New International Version. Isaiah 3:18.** In that day the Lord will snatch away their finery: the bangles and headbands and crescent necklaces,
> 19. the earrings and bracelets and veils,
> 20. the headdresses and ankle chains and sashes, the perfume bottles and charms,
> 21. the signet rings and nose rings,
> 22. the fine robes and the capes and cloaks, the purses
> 23. and mirrors, and the linen garments and tiaras and shawls.

Smith didn't have a clue about the passage and he just copied it. Had God *actually* spoken to Smith in his hat, then we would have a perfect rendition of an original text, transposed into modern day understandable language and items. That would be an impressive indicator that Smith may have been telling the truth. The fact is that *everything* in Smith's work is equally bad and equally as damning, constantly evidencing his fraudulent claims rather than remotely substantiating them as real in *any* way whatsoever. What a difference it would make if everything was grammatically correct and beautifully structured, not to mention authentic in detail and prophetically accurate. ***None*** of it remotely is.

# THE GOSPEL OF JESUS CHRIST

## Mercy and Justice

There is plenty about 'mercy' in the New Testament but 'justice' does not appear there at all. It is confined to the Old Testament where God appears to be a more aggressive character. Although, even then it should be said there is a lot more about mercy than justice. There is actually only one biblical reference to both justice and mercy in the same verse, although the manual does not use it. That reference is:

> **Psalm 89:14.** Justice and judgment are the habitation of thy throne: mercy and truth shall go before thy face.

*Mosiah 15:9* is used to identify the concept that Christ has satisfied the 'demands of justice' and *Alma 42:22-25* goes into detail about laws and punishments, repentance, and mercy due to the atonement which brings about the resurrection of the dead. Once again, carefully worded Mormon scriptures are used to explain the case.

## The First Principle of the Gospel
## Faith in Jesus Christ

In the early Mormon Church, the 'first principles' were described by one apostle as *'The Book of Mormon'* and the 'gathering' to Zion in Nauvoo. The Articles of Faith came later and firmed up a more cohesive set of principles.

The lesson manual *(pp.61-62)* confirms that today, faith in the Lord Jesus Christ is the 'first principle' of the gospel. This involves believing in him after the Mormon fashion, as an entirely separate being from God the Father.

> We recognize that we can return to live with our Heavenly Father only by relying on His Son's grace and mercy. When we have faith in Christ, we accept and apply His Atonement and His teachings. We trust Him and what He says. We know that He has the power to keep His promises. Heavenly Father blesses those who have faith to obey His Son.

Of course, the Mormon missionaries will teach their investigator's what it is they are supposed to 'obey' and it does *not* come from the Bible. This leads into a statement about required *action*. 'Faith', in Mormon terms, is not passive. "Faith in Christ leads to action" proclaims the manual, to "try as hard as we can to learn about and become more like our Savior. It leads to sincere and lasting repentance."

The manual goes on to explain that:

> ***We want to learn what His commandments are and then obey them.*** Even though we will still make mistakes, we show our love for Him by striving to keep His commandments and avoid sin. We believe in Christ, and we believe that He wants us to keep all His commandments. We want to show our faith by obeying Him. ***We pray in faith for strength to conquer temptation.***
>
> We can also ***develop faith in a particular principle, such as the Word of Wisdom or tithing***, by first believing in Jesus Christ strongly enough to obey His commandments. ***As we live a specific commandment, we learn the truthfulness of it by experience.*** *(Page 62).* (Emphasis added).

The psychology is simple and very clever. Mormon missionaries will teach investigators lots of 'commandments'. If they are starting to believe that Smith was indeed a prophet, investigators may accept them all as real. Prayer will provide strength to obey them. Living "such as" the Word of Wisdom or tithing as the manual suggests *(above)*, will help people to learn the truth of them. In point of fact there are *no* other "such as" things to consider. The two main principles investigators *must* live are the *Word of Wisdom* and *tithing*. Investigators who do *not* have the 'faith' to live those principles, generally do not stay long in the Church. Mormon leaders are aware of that fact and thus whilst "such as" *appears* to illustrate just a couple out of *many* other choices, they are in fact the *only* two that really matter at this stage.

Regardless of any other aspect of the gospel, no one usually survives to become an active and long term believing Mormon without giving up tea, coffee, alcohol and tobacco and paying tithing. The rest generally fall by the wayside. A few who begin well, later become 'less-active' Mormons and don't live the Word of Wisdom and in my experience, about half to two-thirds of so-called 'active' members don't actually pay full tithing and will never be called to positions of any significance in the Church.

The idea that living those principles will bring a 'testimony' of their divine nature to investigators is emphasised by using a scripture from *John 17. (See below, p.239).* In a state of willing compliance, of course it is an easy thing for someone to conclude. They have been told to expect it, so they do. People feel good anyway when they achieve something and the 'feel good' factor of giving up things they enjoy, and donating the Lord's tenth to His Church, do feel like good things to have achieved. Thus they obtain a 'testimony' of them.

Sometimes people try, and fail, as such lifestyle habits can be extremely hard to break. Likewise, tithing can for some be an extreme difficulty. Many people are already struggling without the added burden of tithing. I have never

# THE GOSPEL OF JESUS CHRIST

heard anyone suggest a programmed reconstruction of someone's financial position so as to gradually enable tithing to be accommodated into a budget, commencing, say a year following them joining the Church.

As a financial adviser, I often helped people move from one financial structure, and perhaps tax position, to another *over time*; it cannot be achieved *overnight* by everyone. Yet the Mormon Church requires tithing immediately and of *everyone*, regardless of their financial position. *Ability* to pay is never discussed or even considered, unless an investigator mentions it as a problem, when missionaries will invariably teach that faith is all that is required and everything else will follow. Additionally, they will be reminded of how much money they will *save* by living the Word of Wisdom.

Naturally, there are many who claim such 'miracles' as still having enough money to live on even though their budget was already stretched beyond reason when they faithfully added in tithing. Money still went around. The truth is that money is *finite* and can only do so much. Faith changes *nothing* in that respect. Frugal planning does. People restructure or re-evaluate needs, often rationalise their real financial requirements, and sacrifice a great deal to accommodate the payment of tithing, sometimes erroneously coming to conclude the Lord helped them make the available money 'go around'.

He clearly did not, but *believing* He did will enhance a new and still fragile testimony. I was one who managed that over the years and the consequence is that whilst I managed a full tithe and raised a large family, I never did manage to contribute properly to a pension fund. I am now paying the price for that.

Ten percent of my earnings would have funded a sensible pension but I gave it to the Church instead. Money *is* finite and will only go so far, regardless of faith or fanciful thinking. I always thought everything would be alright and I 'trusted' the Lord. It is *not* alright; I am now retired, and I have to suffer the consequences of my decision for the rest of my life – and we live very frugally.

The irony is that for the last two decades and more of my career, I was in financial services, advising clients on pensions and investments; the very things that I had not financially been able to provide for myself over the years; I was too busy paying and serving.

> **John 7:17.** If any man will do his will, he shall know of the doctrine, whether it be of God, or *whether* I speak of myself.

The problem is that John was not talking about such things as the Mormon Word of Wisdom or tithing. He was speaking about the basic New Testament teachings of Christ which did not include such things.

> We also grow in faith by hearing the word of God (see Romans 10:17) and by reading the word of God (see Helaman 15:7–8). *(Page 62).*

# THE MORMON DELUSION

Faith will be increased the more we listen to people speak about the Church and the more we read the scriptures, which in Mormon terms means first and foremost the *Book of Mormon*. Regular cycles of self-induced brainwashing start here.

> As we obey God, He blesses us. He gives us power to meet life's challenges. He helps us change the desires of our hearts. Through our faith in Jesus Christ, He can heal us, both physically and spiritually.

There are scriptures referenced under the heading of faith, regarding 'power' and 'salvation', as a 'doctrine', 'works and obedience', and also 'faith unto repentance'. The overall message is one of *blind* faith in a requirement to do what the Church teaches is *correct*. Once a person displays such 'faith' that they will submissively live the way Mormonism dictates, they will accept any and every new principle and doctrine, regardless of the fact that at the stage of making such a commitment, they knew little of anything that would entail. In the main, they are fed what the Church terms 'milk', and all the 'meat' comes later, by which time it is too late to seriously consider anything new in the cold light of day. By then, they will have the preconceived notion that *whatever* comes next, it is already *known* to be true. Religion is one of the only things that can achieve this phenomenon. One very clever reference which will be familiar to all Mormons is this:

> **1 Nephi 3:7.** And it came to pass that I, Nephi, said unto my father: I will go and do the things which the Lord hath commanded, for I know that the Lord giveth no commandments unto the children of men, save he shall prepare a way for them that they may accomplish the thing which he commandeth them.

Many an investigator, and equally, many a long term Mormon, has taken comfort from that statement and considered they can achieve anything asked of them as long as they have enough faith to do so. In this way, many people are persuaded to do things which in other circumstances they would rather not do at all.

Whilst the header for this section is 'Faith in Jesus Christ', the reality is investigators are being brainwashed into having faith in things the Mormon Church *teaches* are his commandments – but unless Smith *was* a real prophet, really they are not. 'Faith', in Mormon terms takes on a whole new dimension to the traditional Christian concept. It is a ploy to get people to *behave* and *think differently* to mainstream Christians – and to part with huge amounts of money on an ongoing basis. Faith in Christ traditionally did not mean that in Christian terms. Faith in Christ meant simply *trusting* Him to live up to being

# THE GOSPEL OF JESUS CHRIST

what He said He was and *believing* that He would do what He said He could and would do for us. We should be *steadfast* in our *faith*, or *belief*, in that.

> In traditional Christian terms, faith (*Pistis*, fides). In the Old Testament, the Hebrew means essentially *steadfastness.* As signifying man's attitude towards God it means trustfulness or *fiducia*.
>
> But that the word does itself contain the notion of belief is clear from the use of the radical, which in the causative conjugation, or *Hiph'il*, means "to believe", e.g. Genesis 15:6, and Deuteronomy 1:32, in which latter passage the two meanings — viz. of believing and of trusting — are combined. That the noun itself often means *faith* or *belief*, is clear from Habakkuk 2:4, where the context demands it. *(Catholic Encyclopaedia).*

Of course, faith can be considered *objectively* and *subjectively*, thus the way the Mormon Church uses it does fit the correct definitions.

However, it is what the Mormon Church asks people to have faith *in* that becomes the problem. A carefully constructed cocktail of lies presented to the unsuspecting is taken by them to the Lord in prayer and *only* when they believe they have received a positive response is it considered to have been an answer from God. If someone thinks they get an answer saying the Church is *not* true, then the missionaries will claim that came from the adversary rather than God.

If someone does not get an answer at all, they need more *faith* and should sleep on things, study them more and then pray again, with real intent, wanting to *know* it *is* true, until the *correct* answer comes to them. In other words, they must brainwash themselves until they believe it all without further question.

A classic example of this kind of self-induced indoctrination of a new, and unwanted, concept was recorded by a young woman in Mormon history who could not cope with the idea that her beloved prophet wanted to sleep with her in return for salvation for her family. This is what fourteen-year-old Helen Mar Kimball recorded about how she managed to convince herself, against her own will, to accommodate Joseph Smith's objectionable and despicable advances.

> After which he said to me, 'if you take this step, ***it will ensure your eternal salvation & exaltation and that of your father's household and all of your kindred.***'
>
> This promise was so great that I willingly gave myself to purchase so glorious a reward. None but God and his angels could see my mother's bleeding heart - when Joseph asked her if she was willing, she replied 'If Helen is willing I have nothing more to say.'

> She had witnessed the sufferings of others, who were older and who better understood the step they were taking, and to see her child, who had yet seen her fifteenth summer, following the same thorny path, in her mind she saw the misery which was as sure to come as the sun was to rise and set; but it was hidden from me. *(Compton 1997:499).* (Emphasis added).

The thing that was hidden from Helen was that the marriage arrangement was far more than her originally perceived dynastic family link. She had no idea that she would not only be expected to sleep with Smith when he fancied to but also that her teenage years would be stolen from her. She could no longer attend weekly dancing parties at the Smith's Mansion House with her brother William and her friends. Smith had warned her father to keep Helen away from the dances. Being obliged to stay home, Helen was effectively cut off from society and especially from everyone her own age.

> …no girl liked dancing better than I did…and like a wild bird I longed for the freedom that was denied me; **and thought myself an abused child**, and that it was pardonable if I did murmur.

> **I would never have been sealed to Joseph had I known it was anything more than ceremony. I was young, and they deceived me, by saying the salvation of our whole family depended on it.** *(Van Wagoner 1989:53 c: Lewis 1848: 19).* (Emphasis added).

Helen eventually succumbed to the delusion that polygamy was of God in what appears to have been a form of 'Stockholm syndrome'. She recorded: "I had, in hours of temptation when seeing the trials of my mother, felt to rebel. I hated polygamy in my heart." Helen became very ill for three months and typically of the period, took it to be a "punishment which is prepared for those who reject any of the principles of His gospel". Helen then *forced* herself into personal submission and acceptance of the principle. "I fasted for one week, and every day I gained until I had won the victory … I had learned for myself that plural marriage is a celestial principle, and saw … the necessity of obedience to those who hold the priesthood, and the danger of rebelling against or speaking lightly of the Lord's anointed."

Helen's self-deluded mind was now convinced; her conversion to Joseph Smith's required polygamy was complete. Smith had his way with a fourteen-year-old girl through deception and her fear of the eternal consequences of rejecting him, for no other purpose than his own self-gratification. That typifies self-induced brainwashing at its most powerful. In modern-day terms and law, Joseph Smith first groomed and then he raped Helen. *(See: TMD Vol.1:83-85).*

# THE GOSPEL OF JESUS CHRIST

When pre-baptismal 'teachings' are compared with *evidence* of the truth, I personally believe that a conspiracy to deceive can conclusively be shown to have been perpetrated to such a degree that legal action should be possible.

Unfortunately, the very fact that it is all considered just 'a matter of faith' appears to preclude much chance of success of that idea at the present time. Obviously, investigators would be advised by the legal profession to carefully check the teachings with alternative sources before being taken in by such nonsense. Unfortunately, some people are not that careful and not that capable.

## The Second Principle of the Gospel
## Repentance

> Our faith in Christ and our love for Him lead us to repent, or to change our thoughts, beliefs, and behaviors that are not in harmony with His will. Repentance includes forming a fresh view of God, ourselves, and the world. When we repent, we feel godly sorrow, then we stop doing things that are wrong and continue doing things that are right. Bringing our lives in line with God's will through repentance is a central purpose of our lives. We can return to live with God the Father only through Christ's mercy, and we receive Christ's mercy only on condition of repentance. *(Page 62)*.

The principle of repentance is wrapped up very nicely *(above)* and of course 'repentance' really does literally cover 'a multitude of sins' in Mormonism, as the Mormon Church has invented and developed more than you can count. Sins of 'omission' increase the number significantly once you have finished a list of sins of 'commission'. As mentioned previously, sin does not actually exist until and unless a person embraces the concept as reality within a religious mindset.

In the case of Mormonism, investigators are taught to recognise what *is* sin, and then to be sorry for it and repent, which means to forsake such things, even thoughts, and to never do them again. The usual things in religion are included, along with many new Mormon ideas, which although to the rest of the world consist of normal living and behaviour, in Mormonism they become sinful.

Luckily for the rest of the world, some things, such as not living the Word of Wisdom, are only a sin for Mormons. The rest of the world can happily smoke and drink and have tea or coffee and God doesn't mind at all because they know no better. The rest of the world should consider itself lucky in that God is very kind to them in that respect. Seriously though, the Mormon Church concludes that God would never punish people for doing things they have no idea are actually wrong. That of course is as it should be. But then, in reality, the rest of the world is not doing anything wrong anyway; it is the Mormon

Church which has it all wrong. Their Word of Wisdom ideas all stem from a *joke* between Smith's Elders and the 'sisters' and were it not for that, they wouldn't even have such a code. *(See TMD Vol. 2. Ch.10).*

Sins are to be confessed to God rather than to a mere mortal. Forgiveness comes from God and not from man. So-called serious sins are to be confessed to Church leaders however. These would include the obvious, such as murder, rape, robbery, fraud and so forth in addition to the more common sins, adultery and homosexuality, plus the odd case of incest or child abuse, some of which have never been reported outside Church disciplinary councils, as determined in cases where the Mormon Church has been sued by angry parents when such has taken place and been covered up, only later to be discovered and exposed.

If you imagine Mormons do not get involved in such things, you would be entirely wrong. An English Bishop and a couple of other members were jailed a few years ago following an armed bank robbery. They were hopeless at it and were immediately caught. I suspect that being a Mormon Bishop, the man felt he would hardly be considered a suspect, but he left a trail of evidence that led to his immediate arrest and subsequent conviction. I guess, being a Mormon Bishop, he didn't have enough time to watch TV crime programmes and learn not to leave evidence behind. There may unfortunately be some truth in that.

A number of clerks involved in the handling of tithes and offerings end up embezzling money which many 'intend' to repay, but the paper trail usually catches up with them. I am personally aware of instances of embezzlement and whilst there has always been local disciplinary action in such cases; usually temporary disfellowshipment; *none* I that am aware of were ever reported to the police and no legal action was taken. The Church does not like to go public about such things. In at least one case of which I am aware, the individual did not even have to repay all of the money. His 'repentance' included staged repayment of just some of it. He was disfellowshipped for a short period of time. As it happens, he was also a relative of the local authority who decided the case.

Every youngster has a half yearly interview and every adult has a regular 'temple recommend' interview plus further interviews when being called to new positions. Each interview questions, not just belief in God, Jesus and the current prophet; there are also Word of Wisdom, tithing and morality questions which sometimes get pretty specific, especially with youth where there may be morality 'concerns'. Then detail is often explored and probed until a youngster 'cracks'. That is one reason why some of them just stop attending church. I know some instances where entirely inappropriate questions have been asked; some when youth didn't even know what the questions meant, and some where embarrassed youngsters just clammed up, voted with their feet and left the Church. One of my own children had that experience. She considered the

# THE GOSPEL OF JESUS CHRIST

Bishop to be a pervert. To be fair, he wasn't, he was just entirely out of his depth, asking questions well beyond the simple standard suggested.

In a nutshell, Mormonism is pretty much the same as every other religion in respect of its attitude to sin. Identify it; stop doing it; repent and never do it again. Feel better about yourself because you have overcome it and draw ever closer to God. This will make you happy and God will be pleased with you. We will 'feel' God's forgiveness, according to the manual. We will also feel the spirit in 'greater abundance'. The Church has no end of clichés to make us feel we are getting somewhere. "When we pass from this life, we will be more prepared to live with our Heavenly Father and His Son." *(Manual p.62)*. As ever, the rewards for repentance come after we are dead, so there is no measure in this life of the validity or efficacy of such blind faith and obedience. But then, that is not unique to Mormonism of course. In Mormonism, people are promised blessings in this life too, but there is no *real* evidence that any are actually received, making life any different to the way it would have been without such promises.

We are naturally going to sin again (and again) so we should continually try to correct these 'transgressions', so the manual informs the missionaries. As elsewhere stated, we can and will *never* be good enough. In addition, we must continually *improve*. The manual confirms we will come to feel great joy in repenting *daily*. To be honest, I never did find any joy in that at all. I actually tried hard and usually thought I did okay in life. I couldn't really think of much of anything I had really done wrong most of the time and had to think hard as to where I may have underperformed during the day. Ultimately, in the frame of mind that we are all sinners, I would dredge up some sins of omission. There are always things we have *not* done.

That's not to say that I *never* did anything wrong at all. I made one or two huge mistakes earlier in life, some of which I deeply regret, but on reflection, I wouldn't call them *sins*. Sometimes, we are only human and we succumb to circumstance. Often, we hurt people when we don't mean to. We are sorry; we are forgiven; everyone moves on, but not so easily within Mormonism.

It is only when we *create* sin as a concept that our actions become *more* than personally 'regrettable' and without the Church and its concepts, we would more readily forgive ourselves and be able to just forget all about the past. No one needs to know about most things that many people are 'guilty' of at one time or another. The Mormon Church is more than capable of keeping many members in the depths of despair when any good psychologist would confirm they could be far better served by moving on and forgetting the past. They usually have nothing to be sorry for at all after that. In Mormonism, their Saviour wants more:

> As we learn more about what the Savior expects of us, we will want to show our love by obeying Him. Thus, as we repent daily, we will find that our lives will change and improve. Our hearts and our behavior will become more Christlike. We will come to feel great joy in repenting daily. *(Page 63)*.

The lesson manual provides two references regarding the idea that we *all* sin. Surprisingly they are both biblical. If we don't believe we sin, then we are just deceiving ourselves. There are references on repentance; redemption and forgiveness; mercy 'claims the penitent'; the latter confirming the concept that it is mercy that redeems us. If you are happy with the idea you are a sinner and that you need to repent every day, then Mormonism spells it all out in no uncertain terms.

## The Third Principle of the Gospel
## Baptism

The Mormon method of baptism remains true to the biblical account of the Saviour being fully immersed. This is the way the manual expresses Mormon perceptions surrounding the ordinance. It constitutes a covenant between the individual and God.

> Through the ordinance of baptism ... we covenant to take upon ourselves the name of Jesus Christ, always remember Him, and keep His commandments. As we keep our part of the covenant, God promises the constant companionship of the Holy Ghost, a remission of our sins, and being born again. *(Page 64)*.

The manual explains that we give up certain things in order to be baptised and follow Christ in the way Mormonism portrays that He requires us to.

> To keep our covenants, we must give up activities or interests that prevent us from honoring those covenants. For example, we give up shopping and recreational pursuits on Sunday so we can keep the Sabbath day holy. *(Page 63)*.

This is the only way to enter the kingdom of God, and Jesus Christ set the example for us.

> Jesus taught that we must be baptized by immersion for the remission, or forgiveness, of our sins. Baptism is an essential ordinance of salvation. No person can enter the kingdom of God without being baptized. Christ set the example for us by being baptized. *(Page 64)*.

# THE GOSPEL OF JESUS CHRIST

The inherent symbolism surrounding baptism is explained.

> Baptism by immersion is a symbol of the death, burial, and resurrection of the Savior. In a similar way, it represents the end of our old life of sin and a commitment to live a new life as a disciple of Christ. The Savior taught that baptism is a rebirth. When we are baptized we begin the process of being born again and become spiritual sons and daughters of Christ (see Mosiah 5:7–8; Romans 8:14–17). *(Page 64).*

It is interesting that baptism represents "the end of our old life of sin and a commitment to live a new life..." when without such newfound knowledge, many investigators could hardly have been accused of sinning beforehand.

Generally, people are not regular 'sinners' at all. They just live normal lives and are good people, with or without any religious 'direction'. Not knowing what Mormons believe is the 'truth' hardly makes someone a sinner.

However, Mormonism would have people believe they were sinners, so as to control them in the future. It is typical 'guilt complex' propaganda, designed here perhaps more for missionary benefit than investigator self-assessment. I doubt that people are *directly* told they are sinners and must repent. They will be left to decide that for themselves. Given enough time and later information, many will conclude that they were sinners before becoming Mormons.

The concept is that members can 'renew' baptismal covenants each week by partaking of the sacrament. It is in fact a *commandment* for them to do so.

> We also regularly renew the covenants we make when baptized by partaking of the sacrament. Partaking of the sacrament weekly is a commandment. It helps us remain worthy to have the Spirit with us always. It is a weekly reminder of our covenants. Jesus Christ introduced this ordinance to His Apostles just before His Atonement. He restored it through the Prophet Joseph Smith. The Savior commanded that priesthood holders should administer the sacrament in remembrance of His body and His blood, which was shed for us. By partaking of the sacrament worthily we promise always to remember His sacrifice, we renew our promises, and we receive anew the promise that the Spirit will always be with us. *(Page 64).*

When the sacrament was first introduced in Mormonism, it consisted of bread and *wine*. Some years later, it was changed to the use of bread and *water*. Considering Mormonism is supposedly the 'restored' gospel it is surprising that Smith's God didn't direct Smith to use bread and *water* from the very start.

Many things have *evolved* in Mormonism rather than, as is perceived, being *restored* the way God wanted them to be in the first place. In addition to the sacrament, another classic example, which we have already discussed, is the actual name of the Church which took several attempts by Smith before God finally told him what to call it. It doesn't ring true that God would not 'restore' everything in proper order and get it all right – the *first* time. Chopping and changing things is indicative of human ideas evolving rather than deity being remotely involved with a 'restoration' of all things.

In *Section 27* of the *D&C*, God tells Smith not to buy wine from 'enemies'. There are a couple of other aspects that appear there that are worth mentioning in passing. Let's look at v.5-7.

> **D&C 27:5.** Behold, this is wisdom in me; wherefore, marvel not, for the hour cometh that I **will drink of the fruit of the vine with you on the earth, and with Moroni,** whom I have sent unto you to reveal **the Book of Mormon, containing the fulness of my everlasting gospel,** to whom I have committed the keys of the record of the stick of Ephraim;
> **6.** And **also with Elias**, to whom I have committed the keys of bringing to pass the restoration of all things spoken by the mouth of all the holy prophets since the world began, concerning the last days;
> **7.** And also John the son of Zacharias, which Zacharias he (***Elias***) visited and gave promise that he should have a son, and his name should be John, and he should be filled with the spirit of ***Elias***; (Emphasis added).

In 1831, Smith has Jesus Christ saying he will come to earth and drink "the fruit of the vine" with Smith and strangely, also Smith's fictional character Moroni. Christ is not referring to the sacrament and of course in any event Christ would hardly partake in remembrance of himself. He is going to drink wine with Smith. And yet a couple of years later, the Word of Wisdom was revealed. Today, it proscribes the use of *all* alcoholic drinks. Perhaps after this life 'sensible' levels of drinking alcohol will be permitted?

Verse 5 also contains the message that the *Book of Mormon* contains the fullness of the gospel which we address in other chapters of this book. Clearly, the fullness of the Mormon gospel as taught today does *not* appear in the *Book of Mormon* by any stretch of the imagination.

Smith goes on in v.6-7 to speak of *Elias* as a real person to whom Christ committed keys. Mormon apologists try to claim that 'an Elias' is a messenger or forerunner, but this excuse falls flat in the case of him being expressed as an individual to whom keys are committed. Smith just used the name with no idea that it could not be a real person. We have already covered the fact that he is one and the same as Elijah. *(See Pp.200-202)*. In v.9, Smith mentions Elijah as another person to whom other keys are committed, thus evidencing his entire ignorance about the two names. There is much more nonsense we could review regarding this Section of the *D&C* but we must move on.

# THE GOSPEL OF JESUS CHRIST

Likewise, we have discussed the fact that whilst the Mormon Church dismisses other religions that 'sprinkle' rather than baptise by immersion, the Mormon Church now only symbolically washes and anoints members in their temples, when once they were immersed in bathtubs. *(See p.77)*. Mormons like everything their own way and yet allow others no leeway whatsoever.

Baptism is performed by the authority of a 'restored' priesthood, for which restoration there is no properly documented record at all. Coincidentally, such restoration is referred to in *D&C 27* which we have just been reviewing, but no actual verifiable or confirming record exists anywhere. The accounts we have from Smith and Cowdery completely contradict each other as discussed earlier. *(See: Pp.111-20)*. The accounts conflict so dramatically with each other as to be far more than suspect and even then the details are sparse at best.

In respect of the 'baptismal covenant' and 'qualifications' for baptism, one reference for both aspects is *D&C 20:37*.

> **20:37.** *And again, by way of commandment to the church concerning the manner of baptism*—All those who humble themselves before God, and desire to be baptized, and come forth with broken hearts and contrite spirits, and witness before the church that they have truly repented of all their sins, and are willing to take upon them the name of Jesus Christ, having a determination to serve him to the end, and truly manifest by their works that they have received of the Spirit of Christ unto the remission of their sins, shall be received by baptism into his church. (Emphasis in original).

If evidence confirms Joseph Smith a prophet and his Church true, then the above is fair and acceptable for those who wish to avail themselves of the opportunity of commencing a path back to their God. On the other hand, if evidence confirms otherwise, then such a step would be ill advised, as it will lead absolutely nowhere.

Unfortunately for Smith the latter is unquestionably the case and in fact evidence lies within the very same section the Church chooses to use here. *Section 20* was 'received' in April of 1830 and reveals, in v.1, the day (6th April) on which the Church was formally organised. It was one of the several occasions when Smith could have provided details of his astounding First Vision which started the whole restoration. Two glorious beings, God the Father and Jesus Christ appearing as two separate personages with bodies... *No such declaration was made on the auspicious occasion when the Church was officially established.*

However, something *else* is mentioned which casts serious doubt once again on the authenticity of Smith's official First Vision story when he did finally record it eight years later. Smith speaks of a heavenly vision which presumably refers to Moroni.

> **D&C 20:5.** After it was truly manifested unto this first elder that he had received a remission of his sins, he was entangled again in the vanities of the world;
> **6.** But after repenting, and humbling himself sincerely, through faith, *God ministered unto him by an holy angel, whose countenance was as lightning, and whose garments were pure and white above all other whiteness;*
> **7.** And gave unto him commandments which inspired him;
> **8.** And gave him *power from on high*, by the means which were before prepared, *to translate the Book of Mormon;*
> **9.** Which contains a record of a fallen people, and the fulness of the gospel of Jesus Christ to the Gentiles and to the Jews also;
> **10.** *Which was given by inspiration...* (Emphasis added).

If Smith had already made up his First Vision idea, he would certainly have included it here in order to maximise his credibility when the Church was first organised. The fact that he had not yet thought of the concept is manifest in what he said *instead*. In v.6, Smith indicates that he was ministered to by an angel in pure white, who shone like lightening. Verse 5 must relate to the first Moroni visits of 1823 and v.6 to the 1827 visit where Smith claimed to receive the golden plates. Why no account of a glorious First Vision – it if was a *real* foundational experience? Smith would never have held that back if it were true.

In v.10 Smith claims the translation of the *Book of Mormon* was given by *inspiration*, not through direct translation or by dictation into his hat. This confirms Smith just made up what he thought the book should contain while his head was buried in his hat looking at his old money digging seer stone which he had previously used to con people out of money by pretending he could see into the earth. He said it was "given by inspiration" during that process. Bearing in mind the prior use of the pebble, and in addition, the times when he received 'revelations' that he later confessed were *not* of the Lord but either of the devil or his own wishful thinking, such as the failed Canada trip to sell the copyright of the Book of Mormon *(See TMD Vol.3:270-274)*, how on earth would he or anyone else be able to trust *anything* that came out of his hat?

Later on in the same section, we once again find confirmation from Smith that God and Jesus and the Holy Ghost are, still in Smith's then monotheistic mindset, *one* God.

> **20:27.** ...believe in the gifts and callings of God by the Holy Ghost, which beareth record of the Father and of the Son;
> **28.** Which *Father, Son, and Holy Ghost are one God*, infinite and eternal, without end. Amen. (Emphasis added).

# THE GOSPEL OF JESUS CHRIST

This is a far cry from Smith's much later claim that "The Father has a body of flesh and bones as tangible as man's; the Son also; but the Holy Ghost has not a body of flesh and bones, but is a personage of Spirit"; a concept which was eventually, and singularly, to emerge thirteen years later in *D&C 130*. The notions are so divergent that it is impossible for Smith to have considered this 1843 statement to have been the case in 1830 when he declared, for the umpteenth time, that they were 'three in one'. Even when Smith did ultimately come out with his new and controversial claim, it was not encapsulated in a glorious 'thus saith the Lord' revelation; it was tagged on to the end of some 'items of instruction' from Smith to the Church. *(See Ch. 1.pp. 26-27).*

## The Fourth Principle of the Gospel
## The Gift of the Holy Ghost

> Jesus taught that we must be baptized of water and also of the Spirit. Baptism by water must be followed by baptism of the Spirit or it is incomplete. Only when we receive baptism and the gift of the Holy Ghost can we receive a remission of our sins and become completely spiritually reborn. We then begin a new spiritual life as disciples of Christ. *(Page 65).*

In the Jewish religion, God is, and always was, truly monotheistic. Even Satan, as perceived by Christians, is *not* an autocratic character in the Old Testament. As discussed elsewhere, the Jewish HaSaTan is not evil and he sits on God's council, only acting with permission and under the direction of God. God rules and there is *no one* else. To Jews, such a being having any control whatsoever would render their God *not* monotheistic after all. Jesus Christ of course does not even enter the frame for Jews and the 'Holy Ghost' is a New Testament Christian invention entirely. In Judaism, the 'holy spirit' of the Old Testament is the 'mind' of God, or His 'energy'.

Conversely, in Joseph Smith's evolving theology, the Holy Ghost becomes an actual *man*; a being of spirit, without a body. He is the third 'personage' of the godhead and the exclusive companion of 'worthy' Mormons. The lesson manual confirms that in Mormonism, the Holy Ghost testifies of Jesus Christ and helps members recognise the truth. He is the 'comforter' and does comfort in times of trial or sorrow. He warns of spiritual and even 'physical danger'. I have yet to see substantiated physical evidence of that. Anecdotal evidence, where people claim to have been influenced by the Holy Ghost so as to have avoided incident, accident or even death, whilst prolific, falls well short of the many illnesses, accidents and deaths that *have* occurred where members – including several Mormon missionaries – have indeed suffered or been killed.

# THE MORMON DELUSION

Faith provides the anecdotes and religious people just love faith promoting experiences whether imagined or real. Where was the Holy Ghost on all those occasions? Statistically, Mormons appear to suffer and die no more or less frequently than other 'ordinary' people. For there to be any merit in the claim, there should and would be empirical evidence provided. There is *none*. There never has been any and there never will be any.

Unless that is, the Church would care to have prepared, an independent statistical analysis of these areas regarding Mormons, compared with society in general, to prove their case. Such a claim *can* be proved or disproved by such means; not by assessing any *claims*, but simply comparing the *number* of actual incidences of various Mormon illnesses, accidents and deaths, from murder, suicide, accident etc., with the rest of society. If the Holy Ghost, and let's add in Mormon blessings of their sick and afflicted, to help their statistics along, really does help Mormons recover from illness and avoid accidents and even death, it should show up in such a comparative statistical analysis.

The Church will *never* accede to such a request, as they already know what the results would be. One thing that I can predict, at least for Utah, is that the suicide rate within the Church will be higher than the average for the rest of the United States, as that has already been determined for Utah as a whole which includes many non-Mormons of course. Isolate members and evaluate suicides per capita and I predict the incidence will be even more significantly above the national average than it already is when everyone is included. Isolate Mormon and non-Mormon gay suicides and the statistic will escalate even further.

The main reason for this is the numbers of gay suicides that the Church and even some Mormon families effectively cause by the way gay youngsters are treated. Utah also already has the highest 'poor mental health' rate in America. *(See TMD Vol.3:51-52)*. There is no data to support the Church claim and the Holy Ghost is just another imaginary friend to Mormons who believe they can exclusively feel His influence. Collated evidence would prove otherwise.

The rest of the world feels the same emotions about many things, including for some, the equivalent 'spiritual' companionship of their own perception of the same being, spirit or essence, belonging to or being part of the same God.

The fact that billions of other people claim the same experience in different settings does not concern Mormons who continue to assert exclusivity. To them, the rest of the world remains deluded and they can only experience the influence of the 'spirit of Christ' which to Mormons is entirely different, and somewhat inferior to the 'companionship' of their Holy Ghost.

The manual claims that "Through the power of the Holy Ghost we can feel God's love and direction for us" and that it is a "foretaste of eternal joy and a promise of eternal life". I know how it feels to believe you are affected by the Holy Ghost. I have had many such experiences, which at times even brought me to tears. Since leaving the Mormon Church, some may be surprised to learn

# THE GOSPEL OF JESUS CHRIST

that I have also had many such experiences, for entirely different reasons and yet with the same mental and even physical manifestations. Yet I am no longer 'entitled' to them according to the Mormon Church. Indeed, they would claim I do *not* experience them any longer and am deluding myself about such things.

However, the very 'inspiration' that I have often felt whilst writing these books has been powerful and also often 'brought things to mind', but of course I am an apostate and no longer a Mormon, so that cannot be the Holy Ghost. Of course, I know it is *not* the Holy Ghost, but then the experiences are identical or on occasion even *more* profound than those I had when in the Church, thus showing it was *not* the Holy Ghost in the first instance. If there is such a thing, it is certainly not exclusive to Mormons. 'Inspiration' experienced by someone, comes from within and can equally be experienced by anyone and everyone, Mormon or not, religious or not. I know – from extensive personal experience of being both Mormon and non-Mormon. It is identical – except for one simple and singular aspect – personal *perception*.

> Only through membership in the Church can one receive the gift of the Holy Ghost. This authority makes the Church different from any other religion in the world. By the Lord's own declaration, it is "the only true and living church upon the face of the whole earth" (D&C 1:30). *(Page 65)*.

The manual explains to missionaries what they are to teach about this:

> Explain to those whom you are teaching that Satan opposes God and entices people to commit sin. To retain the good feelings they have had while meeting the missionaries, they should read the Book of Mormon, pray, attend church, and obey the commandments. Explain that having the continued guidance of the Holy Ghost is one of the benefits of being baptized and confirmed. *(Page 65)*.

Note once again that Satan opposes God and he will *entice* people to sin. Investigators will have had 'good feelings' while the missionaries were with them and to 'retain' those feelings, they should pray and read the *Book of Mormon* – with no reference to reading the Bible – attend church and obey the Mormon commandments. The psychology is that they will feel they are doing the right things and that will, and I can confirm that it does, feel 'good'. That does not however make it *true*. Many other people equally feel as good about what they are doing and what they believe. And it is often a far cry from Mormonism.

## Endure to the End

> Once we have been forgiven of our sins, we should try every day to remain free from sin so that we can always have the Holy Ghost with us. In the covenant of baptism, we promise our Father in Heaven that we will obey His commandments for the rest of our lives. If we fall short, we must repent in order to retain the blessings of the covenant. We promise to do good works, serve others, and follow the Savior's example. In the scriptures this lifelong commitment is often called "enduring to the end."
>
> Peace and joy come by following this way, and we gradually grow in Christlike attributes. Eventually, as we follow this way and "press forward with a steadfastness in Christ . . . and endure to the end," we are promised, "Ye shall have eternal life" (2 Nephi 31:20). *(Page 66).*

There is nothing wrong with trying every day to be *good* people. Indeed, there is nothing wrong with trying to improve qualities and traits which make us *better* people. It is most important that we are at least *happy* people. If we cannot be *content* with life, there is no point to it. The non-believer would argue – is it not enough to realise how lucky we are to even have a life? For each of us who *are* born, billions of others are *not* born. We are the result of millions of years where our ancestors were the strongest, fastest and sharpest of their kind, surviving long enough to procreate before they died. We can and should treasure our time here and enjoy the moment as it will soon be over, and many humans who have lived, did not remotely enjoy the intelligence or lifestyle or the longevity that we do. Having not existed for billions of years before we were born, why should we expect to wake up once the neurons cease to fire in our brains and we are dead, or once again – non existent?

To the non-believer scientist, the human body is not structured in any way to be resurrected. There are *trillions* of life forms both within and on our bodies, without which neither they nor we could survive. In Mormonism, all life was created by God and all life, *all life,* will be resurrected. In one handful of dirt there are about twenty-five *billion* bacteria that need resurrection and an eternal purpose. That's four times the human population of the earth – in just *one* handful of dirt. There is no logic to the Mormon idea of resurrection for *all* life. Life is cyclical and species live, procreate, and gradually evolve – and die. That's the process. What is God to do with the viruses that affect humans if He resurrects them? Where do they go, and more importantly, why did He create them in the first instance. Some of God's 'creations' remain an absolute horror story which many would scarcely believe. But again, that is another topic for another day.

# THE GOSPEL OF JESUS CHRIST

The question, from the non-believer is, if someone does decide to adopt the early human traits of belief in imaginary beings when they did not understand their world or the universe, turning to the supernatural for answers, do they now need in addition, to bind themselves down with all of the study, prayer, meetings, rules and regulations, that don't affect much of anything, and become subservient to Mormon leaders who continue to tell their members how to behave and even what to wear? Don't have tattoos, and only wear one set of earrings. Would any real God not just be happy that we *believe* in Him and try our best? Christianity in general takes the latter stance; Mormonism dictates far more and expects much more. Whilst believing in supernatural beings clearly transcends reason, once you study the evidence, belief in the Mormon version transcends more; it goes beyond common sense and reason into the realms of complete absurdity; into a world of deep delusion and wishful thinking.

Here's the thing: before 'enduring' to the Mormon 'end', consider this from a non-believers viewpoint:

In the cold light of day, and with such an abundance of evidence available concerning our world and the proven fact of the evolution of life, our growing understanding of the universe and how it is developing, why do modern, and now 'intelligent' humans still turn to the mythical for worship? We are no longer worried about the sun rising or where rain comes from. If there *is* a supreme 'being' of some description, He, She or It is not an archaic being that after all would have required people to kill other life forms and burn them to 'appease' Him as with the God of the Old Testament. That was just superstition by archaic races, even in biblical times. Their concepts stemmed from much earlier pagan ideas. Why do humans still feel the need to follow such traits?

If you believe in a God, do you really think that once He really wanted people to burn animals? If He exists, He is a scientist who sparked life and left it to evolve. What He got was a matter of chance rather than choice, and it was not some grand design. There is no *design* to the animal kingdom. There is a natural 'order' which stems from the survival of the fittest, so to speak. There is a 'pecking order' and certainly a food chain wherein many species kill and eat each other. Thousands of animals suffer terribly as they are ripped apart and die violent and painful deaths every hour of every day and have done for millennia.

Why would any God 'design' such a barbaric and sickening system? Many humans also forget that we kill and eat millions of animals every day for our own sustenance. They think God provided them for us, when in reality we are also animals – that have emerged at the top of the food chain. We are the fifth ape and we are out of Africa. Chimps are our cousins and we have a common ancestor, who looked nothing like a chimp, or us. That's not a bad thing. It is interesting to know where we really came from and fascinating that we know so much that our ancestors just two or three generations ago had no clue about. We must not reject science in favour of faith. We should joyfully embrace *truth* which is reinforced by convincing evidence and set it above provable fiction.

The human body, far from being 'perfect' in its 'design' as creationists would have us believe, falls far short of perfection and humans are already capable of designing it far more adequately than God supposedly ever did. One day they will. Presently, laws forbid a lot of that kind of research to a large degree. Humans, over the centuries, having domesticated dogs, cats, many plants and crops, have redesigned them and bred them to evolve into many new varieties. Genetics are now being employed to further that process even more effectively. So, where does that leave God?

We have the remnants of tails. We have an appendix – well, most of us still do – which is no longer required. Why did God bother with it? There is most certainly an evolutionary reason, but not a 'creation' reason to have one. The inside of the human body is a complete mess and could be far more efficiently designed but you will never hear a creationist say that. You will hear biologists and surgeons talk about it.

Why did God 'design' the path from a giraffes brain to its vocal chords to go all the way down its neck, around the heart and back up again to the throat whilst not connecting to *anything* along the way – a distance of some twelve feet, rather than to just run the few inches from the brain to its throat? That's not a grand 'design'; it's called *evolution* and occurred as the giraffe developed over many hundreds of thousands of years.

Although evolution appears slow, if you could hold hands with your mother and she with her mother and so on back through the generations, how long would the line be before we reached the 'common ancestor' we share with chimps? The answer is three-hundred miles. Not so far back after all then. On the scale of time since life began, if you equate it to a set of piano keys, homo erectus evolved on the very last 'key' and *we* have happened so recently as to cover the width of just a piano string. We are the new-comers on the block and we are highly unlikely to be here for very long in evolutionary terms, before other species replace us forever. It is estimated that some 99.9% of species that have ever existed are now extinct. In the *real* world, the past, present, and confidently predictable future of 'life', is vastly different to any and every religious concept that we could ever imagine, yet we tend to accept what we are *taught* rather than study the scientific *evidence* for ourselves. That is a huge mistake.

If you must believe in a God, believe in one who *used* evolution. To go beyond available evidence and claim each species was individually 'created' beggars belief once you study the evidence of what is *known* to have happened. Confirmed DNA evidence has mapped the tree of all life beyond question. I have a copy of it, provided by the BBC (British Broadcasting Corporation) in conjunction with The Open University. It is accepted scientific *fact*. The fossil record *backs up* the real evidence of evolution but is no longer even needed to

# THE GOSPEL OF JESUS CHRIST

substantiate it. There are several other arms of science that confirm evolution, each from their different disciplines, as a conclusive fact. The Anglican Church accepts evolution; the Pope accepts evolution on behalf of all Catholics. The Mormon Church is neutral about it, but that is simply because they have never decided to face and deal with it. With Hinckley's statement that God doesn't talk to them like he used to, I wouldn't expect an explanation of Smith's clearly erroneous statements any time soon. When and if they do so address the issue, they will run into major problems that Joseph Smith created for them regarding the creation; Adam's altar and fossils found in the stones he used for one thing, and particularly his absolute confirmation of the age of the earth for another.

> **D&C 77:6.** Q. What are we to understand by the book which John saw, which was sealed on the back with seven seals?
> A. We are to understand that it contains the revealed will, mysteries, and the works of God; the hidden things of his economy *concerning this earth during the seven thousand years of its continuance, or its temporal existence.* (Emphasis added).

The Church will somehow have to equate its header to this section, which reads *"This earth has a temporal existence of 7,000 years"*, with the fact that it and life upon it has been around for *billions* of years. This canonised scripture will become increasingly problematic for the Mormon Church in future years.

People who now say they still don't *believe* in evolution simply do not understand that unlike 'God' it is no longer something to 'believe' in. It is simply something *factual* that needs to be **understood**. It is no longer the Darwinian 'theory' that it once was. The *facts* are in. The evidence, established from several different disciplines which all correlate and confirm the same 'tree of life', is **conclusive**. Evolution is established and proven as a scientific *fact*.

Before 'believing' in anything that anyone else ever says or claims the case, especially concerning God, study all the scientific *evidence* and then decide what is true and what is not true. I think I have now strayed far enough from the idea of 'enduring to the end' to call a halt and move on. I hope the reason for my short but necessary diversion can readily be seen and understood, even if it is not 'appreciated' by everyone.

It does take time to understand it all, but the journey is wonderful and thoroughly recommended. Try starting with *Dawkins 2009* if this is unfamiliar territory.

# Chapter 13

## Lesson 4

### Part A

### The Commandments

This is where, if they haven't been divulged previously, investigators will learn what is expected of them in terms of Mormon commandments and lifestyle changes. It will be a shock to many and problematic for some. A small minority of investigators will accommodate them fully and ultimately join the Church. First, the missionaries are prepared.

> Your purpose in teaching the commandments is to help people live the gospel by exercising faith in Jesus Christ and repenting as they prepare for baptism and confirmation. By obeying the commandments, people will grow in their testimony of the gospel, show that they have "broken hearts and contrite spirits," and begin to repent of all their sins. *(Page 71).*

# THE MORMON DELUSION

The manual explains this lesson is organised somewhat differently from the first three. That is because earlier lessons dealt with the 'doctrinal foundation' for the Mormon gospel. Missionaries are given choices regarding how and when they teach the concepts included in this lesson. Some, such as study and prayer may well have been discussed during an earlier lesson; they usually are, in my experience. Missionaries are reminded of a *Book of Mormon* reference which is a favourite among the Mormon faithful.

> **Alma 12:32:** God gave unto them commandments, *after* having made known unto them the plan of redemption. (Italics in manual).

The concept is that you can't teach people commandments until they understand *why* they should live them. Thus, the 'plan of redemption' is taught first so as to confirm the reason behind them and only then are commandments associated with the plan revealed. The following may be taught singularly or combined into one lesson. The manual explains that investigators' lives will be blessed as they "see the gospel of Jesus Christ as a pattern for living".

The fact is that it can indeed be a warm and fuzzy place to be, despite the pressures and obligations. The only problem at the end of the day is that it simply isn't true, which is a crying shame as it would actually be quite nice in many ways if at least some of it were true. Having said that, I am not sure *any* modern Mormon woman would be happy to accommodate her husband having no end of wives in the eternities in order to populate all of his worlds as a God. No woman I have ever met has remotely agreed with the idea that she should 'allow' her own husband to take further wives in the eternities. Whenever it has been raised, without exception, women have indicated that it will be fine for the husbands of *other* women, but not for theirs. None of them will have even begun to notice or understand the 'law of Sarah' as outlined in *D&C 132:65*, or fully comprehend or appreciate the fact that if they *do* object to it when the time comes, they could not only lose their eternal salvation through such a lack of obedience, but also their husband – to who knows how many other women.

So… perhaps it's not a shame after all.

Just to remind any ladies who may be reading this and *not* be aware of just how misogynistic the Mormon God is:

> **D&C 132:65.** Therefore, it shall be lawful in me, if she receive not this law, for him to receive all things whatsoever I, the Lord his God, will give unto him, because she did not believe and administer unto him according to my word; and she then becomes the transgressor; and he is exempt from the law of Sarah, who administered unto Abraham according to the law when I commanded Abraham to take Hagar to wife.

# THE COMMANDMENTS – PART A

The sixth Mormon prophet, Joseph F. (Fielding) Smith, confirmed in the Reed Smoot Senate hearings that indeed this was so. A woman's 'consent' for her husband to marry a further wife, or wives, was no more than that, it was simply her consent which she was *commanded* to give and had no *merit* at all.

    Senator Bailey:    She is commanded to consent, but if she does not, then he is exempt from the requirement?
    Mr. Smith:    Then he is at liberty to proceed without her consent, under the law.
    Sen. Beveridge:    In other words, her consent amounts to nothing?
    Mr. Smith:    It amounts to nothing but her consent.
    *(Reed Smoot Case 1907: Vol. 1:201).*

Sorry ladies; heads you lose – and tails you lose even more. *(See: TMD Vol. 1:26-32).* It is by far, women more so than men, who must be subservient in the Mormon Church even today, whether they can see or fully appreciate it or not.

We have looked at the first 'principles' of the Mormon gospel. Obedience appears as the first 'law' or 'commandment' of the Mormon gospel. Although polygamy is not practiced at present, that is only because the law forbids it. Doctrinally, polygamy, although they really mean *polygyny* – a man with multiple wives, rather than *polygamy* as such, which actually refers to men *or* women with multiple spouses – will most certainly be practiced in the Mormon heaven, which is exaltation in the Celestial kingdom, in the eternities.

Every commandment has an 'or else' connotation. Once you are a Mormon, you immediately become subject to all the commandments they have. If you obey them, there are many 'blessings' attached which are unquantifiable in reality and unrealisable in mortality. As already stated, sins come in both 'commission' and 'omission' categories; penalties are attached to both. Every Mormon is tied to the absolute obligation to be 'obedient' to commandments.

## Obedience

If they convert, the rest of an investigator's life will be wrapped up in this single concept. Perhaps that is why it comes first. 'Obedience' is the key to keeping a convert in the Church and faithful to the commandments.

Accepting that the Lord expects obedience to his commandments means a person is committed to anything and everything that Mormonism subsequently throws at them; from the several soon to be presented commandments, to the many subsequent 'callings' or 'positions' which will consume endless amounts of time, money and energy. The commandments are of course for *our* benefit. God doesn't benefit from anything people do whatsoever. However, it may be difficult to ascertain where, when or how some of the commandments actually benefit *anyone* in reality. This is the deal:

They are **instructions from a loving Father in Heaven** to help us have happy lives. He also **gives us agency**, or the ability and opportunity to **choose between good and evil**. When we obey God, we follow the influence of the Spirit and choose to conform to His will. Obedience to the commandments brings us peace in this life and eternal life in the world to come. **Obedience shows our love for God. Disobedience brings us sorrow.** Heavenly Father knows our weaknesses and is patient with us. He blesses us as we strive to obey His commandments. **He expects us to obey Him so He can bless us.** *(Page 72).* (Emphasis added).

The question missionaries must ask at an early stage is: "Will you obey the laws of God?" Once an investigator accepts the Church and agrees to live the Mormon "laws of God" they are likely to be baptised and confirmed a member.

Commandments are 'instructions' and we are given 'agency' to choose. The choice between doing and not doing something is not seen from the normal human perspective of such things as individual personal ability or affordability. Rather, each 'choice' is determined as being between 'good' and 'evil'. That means obedience is 'good' and disobedience is nothing short of 'evil'. They are the only two alternatives presented. So when a member fails to pay a full tithe or works on a Sunday or forgets to pray, that is *choosing* evil. In the real world, whether God is involved with it or not, such choices are surely a far cry from real 'evil'. Still, that is a Mormon concept – and it is no longer mine. Surely, if a person fails to pay or pray, it is neither good nor evil; it doesn't even *matter*.

Obedience will bring 'peace' and disobedience brings 'sorrow'. Heavenly Father will be patient with us as he knows our weaknesses. That means, when a new member breaks a commandment which is new to them, such as the Word of Wisdom, God won't mind as long as they try again until they get it right.

There are several references provided relating to 'agency' and 'obedience' to help missionaries confirm the concepts to investigators so they in turn can learn what they should do. One, claimed 588-570 BCE, is from the *Book of Mormon*:

> **2 Nephi 2:26.** And the Messiah cometh in the fulness of time, that he may redeem the children of men from the fall. And because that they are redeemed from the fall they have become free forever, knowing good from evil; to act for themselves and not to be acted upon, save it be by the punishment of the law at the great and last day, according to the commandments which God hath given.
> **27.** Wherefore, men are free according to the flesh; and all things are given them which are expedient unto man. And **they are free to choose liberty and eternal life**, through the great Mediator of all men, **or to choose captivity and death**, according to the captivity and power of the devil; for he seeketh that all men might be miserable like unto himself.

# THE COMMANDMENTS – PART A

**28.** And now, my sons, I would that ye should look to the great Mediator, and hearken unto his great commandments; and be faithful unto his words, and *choose eternal life*, according to the will of his Holy Spirit;

**29.** And *not choose eternal death*, according to the will of the flesh and the evil which is therein, which giveth the spirit of the devil power to captivate, *to bring you down to hell, that he may reign over you in his own kingdom*. (Emphasis added).

The above relates to 'agency' and is used to once again direct investigators toward the Mormon Church. That is choosing "liberty and eternal life" rather than the alternative, "captivity and death". We have discussed this concept elsewhere and no one in their right mind would really *choose* captivity and death as an eternal option. Mormon Church leaders would argue that people do that by default if they reject the gospel. Once people have had the true gospel presented to them, if they reject it, they are then responsible, and having *not* chosen the right path, they have *chosen* captivity and death instead. In reality, most people reject Mormonism, but far from choosing captivity and death as their alternate preference, they have simply seen through the entire charade and rightly decided to leave well alone.

The reality for most people who listen to the missionaries is they actually come to consider the very opposite of what the missionaries teach to be the real case, and they say so, by voting with their feet, or rather the missionaries' feet, by asking them not to return. Most people consider that to actually join the Mormon Church would be a kind of 'captivity' from their normal and not essentially sinful way of life, and they prefer to retain their present perception of 'liberty' which suits them just fine. It is all a matter of personal perception and ultimately, missionary persuasion. Many people who do join the Mormon Church are often more captivated by charismatic missionaries than by their message and when those missionaries leave the area, new converts often just drift away. People who reject Mormonism outright are not 'choosing' captivity or death; they are simply seeing through the hoax and rejecting Smith's claims as represented by the missionaries.

An investigator who is religious and who believes in answers to prayer may even feel that he or she had an answer confirming the Mormon Church is *not* true. Thus, to the 'prayer informed' investigator, their God may be telling him or her to *reject* Mormonism. To the missionaries, Satan has answered that prayer rather than God. Something in that process is too unreliable to consider and *all* 'responses' should be rejected and ignored. People should not turn to, nor rely upon, prayer as a suitable method of determining the truth. That is especially the case when there is plentiful *evidence* to consider instead. If there is a God, He hardly needs to be bothered with things we can far more easily determine through a study of abundant available evidence. In fact, where there is *evidence*, answers are far *more* reliable, as prayer is far too delusive to determine the truth.

Note that the devil wants to "bring you down to hell, that he may reign over you in his own kingdom". It is interesting that the *Book of Mormon* is replete with such suggestions, yet the modern Mormon Church considers the lowest of kingdoms to be better than the Earth we live on. If the Telestial kingdom is determined as being the equivalent of the Christian hell, I doubt many people would be weeping and wailing or gnashing their teeth over it, as it would still be the best place they had yet come to know and would certainly be nothing like a lake of fire and brimstone. Smith's inconsistency shines through when considering his *Book of Mormon* descriptions compared with his later theology which survived into modern-day Mormonism.

The Church doesn't comment on the *Book of Mormon* use of 'fire and brimstone' or its descriptions of 'hell'. They are now considered figurative.

The modern Mormon version of 'hell' is in fact 'outer darkness' and *that* is where Satan will go. That place is reserved for the very few who will be sent there for denying the Holy Ghost, which is to deny Christ, having first had a full *knowledge of his divinity*, not just faith or belief, and then *choosing* to reject him and follow Satan. That means that *only* Mormons who once knew the truth and deliberately turned their backs on it – are eligible for admittance.

Ergo; ordinary everyday sinners, deserving of the Christian concept of hell, cannot possibly go there. That very concept makes no sense whatsoever when compared with the *Book of Mormon*.

In February of 1832, Smith penned a revelation in which v.31 states "Thus saith the Lord concerning all those who know my power..." A few verses later Smith has the Lord say this:

> **D&C 76:35.** Having denied the Holy Spirit after having received it, and having denied the Only Begotten Son of the Father, having crucified him unto themselves and put him to an open shame.

This is not just an extremely harsh and devastating statement to be directed *at Mormons* by Smith, it was *plagiarised* from Hebrews – which was a letter from Paul and not directly words of the Lord at all. Smith even made changes to it when he wrote his so-called *Inspired Revision* of the Bible. Smith's utterly pointless alterations are emphasised below.

> **KJV. Hebrews 6:6.** If they shall fall away, to **renew them** again unto repentance; seeing they crucify **to** themselves the Son of God afresh, and put him to an open shame. (Emphasis added).

> **JST. Hebrews 6:6** If they shall fall away, to **be renewed** again unto repentance, seeing they crucify **unto** themselves the Son of God afresh, and put him to an open shame. (Emphasis added).

# THE COMMANDMENTS – PART A

Smith goes on to confirm his belief in the 'lake of fire and brimstone', just as described in his *Book of Mormon*. In 1832 he still considered it literal.

> **D&C 76:36.** These are they who shall go away into the lake of fire and brimstone, with the devil and his angels—
> **37.** And the only ones on whom the second death shall have any power;
> **38.** Yea, verily, the only ones who shall not be redeemed in the due time of the Lord, after the sufferings of his wrath.

But, what did Smith's Nephites believe? They had *no* concept of his much later idea of Celestial, Terrestrial or Telestial kingdoms – the Telestial being equivalent to Christian hell. They only knew and spoke of 'heaven' and 'hell'. Why? Because, Smith still thought that way himself when he wrote it and that is reflected no end of times in his fairy story book of the ancients. There are *dozens* of references to 'hell' in the *Book of Mormon*, along with several that include a lake of fire and brimstone. There are *countless* references to 'heaven' and ***none*** to any other 'kingdoms' or 'degrees' of glory or any other concepts regarding heaven whatsoever.

## Two questions that investigators should ask:

**1.** Joseph Smith taught that there are three heavens and that the top one has three levels of which the highest is exaltation; why then were the Nephites never told of this, despite Christ supposedly visiting them? Everything in the *Book of Mormon* conspires to confirm monotheistic thinking and traditional Christian concepts, including heaven and hell. There is *no* mention of later Mormon concepts or theology. The evidence for *Book of Mormon* fraud is more than compelling from that standpoint alone. Then there are of course all the other impossibilities which combine to prove conclusively that it cannot remotely be a true account of a real people – who knew of only *one* heaven.

**2.** Why does *2 Nephi* twice affirm *(12:11&17)* that "the Lord alone shall be exalted" and the *Book of Mormon **not*** contain the word 'exaltation' at all, when that is *exactly* what all Mormons aspire to achieve? The Nephites knew *nothing* of exaltation. The answer is all too clear and perfectly obvious.

Another reference on 'obedience' from the *Book of Mormon* is this one:

> **Alma 12:31.** Wherefore, he gave commandments unto men, they having first transgressed the first commandments as to things which

were temporal, and becoming as Gods, knowing good from evil, placing themselves in a state to act, or ***being placed in a state to act according to their wills and pleasures, whether to do evil or to do good***— (Emphasis added).

According to the above, people can choose "to do evil or to do good" as they have been placed in a position to act for themselves. To the non-believer, it is a strange phenomenon that it is only within a religious context that even the idea of 'good and *evil*' really exists. In what one might call 'normal' life, there is 'right and wrong' and 'good and bad' but even perceptions of those vary. Sometimes things are described as 'positively evil' to emphasise the severity of something someone may have done wrong. However, such cases are the exception rather than the rule and unaffected by religion. Well, that is not entirely true as many truly 'evil' acts have actually been perpetrated on behalf of God – including the Mormon version of God; Mountain Meadows massacre; Aitken party murders; the assassination attempt on Governor Boggs, etc. People seem equally capable of 'evil' acts whether they are religious or not. Prisons are not full of atheists and many crimes are committed in the name of God. I am not aware of very many crimes committed in the name of Satan. Satan is not exactly 'followed' as extensively as God – regarding killing on his behalf.

Most people do not do truly evil things, regardless of their belief or lack of it. Some are mentally disturbed; some act in revenge; some do indeed do things considered very wrong in law. They are punished if caught and modern society has systems in place to deal with such things. The point is that most people, most of the time, do not 'choose' good *or* evil. Most just live and enjoy their lives, in a complex but fairly well ordered society, and live life without such considerations. Most do not generally deliberately break the law – other than speed limits and such – but you know what I mean, and they try to be 'good' citizens. People don't need to adopt a shed load of new 'sins' to overcome, or new rules where they become guilty of sins of omission, just to please a God.

Some societies have 'positively evil' leaders and even laws which make western society cringe, and yet they are considered 'normal' *in* such societies. For example, study the history and current use of the *full* burka and the place of women in societies that still use it *forcibly* and you will get a clearer picture of the cruel influences of a belief in God. Of course, to Mormons, that would have nothing to do with *their* God. That would be someone else's delusion, related to the Islamic God – who is surely not real? Considering the God of Judaism, of Islam and Christianity is the *same one* as the God of Abraham, who is to say? If there is only *one* God, then He is *everyone's* God irrespective of how any one individual perceives Him or 'obeys' Him. Some obey the Mormon way and others strap bombs to their chests. They are each obeying their own

# THE COMMANDMENTS – PART A

personally perceived will of the very same God and equally anticipate their just reward.

The non-believers' view is humans seem to do well enough on their own without the need for a God. Introduce 'commandments' of a God, Mormon or otherwise, and that's when the problems start. It was the creation of gods and of sin that caused some of the major problems in society in the first place.

Whilst human intelligence has evolved to a stage where we understand so much about life, our planet and the universe, so as to be able to put such historical superstitions into perspective, many people still seem to have been unable to let go of earlier belief systems which stem from fear of the unknown and a desire to live beyond this life.

There is little these days which is so unknown that we need fear it and we should now be intelligent enough to also see that the human body does not represent a viable vehicle to be resurrected in any way. Nor should it be, any more than any other life form. The Mormon God deserves no more respect as a plausible entity than the Greek, Roman or Egyptian gods before Him; no more than the early rain or sun gods; the mountain gods, or the juju at the bottom of the sea. They all stem from the same source and all are equally imaginary.

The one true God of the Israelites evolved out of Hebrew polytheism that preceded Him. Once again, all I can say is that if you feel you must believe in a God, pick one that is at least *plausible* and who doesn't ask too much of you and who will let you keep your money and have some family and leisure time without you feeling guilty.

Another favourite Mormon so-called scripture is provided as a reference regarding 'obedience':

> **D&C 130:20.** There is a law, irrevocably decreed in heaven before the foundations of this world, upon which all blessings are predicated—
> **21.** And when we obtain any blessing from God, it is by obedience to that law upon which it is predicated.

The only problem is that whilst Mormons believe implicitly that their God *is* blessing them for their obedience, the evidence suggests that He is *not*.

Mormons *feel* they are blessed but 'feelings' are emotions and they are very deceptive. Why then are so many Mormons depressed? Depression is just a feeling too, which their God could have equally given them, but Prozac seems to have become the *real* god of tens, if not hundreds of thousands of depressed Mormons. The U.S. 'poor mental health' statistics provide evidence of that in Utah, which has a massive 41.4% incidence of poor mental health; the highest of all the States. *(See: TMD Vol. 2:51-52 n.34).*

There is also evidence concerning huge financial struggles and even high levels of bankruptcy in the Church; high levels of poor mental health and high suicide rates in young Mormon gays; but there is *no* evidence that the Mormon God has actually 'blessed' anyone with anything *ever*. There is just a mountain of, only to be expected, anecdotal evidence which counts for nothing except further confirmation of deep seated delusion.

I was one who used to convince myself I was blessed for faithfully paying my tithing before we even considered paying bills or eating. **Do I have a privately funded pension? No, just the modest state pension that everyone receives in England.** Sometimes we couldn't pay bills and had to re-mortgage our house several times. Was I delusional? Most certainly, or I would have provided for myself rather than my God, who spent my tithing on who knows what more important things than my family's needs and my own retirement – obviously.

The above quote from the *D&C* says a *law* promises unquantified *rewards* for obedience. Mormons, who are faithful and thus obedient, regularly 'feel' blessed for being so. In reality they are not being blessed or rewarded; it is an emotional state brought about through the combined effects of obedience to a multitude of Mormon 'commandments' such as study, prayer and fasting, and programmed delusional thinking. Until someone steps outside that mode and discovers the truth, it is impossible for them to see they have been in a kind of hypnotic religious trance during all of their 'Mormon' lives. Afterwards, it is all too obvious to them and they wonder how and why they did not see through it all before and realise the truth sooner. But, you can't *see* it until experienced.

## Pray Often

God commands us to pray to Him. *(Page73).*

This is the opening gambit in the lesson manual. Prayer is a *commandment*. First, we accept that our imaginary friend, the Mormon version of God, is actually there and we start talking to Him; next we even come to think that He sometimes *responds* in some way; then we become captured in a delusion from which there is little hope of extraction unless and until something forces our mind to consider the possibility of the awful alternative. It does happen, but most people would rather avoid the possibility that they may be wrong, so they abide by counsel and never look outside the Church for the truth.

Prayer is the foundation of the Mormon delusion once we are captured in it. We *must* begin and end our day by talking to our imaginary friend. The more we do so, the more He becomes *real*. The more we *believe* He is there, the more He will *seem* to be there. He becomes very familiar; in times of stress,

## THE COMMANDMENTS – PART A

difficulty or trial, we turn to Him. In our deluded state, we believe He helps and comforts us. The alternative is that we are talking to ourselves and convincing ourselves what to do, rather than receiving actual answers or inspiration from the Mormon God. We don't *want* that to be the case; indeed, we think it would make us feel and look foolish if it were; so we convince ourselves that it is not.

We constantly and voluntarily brainwash ourselves through daily prayer. And that is just the beginning. The manual claims that God will "guide us in our daily lives and help us make good decisions" and that he will "bless us with feelings of comfort and peace". I believed that to be the case as a member, but after several years away from the Church, I can honestly say that those feelings are no different now than they were when I thought God was giving them to me. I no longer talk to him, but I do of course review with myself, important things I would like to sleep on, and as ever, the subconscious mind works on concerns and ultimately provides answers or potential decisions. That is what the brain does – with or without the notion that a God is helping. Results and how they are derived are always just a matter of personal *perception*. The Mormon God is real if you *want* Him to be, and He is *not* if you are honest with yourself. That's what it all boils down to at the end of the day.

The manual asserts that God will warn us of danger and strengthen us to resist. The reality is that so-called danger may be considered things such as not going into a bar in case we are tempted to drink, or avoiding some publications which may contain 'inappropriate' material or even pornography. 'Danger' also comes in the form of 'R' rated (U.K. 18) movies and we should avoid *all* of them for our own safety. We don't need a God to help us decide such things at all. They are personal choices based on human desires and perceptions, having nothing to do with God until his supposed representatives tell us, on His behalf, that He considers such things to be 'sinful' and that we must avoid them.

God did not *tell* these men such things. They thought about them, prayed about them, and then just felt 'good' about them. You can 'feel' good about anything if you want to enough. Thus *we* have to obey *them*, as it 'becomes' God's will. The Mormon God is a very strange God indeed. The prophet John Taylor convinced his twelve apostles that it was the 'mind of the Lord' that his First Counsellor, George Q. Cannon, should skip bail, when he was arrested for polygamy. God said the Church should stump up the $25,000 bond money; well over half a million dollars in today's money; yet Cannon gave himself up a couple of years later and spent the best part of six months in the Utah State Penitentiary anyway. Why did God bother? What was the point? The 'mind' of the Mormon God seems addled to me, so it would be prudent not to trust it at all and rely on our own common sense and reason which will ultimately serve us far better. Decisions to avoid whatever the Church considers to be 'dangers' do *not* come via direct promptings from God; they come from our developing (manipulated) conscience as it starts to accept the idea that certain things are not 'appropriate' – as decided and dictated by God's supposed representatives.

I have never heard of God actually *telling* someone to stop their car when someone else is about to jump a red light and that they will be killed if they continue. Well, on occasion, people do *claim* such things, but considering the number of the faithful who get killed or maimed because God did *not* tell them in time, to avoid an imminent event that would kill or injure, that nullifies the odd claim that God *did* prompt someone and save their life. Intuition or natural indicators that something may not be a good idea explains most things. God is not apparent in anything I have ever heard or seen in that context. The incidence of accident and death within the realms of Mormonism is *no* different to the rest of society. That *evidence* speaks for itself.

People like 'faith promoting' stories and there are plenty of those that come and go. One such was the idea that on the day of 9/11 a missionary group were supposed to meet with their Mission President in one of the twin towers and a series of miraculous events prevented it going ahead, thus 'saving' the lives of the group. There never was such a thing planned and the story was as much of a hoax as Joseph Smith's claims when he started the Church. If someone *claims* God is in something, look for the tangible evidence. You will *never* find any. Everything is sacred, personal, or just feelings.

The manual continues:

> He will forgive our sins. We will feel closer to Him. We must learn to recognize His influence in our lives. We must learn to listen to the still, small voice of the Spirit. We can recognize when the Holy Ghost is teaching us the truth. Our minds will be filled with inspiring and uplifting thoughts. We will be enlightened, or given new knowledge. Our hearts will have feelings of peace, joy, and love. We will want to do good and be helpful to others. These feelings are hard to describe but can be recognized as we experience them. *(Page 73)*.

The first thing that should be said is that this theological reasoning applies to every one of thirty-four-thousand-and-then-some Christian denominations, and also to Judaism, Islam and many other religions and their versions of God. Mormonism does not have exclusivity on the concept of prayer or the claimed experiences of members. Take a trip to Lourdes and you will see first hand on any given day what faith and prayer can achieve in the human mind.

The psychology applied is exactly the same as when missionaries first ask investigators to pray and ask God if the Church is true. Once we accept the idea that the Mormon version of God is there and that He may answer us if we pray, wanting it to be true, it won't take much to *make* it be true and God will ever after be there for us in our minds. That was certainly my experience. After that, the above premise works every time. We *believe* God is there. We believe Mormonism is true, despite the fact we never checked evidence, and therefore

# THE COMMANDMENTS – PART A

we expect to pray. We feel good when we do pray and often believe what we feel inside to effectively consist of *answers* to prayer. We strive to be good people and to serve others, which is a good idea anyway with or without prayer or religion. Life becomes perceived as more fulfilling than it was. We would have felt just the same had we volunteered for a support group or soup kitchen. Doing good – feels good.

It does not make us better people and it does not mean the Mormon God is really there to hear our prayers or answer them. It is a supposition which is accepted and experienced entirely on faith and delusional thinking. And I say that, having had more than my fair share of 'prayer' experiences as a Mormon, including the perception of keeping someone alive through prayer associated with blessings. A child was anointed with oil. Doctors and surgeons concluded he would certainly die during the night. At the time, my faith was strong and I firmly believed I could keep my baby son alive. He did survive the night and I thanked God for 'honouring' my *command* in His name that he should live. My little boy died a few weeks later. I knew even then, that sometimes people just die and sometimes they don't. Prayer and oil make absolutely *no* difference whatsoever, but I *wanted* to think and believe that they could and did.

Some readers who still believe in God may well consider that I just lacked faith but that was not the case at all. I understood the scientific evidence and I also understood that my son was just a vegetable and would never have had a life he could remotely have ever been aware of. He was better off passing on as a baby. I always thought God would serve us better if he helped the thousands of children who die each day for the want of fresh water and a bowl of rice or a mosquito net. Ask yourself these two questions if you pray and ask God for your child to do well in his or her exams and believe He is there and actually listens or even cares about such things… If He does, He really shouldn't, as there are far more pressing matters that deserve His attention.

**1.** Why did over a hundred *more* children die from malaria, or dehydration, malnutrition, or AIDS during the time it took to type that last paragraph? – And I type fairly quickly. I prayed for years that God would somehow find a way for them to be helped and I donated all I could to such causes. I later donated through the Mormon 'Humanitarian Aid' fund for that very purpose, only to discover the money never leaves our country and is held in a reserve fund just in case there is a greater need in the U.K. What greater need could there be than saving a child's life ***now***? *(See TMD Vol 2:346).*

**2.** Why did God create mosquitoes or the parasites (Plasmodium) that some of them carry? Both are life forms and the Mormon God not only created *all* life, He also promised to resurrect it *all*, so where will all the bad bacteria and parasites and wasps – and every other obnoxious species go in

His magical kingdoms of the hereafter? The question is – if God loves his children, why create such completely unnecessary life forms which do nothing but destroy human, and especially young, life? If you were a God, would you create a parasite that multiplies in the liver and then affects the red blood cells? And that is just one of the *many* of God's nasty little inventions. One of His most obnoxious creations remains the loa loa (eye) worm mentioned on p.149 in my view. If God exists, I would like to talk to Him about that one day, as even Satan could not have dreamed up a more evil thing to create than that. These questions *must* be answered. It is not good enough to excuse them as part of any so-called *plan*. That is not much of a plan at all.

I was once one of those who rationalised God's supposed inability to help the masses avoid devastating and catastrophic events, by claiming that we are subject to the laws of nature. However, I never quite saw why, if He could *not* help such people, He *would* help my child pass a driving test through a father's 'blessing'. It never did make any sense that He would answer a prayer request for an elderly person who had suffered a heart attack, to be 'healed', when He could do nothing for hundreds of thousands of children who would never get to live that long – and it still doesn't. A divine being should and would have better things to do. Moreover, His design system should have been far better than it was, so the planet, and some of the species He created, did not end up the way they now are. Some are not very pleasant at all and not worthy of 'creation'.

People are often heard testifying in Mormon Fast and Testimony meetings as to how their prayers have been answered. Most such claims are regarding the mundane and some are positively silly. No one has ever stood and said they are sick of asking God to forget about them and to get on with helping those who *really* need Him.

I was one who *did* end up asking God to do that, once I realised how selfish I had been. I forgot my own small needs and I began to beg God to help resolve real issues as best He could. They have subsequently got worse and worse, and epidemics, weather, and natural disasters are all very hard to keep up with. It was only after realising that for me God did not actually exist at all, and I left the Church, that I finally began to understand there is of course a very good reason *why* such prayer is *not* answered, and equally, exactly *why* wasps and plasmodium *do* exist. It is because God does not; and evolution plays out its own game with no plan, no agenda and no defined destination. Life, in all of its forms, continues to evolve. Species come and go. Intelligent or 'aware' humans have not been here for very long in evolutionary time and terms, and sometime soon, in the not too distant evolutionary future time frame, we too will become extinct, while 'life' in other forms will continue merrily on without us.

# THE COMMANDMENTS – PART A

There is the usual array of references to support the idea that investigators should pray several times a day. One from the *D&C* has the Lord confirming that things which come to mind are from the Holy Ghost and they consist of revelation; He also confirms it is the same spirit by which Moses brought the children of Israel through the red sea on dry ground. That was a *huge* mistake.

> **D&C 8:2.** Yea, behold, I will tell you in your mind and in your heart, by the Holy Ghost, which shall come upon you and which shall dwell in your heart.
> **3.** Now, behold, this is the spirit of revelation; behold, this is the spirit by which Moses brought the children of Israel through the Red Sea on dry ground.

Unfortunately for Smith, whilst he may have assumed the story of Moses to be true, the Lord could not really confirm that to him, or to anyone else for that matter. Even Jewish historians now accept the fact that their tribes were never historically of such a large size; they never were slaves in Egypt; they did not cross the Red Sea or dwell in the Sinai for forty years any more than the walls of Jericho fell at the claimed biblical time of Joshua. Archaeological evidence, in addition to detailed and accurate Egyptian history confirms otherwise. So, if Smith has the Lord telling obvious lies about all that, how can we possibly accept his idea that the Mormon God commands us to pray to him?

Missionaries solidify their visit with the question "Will you kneel and pray daily as individuals and as a family."

## Study the Scriptures

Hand in hand with prayer goes scripture study, and although the manual refers to all of the scriptures, in Mormonism that really does translate to the concept that the *Book of Mormon* should be studied daily as it is considered far more accurate and reliable than the Bible which is only considered valid 'as far as it is translated correctly'. Study and prayer combine to keep the newly converted mind in a constant state of delusion. Much that has been said above about prayer applies equally to 'study'. The more you study, the more you convince yourself it comes from God. Investigators are asked to show faith by "studying, *believing*, and *obeying* God's revealed word".

It is ironic that when you study with an open but *questioning* mind, the truth leaps out from every page. The Church would claim that the former – that is, coming to believe that it is all from God – is achieved through *faith*, and the latter – that God was *not* involved – is achieved through allowing Satan to deceive you because you have not read with faith, actually *wanting* it to be true.

# THE MORMON DELUSION

The reality? We can convince ourselves that *anything* is true if we try hard enough; likewise we can know what the *real* case is if we are sensible enough to compare any claims from within the pages of 'scripture' with other historical evidence using common sense and reason. Anything claimed 'scripture' should stand up to scrutiny; with or without 'faith', the content should be *plausible*.

> *The scriptures are written records of God's dealings with His children as recorded by prophets under the influence of the Holy Ghost.* We show our faith by studying, believing, and obeying God's revealed word. *We diligently search the scriptures to understand the truth.* We *feast upon them because they open the door to revelation* and show us what we need to do and become. We search the scriptures to learn about Jesus Christ and His gospel. Faith in Jesus Christ is a gift from God and comes through studying and living His word and His gospel. The approved scriptures of the Church, also called the standard works, are the Holy Bible, the Book of Mormon, the Doctrine and Covenants, and the Pearl of Great Price. We should study these sacred books daily. (Emphasis added). *(Page 73).*

There are, as ever, several references provided. They talk about reading the scriptures. I would suggest there are quite a number of 'scriptures' which the Church would rather investigators did *not* turn to, until they are fully immersed – but not just in water – in their new delusion, when they may be more able to deal with them. Many *D&C* references, for example, are complete nonsense, unless you are one of the faithful who will believe and accept *anything* and be able to ignore all the obvious and pointless 'filler' Smith invariably included.

Likewise, many *Book of Mormon* passages are completely avoided at the 'teaching' stage and it is left to investigators to find them for themselves later when they are members. By then, they should have learned to gloss over and ignore things that may have, prior to membership, appeared an obvious hoax.

A classic example lies in the several chapters of *Isaiah* which Smith copied directly from the *KJV* into his *Book of Mormon*. Most of *Isaiah* is very boring for most people and quite a chore for them to get through. Many Mormons who start to read the *Book of Mormon* do not get through *2 Nephi* before they give up. Many skip it and read the later, easier to read and understand chapters. Yet Smith copied many complete chapters of Isaiah into his *Book of Mormon*, original translation errors included. **Investigators** will not be directed to study those chapters. Why? They would probably fall asleep. If not, they **may ask**: a) why do they read the *same* as the *KJV* and: b) why are they the *only* chapters in the *Book of Mormon* that are actually grammatically *correct*? These are two good questions – both have *no* satisfactory answers. The Bible is not without its problems either. As I have dealt with the *Book of Mormon* extensively in other chapters, the *Book of Abraham* in *Volume 2*, and a few sections of the *D&C* in

# THE COMMANDMENTS – PART A

*Volume 3* of this work, I will just mention the Bible – and perhaps a little gem from the *D&C* that I have not covered elsewhere, in the following paragraphs.

I am going to deal with two assertions in the manual; "The scriptures are written records of God's dealings with His children as recorded by prophets under the influence of the Holy Ghost" and "We diligently search the scriptures to understand the truth". Regarding the first, I just wanted to show what a strange thing the Holy Ghost is, if it – or He, in Mormonism – actually *was* responsible for some 'scripture' in the Bible. Regarding the second, I agree that if we diligently search the scriptures, we will indeed find the truth – that is, *about* those very so-called scriptures and the fact they are complete nonsense.

That's not what the Church actually *intends* for investigators when making the suggestions, but it is certainly where it gets them if they have the common sense to study *evidence*, as it stands, within the very place the Church suggests we should look.

## 1. The scriptures are written records of God's dealings with His children as recorded by prophets under the influence of the Holy Ghost.

I mentioned Smith's use of Isaiah in his *Book of Mormon*. He copied a number of complete chapters, twenty-one of them to be precise, verbatim from the *KJV*. There are only *six* references to Isaiah in the lesson manual and two contain the same verses, so Isaiah can't be that important to Mormonism in respect of its investigators. From Isaiah, only Chapters 24, 29, 55 and 58 are referred to in the manual. The *only* one of those Smith copied across to the *Book of Mormon* was Chapter 29 *(2 Nephi 27)*. The Mormon Church asserts it is prophesying about the Nephites. The chapter heading in the Mormon edition of the *KJV* claims "*Nephites shall speak as a voice from the dust—The apostasy, restoration of the gospel, and coming forth of Book of Mormon are foretold.*"

Whilst that was Smith's take on *Isaiah 29* so he could use it to support his case from the Bible, it is certainly *not* what the chapter is actually *about* at all. This is discussed more fully in *Chapter 17. (See Pp.428-29)*.

*Isaiah 55:8-9* is used in the manual regarding recognising the spirit.

> **Isaiah 55:8.** For my thoughts are not your thoughts, neither are your ways, saith the Lord.
> **9.** For as the heavens are higher than the earth, so are my ways higher than your ways, and my thoughts than your thoughts.

The manual suggests *(page 95)* that we should trust God to answer our prayers in His own way and in His own time. The manual does not of course reference v.1 of *Isaiah 55*, which clearly states salvation is *free*. In Mormonism it certainly is *not* free; it will cost a fortune over a lifetime.

> **Isaiah 55:1.** Ho, every one that thirsteth, come ye to the waters, and he that hath no money; come ye, buy, and eat; yea, come, buy wine and milk without money and without price.

Tithing is of course mentioned in the Bible, so the verse becomes a possible contradiction. In Mormonism, it would of course be argued salvation, meaning resurrection, is indeed free to all. Immortality is one thing but Mormon 'eternal life', which means living with God, is quite another which must be *earned*. One requirement is a full tithe, so Mormon 'eternal life' is anything *but* free.

In respect to readers who retain a belief in the Bible, rather than get into the contradictions appearing in the Bible, for those who are actually interested, there is a list of 101 Bible contradictions at this link:
http://www.islamway.com/english/images/library/contradictions.htm

There is more analysis available at these links:
http://www.evilbible.com/contradictions.htm
http://www.evilbible.com/Biblical%20Contradictions.htm
http://www.infidels.org/library/modern/donald_morgan/inconsistencies.html

Whilst many claimed Bible contradictions are not essentially contradictions as such but are in fact just not understood in their true context, many do remain unanswered. It is also clear that one or the other, or more, related and clearly contradictory references are incorrect in at least some instances. The point is that it is evident the Holy Ghost was *not* involved with everything in the Bible as Mormonism claims. Some things in fact are so far from any religious or even literary merit, they would have been better not being included. When you consider the number of gospels and the hundreds of epistles that were available and not included in the Bible, although we can see why when we read some of them, some items that were included really should not have made the cut either when you consider them. Question; was the Holy Ghost involved with them?

There are a couple of things included in the Bible which Mormons do not refer to at all. One is the 'Song of Solomon', which hardly constitutes scripture or any influence of the Holy Ghost. Not that the Holy Ghost should be involved at all in *Old Testament* material as it is entirely a *New Testament* concept.

*Song of Solomon* consists of eight short chapters constituting erotic love songs. It was clearly influenced by love alone and has nothing to do with God or the Holy Ghost. No one knows who wrote this book. Personally, I think it is one of the only redeeming features of the Bible, as it expresses a form of poetry unique to the culture of the day. But it is not *religious* by any stretch of the imagination. The text incorporates features that are considered *qualities*, such as excellence, rather than visual; figurative rather than literal – which quickly becomes obvious. The eight chapters create a 'ring comparison', typical of the

# THE COMMANDMENTS – PART A

day – which biblical scholars call *chiasm* (crossing). The text shifts from one speaker to another, from male to female, without warning, and at times, others 'observing' appear to also speak. In literary terms, I think the *Song of Solomon* quite remarkable. However, the question is, in Mormon terms, was the Holy Ghost involved in revealing the will of God to us through such as this? By chapter four it is getting pretty detailed. Here are some excerpts:

> **Song of Solomon 4:5.** Thy two breasts are like two young roes that are twins, which feed among the lilies.
> **6.** Until the day break, and the shadows flee away, I will get me to the mountain of myrrh, and to the hill of frankincense.
>
> **Song of Solomon 5:10.** My beloved is white and ruddy, the chiefest among ten thousand.
> **11.** His head is as the most fine gold, his locks are bushy, and black as a raven.
> **12.** His eyes are as the eyes of doves by the rivers of waters, washed with milk, and fitly set.
> **13.** His cheeks are as a bed of spices, as sweet flowers: his lips like lilies, dropping sweet smelling myrrh.
> **14.** His hands are as gold rings set with the beryl: his belly is as bright ivory overlaid with sapphires.
> **15.** His legs are as pillars of marble, set upon sockets of fine gold: his countenance is as Lebanon, excellent as the cedars.
> **16.** His mouth is most sweet: yea, he is altogether lovely. This is my beloved, and this is my friend, O daughters of Jerusalem.
>
> **Song of Solomon 7:1.** How beautiful are thy feet with shoes, O prince's daughter! the joints of thy thighs are like jewels, the work of the hands of a cunning workman.
> **2.** Thy navel is like a round goblet, which wanteth not liquor: thy belly is like an heap of wheat set about with lilies.
> **3.** Thy two breasts are like two young roes that are twins.
> **4.** Thy neck is as a tower of ivory; thine eyes like the fishpools in Heshbon, by the gate of Bath-rabbim: thy nose is as the tower of Lebanon which looketh toward Damascus.
> **5.** Thine head upon thee is like Carmel, and the hair of thine head like purple; the king is held in the galleries.
> **6.** How fair and how pleasant art thou, O love, for delights!
> **7.** This thy stature is like to a palm tree, and thy breasts to clusters of grapes.
> **8.** I said, I will go up to the palm tree, I will take hold of the boughs thereof: now also thy breasts shall be as clusters of the vine, and the smell of thy nose like apples;
> **9.** And the roof of thy mouth like the best wine for my beloved, that goeth down sweetly, causing the lips of those that are asleep to speak.
> **10.** I am my beloved's, and his desire is toward me.

Yes, the lines really *do* mean what your brain suggested in your mind. If you like erotic poetry, then I would suggest reading the entire text. It is intense and deeply moving. Make of it what you will, if you read the *Song of Solomon*, you will get the implications and I can't see any Holy Ghost being involved with it at all. If it was, the question then becomes *why*? Also; why does the Mormon Church largely ignore it? Clearly, it is of no 'religious' value at all.

There are many things that could be mentioned here regarding what the Holy Ghost most certainly would have wanted to avoid being associated with. I will mention just two, one of which is burned into my memory. Many decades ago my mother was our adult Sunday School teacher. During an Old Testament course of study, she would habitually read parts of the assigned scriptures, aware of the fact that most of her lazy class had not filled the reading assignment. I did usually read them myself and one Sunday, as she started to read some verses, I immediately realised that before that moment she too had not actually read them. Knowing where the chapter was leading, I wondered how she would handle her inevitable forthcoming embarrassment when she finally arrived where she most certainly did not want to go. This is what she *started* to read – but never finished:

> **Genesis 38:1.** And it came to pass at that time, that Judah went down from his brethren, and turned in to a certain Adullamite, whose name *was* Hirah.
> 2. And Judah saw there a daughter of a certain Canaanite, whose name *was* Shuah; and he took her, and went in unto her.
> 3. And she conceived, and bare a son; and he called his name Er.
> 4. And she conceived again, and bare a son; and she called his name Onan.
> 5. And she yet again conceived, and bare a son; and called his name Shelah: and he was at Chezib, when she bare him.
> 6. And Judah took a wife for Er his firstborn, whose name *was* Tamar.
> 7. And Er, Judah's firstborn, was wicked in the sight of the Lord; and the Lord slew him.
> 8. And Judah said unto Onan, Go in unto thy brother's wife, and marry her, and raise up seed to thy brother.
> 9. And Onan knew that the seed should not be his; and it came to pass, when he went in unto his brother's wife, that he spilled *it* on the ground, lest that he should give seed to his brother.
> 10. And the thing which he did displeased the Lord: wherefore he slew him also.

It was the usual boring ramble through uninteresting verses and my very straight-laced Victorian mother was heading for disaster the minute she chose to read the chapter to the class. She was fast approaching 'brother's wife' in v.9 and suddenly exclaimed "Oh! Well; I think that's enough of that" and mid-

# THE COMMANDMENTS – PART A

sentence she swiftly moved on to something else entirely. My wife and I exchanged glances and silent giggles; it was funny then, but now it saddens me that my mother went to her grave, not knowing the truth behind the Church.

The underlying point is that much that is written in the Bible is far from prophetic, revelatory, or even inspirational. Some detail would be better left out altogether. Society records what it records. That doesn't mean it comes from God or that it is written under the influence of the Holy Ghost.

Another example of strange things to include in 'scripture' concerns the story of a man who needed lodgings for the night and was kindly offered help. Meanwhile, a gang came along and wanted to 'know' him. That's Bible speak for wanting the man to be sent out so they could rape him. The host was devastated by such an idea and offered to send out his own daughter and the visitor's concubine to them, so they could spend the night raping them instead, decrying the wicked gang for even contemplating such an evil deed as forced homosexual activity. The rest of the story tells itself in graphic terms. It is hard to understand the ways of the times or the concept of God in early Judaism, but one thing is for certain, if the Mormon Church is right and this recorded 'scripture', kept for posterity, did involve the Holy Ghost, or God, then they should explain why they bothered, as it really isn't material that inspires anything except revulsion.

> **Judges 19:16.** And, behold, there came an old man from his work out of the field at even, which was also of mount Ephraim; and he sojourned in Gibeah: but the men of the place were Benjamites.
> **17.** And when he had lifted up his eyes, he saw a wayfaring man in the street of the city: and the old man said, Whither goest thou? and whence comest thou?
> **18.** And he said unto him, We are passing from Beth-lehem-judah toward the side of mount Ephraim; from thence am I: and I went to Beth-lehem-judah, but I am now going to the house of the Lord; and there is no man that receiveth me to house.
> **19.** Yet there is both straw and provender for our asses; and there is bread and wine also for me, and for thy handmaid, and for the young man which is with thy servants: there is no want of any thing.
> **20.** And the old man said, Peace be with thee; howsoever let all thy wants lie upon me; only lodge not in the street.
> **21.** So he brought him into his house, and gave provender unto the asses: and they washed their feet, and did eat and drink.
> **22.** Now as they were making their hearts merry, behold, the men of the city, certain sons of Belial, beset the house round about, and beat at the door, and spake to the master of the house, the old man, saying, Bring forth the man that came into thine house, that we may know him.

**23.** And the man, the master of the house, went out unto them, and said unto them, Nay, my brethren, nay, I pray you, do not so wickedly; seeing that this man is come into mine house, do not this folly.
**24.** Behold, here is my daughter a maiden, and his concubine; them I will bring out now, and humble ye them, and do with them what seemeth good unto you: but unto this man do not so vile a thing.
**25.** But the men would not hearken to him: so the man took his concubine, and brought her forth unto them; and they knew her, and abused her all the night until the morning: and when the day began to spring, they let her go.
**26.** Then came the woman in the dawning of the day, and fell down at the door of the man's house where her lord was, till it was light.
**27.** And her lord rose up in the morning, and opened the doors of the house, and went out to go his way: and, behold, the woman his concubine was fallen down at the door of the house, and her hands were upon the threshold.
**28.** And he said unto her, Up, and let us be going. But none answered. Then the man took her up upon an ass, and the man rose up, and gat him unto his place.
**29.** And when he was come into his house, he took a knife, and laid hold on his concubine, and divided her, together with her bones, into twelve pieces, and sent her into all the coasts of Israel.
**30.** And it was so, that all that saw it said, There was no such deed done nor seen from the day that the children of Israel came up out of the land of Egypt unto this day: consider of it, take advice, and speak your minds.

Remember, regarding the examples provided above, that the lesson manual claims these "written records of God's dealings with His children as recorded by prophets under the influence of the Holy Ghost".

> **2 Peter 1:20.** Knowing this first, that no prophecy of the scripture is of any private interpretation.
> **21.** For the prophecy came not in old time by the will of man: but holy men of God spake as they were moved by the Holy Ghost.

The concept is supported in *2 Peter* so we can't blame the Mormon Church for its view. However, many other denominations accept the fact that the Bible does contain lots of material which is not entirely in the category of 'inspired writing' and would have been far better left out. The Mormon Church has no wriggle room as it accepts the Bible "as far as it is translated correctly". This *is*.

## 2. We diligently search the scriptures to understand the truth.

> **John 5:39.** Search the scriptures; for in them ye think ye have eternal life: and they are they which testify of me.

# THE COMMANDMENTS – PART A

John 5 is referring to the *Old Testament* of course, as the *New Testament* did not exist when John was written. The *Catholic Encyclopaedia* concludes that John was written around 96 CE. The *New Testament* was settled on in 367 CE in the most part, when the four gospels were selected from *fifty* that were available. Revelation, which was hotly disputed, finally only *just* made the cut a couple of centuries later. It is not used by some churches.

Much of what we find in the Old Testament is pure fiction; this is clearly identified by the very nature of what is claimed. Genesis contains the handed down, from many earlier similar myths and legends, Hebrew, and subsequently Christian, creation 'story' which in light of modern scientific understanding, cannot be taken literally by any stretch of the imagination. I will come back to that later in the chapter, as Smith mentioned something relating to it in the *D&C*. Meanwhile, another fictional story concerns the Israelites being slaves in Egypt, the plagues, two million of them crossing the Red Sea and then dwelling in the Sinai.

Extensive archaeology and detailed Egyptian history tell the real tale. They were simply never there. The Hebrews retrospectively developed their ancestral nomadic tribes into great nations by embellishing their history with fantastical stories of the past. Many modern-day Jewish theologians know and accept this.

The Israelites supposedly ended up at Jericho which God said they could have. God had sky-high walls 'tumble' and told Joshua to kill everyone there. What had the people of Jericho ever done to deserve that? Isn't everyone a child of God? Additionally, Jericho was under the rule of the Egyptians at the time; the very people that the Israelites had been trying to escape from. Had the event really transpired, how long do you think it would have taken before the Egyptians arrived to take revenge on the invading Israelites?

I have visited the Holy Land and many biblical sites. It is perfectly clear, despite what some Christian web sites may claim about their own 'Christian' archaeological research, that things are *not* all as they are claimed in scripture.

For example, I visited Jericho and looked at the digs and the archaeological *evidence* there regarding the early 'walls' of the city. Firstly, it was more of a village than a city in biblical times. Modern Jericho, which is not built on the same site as the old Jericho, is no more than a small town even today, with a population a little over twenty thousand people. Secondly, the original 'walls' were some of the oldest in the world, dating back some fourteen thousand years, several thousands of years *prior* to the biblically claimed date of the creation and of Adam and Eve.

The original 'walls' of Jericho were not 'high' – being two stories at most; they eventually just crumbled, in a time frame several *centuries* different to the claimed event where Joshua supposedly had the Lord make them miraculously 'tumble' so they could take the city with relative ease. Then their God had them kill everyone and also every *thing*. Whether the original walls eventually crumbled due to their age, or earthquake – or even by the wrath of a God, they were certainly *not* destroyed in a *timeframe* even close to the Joshua claim.

Another story that is absolutely impossible is one on which hangs specific Mormon theology and which determines that the Church cannot do what it would undoubtedly like to do, which is to admit that indeed it is just a fictional tale. I refer here to the flood story which Mormons have to accept as a *reality* due to Smith confirming it in context of the Earth needing 'baptism', which is now inextricably part of Mormon theology. *(See: Chapter 10. Pp.195-99)*.

For readers who remain Christian and accept the Bible, again I can only suggest doing so with a 'sensible' hat on. Accepting God and early prophets as real, does not mean you have to believe the fiction as well. Many aspects of the Bible are purely symbolic and serve as lessons or parallels. Modern Jews and Catholics understand and accept this. To consider the Bible absolute, is as bad as considering Mormonism true, after you study the evidence. Many things are scientifically, as well as logically, impossible and clearly myths and legends.

I now want to return to the Adam and Eve story – and Adam's altar. The heading to *Doctrine and Covenants, Section 77* includes the statement *"This earth has a temporal existence of 7,000 years"*, referring to v.5-7.

> **D&C 77:5. Q.** What are we to understand by the four and twenty elders, spoken of by John?
> **A.** We are to understand that these elders whom John saw, were elders who had been faithful in the work of the ministry and were dead; who belonged to the seven churches, and were then in the paradise of God.
> **6. Q.** What are we to understand by the book which John saw, which was sealed on the back with **seven seals?**
> **A.** We are to understand that it contains the revealed will, mysteries, and the works of God; the hidden things of his economy **concerning this earth during the seven thousand years of its continuance, or its temporal existence.**
> **7. Q.** What are we to understand by the seven seals with which it was sealed?
> **A.** We are to understand that the first seal contains the things of the first thousand years, and the second also of the second thousand years, and so on until the seventh. (Emphasis added).

There is no getting away from the fact that Smith believed this Earth was destined for a total of seven thousand years of existence, or that the Mormon Church today accepts this as a theological *fact* by its own admission in the heading to this section.

The Mormon Church has a real problem here, as modern science has not only confirmed evolution of species as an absolute *fact* from several different scientific disciplines, which all *exactly* corroborate the 'tree of life', leaving the

# THE COMMANDMENTS – PART A

fossil record as a kind of bonus, but our Earth is already well over four billion years old. Sharks alone date back several hundreds of thousands of years; so, where are we with the Mormon Church and its archaic theology?

The Church is very quiet about it. It still even remains *neutral* on evolution. I personally think that is because by openly accepting the evidence, it would open up a whole can of worms which then becomes inexplicable; that is, without admitting Smith got a shed load of doctrine entirely *wrong*. Goodness knows what they teach at BYU and how they rationalise now known facts with obvious fiction written by a claimed prophet and held in canonised scripture.

Joseph Smith certainly accepted the concept that Adam built an altar just a few thousand years ago – as he claimed to actually *locate* it – and the 'saints' would go to *see* it. The fact that the so-called altar stones contained *fossils* doesn't seem to bother the Church at all – not that they attempt to *explain* it.

> 7 April 1931. First Presidency instructs Apostle Joseph Fielding Smith and Seventy's president B. H. Roberts: "The subject of Pre-Adamites [is] not to be discussed in public by the brethren either for or against the theory, as the Church has not declared itself and its attitude on the question." *(Quinn 1997:821.)*

A few weeks later:

> May 21, 1931 - Apostle James E. Talmage, a believer in organic evolution, writes to his son: ". . . according to a tradition in the Church based on good authority as having risen from a declaration made by the Prophet Joseph Smith, a certain pile of stones at Adamondi-Ahman, Spring Hill, Mo., is really part of the altar on which Adam offered sacrifices, and that I had personally examined those stones and found them to be fossiliferous, so that if those stones be part of the first altar, Adam built it of stones containing corpses, and therefore death must have prevailed in the earth before Adam's time."

The Church doesn't officially comment on how that deduction is a reality. Was there then death *before* Adam and Eve, or did Smith lie about Adam's altar? As evolution is now established as an absolute scientific fact and as Joseph Smith was a proven and consistently compulsive liar, the answers are clear and all too obvious; Adam was a fictional character and Smith lied about Adam's altar. Today, the Church most certainly allows members to believe that death entered the world *following* the 'fall' of Adam. Many religions now accept evolution as fact, including the Anglican Church. The Pope accepts evolution – and that affects half the Christian world. He is just a little uncertain as to when 'mankind' started having a soul, according to Dawkins' latest book, *The Greatest Show on Earth*. The Mormon Church appears completely quiet about it. The problems such an admission would create are insurmountable.

# THE MORMON DELUSION

If you are looking for the truth in scripture, you may find some, but nothing *reliable* relating to God or to Jesus. The stories are mostly fables, not remotely verifiable as any form of reality. Likewise, in Mormon so-called scripture, you won't find *any* authenticity of Joseph Smith as a prophet. Consider this:

*D&C Section 61* was 'received' from the Lord by Smith on the bank of the Missouri River, McIlwaine's Bend, on 12 August 1831, when he and ten Elders were returning to Kirtland and so far had been travelling in canoes. The heading tells it all really; Smith picked up on the supposed 'vision' and the associated fear and gave the men a detailed revelation. The heading includes:

> **D&C 61 Header:** On the third day of the journey many dangers were experienced. Elder William W. Phelps, in daylight vision, saw the destroyer riding in power upon the face of the waters.

People were always imagining visions of all sorts of things and when it all started to undermine Smith's leadership, more often than not, Smith claimed they were of Satan and that only his visions and revelations counted. This time however, he seized on the opportunity to impress his companions. Apart from the obvious question, why would the Lord bother with such petty detail, when, where and *why* did the servant 'John' *(v.14)* curse the waters? Carefully read the text of this section, asking *why* any God would *ever* get into these mundane and entirely human concerns in such silly and meaningless detail. Joseph Smith clearly made it up so he could get everyone to do what he wanted them to do next without any argument. It became *God's* idea.

> **D&C 61:1.** Behold, and hearken unto the voice of him who has all power, who is from everlasting to everlasting, even Alpha and Omega, the beginning and the end.
> **2.** Behold, verily thus saith the Lord unto you, O ye elders of my church, who are assembled upon this spot, whose sins are now forgiven you, for I, the Lord, forgive sins, and am merciful unto those who confess their sins with humble hearts;

The Lord firstly forgives their sins. In those days and times, that was what everyone sought first and foremost; almost without exception, everyone who claimed to have received visions recorded that they had their sins forgiven.

> **61:3.** But verily I say unto you, that it is not needful for this whole company of mine elders to be moving swiftly upon the waters, whilst the inhabitants on either side are perishing in unbelief.
> **4.** Nevertheless, I suffered it that ye might bear record; behold, there are many dangers upon the waters, and more especially hereafter;

# THE COMMANDMENTS – PART A

> **5.** For I, the Lord, have decreed in mine anger many destructions upon the waters; yea, and especially upon these waters.
> **6.** Nevertheless, all flesh is in mine hand, and he that is faithful among you shall not perish by the waters.

Now God says it is not needful for them to be travelling on the water when the people on each side are 'perishing' in unbelief. Yet He has let them do so to prove a point – that there are *dangers* on the water. Not only that, there will be even more dangers later, because the Lord has 'decreed' in his *anger*, many destructions upon the waters – especially *those* waters. If they are faithful, they won't perish on the waters. Why would God be angry enough to decree such nonsense as 'destructions' on the Missouri River which was to be traversed, not just by the locals but also by many Mormons in the forthcoming years? Where is the record of all the subsequent destruction? There were the usual occasional accidents, but no more than that, so what *was* God going on about? Now God turns to the mundane in a way that is as meaningless as it is pointless.

> **61:7.** Wherefore, it is expedient that my servant Sidney Gilbert and my servant William W. Phelps be in haste upon their errand and mission.
> **8.** Nevertheless, I would not suffer that ye should part until you were chastened for all your sins, that you might be one, that you might not perish in wickedness;
> **9.** But now, verily I say, it behooveth me that ye should part. Wherefore let my servants Sidney Gilbert and William W. Phelps take their former company, and let them take their journey in haste that they may fill their mission, and through faith they shall overcome;
> **10.** And inasmuch as they are faithful they shall be preserved, and I, the Lord, will be with them.
> **11.** And let the residue take that which is needful for clothing.
> **12.** Let my servant Sidney Gilbert take that which is not needful with him, as you shall agree.

Here's the thing; can you imagine any God at any time actually getting into such detail over who takes what *clothes* where? Think *rationally* about this.

The Lord says it is 'expedient' that Gilbert and Phelps 'haste' upon their errand and mission. But before they go, He wants to chasten them for sins that remain undisclosed. Why did Joseph Smith seem to think that everyone always needed chastening by God? Well, God said it was so they wouldn't 'perish' in wickedness. In 'faith' they will now 'overcome', but we don't discover *what* it is that they will actually overcome. Smith's writing is full of such phrases as this which cannot be remotely quantified. Their faith will preserve them. God actually takes the time *and* interest to tell them that everyone else should take the clothing they need and that Gilbert should look after the rest. Why would God get involved in such things as that? ***Why?***

> **61:13.** And now, behold, for your good I gave unto you a commandment concerning these things; and I, the Lord, will reason with you as with men in days of old.
> **14.** Behold, I, the Lord, in the beginning blessed the waters; but in the last days, by the mouth of my servant John, I cursed the waters.
> **15.** Wherefore, the days will come that no flesh shall be safe upon the waters.
> **16.** And it shall be said in days to come that none is able to go up to the land of Zion upon the waters, but he that is upright in heart.
> **17.** And, as I, the Lord, in the beginning cursed the land, even so in the last days have I blessed it, in its time, for the use of my saints, that they may partake the fatness thereof.
> **18.** And now I give unto you a commandment that what I say unto one I say unto all, that you shall forewarn your brethren concerning these waters, that they come not in journeying upon them, lest their faith fail and they are caught in snares;
> **19.** I, the Lord, have decreed, and the destroyer rideth upon the face thereof, and I revoke not the decree.

Here, God is going to reason with them like He used to in olden times. Earlier He blessed the waters – but He doesn't say *why*; then He says John *cursed* the waters *for* Him. Again he doesn't say *why* – or even when. The days will come when no one is safe on the waters going up to the land of Zion. That was a clear reference to that river, as it was the only one that went near their Zion of the day. That was a long time ago and the record of death on that river is no different to any other river, *anywhere*.

The Missouri River flows from the confluence of the Jefferson, Madison and Gallatin Rivers and is the longest river (2,341 miles) in the United States. Taken together, the Jefferson, the Missouri, and the Mississippi form the longest river system in North America. It has been just as 'dangerous' as, but no more than, any other river of its type and there is no evidence that it has been 'cursed' with more than its fair share of incidents and accidents during its history, despite Gods declared but not quantified *anger*. No one else reported the 'destroyer' riding on the waters either. People haven't imagined such things as the devil on a horse riding on water for a very long time. In those days, the gullible may have believed such a notion; today, someone claiming something like that would quite rightly be considered slightly, if not entirely, mad.

In the spring of 1927, the overall river complex broke its banks in 145 places, during the Great Mississippi Flood and inundated 27,000 square miles (70,000 km$^2$) to a depth of up to 30 ft (9.1 m). Was that God's anger, or just the weather? Today (summer 2010), we find ourselves donating money to Pakistan in order to help people there overcome unprecedented of levels of devastation arising from recent flooding.

# THE COMMANDMENTS – PART A

Regarding the Mississippi River complex, on 20 October 1976, a car ferry, *MV George Prince*, was struck by a ship travelling upstream as the ferry attempted to cross from Destrehan, Louisiana, to Luling, Louisiana. Seventy-eight passengers and crew died; only eighteen survived the accident. No God was involved with that and if He was, then He has a lot to answer for and is certainly not worthy of being followed.

Conversely to God now cursing the *waters*, God states that He originally cursed the *land* but now He has blessed it *(v.17)* for the use of His saints "that they may partake the fatness thereof". What kind of a God is this? It did not do His saints much good when they arrived in the Salt Lake valley. Their 'blessed' land may well have derived a faith-promoting story about seagulls saving the day when crickets were devouring the crops in *one* year, and may even have a monument to show for it, but they are quiet about all the other recorded years when God's 'saints' suffered a similar fate and *no* seagulls appeared to save the crops; just as they also are about droughts and other normal problems affecting farmers. The Mormon God is mysterious indeed. Smith was once again just spouting things that were both meaningless and pointless, but they would have *sounded* like God speaking, to the gullible men who were listening to Smith.

God finally *(v.18-19)* says they should warn people not to travel on those waters lest their faith fails them and they get caught in snares. What does that mean exactly and who did they ever tell? As Smith seems to have *accepted* Phelps's daylight vision of the destroyer, which was not always a given, Smith reinforces God's curse by having God say "I, the Lord, have decreed, and the destroyer rideth upon the face thereof, and I revoke not the decree". The whole 'revelation' would never have been given were it not for Phelps and his vivid imagination. Smith either railed on people when such visions were claimed, or he took over and beat their stories with bigger, better and more authoritative revelations. In this case he seems to have developed Phelps's vision and made it into a long 'song and dance' about nothing in particular. Moving on:

> **61:20.** I, the Lord, was angry with you yesterday, but today mine anger is turned away.
> **21.** Wherefore, let those concerning whom I have spoken, that should take their journey in haste—again I say unto you, let them take their journey in haste.
> **22.** And it mattereth not unto me, after a little, if it so be that they fill their mission, whether they go by water or by land; let this be as it is made known unto them according to their judgments hereafter.

Yesterday, God was angry and today he has calmed down again, so he is no longer angry. This is a far cry from God being the same yesterday, today and forever. It is of course indicative of human understanding and traits rather than accepted heavenly ones. God now restates – "let them take their journey in haste", yet if Smith hadn't spent so much time with all his revelatory nonsense, they could have left ages before then. Then, incredibly, having made such a big deal about the waters, God says He doesn't much care whether they go by water or by land; make up your mind God.

> **23.** And now, concerning my servants, Sidney Rigdon, Joseph Smith, Jun., and Oliver Cowdery, let them come not again upon the waters, save it be upon the canal, while journeying unto their homes; or in other words they shall not come upon the waters to journey, save upon the canal.

If you don't laugh at the absurdity of Smith's god-speak, you have to cry – for not seeing through it when you were a Mormon, if indeed like me you were one. God actually says in v.23 that Rigdon, Smith and Cowdery should *not* go upon the waters unless it is the canal, and then adds "in other words" – the very same thing again. Would any God ever really speak like that? **Come on**; how much evidence do we need on this? God actually says to Smith:

> …come not again upon the waters, save it be upon the canal, while journeying … or in other words…
> …they shall not come upon the waters to journey, save upon the canal.

Smith's God often likes to repeat Himself "in other words" and then use virtually the *same* words – for no apparent reason. Would any deity **ever** need to *repeat* Himself and speak in this way? It is perfectly clear that God was *not* speaking in these or other such verses. For examples of God's "in other words" statements, which are really the very *same* things repeated a second time, see *D&C* 10:17; 42:69; 58:20; 63:42, where God says "Let my servant Newel K. Whitney retain his store, or in other words, the store, yet for a little season."; 82:8-9,17; 83:5; 104:5,68-69.

There are many more examples where God 'in other words' does *vary* the wording somewhat, but He does like to use the phrase "in other words" with Smith. Ironically, God **also** used it with the Nephites, but **never** in the Bible. A few *Book of Mormon* examples are 1 Nephi 8:2; 1 Nephi 10:4; Mosiah 7:27; Alma 13:7; Alma 46:21; Alma 48:15; 3 Nephi 3:6-7; 3 Nephi 6:20.

This may be a tough call but should we conclude that God spoke to Smith and to the Nephites in this manner – illuminating His meaning by saying virtually the same thing twice? He didn't seem to feel it necessary to clarify Himself in the Bible at all. Or did Joseph Smith simply make up everything he attributed to God? Not a hard question at all once the evidence is examined.

> **61:24.** Behold, I, the Lord, have appointed a way for the journeying of my saints; and behold, this is the way—that after they leave the canal

> they shall journey by land, inasmuch as they are commanded to journey and go up unto the land of Zion;
> **25.** And they shall do like unto the children of Israel, pitching their tents by the way.
> **26.** And, behold, this commandment you shall give unto all your brethren.

Next God 'appoints' a way for His saints to travel after leaving the canal; that would be by land. What other way could there be? It was a little early for anyone to fly, but now I am being facetious. But a *commandment* to 'pitch tents by the way' – just like the Israelites? I just can't believe I missed all this as a member. I suppose, with the *D&C*, it is because I always struggled with it and my way of dealing with that was to only read it when and where references suggested it. Such references were usually quite familiar and although I did read it all once, I never ventured to properly study or analyse the content in the cold light of day. I think the possible consequences must have subconsciously frightened me. The faithful just don't do that sort of thing.

> **61:27.** Nevertheless, unto whom is given power to command the waters, unto him it is given by the Spirit to know all his ways;
> **28.** Wherefore, let him do as the Spirit of the living God commandeth him, whether upon the land or upon the waters, as it remaineth with me to do hereafter.
> **29.** And unto you is given the course for the saints, or the way for the saints of the camp of the Lord, to journey.

This is Smith's way of saying *he* can command the waters, so he can do as he pleases if he needs to change his mind about travel by land; a clever ploy – and good forward thinking. God can still tell Smith to travel either by water or land and that will be alright, despite all the previous nonsense about cursing the waters. As the Church grew and converts arrived from abroad, although a few ships arrived at eastern ports such as New York or Boston, the vast majority landed at New Orleans during the Nauvoo period. The immigrants travelled up the Mississippi River on river boats that delivered them *directly* to Nauvoo.

New Orleans remained the port of choice for inbound immigrants for a considerable period. This preference was due largely to economic factors and the advantage of New Orleans giving accessibility to the Mississippi River. With no mention of overland travel or of pitching any 'tents by the way', even after the Church moved to Salt Lake, it was often still the preferred route. *(For a short study on Mormon immigration and its perils see: Illness and Mortality in Mormon Immigration. Shane A. Baker, available at the following link:* http://www.mormonhistoricsitesfoundation.org/publications/studies_fall2001/Mhs2.2BakerFall2001.pdf).

> **61:30.** And again, verily I say unto you, my servants, Sidney Rigdon, Joseph Smith, Jun., and Oliver Cowdery, shall not open their mouths in the congregations of the wicked until they arrive at Cincinnati;
> **31.** And in that place they shall lift up their voices unto God against that people, yea, unto him whose anger is kindled against their wickedness, a people who are well-nigh ripened for destruction.

Next, the 'three' are not to speak to anyone before getting to Cincinnati, where they are then to speak 'against' that people who God is strangely angry with. What had the people of Cincinnati done in particular one may ask? God says they are "well-nigh ripened for destruction".

Really? Historically, I can find *no* evidence remotely suggesting what these people in particular may have ever done to deserve God's wrath – and I *have* looked.

In the 1830s, cholera killed thousands of people in the United States, and in Cincinnati, eight thousand people died from the disease. That wasn't from God being angry; it was simply from lack of understanding about what caused the disease. The following, shows that Smith would have served his people *far* better in the forthcoming years had he understood, or had his God bothered to *tell* him instead of talking about who should take what clothing with them, what actually *caused* cholera, as many Mormons also died from the disease. Revelation to assist in avoiding cholera, and also malaria, would have been much more impressive than the content of *D&C 61* that's for sure. This is why:

> People who contract cholera generally suffer from severe, diarrhea, vomiting, and cramps. The disease is spread by drinking water or eating food that is contaminated with human feces. People with this illness can die from dehydration within a few hours after the symptoms first appear.
>
> Cholera first appeared in the United States in 1832. European immigrants apparently brought the disease with them to America. Cleveland residents were the first people in Ohio to contract the illness. Migrants or businessmen who traveled across Lake Erie probably brought the disease. With poor sanitation systems, cholera tended to be most virulent in cities. By the autumn of 1832, the illness had reached Cincinnati, probably brought by people traveling along the Ohio River. The Ohio and Mississippi Rivers allowed the disease to spread quickly across the United States in all directions. Cholera also reached Ohio's interior. Canals provided a relatively stagnant source of water that allowed cholera to fester. As a result of the stagnant water, canal workers commonly died from this illness. While canals, railroads, and steamboats benefited Ohioans economically, these modes of transportation also brought disease. The worst epidemic to affect Ohio

# THE COMMANDMENTS – PART A

occurred in 1849. Eight thousand people in Cincinnati died in this epidemic, including Harriet Beecher Stowe's infant son. Many Cincinnati residents fled the city and ended up in Mt. Pleasant, a community that escaped the illness. The town residents soon changed its name to Mt. Healthy in honor of its good fortune. In Columbus, 116 inmates at the Ohio Penitentiary succumbed to the illness. Former President James Polk, a resident of Tennessee, was the most famous person to die of cholera in 1849. *(Ohio History Central Online Encyclopaedia).*

Next, God tells the rest of Smith's group what they should do. To God, this is apparently far more important than letting Smith know about how to avoid illnesses and diseases which were to kill *thousands* of Mormons during the coming years. Giving an understanding about cholera and malaria would have served them far better than who should go where next. The Mormon version of God is not just mysterious; He is completely ***heartless***.

> **61:32.** And from thence let them journey for the congregations of their brethren, for their labors even now are wanted more abundantly among them than among the congregations of the wicked.
> **33.** And now, concerning the residue, let them journey and declare the word among the congregations of the wicked, inasmuch as it is given;
> **34.** And inasmuch as they do this they shall rid their garments, and they shall be spotless before me.
> **35.** And let them journey together, or two by two, as seemeth them good, only let my servant Reynolds Cahoon, and my servant Samuel H. Smith, with whom I am well pleased, be not separated until they return to their homes, and this for a wise purpose in me.

What was the point of *any* of that? 'Rid their garments' and be 'spotless'? I do get the underlying point, but the language is appalling and the explanation terrible, and this is supposedly the *Lord* talking to them.

Considering remotely, the possibility of God speaking in such a manner and about such things is as utterly *preposterous* as the content is pointless. The same can be said for the rest of the 'Section' which does not even deserve comment. I think at this stage, if I did comment on the last four verses, it would not be professional – or publishable – so it is high time we moved along. These are the final four verses.

> **61:36.** And now, verily I say unto you, and what I say unto one I say unto all, be of good cheer, little children; for I am in your midst, and I have not forsaken you;
> **37.** And inasmuch as you have humbled yourselves before me, the blessings of the kingdom are yours.

> **38.** Gird up your loins and be watchful and be sober, looking forth for the coming of the Son of Man, for he cometh in an hour you think not.
> **39.** Pray always that you enter not into temptation, that you may abide the day of his coming, whether in life or in death. Even so. Amen.

Suffice it to say that we have now 'diligently searched' some scriptures and we 'understand the truth', as requested in the lesson manual.

Once again, missionaries have to commit investigators; "Will you read the scriptures daily as individuals and as a family?" Just don't read anything like *D&C 61* until you are so deluded you will believe and accept any old rubbish.

## Keep the Sabbath Day Holy

> Our Sabbath-day behavior is a reflection of our commitment to honor and worship God. *(Page 74).*

Typical of many religions, the Mormon concept of Sabbath day observance means first and foremost, attending all available church meetings. Members should not go shopping on Sundays or work on that holy day unless the job is in essential services and demands that they do. Ideally, it also means not watching TV and certainly not watching or participating in sporting events.

I found it very strange that Mormon celebrities who were famous golfers or singers would play or perform on Sundays and the Church would promote them as fine examples at 'firesides', taking absolutely no notice of the fact that they broke the Sabbath in order to develop and then maintain their chosen careers.

Partaking of the sacrament is the main Sabbath-day 'purpose' and members are *commanded* to attend. Priesthood meeting attendance is also *commanded*. Sunday School is not a commandment, but as it is invariably placed between Priesthood and Sacrament meetings, active and faithful Mormons will usually attend that as well.

To give an idea of how times change and how things evolve, when I first became a Mormon, Priesthood meeting was held on Sunday 9:00-10:00 a.m; Sunday School followed 10:40-12:30 p.m; Sacrament meeting commenced at 5.00 p.m., running for an hour and a half until 6:30 p.m. There was no time to do anything other than get to and from church and participate in meetings.

On Fast and Testimony Sundays, the first Sunday of the month, the meeting would follow Sunday School, starting at 1:00 p.m. and concluding at 2:30 p.m. In those days, we always had a 'youth fireside' on Fast Sunday evening; there was always *something* to do. Many years ago, long before my time, 'Fast Day' was on a Thursday for some reason.

# THE COMMANDMENTS – PART A

Men would drive or catch a bus to priesthood and those living locally to the chapel would collect their families in time for Sunday school during the forty minutes available. Those of us who lived several miles away would rely on others to bring in our families or they would catch later busses. Many a woman spent her morning in tears, trying to get her young family ready for church, wishing her husband, who was at Priesthood meeting, was there to help her. Sundays were often far from a spiritual feast for many women in those days. When my own first wife, Jan, was a young mother, she had a very difficult time on Sunday. I always cooked dinner on that day during our entire marriage, to give her a break – at least from cooking.

In our early twenties, we lived several miles from the chapel and I owned a van which could carry a dozen people. I used to pick up and drop off several members around our area who had no transport at all and that took a lot of time. These days, 'auxiliary' meetings, that is, anything other than scheduled meetings, are not permitted on Sunday as it is considered a family day, but in the sixties there were forever meetings for leaders and/or teachers of Sunday School, Primary, MIA (Mutual Improvement Association), Relief Society and Priesthood Quorums. Even class presidencies held meetings, so most members, young and old, were involved in extra curricular meetings of some description most Sundays. In those days, what are now 'Young Men' and 'Young Women' mid-week activities were for all members from age 'twelve to one-hundred-and-twelve', so everyone attended. There were forever meetings after Sunday School for some family member, so the others waited, or more usually became members of the choir so they could practice and have something to do.

My own personal typical Sunday in those days consisted of leaving home at 8:15 a.m. to start picking up 'brethren' to get them to Priesthood meeting by 9:00 a.m. My poor wife would meanwhile struggle with three children less than five years old, all on her own, catching two busses to get to church by 10:40 a.m. Following Sunday School, auxiliary meetings would start, but only after people had taken some time to socialise. Things took a slow leisurely pace and filled the day. Those meetings would conclude around 1:30-2:00 p.m. We were usually on the road home by about 2:00-2:15 p.m. By the time people who had crammed into our van had been dropped off, we would arrive home at about 3:00 p.m. or even later. We had to get dinner and be back on the road by 4:00 p.m. to pick people up in time for Sacrament meeting. We rarely had more than an hour or so at home so I usually had a roast dinner slow cooking all morning and it would be ready to eat when we got home. By the time we eventually arrived home in the evening, it was usually getting on for 8:00 p.m., well past a sensible bed-time for such small children.

We were all exhausted but accepted that it was simply the way we lived our religion in nineteen-sixties England. Members generally held at least three or four church callings and some had six or seven. Everyone was always busy.

# THE MORMON DELUSION

Apart from Monday 'Family Home Evening', *every* night was filled with meetings; MIA; Relief Society, which did not then meet on a Sunday; Primary, which also did not then meet on a Sunday, was often on Saturday morning; and of course there were more Presidency meetings and socials. 'Young Marrieds' also had 'evenings' with further lessons and activities in those days too. There were dances every Saturday night, organised in turn by Sunday School, MIA, Relief Society or Elder's Quorum leaders. There was no time for anything *but* church. Sabbath day observance was a given; there was no time to do anything *but* observe it.

Members would faithfully not make purchases on Sunday, to the extent that one man, who held a senior calling which required extensive Sunday travel, found a way of avoiding filling up his car on Sunday. Instead, he would keep a five gallon can of fuel in the boot (trunk) of his car. What he did not realise, until someone explained it to him, was that for safety reasons, it was, and still is, illegal in the U.K. to carry more than a single gallon can of fuel. Thus he unwittingly broke the law of the land in order to obey the law of God. What he did, once he had been informed of the legal position, I don't know. That state of affairs now has a very familiar ring about it regarding the way early Church leaders treated the law of the land – and that was when they *were* aware of it.

Times change, and partly due to a major fuel crisis some years ago, the Church introduced its 'consolidated meeting' schedule. Primary and Relief Society are now held on Sundays during the three hour block of meetings. One exception is the extremely outdated women's home-making meeting, now bearing the exalted title, 'Home, Family and Personal Enrichment Meeting,' and held quarterly. The consolidated schedule is usually between 9:00-12:00 a.m. or 10:00 a.m.-1:00 p.m., unless in a multi-Ward building when it could be later. This leaves the rest of the day free for families to spend time together.

The modern concept of what many members now consider acceptable to do on Sunday is somewhat different to my early years. Quite a few members seem comfortable eating out on Sunday, but when I was young we couldn't afford to do that during the week, never mind consider it on a Sunday. Later, when we could afford to do so, once or twice, I did take the family out for lunch on Mother's Day as a treat. I didn't think God would mind and if He did, well it was just too bad. I tried to be good in other ways that I considered far more important. Even then, I only did that after seeing some General Authorities do the same thing when they were on assignment. They had to eat somewhere of course.

Times and concepts change but basics remain the same. Members should study and pray together as families on Sunday. Children should not 'play out' and truly faithful men would not dream of taking off their suits throughout the day. I always did, as I had been wearing one all week and often on a Saturday too. I needed to relax after Sunday meetings and the first thing that I did was

# THE COMMANDMENTS – PART A

change clothes. I was on the Stake High Council for many years and the men all assumed that like everyone else there, I kept my suit on all day after church and that we did not watch TV on a Sunday. They were quite wrong.

Perhaps I was a rebel, but I saw no wrong in relaxing and enjoying my family time that way. The fact is that in my experience, most Mormons go home from church on Sunday and live the rest of the day just as they would any other day of the week. Only those in more senior positions who feel they must set an example and try to be like 'the brethren' seem to go the extra mile. With young children, you really do have to compromise in order to keep them entertained.

Some Mormon 'leaders' do become over pious and some go to extremes not really necessary. One General Authority reported that he and his wife had 'finally' given up their television – as if it was some sort of redeeming feature.

My own Stake President was chatting to me in the car park (parking lot) one evening some years ago after a Stake meeting, and he mentioned that he had been talking earlier to an old friend of his who was then a Regional Representative (no longer a church position) whom he deeply admired. I actually knew the man too and considered him to be extremely arrogant and not exactly spiritual at all. He always seemed full of himself and his family who could do no wrong. My Stake President said he told his friend that he aspired to become like him one day… I wanted to throw up at that point, but he was my friend and I kept my peace. He then said that his friend replied "You have to remember that when you reach that stage, I will have moved on". Then I really wanted to throw up. My Stake President left that hanging on the air, as if he had shared some of the most powerful revelation he had ever heard. My own thoughts were that if he felt that and was so proud about it that he had to say so, then he wasn't going to move on anywhere. He was nothing but a jumped up arrogant man who was not very nice at all; that was my opinion as a faithful member – now my thoughts about such things and people are not publishable.

I can remember staying with my mother when we were on holiday one year. We always attended church wherever we went on vacation but we did *not* stick to the rule of not buying things on a Sunday. It was an exception for us as we were on holiday and the children usually wanted some sweets (candy) as an afternoon treat, so that was our choice in the matter. My mother, who would not dream of making a purchase on Sunday *ever*, tried to persuade us that even though we were on holiday, we should still not spend money on 'the Sabbath'. When she finally saw that her advice was all to no avail, she said "Well, if you are going to the shop, can you get me a bottle of Lucozade while you are there please". We really had to laugh at that and I asked mother what difference there was in us going and her going herself. She said, "Well, it's not me buying it". We all laughed at that too. I am sure there was some logic in there somewhere.

We bought her item, a British carbonated 'health' drink – which is full of caffeine, and we enjoyed our Sunday in our own way.

Among the scripture references listed in the lesson manual is one from *Exodus* which of course is bound to be harsh and archaic in today's terms. The full reference is *Exodus 31:12-17* and this is something it includes:

> **Exodus 31:14.** Ye shall keep the sabbath therefore; for it is holy unto you: every one that defileth it shall surely be put to death: for whosoever doeth any work therein, that soul shall be cut off from among his people.

God certainly does seem to have mellowed over the centuries, but in all honesty, can you imagine a real God *ever* making such a statement? Requiring that people be put to death for working on the Sabbath day seems somewhat *extreme* at any time and in any culture.

This is another lesson manual reference:

> **D&C 59:9.** And that thou mayest more fully keep thyself unspotted from the world, thou shalt go to the house of prayer and ***offer up thy sacraments*** upon my holy day;
> **10.** For verily this is a ***day appointed unto you to rest*** from your labors, and to pay thy devotions unto the Most High;
> **11.** Nevertheless thy vows shall be offered up in righteousness on all days and at all times;
> **12.** But remember that ***on this, the Lord's day, thou shalt offer thine oblations*** and thy sacraments unto the Most High, ***confessing thy sins unto thy brethren, and before the Lord***.
> **13.** And on this day thou shalt do none other thing, only let thy food be prepared with singleness of heart that thy fasting may be perfect, or, ***in other words***, that thy joy may be full.
> **14.** Verily, this is fasting and prayer, or ***in other words***, rejoicing and prayer.
> **15.** And inasmuch as ye do these things with thanksgiving, with cheerful hearts and countenances, ***not with much laughter, for this is sin***, but with a glad heart and a cheerful countenance— (Emphasis added).

This 'revelation' was given 7 August 1831, at which time Mormons would stand in turn during Sunday meetings to confess their sins. It was a standard early Mormon practice. Some also spoke in tongues and others interpreted.

Some members gave revelations and many made prophecies concerning the 'kingdom'. That hasn't happened in a very long time, so why did God require open meeting confessions *then* and not *now*? To Smith's God, 'much laughter' is yet another 'sin' to add to the list. He appears to have no sense of humour at all.

# THE COMMANDMENTS – PART A

I just can't imagine a God as the 'Master of the Universe' actually speaking to Joseph Smith in such a pitiful manner, let alone with such a disjointed and incorrect language structure. Note that yet another couple of "in other words" 'restatements', that I did not include earlier, also appear in this reference. They are very telling.

The reference finishes at v.15 and it does not include all that God promises for those who keep the Sabbath. The rest of the section does and is interesting:

> **D&C 59:16.** Verily I say, that *inasmuch as ye do this, the fulness of the earth is yours*, the *beasts* of the field and the *fowls* of the air, and *that which climbeth* upon the trees *and walketh* upon the earth;
> **17.** Yea, and *the herb*, and the *good things* which come of the earth, whether *for food* or for *raiment*, or *for houses*, or for *barns*, or *for orchards*, or *for gardens*, or *for vineyards*;
> **18.** Yea, *all things* which come of the earth, in the season thereof, are made for the *benefit and the use of man*, both to please the eye and to gladden the heart;
> **19.** Yea, for *food* and for *raiment*, for *taste* and for *smell*, to *strengthen the body* and to *enliven the soul*.
> **20.** And it pleaseth God that he hath given all these things unto man; for unto this end were they made to be *used, with judgment*, not to excess, *neither by extortion.*
> **21.** And in nothing doth man offend God, or *against none is his wrath kindled, save those who confess not his hand in all things, and obey not his commandments.*
> **22.** Behold, *this is according to the law and the prophets*; wherefore, *trouble me no more concerning this matter.* (Emphasis added).

Reading this strange list of what the Lord promises to Smith for those who keep the Sabbath day holy, leaves me wondering what difference it would have made either way. It also makes me wonder how anyone could consider that it *was* God actually speaking. There is *nothing* listed that measurably belongs to anyone *(v.16 "inasmuch as ye do this, the fulness of the earth is yours")* for keeping the Sabbath, any more than those who do *not*. Nothing is *quantifiable.*

That is a very clever way of using so-called revelation and prophecy. Promise obscure things which can never be measured or quantified – and you are completely safe.

Where is the evidence of the Lord fulfilling this promise? It is in fact such a *stupid* promise that it belittles any God who would actually make it. Clearly, it cannot be fulfilled exclusively to any sector of society and the whole concept is just plain silly. Smith has God say it is according to the law and the prophets. No, it *isn't.*

God says that having said all that, He does not want them bothering Him about it any more. There is not much more that Smith could have God say really, is there? He has already said more than enough for any sane person to immediately see though it all.

Unfortunately, we do not appear to actually *be* sane as members of the Mormon Church, as I certainly never 'saw' this for what it really was – that is, until now. I just didn't consider anything properly if it didn't make sense. I just skipped over it until I found something that I did understand. Mormons are not prone to think for themselves. The thinking has already been done for them.

> **D&C 59:23.** But learn that he who doeth the works of righteousness shall receive his reward, even peace in this world, and eternal life in the world to come.
> **24.** I, the Lord, have spoken it, and the Spirit beareth record. Amen.

So, we all have to settle for 'peace' in this world; not that there is much of that about, and wait for the next life, as usual, for the rest.

The commitment and baptismal questions that apply to investigators include:

> Will you prepare yourself to partake of the sacrament worthily?
>
> What do you understand of the Sabbath day, including partaking of the sacrament weekly and rendering service to others?
>
> Are you willing to obey this law [before your baptism]? *(Page 74).*

The missionaries must obtain a commitment from their investigators of course:

> Will you keep the Sabbath day holy?

# Chapter 14

## Lesson 4

### Part B

### The Commandments

### Baptism and Confirmation

The section on baptism is 'short and sweet' as they say. It doesn't take much to persuade the newly convinced that baptism comes next, and of course the traditional concept that full immersion is the correct method is easy to identify, explain and justify. The manual gives the basic concepts for missionaries.

> The way we show our desire to follow in God's way is through baptism and confirmation. When we are baptized and confirmed, we enter into a covenant that we will take upon ourselves the name of Jesus Christ and that we will always remember Him and keep His commandments. We also promise to stand as witnesses of God at all times and to assist those in need. In return, God promises the constant companionship of the Holy Ghost, a remission of our sins, and being born again. *(Page 75)*.

The above statement from the lesson manual could reflect any number of Christian denominations of course, including the 'sprinklers' as the *method* of baptism is not mentioned here. Naturally, all will be made clear by well trained and experienced missionaries. The concept that people will be 'born again' is a fairly passive one in the Mormon context. Compare the results of being 'born again' in Mormonism, with becoming a 'born again Christian' in a Pentecostal group and you will see a marked difference in exuberance and in subsequent actions, reflecting expression of the euphoric joy people find in their newfound religious state.

I have met a number of such 'born again' people within Pentecostal groups and without exception, they certainly live up to the ideal of their perceived personal experience of *being* 'born again'. Perhaps that is why such religion has grown so quickly compared with Mormonism. There are many faith groups that combine to be considered 'Pentecostal' but the underlying concept, dating from 1901, appears to have captured some 480 million people today overall, compared with fewer than 14 million Mormons; fewer than five million of whom are probably 'active' tithe paying members.

The missionaries are to get the most out of a baptismal service and it is always a good time to have other investigators, and as many friends and family of those getting baptised as possible, in attendance, so the word can be spread and more converts can be obtained.

> Will you be baptized and confirmed?
> Will you invite your friends and family to attend a baptismal service?
>
> If possible, invite investigators to attend a baptismal service and a sacrament meeting during which someone is confirmed.
>
> The invitation to be baptized and confirmed should be specific and direct: "Will you follow the example of Jesus Christ by being baptized by someone holding the priesthood authority of God? We will be holding a baptismal service on [date]. Will you prepare yourself to be baptized on that date?" *(Page 75).*

Confirmation of membership by laying on of hands for the gift of the Holy Ghost has had a varied background during the last fifty years. At times, it has been performed immediately following baptism, as part of the service. At other times it has been performed during Sacrament service the following Sunday. For a period, it was reserved until Fast and Testimony Sunday, the first Sunday of the month, when someone may have had to wait for up to a month for the ordinance. I have known a number of converts not to last the month and they never did have the Holy Ghost conferred on them. I am not sure where that left them as 'members' but perhaps they are still counted. The Church uses all the numbers it can when calculating and publishing membership figures.

# THE COMMANDMENTS – PART B

Baptismal services themselves have ranged from being on any day of the week, to only on Sunday, to any day *but* Sunday over the years. The Mormon prophet David O. McKay declared that it was every child's *right* to be baptised on his or her eighth birthday. That became no longer the case, when at a later stage Sunday baptisms were 'banned' for a while. I actually questioned this apparent departure from a declared *right* by a prophet of God and I was told: "Well, he's dead." I wasn't happy; I wasn't at all happy, and looking back, I actually think that may have been the beginning of the end for me. Things declared by a prophet of God, on behalf of God, should not change – *ever*.

All they had to do, to honour the dictate of an earlier prophet, was to add a rider to the new mandate which said "with the exception of where a child's eighth birthday falls on the Sabbath". That wouldn't have been so hard, now would it? Naturally, when making and updating the 'rules' of the Mormon game, no one ever checks to see what a previous prophet may have declared – they are dead, and only the living prophet counts. 'Consistency' is not a word Mormonism bothers with. God however, if He exists, is the same yesterday, today and forever. The *truth*, so the Mormon Church teaches, is 'ultimate and eternal', yet in reality, day-to-day Mormonism is an ever changing feast. If "truth is knowledge" as the next section declares, then we should question why the Mormon Church often favours fiction instead of the facts.

## Follow the prophet

> ***Truth is a knowledge*** of things as they really are, were, and will be. ***It does not change*** with conditions or time. ***Truth is the same in every age and culture.*** God is the source of all truth. We can have faith in Him because we know ***He will teach us only truth***. Christ's Church is built on the foundation of apostles and prophets, who direct the Church by revelation. *(Page 75 )*. (Emphasis added).

Really? Is that so? Then let's take a look at what the Mormon God has taught is the "truth" which "does not change with time" and is the "same in every age and culture." Remember: "He will teach us *only* the truth" and the "apostles and prophets … direct the Church by revelation" according to the missionary lesson manual.

When Joseph Smith wrote the *Book of Mormon* in 1828-9, he was yet to be unfaithful to his wife Emma, as far as we know, so his take on marriage was entirely monogamous and his *Book of Mormon* therefore reflects that concept throughout. Polygamy is strictly forbidden in that book and classified a major sin. One example of the abomination that polygamy is to God is where the *Book of Mormon* makes reference to the activities of David and Solomon.

> **Jacob 2: 23-24.** For behold, ***thus saith the Lord***: ... Behold ***David and Solomon*** truly had ***many wives*** and concubines, which thing was ***abominable before me***, saith the Lord. *(Book of Mormon – written in 1828-29).* (Emphasis added).

Some years later, when Smith had taken several women as plural wives – some young and single and others who were already married, he needed to somehow justify his actions. He invented revelation permitting his activities and in his defence he called on none other than *God* to now *justify* David and Solomon's very same actions that the *Book of Mormon* declared *abominable*.

> **D&C 132:1.** Verily, ***thus saith the Lord*** ... I, the Lord, ***justified*** my servants Abraham, Isaac, and Jacob, as also Moses, ***David and Solomon***, my servants, as touching the principle and doctrine of their having ***many wives*** and concubines— *(Written in 1843).* (Emphasis added).

If that was not enough to question Smith as a prophet and/or his God as authentic, he – God or Smith, take your pick – went on in both the *Book of Mormon* and the *D&C* to *reinforce* the contradictory position established in each book.

> **Jacob 1:15.** The people of Nephi ... began to ... indulge themselves somewhat in ***wicked practices***, such as like unto ***David*** of old desiring ***many wives*** and concubines, and also ***Solomon***, his son. (Emphasis added).

> **D&C 132:38-39.** ***David*** also received ***many wives*** and concubines, and also ***Solomon*** and Moses my servants ... ***in nothing did they sin*** ... David's wives and concubines ***were given unto him of me***... (Emphasis added).

The *Book of Mormon* confirms the practice "abominable" and the *D&C* states that the practice was "justified". *Both* refer to the wives of David and Solomon and *both* are preceded by *"Thus saith the Lord"*. There is *nowhere* to go on this but admit to the truth.

> I am afraid I can't adequately reconcile these two statements... If the one in Doctrine and Covenants 132:1 had omitted the names of David and Solomon, then I think I could reconcile the two statements. *(Apostle LeGrand Richards, letter to Morris L. Reynolds dated 14 July 1966. Tanner 1987:205).*

**Facts do not cease to exist because they are ignored.** *(Aldous Huxley)*

# THE COMMANDMENTS – PART B

Of course, someone could try to reconcile such statements, but even then it would not be very convincing, if the *names were* removed, but the fact is they were ***not*** removed. Apostle LeGrand Richards, a sustained prophet, seer and revelator, could not reconcile the statements. So, what did he do instead? Did he conclude that the only alternative was to face the facts, realise that if God exists, He is consistent, and therefore Smith's version of God could not be real by any stretch of the imagination and *reject* Smith as a prophet? No, he did not.

There is in fact *no* record that he ever did *anything* other than what all the other leaders have done over the years when faced with indisputable evidence of the truth behind Smith's hoax. He buried his head in the sand and said no more about it. That is to say that I certainly cannot find anything.

No one can justify contradicting statements, especially when they are both purported to have come from *God*. The notion is preposterous. As the names of David and Solomon were *not* omitted from either text, we have absolute and conclusive *proof* of Smith's complete hoax. God, if He exists, is accepted even in Mormonism as *never* changing, and if something is an abomination, He *cannot* change His mind. It was not God; it was Smith who changed *his* mind about it, just to suit his later perverse sexual behaviour. That point is not just a logical conclusion; it is a positively *proven fact*. Smith made a liar out of God in order to cover his own illegal polygamy and polyandry, which all took place well after he wrote the *Book of Mormon* in which Smith had God *condemn* it.

Smith is here self-confessed, self-evidenced – with *reinforced* evidence, and condemned, in his own entirely contradictory writings, as a complete and utter *liar*. His selfish re-use of so-called scripture, altered in an attempt to justify and explain his sexual exploits, does nothing more than conclusively prove Smith to be one of most predatory kinds of human being to have ever lived. Contradicting statements from any real God would be *impossible*. (See *TMD Vol. 1. Ch.3 for an expanded discussion of this area*).

If you want a third option, then the Nephites got *their* revelation about it all wrong – but then, considering God *dictated* it into Smith's hat, we can't blame them, and the con comes back to either Smith and/or his God. You *must* choose one… I suggest *both*, as Smith's *God* is clearly proven to be just as false as Smith was a false prophet. If 'one true God' exists, He *must* be found elsewhere.

> The President of the Church today is a **living prophet**. We are to **have faith** in God's chosen prophet, **gain conviction** of his divine calling, and **follow his teachings**. We have frequent opportunities to sustain Church leaders publicly. *Sustain* means to support. We are to **prepare ourselves** so that when the prophets and apostles speak, the **Holy Ghost can confirm** the truths they teach, and **we can then determine to follow** the counsel they give us. *(Page 75)*. (Emphasis added). (*Sustain* emphasised in original).

Note the Mormon psychology; have faith in the *living* prophet; forget the rest, in case the living one contradicts things that earlier ones have said, which they often do; gain conviction and follow his teachings. We must prepare ourselves so the Holy Ghost can confirm the truth and we can then determine to follow the counsel. We are to programme ourselves to accept *anything* they say as true, and then just blindly follow it.

> Those who listen to and follow the counsel of living prophets and apostles will not go astray. The teachings of living prophets provide an anchor of eternal truth in a world of shifting values and help us avoid misery and sorrow. The confusion and strife of the world will not overwhelm us, and we can enjoy the assurance of being in harmony with God's will. *(Page 75).*

The problem is that a prophet is determined by his *prophesy*. The prophet and apostles are all sustained as prophets, seers and revelators and yet not one of them has 'prophesied' or 'seen' or 'revealed' anything in *this* day. When a supposed prophet of God claims that God doesn't work that way any more – he is *not* a prophet and his God is invented.

Don Lattin, reporter for the *San Francisco Chronicle*, interviewed President Hinckley and asked him about divine revelation. *(See the full quote on p.121).*

> **Q**: And this belief in contemporary revelation and prophecy? As the prophet, tell us how that works. How do you receive divine revelation? What does it feel like?
>
> **A**: Let me say first that we have a great body of revelation, the vast majority of which came from the prophet Joseph Smith. **We don't need much revelation**. We need to pay more attention to the revelation we've already received. Now, if a problem should arise on which we don't have an answer, we pray about it, we may fast about it, and it comes. Quietly. **Usually no voice of any kind, but just a perception in the mind.** *(Interview with President Gordon B. Hinckley, as published on the Web site of the San Francisco Chronicle, 13 April 1997).*

The lesson manual urges investigators to follow the living prophet and accept his teachings. We now know that all he got was *feelings*, which we all get; feelings are of course extremely unreliable. If the Mormon God is no longer appearing, or at least speaking to his prophet, then of what use is he to anyone? The idea that we already have lots of revelation and that we hardly need any now is a cop-out and doesn't cut it at all. The world obviously needs revelation if it is available. Do we not need revelation now more than ever?

God didn't even bother to tell Hinckley that world markets would crash and leave Mormon Church 'final salary' pension schemes short of many millions of

# THE COMMANDMENTS – PART B

dollars. Ironically, I was a Financial Adviser myself and restructured several employee pension schemes to 'defined contribution' arrangements many years ago in order to avoid such an eventuality. Every professional adviser did so, as otherwise most companies would by now have gone bankrupt. Retaining such schemes has long been financially unviable. God didn't tell us as 'non-prophet' Financial Advisers to do that; common sense and financial acumen did. The Church does have *access* to that kind of professional advice too.

God didn't seem to have enough common sense to at least whisper *that* to his prophet or even have the 'thought' come to his mind. That's probably as Hinckley had no idea about finance or pensions, so he would never have had a *question* about it and never have fasted or prayed about it – so no thought could possibly have come to his mind. If Hinckley had to think of a *question* before he could even *get* a revelation consisting of *thoughts* in his mind, he never was going to be able to reveal anything new or essential from God.

Regardless of God, Mormon Church Financial Advisers invariably must have advised the Church to make changes many years ago. It is inconceivable that *any* adviser would have suggested continuing such schemes during the last ten to fifteen years. Church leaders must have ignored such professional advice – and at what cost? It has now cost many tens, if not hundreds, of millions of dollars of faithful members' tithing money just to prop up the funds in recent years. How many members tithed all of their lives just to meet the Mormon pension shortfall?

The Mormon God could have told his prophet to make the change and save tens of millions of dollars which would have been better served saving many thousands of lives in countries continuously beset by one tragedy or another. In 2005, some £11.8 million (over $18.4 million) was injected into the U.K. part of the Mormon Church pension fund *alone. (See TMD Vol 2:342-43).*

One of the recommended references is this familiar *Old Testament* verse:

> **Amos 3:7.** Surely the Lord God will do nothing, but he revealeth his secret unto his servants the prophets.

According to Hinckley, God now keeps His 'secrets' to Himself and doesn't reveal anything worth hearing at all. "Now, if a problem should arise on which we don't have an answer, we pray about it, we may fast about it, and it comes. Quietly. Usually no voice of any kind, but just a perception in the mind." *(See p.304).* The only problem with this method is that they have to first *think* of a question for which they need an answer. A prophet is supposed to *prophesy*. God is supposed to 'reveal' *His* 'secrets' unknown to a prophet until God speaks. A prophet should not have to dream up appropriate questions in order to obtain 'feelings' that are supposed to represent answers from God. It is not supposed to work that way. In reality, of course it *doesn't*.

These are the commitment questions:

Will you meet the bishop?
Will you sustain and follow the counsel of Church leaders?
Do you believe that [current Church President] is a prophet of God?
What does that mean to you?

## Keep the Ten Commandments

Heavenly Father gives us commandments so that we will know what to do and what to avoid in order to receive the blessings He wants to give us (joy, peace of conscience, lasting happiness). God revealed to Moses the Ten Commandments to guide His people: *(Page 76).*

Thou shalt have no other gods before me. (Exodus 20:3).
Other "gods" can include possessions, power, or prominence.
Thou shalt not make unto thee any graven image. (Exodus 20:4)
Thou shalt not take the name of the Lord thy God in vain. (Exodus 20:7).
Remember the sabbath day, to keep it holy. (Exodus 20:8).
Honour thy father and thy mother. (Exodus 20:12).
Thou shalt not kill. (Exodus 20:13).
Thou shalt not commit adultery. (Exodus 20:14).
Thou shalt not steal. (Exodus 20:15).
Thou shalt not bear false witness against thy neighbour. (Exodus 20:16).
Thou shalt not covet. (Exodus 20:17).

The Ten Commandments are still valid today. They teach us to worship and show reverence for God. They also teach us how to treat one another.

According to *Exodus*, God is a jealous God and will punish your children's children if you disobey His commandments; at least, that was the case in the time of Moses. In the modern *Tanakh*, God is *zealous* rather than *jealous* but results are similar and the children still get punished for things they didn't do.

> **Exodus 20:5.** ...for I the Lord thy God am a ***jealous*** God, visiting the iniquity of the fathers upon the children unto the third and fourth generation of them that hate me; (Emphasis added).

The manual lists the Ten Commandments as they appear in *Exodus*. These are of course widely known. There are actually several more commandments in Exodus but as they are not mentioned by the Mormon Church there is no point

# THE COMMANDMENTS – PART B

in referencing them here as they do not impact on this little section. What does impact on it is the fact that the manual not only references *Exodus*, it also references *Mosiah 13* where Abinadi apparently "teaches" the Nephites the Ten Commandments in about 148 BCE. The manual does not reference two earlier verses in *Mosiah 12:35-36* which contain the first two commandments, but they are virtually identical to the *KJV*.

Despite the fact that the *Pentateuch* for Christians, or *Torah* for Jews, is often referred to as the five 'Books of Moses', particularly in Mormonism, many scholars think they were written later by different people – and certainly *not* by Moses. An indication of the probability of this lies in the duplication of several aspects, including the Ten Commandments. They are repeated in *Deuteronomy 5:6-21*, but there, the wording is somewhat different, as you would expect when recounted by a different author. Every 'telling' would vary, and records, unless copied, will always have differences. Smith *copied* the *KJV* of the *Exodus* account and pretended Abinadi was *reading* it.

Abinadi's 'reading' was presumably from the brass plates. God supposedly had Nephi *murder* Laban in order to obtain them so Lehi could take them with him when he left Jerusalem. That act appears to conflict with at least two of the Ten Commandments. First, Nephi commits a premeditated and cold-blooded murder under a contradictory instruction from God; thou shalt not murder – go and murder Laban; then he steals the plates; thou shalt not steal – steal the plates, which do not belong to him. The *Book of Mormon* claims *God* was responsible for both of these acts which defy two of His own commandments.

God seems to be living by different 'rules':

> **1 Nephi 4:13.** Behold the Lord slayeth the wicked to bring forth his righteous purposes. It is better that one man should perish than that a nation should dwindle and perish in unbelief.

Many Mormons have a very hard time getting their heads around this idea but usually they eventually manage to do so. It is understandable why it can be a struggle, as it makes no theological sense whatsoever. Humans can't murder each other but God can instruct them to do so. He supposedly did so at Jericho and God Himself killed first-born Egyptians, according to the Bible. This early *Book of Mormon* 'confession' is just the beginning of the 'hang on a minute' moments that people have when they start to look at what the book contains.

If the entire *Book of Mormon* were to be properly studied and considered, rather than reading only selected verses *prior* to obtaining a 'testimony' that it is true by ethereal means, then ultimately so many more such 'moments' would arise that any investigator would eventually just reject the whole thing out of hand. No prayer would be needed as there would be nothing left to verify. A testimony is gained by wishful thinking that overall concepts of Mormonism could be true. That would be very nice. So, it 'becomes' true in the mind and that is considered an answer to prayer. The 'detail' in the *Book of Mormon* however, *proves* otherwise. If someone thoroughly *studies* Mormonism *before* a delusion is entered into, rather than afterwards, they do *not* join the Church.

Ignore the fact that the Hebrews only ever used papyri for their scriptures. There was an unusual and unique single 'copper' document among the Dead Sea Scrolls found at Qumran, but this also was a *scroll*. It looks a bit like 'plates' now, as it was carefully cut into segments in order to decipher it. This is a far cry from brass plates supposedly owned by Smith's fictional Laban.

If Abinadi was reading from plates inscribed long before 600 BCE, then as mentioned elsewhere, they certainly should *not* read *exactly* the same as the *KJV* for a number of reasons. The Jews wrote and rewrote their scriptures on papyri, destroying an entire scroll and starting again if they made a single error. The *Pentateuch* was constructed in the format in which it then moved forward into the Common Era, long after Lehi left Jerusalem while the Jews were in exile, but anything Lehi had should have still *matched* such documents exactly. The textual journey of the 'Christian' version, culminating in what eventually became the *Old Testament*, constructed by comparing several earlier versions in 1611, could not possibly be translated into exact words derived from plates predating 600 BCE. These were then supposedly transcribed into 'reformed' Egyptian hieroglyphs (picture language) and then into early modern English by God for Smith. Yet Smith, as ever, seemed content to copy, in the main, into his *Book of Mormon*, word for word details as they *now* appear in the *KJV*.

Check any other translation and note the small differences that start to creep in and you will immediately understand the *impossibility* of Smith's *Book of Mormon* version having come from early original texts predating 600 BCE.

The *New International Version* of the Bible contains classic examples of how wording changes, retaining the original message but presented in a format to suit the current generation. Instead of saying "Thou shalt not kill", it says "Thou shalt not murder" – as does the Tanakh, as it happens. There is an inherent difference in connotation. Instead of saying "Thou shalt not take the name of the Lord thy God in vain", the *NIV* explains "You shall not misuse the name of the Lord your God". Instead of saying "Thou shalt not bear false witness..." it urges "You shall not give false testimony...", so it is clear to see how explanations are structured by translators to suit their *current* audience. Other than Smith, no one used archaic language forms that they neither understood properly nor could write correctly.

In Smith's attempted use of Early Modern English language and grammar alone, his hoax is exposed *thousands* of times in the *Book of Mormon*, the *Book of Moses*, the *Book of Abraham* and the *Doctrine and Covenants*. The only parts of the *Book of Mormon* which are grammatically *correct* are the portions

# THE COMMANDMENTS – PART B

he *copied* from the *KJV*. When we consider that fact alone, does anything more need to be said or considered in order to determine that Smith was a fraud?

I am sure readers would agree that whilst the meaning was fairly clear in the *KJV*, the updated wording sits better in our modern language and thought processes. This kind of updating of concepts and ideas is of course not unique to the last four centuries. It has gone on for thousands of years, so what we read today is, in some instances, not even close to the original concepts, let alone the exact words used in any original texts. Having been translated through different routes and languages, as ever, what Smith claims is entirely impossible. The details should incorporate *similar* ideas but be expressed somewhat differently, due to the language and cultural differences of each era, for them to stand any chance of being considered authentic. Otherwise – a copy is a copy is a copy.

Apologists have tried to con Mormons into believing, regarding the many chapters of Isaiah in the *Book of Mormon*, that when Smith came across them in the book, he may have just used the *KJV* rather than bother to translate them again. I have mentioned elsewhere the fact that that is hardly plausible, as God was dictating everything into Smith's hat. God would have provided a much clearer and more accurate original account for Smith during such a process and Smith would not have turned to the *KJV* in preference. The notion is absurd, but then of course the very idea that God spoke to Smith via a stone in his hat is also absurd. An original version from a God would *be* original, and beautiful.

The point is that if the Mormon Church wishes to use the same argument here – that Smith noticed the commandments, so he copied them from the *KJV* – it would in fact be ridiculous, as here we have Abinadi, not just reading them out, but interspersing them with his own thoughts. This is an important issue, so I have included the relevant chapters from Mosiah as an appendix, isolating the *KJV* narrative for reference. It is clear from *Book of Mormon* text that the words were *supposedly* original, read from brass plates to King Noah and his people, and it is also clear that they are anything *but* original. *(See: Apx B).*

In order to quantify that, compare the *KJV*, which Smith virtually *copied*, with a direct Early Modern English translation of the *Tanakh* and the point will more easily be seen. If the 1830 *Book of Mormon* included the translation of an original pre-600 BCE text, then it should more closely resemble the *Tanakh* and most certainly not be almost identical to the *KJV*. Differences are slight, as would be expected, but they are nevertheless extremely significant.

In the following comparison of texts, look for significant flaws in Smith's work too. For example, in the first commandment, the *KJV* mentions 'gods' in the plural but lower case, signifying the Jews had been worshiping multiple gods, which to the one true 'God' were the false gods of 'others'. Smith uses 'God' in the *singular* and it is *capitalised*. Both the singular and capitalisation offend the original text of the *KJV and* the *Tanakh*. Smith doesn't stop there...

# THE MORMON DELUSION

I have emphasised a few of the more significant differences in the text of the *Tanakh* and Smith's *Book of Mormon* version. There are some instances where the *KJV* and the *Tanakh* are *identical* but Smith uses different words altogether. At those *converging* points, Smith's, Abinadi's or God's, words should of course definitely be *exactly the same* but they are *not*. Smith also leaves some words out completely which appear in both the *KJV and* the *Tanakh*. This is also very telling in context of evidence contained in multiple sources of an original text. Although most of the *KJV* translates the same as the *Tanakh*, where there are differences, Abinadi 'reads' words that match the *KJV* rather than the *Tanakh*. This should not be the case. Modern verse numbers have been inserted into the original *Book of Mormon* text for reference.

| King James Version. Exodus 20 | 1830 Book of Mormon. Mosiah 12 & 13 | Tanakh – English Translation Exodus 20 |
|---|---|---|
| 3. Thou shalt have no other gods before me. | 12:35. Thou shalt have no other **God** before me. (Below is all Chapter 13). | 3. Thou shalt have no other gods before **Me**. |
| 4. Thou shalt not make unto thee any graven image, or any likeness of any thing that is in heaven above, or that is in the earth beneath, or that is in the water under the earth: 5. Thou shalt not bow down **thyself** to them, nor serve them: for I the LORD thy God am a jealous God, visiting the *iniquity* of the fathers upon the children unto the third and fourth generation of them that hate me; 6. And shewing mercy unto thousands        of them that love me, and keep my commandments. | 12. ...Thou shalt not make unto thee any graven image, or any likeness of **things which is** [later changed to ***are***] in heaven above, or **which is** [later changed to ***are***] in the earth beneath, or **which are** in the water under the earth. 13. ***And again***: Thou shalt not bow down **thyself** unto them, nor serve them; for I the Lord thy God am a jealous God, visiting the ***iniquities*** of the fathers upon the children, unto the third and fourth generation*s* of them that hate me; 14. And shewing mercy unto thousands        of them that love me and keep my commandments. | 4. Thou shalt not make unto thee ***a*** graven image, ***nor any manner*** of likeness, of any thing that is in heaven above, or that is in the earth beneath, or that is in the water under the earth; 5. thou shalt not bow down unto them, nor serve them; for I the LORD thy God am a jealous God, visiting the ***iniquity*** of the fathers upon the children unto the third and fourth generation of them that hate ***Me***; 6. and showing mercy ***unto the thousandth generation*** of them that love Me and keep ***My*** commandments. |
| 7. Thou shalt not take the name of the Lord thy God in vain; for the | 15. Thou shalt not take the name of the Lord thy God in vain: for the | 7. Thou shalt not take the name of the LORD thy God in vain; for the |

# THE COMMANDMENTS – PART B

| | | |
|---|---|---|
| Lord will not hold him guiltless that taketh his name in vain. | Lord will not hold him guiltless that taketh his name in vain. | LORD will not hold him guiltless that taketh His name in vain. |
| 8. Remember the sabbath day, to keep it holy. 9. Six days shalt thou labour, and do all thy work: 10. But the seventh day is the sabbath *of the* Lord thy God: *in it* thou shalt not do any work, thou, nor thy son, nor thy daughter, thy manservant, nor thy maidservant, nor thy cattle, nor thy stranger that is within thy gates: 11. For in six days the Lord made heaven and earth, the sea, and all that in them is, *and rested the seventh day*: wherefore the Lord blessed the sabbath day, and hallowed it. | 16. Remember the sabbath day, to keep it holy. 17. Six days shalt thou labor, and do all thy work: 18. but the seventh day, the sabbath *of the* Lord thy God, thou shalt not do any work, thou, nor thy son, nor thy daughter, thy man-servant, nor thy maid-servant, nor thy cattle, nor thy stranger that is within thy gates: 19. For in six days the Lord made heaven and earth, and the sea, and all that in them is; wherefore the Lord blessed the Sabbath-day, and hallowed it. | 8 Remember the sabbath day, to keep it holy. 9 Six days shalt thou labour, and do all thy work; 10 but the seventh day is *a* sabbath unto the LORD thy God, *in it* thou shalt not do any *manner of* work, thou, nor thy son, nor thy daughter, *nor* thy man-servant, nor thy maid-servant, nor thy cattle, nor thy stranger that is within thy gates; 11. for in six days the LORD made heaven and earth, the sea, and all that in them is, *and rested on the seventh day*; wherefore the LORD blessed the sabbath day, and hallowed it. |
| 12. Honour thy father and thy mother: that thy days may be long upon the land which the Lord thy God giveth thee. | 20. Honor thy father and thy mother, that thy days may be long upon the land which the Lord thy God giveth thee. | 12. Honour thy father and thy mother, that thy days may be long upon the land which the LORD thy God giveth thee. |
| 13. Thou shalt not kill. | 21. Thou shalt not kill. | 13. Thou shalt not *murder*. |
| 14. Thou shalt not commit adultery. | 22. Thou shalt not commit adultery. | 13. Thou shalt not commit adultery. |
| 15. Thou shalt not steal. | 22. Thou shalt not steal. | 13. Thou shalt not steal. |
| 16. Thou shalt not bear false witness against thy neighbour. | 23. Thou shalt not bear false witness against thy neighbor. | 13. Thou shalt not bear false witness against thy neighbour. |
| 17. Thou shalt not covet thy neighbour's house, thou shalt not covet thy neighbour's wife, nor his manservant, nor his maidservant, nor his ox, | 24. Thou shalt not covet thy neighbor's house, thou shalt not covet thy neighbor's wife, nor his man-servant, nor his maid-servant, nor his ox, | 14. Thou shalt not covet thy neighbour's house; thou shalt not covet thy neighbour's wife, nor his man-servant, nor his maid-servant, nor his ox, |

| nor his ass, nor any thing that is thy neighbour's. | nor his ass, nor any thing [later changed to ***anything***] that is thy neighbor's. | nor his ass, nor any thing that is thy neighbour's. |

Smith has yet another *Book of Mormon* problem. Regarding keeping the Sabbath day holy, the commandments confirm that even "thy cattle" should do no work. Also, regarding 'coveting' they should not covet their neighbour's "ox nor his ass". Unfortunately, the Nephites did not *have* any cattle, or oxen or asses *to* covet. They would not have had a clue what they were. Abinadi could not explain the animals, as he was born several hundreds of years after Lehi left Jerusalem and no one had seen such beasts since that time. He could have changed the names to other animals of possible ownership in order to make the point – or better yet, simply have just left out those words altogether – as they didn't actually have *any* domesticated animals to covet – unless any of them managed to domesticate turkeys. Such animals simply did *not* exist there.

The following are some, but not all, of the animals that *were* in existence in various parts of the Americas during the *Book of Mormon* era: alpaca; bear; boar; bison; coati (which resembles a raccoon); coyote; deer; duck; guinea-pig; jackrabbit; pronghorn (*Antilocapra americana*, often mistakenly termed an antelope); mountain sheep; jaguar; llama; monkey; reindeer; sloth; tapir; wild turkey and the domesticated turkey from about 3000 BCE; and the turtle. Take your pick. They would hardly be 'coveted' as no one's neighbours would have 'owned' any.

A recent study identified that Native Americans domesticated turkeys about 800 BCE, long before Lehi left Jerusalem to inhabit a supposedly *empty* America, in south-central Mexico. They were domesticated a second time in what is now the south-western U.S. around 200 BCE. They were not raised for food however, but rather for their feathers which were used in rituals and ceremonies, as well as to make feather robes or blankets. It was not until about 1100 CE that Puebloans started to use them for food. Therefore, if the Nephites ever existed, it is unlikely that turkeys were ever used for sacrifices. That doesn't leave much of anything for them to have used for such purposes.

> Their investigations revealed that pre-Aztec people around south-central Mexico first domesticated turkeys. The birds appear to either have either been penned or "allowed to roam around the village," (http://www.msnbc.msn.com/id/35186605/)

On that evidence, even domesticated turkeys could hardly have been used by Smith's fictitious BCE Nephites for any "sacrifice and burnt offerings". In any event, the *Book of Mormon* claims they took "the firstlings of their flocks", but they didn't *have* flocks of *any* animals whatsoever in the Americas BCE.

# THE COMMANDMENTS – PART B

> **Mosiah 2:3.** And they also took of the firstlings of their flocks, that they might offer sacrifice and burnt offerings according to the law of Moses;

Following Abinadi 'reading' the Ten Commandments in 184 BCE, Smith then goes on to describe how the atonement will work.

> **Mosiah 13:28.** And moreover, I say unto you, that salvation doth not come by the law alone; and *were it not for the atonement, which God himself shall make* for the sins and iniquities of his people.
>
> **13:32.** …there could not any man be saved except it were *through the redemption of God.*
>
> **13:34.** Have they not said that *God himself should come down among the children of men, and take upon him the form of man,* and go forth in mighty power upon the face of the earth?
> **13:35.** Yea, and have they not said also that *he should bring to pass the resurrection of the dead, and that he, himself, should be oppressed and afflicted?* (Emphasis added).

These verses are of course, yet again, entirely *monotheistic*. It is God Himself who will come down "in the form of a man" and *become* the Messiah, or Jesus, the Christ, in order to redeem humankind. They are one and the same being in these descriptions.

## Religious 'Objects'

The missionaries must teach investigators that even innocent tokens of their faith are not appropriate and should be removed from their homes.

> People in many cultures own or pay respect to objects that remind them of Deity or ancestors. Sometimes those objects, such as statues, religious emblems, or small shrines, might also be the focus of their worship. Help them understand that the Lord has commanded us not to worship idols. Encourage them to remove from their home any object they worship or to which they pray. Help them focus their faith and worship on their Heavenly Father and Jesus Christ.

The obvious commitment question is asked:

> Will you keep the Ten Commandments?

## Live the Law of Chastity

This area is becoming increasingly problematic for the Mormon Church as well as several other denominations, as they adhere to the perceived biblical concept that people should be married before having sex, and that even then couples should exclusively be of the opposite sex. Although it is not mentioned these days, in my early years in the Church it was still taught very strongly that we should marry someone of our own race and colour, our own 'social class' and of course our own religion. Inter-racial marriages were more than frowned upon and the concept of what were then known as 'half-caste' babies bore a Mormon stigma that could not be avoided. Thankfully, times do change.

Modern society, in Mormon terms, has 'become' corrupt. The fact that it has always been more or less the way that it is now, seems to escape the current generation of Church leaders. There really is nothing new under the sun. In a society which now not only tolerates but generally also accommodates couples, from a legal rights perspective, who decide *not* to enter into the formality of a marriage, and which also much more readily understands and accepts the gay community, churches in general have to rethink their position or enjoy fewer converts to their faith. This is especially true of Mormonism which has zero 'tolerance' for premarital sex, and as the manual explains, also "homosexual or lesbian relations." (The word 'homosexual' actually relates to *both* sexes and is not an exclusively masculine word). The Church understands little of this area.

> God delights in chastity and hates sexual sin. Chastity includes strict abstinence from sexual relations before marriage and complete fidelity and loyalty to one's spouse after marriage. Those who live the law of chastity enjoy the strength that comes from self control. They enjoy confidence and trust in their family relationships. They can enjoy more fully the influence of the Holy Ghost in their lives. Those who break this law are subject to a lasting sense of shame and guilt that burdens their lives. *(Page 77).*

Unfortunately, within the Mormon Church, that "sense of shame and guilt" is actually piled upon 'guilty' members by the Church itself through interviews, confessions and disciplinary councils. It is a terrible ordeal for people, who, if not Mormon, could quickly and easily put things behind them and just move on. That is, assuming someone even considered what they may have done to actually be *wrong* in the first place. Once again, many things considered to be 'sin' are inventions of the religious. Premarital sex is *not* a 'sin' unless you happen to be a member of a religious sect which determines for you that it is.

The Church decides what God does and does not approve of, and members are obliged to obey those man-made rules which are attributed to God. Modern

# THE COMMANDMENTS – PART B

thinking couples, who decide to live together, cannot become Mormons unless they separate or marry. Gays have no chance of becoming Mormon unless they forsake the whole idea of same sex love and remain celibate or more preferably marry a member of the opposite sex and try to 'overcome their problem.' I do know people who have obediently tried that idea, only to later regret it. Such obedience can destroy lives, but the Mormon God does not tolerate gays at all.

As expressed elsewhere, considering the fact that we now understand *why* many people *are* gay, if it is wrong in the sight of the Mormon God, is it not His 'fault' that such people are that way in the first place? How then can He decree it *wrong*, when He *made* them that way? Hardwiring the wrong sexual orientation into the brain is a despicably cruel trick for a God to play on some 5-8% of the world population. Being *responsible*, He should just *accept* them.

Once we understand that evolution isn't perfect in *exactly* replicating any species – the very reason why evolution *works* – every new divergence can be understood, explained and indeed more readily appreciated and accepted. God doesn't need to get involved at all. Progressive religions accept gays with open arms. To me, that at least does seem to mirror original concepts of Christianity.

Mormonism is always decades to centuries behind everyone else but it will be obliged to get there eventually. Give Mormonism another century or two to accept gays. One day their God will decide to love and accept them after all, just as many other churches and their versions of God already do.

> Baptismal candidates are to live the law of chastity, which prohibits any sexual relations outside of a legal marriage between a man and a woman. They are not to participate in abortions or homosexual or lesbian relations. Those who have committed sexual sin can repent and be forgiven.
>
> Men and women who are living together but are not married may not be baptized without first getting married or separated. Those who are married to more than one person at a time may not be baptized. Seek counsel from your mission president, who will give you specific direction in each case. *(Page 77).*

The above means not just what it *says*, 'sexual relations' in Mormonism means a couple must do no more than kiss or hold hands – and possibly have a hug, prior to marriage. Anything more than that is considered 'petting' and 'inappropriate' as it can lead to other things. Youngsters do not attend dances until age fourteen; they do not date until age sixteen, when they are encouraged to 'double date' and never be alone together. They should be chaperoned. Over eighteens date, but young men should not get serious until after serving their mission. It doesn't always work that way of course, but that is the idea.

The Mormon Church stand on abortion is clearly identified here. Abortion is a grave sin in Mormonism and even aborting following pregnancy caused by rape is a very serious consideration and one not to be undertaken unless it would affect the mental or physical health of the mother. Indeed, rape victims in the Mormon Church have often been treated as if *they* were partly responsible, as they must have somehow encouraged the attack by their dress or their actions.

Whether abortion is actually 'right' or 'wrong' calls for opinion and I think that should remain a personal, as well as legal, matter for each individual to consider and certainly not be dictated by any religion or their God. I will leave it at identifying the Mormon stance on the matter. It is yet another aspect of life in which religion tends to interfere, and the results are not always helpful.

References provided in support of 'morality' include the Bible and *Book of Mormon* and there are also a couple from the *D&C*. Considering Smith's own track record, it is worth considering what he had to say about the subject himself. On 9 February 1831, when he was, as far as we know, still loyal to Emma, Smith penned the following:

> **D&C 42:22.** Thou shalt love thy wife with all thy heart, and shalt *cleave unto her and none else.*
> **23.** And *he that looketh upon a woman to lust after her shall deny the faith, and shall not have the Spirit; and if he repents not he shall be cast out.*
> **24.** Thou shalt not commit adultery; and *he that committeth adultery, and repenteth not, shall be cast out.* (Emphasis added).

Obviously Smith's polygamy was to come later. However, the above was supposedly a 'revelation' from God, so God should have revealed His ideas on polygamy *then*. The next two verses are not referenced, but they do concern Mormon 'rules' on adultery.

> **25.** But he that has committed adultery and repents with all his heart, and forsaketh it, and doeth it no more, thou shalt forgive;
> **26.** But if he doeth it again, he shall not be forgiven, but shall be cast out.

These verses make it clear that someone can return to fellowship after an adulterous relationship, provided they repent and they don't do it again. This supposedly includes putting things right with a wronged spouse. I have known cases where this was *not* the case at all, including one where a Bishop had an adulterous affair with his Young Women President. He was excommunicated; he left his wife, the adulterous couple lived together, he got divorced, married the other party and once they were readmitted to the Church, they went to the temple and were sealed for eternity. His first wife had to suffer, not just his adultery and abandonment, she then had to endure the indignity of seeing them together in the temple. That doesn't square with the concept of 'repentance' as the 'rules' were not met. There was a time when a man could *not* be sealed to a woman with whom he had committed adultery, as *forsaking* the woman was considered part of the *repentance* process, whether or not the first marriage survived. Times change and the Church seems to have softened its approach.

I was also involved in many disciplinary councils over the fifteen years or so that I spent on a Stake High Council and I saw at least one man readmitted to membership after his *second* excommunication for adultery. He was told if it happened a *third* time he would not be baptised again. I could not understand the way rules were interpreted at different times in different ways for different people, considering the *D&C 42:25-26* directive was supposedly a revelation from God. Either people *do* get excommunicated for life following a second 'offence' or they do not. Once again, far from being the same yesterday, today and forever, the Mormon God seems to forever chop and change the revealed rules of His ever evolving and entirely unpredictable game. Or is that just the modern Church perpetuating the same tactics as Joseph Smith and continuing to make things up as they go along, depending on what suits them at the time?

The Church keeps a 'black list' of such people who are readmitted to the Church and they will *never* be called anything as 'high' as the office of Bishop or Stake President, but the Church never informs the member that they are on the list and many think they can still be called to *any* position within the Church. When someone receives an ordinance termed the 'restoration of all former blessings' they are in fact told that it is then as if the sin had never been committed. That is not the case at all. All proposed Bishops and Stake Presidents must be submitted to the First Presidency for approval and all such individuals are invariably declined.

Until recently, a man who had divorced and remarried, and where he had been a completely innocent party, could nevertheless not be called as a Mission President or a General Authority due to the 'example' required. I know this has now changed, as someone whom I know personally, who was an 'innocent' in his first marriage failure, was subsequently called, along with his second wife. I think they deserved the call.

Late in August of 1831, some eighteen months before he had his own first affair with Fanny Alger, Smith wrote the following, which the manual also references:

> **D&C 63:16.** And verily I say unto you, as I have said before, he that looketh on a woman to lust after her, or if any shall commit adultery in their hearts, they shall not have the Spirit, but shall deny the faith and shall fear.

Naturally, the lesson manual does *not* mention *D&C 132* which advocates polygamy and includes such things as the 'Law of Sarah', where a first wife was considered out of tune with the spirit if she refused to agree to her husband's latest choice in a further wife. He could go ahead and marry again regardless, and the first wife's salvation was considered to be in jeopardy for not consenting to the marriage. Such 'consent' meant absolutely *nothing*.

That's a far cry from the monogamy *dictated by God* just a few years earlier. Now Smith can do no wrong if he marries 'ten virgins' who are given to him. There really is some nonsense in the *D&C* and Section 132 is no exception; it is one of the *worst*. Consider the following:

> **D&C 132:59.** Verily, if a man be called of my Father, as was Aaron, by mine own voice, and by the voice of him that sent me, and I have endowed him with the keys of the power of this priesthood, *if he do anything in my name*, and according to my law and by my word, he will not commit sin, and *I will justify him*. (Emphasis added).

This is the set up for a 'sting' regarding Joseph Smith forcing his wife Emma to accommodate her husband's plural wives, but that is not why we are reviewing it here. Smith has God say that whatever Smith does in His name is not a sin and He will 'justify' him. The next verse, and remember this is *God* speaking, says:

> **132:60.** Let no one, therefore, set on my servant Joseph; for I will justify him; for he shall do the sacrifice which I require at his hands for his transgressions, saith the Lord your God.

Can you imagine a God actually saying "Let no one, therefore, **set on my servant** Joseph"? It is hardly 'heavenly' language to say the very least, and just reflects nineteenth century words that Smith himself would have used. God would be more dignified. Far from 'justifying' Smith, when Smith got himself arrested on charges of treason, having had the Law brothers' printing press destroyed, he wasn't to live very long. Less than a year after Smith's God supposedly said he would 'justify' Smith and that *no one* should 'set on him', Joseph Smith was very dead.

What the revelation said about virgins allowed Smith his way with anyone he fancied who would have him. Surprisingly, he chose several married women as well, even though the 'revelation' does not accommodate that at all and the Church today has confirmed the very concept of polyandry entirely contrary to doctrine. Compare the following with Smith's earlier 'revelations' concerning monogamy and being faithful to one wife.

# THE COMMANDMENTS – PART B

> **132:61.** And again, as pertaining to the law of the priesthood—*if any man espouse a virgin, and desire to espouse another*, and *the first give her consent*, and if he espouse the second, *and they are virgins, and have vowed to no other man, then is he justified*; he cannot commit adultery for they are given unto him; for *he cannot commit adultery with that that belongeth unto him and to no one else.*
> **62.** And if *he have ten virgins given unto him by this law, he cannot commit adultery, for they belong to him, and they are given unto him; therefore is he justified.*
> **63.** But if one or either of the ten virgins, after she is espoused, shall be with another man, she has committed adultery, and shall be destroyed; for *they are given unto him to multiply and replenish the earth*, according to my commandment, and to fulfil the promise which was given by my Father before the foundation of the world, and for their exaltation in the eternal worlds, that *they may bear the souls of men*; for *herein is the work of my Father continued*, that he may be glorified.
> **64.** And again, verily, verily, I say unto you, if *any man have a wife, who holds the keys of this power, and he teaches unto her the law of my priesthood*, as pertaining to these things, *then shall she believe and administer unto him, or she shall be destroyed, saith the Lord your God; for I will destroy her*; for I will magnify my name upon all those who receive and abide in my law.
> **65.** Therefore, it shall be lawful in me, *if she receive not this law*, for him to receive all things whatsoever I, the Lord his God, will give unto him, because she did not believe and administer unto him according to my word; and *she then becomes the transgressor*; and *he is exempt from the law of Sarah*, who administered unto Abraham according to the law when I commanded Abraham to take Hagar to wife.
> **66.** And now, as pertaining to this law, verily, verily, I say unto you, I will reveal more unto you, hereafter; therefore, let this suffice for the present. Behold, I am Alpha and Omega. Amen. (Emphasis added).

It is probably as well that God did *not* reveal more, as promised in v.66, as that was quite enough as it was. The Mormon God is entirely misogynous in His views according to this, and women in Mormonism are mere chattels.

One of Smith's problems was that several of his wives were indeed given to someone else *before* he married them. That doesn't fit with the revelation at all.

There wasn't exactly much of any 'multiplying' or 'replenishing the earth' in Smith's case either. He certainly enjoyed sex with a number of women, as they, and others who accommodated Smith and his latest 'bride' recorded the fact in their journals. To date, there are no resulting Smith polygamous children which have been confirmed through DNA testing, although such research is still ongoing.

The obvious qualifier is asked:

Will you live the law of chastity?

**Baptismal Interview Questions That Apply:**

What do you understand of the law of chastity, which prohibits any sexual relationship outside the bonds of a legal marriage between a man and a woman?

Are you willing to obey this law [before your baptism]?

Have you ever participated in an abortion?

A homosexual relationship?

[Note: A person who answers yes to either of these questions must be interviewed by the mission president before being baptized.]

In Mormonism, you never really can put the past behind you, even a pre-membership past. It must be disclosed and reviewed, and possibly recorded by the Church, before you are allowed to move on. People must *feel* guilt.

## The Word of Wisdom

The Lord revealed to the Prophet Joseph Smith a law of health called the Word of Wisdom. This law teaches us what foods and substances we should and should not use to maintain the health of our bodies and to keep us *free from evil influences*. The Lord promises blessings of health, strength, *protection against evil*, and greater receptiveness to spiritual truths. (Emphasis added). *(Page 78)*.

This can be a difficult area for people to adapt their lives to, especially if they are not young and have been smoking and drinking alcohol, tea and coffee for many years. Missionaries are advised on ways they can help investigators adapt their lifestyle and those who are willing, somehow manage to change. "Evil influences" no doubt refers to the environment of bars and such like. The actual *use* of such things hardly constitutes an evil influence. Chapter 10 *(Pp.188-90)* of the lesson manual has more suggestions to aid investigators in overcoming addictions, but it is easy to guess what it contains and not worth repeating here.

Naturally, *Section 89* of the *D&C* is referenced, but some aspects will of course *not* be covered with investigators as they are completely disregarded by the modern-day Church. No explanation is given to rank and file members as to why some of *Section 89* is completely ignored today, but they just accept the current 'interpretation'. In addition to the idea of abstaining from tobacco,

# THE COMMANDMENTS – PART B

*Section 89* does not actually proscribe alcohol *completely*, and it also doesn't specifically mention *tea* or *coffee* either. That is a more recent 'interpretation'.

Before going into the detail of what *is* included in *D&C 89*, it is worth reminding the reader that as mentioned on p.243, it would never have been given at all, were it not for a simple joke between the Elders and some of the 'sisters'. A few of the following paragraphs and quotes concerning the Word of Wisdom and the way it impacted the early years of the Church appear in *Whitefield 2009b. (For a detailed review of this area see TMD Vol. 2. Ch.10).*

The situation that arose to evoke the 'revelation' started with a combination of efforts of the Kirtland Temperance Society, founded in 1830, predominantly non-Mormon, who were opposed to alcohol, tobacco and eating too much meat, and Smith training men in his 'School of Elders' every day, meeting in a small smoke filled room above Emma's kitchen, with tobacco juice being spit all over the floor. Emma had the job of cleaning up following the meetings. The situation and results are available from several sources. This is just one:

> Thus Emma, faced almost daily with "having to clean so filthy a floor" as was left by the men chewing tobacco, spoke to Joseph about the matter. David Whitmer's account supports Brigham Young's description. "Some of the men were excessive chewers of the filthy weed, and their disgusting slobbering and spitting caused **Mrs. Smith … to make the ironical remark that 'It would be a good thing if a revelation could be had declaring the use of tobacco a sin, and commanding it's suppression.' The matter was taken up and joked about**, one of the brethren suggested that **the revelation should also provide for a total abstinence from tea and coffee** drinking, intending this **as a counter 'dig' at the sisters**." Sure enough the subject was afterward taken up in dead earnest, and the 'Word of Wisdom' was the result. *(David Whitmer). (Des Moines Daily News, 16 Oct 1886:20 c. in: Newell & Avery 1994:47, also c: An Historical Analysis of the Word of Wisdom, Paul H. Peterson - Masters Thesis, [no location provided]; Also: c. in Tanner 1987:406. See also Tanner 1987: Ch. 26 for excellent coverage).* (Emphasis added).

*Section 89* of the *D&C* is one of many sections written to appear, not just as inspired words but rather, as if it was direct from the mouth of the Lord, as verse 4 includes "…thus saith the Lord unto you…". It is very difficult to accommodate the idea that God *coincidentally* wanted the saints to comply with all aspects of discussions that were in reality, no more than a joke at the time. As with everything connected with his religion though, it gave Smith more control over people and bound them more into the web of Mormonism. It was more new revelation and something the saints could do to show obedience to their God.

Smith often seems to have picked up on what was popular in his day, such as the ideas in *View of the Hebrews* for his *Book of Mormon*, and he may have seen the 25 August 1830 edition of the *Journal of Health*, published in Philadelphia. It had been running a series of articles written strongly against the use of spirits, alcohol, tobacco, tea and coffee; plus it advised substitution of vegetables for animal products. *D&C 89*, reflecting *all* of the above ideas, was dated 27 February 1833. Smith's Word of Wisdom was not out of harmony with current health issues of his day, even if they were the more radical views.

I always thought the revelation was originally given as advice, becoming a commandment later, in the early twentieth century, but Wilford Woodruff records that initially it *was* a commandment which, being extremely unpopular quickly *devolved* into a matter of choice.

> [Footnote: The Word of Wisdom--Section 89 of the Doctrine and Covenants (D&C 89)--as given in the spring of 1833 ***commanded*** that the Saints totally abstain from the use of alcohol, tobacco, and hot drinks (tea and coffee). However, because of wide-spread use of and deep-seated attachment to these substances by members, this revelation, ***by 1834, was changed from a direct commandment to general advise*** only. Even so, zealous leaders and members pressed for compliance with the original meaning of the revelation, and ***in early December 1836, a unanimous vote of the Saints in Kirtland supported the complete abstinence of "all liquors from the Church in Sickness & in health except wine at the Sacraments & for external washing"*** (Journal of Wilford Woodruff, 4 December 1836).]
> *(Kirtland Elders' Quorum Record: 15 Oct 1837).* (Emphasis added).

This indicates a perception that God *commanded* abstinence, yet the idea was quickly diluted, so what did God really have to do with it? Evidence that Smith did not take his Word of Wisdom revelation too seriously himself, is firmly established in the following quote about the day he rode through town on a horse smoking a cigar. He drank beer of course and, although apparently moderately, also wine, up until and including the very day he was killed.

> Joseph Smith tried the faith of the saints many times by his peculiarities. At one time he had preached a powerful sermon on the Word of Wisdom and immediately thereafter, he rode through the streets of Nauvoo ***smoking a cigar***. Some of the brethren were tried as was Abraham of old. *(Tanner 1987:6 c: Joseph Smith as an Administrator, Gary Dean Guthrie, M.A. thesis, Brigham Young University, May 1969:161, in turn c: the diary of Apostle Abraham H. Cannon. V.19. 1 Oct 1895. Special Collections Dept. BYU Library).* (Emphasis added).

# THE COMMANDMENTS – PART B

There are various references to Smith also being fond of a drink:

> Called at the office and **drank a glass of wine** with Sister Jenetta Richards, made by her mother in England, and reviewed a portion of the conference minutes. *(HC V.5:380. Incident date: 2 May 1843).* (Emphasis added).

> He was partial to a well supplied table and he **did not always refuse the wine** that 'maketh the heart glad.' *(Tanner 1987:407 c: A letter by Benjamin F. Johnson to Elder George S. Gibbs, 1903, printed in The Testimony of Joseph Smith's Best Friend, p 4).* (Emphasis added).

> We then partook of some refreshments, and our hearts were made glad **with the fruit of the vine**. *(HC V.2:369. Incident date: January 1836; Also c. in Tanner 1987:407).* (Emphasis added).

The Word of Wisdom was ultimately then, not confirmed a commandment, but rather as advice and there was no actual obligation to obey; it was a matter of individual choice. Neither Joseph nor Emma appeared to completely adhere to it but it did keep the room used for the *School of Elders* free from smoke and tobacco spit and that would have at least kept Emma happy.

On the day that Joseph Smith died, he and his companions drank wine to revive their spirits:

> Sometime after dinner we sent for some wine. It has been reported by some that this was taken as a sacrament. It was no such thing; our spirits were generally dull and heavy, and it was sent for to revive us. I think it was Captain Jones who went after it, but they would not suffer him to return. I believe we all drank of the wine, and gave some to one or two of the prison guards. (John Taylor). *(HC V.7:101).*

John Taylor became the third prophet and President of the Church. The Tanners take up Taylor's later attitude towards alcohol, which remained liberal:

> It is interesting to note that the Apostle John Taylor continued to use alcoholic beverages after Joseph Smith's death. Hosea Stout recorded the following in his diary on June 3, 1847: While I was explaining this **prests O. Hyde P. P. Pratt and John Taylor** also came in so I stoped saying I had been catched twice. Elder Taylor replied to go on and not stop for them. I told him it was nothing but a police meeting and not interesting to them. 'Never mind says he we are police men too.' Says I. 'I hope you will all conform to the rules of the police then.' 'Certainly' says **Taylor**. 'Bring on the **jug**' says I at which they were presented with a **large jug of whiskey**. This was such an unexpected

turn that it was only answered by a peal of laughter & they all paid ***due respect to the jug...*** After ***drinking*** says Parley 'I have traveled these streets all times of the night & never before have I saw a police man but now I know where to find them hereafter' alluding to the ***jug***. 'Parley' says I 'do you not know that some things in this kingdom are only spiritually discerned & so with the police.' *(Tanner 1987:407 c: On the Mormon Frontier, The Diary of Hosea Stout, 1844-1861, V.1:259. For more references, see Tanner 1987: Ch 26).*

*Section 89* includes the following aspects relating to alcohol in the 'Word of Wisdom'.

> **D&C 89:5.** That inasmuch as any man drinketh ***wine or strong drink*** among you, behold ***it is not good***, neither meet in the sight of your Father, ***only in*** assembling yourselves together to offer up ***your sacraments*** before him.
> **6.** And, behold, this should be wine, yea, pure wine of the grape of the vine, of your own make.
> **7.** And, again, strong drinks are not for the belly, but for the washing of your bodies. (Emphasis added).

This section was recorded 27 February 1833. At that time God was more than happy for wine to be used for the sacrament and He says so. It is not to be used other than that, although Smith himself clearly did. Later, the Church changed the sacrament requirement and it is now bread and *water*. Why God didn't just let them use water in the first place is not explained. Beer was not considered a 'strong drink' and was freely used well into the twentieth century.

Even after the turn of the century, the First Presidency and Twelve were facing dilemmas concerning what to include in the Word of Wisdom. On 1 February 1901, the first Presidency decided to suspend a ten-year policy allowing the sale of alcohol at Saltair, a Church owned amusement park and resort. *(Quinn 1997:803)*. During a meeting on 11 July 1901, consideration was given as to whether they should continue to sell beer at Saltair or whether stopping would invade the rights of the old saints who would go there and smoke their pipes and drink alcohol. They talked of the revelation speaking of barley for mild drinks and considered whether beer that was intoxicating would be considered a mild drink. They felt it needed serious thought and wondered if they had an extreme view of the word of the Lord.

They considered German beer very light and mild, which would not intoxicate, whereas American beer was much stronger and would cause drunkenness. Eventually, they agreed Danish beer was not harmful or in violation of the Word of Wisdom and released an official statement to that effect. No revelation appears to have been sought to clarify the Lord's desires for His people. They just chose what it meant to them at that time. On 14 April

# THE COMMANDMENTS – PART B

1904, the First Presidency and apostles also decided to resume the sale of liquor at Saltair due to the need for non-Mormon patronage.
Many early leaders had a strange approach to living the Word of Wisdom.

> 28 Sept 1883. "A number" of First Presidency and apostles "confessed to breaking the Word of Wisdom" and vote to obey it. However, this vote does not apply to wine which members of School of Prophets drink by glassful at their meeting on 12 Oct. *(Quinn 1997:782).*

> I was quite restless all night. Felt chilly. Took a little Brandy sling and a cup of coffee, and slept some before daylight and until 9 am... *(Wilford Woodruff Journal, 9 Jun 1897).*

Woodruff had been the Prophet and President of the Church for several years (1889-1898) when he wrote that note in his journal.

Strong drinks are not for drinking but "for the washing of your bodies". Perhaps that is why whisky was added to fragrance baths in which members were originally *immersed* during the *washing and anointing* (initiatory) ceremony in early Temples, another eternal unchangeable principle which has continually changed until it has in fact completely disappeared, the remaining ordinance being *entirely* symbolic. *(See TMD Volume 3, Section 3, Temple Ceremonies).* Whatever people did or did not then do regarding the normal 'washing' of their bodies, strong drinks most certainly are not used for that purpose these days.

In the real world? – A glass of red wine each day is considered healthy. It contains resveratrol which is a strong antioxidant and is heart-*healthy*.

> **89:8.** And again, tobacco is not for the body, neither for the belly, and is not good for man, but is an herb for bruises and all sick cattle, to be used with judgment and skill.

The Word of Wisdom seems to have been lived by a minority of the saints rather than the majority by all accounts. On 5 May 1870, in a testimony meeting in the Tabernacle, Brigham Young requested mothers leave children at home if possible so as not to disturb the meeting, and also:

> that Gentlemen will desist besmearing the floors with tobacco spittle &c. Tabernacle installs dozens of tobacco spittoons." *(Quinn 1997: 766).*

> 7 October 1894. Wilford Woodruff instructs conference priesthood meeting that all presiding officers should live Word of Wisdom, and he threatens to drop Presiding Patriarch John Smith from office if he continues using tobacco and alcohol. *(Quinn 1997:796).*

That was rich, coming from the prophet Wilford Woodruff, when three years later he recorded in his own journal that he drank coffee and had a 'brandy sling' *(see page 325)*. There are rules for some and rules for others it seems. No doubt Woodruff considered 'medicinal' use of brandy and coffee to be acceptable. That's not what Smith claimed God said, and certainly not how the Church sees things today. So much for the Mormon God being the same yesterday, today and forever; things seem to change every five minutes.

Tobacco is only for use in treating bruises and to heal sick cattle; "with judgment and skill" – if ever anyone can ever discover how that works.

> **89:9.** And again, hot drinks are not for the body or belly.

The concept of the Word of Wisdom, as it applied in the mid-eighteen hundreds, is evidence of yet another evolving, rather than specific, principle which is here expressed differently to that which is accepted today. Early saints considered hot chocolate, cocoa, hot soup and pig's meat included in the list of proscribed items. Nothing anywhere explains why they were once included, any more than why they are now found to be perfectly acceptable.

> We are told, and very plainly too, that hot drinks - tea, coffee, **chocolate, cocoa and all drinks of this kind** are not good for man. We are also told that alcoholic drinks are not good, and that tobacco when either smoked or chewed is an evil. We are told that **swine's flesh is not good, and that we should dispense with it; and we are told that flesh of any kind is not suitable to man in the summer time, and ought to be eaten sparingly in the winter...**
>
> ...we must feed our children properly.... We must not permit them to drink liquor or **hot drinks, or hot soups** or to use tobacco or other articles that are injurious. *(JD. V.12:221&223. George Q. Cannon 7 Apr 1868).*

When you consider that the tenth Prophet, Joseph Fielding Smith, declared the habit of drinking tea, coffee or smoking can 'bar' a person from the 'celestial kingdom of God' it appears that not so many of the early members, and almost none of their leaders, will make it there after all, as they took little, if any, notice of the Word of Wisdom. *(See: Tanner 1987:406 c: Smith, Joseph Fielding 1954: Vol. 2:16; also c: Stewart 1966, who claimed Joseph Smith "carefully observed the Word of Wisdom").*

The Tanners thus identified that you cannot believe much of anything you read without checking the facts for yourself. But then Joseph Smith never said anything about it being completely mandatory, or of disobedience having an eternal consequence; Joseph Fielding Smith was using *fear* to keep members in

# THE COMMANDMENTS – PART B

line, while Joseph Smith Jr. was originally just keeping his wife happy. It is inconceivable that any God would bar some people from heaven for drinking tea and allow his own prophet, who 'revealed' the idea yet still drank tea, to enter. As previously stated, times change – but God's doctrines should not.

In the real world? – Twenty-four ounces of coffee a day is shown to reduce liver cancer and to be effective with symptoms of Alzheimer's and Parkinson's diseases; so that too is considered *healthy*.

> **89:10.** And again, verily I say unto you, all wholesome herbs God hath ordained for the constitution, nature, and use of man—
> **11.** Every herb in the season thereof, and every fruit in the season thereof; all these to be used with prudence and thanksgiving.

Apparently, we are free to use herbs and to eat fruit. This is just as well, as in the following verses not much else *is* permitted – except in times of famine.

> **89:12.** Yea, *flesh also of beasts and of the fowls of the air*, I, the Lord, have ordained *for the use of man* with thanksgiving; nevertheless *they are to be used sparingly*;
> **13.** And it is pleasing unto me that *they should not be used, only in times of winter, or of cold, or famine.* (Emphasis added).

Today, the Church completely *ignores* aspects of the revelation that relate to meat, which is designated to be eaten "sparingly" and even then "*only* in times of winter, or cold, or famine." Now, it is freely eaten and never gets mentioned at all. I don't know that anyone ever did take much notice of it. We may wonder why the Mormon God bothered to include it. Remember, this section includes "Thus saith the Lord" *(v.4)*. Perhaps modern leaders like their meat too much to obey their God. There has been no revelation whatsoever rescinding any part of *Section 89* since it was given.

> **89:14.** *All grain* is ordained for the *use of man* and *of beasts*, to be the staff of life, not only *for man* but for *the beasts* of the field, and *the fowls* of heaven, *and all wild animals that run or creep on the earth;*
> **15.** And these hath God made for the use of man *only in times of famine and excess of hunger.*
> **16.** All *grain is good* for the food of man; as also the *fruit of the vine*; that which yieldeth *fruit, whether in the ground or above the ground—*
> **17.** Nevertheless, *wheat for man*, and *corn for the ox*, and *oats for the horse*, and *rye for the fowls and for swine, and for all beasts* of the field, and *barley for all useful animals, and for mild drinks, as also other grain*. (Emphasis added).

In v.14, God provides *all* grain for the use of man, beasts, birds and *all* wild animals. The trouble is that many animals are entirely carnivorous and cannot comply with this idea at all. Their systems have simply not evolved to be able to accommodate a vegetarian diet, any more than their temperaments have, and many of them would simply die if they changed diet. Smith was clearly not thinking this through – unless you would prefer to argue that God forgot the diet of some of the animals He had 'created'. Many animals form part of a food chain and they eat each other. Many do not eat any grain at all. Some of the wild animals that graze do not eat grain either. Even some exotic plants are carnivorous, but then Smith's God doesn't mention the fact that some plants effectively need to 'eat' either.

In v.15 God declares very clearly that even "all grain" is to be used "only in times of famine and excess of hunger", so we are left with fruit, vegetables and herbs to eat in 'normal' times. I don't think anyone has ever taken *any* notice of that idea at all and yet here we have Smith's God 'thus saying' this is indeed His requirement. So, *why* are Mormons *not* taught to obey their God in the matter, when He *commanded* it?

In v.17 we get a breakdown of the uses for grain from *God*. Smith lived and worked on a farm so he had a rough idea of which animals ate what, but he wasn't very good at defining the list properly. Perhaps they were nearer to being correct in Smith's day than they are today, but somehow I very much doubt things were that much different, which means God's list was pretty pathetic really.

Some of the following foodstuffs apply to the U.K. and may differ slightly in the U.S. but the main items are the same. The point here is that the list is really unimportant but unfortunately, although some items sit reasonably well, some are not suited at all and so it makes absolutely no sense overall, isolating specific crops for specific animals in this way. It is typical of the sort of thing a feeble human mind (i.e. Joseph Smith) would dream up, as filler for his new 'revelation', but surely it is *not* the sort of thing any God would ever bother with? The question is what would be the *point* of such a list as this; where is the reason for it?

Smith has his God state, in v.14, that "*All grain* is ordained for the *use of man* and *of beasts*" – and that needs *no* further explanation. But then in v.17, Smith has God say "nevertheless", and then Smith's God makes a list. The detail therefore has no real point to it and as it is not *absolutely* correct, it is another clear evidence of Smith 'padding' rather than something that would ever be dictated by any God for any practical purpose or reason. Why would He bother?

Out of sheer idle interest, this then is Joseph Smith's record of *God's* "nevertheless" suggested uses and a summary of the *actual* uses in each case –

# THE COMMANDMENTS – PART B

God having already stated that "*All grain* is ordained for the *use of man* and *of beasts.*"

Nevertheless, says God…

**Wheat for man.**

Wheat is indeed used by humans of course. It is the world's number one crop. Archaeological evidence of wheat being cultivated dates back some 9,000 years, long before Adam was supposedly born. Wheat used for livestock and poultry feed is a by-product of the flour milling industry. God failed to mention that livestock and poultry could also have wheat. God also did not mention that wheat could be used in the production of pet foods and many non-food items such as cosmetics, newsprint, paperboard, soap, rubbish (trash) bags, concrete, paste etc. If they weren't all available in Smith's time, they would have made for excellent 'prophecy' of some future uses but Smith's God wasn't that good.

**Corn for the ox.**

Smith probably saw oxen being fed on corn and indeed it is a fine feed. Some breeds of cattle fed on corn (maize) are rich in omega-6. However, corn is also fed to most other livestock, and chickens are often fed on corn. The ox is just one of several animals to benefit from corn feed. Humans also use a lot of corn and also cornstarch, so the idea that corn is 'for the ox' is extremely limiting. It is 'for' a lot more besides. It is in general use across a broad spectrum of animals. It is also used to produce alcohol and of 10,000 items in a typical supermarket, at least 2,500 items use maize in some form during production or processing. God doesn't expand things or indicate the extent to which they are really used or will be used in future. Yet another 'prophesy moment' is wasted.

**Oats for the horse.**

Once again, Smith was probably familiar with horses being fed oats in his day and indeed oats are the cereal of choice for horses as they like them so much. Horses are also fed barley and corn, and of course hay and grass. Once again, oats are not just for the horse and they are used in a variety of ways, including human consumption.

**Rye for birds and pigs (and all beasts of the field).**

Many people would immediately suggest the best use for rye is to make whisky or vodka. Rye is another cereal used in animal feed and covers a variety of uses. Although rye has a higher feed value than oats or barley and has a feeding value of 85% to 90% of corn, its high soluble fibre content makes it better suited to ruminants, i.e. cud chewing cattle, sheep and goats – with multiple stomachs, than monogastrics, i.e. *pigs* and chickens – with one stomach, so it is not really suited to "all beasts of the field" at all. Pigs are certainly fed on rye in some areas where it is a prolific crop, although it is not considered by some experts to be ideal for them. In Joseph Smith's day, the availability of rye in his area possibly dictated that as a choice of feed.

Pigs are omnivores and will pretty much eat anything, animal or vegetable. Rye is hardly a stock feed for pigs in most areas of the world today but in Smith's day and location it was probably readily available. Pig diets typically include cereal grains, oilseed meals, and other by-products of the human food industry. Pigs reared outdoors may also be fed root crops such as swedes, turnips and mangolds. The rest of the 'beasts of the field' aren't particularly fed on rye in preference to other feeds.

'Rye for birds' is another strange thing to claim. Birds eat all food sources, though individual birds do not use all the foods available. Some, such as crows and jays, are generalists able to use a variety of foods; birds like eagles eat only meat, warblers only insects, and cardinals only seeds. Birds can eat seeds, insects, nectar, meat, berries, and plant material, depending on their physical adaptations to do so. Rye will be in there somewhere for some birds, among some ten-thousand species, but as a singular specific for all birds? No.

**Barley for all useful animals.**

God doesn't deign to mention which animals are *not* useful and therefore should not be fed barley. It is a strange thing to say and again typical 'Smith-speak' rather than plausible words from deity. Barley is indeed an important grain in many areas of the world. It is the principal feed grain in Canada, Europe, and in the northern United States. Dairy cows and beef cattle are usually fed grass during the summer months and conserved forage – grass or maize silage, or hay in the winter. These forages may be supplemented with cereals and other by-products to increase milk yield or 'live weight' gain. The diets of both may also include, as available, forage crops such as kale and rapeseed, root crops – turnips and fodder beet, and the pulp remaining from the processing of sugar beet or citrus fruit.

Sheep and goats spend less time indoors than cattle. Their diet is similar to that of cattle, although *barley* and other cereals are usually fed *only* to pregnant and lactating ewes and to young lambs. During winter months they may also be fed on root crops, including swedes, mangolds and fodder beet, which may also be grazed in the fields in which they are grown.

# THE COMMANDMENTS – PART B

Poultry – chickens, turkeys, quails, ducks and geese – are typically fed on cereal grains, especially those reared in poultry houses. Free range poultry, geese and ducks in particular, will also graze on grass.

**Barley (and other grain) for mild drinks.**

Barley can indeed be used to make mild hot drinks and also mild beer which Mormons once drank – well into the twentieth century. Barley and other grains can also be used for making stronger alcoholic drinks. It is used in soups and stews, and also in 'barley bread' which is made in various cultures ranging from Africa to Scotland.

God doesn't mention rice or pulses. Perhaps Smith wasn't really familiar with them but God should be. He doesn't mention fish either in conjunction with, or as an alternative to meat, and yet fish is now used in many more ways than just feeding humans. It is also used in many modern animal feeds. Clearly Smith was trying to have God say something useful and intelligent *sounding*, and we could forgive God for not mentioning rice or fish, but He still got some of the other things muddled and He shouldn't have; He is, after all – God.

Today, members abstain from tea, coffee, alcohol of all types and tobacco. Some years after I joined the Church, we were advised against all forms of Cola drinks. No specific reason was given. It was rumoured that the Church used the term Coca-Cola in advice letters and the Coca-Cola company threatened to sue the Church, so it was changed to 'all forms of Cola drink'. I don't know if that rumour was true, but it wouldn't surprise me. As chocolate also contains caffeine, and we could happily eat and drink as much of that as we pleased, I always thought it may be the phosphoric acid that was most harmful in Cola drinks, but then later, articles started to appear in Church youth magazines that referred to caffeine in Cola. I never did understand the idea but when *revealed*, my family and I faithfully abstained from Cola drinks.

The concept that it is preferable to avoid Cola drinks is *not even mentioned* in the lesson manual at all. It seems the Church has now gone quiet about it and new converts will become Mormons having no idea concerning it. Perhaps God has changed His mind about that now? Given as a 'word of advice', it seems to have now been completely abandoned. The thing is with the Church, they don't retract such things; they say absolutely *nothing*, so Mormons who have been members for years believing God doesn't want them to drink Cola, will end up telling new converts about such things which will confuse them completely as they were not taught it by missionaries. As I have mentioned elsewhere in my work, the most consistent thing about the Mormon Church is its inconsistency.

Commitment question:

    Will you live the Word of Wisdom?

# THE MORMON DELUSION

## The Law of Tithing

Quite naturally, the manual proclaims tithing one of the greatest 'blessings' associated with Church membership. As a Mormon, you do buy into that concept and quickly rationalise away any and all problems you ever face regarding finance. You never fully appreciate or understand that tithing is in reality for many Mormons an extremely hard burden to bear on top of all the other costs of living – and living the gospel. Only when you look *back* at what you put yourself through during a lifetime of such a commitment do you begin to see and realise the damage that living such a principle can cause to some people. The fact is that a large number of Mormons are not affluent and can ill afford such donations on a continuing basis. Faith is one thing but money *is* finite and it only goes so far.

> One of the great blessings of membership in The Church of Jesus Christ of Latter-day Saints is the privilege of contributing to the growth of the kingdom of God through paying tithing. Tithing is an ancient, divine law. For example, the Old Testament prophet Abraham paid tithes of all he possessed (see Alma 13:15). *(Page 78)*.

The initial reference mentioned is not biblical. It is in fact from the *Book of Mormon* where Smith has it related by Alma.

> **Alma 13:15.** And it was this same Melchizedek to whom Abraham paid tithes; yea, even our father Abraham paid tithes of one-tenth part of all he possessed.

Incidentally, *Alma 13* is a chapter where Smith has Alma 'cite' the minds of the people *forward* to something yet to happen and then speak of it in the *past* tense.

Smith's mistake once again exposes his hoax. For someone to cite minds forward, the text should of course remain in the *future* tense. If someone is looking *back* and *pretending* someone else is looking forward, then it would be easy to slip into the trap, which Smith obviously does, and inadvertently start speaking in the *past* tense.

> **Alma 13:1.** And again, my brethren, I would cite your minds forward to the time when the Lord God ***gave*** these commandments unto his children… (Emphasis added).

At least the names in *Alma 13* in reference to tithing are biblical and should convince an investigator that tithing comes from a commandment in the Bible. Unfortunately, the Abraham references in *Genesis 14* are in fact the very *first* references to tithing in the Bible. Whilst Adam sacrificed with burnt offerings,

# THE COMMANDMENTS – PART B

he is not recorded as having been given the law of tithing. After all, who would he have paid it to? The following generations did not pay tithing either. From the time of Adam to Abraham, a period of well over two thousand years, long after the supposed flood and the Tower of Babel, there is no mention of tithing whatsoever, then we finally, seemingly, have the introduction of tithing as we know it today. But then, do we?

Whilst many churches jump on the tithing bandwagon and make a fortune by requiring their members to faithfully donate ten percent of their income every year, that does not mean that is what Abraham did, nor does it mean God actually wants people to. It is what modern-day churches need to bankroll their future operations, so it is a useful reference.

Scholars are divided on what it actually meant and even how much was paid. Was it just a tithe given by Abraham as a *voluntary* gift from the spoils of war; was it of *all* he possessed, or an *ongoing* yearly commitment commanded by God? The first mention of tithing is at the time he was called Abram. The following is an extract from www.stopthinkrepeat.com on the tithing question:

> **Gen 14:17-20:** "at the Valley of Shaveh (that is, the King's Valley), after his return from the defeat of Chedorlaomer and the kings who were with him. Then Melchizedek king of Salem brought out bread and wine; he was the priest of God Most High. And he blessed him and said: "Blessed be Abram of God Most High, Possessor of heaven and earth; And blessed be God Most High, who has delivered your enemies into your hand." And he gave him a tithe of all."
>
> Is the tithe of all in reference truly a tithe of all Abram possessed? Not if taken in context; consider the previous verse.
>
> **Gen 14:16**: "And he brought back all the goods, and also brought again his brother Lot, and his goods, and the women also, and the people."
>
> The "*tithe of all*" is really the spoils of war they received after rescuing Lot and defeating Chedorlaomer and the kings that were with him as further demonstrated in **Hebrews 7:4**: *"Now consider how great this man was, unto whom even the patriarch Abraham gave the tenth of the spoils"*.
>
> In fact this is the only recorded instance of Abram paying tithing and it was not at the admonition of god but rather as thanks for the safe return of those taken captive. *(See* http://www.stopthinkrepeat.com/religion/pondering-the-origin-concept-and-meaning-behind-tithing/ *from where this extract is drawn, for a concise article on the origins and use of tithing in the Old Testament).* (Emphasis in original).

You could write a whole book on tithing, once you get into the details. In fact several people have, so I will not wander further from the point and simply recommend one. *(Kelly, Russell Earl. PhD. 2000. Should the Church Teach Tithing? A Theologian's Conclusions about a Taboo Doctrine. Lincoln, NE: Writers Club Press, iUniverse).*

> To those who pay tithing, the Lord promises that He will "open . . . the windows of heaven, and pour . . . out a blessing, that there shall not be room enough to receive it" (Malachi 3:10). These blessings may be temporal or spiritual, but they will come to those who obey this divine law. *(Page 79).*

It surprises me that the manual claims these blessings may be "temporal or spiritual" without mentioning what the Church once taught. My understanding was that the 'windows of heaven' *specifically* referred to the heavens opening for an individual to receive personal *revelation*, and *that*, above all else, was the promised blessing in return for the payment of tithing. Such a gift is not even mentioned in the manual. Either the manual writers had no idea that such was the case, as they are of a new generation and didn't refer back to what was previously promised, or God has once again changed His unchangeable mind about that gift.

A Mormon Apostle mentioned blessings being 'temporal or spiritual' but even he didn't mention that the windows of heaven are meant to mean personal *revelation*.

> His promise is sure: "I will ... pour you out a blessing, that there shall not be room enough to receive it." Although tithing carries with it both temporal and spiritual blessings, the only absolute promise to the faithful is "ye shall have the riches of eternity. *(James E. Faust. 2nd Counsellor, 1st Presidency. Ensign, Nov. 1998:54 ). (Page 79).*

There we go again – the only thing we can be *sure* of is what we will get in the *next* life in return for a lifetime of tithing – convenient, as no one benefits in *this* life – unless they are living the delusion of course, when imagination will accommodate practically anything. A next life, and any 'promises' concerning it, is in fact the only thing that we can *not* be sure of. Tithing is a high price to pay for such an unquantifiable promise. Faith is always the Mormon answer of course – just have faith. As Steve Benson, grandson of the prophet Ezra Taft Benson, coined: "pay, pray and obey" and everything will be okay – one day – in the next life.

Next comes the guilt trip…

> Those who do not pay tithing rob God (see Malachi 3:8). They keep for themselves something that rightfully belongs to Him. *(Page 79).*

# THE COMMANDMENTS – PART B

When you become a Mormon, you simply accept the law of tithing as another one of God's requirements. It seems to make sense, as that is how the Church can operate and build new meeting houses and temples. It is not something that tends to be questioned. The thing is, the Church doesn't actually ever disclose what it does with the money. When the prophet, Gordon B. Hinckley, was questioned about this financial secrecy, he explained why there are no published accounts.

> **Helmut Nemetchek of German ZFT Television:** In my country we say the people's churches, the Protestants, the Catholics. They publish all their budgets annually to all the public. Why is not this possible for your church?
>
> **Hinckley:** Well, we simply think that information belongs to those who make the contributions, not to the world. That's the only thing. Yes. *(Gordon B. Hinckley Interview – ZDF German Television Salt Lake City, Utah January 29, 2002 Conducted by Helmut Nemetschek at 47 East South Temple - Church Administration Building).*

The only problem is that what Hinckley said is entirely untrue. To be blunt, it was an absolute *lie*. Members and donors have no more idea about these things than the general public, as the details are completely hidden from them too. In countries such as the U.K. and Canada, local accounts do have to be published by law but they are limited to that country and details are sparse. *(For examples see TMD Vol. 2. Ch. 17).* The missionary manual tries to bring investigators to a position of understanding that all the tithing is used for good purposes and it is not used to pay 'local Church leaders'. It is all very carefully 'managed'. There is no need to worry.

> Tithing does not pay local Church leaders, who serve without receiving payment of any kind. Local Church leaders send the tithing received each week directly to Church headquarters. A council comprised of the First Presidency, the Quorum of the Twelve, and the Presiding Bishopric determines specific ways to use the sacred tithing funds. *(Page 79).*

The idea that there should be no paid ministry in the Lord's Church is a well established concept in the minds of modern-day rank and file Mormons.

The idea that local leaders serve "without receiving payment of ***any*** kind" is not entirely true, as Bishops and Stake Presidents can and do claim generous travel and associated expenses. Has it always been that way in Mormonism? Of course not! Pretty much everything in Mormonism today stems from a trail of earlier ever changing history which the Church now keeps quiet about.

The perception is that absolutely no one in the Church, apart from essential administrative staff – where people are *employed* by the Church, outside the ecclesiastical structure, receives any pay for their service. That is almost true, but not just Bishops and Stake Presidents can claim expenses, so can some Seminary and Institute teachers, for costs of travel and expenses. I personally received generous travel expenses as a Stake Institute teacher for several years. Full time professional Seminary and Institute staff are exceptionally well paid and they also receive extremely generous final salary based pensions.

General Authorities now get what they term a 'stipend' to enable them to cover their living expenses, as full time employees. The Church effectively provides them a salary which, from first hand knowledge, is more than enough to make mortgage payments as well as live comfortably, in addition to which, when on assignment, cars, houses, utilities, travel and related expenses are also provided. Figures regarding these salaries have been suggested, but as I have no evidence to corroborate the amounts and they are really quite unimportant, I will not mention them here. They would not be considered excessive.

Nineteenth century apostles *negotiated* their 'allotments' individually with the Trustee-in-Trust, until 8 September 1887, when formal fixed *salaries* were agreed by Wilford Woodruff and the twelve. *(Quinn 1997:787).*

What is interesting is that whilst the Church today claims paid ministry is not appropriate and that early missionaries went out 'without purse or scrip', unpaid ministry was not always the case regarding local ecclesiastical leaders.

Today, unpaid Bishops and Stake Presidents are called and later released, usually after about five and ten years respectively. In the early Church, they usually stayed in office for several decades, if not for life, and were paid for their services. Bishops, whom Brigham Young criticised for spending too much of the tithing on their own families and not forwarding it, were entitled to keep 8% of all the tithing they collected. Stake Presidents kept 2% of the total tithing from their Stake 'in payment for their services'. *(Quinn 1997:783).*

> 8 Oct 1860. Brigham Young preaches "he was contending against the principle in many of the Bishops to use up all the tithing they could for their own families." *(Quinn 1997:760).*

It should be remembered that much was then given 'in kind' and record keeping regarding some of the donations would have been extremely arbitrary. Effectively, if they could get more members to faithfully pay their tithing, then Bishops' own income and lifestyles increased. Members were initially expected to give up 10% of all they owned upon joining the Church and thereafter pay 10% of their 'increase' annually.

Later, presumably due to disparity created by the income of different Ward and Stake leaders, which would largely depend on the size and affluence of

# THE COMMANDMENTS – PART B

their congregations, the percentage income for Bishops and Stake Presidents was stopped and replaced by a fixed salary.

> 6 April 1888. letter of Wilford Woodruff and apostles establish annual salaries for the stake presidents and end President John Taylor's provisions for local bishops to receive fixed percentage (8 percent) and stake presidents (2 percent) of collect tithing as salary. Until 1896 stake committee apportions this 10 percent of tithing between stake tithing clerk and bishops. On same day apostles approve salary for First Council of Seventy, to which one of its members responds: "I would prefer to receive no salary." *(Quinn 1997:788)*.
>
> At a meeting of the apostles (3 May 1880), 'The question of over running salaries was brought up. Several of the brethren had overdrawn their allowance.' They vote to forgive overdrafts, to increase their annual allowance, and give allowance to Presiding Patriarch. *(Quinn 1997:778)*.
>
> The custom of paying local leaders was discontinued in April 1896. *(Quinn 1997:797)*.

Yet in *Book of Mormon* times, apparently God didn't want the Priests (they didn't have Bishops) to receive any money, so why did Mormon Bishops and Stake Presidents get paid? It doesn't seem very consistent of the Mormon God.

> **Mosiah 18:26.** And the priests were not to depend upon the people for their support; but for their labor they were to receive the grace of God, that they might wax strong in the Spirit, having the knowledge of God, that they might teach with power and authority from God.

Modern-day Mormons generally have no idea about the past. It is clear that at no time was any 'direction' sought from or given by God regarding such matters. They were ever changing and the 'rules' were just made up as they went along.

Surprisingly, the manual doesn't mention "he that is tithed shall not be burned at his coming" which is found in *D&C 64:23*. In my younger days, members would often joke about tithing being their 'fire insurance'. It is not so much of a joke to consider the idea a reality, in that God would actually *burn* anyone – whether they pay their fire insurance or not. What kind of father would burn his children to death, no matter how bad they were?

The manual references *3 Nephi 24* in which Joseph Smith pretends Jesus Christ spoke to the Nephites in 34 CE. We know this to be an impossible claim as the proper name of 'Jesus' was not the Saviour's real name. It may have been '*Yeshua* (Yahshua or Yehoshua) Ben Yosef' (meaning *Joshua, son of Joseph*) and the English name 'Jesus' was not allocated to the Saviour until centuries *after* the time Smith has Jesus supposedly speaking to the Nephites.

The New Testament was written in Koiné (common) Greek, but as the gospel spread into areas where Greek was not spoken, missionaries made translations in other languages such as Coptic, Slavic, and Latin. It wasn't until 382 CE when Jerome translated a standardised Latin Bible (The Vulgate, or common Bible) that the transliterated Greek name of Jesus came about by incorporating all the Greek sounds in his name. It was written 'IESUS'. The Latin and Greek alphabets are not identical but the Latin pronunciation was identical to the Greek 'ee-ay-soos'. Theodosus made Christianity the official religion of the Roman Empire in 391. Jerome's Latin Vulgate became the undeclared 'official' text of the Roman Church. In 1229, the Council of Toulouse made the Latin Bible official by "expressly forbidding it's translation into vulgar tongues." The Latin spelling and pronunciation of **Iesus** dominated the Western Christian world for almost *1,000 years. (See also Ch. 4, pp.75-6)*.

> The Norman invasion of 1066 introduced the letter "j" to England but the sound of the letter did not exist in the Old English language until the early 1200's. Over the next 300 years the hard "J" sound started to replace male names that began with I or Y because it sounded so masculine. Names like Iames became "James," Iakob became Jacob, and Yohan became "John." During the time the letter J was starting to gain acceptance, John Wycliffe became the first person to translate the New Testament from Latin into English in 1384. He preserved the Latin spelling and pronunciation of IESUS but his translation was unread by the common man because only a few hand-written copies of his Bible were produced which were quickly banned by the Church.
> 
> When Gutenburg invented the printing press the Latin Vulgate Bible became the first book ever printed in 1455. The first printed bible in a foreign tongue was the German Mentel Bible of 1466 followed by the Martin Luther bible of 1522.
> 
> After William Tyndale was denied permission to print an English bible he went to visit Martin Luther and completed his translation of the New Testament in 1525. Tyndale had 18,000 copies printed at Worms and smuggled into England of which only two copies survive. After printing his revised edition of 1534 he was captured in Belgium, tried for heresy by order of the pope, and put to death in 1536 by strangulation after which his body was burned at the stake.
> 
> By the year 1611 the letter "J" was officially part of the English language and the King James Bible was printed along with

pronunciation guides for all proper names like Jesus, Jew, Jeremiah, Jerusalem, Judah, and John. The name "Jesus" has been in use ever since. *(See The Evolution of the name Jesus at the following link:* http://webcache.googleusercontent.com/search?q=cache:oDwaO2AZF x8J:www.jesus8880.com/chapters/gematria/yehoshua.htm+when+was+ the+name+jesus+originate&cd=9&hl=en&ct=clnk&gl=uk).

The point is that the **name Jesus** was *not* in use *before* that time.

Not only that, the *title* 'Christ' was not to appear for many centuries either and it is an **English** invention. It first appeared in the fourteenth century. The spelling of *Christ* (Greek genitive): τοῦ Χριστοῦ, *toú Christoú*; Nominative: ὁ Χριστός, *ho Christós* in English was not standardised until the 18<sup>th</sup> century. Prior to this, in Old and Middle English, the word was usually spelt *Crist* (as in Christmas). The spelling "Christ" is attested from the 14th century.

Once again, the point is that it was **not** known *before* the 14<sup>th</sup> century. If this had been a remotely true account, it would have used the term *Messiah* as that was the *only* term known to the Jews and therefore to Lehi when he left Jerusalem. The Saviour Himself could *not* tell the Nephites he was 'Jesus Christ' in 34 CE, as neither the name nor the title had yet been invented. If Mormons want to play the – he knows all things, past, present and future, so the Saviour would know what he would later be known as – 'card', the point is, *why* would the Saviour refer to himself by a name and a title yet to be invented, in England, centuries after the Nephites were all long dead, at a time when they would have had no idea what they meant whatsoever? If he had said call me *Yeshua*, they may have understood that but there would equally have been no point. He would undoubtedly have confirmed he was the *Messias*. All the claim does is to bring obvious dispute to the possible veracity of the record.

And no, God would *not* have retranslated it from Messiah to Jesus Christ in Smith's hat so we would more readily recognise him, as we equally recognise 'Messiah' or 'Messias', and God didn't exactly translate 'cureloms', 'cumoms', 'neas' or 'sheum' for us *(Ether 9:19; Mosiah 9:9)* now did He? The Mormon God would have known very well that people like me would come along and question the absurdity of including 14<sup>th</sup> and 17<sup>th</sup> century English words in a supposed 34 CE text. God is *not* that stupid, but Joseph Smith was, and *he **did***.

> **3 Nephi 23:6.** And now it came to pass that when ***Jesus*** had said these words he said unto them again, after he had expounded all the scriptures unto them which they had received, he said unto them: ***Behold, other scriptures I would that ye should write, that ye have not.***

# THE MORMON DELUSION

> **3 Nephi 24:1.** *And it came to pass that he commanded them that they should write the words which the Father had given unto Malachi, which he should tell unto them.* And it came to pass that after they were written he expounded them. And these are the words which he did tell unto them, saying: Thus said the Father unto Malachi—

So, *Jesus* is speaking the words the *Father spoke to Malachi in Israel circa 450 BCE...*

The Mormon Church now teaches that Jesus Christ was the God of the Old Testament, so would they not have been *his* words? A big question is **why** does the recorded text, include reference to the 'sons of Levi' *(v.3)*; the 'offering of Judah and Jerusalem' (v.4), and 'all nations shall call you blessed', referring specifically to His 'chosen', the *Jews (v.12)*? Jesus apparently 'recited' this to them, and he claims his *Father* spoke to Malachi. It should have been Jesus speaking – according to modern Mormon theology.

No nations have ever called the Nephites 'blessed'; that was for the Jews. No one, other than devout Mormons, even believes the Nephites ever *existed*, so why include that statement just as given to Malachi? The Nephites had purportedly been in the Americas for hundreds of years and it had nothing whatsoever to do with them. Moreover, they would not have had a clue what most of it meant. Smith conveniently has Jesus 'expound' things in *3 Nephi 24:1 (see above)*, but considering the fact that the context applied to other people on another continent, what was the *point*? As with nonsense that Smith claimed Moroni related to him from scripture, wouldn't the Saviour have found something more important and meaningful to say rather than relate Old Testament references matching directly with a then futuristic *KJV*?

In addition to *3 Nephi 24*, the manual actually references *Malachi 3:7-12*.

*3 Nephi 24* **is** *Malachi 3* and the written text is *identical* to the *KJV* with the following very minor exceptions. Three bracketed words in v.5., which are italicised in the *KJV* for clarification, were not included by Smith, but they do appear in the *Tanakh*. The word 'say' in v.7; the *KJV* uses the word 'said'. The 1830 edition of the *Book of Mormon* also included the word 'said' but it was *later* altered to read 'say'. In v.14, the *KJV* has 'ordinances' in the plural. The 's' was missed in the 1830 edition of the *Book of Mormon* but later editions added it back, so it now *matches* the *KJV*. The word 'purifier' in v.3 was misspelled in the 1830 edition of the *BOM* and later 'corrected'. The word 'mine' was changed *(v.10)* to 'my' in the 1830 *BOM* but later changed back to *match* the *KJV* 'mine'. So, the 'translation' of *3 Nephi 24* in the *Book of Mormon* now mirrors the 1611 *KJV* almost *exactly*.

There are noticeable changes that also *prove* the work was *copied* directly from the *KJV* rather than it being a translation of words spoken by Christ in Hebrew (or Aramaic), written in reformed Egyptian hieroglyphs, and translated

# THE COMMANDMENTS – PART B

by Smith. In v.2, the *KJV* uses the word – fullers' – with the apostrophe *after* the 's'. This was originally faithfully *copied* into the *Book of Mormon* in exactly the same way. Later, someone clearly thought that the soap related *to* fuller and altered it to – fuller's – so it no longer matches the *KJV*. But it once *did* and the hoax is thus exposed.

In point of fact, the Tanakh also translates as 'fullers' soap' and in the *KJV* it is *not* a grammatical error. It does not relate to the singular person. A 'fuller' was someone (anyone) who used the soap in **an ancient process used to clean woollen cloth before it was made into garments,** so *fullers'* is the correct translation in the context used in the *KJV*. Young's Literal Translation renders it **"And as soap of a fuller" which puts things in perspective.** This is despite the fact that if you look it up, invariably it is referred to as 'Fuller's soap' as if it was invented by someone *called* Fuller. The word *fullers'* was *copied* into the *Book of Mormon* from the *KJV* but it was later 'corrected', or at least altered, to read *fuller's*, thus exposing Smith's source of *3 Nephi 24*.

Turning to the punctuation, the original 1830 *Book of Mormon* text also mirrors the *KJV* which has about eighty-eight apostrophes, commas, full-stops (periods), semi-colons, colons and question-marks. The question is, considering how the Early Modern English language was then structured, how *closely* did Smith *copy* the punctuation? He was, or at least his scribes were, hopeless at Early Modern English language and grammar and some of the original *Book of Mormon* grammatical structure was positively appalling. Several *thousands* of subsequent changes had to be made for it to remotely sound close to sensible.

The only *consistently correct* textual structure and grammar in the *Book of Mormon* belongs to material that Smith copied directly from the *KJV*. This more than suggests that his scribes were complicit in *copying* the text from the Bible. Some punctuation has been altered in *3 Nephi 24* since the 1830 edition of the *Book of Mormon*.

It is difficult to picture this so I am including the text below, identifying each point so the reader can see how Smith *copied* the text he claimed Christ related to the Nephites.

Original *KJV* punctuation is in (round brackets).
The 1830 *Book of Mormon* (Pp.502-505) punctuation is in [square brackets].
The *Book of Mormon* as it reads today is in {braces – or 'curly' brackets}.
Where *no* brackets appear, the text and grammar are *identical* in each book.
Where no *punctuation* appears *in* the brackets, it was missing in that instance.
The sequence in each instance, left to right, is: KJV; BOM 1830; BOM today.
An exception to the 'left to right' rule occurs with a moved apostrophe.

I will repeat the above seven lines on the next page just above the scriptural text referenced so the reader can more easily identify each classification.

# THE MORMON DELUSION

Where some punctuation appears the *same* in brackets, it identifies *when* any changes were made. For example in v.1 we have "...delight in (:)[:]{;} behold...", identifying the (*KJV*) was *matched* in the [1830 *Book of Mormon*] but the {modern-day *Book of Mormon*} contains *altered* punctuation. Likewise, in v.13, we have "Yet ye say (:)[,]{:} What have..." showing the (*KJV*) colon changing to a comma in the [1830 *Book of Mormon*] and then later editions of the {*Book of Mormon*} reverting to the use of the *KJV* colon.

This may all sound a little complex and detailed but I hope it will be clear below. It is an extremely important point, as it indisputably identifies the fact that Smith not only *copied* the *entire text* directly from the *KJV* but that the incidence of plagiarised punctuation is far too high to be a coincidence by any stretch of the imagination. The probability of Jesus Christ dictating in Hebrew or Aramaic, words that were transcribed into 'Reformed Egyptian' and then centuries later translated into English – turning out to be *exactly* the same as in the *KJV*, punctuation and all, is as close to absolute ***zero*** as it can possibly get.

Here is the legend reminder: Original *KJV* punctuation is in (round brackets). The 1830 *Book of Mormon* (Pp.502-505) punctuation is in [square brackets]. The *Book of Mormon* as it reads today is in {braces – or 'curly' brackets}. Where *no* brackets appear, the text and grammar are *identical* in each book. Where no *punctuation* appears *in* the brackets, it was missing in that instance. The sequence in each instance, left to right, is: KJV; BOM 1830; BOM today. An exception to the 'left to right' rule occurs with a moved apostrophe.

**3 Nephi 24:1.** Behold, I will send my messenger, and he shall prepare the way before me (:)[:]{,} and the Lord (,)[,]{ }whom ye seek (,)[,]{ } shall suddenly come to his temple, even the messenger of the covenant, whom ye delight in (:)[:]{;} behold, he shall come, saith the Lord of Hosts.
**2.** But who may abide the day of his coming (?)[?]{,} and who shall stand when he appeareth? For he is like a refiner's fire, and like fuller{'}s(')['] soap(:)[.]{.}
**3.** And he shall sit as a refiner and purifi[y]er of silver (:)[:]{;} and he shall purify the sons of Levi, and purge them as gold and silver, that they may offer unto the Lord an offering in righteousness. ( )[—]{ }
**4.** Then shall the offering of Judah and Jerusalem be pleasant unto the Lord, as in the days of old, and as in former years.
**5.** And I will come near to you to judgment (;)[:]{;} and I will be a swift witness against the sorcerers, and against the adulterers, and against false swearers, and against those that oppress the hireling in his wages, the widow (,)[,]{ } and the fatherless, and that turn aside the stranger *(from his right)*[ ]{ }, and fear not me, saith the Lord of Hosts.
**6.** For I am the Lord, I change not; therefore ye sons of Jacob are not consumed.

# THE COMMANDMENTS – PART B

7. Even from the days of your fathers ye are gone away from mine ordinances, and have not kept them. Return unto me (,)[,]{ } and I will return unto you, saith the Lord of Hosts. But ye (said,)[said,]{say:} Wherein shall we return?

8. Will a man rob God? Yet ye have robbed me. But ye say (,)[,]{:} Wherein have we robbed thee? In tithes and offerings.

9. Ye are cursed with a curse (:)[:]{,} for ye have robbed me, even this whole nation.

10. Bring ye all the tithes into the storehouse, that there may be meat in (mine) [my] {mine} house (,)[,]{:} and prove me now herewith, saith the Lord of Hosts, if I will not open you the windows of heaven, and pour you out a blessing (,)[,]{ } that there shall not be room enough to receive it.

11. And I will rebuke the devourer for your sakes, and he shall not destroy the fruits of your ground; neither shall your vine cast her fruit before the time in the field{s}, saith the Lord of Hosts.

12. And all nations shall call you blessed (:)[:]{,} for ye shall be a delightsome land, saith the Lord of Hosts.

13. Your words have been stout against me, saith the Lord. Yet ye say (:)[,]{:} What have we spoken against thee?

14. Ye have said (:)[,]{:} It is vain to serve God (,)[:]{,} and what doth it profit that we have kept his ordinance(s)[ ]{s} and that we have walked mournfully before the Lord of Hosts?

15. And now we call the proud happy; yea, they that work wickedness are set up; yea, they that tempt God are even delivered.

16. Then they that feared the Lord spake often one to another (,)[:]{,} and the Lord hearkened ( )[,]{ } and heard (;)[:]{;} and a book of remembrance was written before him for them that feared the Lord, and that thought upon his name.

17. And they shall be mine, saith the Lord of Hosts, in that day when I make up my jewels; and I will spare them ( )[,]{ } as a man spareth his own son that serveth him.

18. Then shall ye return and discern between the righteous and the wicked, between him that serveth God and him that serveth him not.

Results of analysis on the above text show that of eight-eight punctuation marks, Joseph Smith faithfully copied across seventy-seven of them *exactly*. Incredibly, of the eleven he *altered* in the 1830 *Book of Mormon*, **ten** were later **changed back** to *match* the *KJV*, increasing the incidence of *exact* punctuation to *all but one*, bringing text and punctuation to an **almost ninety-nine percent match**. That is **not** a coincidence and God was **not** involved. Notwithstanding that, later editions of the *Book of Mormon* were further altered and today the book contains a further sixteen subsequent alterations, which are different to Smith's, to the punctuation and text, when compared with the *KJV*.

# THE MORMON DELUSION

The fact is that if Jesus really did dictate words that his Father had given to Malachi almost five hundred years before his visit to the Americas, the final English translation should be a closer match to the *Tanakh* than the *KJV*, as that has only been translated from original Hebrew into English, whereas the *KJV* is the result of several earlier translations from Hebrew to Latin to Greek and then a committee of scholars deriving their take on it from a variety of sources. The *Book of Mormon* could not therefore possibly match the *KJV*, which it does, almost exactly, as we have discovered, but it should be closer to the *Tanakh*. It ***isn't***. *(See Appendix C for a full comparison).*

It gets WORSE...

Jesus also relates *Malachi 4* in the following chapter of the *Book of Mormon (3 Nephi 25)*, although it is not referenced in the lesson manual in connection with tithing of course. If we were to analyse it here, we would discover *exactly* the same consistency with the *KJV*, and inconsistency with the *Tanakh*, that we discovered when comparing *3 Nephi 23* with *Malachi 3*.

What really uncovers Smith's hoax in the case of his *Malachi 4* plagiarism in the *Book of Mormon* though, is a mistake he made in 1838 when he recorded supposed scriptures related by the Angel Moroni, formerly known as Nephi, when Smith was supposedly visited by the angel in 1823. Smith apparently remembered, in 1838, word for word *exact* supposed *corrections* to Malachi 4 made by the visiting angel – but he obviously forgot that he had had Jesus relate it all to the Nephites, word for word the same as the *KJV*, in his *Book of Mormon*, when he wrote that a few years earlier.

Either that or he simply didn't care, as it was not the only time he changed scripture, declared it *corrected*, later reverting to the original version, declaring *that* to be correct. For example, *Revelation 1:6* in Smith's *Inspired Revision*, compared to his use of the *KJV* version some years later during his King Follett Sermon, when he then declared the *KJV* version of it to be 'correct'. Smith had changed the very *context* of that verse some years earlier in his *I.R. (See Ch. 5, p.103). (See: TMD. Vol.2. Ch.6 for coverage of Moroni's altered scriptures).*

The *only* references to tithing in the *Book of Mormon* are in *Alma 13*, regarding Abraham *(see p.332)*, and *3 Nephi 24:8,10 (see p.343)* where Jesus supposedly quotes Malachi. There is no record of anyone, Jaredites or Nephites, or any of their descendants, ever being commanded to live the law of tithing themselves.

The closest it gets is in Mosiah in 147 BCE but even then, it is not tithing.

> **Mosiah 18:27.** And again Alma commanded that the people of the church should impart of their substance, every one according to that which he had; if he have more abundantly he should impart more

abundantly; and of him that had but little, but little should be required; and to him that had not should be given.
**28.** And thus they should impart of their substance of their own free will and good desires towards God, and to those priests that stood in need, yea, and to every needy, naked soul.

There is no tribe or civilisation anywhere in the Americas today which has a history, or even legends of such a practice, any more than any other *Book of Mormon* claimed way of life or theocracy. If it was an ancient law in biblical times, surely Lehi knew of it and practiced it himself? Once his family grew and spread, why then was it not continued, along with all the laws of Moses they supposedly lived? Once again, it all comes down to what was in Smith's imagination when he wrote the *Book of Mormon*. He didn't think of tithing.

Early Mormons were expected to donate ten percent of all they owned upon joining the Church and then ten percent of their increase, or 'work' equivalent, where they would work for the Church one day in ten each year. Today, new converts are only required to pay ten percent of their gross income or increase (interest etc.,) per annum in tithing once they are baptised.

> Tithing has variously been described as the donation of (1) a tenth of what people owned when they were converted; (2) a tenth of their "increase" or income each year; and (3) one workday in ten of their labor, teams, and tools to public projects. Today, tithe payers pay a tenth of their "increase" or income. *(Encyclopaedia of Mormonism p.1582).*

The thing is that the Mormon God is once again being completely, or at least in part, ignored by Church leaders today. Why do they not 'require' new converts to give up ten percent of their assets when they join the Church now?

This reference from the *D&C* explains what God wants – but doesn't get.

> **D&C 119:1.** Verily, thus saith the Lord, *I require all their surplus property* to be put into the hands of the bishop of my church in Zion,
> **2.** For the building of mine house, and for the laying of the foundation of Zion and *for the priesthood, and for the debts of the Presidency of my Church.*
> **3.** And this shall be the beginning of the tithing of my people.
> **4.** And *after that, those who have thus been tithed shall pay one-tenth of all their interest annually;* and this shall be *a standing law unto them forever,* for my holy priesthood, saith the Lord.
> **5.** Verily I say unto you, it shall come to pass that *all* those who gather unto the land of Zion *shall be tithed of their surplus properties, and*

*shall observe this law, or they shall not be found worthy* to abide among you.

**6.** And I say unto you, if my people observe not this law, to keep it holy, and by this law sanctify the land of Zion unto me, that my statutes and my judgments may be kept thereon, that it may be most holy, behold, verily I say unto you, it shall not be a land of Zion unto you.

**7.** And this shall be an ensample unto all the stakes of Zion. Even so. Amen. (Emphasis added).

A tithe of all surplus property is to be given by all converts who gather to Zion as a "standing law unto them forever." That 'gathering' of converts went on until shortly before I joined the Church in 1960, but no one then gave up anything upon joining. So, we may wonder, what happened to that idea?

Nothing ever remains the same forever, despite the fact that the Mormon God keeps saying everything *is* forever.

The qualifying question:

Will you live the law of tithing when you are baptized?

## The Law of the Fast

Great blessings are available to those who obey God's commandment to fast. Fasting means going without food and drink for a period of time. Usually the first Sunday of each month is set aside as a special day to fast for two consecutive meals, pray, and bear testimony. *(Page 79).*

The fast usually runs from after lunch on Saturday, through until lunchtime on Sunday when most members eat when they return home from Church. This can vary, depending on meeting times. No food or any drink is usually consumed during a twenty-four hour fast, with the exception of partaking of the sacrament where that occurs during a fast period. The sacrament is not considered the end of a fast, which may continue beyond it. Children under the age of eight are not expected to fast. Older children may participate, but usually not for longer than they feel comfortable. Some people cannot fast for various medical reasons and pregnant women may be advised not to fast. It is considered very much an individual thing and no one is ever asked about their fasting in practice. The fast is not considered 'complete' until a suitable 'fast offering' has been made which should at least equal, if not significantly exceed, the cost of the missed meals. The donations are designated for the 'poor and needy'. I took a closer look at this area, as it relates to the U.K., when writing *TMD Volume 2.*

# THE COMMANDMENTS – PART B

As of the end of 2005, the U.K. figures show income to the 'fast offering' fund of over £1.5 million during that year. The 'expenditure and transfers' of just half a million left a balance carried forward to 2006 in excess of £3.1 million. People are starving and dying *now*, so why the huge reserve? It won't get better, unless something is done now, and members believe their donations are helping people immediately. It is, after all, a natural assumption, as there is constantly dire need in several locations. The 'Fast Offering Fund' is listed as "contributed by members of the Church to be used in the relief of the poor and needy". Yes, that is the *relief* of the poor and needy. The perception is that the relief is given immediately to those who are in most need. The £500,000 'expenditure' was actually transferred to the 'Welfare Fund' which has broader scope for use than members may imagine for their fast offerings.

The Welfare Fund does far more than provide food and necessities to those who desperately need immediate help to survive (the poor and needy); its full range and scope of expenditure, specified to achieve the goal of helping the poor and needy, includes the following: "Invests in farms which it rents out to subsidiary companies", profits from which are returned to the charity of course, "acquires land and builds purpose built meeting houses, for a fellow subsidiary, in which members of the Church and members of the public can meet together for religious instruction and worship" and "assists individuals suffering through hardship, sickness and distress as needed" and "provides advice and guidance to Church members on the Church's worldwide welfare and humanitarian aid programmes". So, the fund that actually runs farms and pays for the construction of chapels is somewhat supported from funds donated by members who think 'fast offering' donations go to *feed* the poor and needy. *(TMD Vol. 2:341).*

Mormons generally have no idea what happens to any of their offerings and most don't really care; they just know they have obeyed the Lord and trust their leaders to use the money 'wisely'. I personally would not have been happy had I known what some of the donations really got used for, but the 'rule' is that they are voluntary donations, and as a member, you don't really consider anything further than that.

There are several references provided in the manual dealing with giving fast offerings to assist the poor, and several relating to the actual concept of fasting. One of these is supposedly from 361-130 BCE, and although it seems innocuous enough in referring to fasting, it is also yet another which refers to *Christ* in the BCE period. There are so many of these anachronisms in the *Book of Mormon* that it is hard to research any other aspect without stumbling over even more of them.

> **Omni 1:26.** And now, my beloved brethren, I would that ye should come unto Christ, who is the Holy One of Israel, and partake of his salvation, and the power of his redemption. Yea, come unto him, and offer your whole souls as an offering unto him, and continue in fasting and praying, and endure to the end; and as the Lord liveth ye will be saved.

A couple of other references to fasting found in the *Book of Mormon* come from *Alma 6:6* and *Moroni 6:5*, both of which seem straight forward enough at first glance:

> **Alma 6:6.** Nevertheless the children of God were commanded that they should gather themselves together oft, and join in fasting and mighty prayer in behalf of the welfare of the souls of those who knew not God.

> **Moroni 6:5.** And the church did meet together oft, to fast and to pray, and to speak one with another concerning the welfare of their souls.

Alma was supposedly written 83 BCE and Moroni 400-421 CE, some *five centuries* later, yet the wording here is remarkably similar. Looking at the surrounding verses, it is difficult to reach any other conclusion than that they were in all probability both written at a similar time, by the *same* person. The Church would no doubt claim this to be mere speculation, and as I like to deal exclusively with *evidence* I will just mention a couple of other verses that look extremely suspicious and leave the reader to compare *Alma 6* with *Moroni 6* and consider what they make of the similarities.

> **Alma 6:3.** …the same were rejected, and their names were blotted out, that their names were not numbered among those of the righteous.

> **Mor. 6:7.** …if they repented not, and confessed not, their names were blotted out, and they were not numbered among the people of Christ.

I will just mention that Alma 6:8 contains yet *another* reference to Jesus Christ in the BCE period and ask, **what** "testimony of Jesus Christ", who was *yet* to be born, and well over a thousand years away from being named and titled that way – in England?

> **Alma 6:8.** And Alma went and began to declare the word of God unto the church which was established in the valley of Gideon, according to the revelation of the truth of the word which had been spoken by his fathers, and according to the spirit of prophecy which was in him, *according to the testimony of Jesus Christ, the Son of God*, who should come to redeem his people from their sins, and the holy order by which he was called. And thus it is written. Amen. (Emphasis added).

# THE COMMANDMENTS – PART B

Commitment questions:

Will you fast and pray on the next fast Sunday for some special need?
Will you donate a generous fast offering [after you are baptized]?

## Obey and Honour the Law

Latter-day Saints everywhere believe in obeying the laws of the country in which they live. Members of the Church are counselled to be good citizens, to participate in civil government and the political process, and to render community service. They do so, however, as concerned citizens, not as representatives of the Church. *(Page 80)*.

Considering what has gone on within the leadership of the Mormon Church since the very beginning, it is hard to see how they can even begin to teach members how to behave regarding the law. Most faithful Mormons would, I am sure, try to obey the law, irrespective of such a command.

I have covered a number of cases of the unlawful activities of Mormon leaders elsewhere in this and especially my earlier volumes; from the illegal practice of polygamy and polyandry, to the bribery of government officials and newspaper editors in respect of trying to get Utah admitted as a State; from prophets on the run from the law, to the modern-day monetary and activist support for Proposition 8 in California, for which the Church was fined $5,000.

Notwithstanding all the illegal activities of Mormon leaders over the years and all of the lies and deceptions committed against the United States as well as its own rank and file members, the Mormon Church still puts on a pious 'face' and dictates the standards of 'law abiding' and 'truth telling' in no uncertain terms. Evidence proves time and time again that there is one rule for rank and file Mormons and entirely another for their leaders, who do just as they please.

Articles of Faith 12 and 13 are prolifically referred to by the Mormon leaders. I mentioned them in the 'Prelude', on page 12. They are worth repeating again:

**12.** *We believe in being subject to kings, presidents, rulers, and magistrates, in obeying, honoring, and sustaining the law.*

**13.** *We believe in being honest, true, chaste,* benevolent, virtuous, and in doing good to all men; indeed, we may say that we follow the admonition of Paul - We believe all things, we hope all things, we have endured many things, and hope to be able to endure all things. If there is anything virtuous, lovely, or of good report or praiseworthy, we seek after these things. (Emphasis added).

The Church also publishes extensive material in lesson manuals concerning the principles of honesty and integrity which members are expected to live by.

The track record of Mormon leaders since the very beginning does not even come close to the analysis of concepts provided for members to adhere to.

The following, also referenced in the 'Prelude' *(p.15)* is just one example of published expectations and cannot be emphasised enough; not just as a classic example of how things should be, but how they are ***not*** for Mormon leaders.

### Honesty and Integrity

Honest people love truth and justice.
They are honest in their words and actions.
Lying is intentionally deceiving others.
We can also intentionally deceive others by a gesture or a look,
by silence, or by telling only part of the truth.
Whenever we lead people in any way to believe something
that is not true, we are not being honest.

*(Mormon Church Lesson Manual 'Gospel Principles'*
*Chapter 31. Honesty. 1979 Edition).*

# Chapter 15

## Lesson 5

### Laws and Ordinances

This lesson is designed to be taught to new converts as soon as possible after they are baptised and confirmed members. The immediate question that springs to mind is; why are these not *mandatory* teachings prior to a commitment to be baptised? Surely a more complete picture of requirements is necessary before anyone makes such a long term and life changing decision? The lesson manual indicates that some of these things *may* be taught prior to baptism or early afterwards, but there is no specific pre-baptismal requirement.

> This lesson should be taught to new members soon after they are baptized and confirmed. You may begin teaching them about these laws and ordinances between their baptism and confirmation or even before baptism. Baptismal candidates should at least be aware of these laws and ordinances before baptism. *(Page 82).*

There are suggested ways in which some of the material could be included within earlier discussions. The manual gives missionaries ideas about how this may be achieved, indicating that it works much like Lesson 4 and can be integrated elsewhere. There is therefore a lot of leeway for missionaries.

> Ideas include: Teaching the new member each of the laws and ordinances from this lesson while reviewing "The Message of the Restoration," "The Plan of Salvation," and "The Gospel of Jesus Christ" lessons. For example, while reviewing the message of the Restoration you may want to teach about priesthood and missionary work; while reviewing the plan of salvation you may teach about eternal marriage, temples and family history work, and teaching and learning in the Church. When reviewing the gospel of Jesus Christ you may want to teach about the strait and narrow way and serving in the Church. Teaching two or three of the laws and ordinances as a single lesson. Teaching a single law or ordinance as a lesson. *(Page 82).*

Missionaries are instructed to help new converts recognise that by keeping God's laws they will retain a "remission of their sins" and stay on the "pathway to eternal life".

They will experience "greater peace and joy" and find answers to life's questions. They will feel secure in the "knowledge" that they belong to the "true Church of Jesus Christ." This of course is how it is spelled out to the missionaries in the manual. Investigators, or by now, possibly new converts, don't actually see it, but the message will be presented to converts in a similar manner. They therefore ultimately conclude, not just that they *believe* the Church is true, but rather, they somehow ethereally come to *know* that it is true.

This completely unquantifiable concept will be constantly reinforced by the many other members who continually affirm in 'testimony meetings' that they "Know the Church is true, know Joseph Smith was a prophet of God, and know the Book of Mormon to be the word of God". These kinds of statements are repeated almost by rote by most Mormons from the time they begin to speak as small children. Once a new member starts to repeat the same things, the initial stages of 'conditioning' a new convert are well under way.

## Priesthood and Auxiliaries

The manual explains that the priesthood is the authority for men, and only men, to run the Lord's Church. No women in Mormonism hold the priesthood or *any* positions of *authority* whatsoever and have *no* say in the running of the Church, even at a local level. Men alone act in God's name; women do as they are told. The Church is quiet about the fact that there were *prophetesses* in the Bible.

> The Church of Jesus Christ of Latter-day Saints is led by Jesus Christ through apostles and prophets. These are righteous men who are called of God and given the priesthood. Anciently Christ ordained His Apostles and gave them the priesthood. That authority was lost when

the people rejected the gospel and killed Christ and the Apostles. Priesthood authority was restored in 1829 when John the Baptist appeared to the Prophet Joseph Smith and Oliver Cowdery. He laid his hands on their heads and conferred on them the Aaronic Priesthood (see D&C 13). A short time later Peter, James, and John of the original Twelve Apostles laid their hands on Joseph Smith and Oliver Cowdery and conferred upon them the Melchizedek Priesthood, which Peter, James, and John had received from Jesus Christ (see D&C 27:12–13). *(Page 83)*.

Many Mormon historians struggle to validate these claims as there is no properly accredited record accounting for the events whatsoever. *D&C 13* and *D&C 27* were covered earlier in respect of priesthood restoration in Chapter 5. *(See: pp.111-19)*. The manual affirms that receiving the priesthood is a 'marvellous' opportunity.

> He enters a covenant to fulfill sacred duties, serve others, and help build up the Church. He must have a desire to serve God and must be ordained to this power (see D&C 4:3; 63:57). *(Page 83)*.

New converts will learn from missionaries or local members about Aaronic and Melchizedek Priesthood offices and responsibilities, and male converts will soon be on a priesthood path leading to temple ordinances. The manual points out who leads the Ward and Stake and explains how they are the local 'judges' of the people.

> Bishops and stake presidents are judges in the Church. They have the authority to help Saints who have sinned to repent and enjoy the full blessings of Church membership. They interview people to ensure their worthiness to enter the temple. *(Page 83)*.

Whilst day to day religious 'misdemeanours' generally remain between a member and the Lord, anything that violates commandments that are reviewed in a recommend interview must be confessed to a Bishop or Stake President.

That generally means sexual transgressions or any kind of illegal activity. It also means apostasy which usually only becomes evident if someone speaks out or publishes historical facts which are considered 'unhelpful' by the Church. Disciplinary action may well follow such publication, despite the fact that the individual concerned may not feel they are actually apostate.

Church discipline may consist of a cautionary warning; probation, usually lasting from a few months to a year or so; disfellowshipment, usually for a year, possibly longer; or excommunication, when it will take two to four years, sometimes longer, for a person to return to full membership should they wish to do so. So called 'apostates' are not usually invited back into the Church, as their published work remains in the public arena and the Church cannot be seen to be associated with such things. Many historians who get excommunicated did not 'confess' as such and did not ask to be disciplined. They were simply historians who published the truth. They may even have thought their work supported the very integrity of the Church in which they still believed. But the Church sees things differently. It firmly believes that some things, whilst *true*, are best not *said*, so if someone decides to disclose the way things really were regarding Mormon history, such news is not at all well received by leaders.

Obedience, in Mormon terms, includes *not* saying anything of which the leaders would not approve, irrespective of whether or not it is true. Truth does not enter into the equation. Among Mormon Church leadership, 'integrity' is not a common feature at all, despite the fact that they teach it prolifically as a principle. That's for the rank and file, and evidently not for the leaders.

Auxiliary organisations and their various purposes are explained. I have included the text from the manual below, for readers unfamiliar with the ways of Mormonism. Note, absolutely *everything* is "under priesthood direction" meaning that men run the show and women are mere spectators. Some women *think* they have leadership roles in Relief Society and somewhat in Primary, but really they don't, as everything is still run under priesthood dictatorship and women are allowed to lead those auxiliaries only under direction, supervision and tight control. There is no autonomy for women. Years ago, the Relief Society had its own funds and bank accounts in each Ward and could raise money for its own use. Even that level of autonomy was removed and all finances placed under priesthood control. The women do not handle money. They have no say in *anything*.

> Under priesthood direction, auxiliary organizations assist in strengthening members. They are a great resource in missionary work as they assist in finding and teaching investigators and fellowshipping new converts. Women age 18 and older are members of the Relief Society, which reaches out in service to families, individuals, and the community. Young women ages 12 to 18 are members of the Young Women program. Boys of similar ages participate in the Young Men program. All children ages 3 to 11 are part of the Primary organization. All members age 12 and older are enrolled in Sunday School classes. *(Page 84).*

Several references are provided, one of which is *Mosiah 18:17*.

> **Mosiah 18:17.** And they were **called the church of God, or the church of Christ**, from that time forward. And it came to pass that whosoever was baptized by the power and authority of God was added to his church. (Emphasis added).

## LAWS AND ORDINANCES

When Mormons read through that verse, they may feel slightly confused but probably not consciously so, and will just move on past it. But when you stop and look at what it *says*, it begs the question, which was it then? Did they call it the *Church of God* or did they call it the *Church of Christ*? You can't call it *both* – even if Smith thought God and Christ *were* one and the same being when he wrote it. The statement leaves ambiguity where none should exist. But then, Joseph Smith seemed to have the same problem. *(See pp.120-1)*.

Regarding baptism in the *Book of Mormon*, *Mosiah 18:13-15* contains the following method and words, which yet again include the word 'Christ' 148-145 BCE:

> **Mosiah 18:13.** And when he had said these words, the Spirit of the Lord was upon him, and he said: *Helam, I baptize thee, having authority from the Almighty God, as a testimony that ye have entered into a covenant to serve him until you are dead as to the mortal body; and may the Spirit of the Lord be poured out upon you; and may he grant unto you eternal life, through the redemption of Christ, whom he has prepared from the foundation of the world.*
> **14.** And after Alma had said these words, both Alma and Helam were buried in the water; and they arose and came forth out of the water rejoicing, being filled with the Spirit.
> **15.** And again, Alma took another, and went forth a second time into the water, and baptized him according to the first, only he did not bury himself again in the water. (Emphasis added).

Contrast those baptismal words with what the Mormon Church uses today, which is taken from Third Nephi. There is no consistency with the Mormon God's ideas.

> **3 Nephi 11:25.** Having authority given me of Jesus Christ, I baptize you in the name of the Father, and of the Son, and of the Holy Ghost. Amen.

Note that two verses later, yet again, an entirely monotheistic statement is included.

> **3 Nephi 11:27.** And after this manner shall ye baptize in my name; for behold, verily I say unto you, that the Father, and the Son, and the Holy Ghost are one; and I am in the Father, and the Father in me, and the Father and I are one.

In v.18 of *Mosiah 18*, Alma ordained one priest to preach to every fifty people. Today, priests are sixteen and seventeen-year-old boys who can bless the sacrament and be junior Home Teaching companions, but that's about it.

# THE MORMON DELUSION

**Mosiah 18:18.** And it came to pass that Alma, having authority from God, ordained priests; even one priest to every fifty of their number did he ordain to preach unto them, and to teach them concerning the things pertaining to the kingdom of God.

*D&C 107* is referenced in its entirety. One part has always seemed strange to me, as no one has ever been able to establish a direct and literal link back to Aaron. What would be the case if such a person were located and found to be a complete reprobate? In any event, the notion seems quite pointless as it has never amounted to anything and I doubt it ever will. But, should such a person ever be identified, what are the chances of future sons and grandsons all being 'suitable' Bishops? How far would this 'right' then extend? 'Get out' clauses would inevitably be introduced. Yet, in theory, they would have the inherent 'right' to run a Ward without counsellors and do just as they pleased. As the possibility of such a thing happening would never be risked by the Church, it seems unlikely a link will ever be pursued in earnest, despite DNA testing now being available. It then begs the question why such detail as this was bothered with by Smith and his God; it has never been needed and it never will be.

**D&C 107:69.** Nevertheless *a bishop must be chosen from the High Priesthood, unless he is a literal descendant of Aaron*;
**70.** For *unless he is a literal descendant of Aaron he cannot hold the keys of that priesthood.*
**71.** Nevertheless, a high priest, that is, after the order of Melchizedek, may be set apart unto the ministering of temporal things, having a knowledge of them by the Spirit of truth;
**72.** And also to be a judge in Israel, to do the business of the church, to sit in judgment upon transgressors upon testimony as it shall be laid before him according to the laws, by the assistance of his counselors, whom he has chosen or will choose among the elders of the church.
**73.** This is the duty of a bishop who is not a literal descendant of Aaron, but has been ordained to the High Priesthood after the order of Melchizedek.
**74.** Thus shall he be a judge, even a common judge among the inhabitants of Zion, or in a stake of Zion, or in any branch of the church where he shall be set apart unto this ministry, until the borders of Zion are enlarged and it becomes necessary to have other bishops or judges in Zion or elsewhere.
**75.** And inasmuch as there are other bishops appointed they shall act in the same office.
**76.** *But a literal descendant of Aaron has a legal right to the presidency of this priesthood, to the keys of this ministry, to act in the office of bishop independently, without counselors*, except in a case where a President of the High Priesthood, after the order of Melchizedek, is tried, to sit as a judge in Israel. (Emphasis added).

## LAWS AND ORDINANCES

*Alma 13:1–19* is also referenced in connection with the priesthood. It contains another one of those meaningless speeches that go on and on whilst saying absolutely nothing of any sense or use whatsoever. It is the one that starts by citing minds forward and then speaking in the *past* tense, which we have discussed elsewhere *(see: p.332)*. It then goes on to supposedly give an explanation of "the manner after which they were ordained", as if it will help investigators to understand the process. I don't think it will at all.

Try to make sense of why this is included in the *Book of Mormon*, let alone referenced in missionary lessons. Not only is the text completely boring, much of the grammar, flow, context and structure is positively *dreadful*. I am sure the reader will quite easily notice them without me pointing them out. Remember, once again, that this is what *God* supposedly dictated word for word, and word by word – into Joseph Smith's hat.

> **Alma 13:3.** And this is the manner after which they were ordained—being called and prepared from the foundation of the world according to the foreknowledge of God, on account of their exceeding faith and good works; in the first place being left to choose good or evil; therefore they having chosen good, and exercising exceedingly great faith, are called with a holy calling, yea, with that holy calling which was prepared with, and according to, a preparatory redemption for such.
> **4.** And thus they have been called to this holy calling on account of their faith, while others would reject the Spirit of God on account of the hardness of their hearts and blindness of their minds, while, if it had not been for this they might have had as great privilege as their brethren.
> **5.** Or in fine, in the first place they were on the same standing with their brethren; thus this holy calling being prepared from the foundation of the world for such as would not harden their hearts, being in and through the atonement of the Only Begotten Son, who was prepared—
> **6.** And thus being called by this holy calling, and ordained unto the high priesthood of the holy order of God, to teach his commandments unto the children of men, that they also might enter into his rest—
> **7.** This high priesthood being after the order of his Son, which order was from the foundation of the world; or in other words, being without beginning of days or end of years, being prepared from eternity to all eternity, according to his foreknowledge of all things—
> **8.** Now they were ordained after this manner—being called with a holy calling, and ordained with a holy ordinance, and taking upon them the high priesthood of the holy order, which calling, and ordinance, and high priesthood, is without beginning or end—

**9.** Thus they become high priests forever, after the order of the Son, the Only Begotten of the Father, who is without beginning of days or end of years, who is full of grace, equity, and truth. And thus it is. Amen.
**10.** Now, as I said concerning the holy order, or this high priesthood, there were many who were ordained and became high priests of God; and it was on account of their exceeding faith and repentance, and their righteousness before God, they choosing to repent and work righteousness rather than to perish;
**11.** Therefore they were called after this holy order, and were sanctified, and their garments were washed white through the blood of the Lamb.
**12.** Now they, after being sanctified by the Holy Ghost, having their garments made white, being pure and spotless before God, could not look upon sin save it were with abhorrence; and there were many, exceedingly great many, who were made pure and entered into the rest of the Lord their God.
**13.** And now, my brethren, I would that ye should humble yourselves before God, and bring forth fruit meet for repentance, that ye may also enter into that rest.

So, the upshot is that they were foreordained, had faith, chose good, got called as High Priests, and lived happily ever after. The passage then continues to speak about Melchizedek and tithing, but I expect the reader is by now completely bored by the text. The point having been made, I will move on.

The *D&C* is referenced regarding what the offices in the priesthood are and who does what. However, no one seems to account for, or comment on, the obvious differences in what God apparently told Smith and what the Church now does in each case.

**D&C 20:38.** The duty of the elders, priests, teachers, deacons, and members of the church of Christ—An apostle is an elder, and it is his calling to baptize;
**39.** And to ordain other elders, priests, teachers, and deacons;
**40.** And to administer bread and wine—the emblems of the flesh and blood of Christ—
**41.** And to confirm those who are baptized into the church, by the laying on of hands for the baptism of fire and the Holy Ghost, according to the scriptures;
**42.** And to teach, expound, exhort, baptize, and watch over the church;
**43.** And to confirm the church by the laying on of the hands, and the giving of the Holy Ghost;
**44.** And to take the lead of all meetings.
**45.** The elders are to conduct the meetings as they are led by the Holy Ghost, according to the commandments and revelations of God.

## LAWS AND ORDINANCES

**46.** The priest's duty is to preach, teach, expound, exhort, and baptize, and administer the sacrament,

**47.** And visit the house of each member, and exhort them to pray vocally and in secret and attend to all family duties.

**48.** And he may also ordain other priests, teachers, and deacons.

**49.** And he is to take the lead of meetings when there is no elder present;

**50.** But when there is an elder present, he is only to preach, teach, expound, exhort, and baptize,

**51.** And visit the house of each member, exhorting them to pray vocally and in secret and attend to all family duties.

**52.** In all these duties the priest is to assist the elder if occasion requires.

**53.** The teacher's duty is to watch over the church always, and be with and strengthen them;

**54.** And see that there is no iniquity in the church, neither hardness with each other, neither lying, backbiting, nor evil speaking;

**55.** And see that the church meet together often, and also see that all the members do their duty.

**56.** And he is to take the lead of meetings in the absence of the elder or priest—

**57.** And is to be assisted always, in all his duties in the church, by the deacons, if occasion requires.

**58.** But neither teachers nor deacons have authority to baptize, administer the sacrament, or lay on hands;

**59.** They are, however, to warn, expound, exhort, and teach, and invite all to come unto Christ.

**60.** Every elder, priest, teacher, or deacon is to be ordained according to the gifts and callings of God unto him; and he is to be ordained by the power of the Holy Ghost, which is in the one who ordains him.

**61.** The several elders composing this church of Christ are to meet in conference once in three months, or from time to time as said conferences shall direct or appoint;

**62.** And said conferences are to do whatever church business is necessary to be done at the time.

**63.** The elders are to receive their licenses from other elders, by vote of the church to which they belong, or from the conferences.

**64.** Each priest, teacher, or deacon, who is ordained by a priest, may take a certificate from him at the time, which certificate, when presented to an elder, shall entitle him to a license, which shall authorize him to perform the duties of his calling, or he may receive it from a conference.

**65.** No person is to be ordained to any office in this church, where there is a regularly organized branch of the same, without the vote of that church;

This section was a supposed revelation from God. An *apostle* is an elder and is to *baptise (v.38)*, to ordain other elders, priests, teachers and deacons *(v.39)*, to administer the sacrament *(v.40)*, *confirm* new members *(v.41)*, teach, expound, exhort, *baptise* (again), and watch over the church *(v.42)*, despite *baptise* already appearing in v.38, and to *confirm* new members *(v.43)*, despite having just been told the same thing in v.41, to take the lead of all meetings *(v.44)*, as they are led by the Holy Ghost *(v.45)*. God, or rather Joseph Smith, seems to keep forgetting what he has already said and then repeating himself.

Today, it would be rare to see an apostle involved at those levels very often and all are High Priests, a higher priesthood 'rank', rather than just elders.

Likewise, there are now 'Seventies' who are all General Authorities these days. Earlier in my church life, there were Seventies quorums in every single Ward of the Church. This was a local missionary calling and priesthood office, above that of Elder but below High Priest. These quorums have long since been disbanded, when all Seventies were absorbed into existing Elder's quorums. That was a strange change.

In 1830, when this detail was originally 'revealed', there was no mention of Seventies or High Priests. These came later as the Church evolved. Likewise, early Priests, Teachers and Deacons were usually adults who were to do things that the modern equivalent are very unlikely to ever do today – such as 'lead meetings' and 'see that the church meet together often, and also see that all the members do their duty'.

Now, young boys are ordained Deacons at age twelve, Teachers at fourteen and Priests at sixteen. We have to remember that they just made up the rules as they went along – and they still do. Brigham Young ordained *four* of his own sons *apostles*, even though they were not members of the Quorum of Twelve. One son was just eleven years old; John W. Young was ordained an apostle on 22 November 1855. The Quorum of Twelve did not discover this until 1864. *(See Quinn 1997:752-3)*. Times change. Positions such as 'Bishop' and 'Stake President' were not mentioned in this revelation either.

There are always commitment questions:

> Will you prepare to receive the Aaronic Priesthood (eligible and worthy males age 12 and over)?
>
> Will you prepare to receive the Melchizedek Priesthood (eligible and worthy adult males)?
>
> Will you participate actively in the appropriate auxiliary organization?

# LAWS AND ORDINANCES
## Missionary Work

Mormon Church leaders are aware that the best time to get 'referrals' from members is when they are first converted, full of enthusiasm and keen to tell everyone they know, that they have discovered the one true Church. As time goes by, the 'novelty', if it can legitimately be called that, does wear off, in the sense that most people become more accustomed to what they have joined and less enthusiastic about sharing it with all and sundry. Eventually, if they are honest with themselves, it is something that many members actually tend to avoid, even if subconsciously, unless circumstances provide an opportunity to discuss aspects that may interest someone without them first having to raise the question.

Missionaries teach new converts how to share the gospel with others and to provide referrals for them to teach. The psychology is extremely simple. God *commands* it of His followers.

> The Lord commanded His followers to preach the gospel in all the world, giving every person the opportunity to accept or reject it. When people are baptized, they make a covenant to always stand as witnesses of God. They are commanded to share the gospel with those who have not yet received it. As they live the gospel faithfully, they will set an example, showing their family members and friends the great blessings that come from living the gospel. They should also take advantage of opportunities to answer questions, share printed or audiovisual materials, and invite others to learn more about the message of the restored gospel. Members should pray for those who are not members of the Church. They should pray for missionary opportunities—to serve those who are not of our faith and share what they believe. The Lord promises to help members know what to say and do as they share the gospel. *(Page 84)*.

Several references are provided to convince converts of their obligation to God. This one should convince new converts of what their responsibility is:

> **D&C 88:81.** Behold, I sent you out to testify and warn the people, and it becometh every man who hath been warned to warn his neighbor.

Two of the references provided are from the *Book of Mormon* and another seven from the *D&C*. There are no biblical references regarding this concept.

One of the *Book of Mormon* references concerns a parable of working in a vineyard, getting the best out of it. In part, it actually sounds quite compelling, suggesting to the sceptic that perhaps, as Smith wasn't very good at writing these things himself, that it was probably not in fact Smith's original idea; so, where could it have come from?

# THE MORMON DELUSION

It doesn't take long to locate the original source. In fact, the material Smith plagiarised for this appears to have come from *two* sources, and he gets a little mixed up between them in his telling of the tale. But first, this is the text referenced by the missionary lesson manual.

*Jacob 5:70-75* was supposedly written 544-421 BCE. *Jacob 5* has 77 verses and the whole chapter deals with the parable. It is essentially an allegory about olive trees. Verse 1 prefaces the story.

> **Jacob 5:1.** Behold, my brethren, do ye not remember to have read the words of the prophet Zenos, which he spake unto the house of Israel, saying:

This highlights Smith's first of many problems. There was no such prophet as *Zenos* in the Old Testament. Here, Jacob is asking if his audience remembers 'reading' Zenos's words. Lehi supposedly had Laban's 'brass plates' which contained scriptures. There was no record of Zenos copied from them into the *Book of Mormon* and no record appears in the Tanakh or Old Testament. Zenos remains a fictional character. He is mentioned about a dozen times in the *Book of Mormon*, and *only* in the *Book of Mormon*, and here he appears along with two other equally fictional characters created by Smith, *Zenock* and *Neum*.

> **1 Nephi 19:10.** ...according to the words of *Zenock*, and to be crucified, according to the words of *Neum*, and to be buried in a sepulchre, according to the words of *Zenos*, which he spake concerning the three days of darkness,...

Jacob 5 contains material from *Isaiah 5* which is about a 'vineyard' and also from *Romans 11*, where Paul is speaking to the Romans about an 'olive tree'. In *Jacob 5*, Smith refers to *olives* **nine** times and yet throughout, he is talking about 'vineyards', with no less than **ninety** references. Vineyards produce *one* thing and one thing **only** – and that is **grapes**, which grow on **vines**. Olives grow on the branches of **trees**, not on vines *or* in a vineyard.

Olive trees grow in groves or perhaps in fields or even in gardens. The Garden of Gethsemane has several ancient olive trees in it. I know – I have walked among them. That doesn't mean that every olive tree is in a garden or that every garden has olive trees. But; we do know for sure *vineyards* contain *vines* on which grow *grapes* and the last things you will find in a vineyard are olives growing on any vines. Smith correctly states that olives grow on trees and yet claims they constitute a 'vineyard' time and time again. When Smith copied across 'olive tree' from the *KJV* into the *Book of Mormon*, he correctly left the expression just as it was in the 1830 edition. The modern day internet version of the *Book of Mormon* has olive-tree quite unnecessarily hyphenated. I have no idea why such falsification has been made to Smith's original work.

## LAWS AND ORDINANCES

Considering, once again, that God is supposed to have dictated this into Smith's hat, surely He should have known the difference between a vineyard and an olive grove – even if Joseph Smith was ignorant about it. It does no good for the Mormon Church to claim that there may have been the odd olive tree in a vineyard, which was otherwise occupied by vines and grapes, because Jacob 5:47, and also an earlier verse, clearly states the so-called vineyard consisted *entirely* of olive trees. A 'vineyard' has vines; there are *no* trees and *no* olives.

> **Jacob 5:47.** ...And it grieveth me that I should hew down all the trees of my vineyard, and cast them into the fire that they should be burned.

There is excellent coverage of this problem in an article on "The Bible in the Book of Mormon" by Curt van den Heuvel at the following link *(scroll down to "Fatigue in the Book of Mormon" and then on to Jacob 5:3)*. The article also includes some nonsense apologetic response material that does no more than make Mormon Church historians and apologists look very silly.

http://www.infidels.org/library/modern/curt_heuvel/bom_bible.html

You will find within the article, reference to B.H. Roberts 'addressing' the 'problem'.

> B. H. Roberts addressed the question of protracted KJV quotes in the Book of Mormon. Quoting then president Joseph Fielding Smith, Roberts wrote the following:
>
> When Joseph Smith saw that the Nephite record was quoting the prophecies of Isaiah, of Malachi, or the words of the Savior, he took the English Bible and compared these passages as far as they paralleled each other, and finding that in substance, they were alike, he adopted our English translation; and hence, we have the sameness to which you refer. *(B. H. Roberts, New Witnesses for God (Vol. III) (Salt Lake City: George Q. Cannon & Sons Company, 1895:428).*

I have mentioned previously that this was a typical response to any *KJV* plagiarism by Smith. As stated above, considering the fact God was dictating the words into Smith's *hat*, what would Smith be doing 'comparing' what was *on* the plates, which he was not actually looking at and clearly could not translate himself, with the Bible? How would Smith come to 'see' that the words were *similar* to Isaiah, or other scriptures, and moreover, even if he somehow did, why on earth would he use the *KJV* instead of a more correct early translation that had been *dictated* to him – by God no less? The answer is just as clear and obvious here as it was when mentioned previously. The notion is preposterous; unless that is, the Mormon Church now wishes to refute the idea that Smith translated with his face in his hat whilst not even looking at the gold plates, as confirmed was the case in an Ensign article by a modern-day Mormon apostle. *(See: Russell M. Nelson, A Treasured Testament, Ensign, Jul 1993:61).*

The header to *Jacob 5* tells what the chapter is about and that the fictitious *Zenos* spoke about it *before* 600 BCE. Joseph Smith mixes up the 'vineyard song' in *Isaiah 5* with the real 'allegory of the olive tree' which comes much later, from *Romans 11* in the New Testament.

> *Jacob quotes Zenos relative to the allegory of the tame and wild olive trees—They are a likeness of Israel and the gentiles—The scattering and gathering of Israel are prefigured—Allusions are made to the Nephites and Lamanites and all the house of Israel—Gentiles shall be grafted into Israel—Eventually the vineyard shall be burned. Between 544 and 421 B.C.*

Compare details in *Jacob 5* with *Isaiah 5* – which is about vineyards, and *Romans 11* – which is the allegory of the olive tree, and Smith's plagiarism, as well as his ***ninety*** errors about olive trees constituting a 'vineyard' immediately jump out. These are verses 'referenced' but the whole chapter is worth reading.

> **Jacob 5:70.** And it came to pass that the Lord of the **vineyard** sent his servant; and the servant went and did as the Lord had commanded him, and brought other servants; and they were few.
> **71.** And the Lord of the **vineyard** said unto them: Go to, and labor in the **vineyard**, with your might. For behold, this is the last time that I shall nourish my **vineyard**; for the end is nigh at hand, and the season speedily cometh; and if ye labor with your might with me ye shall have joy in the fruit which I shall lay up unto myself against the time which will soon come.
> **72.** And it came to pass that the servants did go and labor with their **mights**; and the Lord of the **vineyard** labored also with them; and they did obey the commandments of the Lord of the **vineyard** in all things.
> **73.** And there began to be the natural fruit again in the **vineyard**; and the natural **branches** began to grow and thrive exceedingly; and the wild **branches** began to be plucked off and to be cast away; and they did keep the root and the top thereof equal, according to the strength thereof.
> **74.** And thus they labored, with all diligence, according to the commandments of the Lord of the **vineyard**, even until the bad had been cast away out of the **vineyard**, and the Lord had preserved unto himself that the **trees** had become again the natural fruit; and they

## LAWS AND ORDINANCES

became like unto one body; and the fruits were equal; and the Lord of the *vineyard* had preserved unto himself the natural fruit, which was most precious unto him from the beginning.

**75.** And it came to pass that when the Lord of the *vineyard* saw that his fruit was good, and that his *vineyard* was no more corrupt, he called up his servants, and said unto them: Behold, for this last time have we nourished my *vineyard*; and thou beholdest that I have done according to my will; and I have preserved the natural fruit, that it is good, even like as it was in the beginning. And blessed art thou; for because ye have been diligent in laboring with me in my *vineyard*, and have kept my commandments, and have brought unto me again the natural fruit, that my *vineyard* is no more corrupted, and the bad is cast away, behold ye shall have joy with me because of the fruit of my *vineyard*. (Emphasis added).

Note that the referenced text carefully avoids any of the verses that mention *olives* although it does give the game away by mentioning trees and branches. There are extensive references to vineyards in the text and the rest of the chapter affirms that this consisted of *trees* and that they bore only *olives*.

There is *no* reference to *vines* or to *grapes* in the 'vineyard'. The whole chapter thus comprises a completely *impossible* scenario. Smith also shows his grammatical ignorance by using the word 'mights' in v.72 instead of 'might' which serves the plural as well as singular in this context.

Compare this with Romans 5:16-26 and the source and similarity become immediately apparent.

> **Romans 11:16.** For if the firstfruit be holy, the lump is also holy: and if the root be holy, so are the branches.
> **17.** And if some of the branches be broken off, and thou, being a wild olive tree, wert graffed in among them, and with them partakest of the root and fatness of the olive tree;
> **18.** Boast not against the branches. But if thou boast, thou bearest not the root, but the root thee.
> **19.** Thou wilt say then, The branches were broken off, that I might be graffed in.
> **20.** Well; because of unbelief they were broken off, and thou standest by faith. Be not highminded, but fear:
> **21.** For if God spared not the natural branches, take heed lest he also spare not thee.
> **22.** Behold therefore the goodness and severity of God: on them which fell, severity; but toward thee, goodness, if thou continue in his goodness: otherwise thou also shalt be cut off.
> **23.** And they also, if they abide not still in unbelief, shall be graffed in: for God is able to graff them in again.

> **24.** For if thou wert cut out of the olive tree which is wild by nature, and wert graffed contrary to nature into a good olive tree: how much more shall these, which be the natural branches, be graffed into their own olive tree?
> **25.** For I would not, brethren, that ye should be ignorant of this mystery, lest ye should be wise in your own conceits; that blindness in part is happened to Israel, until the fulness of the Gentiles be come in.
> **26.** And so all Israel shall be saved: as it is written, There shall come out of Sion the Deliverer, and shall turn away ungodliness from Jacob:

Note, not just the similarity of detail Smith penned in his *Book of Mormon*, but also the beauty of the *KJV* text and grammar compared with the nonsense Smith ended up with in his version. There is *every* similarity – but there is *no* comparison – in *quality*. A clearer picture of the overall plagiarism of Smith's ideas and his mixing a vineyard with olive trees can be gained by comparing *Jacob 5*, *Isaiah 5* and *Romans 11* in their entirety. There is insufficient space to do so here, but they are all available to reference and compare online.

The following is a bit harsh for a God to say to people who just *cannot* see that Mormonism is actually true. But then, considering all the evidence *against* the possibility that it is, why would God be so cruel as to expect people to enter what appears to them to be such an obvious delusion, or be damned if they don't? As with so much else regarding Mormonism, once you know the truth, the answer is of course more than obvious. However, the psychology behind the statement is effective in ensuring members consider it their duty to try to convert people and see that missionary work continues. The fear factor is hard at work here once again.

> **D&C 84:74.** Verily, verily, I say unto you, **they who believe not** on your words, and are not baptized in water in my name, for the remission of their sins, that they may receive the Holy Ghost, **shall be damned**, and shall not come into my Father's kingdom **where my Father and I am.** (Emphasis added).

Note Smith uses the phrase "where my Father and I *am*." This was an 1832 monotheistic statement, *am* being singular, inferring the Father and Christ are one and the same being, as it should otherwise have read 'are', if they were two separate beings. Either that, or God used extremely bad language structure.

The following verse is also quoted:

> **D&C 84:88.** And whoso receiveth you, there I will be also, for I will go before your face. I will be on your right hand and on your left, and my Spirit shall be in your hearts, and mine angels round about you, to bear you up.

# LAWS AND ORDINANCES

Some verses that are *not* referenced which follow on after v.88 are these:

> **84:89.** Whoso receiveth you receiveth me; and the same will feed you, and clothe you, and give you money.
> **90.** And he who feeds you, or clothes you, or gives you money, shall in nowise lose his reward.
> **91.** And he that doeth not these things is not my disciple; by this you may know my disciples.
> **92.** He that receiveth you not, go away from him alone by yourselves, and cleanse your feet even with water, pure water, whether in heat or in cold, and bear testimony of it unto your Father which is in heaven, and return not again unto that man.
> **93.** And in whatsoever village or city ye enter, do likewise.

These verses are very similar to several others Smith used regarding early Mormon missionaries. The idea of going off on a mission without money soon became redundant, as missionaries were often half starved and getting nowhere and had to resort to paying their own way most of the time. The concept of washing, or shaking dust from, their feet was used elsewhere by Smith.

> **D&C 60:15.** And shake off the dust of thy feet against those who receive thee not, not in their presence, lest thou provoke them, but in secret; and wash thy feet, as a testimony against them in the day of judgment. *(See also D&C 24:15; 75:20).*

Smith simply copied the concept from the New Testament.

> Matthew 10:14. And whosoever shall not receive you, nor hear your words, when ye depart out of that house or city, shake off the dust of your feet. *(See also Mark 6:11; Luke 9:5; Acts 13:51; )*

The other *Book of Mormon* quote is this one, apparently from 92 BCE:

> **Mosiah 28:3.** Now they were desirous that salvation should be declared to every creature, for they could not bear that any human soul should perish; yea, even the very thoughts that any soul should endure endless torment did cause them to quake and tremble.

The question is that if they were *that* keen on converting people to the truth, and as with all religious groups where the generations that follow generally continue on a similar path, what happened to the belief system? The *Book of Mormon* speaks of their religion well into the CE period and yet there is *no* trace of any form of Christianity, or the claimed earlier Judaism, in any later culture *anywhere* in the Americas. But then neither are remnants of the Hebrew or even Aramaic language, culture, traditions, Nephite monetary system, tools, weapons, wheels, buildings, agriculture or claimed animals to be found. Once again, this leads to one and *only* one conclusion.

# THE MORMON DELUSION

Another 1830 reference from the *D&C* suggests just *how* they should call people to repentance.

> **D&C 33:8.** Open your mouths and they shall be filled, and you shall become even as Nephi of old, who journeyed from Jerusalem in the wilderness.
> **9.** Yea, open your mouths and spare not, and you shall be laden with sheaves upon your backs, for lo, I am with you.
> **10.** Yea, open your mouths and they shall be filled, saying: Repent, repent, and prepare ye the way of the Lord, and make his paths straight; for the kingdom of heaven is at hand;
> **11.** Yea, repent and be baptized, every one of you, for a remission of your sins; yea, be baptized even by water, and then cometh the baptism of fire and of the Holy Ghost.

If anyone actually did try to entice people to repent and be baptised in such a manner today, they would probably be locked away and considered entirely insane. In Smith's day, I doubt that they actually spoke *exactly* like that about things either, and they were undoubtedly much more subtle in their approach.

Although, if you go to 'Speaker's Corner' in Hyde Park, London, England, even today you may still hear similar preaching on occasion. Such speakers don't usually get very far with their audience though. It begs the question as to why God would speak that way in 1830, as it is neither sensible nor is it likely to be helpful in regard to the conversion process. Smith just stole the idea from the *KJV* as usual. It appears a couple of times in the Bible. This is Peter:

> **Acts 2:38.** Then Peter said unto them, Repent, and be baptized every one of you in the name of Jesus Christ for the remission of sins, and ye shall receive the gift of the Holy Ghost.

In biblical times, and the manner in which Peter approached it, the text comes over as sane and sensible. Peter gives a reason and promised reward for considering baptism. Not so with Smith, who used the idea with a zeal that has the appearance of bordering on religious insanity. He uses the *same* idea several times in the *Book of Mormon* and also in the *Doctrine and Covenants*.

Commitment to share the gospel is specific:

> Will you prepare to invite friends and relatives who do not belong to the Church to meet with the missionaries to be taught the gospel?

> Will you pray for the missionaries and for opportunities to share the gospel?

> Will you prepare to serve a mission?

# LAWS AND ORDINANCES
## Eternal Marriage

When Mormon missionaries taught my mother and me about the Church, this concept was one thing that most impressed me. The idea we could be together forever was very compelling. I imagined when I grew up and got married how wonderful it would be for it to last forever. Along with the idea of becoming a God and creating worlds, these were incredible concepts to find in religion. To a young boy, creating planets sounded like the best building set ever.

The manual affirms that the family, marriage between a man and a woman *only*, is 'central' to God's eternal *plan* and the basic 'unit' of the Church. It is what everything is based on, and singles, especially older singles, often feel very lonely and neglected as they simply don't fit in anywhere, despite some organised 'singles' conventions and activities. This basic family 'unit' leaves out hundreds of thousands of singles who simply do not count in the eternal sense. This will of course be sorted out *after* this life (isn't everything) and all will be well in the end. But the here and now remains *here* and *now*. And, it is not always well in *this* life, but it *should* be. Many Mormon singles could, and would, find love if they just looked beyond the Church, but those who remain faithful stick to the Church mandate that temple marriage is all that is worth having. I know many people who have lived somewhat lonely and miserable lives due to simply *not* looking beyond Mormonism for marriage which eluded them within the Church.

A lady of my own age, whom I have known for over fifty years, turned down more than one opportunity to marry simply because her suitors were not Mormon. On one occasion she was desperately in love, but nevertheless she stayed true to the principle that only a temple marriage would do. She so much wanted marriage and children. At one point she convinced herself that she 'knew' she would marry within the year and even planned and prepared for the event. No one ever turned up to make the dream come true and then gradually, over the years, she began to accept her fate. Today, she remains a faithful, yet desperately lonely spinster.

> Marriage between a man and a woman is ordained of God and is central to God's eternal plan for the salvation of His children. The means by which mortal life is created is divinely appointed and is safeguarded by marriage. The divine plan of happiness enables family relationships to endure beyond the grave. Marriage, however, can be eternal only when authorized priesthood holders perform the sealing ordinance in sacred temples and when husbands and wives who have been sealed together keep the covenants they have made. Husbands and wives are to love each other. As they keep the commandments and live gospel principles, they are to honor their marital vows with complete

fidelity (see "The Family: A Proclamation to the World," *Ensign,* Nov. 1995, 102; see also D&C 42:22). (Emphasis added. *(Page 85).*

It should be noted that the *D&C* reference provided was written by Joseph Smith in 1831, a couple of years *before* he had his first affair with his teenage housemaid, Fanny Alger, so naturally Smith would have his God say this. It is listed as 'revelation' from God:

> D&C 42:22. Thou shalt love thy wife with all thy heart, and shalt cleave unto her and none else.

It wasn't long after this of course that Smith was 'cleaving' to anyone and everyone, single or married, who would have him, in addition to his first wife Emma, so it begs the question, did the Mormon God lie about 'none else' – or was it just Joseph Smith's own monogamous thought of the day? The Mormon God certainly seemed content for Smith and his cohorts to later devise so-called and definitely false 'scripture', in the form of *D&C 101*, as a cover for the ever evolving polygamy and polyandry, as discussed earlier. Smith's deity was as devious as Smith – if He is indeed a real God.

The manual next explains how happiness is derived and states that "By divine design, fathers are to 'preside' over their families" and mothers are "primarily responsible for the nurture of their children" *(c: Ensign, Nov. 1995: 102).* The divine mandate that men run the Church *and* the family still prevails, although it is generally expressed in softer terms than years ago. But women should still know their place, which is in the home, and they should not work unless and until the children have all left home. This is completely ignored by many modern Mormons but is certainly still the teaching and in my young day was as good as a commandment to us. My own first, now deceased wife, Jan, and subsequently our five active Mormon daughters, would not dream of going out to work unless they absolutely had to. Each has skills or qualifications they can draw on if the need arises, but they know their place; although they would no doubt argue about who actually 'runs' the home and family.

Next, the fear factor is introduced and Satan becomes 'responsible' for family troubles as he is apparently constantly 'attacking' families. The fact that Satan only exists in the imagination of those who choose to believe in the fictional character never dawns on the faithful. It certainly never did on me, until I learned of the origins of Satan. As discussed elsewhere, he is an entirely Christian concept, created in the CE to frighten early Christians into living by Christian principles and forsaking other gods. The Jews never believed in such a creature and he did not exist in the *Tanakh*.

Nevertheless, the Mormon Church today makes good use of putting fear into peoples' hearts by citing Satan's 'role' in their lives.

## LAWS AND ORDINANCES

> Satan is making a concentrated attack on families. Years ago Church leaders set aside Monday evening as a time for family home evening. Parents should use this time to teach their children the gospel, strengthen their relationships with them, and have fun together. Other ways of strengthening the family include daily family prayer and scripture study, worshiping at church as a family, and serving others. ***Heaven is a continuation of the ideal home***. Through priesthood ordinances and righteous living, we can live as families in God's presence eternally. *(Page 85)*. (Emphasis added).

Note that all of these things are really to do with Mormon 'worship' in one form or another. They are mostly not much fun for children at all in my own extensive experience, although we tried hard to do all this stuff. If heaven is a continuation of an ideal home, then what we look for as we get older is not kids running around wanting to do anything *but* any of the above; we would rather play golf, watch favourite movies, read good books, eat out at nice restaurants and have good conversation with friends, ending the day perhaps with a quiet walk along the cliffs in the evening breeze. We've earned it, after years of sacrificing for our children, and that's what we get – in the here and now.

Eternity would be no fun unless it was similarly quiet and peaceful for those who have 'been there and done that' with a family. The concept "Heaven is a continuation of the ideal home" may appeal to young parents, but to those who have passed through that stage, they hardly want go through it all again.

I can't imagine spending eternity *praising* someone. If I ever *were* a God, I certainly would not want people in churches, praying or singing to *me*. Unless they could form a really good 1960s rock band – you get the drift. I would want people to enjoy life and each other, and to know who I was, but not have so much to fear or guess at, through vague and hardly convincing supposed revelations that only came from what other humans *claimed* to be the case.

Anyone can do that. I would want people to understand me and their place in the not so grand scheme of things, without the nonsense that some religion, notably Mormonism, demands on supposed faith. What that really means is that men make up *stuff*, and their God will reward you in the next life, *if* you have faith to believe *their* story in this life – and inevitably also pay them a lot of money for the privilege of living in a way you would rather *not*. Still, that more than borders on opinion, so the reader must ignore it if they are Christian and find their own way in that respect. Atheists will no doubt concur.

The concept of marriage extending beyond death is not a mainstream Christian one and is *nowhere* mentioned in accepted scripture. All references on marriage are from Mormon sources, except two, and the two biblical verses provided do not have *anything* to do with marriage extending beyond mortality. *(Genesis 2:24; Ephesians 5:25)*.

# THE MORMON DELUSION

The reference that seems to explain this actually sounds more like a legal document than God's idea, and it is contained within the revelation that advises polygamy is the way forward, although such verses that refer to the doctrine are of course not referenced in the manual. The entire subject of polygamy is very carefully avoided in the manual and missionaries get no training whatsoever on how to answer any questions that arise concerning it. Goodness knows what they make of anyone like me who may question them about polyandry. They probably wouldn't even know what it means.

As you read the following, ask yourself, in all honesty, exactly what kind of nonsense is this?

> **D&C 132:7.** And verily I say unto you, that the conditions of this law are these:
>
> All covenants, contracts, bonds, obligations, oaths, vows, performances, connections, associations, or expectations, that are not made and entered into and sealed by the Holy Spirit of promise, of him who is anointed, both as well for time and for all eternity, and that too most holy, by revelation and commandment through the medium of mine anointed, whom I have appointed on the earth to hold this power (and I have appointed unto my servant Joseph to hold this power in the last days, and there is never but one on the earth at a time on whom this power and the keys of this priesthood are conferred), are of no efficacy, virtue, or force in and after the resurrection from the dead; for all contracts that are not made unto this end have an end when men are dead.

The Mormon God is getting a bit complicated here don't you think? What has He become; a lawyer? Ironically, the very next verse claims "Behold, mine house is a house of order, saith the Lord God, and not a house of confusion." Really?

You could have fooled me with v.7, which is more than confusing, not just in what it says, but the way it is said and in the construction of the sentence. It isn't exactly well written. The structure is as ever, simply *appalling*. After the introductory first phrase, believe it or not, the entire paragraph of one-hundred-and-thirty-nine words comprises one single solitary, and awfully constructed *sentence*, and it is supposedly *revelation* – from *God*. In the cold light of day – *really*, could this even remotely be a *God* speaking?

Another *D&C* reference from the manual claims marriage is ordained of God. Verse 15 is referenced but not v.16, which speaks once again about only having *one* wife. Well, it would, as Smith wrote it in 1831, *before* his affair with Fanny Alger in 1833.

## LAWS AND ORDINANCES

> **D&C 49:15.** And again, verily I say unto you, that whoso forbiddeth to marry is not ordained of God, for marriage is ordained of God unto man.
> **16.** Wherefore, it is lawful that he should have one wife, and they twain shall be one flesh, and all this that the earth might answer the end of its creation;

*D&C 131* explains eternal marriage and it is referenced. It was penned in 1843.

> **D&C 131:1.** In the celestial glory there are three heavens or degrees;
> **2.** And in order to obtain the highest, a man must enter into this order of the priesthood [meaning the new and everlasting covenant of marriage];
> **3.** And if he does not, he cannot obtain it.
> **4.** He may enter into the other, but that is the end of his kingdom; he cannot have an increase.

This provides the fundamental Mormon doctrine on eternal marriage. Only couples whose marriages have been 'sealed' in a Mormon temple have the eligibility to enter the highest of the three heavens or degrees in the Celestial kingdom. Only they will have 'spirit' children. Anyone in a lower degree or kingdom will never be able to procreate spirit children in the eternities. Indeed, they will not even be married. That's quite an incentive if you like the idea of continuing your marriage in the hereafter. Interestingly, I have actually heard some members, usually women, declare that their partners were hard enough to live with in this life and the last thing they wanted was to be with them forever. However, I expect that may be a minority view.

Naturally, as they would never begin to understand it, especially at this stage (milk before meat), there is no mention to new converts that to enter the highest 'degree' of glory, men must have a shed-load of wives and if their first wife objects, the law of Sarah applies; she will lose her place as well as her husband and end up in a lower kingdom. *(See: D&C 132; TMD Vol. 1:27-31)*.

You wouldn't want to try saying that to most women who have been *born into the Church*, let alone a new convert. Any active Mormon woman that I have ever asked about it just doesn't believe it will apply to *her*. They have no idea about the truth. Well, luckily for them, what Mormons declare *is* the truth clearly isn't, so it doesn't really matter at all. But, the deluded mind accepts what it *likes* and 'shelves' what it doesn't. Then they can somehow manage to 'keep the faith' as they say.

However, as it is fundamental and eternal Mormon doctrine that will affect a convert for billions upon billions of years in the eternities following a short earth life consisting of a few remaining decades at most, is it not reprehensible

# THE MORMON DELUSION

*not* to explain what the Mormon God will actually require of men – and more especially of women *after* this life – *if* they are 'worthy' enough?

These are the commitments:

> Will you hold weekly family home evening, daily family prayer, daily family scripture study, and other family activities?
>
> Will you prepare to enter the temple to (1) receive your endowment? (2) be married for time and eternity? (3) if married, be sealed for eternity as husband and wife? and (4) have your children sealed to you?
>
> Will you worship on the Sabbath as a family?
>
> Will you serve others?

## Temples and Family History

The manual explains that temple ordinances make it possible for couples to be married for eternity and for families to be 'sealed' together forever and live in God's presence. New converts must be members for a minimum of a year before being considered for eligibility to attend the temple and receive their 'endowment'. After that, they can return as often as they please and repeat identical ordinances for ancestors and others, who, it is believed, may or may not accept them, just as they please. The obligation is upon Mormons to do the 'work' for deceased ancestors here on earth, otherwise they will never have the opportunity to progress from the 'spirit prison' *(covered in Chapter 10, page 185 on)*, although recipients are under no obligation to accept the 'gift'. As people who did not have the chance to hear and accept the gospel in this life have the gospel preached to them in the spirit world, if they accept the gospel, the work done for them on earth validates their progression into paradise. That is God's system for saving souls after this life. *(See: TMD Vol 3. Section 3, for details of temple ordinances and rituals and their evolution, including copied Masonic signs, tokens, oaths and blood penalties,).*

> For this reason, Church members search for information about their ancestors. They complete pedigree charts and family group records and submit the names of deceased relatives who need to have saving ordinances performed on their behalf in sacred temples. This is family history work. Worthy members ages 12 and over, including new members, may receive from their bishop a recommend to perform baptisms for the dead. *(Page 86).*

## LAWS AND ORDINANCES

Missionaries are encouraged to take new converts to their local Mormon run Family History Centre and help them get started on their family history. In reality, most Family History Centres are used prolifically by the general public for research. By comparison, certainly in England, very few Mormons actually use the facilities very often.

Commitment questions:

> Will you prepare to receive temple ordinances? (Soon after baptism and confirmation, worthy members over age 12 can receive a recommend to go to the temple and participate in baptisms for the dead.)

> Will you participate in family history work and submit the names of ancestors to receive proxy temple ordinances?

## Service

Part of the psychology, very cleverly used within Mormonism, to keep people active in the Church once they join, is to almost immediately give them some responsibilities so they are somewhat obliged to be there. Every member has something to do. Mormons are taught to give service and it starts by helping to actually run the Church. No one is paid to do this at a local level and everyone participates in one way or another. They feel part of the system and it quickly becomes not just a Church they 'attend' or even 'belong' to; it is very soon perceived by an individual as 'my' Church. There feels a degree of common ownership and this is a deliberate ploy, although it is seen rather as a God-given *opportunity* to members.

Heads of auxiliaries will pray about names for an available calling and then ask the Bishop for people they feel they have been inspired to 'call' and who are able to fill the role. The Bishop either approves or refuses the call in order to retain control over who does what. It is supposed in the Church that God himself approves every new call and release through inspiration given to each of the leaders as part of their own calling. People are set apart for their callings by the laying on of hands which includes a blessing, wherein leaders are also given the gift of such inspiration by the Lord. Often, especially with women, a Bishop or Stake President refuses a proposed call. The person may be 'needed' elsewhere. I could write a another book about what really happens most of the time, as many supposedly 'inspired' callings are refused by a Bishop or Stake President – who must presumably be even *more* inspired, in order to refute the inspiration of the leader who requested the person concerned, following earnest prayer which they, and usually also their counsellors, participated in and subsequently felt inspired to make the call.

Where is God in all of that? But that is another matter for another time.

> One of the great blessings of membership in the Church is the opportunity to serve. When we give loving service to others, we are serving God. When we are baptized, we covenant to give such service (see Mosiah 18:8–10). We are to become aware of others' physical and spiritual needs. We then give of our time, talents, and means to help meet those needs. We follow the example of the Savior, who came to serve others. We are to do what Jesus did and become like Him. *(Page 87)*.

All 'worthy' male Mormons over the age of twelve years are given the priesthood. They meet in various quorums and soon gain leadership experience as every quorum, from twelve to thirteen-year-old Deacons upwards, has a Quorum Presidency, consisting of a President and two counsellors as well as a secretary. They meet and plan activities. The training in Mormonism is extensive and effective. It actually provides experience in areas of public speaking, teaching and leadership. This assists in other aspects of life and many Mormon youth go on to do well in life due to the confidence and experience they gain in early church life. Although this in itself is admirable, it would of course be much better if it were achieved within something that at the end of the day was actually true rather than a cruel hoax.

> All callings are important and help build God's kingdom. We are to accept such callings and work diligently to learn and fulfill our duties. As we do so, we grow in faith, develop new talents and a greater ability to serve, and receive numerous other blessings. *(Page 87)*.

Priesthood holders are assigned in pairs to visit a number of families each month. This is called Home Teaching. It is supposed to consist of a ten minute visit comprising a message, checking family welfare and leaving with a prayer to bless the home and family. In my experience, many men never bother to do this and those who enthusiastically do, sometimes overstay their welcome – by hours rather than minutes. Some members dread the Home Teachers visiting as they can't get rid of them and they have better things to do. Some however, welcome them, especially the elderly who otherwise may have no one to talk to. Women also go Visiting Teaching to fellow 'sisters'. All this is in addition to any other callings and assignments they may be given.

> Priesthood holders may be called as home teachers. Home teachers make at least monthly visits to the homes of assigned member families. They teach the gospel, support parents, nurture friendships, and help families prepare to receive and keep temple covenants. Visiting

## LAWS AND ORDINANCES

teachers represent the Relief Society by making monthly visits to each adult sister as assigned. *(Page 87)*.

The manual provides several references on the areas of charity, care for the poor, and service. The concept is that by being involved in such areas of service, Mormons are "only in the service of your God" *(Mosiah 2:17)*. A convincing reference comes from a much less frequently used biblical source. Whatever Mormons are asked to do, it is *always* for the Lord.

> **Matthew 25:40.** Verily I say unto you, Inasmuch as ye have done it unto one of the least of these my brethren, ye have done it unto me.

Another Bible reference is a reminder of the second 'great commandment' to love your neighbour as yourself *(Matthew 22:36-40)*; as if the convinced still need convincing.

Naturally the carrot always needs a complimentary 'stick' in Mormonism. The pressure is on.

> **D&C 107:99.** Wherefore, now *let every man learn his duty*, and to act in the office in which he is appointed, in all diligence.
> **100.** *He that is slothful shall not be counted worthy to stand*, and he that learns not his duty and *shows himself not approved shall not be counted worthy* to stand. Even so. Amen. (Emphasis added).

Commitment questions:

> Will you accept and fulfill the duties of a calling (including an assignment as a home teacher or visiting teacher)?

> Will you support others in their callings?

## Teaching and Learning in the Church

> The Church is organized to perfect and bless the lives of the members. It gives us opportunities to teach one another the gospel, fellowship and serve one another, and support one another in our quest for salvation. In the family and through the Church, each member is taught the doctrines of the gospel. When members are called to teaching assignments, they are provided materials and help to enable them to succeed. *(Page 88)*.

A *D&C* reference describes what Joseph Smith considered members should teach one another in 1832. It includes a lot more than just the doctrine of the kingdom. You won't hear any talk in Mormon Church classes these days about things in and under the earth from the past or we would perhaps see discussion on the *fact of evolution*, about which the Church remains noncommittal.

News from home or abroad, about wars or the perplexities of the nations are *never* discussed, any more than 'knowledge' of countries and kingdoms. In fact, all lessons are carefully constructed and monitored through the use of specific manuals for teachers and students in every area of the Church. The only 'judgements' mentioned come from such material, and members never discuss anything that has not been both approved and prepared by the Church.

> **D&C 88:77.** And I give unto you a commandment that you shall ***teach one another*** the ***doctrine of the kingdom***.
> **78.** Teach ye diligently and my grace shall attend you, that you may be instructed more perfectly in theory, in principle, in doctrine, in the law of the gospel, in all things that pertain unto the kingdom of God, that are expedient for you to understand;
> **79.** Of things both ***in heaven and in the earth***, and ***under the earth***; things ***which have been***, things ***which are***, things which must ***shortly come to pass***; things which are at ***home***, things which are ***abroad***; the ***wars*** and the ***perplexities of the nations***, and the ***judgments*** which are on the land; and a knowledge also of ***countries and of kingdoms***— (Emphasis added).

Times do change. The manual cites *Ephesians 4:11-14*.

> **Ephesians 4:11.** And he gave some, apostles; and some, prophets; and some, ***evangelists***; and some, ***pastors*** and teachers;
> 12 For the perfecting of the saints, for the work of the ministry, for the edifying of the body of Christ:
> 13 Till we all come in the unity of the faith, and of the knowledge of the Son of God, unto a perfect man, unto the measure of the stature of the fulness of Christ:
> 14 That we henceforth be no more children, tossed to and fro, and carried about with every wind of doctrine, by the sleight of men, and cunning craftiness, whereby they lie in wait to deceive; (Emphasis added).

The *Articles of Faith* (6) also references 'pastors' and 'evangelists' which do not actually appear in the Mormon Church at all. The Church does however try to explain this away.

> **AoF: 6.** We believe in the same organization that existed in the Primitive Church, namely, apostles, prophets, ***pastors,*** teachers, ***evangelists***, and so forth. (Emphasis added).

# LAWS AND ORDINANCES

The Mormon Church claims it has the exact same organisation that Jesus Christ had in his day, yet Christ never personally formed an organisation of *any* description. Perhaps we should say that the Church just claims the same organisation, or at least offices, that appear in the New Testament. The church that later evolved in early Christianity had a variety of officers but not all the ones the modern Mormon Church has, and they were not used in the same way either. Even the early Mormon Church was organised entirely differently to the modern-day Mormon Church and had no more than a 'First' and 'Second Elder' to begin with. That idea was soon dropped when Smith started to lose control and a whole new hierarchy developed with Smith always carefully at the top of the tree and in total control.

In Mormonism, 'Pastor' equates to a Mormon 'Bishop', although the word 'Pastor' is redundant and has never been adopted. The first and most important thing to notice in *Ephesians 4:11 (above, p.378)* is that "pastors and teachers" refers to *one* office, not *two*. The way the nouns are grouped in Greek makes this perfectly clear. Pastors **are** teachers; it is an integral part of their job. A Pastor is a Shepherd; he guides, protects, leads, and feeds his flock. In the Mormon Church, a 'Teacher' becomes an ordained 'office' in the Aaronic Priesthood. This is *not* biblical. There is no such thing as a priesthood 'office' of Teacher in the Bible. In the Mormon context 'Teacher' is a *title* and they do not actually *teach*; Teachers are 14-15 year old boys and their main role is to prepare the sacrament and sometimes assist as 'junior companions' to Home Teachers. That doesn't mean they actually *teach* anything. Actual *teachers* of classes in the Mormon Church are not ordained; they are 'set apart' and this includes a blessing for the duration of their call, which is usually indeterminate.

Smith however, introduces the concept into his *Book of Mormon* in several places. This is just one of them:

> **Moroni 3:1.** The manner which the disciples, who were called the elders of the church, **ordained** priests and **teachers**—
> **2.** After they had prayed unto the Father in the name of Christ, they laid their hands upon them, and said:
> **3.** In the name of Jesus Christ I ordain you to be a priest, (or, if he be a teacher) I **ordain you to be a teacher**, to preach repentance and remission of sins through Jesus Christ, by the endurance of faith on his name to the end. Amen.
> **4.** And after this manner **did they ordain** priests and **teachers**, according to the gifts and callings of God unto men; and they ordained them by the power of the Holy Ghost, which was in them. (Emphasis added).

An 'Evangelist' equals a 'Patriarch' according to the *Encyclopaedia of Mormonism (p.1065)*, where it states "The Doctrine and Covenants speaks of "evangelical ministers", which is understood to refer to patriarchs." *(c: D&C 107:39).*

> **D&C 107:39.** It is the duty of the Twelve, in all large branches of the church, to ordain evangelical ministers, as they shall be designated unto them by revelation—

The *E.M.* doesn't state *who* it is that understands an *Evangelist* is the same thing as a *Patriarch*. It isn't even *close*, and although I was always aware of the 'excuse' use of this in Mormonism, I never did understand *why* it was claimed, as it is clear that it means no such thing. *D&C 107* was penned in 1835 and designated 'evangelical ministers' were to be ordained and established in every 'large branch' of the Church. It clearly *meant* what it *said*. It certainly did **not** mean that Patriarchs should be ordained in *every* branch, regardless of what the *E.M. or* the Mormon Church may now claim. There was never more than one Church Patriarch at a time for a very long time in Mormonism.

Today sees one, and sometimes two, in each Stake but Patriarch's certainly don't do anything remotely *evangelical*. It is a complete misuse of the term. But then it is just an excuse for not actually having any evangelists in the Mormon Church and still be able to claim they have all the 'offices' mentioned in the New Testament.

All a Mormon Patriarch does is to lay hands on the heads of members and give them a 'patriarchal blessing' which is supposedly a personal revelation from God telling them their potential future in this life, and sometimes even the next, *if* they remain faithful and worthy. It is a kind of religious form of fortune telling and to a degree even blackmail. That is because the concept is that if things do *not* work out as per their blessing, then the member must be doing something *wrong* and as ever, needs to repent and 'improve'. I have seen, for example, the heartache when young women who were promised marriage and children later didn't get asked to marry, or did marry, only to discover that they could not have children.

That is no ones fault, but it is a misdiagnosed, for the want of a word, blessing – supposedly from God. If things that should work out don't, then it was meant for the next life rather than this one. There are always standard excuses for any perceived lack of fulfilment of the Mormon God's promises.

Patriarchal blessings are full of unfulfilled promises. In the early days, many members were promised they would be *alive* when Jesus returned. That was because they expected him around 1891. All such people are of course long since dead. Now, the Church claims that it may have meant they would be spirits 'caught up to meet him' when he does come. Uh-huh. It's funny that such promises *never* appear in blessings these days. Blessings are usually much

## LAWS AND ORDINANCES

more mundane now, than some early blessings which made many glorious and largely unfulfilled promises.

Promises that were made to one faithful couple I knew, ended when the young husband died following a car crash. It wasn't exactly the injuries that killed him; he actually died from the effects of a disease he had caught, which had gone undetected, when he was on a mission in Italy a few years earlier. It was discovered while he was in hospital following the accident. The promises in his patriarchal blessing remained completely unfulfilled and must therefore have somehow related to the hereafter. The only problem was that they really *didn't* and that was clear, not just to me but also to his devastated wife. She remained faithful though. She remarried some time later but as she had only been married to her first husband for a year or two before he died, she annulled their eternal sealing so she could be sealed to her new husband. So, the poor young man lost his life, and also his love – forever. That has happened with other women I know, whose young husbands died in accidents; temple annulment and a new eternal companion. The problem is that Mormon men can marry as often as they like in the temple if an earlier wife has died, but women can only ever have *one* husband – that's it. They tend to choose the latest one.

The patriarchal 'blessing' also designates which 'tribe' of Israel the person came from. When members of the same family have patriarchal blessings at different times, and perhaps from different patriarchs, they may be designated as having come from *different* tribes of Israel – which regularly happens. This is excused by the idea that blood lines are now so diluted, one tribe may appear more dominant in one person, and yet another tribe may do so in their very own sibling. Mormons will invariably swallow that bizarre concept without due consideration. Doing so is yet another classic example of the very deep seated delusional state in which Mormons live. They generally understand nothing about DNA. God should *know* the tribe as He *created* the DNA, and the Patriarch should get it *right* – every time, as the Lord is supposed to reveal it.

In the above reference *(D&C 107:39)* the word 'evangelical' is cross referenced with *D&C 124:91* which was written a few years later, in 1841.

> **D&C 124:91.** And again, verily I say unto you, let my servant William be appointed, ordained, and anointed, as counselor unto my servant Joseph, in the room of my servant Hyrum, that my servant ***Hyrum may take the office of Priesthood and Patriarch***, which was ***appointed unto him by his father, by blessing and also by right;***
> **92.** That from henceforth ***he shall hold the keys of the patriarchal blessings*** upon the heads of all my people,

That is a far cry from establishing 'evangelical ministers' in every large branch of the Church and entirely different in concept. How the Church today can hide 'evangelists' under the umbrella of 'patriarchs' is beyond me. But that they do, despite the fact that Joseph Smith was very clear about the two entirely different roles.

The role of Church Patriarch immediately became a kind of hereditary 'Smith family' *right*, starting with Joseph Smith's own father, Joseph Smith Senior and continuing with Joseph's brother Hyrum. It will be seen from this list that the position was entirely unrelated to evangelical ministers whatsoever. Additionally, it was a position second only to that of President of the Church.

## Church Patriarchs.

| Name. | Called. | Released. |
|---|---|---|
| 1. Joseph Smith Sr. (Joseph's father). | 18 Dec 1833. Age 62. | Died 14 Sep 1840. |
| 2. Hyrum Smith. (Joseph's brother). | 24 Jan 1841. Age 40. | Died 27 Jun 1844. |
| 3. William Smith. (Joseph's brother). | 24 May 1845. Age 34. | Rejected 6 Oct 1845. |

William was one of the several contenders for the presidency of the Church following the death of Joseph Smith. Brigham Young used various tactics to get rid of competition and his way of 'dealing' with William was to make him Church Patriarch. It seemed like a very high office to William, so he accepted it instead of contending for the leadership, but once he realised he had effectively been sidelined and had absolutely no 'say' in anything, he started to speak out and that didn't go down at all well, hence his demise. He was rejected by the Church membership at the 6 Oct 1845 General Conference and then quickly excommunicated from the Church on 19 Oct 1845. William died 13 Nov 1893. The Church *Almanac* skips William with regard to a 'number' and allocates 'Patriarch 3' to John Smith, who I have numbered 4 below.

| 4. John Smith. (Joseph's uncle). | 1 Jan 1849. Age 67. | Died 23 May 1854. |
|---|---|---|

*The Church Almanac (2007)* contains inadvertent misinformation regarding John Smith. *(No.4)*. In the 'Patriarchs to the Church' section, under 'William Smith', it correctly states that there was then *no* Patriarch until the ordination of John, on 1 Jan 1849. Under "Assistant Counselors in the First Presidency",

# LAWS AND ORDINANCES

where his details actually appear, it *incorrectly* states John Smith was ordained Patriarch on 10 Jan 1845 which was impossible; although it *correctly* states his age was 67 when he was called – but that was 1 Jan 1849, just as shown above.

Everyone makes mistakes.

The list continues:

5. John Smith.           18 Feb 1855. Age 22.        Died 5 Nov 1911.
   (Hyrum's son).

6. Hyrum Gibbs Smith.    9 May 1912. Age 32.         Died 4 Feb 1932.
   (Grandson of John – No.4 above).

From 1932 to 1937 there was no Church Patriarch, according to the Church *Almanac*, although the function of remaining responsibilities was carried out in the background, first by Nicholas G. Smith (1932-1934) and then Frank B. Woodbury (1934-1937) according to the *E.M.* These men were not actually called or set apart, so they are not mentioned in the *Almanac*. They were not Smith 'family'.

7. George Franklin Richards.  8 Oct 1937. Age 76.    Released 3 Oct 1942.
   (Sustained *acting* Patriarch).

The *Almanac* once again skips a number for Richards, as he was an interim *acting* Patriarch rather than in the family hereditary line. Joseph Fielding Smith is listed as No. 6 *(my No.8 below)*. To place *this* 'Joseph Fielding Smith' in the Smith family tree, as there are several, he was the son of Hyrum Mack Smith and grandson of the sixth prophet, Joseph Fielding Smith, who was the son of Hyrum, Joseph Smith's brother. *(No.2 above)*.

8. Joseph Fielding Smith.    8 Oct 1942. Age 43.    Released 6 Oct 1946.
   (Great-grandson of Hyrum).

Smith was called as Patriarch, disappointing Eldred G. Smith, who felt it his right in the 'succession' process. Was the choice that the 'brethren' made divinely inspired or just 'family' oriented? Apparently the *brethren* chose, and God *did not* choose Smith, because the Mormon God *hates* gays. Smith had long been, and although married he still was, a practicing gay when he was called, and he continued to be so until the fact was eventually discovered and he had to be released. Smith's closest friends and immediate family were aware of his orientation but everyone kept quiet and God didn't bother to reveal the truth to his prophet.

383

It wasn't the only time when the 'brethren' didn't *see* anything wrong with a Church leader and their God didn't bother to tell them about it. One apostle managed to have an adulterous affair, for eighteen years, during the twentieth-century, before he eventually got caught. Richard Roswell Lyman considered it a 'personally covenanted' polygamous marriage which no one discovered until 1943. He was then excommunicated. *(See TMD Vol. 2:213-4 for more details).*

The Church *Almanac* as well as the *E.M.* claims Joseph Fielding Smith was released "due to ill health" and although sidelined for several years and exiled to Hawaii, he was never actually disciplined. There is one rule for the rank and file and entirely another for 'family' it seems. *(For more details of the Smith case, see: TMD Vol. 2:261-3).*

9. Eldred G. Smith.    10 April 1947. Age 40.    Emeritus. 6 Oct 1979.
(Son of Hyrum G. Smith – No. 6 above).

In 1979, the Mormon Church finally dispensed with the position of Church Patriarch and none have since been called. Meanwhile, within the Church, local patriarchs had been ordained and today there is at least one in each Stake. Once presided over by a 'Church Patriarch', the Mormon God clearly learned his lesson and discontinued the idea.

In the real world, as discussed, patriarchs are not remotely connected with evangelists and they never were – even in the Mormon Church, despite what the *E.M.* may claim.

Evangelists always were, and still are, gifted people with special talent for explaining the Gospel and calling people to commit to Jesus Christ. Today, some evangelists are officers of a church and others are as informal as Jesus was in his day. Consider Billy Graham as just one famous example.

Commitment question:

Will you attend church?

## Endure to the End

Naturally, once an investigator becomes a convert, is captured in the web of lies and deception, and embraces the delusion that is Mormonism, the Church hardly wants to lose them again, so the rule is – they must 'endure to the end'.

Instead of saying they should *enjoy* the gospel to the end, they must *endure* it to the end, suggesting that the journey through life is hard and that endurance is needed. Life generally is hardly a marathon run where people just want to give up. If someone is not experiencing some kind of joy from their religion, of what use is it to them? I did find church very tiring – and also expensive, but

## LAWS AND ORDINANCES

nonetheless much of the time we thoroughly enjoyed the things we were doing. The idea of *endurance* seemed foreign to me but I suppose it is typical religious speak to keep the faithful worried that they are still not doing enough and that they must be ultra cautious, so they don't fall by the wayside in some way.

> As we continue to exercise faith in Christ, **repent,** and **renew our covenants**, we enjoy continued guidance from the Holy Ghost. If we **endure to the end** of our lives in being true to our covenants, we will receive eternal life. ***A few members do not endure or remain fully active.*** However, enduring to the end is a ***personal responsibility***. We "work out [our] own salvation" (Philippians 2:12), and we ***serve and love those whose faith has grown weak through inactivity.*** *(Page 88).*

Once again, we must always 'repent' and 'endure' and now we must also "serve and love those whose faith has grown weak through inactivity". There is always a 'reactivation' programme of one sort or another going on in the Mormon Church. When we were young, the Sunday School ran an 'enlistment programme' where youngsters would visit inactive class members and try to persuade them to return to church. My own then future wife was reactivated in this way when she was about eleven years old after her father stopped attending when his wife died from Hodgkin's Disease. His excuse was that he wanted to stop learning when his wife did. The problem is that in Mormon theology, she would still be 'learning' in the spirit world. The reality was that he remarried and slowly drank himself to death over the next few decades.

The manual suggests that "A few members do not endure or remain fully active." A few? That is really stretching things. The fact is that a vast *majority* of people never convert in the first place. Of those who do, again the *majority* do *not* stay, and in addition, with the advent of the internet, lots of long term converts, along with many who were born into the cult, are starting to vote with their feet once they learn the truth. As things stand today, the truly active, tithe-paying worldwide Mormon Church membership stands somewhere around the five million mark, give or take half a million, out of a claimed close to fourteen million members on paper. The Church should be honest and confess that most members in fact do *not* endure at all. They realise the truth and they *leave*.

The final commitment question is this:

> Will you continue to live the gospel by keeping baptismal covenants throughout your life?

# Chapter 16

## Post Lesson Material for Missionaries

Chapters 4–13 of the lesson manual consist of additional material designed to assist missionaries in their work. Much of it is unrelated to the delusion itself or directly to the conversion process and of little interest to anyone other than Mormon missionaries. In effect, it is a 'sales' manual and the content is not dissimilar to the psychology used in ordinary everyday sales training. In the manual however, despite extensive earlier coverage in the missionary lessons, Chapter 5 is dedicated to the role of the *Book of Mormon* in the conversion process. This is dealt with separately in the next Chapter *(Ch.17)*. This chapter contains comments and notes relative to some of the other aspects covered in the remaining chapters of the lesson manual that are of some relevance. Manual page numbers rather than specific chapters are noted for ease of reference.

# THE MORMON DELUSION

## How Do I Recognize and Understand the Spirit?

## Personal Revelation

> Joseph Smith said, "Salvation cannot come without revelation; it is in vain for anyone to minister without it" (*History of the Church*, 3:389). You will succeed in your work as you learn to receive and follow personal revelation. *(Page 89).*

Mormons firmly believe that if worthy they can ask the Lord for and receive personal revelation on a variety of things. Missionaries are assured that as they are in the service of their God they will most certainly receive revelation and inspiration, designed by the Lord to assist them in the process of converting investigators.

The only problem with the concept is that it is not quantifiable. A member may well feel they receive personal revelation. My own experiences, when I was a believing Mormon, confirmed to me that God did sometimes appear to guide my thoughts and actions through inspiration. Things 'felt' right when I had prayed for guidance through the day. I also assumed that I was receiving personal revelation when on occasion things just came to mind. The applied psychology that this is God 'revealing' things to us works very well and also, as it happens, is accepted very easily by people, Mormon and otherwise as true. All it takes is their religion to teach them that this is what they are experiencing when it happens.

What such people do not account for is that *everyone* experiences similar phenomenon whether they are religious or not. We often feel good about decisions or things that are happening and we often have things spring to mind. We sleep on ideas and often feel 'inspired'. That applies to *everyone*. Religion does not enter into it at all. It is just a false perception induced by a belief that it is God communicating with us in some way. All that happens is that if we *are* religious and we talk to God, then to us, it is clear that it is He who is 'blessing' us with such inspiration and revelation. If not, similar experiences still happen.

As explained elsewhere, I resigned from the Mormon Church simply because, try as I might, I could no longer hold to a belief in God. Although the conclusion was a reluctant one, once accepted, naturally I no longer prayed to Him and did not recognise such a being as real. Again, I must point out, for those who are religious, that this was for *me* and me alone, with due respect to everyone else to believe what they will.

However, it will not astonish fellow atheists to learn that my 'inspiration' and my 'revelation' did not *stop*. Not for one moment did it stop. I have experienced the same emotions, the same level of inspired thoughts, and indeed what people in religious fraternities would consider personal revelation. Many

## POST LESSON MATERIAL

things have come to me out of the blue as I have been researching and writing my work. It has at times been so prolific and so continuous that it felt like I was guided as I expressed my thoughts.

Had I still *believed* in God, I would have been absolutely convinced that He was guiding my thoughts and my hands as I converted the 'revealed' thoughts into words on my computer. It has been an absolutely amazing experience and one which has confirmed completely that the whole concept of inspiration and so-called revelation being exclusively introduced into our minds by God, to be a ludicrous notion. The Mormon faithful consider that Satan's influence, while other Christians may think God is actually helping me expose a false religion.

How would we ever tell the difference between what we have experienced since leaving the Church, with what we thought was from God while we were in it? This alone tells us that there is something alarmingly wrong with the supposition that God is involved. Having left the Church, we have 'lost the spirit'; Satan is deceiving us, making us think this way. There is always a Mormon cliché to cover all eventualities and to a believer, the Church therefore remains true. Whilst anyone outside the Church sees through that immediately, someone inside the delusion remains protected from the truth of the matter. Thus the delusion prevails.

Irrespective of the above, which the reader can take or leave, in point of fact, the 'results' of God's promised 'personal revelation' and 'inspiration' given to Mormon missionaries *can* actually be *measured and quantified* – as with any sales process – by *results*.

> God loves you and all His children. He is anxious to support you in your practical and specific challenges. **You have been promised inspiration** to know what to do and have been **given the power** to do it (see D&C 43:15–16). **He will help you** as you try to recognize and understand the Spirit through diligent scripture study. **He will guide you to people who will receive the message** of the Restoration. He will **give you power to deliver the message** and to testify of Christ and His gospel. He **will shower His blessings upon you** through the gift of the Holy Ghost. He asks that you remain worthy of this gift and that you ask, seek, and knock (see D&C 4:7; Matthew 7:7–8). *(Page 89).* (Emphasis added).

So, God promises missionaries help, inspiration, power, guidance and a shower of blessings. In that case, conversions should be prolific and numerical development of the Mormon Church year on year should be staggering. Yet the reality is that missionaries tract (knock on doors) hour after hour, day after day and week after week in order to find someone to teach. Then most people do not proceed beyond the first 'lesson'. This has been the case for many years and the Mormon Church 'message' is simply not as popular any more.

It begs the question that if this is the result when the Mormon God *is* giving such supposed abundant revelatory help to missionaries, what on earth would statistics look like without it? Also, why is it that so many other denominations are experiencing vastly superior conversion rates than the Mormon Church? Is that Satan helping them? If so, he is much better at it than the Mormon God, who may want to reconsider His methods. The reader can no doubt see the point. In the early Mormon Church, they could get away with more than is now the case but in the modern day, a non-Mormon can easily discover the truth – and they usually do, long before they get to the end of the lessons.

Statistically, many more missionaries are needed these days to obtain the *same* number of converts that *fewer* missionaries achieved in earlier years. The percentage of young men who serve missions is much lower than it was. What then is the result of all this claimed help which is coming directly from God?

> A look at the number of missionaries called each year, as recorded in the Church Almanac over the last few years, gives an idea of the falling missionary activity at a time when growth is still being recorded as increasing. After peaking, it was steady at around 25,000 missionaries called per year from 1989 to 1991 and then leapt to 30,000 in 1992. After that it fell and didn't climb above 30,000 again until 1996. It struggled up to 36,000 in 2001 and since then, it has declined rapidly. The 2005 figure was 30,587, right back to where it was in 1992 when there were 8.4 million members. So, with one and a half times as many (claimed) members as there were in 1992, the *same* numbers of missionaries are going out. This is proportionately a decline of 33% per capita.
>
> The total actually serving at the end of 2007 is shown as 52,686, a number which has remained fairly static for several years. As a mission is for two years that's a real yearly average of much less than the 30,000 shown as called, in changeover terms. This does not statistically support a substantial positive growth potential, unless the missionaries are proportionately converting many more people than before, which clearly they are not. More missionaries per capita need to go out, to achieve the *same* previous growth rate, and this has been the case for several years. The combination of these data confirms some of the first signs of true decline in a religious movement.
>
> The Church boasts a total of 13,193,999 members as of 31 December 2007. There were 279,218 converts in 2007 (2.2% growth) which is only 6,373 more than in 2006. There are a number of much faster growing religious movements, Christian and otherwise, but in the world of Christianity, the truly fastest *growing* movement, by far, is actually Pentecostalism. This group started in the early twentieth century and already boasts close to 100 million members. Claimed

## POST LESSON MATERIAL

> affiliations bring that figure to the much larger total of 480 million. Now, for me personally, having the biggest number doesn't make anything actually *true*. That would mean the Roman Catholic Church already wins without a race. In overall 'religious' terms, Christianity itself is a minority faith (inasmuch as it accounts for only one third of the world population) so you can't go by size. *(TMD Vol.2:333-4). (See TMD Vol. 2. Ch. 17 for further analysis and statistical detail).*

Nevertheless, the Mormon God wants His missionaries to labour under the delusion that He is actually helping and guiding them. The results of their labours, compared with those of other religious groups, regarding conversions and growth do not stack up at all. The Roman Catholic Church grows *each year* by fourteen million members; more than the *total* claimed membership of the Mormon Church. Every *ten days* it grows by as much as the *annual* growth of the Mormon Church. The Jehovah's Witnesses passed the seven million member mark in 2009. Even so, they only even *count* those who are actively involved in the missionary 'public Bible educational work' programme as true *members*. They have no full time missionaries – all *members* proselytise.

Those who actually attend the Jehovah's Witness 'Annual Memorial of Christ's death' number close to eighteen million. The Jehovah's Witness 'member' conversion programme produces about *twice* as many converts each year as Mormonism. The Mormon Church has tens of thousands of full time trained missionaries and yet the *active* membership in Mormonism is much lower than the seven million active Bible teaching members that the Witnesses now claim.

> You need to **seek and receive personal revelation** through the Holy Ghost as you help people become baptized and confirmed. Have faith that **you will receive personal revelation to guide** you from day to day. The Holy Ghost will help you in every aspect of your work. *(Page 90).*

Missionaries who believe they do receive revelation have no idea about the truth. They are called to serve and they just go, believing it is God's will that they do so. They also believe that God is indeed inspiring them and revealing to them the things they need to do in order to find, teach and convert people the Lord has 'prepared'. Clearly, the Mormon God needs to take lessons from the likes of Jehovah's Witnesses and Roman Catholics if He wants the Church to grow in the way theirs do. As I previously stated somewhere, He would have been better off ensuring that His son got things right in the first instance so the original Church did not go into apostasy and even *require* a restoration. What a waste of thousands of years of nothing but false religion being available to the children of a God who didn't love them enough to ensure they had true light and direction in their all too often, very short and extremely difficult lives.

# THE MORMON DELUSION

## The Light of Christ

The manual explains the difference between the Light of Christ and the Holy Ghost. The gift of the Holy Ghost is reserved for Mormons and Mormons *alone*, although it will testify to a potential convert, through the Light of Christ, that the Mormon Church is indeed true. Other than that, the rest of the world can only experience the Light of Christ.

> A person is capable of receiving spiritual guidance before being baptized and confirmed. This spiritual influence begins with the Light of Christ, which "is given to every man, that he may know good from evil" (Moroni 7:16; see also verses 14–19). "The light of Christ is just what the words imply: enlightenment, knowledge, and an uplifting, ennobling, persevering influence that comes upon mankind because of Jesus Christ. . . . "The light of Christ should not be confused with the personage of the Holy Ghost, for the light of Christ is not a personage at all. Its influence is preliminary to and preparatory to one's receiving the Holy Ghost. The light of Christ will lead the honest soul who 'hearkeneth to the voice' to find the true gospel and the true Church and thereby receive the Holy Ghost" *(Page 90)*.

> President Boyd K. Packer said, "It is important for a . . . missionary . . . to know that the Holy Ghost can work through the Light of Christ. A teacher of gospel truths is not planting something foreign or even new into an adult or a child. Rather, the missionary or teacher is making contact with the Spirit of Christ already there. The gospel will have a familiar 'ring' to them" ("The Light of Christ," address delivered at the seminar for new mission presidents, 22 June 2004, 2). *(Page 90)*.

To most of the rest of the Christian world, the Holy Ghost is the Third Person in the Trinity that makes up the Christian's One God. To Jews, the Holy Spirit is the mind Of God, who is distinctly and absolutely a *singular* God. Theirs is a true Monotheism. The Holy Ghost is not a *personage* at all in Judaism.

## The Holy Ghost

The manual explains that there is a difference between the Holy Ghost, which may witness the truth to lead someone to the Church, and the 'gift' of the Holy Ghost which is received by laying on of hands following baptism. Remaining worthy, ensures that companionship is ongoing for faithful Mormons – but no one else.

# POST LESSON MATERIAL

> The gift of the Holy Ghost comes after one repents and becomes worthy. . . . The Holy Ghost bears witness of the truth and impresses upon the soul the reality of God the Father and the Son Jesus Christ so deeply that no earthly power or authority can separate him from that knowledge. – PRESIDENT JAMES E. FAUST "THE GIFT OF THE HOLY GHOST—A SURE COMPASS," ENSIGN, APR. 1996, 4). *(Page 91).*

You can immediately see the psychology behind that statement. The Holy Ghost bears witness to someone that the Mormon God is real; so deeply, that "no earthly power or authority can separate him from that *knowledge*". The delusion is complete once someone *feels* they recognise such a thing as 'the spirit' and they then cling to the Church without questioning anything ever again. It is *not knowledge*; it is something else – it is a deluded state of mind. *Nothing* can separate them from it, as the *decision* that it is true prevails. And, it *is* a *decision*. That's how it works. It is not revelation; it is not God speaking; it is not even inspiration; it is purely *emotion* which is created in the mind due to *conditioning* and *expectation*, and that is the key to it all. Once the emotions trigger a belief system, people are permanently captured in a delusional state.

The subconscious mind *decides* it is true and thus it *becomes* true. The *information* in the brain *becomes* reality – until and unless something upsets the brain enough to force the conscious mind to consider matters further. The brain is in effect a sponge which absorbs information. What is true and what is not true is irrelevant and an entirely different matter. At first, to the brain, it is simply 'information'. An individual then 'decides' what is and is not 'true'.

Facts based on evidence are accepted as true; that is, until religion takes over and dictates to the brain a set of predetermined parameters around which everything after that must 'fit'. Then, new information which *is* true and yet offends the perceived 'testimony' will be rejected out of hand, regardless of the fact that it is actually true and the Mormon *perception* of truth is *not*. The brain can be fooled. It takes conscious effort to question *perception*.

That is what happened to me. Years of my subconscious mind trying to tell my conscious mind that I was not being sensible about my 'faith' and that it was based on a fallacy ended one morning when the truth finally burst through. I broke down and wept my heart out; it was the last thing that I ever wanted.

## The Holy Spirit of Promise.

There is a further concept in Mormonism that the Holy Ghost is also the 'Holy Spirit of Promise'. It *seals* promises made in this life in preparation for the next – as long as the person remains worthy of them, otherwise that *sealing* will be broken. You have to stay faithful. You have to remain worthy. You have to endure to the end. One slip and eternal happiness may be forfeit.

> The Holy Ghost is also referred to as the Holy Spirit of Promise. All covenants and performances must be sealed by the Holy Spirit of Promise if they are to be valid after this life (see D&C 132:7, 18–19, 26). Breaking covenants may remove the sealing. *(Page 91).*

This concept keeps people safely in the delusion as the fear of not 'making it' to the Celestial kingdom becomes real – and feared. Break a covenant or commandment and it could be all over – not only during this life – but for *eternity*. That is a *real* and fear promoting threat.

## Gifts of the Spirit.

There is a commonly held belief in Mormonism that everyone is bestowed with different 'gifts of the Spirit' which range from such things as a natural ability to play a musical instrument or to sing well, through to more spiritual abilities such as the gift of tongues or of prophecy or leadership skills.

> The gifts of the Spirit are special spiritual blessings that the Lord gives to worthy individuals for their own benefit and for their use in blessing others. For example, missionaries who must learn a new language may receive the gift of tongues to give them divine help in learning a language. Several gifts of the Spirit are described in Moroni 10:8–18; Doctrine and Covenants 46:11–33; and 1 Corinthians 12:1–12. These are only some examples of the many gifts of the Spirit. The Lord may bless you in other ways depending on your faithfulness, your needs, and the needs of those you serve. You should desire spiritual gifts and earnestly seek for them (see D&C 46:8; 1 Corinthians 12:31; 14:1, 12). These gifts come by prayer, faith, and works, according to God's will (see D&C 63:9–12; 84:64–73). *(Page 91).*

Statements such as the above always seem to include the same 'example' of the 'gift of tongues'. That is hardly the case, as missionaries go to the MTC (Missionary Training Centre) where they will learn to speak another language if they are to serve in a foreign country. Experience of using it in the 'mission field' may lead many a delusional missionary to conclude that the 'gift of tongues' is what helps them to have an intelligent conversation. It is no such thing; it is education and knowledge, practice and experience. No one suddenly speaks in a language which is unknown to them. However, what the manual does *not* mention of course is that the gift of tongues once meant something entirely different to that. The modern interpretation of the gift obscures the past connotation as it has become somewhat of an embarrassment to Mormonism in the modern age. *(See: Pp.397-9).*

## POST LESSON MATERIAL

> Elder M. Russell Ballard spoke of the power of the Spirit: "True conversion comes through the power of the Spirit. When the Spirit touches the heart, hearts are changed. When individuals . . . feel the Spirit working with them, or when they see the evidence of the Lord's love and mercy in their lives, they are edified and strengthened spiritually and their faith in Him increases. These experiences with the Spirit follow naturally when a person is willing to experiment upon the word. This is how we come to *feel* the gospel is true" ("Now Is the Time," *Ensign*, Nov. 2000, 75). *(Page 93).*

The above statement by Ballard becomes a truism when someone *decides* they want the Church to be true and subsequently concludes that it is through perceived inner feelings which correspond with a *desire* for it to be so. Many a person experiences a very strong feeling that they are about to win the lottery… but they do not. The odd one that does may conclude God was telling them, but of course He was not. That may not be a very good example but there are many others and I am sure you get the idea. First, there must be a desire and then a feeling. Everyone gets them. Millions of people in thousands of denominations have experienced the very same thing that Ballard is talking about.

Mormons think they are different, and that is part of the delusion. As more perceived experiences occur, it is not *faith* as such that increases, it is the state of *delusion* that *deepens*, which is perceived as faith. I speak from personal experience.

Under the heading 'Pray with Faith' *(Manual pp.93-95)* missionaries are encouraged to use the 'language of prayer' and this is also what they will teach investigators.

> For example, in English use scriptural pronouns such as *Thee, Thou, Thy,* and *Thine.*

In my forty-three years as a Mormon, I always obeyed this 'rule' and never deviated from the designated format, yet always felt it a very strange thing to do. Why would God want us to talk to Him using Jacobean (Early Modern) English? It is supposedly a mark of respect – but really it isn't. It is far more natural to pour out heartfelt concerns to a perceived God using the language with which you are familiar and comfortable. Question: How does this work with other languages that may not have the equivalent of thee, thou, thy, etc? Does God consider only Jacobean English (or its equivalent) respectful? With some six-thousand-five-hundred known spoken languages to consider, are there alternate 'respectful' words acceptable to the Mormon God in them all? Or was it the archaic language of the *KJV* that led the Church to dream up another 'rule' for English speaking members. Within Mormonism, the more 'instructions' and 'requirements' that there are, the more its members can be controlled. The 'language of prayer' did not come from God; it is another Mormon 'invention'.

# THE MORMON DELUSION

**Learn to Recognize the Promptings of the Spirit.** *(Manual p.96 on).*

As mentioned elsewhere, what are perceived within Mormonism as promptings of the spirit are no different in any way to the feelings everyone gets, regardless of religion. This can only be experienced once you leave the fold and carry on with life. Then you begin to understand that no promptings of any exclusive Mormon 'spirit' attended you within the Church; it was the normal and natural result of the brain and subconscious mind helping you along. You have to experience both the perception within the Church as a member and perceptions outside it before you can begin to realise that *nothing* changes.

All this means is that the Church takes credit, or gives credit to God or to the spirit, for things which happen quite naturally – either way. Yet the Church captures people with the delusion that this is something new and special. If you *believe* that, it will *seem* true and so *become* true for a member. Unfortunately, almost everything the 'spirit' supposedly confirms *as* true is provably false, so clearly any form of 'confirmation' is nothing more than wishful thinking – or confirmation bias.

That is the ultimate test. The spirit appears to *confirm* something which is later discovered as positively *false*. Fact trumps faith. Ergo, the spirit did *not* 'whisper' anything at all. It was wishful and delusional thinking; nothing more.

Nevertheless, the manual instructs missionaries on such matters to first firm up the idea in their minds, and then teach investigators, that they *can* have such experiences. And they do; or at least they *perceive* they do – because they *want* to. The absolute *fact* that many things that are taught are demonstrably fictional proves conclusively *no* spirit has ever confirmed anything of the sort to anyone at all. The perception of truth was a delusional state of mind created by false information, coupled with a desire which the brain then interpreted as 'truth', because it will accept whatever you *decide* is the case. It is that simple.

> The Spirit is always available to guide and direct you. However, the Spirit speaks quietly, through your feelings as well as your mind. One great challenge for you and those you work with is to recognize the quiet, subtle promptings of the Holy Ghost. *(Page 96)*.

Many of those who have experienced such things and later realise that they are equally moved by music, art, poetry, particular movies or life experiences, may conclude such feelings are not dissimilar, and at times even more realistic than those experienced within the Church which were at the time attributed to the spirit. Naturally, the manual differentiates between *emotion* and the *spirit*.

> I get concerned when it appears that strong emotion or free-flowing tears are equated with the presence of the Spirit. Certainly the Spirit of the Lord can bring strong emotional feelings, including tears, but that

# POST LESSON MATERIAL

outward manifestation ought not to be confused with the presence of the Spirit itself" (*The Teachings of Howard W. Hunter*, 184). *(Page 99)*.

So, emotions should not be confused with the spirit. I agree, but then what *is* the difference? When something comes to mind, is that the spirit or just the brain working? On the basis that the experience is *no* different, in or out of the Church, it is clear that it is just the brain and the influence of the human mind.

> President Boyd K. Packer counseled: "I have learned that strong, impressive spiritual experiences do not come to us very frequently. And when they do, they are generally for our own edification, instruction, or correction. Unless we are called by proper authority to do so, they do not position us to counsel or to correct others. "I have come to believe also that it is not wise to continually talk of unusual spiritual experiences. They are to be guarded with care and shared only when the Spirit itself prompts you to use them to the blessing of others" (*Ensign*, Jan. 1983, 53).

There is a reason for that; whenever anyone in a local Mormon community does talk about such experiences – few will usually believe them – a prophet is definitely not known in his own home. Members should keep quite about perceived experiences. As the Lord doesn't give the prophet revelations like He used to, it simply would not do for mere members to receive more revelations than their prophets.

More 'post lesson' material follows the manual chapter on the *Book of Mormon*. It includes the following aspects which may be of interest.

## How can I better learn my mission language?

## The Gift of Tongues

> Seek the gifts of the Spirit, including the **gift of tongues** and the interpretation of tongues. More than anything else, this **will help you speak and understand the language** of the people in your mission. You will not obtain this gift without effort on your part; you need to actively seek it. Part of seeking the gift of tongues is to **labor and struggle and to do all you can to learn the language**. Trust that the Spirit will help you as you live the way you should and do your very best. Have faith that you can **have the gift of tongues in its true and most comprehensive sense**. (Emphasis added). *(Page 133)*.

According to the modern Mormon Church, the gift of tongues is no more than the ability to learn a required new language well and to be prompted to speak it when you may not have a full knowledge of what you are saying. To have the 'gift', of course the missionary must "labor and struggle and do all he can to learn the language", in which case no 'spirit' is even needed of course. The manual goes on to say that the 'spirit' will speak to people in *any* language.

The problem is that the most "comprehensive sense" of the gift of tongues originally meant one of two things – and one of them was *not* just the ability to learn a new language well.

Biblically, it meant speaking in a completely unknown tongue where the speakers had no idea what they were saying and yet the audience heard it in their own language. In the early Mormon Church it explicitly meant *glossolalia* which was used extensively, especially among the women who even held their own 'glossolalia meetings'. It involved one person first standing and speaking gobbledegook and then another would stand and 'interpret' what had been said.

Many women today feel deprived of privileges afforded to early 'sisters' who would practice glossolalia and also anoint with oil and give blessings. Most modern-day Mormons have no idea that originally, women could just as equally as men, anoint with oil and give blessings to the sick. Brigham Young sometimes even sent his carriage, so his wives could go and give blessings.

> I want a wife that can take care of my children when I am away, who can pray, lay on hands, anoint with oil, and baffle the enemy; and this is a spiritual wife. *(Brigham Young. HC. V.6 Ch. 15. Monday 8 April 1844. Conference report).*

It was an era of superstition and magic; people dreaming dreams, seeing visions and speaking in tongues was commonplace. The Mormon Church was a wonderful new outlet for them. In the late 1800s, giving blessings became the exclusive prerogative of the Priesthood and women were no longer permitted to perform such ordinances. Recognising that the first two prophets not only permitted, but actively encouraged women to perform blessings, we may wonder when and why the Mormon God changed his mind about that.

The once prominent and popular feature of glossolalia eventually died out. Was it ever real, or just an imagined ability? If it was real, where did that idea go and why does God not require its use today? If it was imagined, why did Smith not nip it in the bud? It lasted for several decades in the Church until almost the end of the nineteenth century. At first, church meetings were not as they are today. Anyone could stand up and make confessions (which were encouraged) and anyone could also give revelations. Often these were spoken in tongues and someone would then stand and interpret. Today, no one can claim revelation and no one speaks in 'tongues'. *(See: TMD Vol. 2:265; 332).*

# POST LESSON MATERIAL

## How do I use my time wisely?

Missionaries do lots of planning, hold planning meetings, complete numerous written reports and make phone-in reports. Then there is goal setting, coupled with constantly measuring achievements. It is surprising they have any time left to actually teach anyone. The 'fear factor' is as ever, very carefully integrated into their work under the subtle title of 'accountability'.

They are going to be judged by none other than the Lord for what they do or do not achieve while on their mission.

> The principle of accountability is fundamental in God's eternal plan. We will all stand before the Lord at the last judgment and give an accounting for what we have done with the opportunities He has given us (see Alma 5:15–19; D&C 137:9). There is much you can learn about accountability on your mission that will benefit you throughout your life.
>
> The principle of accountability will bless you if you:
>
> Approach your goal setting and planning with the idea that you will account for your efforts to your mission leaders and to the Lord through prayer.
>
> Feel personal responsibility for the sacred trust the Lord has given you.
>
> Set meaningful goals.
>
> Choose to be proactive in accounting for your work to the Lord and to your mission leaders. Don't wait to be asked. Don't require others to follow up with you frequently. Have a desire to account for your labor. Accept full responsibility for your efforts. Never blame others for difficult circumstances or lack of progress.
>
> Seek to learn from your leaders, and invite them to suggest ways you can improve.
>
> Be motivated to do your best work.
>
> Accountability does not come only at the end of your mission. It is a principle that influences how you begin, how you think and feel about the responsibility the Lord has given you, how you approach your work, and how well you endure. The attitude you have toward your mission experience is a reflection of your love toward your Heavenly Father and His Son and your respect for the priesthood. As you pray personally and in your companionship, seek inspiration on what you

should do each day. As you follow your plans, pray and ask the Lord for guidance. Have a prayer in your heart throughout the day that the Spirit will help you know where to go, what to do, and what to say. Ask yourself, "What more can I do?" In your prayer at the end of the day, give an accounting of your work.

You will give an accounting each week to your mission leaders using the Call-In Summary Report. If you are a mission leader, you will receive this information from other missionaries. Show an interest in their lives and in the lives of those they teach rather than simply in numbers. Do not use these tools or the information you receive as ways to control or manipulate. The information you receive through these tools will provide you with opportunities to praise missionaries for their dedication and to see opportunities for future training. *(Manual pp. 150-151)*.

I was involved in sales management for many years before I retired and have never seen a more pressurised 'sales' environment than this. These young men, if they take everything seriously, are constantly under a great deal of pressure to perform.

As always, there are Mormon so-called scriptures provided to back up and support requirements, including the ever popular *D&C 58:26-33* which says it is a slothful servant who has to be commanded in all things and that rewards come to those who act without being commanded. Naturally, it also says woe betide anyone who doesn't perform. The same is "damned" in fact *(v.29)*. In v.30 Smith has the Lord actually say "Who am I that made man, saith the Lord, that will hold him guiltless that obeys not my commandments?" That's pretty heavy stuff for volunteer unpaid Mormon missionaries.

### How do I find people to teach?

Talk with everyone you meet…

### Addressing the Importance of the Family

The following is the approach the Church asks missionaries to take regarding families. Apparently, families are the most important people to 'find'. Never mind the fact that many 'families' now consist of single parents or unmarried couples, and these days of course, gay couples, some with children. The field the Mormon Church aims at is becoming narrower every year as times and attitudes change.

# POST LESSON MATERIAL

The Restoration of the gospel of Jesus Christ **blesses families**. By living the principles of the restored gospel, **families are strengthened** and can experience peace, joy, and a sense of belonging and identity. Addressing **the importance of the family** with those you meet each day will help you find people to teach. Most people have a natural **interest in families**. In many finding situations, you can quickly relate what most people know about the family to the message of the Restoration. When finding, you might say something like the following:

*There is **nothing more important to us than our families**. Our family **ties** us to one another, gives us a name, and helps us feel needed and loved. From **our families** we inherited personality traits, attributes, and physical characteristics, giving us some unique identity. Having **a strong, happy family is the highest priority** for many people throughout the world. Accomplishing this goal is often difficult. Raising children and having a strong marriage in today's world can almost seem impossible at times **with the evils that are all around us**.* (Emphasis added). *(Pp 159-160).*

It is all about *families*; to the extent that many singles in the Mormon Church often feel very lonely and left out. My personal question – which I would never have even thought of as a believer – is *what* "evils"?

The Church will *tell* you what is and is not *evil*, but as stated elsewhere, the very *concepts* of *evil* and *sin* are ones which were invented by the early church and they are not actually real. There is good and bad, legal and illegal, people commit 'crimes' and indeed descriptively, something can even be considered 'positively evil' as I have mentioned previously. That does not mean that *Satan* or related *evil* or *sin* actually exist, or that anyone will be held to account to a God for what they do. That is simply a matter of personal *belief*, which at the end of the day is *always* based on faith in what someone *else* claims is the case.

You could then make a transition to the message of the Restoration:

*The feelings of love and concern that we have for our families are eternal and rooted deep within our souls. They are centered in our relationship with God. You have been part of God's family since before you were born. He is our Father. Because He is our Father, we are brothers and sisters. Heavenly Father wants us to return to live with Him as part of His family. Families here on earth are a tie to God's family. Families can live together after this life. We know this because after centuries of being lost, true doctrines and ordinances such as baptism by immersion have been restored to the earth by our loving Heavenly Father through a living prophet. These restored truths not only help us understand our place in God's family, but they are the greatest hope we have for a strong, happy family in this life. May we teach you more about . . .*

> The same thing can be done with other topics, such as happiness, adversity, the purpose of life, or death. Whatever your finding approach, remember to connect it quickly to our unique message to the world. (Emphasis in original). *(Pp.159-60).*

The Mormon Church continues to seek out married couples with families and whatever approach the missionaries take, the goal is for families to quickly be introduced to the concept that they can be together forever. That doesn't mean they won't teach anyone else who will listen. They will, but they actively seek out families. I remember some years ago, the missionaries were teaching a single young man and one evening he answered the door wearing a very pretty dress… he never did reject the missionaries or the Church, but for some reason the missionaries just didn't go back to see him after that.

## How can I improve my teaching skills?

### Leave Something Behind

> At the conclusion of each teaching visit, provide the investigator with something to read and ponder in preparation for the next meeting. You might assign them chapters from the Book of Mormon. You might give them a brochure addressing what has been taught or what you are going to teach in your next visit, or it may be other literature or an audiovisual presentation. If they have access to the Internet, encourage them to go to www.mormon.org. They should always be given something to think about, to ponder, and to pray about. This can become an opening topic of discussion the next time you meet. *(P.190).*

I was somewhat surprised to see reference to a Mormon Church web site at the discussion stage. It is now so easy for someone to find what the Church terms 'anti-Mormon' web sites that anyone who searches the internet is highly likely to come across some even by accident and quickly discover the truth before the delusion takes over. Still, that fact is at least encouraging.

There are other aspects in the lesson manual which readers can review for themselves. They are of no real significance to what is actually taught. These include such things as:

How do I help people make and keep commitments? This section includes:

> Extend Commitment Invitations

# POST LESSON MATERIAL

Ask Direct Questions

Promise People Blessings

Bear Testimony Frequently

Follow Up

How the missionaries can make promises to people about blessings, only the Mormon God knows. They are of course completely unquantifiable, so I suppose they are on safe ground. They never have to step up and account for the non-deliverance of any promises. Other material in the manual includes aspects such as:

How do I prepare people for baptism and confirmation?

Working with local members.

# Chapter 17

## What Is the Role of the Book of Mormon?

Among the post-lesson material provided for missionaries is an entire chapter dedicated to the role of the *Book of Mormon* in teaching investigators. In part, it at least answers the question why there are so many *Book of Mormon* references and so few biblical ones in the lesson material.

> The Book of Mormon is ***powerful evidence of the divinity of Christ***. It is also ***proof of the Restoration through the Prophet Joseph Smith.*** An essential part of conversion is receiving a witness from the Holy Ghost that the Book of Mormon is true. As a missionary, you must first have a personal testimony that the Book of Mormon is true. (Emphasis added). *(Page 103).*

Unfortunately, neither of the above emphasised statements is true. The claims are unsubstantiated, and in that context it doesn't much matter whether it was written by Smith *or* the ancients. Just because a book *states* something, regardless of when it was written and by whom, that does not constitute actual "evidence" nor is it "proof" of *anything*. Likewise, the book most certainly does not contain any *proof* of a restoration through Joseph Smith; none whatsoever. There is actually plenty of *evidence* in the book to more than suggest it is entirely fictional and that it was not ancient at all. There is absolutely *nothing* concrete to remotely suggest that it was. If anything, it also contains *proof* that Joseph Smith was an utter fraud.

The Mormon Church looks at the *Book of Mormon* one way with rose coloured faith driven spectacles; the rest of the world looks at the *facts*. The evidence and proof contained within the pages of Smith's *Book of Mormon* is quite conclusive and points in only one direction – as discussed in *Chapter 6*. *(See also TMD Vol. 2. Chs: 7-9, 11,12 & 15)*.

Nonetheless, the Mormon Church claims the *Book of Mormon* to be the 'keystone' of its religion.

> The Prophet Joseph Smith taught that the Book of Mormon is "the keystone of our religion" (introduction to the Book of Mormon). On another occasion he stated: "Take away the Book of Mormon and the revelations, and where is our religion? We have none" (*History of the Church*, 2:52). *(Page 103).*

A study of the so-called revelations and prophesy in the *Book of Mormon*, and more particularly in the *D&C*, shows that they were all in the main entirely unfulfilled and/or utter nonsense *(See: TMD Vol. 3, Section 6, for examples)*. The *Book of Mormon* has no theological position of merit other than to deluded Mormons who cannot see the wood for the trees.

A comprehensive 'deforestation' of the *Book of Mormon* has already been undertaken in *TMD Vol. 2* and in *Chapter 6* of this book, but we will address here, the claims of authenticity made in *Chapter 5* of the Lesson Manual, just to stave off any remaining question regarding the facts.

> When Joseph Smith called the Book of Mormon "the keystone of our religion," he taught that the Book of Mormon holds our religion together. President ***Ezra Taft Benson said that the Book of Mormon is the keystone in at least three ways.*** (Emphasis added). *(Page 104).*

Benson's "three ways" were a 'witness of Christ', a 'fullness of doctrine' and the 'foundation of testimony'. Referring to what he said in each case, we will address the facts behind each of the three claims.

### Benson's First way. The *Book of Mormon* is a 'witness of Christ'.

> The Book of Mormon is the keystone in our witness of Jesus Christ, who is Himself the cornerstone of everything we do. It bears witness of His reality with power and clarity. *(Page 104).*

# WHAT IS THE ROLE OF THE BOOK OF MORMON?

The *Book of Mormon* does indeed "bear witness of His reality". Any book could do that, but it means nothing unless it can be substantiated, or refuted, by existing and accepted alternative evidence. Outside Mormonism, Christianity in general dismisses *all Book of Mormon* claims. If the book is a 'witness' to Christ's reality, then why do all other religions entirely reject it? Could they not at least accept the concept that it 'testifies' of Christ? Well, the answer to that is absolutely *no* for many reasons. Not least of those is the *Book of Mormon* idea that Christ appeared to a fictional people in America – that just doesn't sit well in mainstream Christianity at all. Worse however, is the fact that the *Book of Mormon* speaks of 'Christ' and 'Jesus' in the BCE period, before such words were known or invented. It even claims that prophets from the time of Adam worshipped God in the *name* of Jesus Christ. Not only is that problematic in terms of historicity, it just gets a roll of the eyes and instant dismissal from *all* Jewish and Christian theologians alike. The concept is completely impossible.

**Benson's second way. The *Book of Mormon* is a 'fullness of doctrine'.**

> The Lord Himself has stated that the Book of Mormon contains the 'fulness of the gospel of Jesus Christ.' (D&C 20:9 [;27:5].) . . . In the Book of Mormon we will find the fulness of those doctrines required for our salvation. And they are taught plainly and simply so that even children can learn the ways of salvation and exaltation. *(Page 104).*

The idea that the *Book of Mormon* contains the 'fullness of the gospel' was addressed in *Chapter 6*. But here, missionaries are provided with details of what that apparently constitutes.

| Missionary Lesson | Doctrines | References |
|---|---|---|
| The Message of the Restoration of the Gospel of Jesus Christ | Apostasy, Restoration, Joseph Smith, priesthood authority | 1 Nephi 12–14<br>2 Nephi 3; 26–29<br>Mosiah 18 |
| The Plan of Salvation | The "great plan of the eternal God," including the Fall of Adam, the Atonement, the Resurrection, and the Judgment | 2 Nephi 2; 9<br>Mosiah 3; 15<br>Alma 12; 40–42 |
| The Gospel of Jesus Christ | Faith in Christ, repentance, baptism, the gift of the Holy Ghost, and enduring to the end | 2 Nephi 31–32<br>3 Nephi 11; 27 |
| The Commandments; Laws and Ordinances | Ordinances such as baptism, confirmation, priesthood ordination, and the sacrament | 3 Nephi 11:22–28; 18<br>Moroni 2–6 |

# THE MORMON DELUSION

What immediately jumps out of the above in the first box under 'Doctrines' is the fact that the *only* aspects exclusive to Mormonism are 'Apostasy', 'Restoration', and 'Joseph Smith'. The rest are common Christian teachings with one or two slight variations. The 'great plan' is no different to the concepts of other Christian religions. Smith threw in his ideas on priesthood ordination and sacrament prayers that he wanted to use in his new Church which was about to be formed. He inserted wording into the latter part of the *Book of Mormon* which he decided to use. Nothing else that he invented later appears in the book at all.

The references cover prophesies of things yet to happen which are then recorded later in the very book that those prophecies are in. They include the 'land of promise', the 'Lamb of God', 'twelve apostles' and 'disciples', 'wars and rumours of wars', etc. In fact, they more or less describe the rest of the book. That is not exactly convincing 'prophesy', it is more a list of contents.

They also 'prophesy' of Joseph Smith and the *Book of Mormon* coming about. So Smith predicts that he will restore the true gospel and bring the *Book of Mormon* into play and simply backdates it *into* the *Book of Mormon* which he pretends was written by ancients. One problem is that he has it written in about 600 BCE which unleashes innumerable problems concerning historicity, viability and believability; to say nothing of Smith's own credibility. *Mosiah 18* is supposed to quantify 'priesthood authority'. When Smith wrote the *Book of Mormon*, it was 1828-9. The Church was formed the following year, in 1830, with a First and Second 'Elder'. Several other Mormon 'offices' came later. So, do we see *all* of these in *Alma 18*, or anywhere else in the *Book of Mormon* for that matter? No, we don't. In Alma, he ordains only 'Priests'.

In the Mormon Church today, you will find Deacons, Teachers, Priests, Elders, Seventies, High Priests, Bishops and Patriarchs, as well as Presidents of this, that and the other. Even the so-called prophet is identified as the President of the Corporation of the Church of Jesus Christ of Latter Day Saints. Once there were 'Superintendents' of Sunday School and youth programmes, but these went by the board some time after I joined the Church. I remember one Ward having a female Sunday School Superintendent for a couple of years. The Stake President kept telling the Bishop that he thought it should be a man, but the Bishop saw no reason for it not to be a woman. Now, the equivalent position is Sunday School President and women are not allowed near that role.

There is no theological reason why not, other than the Mormon Church essentially being an alpha-male organisation. Since the Relief Society had their finances 'consolidated' within general Church funds *(see p.354)*, they have had to beg for their 'budget' each year. Women are held in tight control within the Church and its hierarchy. In the *Book of Mormon*, we find *no* Deacons or Seventies, no Bishops and no Patriarchs, but there are 'Priests' who 'supported themselves'. Today, Priests are sixteen to seventeen-year-old boys.

# WHAT IS THE ROLE OF THE BOOK OF MORMON?

In the middle of a reference on baptism, once again we find confirmation of Smith's monotheistic outlook of the day. The *Book of Mormon* is saturated with such evidence. As mentioned elsewhere, the Church claims that God and Jesus are 'one in purpose' rather than one and the same being. Members accept this and thus rationalise away all such references. It may be what Smith started to believe later and what the Church believes today, but it most certainly was *not* what Smith believed when he wrote the book.

> **3 Nephi 11:27.** And after this manner shall ye baptize in my name; for behold, verily I say unto you, that the Father, and the Son, and the Holy Ghost are one; and I am in the Father, and the Father in me, and the Father and I are one.

So, the *Book of Mormon* does *not*, after all, contain the 'fullness' of the Mormon gospel. In fact, outside of aspects that most other Christians believe, it really contains *none* of it at all. We might ask; where does the *Book of Mormon* speak of such things as the organisational structure of the Church – among many other things?

---

"The Book of Mormon contains the fulness of the gospel of Jesus Christ."

Plural gods are not in the *Book of Mormon*.
Polygamy is expressly *forbidden* in the *Book of Mormon*.
God is *not* described as an exalted *man*.
Celestial marriage is *not* there.

---

"The Book of Mormon contains the fulness of the gospel of Jesus Christ."

Nephite men could *not* become Gods –
at least God didn't tell them that they could.

---

"The Book of Mormon contains the fulness of the gospel of Jesus Christ."

There are no 'degrees of glory',
no Celestial, Terrestrial or Telestial kingdoms –
but there *is* heaven and hell.

---

"The Book of Mormon contains the fulness of the gospel of Jesus Christ."

Baptism for the dead does *not* get a mention
yet Mormons claim it biblical, citing *1 Corinthians 15:29*.
If it was good enough for people on one side of the world –
then why not on the other?

> "The Book of Mormon contains the fulness of the gospel of Jesus Christ."
>
> Whilst there are 'Priests', there is *no* 'Aaronic Priesthood'.
> There is *no* eternal progression.
> There are *no* temple ordinances (washing, anointing, endowment, sealing) yet they supposedly built temples.
> Smith claimed the ordinances were performed from the time of Adam.

> "The Book of Mormon contains the fulness of the gospel of Jesus Christ."
>
> The Mormon concept of the Godhead is *not* there –
> but Smith's monotheism shines through, page after page.
> A 'mother' in heaven is absent from the book.
> Each 'dispensation' had a 'word of wisdom' yet the Nephites did not.
> That is strange really, as Lehi and his family were Jews and according to the *Book of Mormon* they continued to practice Jewish traditions. That would include an entire health code which does not appear in the book.

The Mormon Church claim that the fullness of the gospel is contained in the *Book of Mormon* is a far cry from the truth. In reality, just the opposite is the case. In fact, some modern Mormon doctrine is completely *contradicted* in the *Book of Mormon*, as has been demonstrated several times in this volume.

Additionally, there are many things in the book which at first may appear innocuous enough but upon inspection are completely wrong when compared to known history – with or without faith. I covered many such things in *TMD Vol. 2* but one thing I did not mention in that volume is an extraordinary idea mentioned in Mosiah 13:18-19.

> **Mosiah 13:18.** But the seventh day, the sabbath of the Lord thy God, thou shalt not do any work, thou, nor thy son, nor thy daughter, thy man-servant, nor thy maid-servant, nor thy cattle, nor thy stranger that is within thy gates;
> **19.** For in six days the Lord made heaven and earth, and the sea, and all that in them is; wherefore the Lord blessed the sabbath day, and hallowed it.

I said this was extraordinary but at first glance the reader may wonder why. Surely the Old Testament confirms the basis of the above thinking. I agree that indeed it does – but that is *not* the problem. The problem is that *all* the cultures discovered in the Americas used anything *but* a seven day week. Calendars used in Mesoamerica vary, but *none* match the Old World calendar. We wouldn't expect them to, unless we believed that they came from there. Then *someone* in the Americas should have had a seven day week and the absence of

# WHAT IS THE ROLE OF THE BOOK OF MORMON?

such is what causes the problem. The Maya had various calendars. One consisted of a two-hundred-and-sixty day cycle divided into thirteen periods of twenty days. Moreover, each day was represented by its own god. These people could hardly have 'evolved' from one God who created the world in seven days, to twenty gods, each with their own day of the 'month'.

Another calendar did have three-hundred-and-sixty-five days in its cycle. However, it was also divided into periods of twenty days. A quick calculation will tell you there must have been eighteen of them, leaving five spare days. These surplus days were called the 'sleep' or the 'rest' of the year. No 'seven day' periods were used. Yet another calendar consisted of a 3276 day cycle. This was sub-divided into four 'quadrants' of 819 days – the product of 7, 9 and 13, which were all sacred numbers to the Maya. The 'long count' calendar simply counted days from the creation of the world – which in our own terms was 11 August 3114 BCE. None of that sounds much like Old World dating to me. *(See: Schele, L&F. 1990:78)*.

No pre-Columbian Native American calendars have been discovered which match Old World traditions, providing yet more evidence that the *Book of Mormon* was nothing but a nineteenth century work of pure fiction.

Likewise, many other Smith mistakes are just glossed over in the *Book of Mormon* by the 'faithful' reader as if they are of no importance. Mormons just don't 'see' all the errors. The *Book of Mormon* claims, in 83 BCE, that Jesus will be born 'at' *Jerusalem*.

> **Alma 7:10.** And behold, **he shall be born of Mary, at Jerusalem** which is the land of our forefathers, she being a virgin, a precious and chosen vessel, who shall be overshadowed and conceive by the power of the Holy Ghost, and bring forth a son, yea, even the Son of God. (Emphasis added).

The fact that Jesus was recorded as having been born in *Bethlehem* means one of three things. Either Alma got his 'prophecy' wrong and he was a false Nephite prophet; Smith got it wrong and he was a false prophet; or, the Bible got it wrong and he *was* born 'at' Jerusalem. No doubt Mormon apologists, clutching at straws, will have postulated the latter option at some stage – as the other two leave them high and dry. Such nonsense wouldn't surprise me at all. They have postulated that Bethlehem was in the district of Jerusalem and so could have been a generalisation. But this was supposedly a prophecy made in 83 BCE and should be consistent with the later biblical record. It is not very convincing when a prophecy says in effect – he will be born around there somewhere. The mistake Smith made is perfectly clear to all but the deluded. Evidence of the false nature of the *Book of Mormon* is prolific from within its own pages. This is just another of the countless insurmountable problems.

**Benson's third way. The *Book of Mormon* is 'the foundation of testimony'.**

> Just as the arch crumbles if the keystone is removed, so does all the Church stand or fall with the truthfulness of the Book of Mormon. The enemies of the Church understand this clearly. This is why they go to such great lengths to try to disprove the Book of Mormon, for if it can be discredited, the Prophet Joseph Smith goes with it. So does our claim to priesthood keys, and revelation, and the restored Church. But in like manner, if the Book of Mormon be true—and millions have now testified that they have the witness of the Spirit that it is indeed true—then one must accept the claims of the Restoration and all that accompanies it (*A Witness and a Warning* [1988], 18–19). *(Page 104).*

So-called 'enemies' of the Church don't actually have to go to "such great lengths to try to disprove the Book of Mormon". Many who have authored books and articles on the subject of the Church and the *Book of Mormon* were originally faithful members and the last thing they wanted was for it *not* to be true. In addition, there are people such as Thomas Stuart Ferguson, who spent twenty-five years and hundreds of thousands of Mormon Church dollars, trying to *substantiate* it. It was only when it finally became clear to him that far from validating the *Book of Mormon* claims, all the archaeology that they undertook completely discredited it, that he lost faith in the book. That hardly constitutes the work or attitude of an enemy. *(See: UTLM. Salt Lake City Messenger. #69. September 1988. Available at:* http://www.utlm.org/newsletters/no69.htm).

The fact that millions have testified of a "witness of the Spirit that it is indeed true" of course does not actually *make* it true. Many *more* millions of Catholics, Muslims and Jews etc., will tell you their religion, beliefs and books are equally true; each 'witness' being obtained through the very same method.

A 'spirit' or 'feeling' tells them so. I count myself as having been in the category of having had such a 'testimony' during my many years of Mormon Church membership. I would read the *Book of Mormon* almost daily, on the basis that it was true. Clearly, it did not make it so; I was reading with my rose-coloured spectacles on, or rather, delusional reasoning. When my faith in God was failing, I spent a full year trying to 'make' the Church be true and avidly read *every* morning from the *Book of Mormon* as part of that process. The day I broke down and sobbed my heart out, knowing for a fact that it was anything other than true, I had earnestly been trying to convince myself of just the opposite. I suspect that many others have been through a similar experience.

I didn't know *why* it wasn't true at that stage; nevertheless, I *knew*. That was through no 'spirit' witnessing it one way or the other, despite my best attempts; it was simply a *fact* that my brain finally accepted, in spite of all my efforts to make it think otherwise. There are equally, many more millions of people who have 'testified' that it is *not* true, who have also prayed about it and

# WHAT IS THE ROLE OF THE BOOK OF MORMON?

then rejected it, along with the Mormon Church. As missionaries teach investigators, for each person who finds the *Book of Mormon* to be true, many hundreds, if not thousands, find *against* the idea and then reject it completely.

Mormons would argue that they were not 'ready' or they did not pray with an 'open mind and a sincere heart', *wanting* to know it is true. They should try again – until they get the *right* answer. People have to *want* it to be true before it can become so in their minds. Only then can they feel that the 'spirit' has witnessed it to them. That should tell them something – but it doesn't. I *wanted* the story to be true at age fourteen and thus it became so. The reality is that most people are just not that gullible and immediately see through the hoax.

Read as faith-promoting 'scripture', coupled with the preconceived notion, already firmly established in the mind by the 'spirit' – otherwise known as wishful thinking – that it is true, no one notices anything *wrong* with the book.

Once again, that is the power of delusion. It is only when a person reviews the book objectively and without prior indoctrination, that they can find *no* evidence supporting it from within its pages, and every evidence discrediting it jumps out at them over and over again – whether they are looking for it or not.

### The Book of Mormon Testifies of Christ

> A central purpose of the Book of Mormon is to convince all people that Jesus is the Christ (see title page of the Book of Mormon). It testifies of Christ by affirming the reality of His life, mission, and power. It teaches true doctrine concerning the Atonement— the foundation for the plan of salvation. Several of those whose writings are preserved in the Book of Mormon saw Christ personally. The brother of Jared, Nephi, and Jacob saw the premortal Christ. Mormon and Moroni saw the risen Christ. In addition, multitudes were present during the Savior's brief but powerful ministry among the Nephites (see 3 Nephi 11–28). Those who know little or nothing about the Savior will come to know Him by reading, pondering, and praying about the Book of Mormon. The testimony of the Book of Mormon confirms the testimony of the Bible that Jesus is the Only Begotten Son of God and the Savior of the world. As you teach the fulness of the gospel of Jesus Christ, you will testify often about the Savior and Redeemer of the world. By the power of the Holy Ghost, you will add your living witness of the truthfulness of this message. *(Page 105).*

The above statement will be taken as read by Mormon missionaries. Indeed, all Mormons who are faithful will immediately recognise what they believe and will support the claims.

Once again, the mind and judgement of believers is clouded by delusional thinking attained by daily reading of the book which they already accept as word for word the most reliable scripture ever written. They don't need to *think* about it at all. For them, it is too late to see beyond the words. Investigators certainly *should think* about it very carefully though, as for them it is not yet too late to discover the truth. A book can be easily written confirming Christ and his life. Everything you need to know is already in the Bible.

So, is the *Book of Mormon* really a reliable witness of Christ, or is it just a nineteenth-century book of fairy stories? One problem in the *Book of Mormon* regarding Jesus Christ is that it not only has him appearing in the Americas following his resurrection, it has him speaking some exact words that appear in the New Testament which were *ascribed* to apostles and would have been nothing remotely close to the actual words of the Saviour himself. There are mentions of Christ later in the *Book of Mormon* but the other real problem is that he is spoken of prolifically BCE, using words and names that were then unknown in *any* language and yet to be invented.

Naturally, in the missionary manual, references are provided concerning Christ in the *Book of Mormon*. Obviously the Mormon Church will pick out what they consider the best ones available, so let's just review some. At this stage, references are provided in the manual to answer the question why the *Book of Mormon* prophets wrote what they did. Several verses just say they 'delighted' in the scriptures.

> **2 Nephi 33:13.** And now, my beloved brethren, all those who are of the house of Israel, and all ye ends of the earth, I speak unto you as the voice of one crying from the dust: Farewell until that great day shall come.
> **14.** And you that will not partake of the goodness of God, ***and respect the words of the Jews, and also my words, and the words which shall proceed forth out of the mouth of the Lamb of God***, behold, I bid you an everlasting farewell, for these words shall condemn you at the last day.
> **15.** For what I seal on earth, shall be brought against you at the judgment bar; for thus hath the Lord commanded me, and I must obey. Amen. *(Between 559 and 545 BCE).* (Emphasis added).

Note that Smith has Nephi speak of respecting the "words of the Jews" and also his own "words" and those of "the Lamb of God" – who was yet to say anything of course. But Nephi ***was*** a Jew; they had only just left Jerusalem a few years previously and in theory were yet to develop ideas beyond Judaism.

I recently read an email from my son-in-law to my grandson who is serving a mission in Brazil. He mentioned that in Sunday School, the teacher pointed out Lehi was 'converted' by Jeremiah. What on Earth was he converted from or to? Lehi and family were Jews; the *Book of Mormon* explains they continued to observe Jewish culture and customs. Jews were not *converted* in the BCE, they were born. It was not just a religion, it was a nation. Perhaps the Sunday School

# WHAT IS THE ROLE OF THE BOOK OF MORMON?

teacher was intimating Lehi was converted *from* Judaism to Christianity, but there were no Christians and the *Book of Mormon* confirms otherwise. Here we see yet another example of typical Mormon Sunday School nonsense. The earliest historical record of any conversion *to* Judaism is in fact the *forcible* conversion of the Idumeans by John Hyrcanus (135-104 BCE).

The *Book of Mormon* explicitly states that they continued in their Jewish customs. It is worth reading *2 Nephi 33* it its entirety to capture the absurdity of Nephi's claim they should "believe in these words, for they are the words of Christ".

In the above verses, the idea of 'crying from the dust' is introduced. Smith of course claimed to translate these words from gold plates, thus fulfilling that idea. All you have to do is write what you claim *has* happened into a book supposedly written long ago, to self-fulfil anything you like. Smith was very good at doing that. If people don't listen to the words in the book, they will be condemned. The 'Lamb of God' is mentioned around five-hundred-and-fifty years BCE. *Only* delusional thinking will make a belief in that possible.

According to the *Book of Mormon*, some prophets apparently had no idea whatsoever *why* they were writing what they did.

> **1 Nephi 9:5.** Wherefore, the Lord hath commanded me to make these plates for a wise purpose in him, which purpose I know not.
>
> **Alma 37:2.** for it is for a wise purpose that they are kept.
> **14.** a wise purpose in him, that he may show forth his power unto future generations.

Another reference *(below)* is claimed to have been written to persuade their children and 'brethren' to believe in Christ. It was supposedly written about 550 BCE and there were only a small handful of them at the time. It goes on to say that they believed in Christ yet kept the laws of Moses. You won't find any references in the *Book of Mormon* actually describing any of the laws of Moses that they kept. 'Offerings', or at best 'burnt offerings', is as close as it ever gets. Smith simply didn't know what the Old Testament Jewish traditions were.

Naturally, you won't find any references to 'Christ' in the Old Testament either; so, the question is if this was a true record of a real people, where did they get that idea from? The answer is, as ever, all too obvious.

> **2 Nephi 25:23.** For we labor diligently to write, to persuade our children, and also our brethren, to believe in Christ, and to be reconciled to God; for we know that it is ***by grace that we are saved, after all we can do.***

**24.** And, ***notwithstanding we believe in Christ, we keep the law of Moses***, and look forward with steadfastness unto Christ, until the law shall be fulfilled.

**25.** For, for this end was the law given; wherefore ***the law hath become dead unto us, and we are made alive in Christ because of our faith***; yet we keep the law because of the commandments.

**26.** And we talk of Christ, we rejoice in Christ, we preach of Christ, we prophesy of Christ, and we write according to our prophecies, that our children may know to what source they may look for a remission of their sins.

**27.** Wherefore, we speak concerning the law that our children may know the deadness of the law; and they, by knowing the deadness of the law, may look forward unto that life which is in Christ, and know for what end the law was given. And after the law is fulfilled in Christ, that they need not harden their hearts against him when the law ought to be done away.

**28.** And now behold, my people, ye are a stiffnecked people; wherefore, I have spoken plainly unto you, that ye cannot misunderstand. And ***the words which I have spoken shall stand as a testimony against you***; for they are sufficient to teach any man the right way; for the right way is to believe in Christ and deny him not; for by denying him ye also deny the prophets and the law.

**29.** And now behold, I say unto you that the right way is to believe in Christ, and deny him not; and ***Christ is the Holy One of Israel***; wherefore ye must bow down before him, and worship him with all your might, mind, and strength, and your whole soul; and if ye do this ye shall in nowise be cast out. (Emphasis added).

The traditional Christian concept of being 'saved by grace' after all we can do appears clearly in v.23. This was to later change in Mormonism. The *Book of Mormon* contains hundreds of references to standard Christian concepts that are now *manipulated* to fit modern Mormon theology. The book came first; then the Church was organised; then the theology evolved. Consequently, not much of anything that became the eventual foundation of Mormonism actually appears *in* the *Book of Mormon*. However, many things that *contradict* it are still there for everyone to see and read. Only a mind 'conditioned' to see what the Church actually teaches, rather than the real and obvious meaning of the original words, can read the book without seeing the truth – which is hidden in plain sight.

The Nephites believe in, and describe themselves as 'alive in', Christ and yet keep the Law of Moses – a law which has become 'dead' to them *(v.24-25)*. This is a very strange way to behave. Once again, the words will stand as a testimony against the people – who are their own children *(v.28)* and in v.29 "Christ is the Holy one of Israel". This is consistent with the *New Testament*.

# WHAT IS THE ROLE OF THE BOOK OF MORMON?

In Mormonism, later doctrine emerged which defined Christ as the God of the *Old Testament* under the direction of God the Father, once Smith decided, several years *later*, that they were two separate entities. In Christianity, Christ *is* also God, so naturally He is the Holy one of Israel. They are one and the same being. When Smith wrote the *Book of Mormon*, that was also *his* belief, and every associated reference in the *Book of Mormon* still confirms that to be the case, with the notable exception of the four verses that he later falsified. *(See: Chapter 5, p.98).*

> **2 Nephi 26:15.** After my seed and the seed of my brethren shall have dwindled in unbelief, and shall have been smitten by the Gentiles; yea, after the Lord God shall have camped against them round about, and shall have laid siege against them with a mount, and raised forts against them; and after they shall have been brought down low in the dust, even that they are not, yet the words of the righteous shall be written, and the prayers of the faithful shall be heard, and all those who have dwindled in unbelief shall not be forgotten.
> **16.** For those who shall be destroyed shall speak unto them out of the ground, and their speech shall be low out of the dust, and their voice shall be as one that hath a familiar spirit; for the Lord God will give unto him power, that he may whisper concerning them, even as it were out of the ground; and their speech shall whisper out of the dust.

Around 550 BCE, when there were only a few dozen of them and all were Jews, still practicing Judaism, we have prophecies that they will 'dwindle in unbelief' and be 'smitten by the Gentiles'. They will all be killed off but will have written things down and 'speak out of the ground'. Here Smith creates the plot for the latter part of the story and also his own role in bringing the voices 'out of the dust'. It is a clever ploy by Smith, but predicting things from the distant past to be fulfilled in the recent past, all written down in the modern day, doesn't constitute anything more than a fairy story – unless *evidence* of an early origin is produced. In addition, *why* would such a prophecy be made?

The family was relatively small and at the time there were no 'Gentiles'. It says "After my seed and the seed of my brethren shall have dwindled in unbelief, and shall have been smitten by the Gentiles..." The overall idea of 'seed' appears to refer to everyone there. **They were supposedly alone in the land, although today due to overwhelming evidence to the contrary, the Church supposes the land may have already been highly populated.** So, who were these Gentiles? In the end, the so-called Gentiles were to be Lamanites, descendants of their own family. They had gone from being practicing Jews in 550 BCE, to Christians, when Christ visited them after his resurrection, to wicked pagans who then killed everyone else off less than four hundred years later. The claims and the sequence of events are equally absurd – and culturally impossible.

Next, we have reference to all the books that are to be written.

**A question for the investigator to ask is – where are they all?**

> **2 Nephi 29:11.** For I command *all men, both in the east* and in *the west*, and in *the north*, and in *the south*, and in the *islands of the sea*, that *they shall write the words which I speak unto them*; for out of the books which shall be written I will judge the world, every man according to their works, according to that which is written.
> **12.** For behold, *I shall speak unto the Jews* and they shall write it; and I shall also *speak unto the Nephites* and they shall write it; and I shall also speak unto the *other tribes of the house of Israel*, which I have led away, and they shall write it; and I shall *also speak unto all nations of the earth* and they shall write it.
> **13.** And it shall come to pass that *the Jews shall have the words of the Nephites*, and the *Nephites shall have the words of the Jews*; and the *Nephites and the Jews shall have the words of the lost tribes of Israel*; and the *lost tribes of Israel shall have the words of the Nephites and the Jews.*
> **14.** And it shall come to pass that *my people, which are of the house of Israel, shall be gathered home unto the lands of their possessions; and my word also shall be gathered in one.* And I will show unto them that fight against my word and against my people, who are of the house of Israel, that I am God, and that I covenanted with Abraham that I would remember his seed forever. (Emphasis added).

If this is 'scripture' then the 'prophecy' must be *seen* to be fulfilled. Just take a look at what it is claiming. *All men,* from the east, west, north and south, as well as all the islands of the sea, will keep records of what God says to them.

The Jews will keep records – that one wasn't too hard to work out. The Nephites will keep records. Smith was in the process of writing them, so that wasn't hard to work out either. Smith has Nephi prophesy that the ten lost tribes will make records of what God says to them. *(See below).* God says he will speak to *all* nations of the earth. Every one of them was going to write down what God said to them.

"The Jews shall have the words of the Nephites." Well, I suppose today, Jews could read the *Book of Mormon.* So far – so good. The "Nephites shall have the word of the Jews." Lehi supposedly took records with him, but Nephi is speaking of the period *after* 550 BCE so I fail to see when the Nephites ever had the words recorded by *subsequent* Jews. The Nephites were entirely wiped out by about 421 CE. The "Nephites and Jews shall have the words of the lost tribes of Israel." Again, as the Nephites have long since been wiped out, and in Mormonism the ten lost tribes are a supposed group yet to be located and

# WHAT IS THE ROLE OF THE BOOK OF MORMON?

identified, the Nephites never had any such thing. Likewise, the Jews certainly do not have words of the lost tribes as there aren't any to have.

Similarly, the lost tribes will not have the words of the Nephites or the Jews as there are no lost tribes today as such. Verse 14 loosely speaks of the gathering before claiming that "my word also shall be gathered in one."

Unfortunately, most of what the reference claims will be written, has not been gathered into one, from – all men from the east, west, north and south, isles of the sea, the 'other' tribes of Israel, and *all* the nations of the earth – and they never will be gathered together in one. Most have never written anything that God supposedly said to them because He has never spoken to them. The 'prophecy' is complete and utter demonstrable nonsense.

In the modern day, the history of the Hebrews is pretty well understood. We know that the ten 'lost tribes' were simply dispersed and absorbed into other cultures. They did *not* migrate to another location as a group, remaining undetected and alone and yet to be located as a people which God 'led away', as described in *2 Nephi 29:12* above.

> The Assyrians conquered the kingdom of Israel some 2,730 years ago, scattering 10 of the 12 tribes into exile, supposedly beyond the mythical Sambation river. The two remaining tribes, Benjamin and Judah, became the modern-day Jewish people, according to Jewish history, and the search for the lost tribes has continued ever since. Some have claimed to have found traces of them in modern day China, Burma, Nigeria, Central Asia, Ethiopia and even in the West.
>
> But it is believed that the tribes were dispersed in an area around modern-day northern Iraq and Afghanistan, which makes the Pashtun connection the strongest.
>
> "Of all the groups, there is more convincing evidence about the Pathans than anybody else, but the Pathans are the ones who would reject Israel most ferociously. That is the sweet irony," said Shalva Weil, an anthropologist and senior researcher at the Hebrew University of Jerusalem.
>
> The Pashtuns have a proud oral history that talks of descending from the Israelites.
>
> Their tribal groupings have similar names, including Yusufzai, which means sons of Joseph; and Afridi, thought by some to come from Ephraim. Some customs and practices are said to be similar to Jewish traditions: lighting candles on the sabbath, refraining from eating certain foods, using a canopy during a wedding ceremony and some similarities in garments.

Weil cautioned, however, that this is not proof of any genetic connection. DNA might be able to determine which area of the world the Pashtuns originated from, but it is not at all certain that it could identify a specific genetic link to the Jewish people. *(Extract from an article in The Observer. (London, England.) Sunday 17 January 2010).*

The article concerns a new DNA research programme being undertaken in this area. The actual story of the 'ten lost tribes' is just a myth. It is interesting that customs and practices of this people resemble Jewish traditions, as well as names being similar. In and of itself, of course it proves nothing. However, at least it is a start. It should be noted that in contrast, anything and everything ever discovered in any culture existing in the Americas, bears absolutely *no* resemblance whatsoever to either the Hebrew language, or Jewish or Christian beliefs, traditions, or culture.

In verses leading up to *2 Nephi 29:11-14* reviewed above *(p.418)*, Smith has Nephi prophesy that people will say: "A Bible! a Bible! We have got a Bible..." – a well known 'scripture' in Mormonism *(2 Nephi 29:3; See also: pp.437-9)*. It is preceded in v.2 by this:

> **2 Nephi 29:2.** And also, that I may remember the promises which I have made unto thee, Nephi, and also unto thy father, that I would remember your seed; and that ***the words of your seed should proceed forth out of my mouth unto your seed;*** and my words shall hiss forth unto the ends of the earth, for a standard unto my people, which are of the house of Israel; (Emphasis added).

This is another Smith manipulation, claiming words written by those who follow after Nephi will 'proceed' from God's mouth to even later descendants.

Once again, in the mind of the faithful, that will be nothing less than a confirmation of the authenticity of the *Book of Mormon*. Unfortunately, according to the *Book of Mormon* itself, all of Nephi's seed were dead many centuries before it was published and only Laman's and Lemuel's seed existed to hear about it. It was always assumed that the Lamanites were Native North Americans but that thinking had to change, due to major DNA evidence among other things.

> **2 Nephi 29:6.** Thou fool, that shall say: *A Bible*, we have got a *Bible*, and we need no more *Bible*. Have ye obtained a *Bible* save it were by the Jews?
> 7. Know ye not that there are more nations than one? Know ye not that I, the Lord your God, have created all men, and that I remember those who are upon the isles of the sea; and that I rule in the heavens above and in the earth beneath; and ***I bring forth my word unto the children of men, yea, even upon all the nations of the earth?***

## WHAT IS THE ROLE OF THE BOOK OF MORMON?

> **8.** Wherefore murmur ye, because that ye shall receive more of my word? Know ye not that *the testimony of two nations is a witness unto you that I am God*, that I remember one nation like unto another? Wherefore, *I speak the same words unto one nation like unto another*. And when the two nations shall run together the testimony of the two nations shall run together also.

As briefly mentioned in *Chapter 6*, Smith uses the word *Bible*, over and over again in references supposedly written hundreds of years BCE. The English word 'Bible' is a manufactured word. The word Bible does not occur *in* the Holy Scriptures. It originated from the Greek word for the papyrus (pa-Pie-rus) plant that Egyptians used to make paper. The Greeks called the plant 'biblos' and eventually writing products derived from the plant, such as scrolls, became known as biblos. An ancient Phoenician city named 'Byblos' derived its name from extensive manufacture and trade in writing materials. To invent the word *Bible*, scholars borrowed the plural Greek word 'biblia' meaning scrolls, or 'little books' and *created* the English word 'Bible'. Greeks still use 'biblia' (βιβλίο) today; it simply means 'book'. Early writings (scrolls) were circulated individually or in groups. It was not until the 4th century CE that the 'books' were all put in a single volume which *became* the 'Bible' in English. BCE, there was *no* Hebrew word for 'Bible' as it had yet to be invented.

In v.8 above, Smith has the Lord say "the testimony of two nations is a witness unto you that I am God" and he adds "I speak the same words unto one nation like unto another." This supposedly BCE statement was to quantify the reason why many *exact* New Testament words attributed to Jesus Christ would later appear prolifically in his book. Unfortunately, we now know that the gospels were not written until decades to centuries after Christ lived and they were written by people who never met or knew Jesus. For authenticity, they were ascribed (according) to Apostles. Therefore, even assuming there to be some truth in them, they most certainly do not contain words that are *exactly* the same as spoken by the Saviour. They might bear a *resemblance* to what he may have said but that is all. To have Christ speak words in the Americas that were *identical* to those appearing in the 1611 New Testament is tantamount to an admission that they are a hoax as it is completely impossible.

> **Jacob 4:1.** NOW behold, it came to pass that I, Jacob, having ministered much unto my people in word, (and *I cannot write but a little of my words*, because of the difficulty of engraving our words upon plates) and we know that the things which we write upon plates must remain;
> **2.** But whatsoever things we write upon anything save it be upon plates must perish and vanish away; but we can write a few words upon

> plates, which will give our children, and also our beloved brethren, a small degree of knowledge concerning us, or concerning their fathers—
> **3.** Now in this thing we do rejoice; and we labor diligently to engraven these words upon plates, hoping that our beloved brethren and our children will receive them with thankful hearts, and look upon them that they may learn with joy and not with sorrow, neither with contempt, concerning their first parents.
> **4.** For, for this intent have we written these things, that they may know that **we knew of Christ**, and we **had a hope of his glory many hundred years before his coming**; and not only we ourselves **had a hope** of his glory, but also all the holy prophets which were before us.
> **5.** Behold, they believed in Christ and worshiped the Father in his name, and also we worship the Father in his name. And for this intent we keep the law of Moses, it pointing our souls to him; and for this cause it is sanctified unto us for righteousness, even as it was accounted unto Abraham in the wilderness to be obedient unto the commands of God in offering up his son Isaac, which is a similitude of God and his Only Begotten Son.
> **6.** Wherefore, we search the prophets, and we have many revelations and the spirit of prophecy; and having all these witnesses we obtain a hope, and our faith becometh unshaken, insomuch that we truly can command in the name of Jesus and the very trees obey us, or the mountains, or the waves of the sea. (Emphasis added).

An objective reading of the above verses leads to the conclusion that if it was so difficult to write on plates and therefore they couldn't write very much, it would have been a good idea not to have written the first three verses at all. No matter how many times you read them and try to get something out of them, they remain entirely superfluous and utterly pointless. That's to say nothing of umpteen chapters of Isaiah painstakingly transcribed from the brass plates onto the gold plates which Smith never used, preferring to copy them straight from the *KJV*. Why bother?

God's English is awry once again too when dictating to Smith, as he says *(v.1)* "I cannot write but a little of my words", which means he will actually write a lot of them. To be correct, it should read "I *can* write but a little, or better yet – 'few', of my words." Once again, we see the slightly illiterate hand of Smith rather than God in the writing of this nonsense. In addition, the word 'engraven' is used in v.3. Even in Smith's time it should have been 'engrave' in order to convey the correct context.

Verse four indicates they wrote so their children would know that they, the writers, and all the prophets before them knew of Christ. This was supposedly written between 544 and 421 BCE, but Smith's mistake is that it is written in the *past tense* at a time which was the *present* for them. Another reference, *Jacob 1:6-7* says much the same thing, again in the past tense. This would not

# WHAT IS THE ROLE OF THE BOOK OF MORMON?

happen in a real setting. Once again, we have an affirmation that earlier prophets worshipped in Christ's *name* and that idea completely cuts across Judaism; not to mention the fact that the name didn't even exist then. The concept in v.6 that they could 'command' trees, mountains and waves, is of course further nonsense for which no evidence, or reason for it, has ever been seen in any era. It is just more Joseph Smith hype.

> **Enos 1:13.** And now behold, this was the desire which I desired of him—that *if it should so be, that my people, the Nephites, should fall into transgression, and by any means be destroyed, and the Lamanites should not be destroyed, that the Lord God would preserve a record of my people, the Nephites*; even if it so be by the power of his holy arm, *that it might be brought forth at some future day unto the Lamanites*, that, perhaps, they might be brought unto salvation—

In about 544-420 BCE, there were still only a very few people in the group. Nevertheless, Enos prays to ask that if by any chance his descendants, who are already called Nephites, should fall into transgression and get destroyed, but the Lamanites do not get destroyed, could the Lord please preserve a record of them which may then later be 'brought forth' and perhaps *convert* residual Lamanites. Think very carefully about this claim – the irrationality will dawn.

Smith already knew the plot of his book and here he plays out the final pages, as well as the book 'coming forth', so he could 'prophesy' what would happen. It was a bit too soon really, but that was Smith for you. Remember, he was writing the book in 1828-9 and 'bringing it forth' right there and then.

Writing that verse tells us more than the story Joseph Smith intended. It just typifies his arrogance and his innovation. I have often wondered, as they could all apparently record what went on, why the Lamanites didn't keep their own records and tell their side of the story. But then, they were the bad guys and lost the ability to read and write in the way the Nephites managed to. Perhaps they were Cherokee, as the Cherokee nation had no alphabet or written language until someone later worked it out for them. (That was obviously not a serious comment). I have studied all Native North American tribes and *none* match, or even resemble, the remotest of *Book of Mormon* language possibilities.

> **Omni 1:25.** And it came to pass that I began to be old; and, having no seed, and knowing king Benjamin to be a just man before the Lord, wherefore, I shall deliver up these plates unto him, exhorting all men to **come unto God, the Holy One of Israel**, and believe in prophesying, and in revelations, and in the ministering of angels, and in the gift of speaking with tongues, and in the gift of interpreting languages, and in all things which are good; for there is nothing which is good save it comes from the Lord; and that which is evil cometh from the devil.

> **26.** And now, my beloved brethren, I would that ye should **come unto Christ, who is the Holy One of Israel**, and partake of his salvation, and the power of his redemption. Yea, come unto him, and offer your whole souls as an offering unto him, and continue in fasting and praying, and endure to the end; and as the Lord liveth ye will be saved.

This was in about 200 BCE. Christ is once again spoken of in an impossible timeframe. Note that in v.25, God is the 'Holy one of Israel', and in v.26 it is Christ who is. Once again, we see here Smith theology of 1828-9. He believed they were one and the same being, whichever way he described things.

In July of 1828, Smith was writing the *Book of Mormon* and in a supposed revelation which became *D&C 3*, he included the following. We have already reviewed several references on this area from the missionary lesson manual. This is yet another one.

> **D&C 3:16.** Nevertheless, *my work shall go forth*, for inasmuch as the knowledge of a Savior has come unto the world, through the testimony of the Jews, even so shall the ***knowledge of a Savior come unto my people***—
> **17.** And to ***the Nephites, and the Jacobites, and the Josephites, and the Zoramites***, through the testimony of their fathers—
> **18.** And this testimony shall come ***to the knowledge of the Lamanites, and the Lemuelites, and the Ishmaelites***, who dwindled in unbelief because of the iniquity of their fathers, whom the Lord has suffered to destroy their brethren the Nephites, because of their iniquities and their abominations.
> **19.** And *for this very purpose are these plates preserved*, which contain these records—that *the promises of the Lord might be fulfilled, which he made to his people*;
> **20.** And *that the Lamanites might come to the knowledge of their fathers*, and that *they might know the promises of the Lord, and that they may believe the gospel* and rely upon the merits of Jesus Christ, and be glorified through faith in his name, and that through their repentance they might be saved. Amen.

Here we have a Smith *revelation* which distinctly states "my work shall go forth" to the *Nephites*, who were actually all destroyed in the end, but Smith hadn't written that part of the *Book of Mormon* when he wrote this revelation to the Jacobites, Josephites, Zoramites, Lamanites, Lemuelites and Ishmaelites.

At the time (1828-29), and indeed even when I was a Mormon, these were considered to consist of *all* Native North American tribes, as *Book of Mormon* characters were considered to be the *only* ones there. Many people over the years have been sent on missions *to* the 'Lamanites', both in North America and the Islands of the Pacific. *(See also pp. 436-7).*

# WHAT IS THE ROLE OF THE BOOK OF MORMON?

> With pride I tell those who come to my office that *a Lamanite is a descendant of one Lehi who left Jerusalem six hundred years before Christ* and with his family crossed the mighty deep and landed in America. And Lehi and his family became the *ancestors of all of the Indian and Mestizo tribes in North and South and Central America and in the islands of the sea,* for in the middle of their history there were those who left America in ships of their making and went to the islands of the sea. Not until the revelations of Joseph Smith, bringing forth the Book of Mormon, did anyone know of these migrants. It was not known before, but *now the question is fully answered.* Now *the Lamanites number about sixty million; they are in all of the states of America from Tierra del Fuego all the way up to Point Barrows, and they are in nearly all the islands of the sea from Hawaii South to New Zealand ... The descendants of this mighty people were called Indians by Columbus in 1492* when he found them here. *The term Lamanite includes all Indians and Indian mixtures, such as Polynesians, the Guatemalans, the Peruvians, as well as the Sioux, the Apache, the Mohawk, the Navajo, and others.* It is a large group of great people. *(Spencer W. Kimball. Of Royal Blood. Ensign: July 1971:7).* (Emphasis added) *(See also TMD Vol. 2:174-183).*

Today, Mormon apologists cannot sustain what was once considered to be absolute truth and they postulate all sorts of nonsense instead. Mormon leaders, as ever, just keep quiet. Judging by the above now embarrassing comments by Kimball, perhaps they may have learned some harsh lessons from the past.

Kimball was supposed to be a prophet and yet is now proven to have been entirely mistaken about who the Lamanites were. It has been conclusively proven through extensive DNA testing that they are 'none of the above'.

Mormon apologists are still searching in vain for plausible alternatives.

In the summer of 1828, following the loss of the first 116 pages of the *Book of Mormon,* Joseph Smith penned another revelation, including the following recommended reading mentioned in the lesson manual. Again, the gospel was to go to the Lamanites – and Smith *knew* who they were.

> **D&C 10:46.** And, behold, all the remainder of this work does contain all those parts of my gospel which my holy prophets, yea, and also my disciples, desired in their prayers should come forth unto this people.
> **47.** And I said unto them, that it should be granted unto them according to their faith in their prayers;
> **48.** Yea, and *this was their faith—that my gospel, which I gave unto them that they might preach in their days, might come unto their brethren the Lamanites*, and also all that had become Lamanites because of their dissensions.

# THE MORMON DELUSION

## The Book of Mormon and the Bible Support Each Other

> The LDS edition of the King James Version of the Bible and the Book of Mormon have cross-references and study aids that make *the stick of Judah (the Bible) and the stick of Joseph (the Book of Mormon) one in our hands* (see Ezekiel 37:15–17; see also 1 Nephi 13:34–41; 2 Nephi 3:12; 29:8). *Give priority to Book of Mormon passages when you teach*, but also show how the Book of Mormon and the Bible teach the same principles. (Emphasis added). *(Page 105).*

Missionaries are advised to "give priority to *Book of Mormon* passages when you teach." The idea that the *Book of Mormon* and the Bible support each other is somewhat short lived in many ways when you discover that the *Book of Mormon* claims Jesus Christ was known in Old Testament times and all the prophets prayed to God in the name of Jesus. Naturally, the Bible does not support that idea, or indeed many other Mormon ideas, at all. Nevertheless, the Church continues to maintain that each supports the other. Members do not see through the many obvious contradictions.

Not least of the liberties taken with the Bible by the Mormon Church is the concept that the Bible is the 'stick of Judah' and the *Book of Mormon* is the 'stick of Joseph' in Ezekiel 37:15-17. Thus the Bible and *Book of Mormon* can be *one* in our hands. I simply accepted this as a member and found great comfort in my 'quad' when the Church started to produce them. That is a quadruple combination of all the scriptures, including the *King James Bible, Book of Mormon, D&C* and *Pearl of Great Price*, all in one handy volume – 'one in our hands'. Let's look at what Ezekiel says and what he *really* means.

> **Ezeliel 37:15.** The word of the LORD came again unto me, saying,
> 16. Moreover, *thou son of man, take thee one stick, and write upon it*, For Judah, and for the children of Israel his companions: *then take another stick, and write upon it*, For Joseph, the stick of Ephraim, and for all the house of Israel his companions:
> 17. And join them one to another into one stick; and they shall become one in thine hand. (Emphasis added). *(See also: NIV, p.525).*

The above is from the *KJV* which Joseph Smith had access to. He used the idea to justify the *Book of Mormon* in an 1830 *D&C* revelation *(D&C 27:5).*

Only now do I begin to understand the real meaning of Ezekiel and what nonsense the Mormon claim is. Ezekiel was not speaking about *books* at all in the way the Mormon Church claims. It is actually quite clear when you read more of Chapter 37 even in the *KJV*, but as Mormons, we just don't put it all together. Ironically, v. 18 actually *asks* what the previous verses really mean and then an explanation is proffered. The truth is right there in black and white.

# WHAT IS THE ROLE OF THE BOOK OF MORMON?

**Ezekiel 37:18.** And when the children of thy people shall speak unto thee, saying, *Wilt thou not shew us what thou meanest by these?*
**19.** Say unto them, Thus saith the Lord GOD; Behold, I will take *the stick of Joseph*, which *is* in the hand of Ephraim, and *the tribes of Israel his fellows*, and will *put them with him, even with the stick of Judah*, and make them one stick, and they shall be one in mine hand.
**20.** And *the sticks whereon thou writest* shall be in thine hand before their eyes.
**21.** And say unto them, Thus saith the Lord GOD; Behold, *I will take the children of Israel from among the heathen, whither they be gone, and will gather them on every side, and bring them into their own land:*
*22. And I will make them one nation in the land upon the mountains of Israel; and one king shall be king to them all: and they shall be no more two nations, neither shall they be divided into two kingdoms any more at all:* (Emphasis added).

So, we see that rather than remotely speaking about two 'books' it relates to two *kingdoms* being brought together under one king. So, what was the writing all about? A clearer translation gives a much better idea. The *New International Version* of the Bible helps with this and reads:

**One Nation Under One King.**

**NIV. Ezekiel 37:15.** The word of the LORD came to me:
**16.** "Son of man, take a stick of wood and write on it, 'Belonging to Judah and the Israelites associated with him.' Then take another stick of wood, and write on it, 'Ephraim's stick, belonging to Joseph and all the house of Israel associated with him.'
**17.** Join them together into one stick so that they will become one in your hand.
**18.** "When your countrymen ask you, 'Won't you tell us what you mean by this?'
**19.** say to them, 'This is what the Sovereign LORD says: I am going to take the stick of Joseph—which is in Ephraim's hand—and of the Israelite tribes associated with him, and join it to Judah's stick, making them a single stick of wood, and they will become one in my hand.'
**20.** Hold before their eyes the sticks you have written on
**21.** and say to them, 'This is what the Sovereign LORD says: I will take the Israelites out of the nations where they have gone. I will gather them from all around and bring them back into their own land.
**22.** I will make them one nation in the land, on the mountains of Israel. There will be one king over all of them and they will never again be two nations or be divided into two kingdoms.

## THE MORMON DELUSION

The Mormon Church would have it that the two 'sticks' were *scrolls* or *books*; one being the Bible and the other, the *Book of Mormon*. However, the scripture clearly states that it was *Ezekiel* who was to do the writing in *both* cases. *(See emphasised text in KJV Ezekiel 37:15-17 on p.426)*. He was also told exactly *what* to write on each stick and the above *NIV* translation tells it all really.

One stick was to have written on it the words:

> For Judah, and for the children of Israel his companions.

The other stick was to say:

> For Joseph, the stick of Ephraim, and for all the house of Israel his companions.

In each case, the letter 'F' in the word 'For' is capitalised, signifying the start of what to actually *write on* each *stick*. It is not an indication of what is to be written 'for' or on behalf of the tribes in books, as is the Mormon claim.

There are forty writers and sixty-six scrolls forming the Bible, and many authors supposedly contributed to the *Book of Mormon*. It is *Ezekiel* who is to write *on* both *sticks* in Ezekiel 37. It is only the Mormon Church that disagrees.

The Mormon Church claims 'stick' means 'scroll' in Ezekiel. Never mind that the *Book of Mormon* was supposedly written on gold plates and *not* scrolls. In any event, Ezekiel clearly identifies that he knows the difference between an actual stick and a scroll. In an entirely different context, Ezekiel writes:

> **Ezekiel 2:9.** And when I looked, behold, an hand was sent unto me; and, lo, a roll of a book was therein;

From what I now understand, following some research, the Hebrew word translated as 'stick' in Ezekiel is pronounced 'ets'. There are quite a variety of English words appearing in the Old Testament translated from 'ets', depending on the context. Alphabetically, these are: gallows, helve, plank, staff, stalk, stick, stock, timber, tree and wood. It is *never* translated as: book, roll, scroll, parchment or papyri, let alone metal plates of gold, brass or any other material.

'Stick' did *not* mean 'scroll' as the Mormon Church now claims. A cursory glance at Ezekiel as a Mormon leaves you feeling warm and fuzzy because you trust your leaders and the Lord has revealed the truth to them. In fact, it can bolster a testimony. Likewise, an investigator may be convinced by a Mormon missionary explanation of *Ezekiel 37*. However, an objective review of the real meaning, translation and explanation provides, once again, quite an opposite conclusion to the Mormon claim.

# WHAT IS THE ROLE OF THE BOOK OF MORMON?

Back to the lesson manual...

> As you use the **Book of Mormon and the Bible as companion volumes** of scripture, they ***will overcome contention and correct false doctrine*** (see 2 Nephi 3:12). The Bible teaches the following about the law of witnesses: "In the mouth of two or three witnesses shall every word be established" (2 Corinthians 13:1). In harmony with this law, **both the Book of Mormon and the Bible testify of Jesus Christ**. (Emphasis added). *(Page 106).*

How the Church can claim that *together* the Bible and *Book of Mormon* "will overcome contention and correct false doctrine" is beyond me, as much of the modern-day Mormon theology does not match the Bible by any stretch of the imagination. In point of fact, it doesn't match the *Book of Mormon* either, as so much evolved and changed after Joseph Smith wrote it. The above statement from the lesson manual refers to *2 Nephi 3:12*.

> **2 Nephi 3:12.** Wherefore, the *fruit of thy loins* shall write; and *the fruit of the loins* of Judah shall write; and that which shall be written by the *fruit of thy loins*, and also that which shall be written by the *fruit of the loins* of Judah, shall grow together, unto the confounding of false doctrines and laying down of contentions, and establishing peace among the *fruit of thy loins*, and bringing them to the knowledge of their fathers in the latter days, and also to the knowledge of my covenants, saith the Lord. *(Between 588 and 570 BCE).*

This is supposed to support the Mormon concept that it was prophesied both the Nephites and the tribe of Judah would keep written records. It isn't difficult to write that in 1828-9 when you have the Bible to hand, and claim it was written hundreds of years BCE. Smith has this set hundreds of years before someone else coined the phrase "fruit of his loins" so, was Smith's use of it just coincidence or was it evidence of further plagiarism? Smith was in the habit of constantly repeating pet phrases and this one is no exception. Once he had used it once, he couldn't resist repeating it over and over in the same chapter.

2 Nephi 3:12 is one single sentence in which Smith uses the phrase no less than five times. He uses a similar phrase some *twenty times* in 2 Nephi 3, then in *Jacob (2:25)*, and in the *D&C (132:30)* where Smith has God say that he, Smith, was himself of the 'fruit of the loins' of Abraham, and also in the *Book of Moses (8:2)*. Smith plagiarised the phrase from the New Testament:

> **Acts 2:30.** Therefore being a prophet, and knowing that God had sworn with an oath to him, that *of the fruit of his loins*, according to the flesh, he would raise up Christ to sit on his throne; (Emphasis added).

Acts was probably written by the same *author* as Luke, but unlikely written *by* Luke, and in any event, certainly not before 70-90 CE.

## What does the Bible say about the Book of Mormon?

Of course, the Bible doesn't say *anything* about the *Book of Mormon* at all as the *Book of Mormon* is a work of pure nineteenth-century fiction, but nevertheless the Church tries to make three references fit the bill:

> **John 10:16.** And other sheep I have, which are not of this fold: them also I must bring, and they shall hear my voice; and there shall be one fold, and one shepherd.

The Mormon Church claims this refers to the Nephites, but that of course is pure supposition and even then only *if* you already believe the *Book of Mormon* to be a true account of a real people. In the Bible, Jesus seemed to become 'aware' at some stage, perhaps at age twelve in the temple, that He was the Son of God. Would he also have had specific knowledge, or memory, of the Nephites? It is a question that doesn't even deserve consideration, as the fact is that the entire world was already well populated and the reference that Christ made was to people living outside the immediate area that he considered also needed teaching.

His new radical ideas and gospel teachings, most of which diametrically opposed the Law of Moses, weren't just for Jews, they were also for 'Gentiles'. The apostles took up the challenge of teaching others, hence the travels and the churches later established by disciples in other locations. No one even knew the Americas existed at that time in the Holy Land. It doesn't take much common sense to understand the scripture. It *only* means what the Mormon Church *claims* it means, to deluded Mormons who *decide* to believe it. To everyone else in the world, the real meaning is perfectly clear and glaringly obvious.

The second scripture claimed to be speaking of the *Book of Mormon* is from *Ezekiel 37* which was covered earlier in this chapter. *(See: pp.426-8)*.

Finally, we have *Isaiah 29:4, 11-18*. This is one of the chapters of Isaiah Smith copied directly from the *KJV* into the *Book of Mormon* where it becomes *2 Nephi 27*. In the Mormon edition of the *KJV*, the header makes an outrageous claim that the –

> *Nephites shall speak as a voice from the dust—The apostasy, restoration of the gospel, and coming forth of Book of Mormon are foretold—Compare 2 Nephi 27.* (Italics in original).

# WHAT IS THE ROLE OF THE BOOK OF MORMON?

**Isaiah 29:4.** And thou shalt be brought down, and shalt speak out of the ground, and thy speech shall be low out of the dust, and thy voice shall be, as of one that hath a familiar spirit, out of the ground, and thy speech shall whisper out of the dust.

**11.** And the vision of all is become unto you as the words of a book that is sealed, which men deliver to one that is learned, saying, Read this, I pray thee: and he saith, I cannot; for it is sealed:

**12.** And the book is delivered to him that is not learned, saying, Read this, I pray thee: and he saith, I am not learned.

**13.** Wherefore the Lord said, Forasmuch as this people draw near me with their mouth, and with their lips do honour me, but have removed their heart far from me, and their fear toward me is taught by the precept of men:

**14.** Therefore, behold, I will proceed to do a marvellous work among this people, even a marvellous work and a wonder: for the wisdom of their wise men shall perish, and the understanding of their prudent men shall be hid.

**15.** Woe unto them that seek deep to hide their counsel from the Lord, and their works are in the dark, and they say, Who seeth us? and who knoweth us?

**16.** Surely your turning of things upside down shall be esteemed as the potter's clay: for shall the work say of him that made it, He made me not? or shall the thing framed say of him that framed it, He had no understanding?

**17.** Is it not yet a very little while, and Lebanon shall be turned into a fruitful field, and the fruitful field shall be esteemed as a forest?

**18.** And in that day shall the deaf hear the words of the book, and the eyes of the blind shall see out of obscurity, and out of darkness.

The topic of the 'sealed book' has already been fully covered *(TMD Vol.2: 99-108)*, but realising that some readers may not have that volume, I have included it as *Appendix D* so as not to leave out relevant information. It is clear that Smith tried to use biblical scripture to validate his work and Martin Harris tried to make his efforts somehow fulfil that scripture. The reality however was something else entirely as will be seen from *Appendix D*.

Next, the manual puts the question the other way round:

## What does the Book of Mormon say about the Bible?

This time there are four references from the *Book of Mormon* that supposedly speak of the Bible. These should actually at face value be quite convincing, as Smith penned the words of his *Book of Mormon* around 1828-9 when he had the *KJV* to hand. In order for anything to be verified, then of course further evidence would be required. But what can we make of what *is* claimed to be said about the Bible in the *Book of Mormon*?

The first reference provided for us is *1 Nephi 13:20-29, 40-41*. The header confirms the Mormon Church's interpretation of the text and what it refers to. Smith was well aware of the earlier discovery of the Americas of course and simply wrote about it in his book and backdated it to around 600 BCE. It should also be noted that if Smith believed many "plain and precious parts of the Bible" had been lost, he didn't exactly *restore* any of them when he wrote his so-called 'Inspired Revision' of the Bible between 1831 and 1834.

> *Nephi sees in vision: the church of the devil set up among the Gentiles; the discovery and colonizing of America; the loss of many plain and precious parts of the Bible; the resultant state of gentile apostasy; the restoration of the gospel, the coming forth of latter-day scripture, and the building up of Zion. Between 600 and 592 B.C.*

**1 Nephi 13:20.** And it came to pass that I, Nephi, beheld that they did prosper in the land; and I beheld a book, and it was carried forth among them.

**21.** And the angel said unto me: Knowest thou the meaning of the book?

**22.** And I said unto him: I know not.

**23.** And he said: Behold it proceedeth out of the mouth of a Jew. And I, Nephi, beheld it; and he said unto me: The book that thou beholdest is a record of the Jews, which contains the covenants of the Lord, which he hath made unto the house of Israel; and it also containeth many of the prophecies of the holy prophets; and it is a record like unto the engravings which are upon the plates of brass, save there are not so many; nevertheless, they contain the covenants of the Lord, which he hath made unto the house of Israel; wherefore, they are of great worth unto the Gentiles.

**24.** And the angel of the Lord said unto me: Thou hast beheld that the book proceeded forth from the mouth of a Jew; and when it proceeded forth from the mouth of a Jew it contained the fulness of the gospel of the Lord, of whom the twelve apostles bear record; and they bear record according to the truth which is in the Lamb of God.

**25.** Wherefore, these things go forth from the Jews in purity unto the Gentiles, according to the truth which is in God.

There is a major problem for Smith here, in that there was no such thing as a *book* containing *all* the scriptures at the time of Christ. What was eventually to become the *Old Testament* simply consisted at that time of many individual papyrus scrolls. These were in effect individual 'books' but 'Bible' was not a known word at that time. It was centuries later when some of the scrolls were

# WHAT IS THE ROLE OF THE BOOK OF MORMON?

integrated into one compilation which became the 'Bible' as we now know it. The invented term was taken from Greek 'biblos' which actually *means* 'book'.

> **1 Nephi 13:26.** And after they go forth by the hand of the twelve apostles of the Lamb, from the Jews unto the Gentiles, thou seest the formation of that great and abominable church, which is most abominable above all other churches; for behold, they have taken away from the gospel of the Lamb many parts which are plain and most precious; and also many covenants of the Lord have they taken away.
> **27.** And all this have they done that they might pervert the right ways of the Lord, that they might blind the eyes and harden the hearts of the children of men.
> **28.** Wherefore, thou seest that after the book hath gone forth through the hands of the great and abominable church, that there are many plain and precious things taken away from the book, which is the book of the Lamb of God.
> **29.** And after these plain and precious things were taken away it goeth forth unto all the nations of the Gentiles; and after it goeth forth unto all the nations of the Gentiles, yea, even across the many waters which thou hast seen with the Gentiles which have gone forth out of captivity, thou seest—because of the many plain and precious things which have been taken out of the book, which were plain unto the understanding of the children of men, according to the plainness which is in the Lamb of God—because of these things which are taken away out of the gospel of the Lamb, an exceedingly great many do stumble, yea, insomuch that Satan hath great power over them.

It does seem strange to me that Smith could make such claims and that we could be gullible enough not to see through them. It is all so obvious when you step back and look at the reality. The Old Testament, which is all that Smith could be considering as he places the words of *1 Nephi* to hundreds of years BCE, pretty much mirrors the *Tanakh*, which also includes writings not in the Old Testament and which Joseph Smith could have drawn on, had he been a real prophet and considered them worthwhile. Original Hebrew texts in the *Tanakh* which *do* mirror the Old Testament and are still used today by Jews, do not vary that significantly from the *KJV* or other even more recent translations of the Bible, indicating that there are *no* plain and precious parts that were removed after the time of Jesus.

If that actually had been the case, then surely the Lord would have simply instructed Smith to use an English translation of the *Tanakh* instead of the *KJV*. He didn't. Additionally, when the Bible was first constructed, well into the CE, hundreds of texts were available from which to draw and some of those not included are still accessible, so Smith could have researched them and included them. The fact is that Smith did not consider the non-inclusion of entire books, but rather the alteration of a few generally meaningless words within the Bible he was familiar with and we also have in the form of the *KJV*. It is fascinating that Smith claimed the Bible was effectively 'tampered' with when in reality it is not the Bible but the *Book of Mormon* which has had many *thousands* of alterations to text, grammar and punctuation since the first edition.

> **1 Nephi 13:40.** And the angel spake unto me, saying: These last records, which thou hast seen among the Gentiles, shall establish the truth of the first, which are of the twelve apostles of the Lamb, and shall make known the plain and precious things which have been taken away from them; and shall make known to all kindreds, tongues, and people, that **the Lamb of God is the Son of the Eternal Father, and the Savior of the world**; and that all men must come unto him, or they cannot be saved. (Emphasis added).

The above verse *(40)* is in fact one of those we covered in *Chapter 5* which originally read "the lamb of God *is* the Eternal Father, and the Savior of the world" *(See: p.98)* which Smith later *changed* to match new theological ideas.

The missionaries are of course not told about this, let alone instructed to make investigators aware of such *falsifications* prior to them making a lifelong commitment to a Church spawned from Smith's fraudulent claims. It is, at least to me, ***an absolute conspiracy to deceive*** and ***defraud*** people, luring them into a false religion through equally false accounts, not to reveal *original* wording.

> **1 Nephi 13:41.** And they must come according to the words which shall be established by the mouth of the Lamb; and the words of the Lamb shall be made known in the records of thy seed, as well as ***in the records of the twelve apostles of the Lamb***; wherefore they both shall be established in one; for there is one God and one Shepherd over all the earth.

Unfortunately for Smith, there are no 'records' made by all 'twelve apostles of the lamb'. He obviously thought the gospels were written by the very people they were later 'ascribed' to, when in fact none of the twelve apostles recorded anything at all as far as has been verified to date. Matthew did not write the book of Mathew. Mark and Luke were not apostles, and even then did not write those books directly. John, the apostle, did not *write* John; it was a construct by the Romans to describe the character they would have liked the Saviour to have been. Revelation is considered by many theologians to be the work of a lunatic which never should have scraped its way into the final canon of the Bible in the fourth century CE. Orthodox churches do not use it for readings. There is wide agreement that Acts was by the same *author* as Luke, but it wasn't Luke. Saul, who became Paul, never met Jesus, except in a supposed visionary experience.

# WHAT IS THE ROLE OF THE BOOK OF MORMON?

I could go on, but the fact of the matter is that the gospels were written decades to centuries after the death of Christ by people who never met or knew Jesus, so Smith's *Book of Mormon* claim is not plausible or sustainable.

The next reference is *3 Nephi 23:1* dated to 34 CE.

> **3 Nephi 23:1.** And now, behold, I say unto you, that ye ought to search these things. Yea, a commandment I give unto you that ye search these things diligently; for great are the words of Isaiah.

There is not a lot that can be said about that reference. The Mormon Church considers it 'evidence' that the *Book of Mormon* supports the Bible, when in fact all it does is show that Smith *copied* huge chunks of *Isaiah* into the *Book of Mormon*. Anyone can do that and it *proves* nothing – other than Joseph Smith's plagiarism, as he also copied translation errors and almost identical grammar, identifying conclusively the *exact* origin of the material.

As mentioned elsewhere, apologists who claim Smith may have noticed the similarity and just used the *KJV* for that instead of translating the plates, fail to remember the Church accepted fact that Smith was reading words dictated into his hat by God while the supposed gold plates were wrapped up or even buried elsewhere and he didn't even look at them. To suggest Smith then said "Never mind God, I will just copy that from the Bible" is of course equally ludicrous and the hoax is once again thoroughly exposed.

The third reference is *Mormon 7:8-9*. The header to that chapter reads:

> *Mormon invites the Lamanites of the latter days to believe in Christ, accept his gospel, and be saved*—***All who believe the Bible will also believe the Book of Mormon.*** *About A.D. 385.* (Bold added).

The idea that those who believe the Bible will also believe the *Book of Mormon* has turned out to be a bit of a non-starter for the Church. More so, is the idea this is prophecy that Native Americans will have the Bible and the *Book of Mormon* – which was once considered to be about their ancestors, whereupon they will join the Church. Not only does every single word of any Native North, Central or South American history, myth or legend, completely contradict the *Book of Mormon*, they also contradict Christianity and Judaism.

> **Mormon 7:8.** Therefore repent, and be baptized in the name of Jesus, and lay hold upon the gospel of Christ, which shall be set before you, not only in this record but also in the record which shall come unto the Gentiles from the Jews, which record shall come from the Gentiles unto you.
> **9.** For behold, this is written for the intent that ye may believe that; and if ye believe that ye will believe this also; and if ye believe this ye will

> know concerning your fathers, and also the marvelous works which were wrought by the power of God among them.

Smith claims Native Americans will believe the Bible – and therefore the *Book of Mormon* as it concerns their ancestors. The Church long believed that all Native Americans and peoples of the islands were Lamanites. They play this down now to the extent that *none* can be located – they somehow 'integrated' into existing cultures. The Church appears to erroneously believe that MtDNA becomes 'diluted' – so much so that it cannot be identified. They should check, and accept, the underlying science, which they clearly do not understand at all.

Times do change within Mormonism. I previously went into detail about the statement made by Mormon prophet, Spencer W. Kimball *(See: p.425)*. Just to expand a little on that statement; Kimball's remarks were preceded by an introduction entitled "Lamanites".

That introduction included the statement:

> "Most members of the Church know that the Lamanites, who consist of the Indians of all the Americas as well as the islanders of the Pacific, are a people with a special heritage."

So, the *direct* descendants of Lehi (then sixty million of them) are then, *everywhere*. Kimball claimed that **all** the Native American Indian and Mestizo tribes covering the Americas and the islands had descended from Lehi. That idea is now proven (and accepted) as entirely ***false*** in every way. Two years later, Kimball became prophet. As early as 1954, when Kimball was an apostle, he was already convinced as to who the Lamanites were:

> "…the Indian or Lamanite, with a background of twenty-five centuries of superstition, degradation, idolatry, and indolence… a people who, according to prophecies, have been scattered and driven, defrauded and deprived, who are a "branch of the tree of Israel - lost from its body - wanderers in a strange land" - their own land… They may be Navajos or Cherokees… Mayas or Pimas… Piutes or Mohicans… these living descendants… will be redeemed, will rise and will become a blessed people. God has said it." *(Spencer W. Kimball, Conference Report, Apr. 1954:106-108).*

Kimball later made similar remarks, in 1975, when he was actually the prophet of the Church. He then stated: "When the Navajos returned from Fort Sumner after a shameful and devastating captivity, there were only 9,000 of them left; now there are more than 100,000. ***There are nearly 130 million Lamanites worldwide.***" He also said that: ***"There are now more than 350,000 Lamanite members of the Church."*** *(See: TMD Vol. 2:176-77).*

# WHAT IS THE ROLE OF THE BOOK OF MORMON?

In 1971, Kimball declared there were sixty million Lamanites *(see p.425)* and by 1975 he increased this number to one-hundred-and-thirty million; such was his confidence that anyone and everyone in the Americas was included.

The only way that the Mormon Church today can wriggle out of the mess created by Kimball, is to revert to the age old Mormon trick of claiming a prophet doesn't always speak *as* a prophet and all that was just his own, clearly scientifically very wrong, personal opinion. Nevertheless, when Kimball spoke those things *he* clearly believed they *were* true, through his own faith in Joseph Smith and the *Book of Mormon*. The Church cannot have it both ways. Either, a prophet *is* a prophet and when he speaks from the stand he speaks *as* a prophet, or he is no such thing at all. How would rank and file Mormons ever know what the truth was otherwise? I *heard* and *read* that *in* 1971/5 and **believed** it.

Judging by evidence of the constructed lies to their own converts, as taught by early Mormon apostles when they were in England, defending the Church against claims of polygamy whilst each having several wives back in Salt Lake City – it is clear that nothing changes in Mormonism and things are still made up as they go along, even today. What was accepted by *everyone* as the truth in 1970/5 is now embarrassingly refuted through documented scientific evidence.

The final reference is *2 Nephi 29:3-14*. The chapter heading reads:

> *Many gentiles shall reject the Book of Mormon—They shall say: We need no more Bible—The Lord speaks to many nations—He will judge the world out of the books thus written. Between 559 and 545 B.C.*

This aspect was somewhat covered earlier in this chapter *(See: Pp.420-21)* identifying the impossibility of Smith's *Book of Mormon* claim set hundreds of years BCE, that future people would mention the then unknown word 'Bible'.

If the Church should claim the word was simply a modern day 'translation' from 'reformed Egyptian', I would be interested to know what it was translated *from*, as there was no such equivalent word at that time in *any* language at all. The whole *concept* was yet to be invented. These are more verses now quoted by the manual, which, apart from v.6, were not included earlier in this chapter.

> **2 Nephi 29:3.** And because my words shall hiss forth—many of the Gentiles shall say: A Bible! A Bible! We have got a Bible, and there cannot be any more Bible.
> **4.** But thus saith the Lord God: O fools, they shall have a Bible; and it shall proceed forth from the Jews, mine ancient covenant people. And what thank they the Jews for the Bible which they receive from them? Yea, what do the Gentiles mean? Do they remember the travails, and the labors, and the pains of the Jews, and their diligence unto me, in bringing forth salvation unto the Gentiles?

> **5.** O ye Gentiles, have ye remembered the Jews, mine ancient covenant people? Nay; but ye have cursed them, and have hated them, and have not sought to recover them. But behold, I will return all these things upon your own heads; for I the Lord have not forgotten my people.
> **6.** Thou fool, that shall say: A Bible, we have got a Bible, and we need no more Bible. Have ye obtained a Bible save it were by the Jews?

It is interesting that Smith not only claims this was written BCE but that he confirms, or claims God is confirming, that the Jews are His covenant people.

Surely the correct 'message' then would be to become a Jew? Whatever the case, Smith impossibly claims 'Bible' a known word and creates the notion that people will reject the *Book of Mormon* on the basis that they already have the Bible and that is enough. That is an easy construct when you are in 1828-9 with the Bible to hand and you want to sell your new book. The hoax is exposed by the use of impossibilities.

> **9.** And I do this that I may prove unto many that I am the same yesterday, today, and forever; and that I speak forth my words according to mine own pleasure. And because that I have spoken one word ye need not suppose that I cannot speak another; for my work is not yet finished; neither shall it be until the end of man, neither from that time henceforth and forever.
> **10.** Wherefore, because that ye have a Bible ye need not suppose that it contains all my words; neither need ye suppose that I have not caused more to be written.

In the above verses, Smith is setting out his stall to sell copies of the *Book of Mormon* by predicting (BCE) that the book will eventually come about. The whole original objective Joseph Smith had was simply book sales. It was to be a money making project. Another thing is – would God *really* speak that way?

In the next verses *(v.11-14)* which we covered on p.418, Smith claims that God commanded the 'Jews' and the 'Nephites', the 'ten lost tribes' and 'all nations', plus people of 'the islands of the sea' to ***all*** write down the things He tells them. These will then be shared with each other so everyone will know all about God and make records of what He has told them.

There is only one, and glaringly obvious, problem with this idea – it never happened. There are *no* records from all the nations or islands where God has spoken to them. Most areas and islands are replete with diverse religions and customs that bear absolutely no resemblance to either Christianity or Judaism.

Does Joseph Smith wish us to embrace the concept that God *did* speak to Mohammed, the prophet of Islam, along with all other religious leaders around the world over the centuries. The 'records' that *are* available from any area of the world bear *no* resemblance to Smith's teachings, and the lost tribes don't exist as such, so we would not expect their records to turn up any time soon.

# WHAT IS THE ROLE OF THE BOOK OF MORMON?

Whatever Smith claimed should be *shared* is not consistent with his belief system. There are thousands of Christian denominations, before even starting to count those following entirely different religious belief systems. It would not exactly be helpful if all the records compiled by all the religions were shared and accepted as coming from God. They are diverse and contradictory. No one God could have been involved with many of the conflicting Christian concepts, let alone the rest. Either Smith got it wrong; or God is very devious; or – there are hundreds of gods, all touting for business among various different cultures.

## In what ways do both books serve as testaments of Christ?

There are three references for this question; one from the *Book of Mormon* and two from the Bible. *(See manual p.106)*. The *Book of Mormon* reference is:

> **2 Nephi 29:8.** Wherefore murmur ye, because that ye shall receive more of my word? Know ye not that ***the testimony of two nations is a witness unto you that I am God***, that I remember one nation like unto another? Wherefore, ***I speak the same words unto one nation like unto another.*** And when the two nations shall run together the testimony of the two nations shall run together also.

Note that despite the heading, this verse doesn't mention Christ at all. The Bible verses have to accommodate that aspect. Meanwhile, it contains major problems for the Mormon Church. We looked at this verse earlier *(See p.421)*, but it is additionally interesting to note that Smith now claims God will speak the *same words* to each nation. We have just reviewed the fact that Smith has his God claim He will speak to *all* nations and islands and have them write what He says, when in fact *none* ever have. Well, that is not entirely true according to some nations of course, but where they claim He *has* spoken, their Gods have apparently told them entirely conflicting things which have resulted in many different religions across the world. Smith's 'Book of Mormon' God is extremely inconsistent if such concepts all stem from Him.

If God *did* speak to *all* nations and Islands, then where are the records from Australia, Africa, Hawaii, Europe, Iceland etc? And why do such records that religious groups in some other nations *do* claim came from their God, conflict so dramatically with Smith's claims? The Mormon Church cannot answer those questions, although no doubt apologists will make their usual vain attempts at skirting around the obvious truth to keep members in the fold. It is perfectly clear that Smith was making up nonsense, but what he really wanted to achieve was the idea that God did indeed provide the same message to the Nephites that He had given in the Holy Land. It simply does not work.

# THE MORMON DELUSION

The biblical references contain standard comments in reference to Jesus:

> **John 20:31.** But these are written, that ye might believe that Jesus is the Christ, the Son of God; and that believing ye might have life through his name.
>
> **Acts 10:43.** To him give all the prophets witness, that through his name whosoever believeth in him shall receive remission of sins.

According to the lesson manual, the *Book of Mormon* can answer many of life's questions…

## The Book of Mormon Answers Questions of the Soul

> President Ezra Taft Benson said that missionaries "need to show how [the Book of Mormon] answers the great questions of the soul" ("Flooding the Earth with the Book of Mormon," *Ensign*, Nov. 1988, 5). *(Manual page 107).*
>
> "The great questions of the soul" may include such questions as these: Is there really a God? Did I exist before I was born? Will I live after I die? What is the purpose of life? Is Jesus really the Savior? Other questions may focus on more temporal needs: How can I improve my relationship with my spouse? How can I help my teenagers avoid drugs or immorality? How can I find work to support my family? The gospel of Jesus Christ helps us answer both kinds of questions. As we gain faith that the Book of Mormon is true, we can begin to answer questions about the purpose of life and the hope of eternal life. The Book of Mormon describes the plan of happiness, which gives meaning and perspective to life. Answers to questions such as the following are clearly taught in the Book of Mormon.

The manual then lists an array of questions and provides *Book of Mormon* references to answer them:

> Is there a God? (Alma 22).

I am absolutely astounded that the answer to the question "Is there a God" is supposed to be found in *Alma 22*. I would have thought the Church would avoid using that chapter. We discussed *Alma 22* earlier *(see: pp.70-76)* as it is one of the chapters that refer explicitly to God as a *spirit* with no body, in line with Smith's monotheism when he wrote the *Book of Mormon*. Just to review the relevant verses:

# WHAT IS THE ROLE OF THE BOOK OF MORMON?

> **Alma 22:9.** And the king said: *Is God that Great Spirit* that brought our fathers out of the land of Jerusalem?
> **10.** And Aaron said unto him: Yea, *he is that Great Spirit*, and he created all things both in heaven and in earth. Believest thou this?
> **11.** And he said: Yea, *I believe that the Great Spirit* created all things, and I desire that ye should tell me concerning all these things, and I will believe thy words. (Emphasis added).

If missionaries actually decide to use this to convince an investigator that God *is* real – then they also confirm, in no uncertain terms, that God is also expressly a *spirit*, in line with Joseph Smith's monotheistic thinking when he wrote it in 1828-9. If missionaries do not pick up on that, investigators should.

What does Jesus Christ expect of me? (2 Nephi 9).

*2 Nephi 9* covers lots of things we should *not* do, which most people wouldn't do anyway, and it doesn't hold back on what will happen if someone does not obey what God *commands* them to do. It confirms the two states, in what was once termed the 'Spirit Prison', now referred to as the 'Spirit World'. They are called 'Paradise' and 'Hell' – just as I was taught as a youngster. The chapter heading confirms it. The chapter contains several references *(about eight)* to 'hell', but only one to 'paradise', as ever reinforcing the fear factor.

The chapter heading also confirms that the atonement saves people from "death, hell, the devil and endless torment" when to Mormons, the only hell is 'outer darkness' which is reserved specifically for the very few who 'deny the Holy Ghost'. Mormons are taught that such people could probably be counted on one hand. The Christian equivalent of hell, in Mormonism, is their 'Telestial kingdom' which is described as being nicer than this Earth, so I am not entirely sure what kind of 'endless torment' people should actually expect there.

The chapter *(2 Nephi 9)* contains one of the many accounts confirming God Himself would come to Earth in the form of a man, providing further evidence of Smith's early monotheism.

> **2 Nephi 9:4.** ...nevertheless, in our bodies *we shall see God*.
> **5.** Yea, I know that ye know that *in the body he shall show himself* unto those at Jerusalem, from whence we came; for it is expedient that it should be among them; for it behooveth *the great Creator that he suffereth himself to become subject unto man in the flesh, and die for all men, that all men might become subject unto him.* (Emphasis added).

Smith's monotheism of the day is further reinforced in *v.20-21*.

> **9:20.** O *how great the holiness of our God!* For he knoweth all things, and there is not anything save he knows it.
> **21.** And *he cometh into the world that he may save all men* if they will hearken unto his voice; for *behold, he suffereth the pains of all men...* (Emphasis added).

We get to *v.16* without a single word about what is expected of us, but God certainly lets us know what will happen if we don't perform. I am still unsure, in terms of modern Mormon theology, where the *place* actually exists so this can happen.

> **9:16.** And assuredly, as the Lord liveth, for the Lord God hath spoken it, and it is his eternal word, which cannot pass away, that they who are righteous shall be righteous still, and *they who are filthy shall be filthy still; wherefore, they who are filthy are the devil and his angels; and they shall go away into everlasting fire, prepared for them; and their torment is as a lake of fire and brimstone, whose flame ascendeth up forever and ever and has no end.* (Emphasis added).

It is only when we get to v.23 that we begin to learn what Jesus Christ expects, or commands, in terms of Mormonism.

Repent, be baptised and have faith *(v.23)*; verse 24 of course reminds us yet again that if we *don't*, we will be *damned*. This is followed by a rant about the 'evil one' and a whole list of 'woe unto' statements which are a far cry from telling us what we *should* do. We get to v.45 and then learn we must turn away from sin and "shake off the chains of him who would bind us fast". Then, apart from v.46 explaining that people must "Prepare your souls for that glorious day when justice shall be administered unto the righteous", the entire chapter never actually gets round to explaining exactly what it is that Jesus *does* expect of us.

How can a belief in Jesus Christ help me? (Alma 36).

In *Alma 36*, Smith has Alma talking to his son Helaman about how he was going around with the sons of Mosiah, 'seeking to destroy the Church of God' when he was accosted by an angel who put him straight. The whole sequence bears an uncanny resemblance to the experience of Saul, who became Paul, in the Bible. *(Compare Alma 36 with Acts 9).* I doubt that belief in the Mormon version of Jesus would promote visionary experiences today, especially as the last Mormon prophet, Gordon B. Hinckley, publicly declared that God didn't even communicate with him other than by 'thoughts' in his mind. The chapter doesn't really answer the question posed as it would relate to people today.

# WHAT IS THE ROLE OF THE BOOK OF MORMON?

Is there life after death? (Alma 40).

Strangely, the chapter heading confirms the wicked go to "outer darkness" to await the resurrection. Doctrinally that was 'hell' in my early years and now it is just a 'spirit prison', so times and definitions do change in Mormonism.

*The righteous dead go to paradise and the wicked to outer darkness to await the day of their resurrection...* (Italics in original).

**Alma 40:12.** And then shall it come to pass, that the spirits of those who are righteous are received into a state of happiness, which is called paradise, a state of rest, a state of peace, where they shall rest from all their troubles and from all care, and sorrow.
**13.** And then shall it come to pass, that the spirits of the wicked, yea, who are evil—for behold, they have no part nor portion of the Spirit of the Lord; for behold, they chose evil works rather than good; therefore the spirit of the devil did enter into them, and take possession of their house—and ***these shall be cast out into outer darkness; there shall be weeping, and wailing, and gnashing of teeth, and this because of their own iniquity, being led captive by the will of the devil.*** (Emphasis added).

There are major problems with this concept, as definitively within Mormon theology, there are only *two* places where people can go in the post-mortal 'spirit world'. Those are Paradise, reserved exclusively for faithful Mormons, and the 'Spirit Prison', previously known as 'hell' – and in *Alma 40* as 'outer darkness'. There are not that many truly *evil* people in the world. Some are bad but most are reasonably *good* people. They all appear to go to the same place.

This state applies to everyone else *other* than Mormons; unless there is a third, and yet undisclosed, place for otherwise good people to reside until the resurrection. Not everyone is Mormon and not that many non-Mormons can be described as evil. Mormonism accounts for just a few million people out of the several billions on the Earth at present. A few million others may well be described as 'evil' if you will, but the majority of people are equally as good as Mormons supposedly are, and also in many instances, equally faithful to some God or other who they believe will reward them for that faithfulness.

This incorporates *billions* of wonderful people who are religious, including Muslims (1.4 billion), Hindus (887 million), Buddhists (391 million), Chinese Universalists (387 million), Ethnoreligionists (261 million), Neoreligionists (106 million), Sikhs (23 million), Jews (15 million), Spiritualists (12 million), Baha'I Faith (7.4 million), Confucianism (6.3 million), Jainism (4.3 million), Zoroastrianism (2.7 million), Shintoism (2.7 million) and Taoism (2.7 million); before even *considering* Christian denominations of which there are over thirty-four thousand, with dozens of new ones emerging every *month*.

# THE MORMON DELUSION

There are 1.15 billion Roman Catholics, and their religion grows every ten days by the equivalent annual supposed growth in Mormonism. In fact, some 14 million Catholics are added to their numbers *every year* and that is more than the entire claimed membership of the Mormon Church. Then there are several hundred million Orthodox Christians and several hundred million Pentecostals before we get to the rest. *(See TMD Vol.2.Ch.17 for full analysis)*.

Why is it that the Mormon God wants to send everyone, other than just a handful of Mormons, by comparison, to *hell* until they are resurrected?

Something is very wrong with Mormon theology regarding what happens after death and before resurrection. The Mormon Church will no doubt claim that other people are simply held in a state of 'unhappiness' due to not having the gospel, but the very concept of Mormonism is so far distant from what the majority of the world perceives to be the case, how and why would any of them ever accept Smith's nonsense in this life *or* the next? In any event, if they are just as faithful to what they perceive their God requires of them as Mormons are regarding theirs, what have they ever done to deserve such treatment? No matter what the ultimate truth is, God is supposed to love all of His children equally and He will reward them according to their adherence to the dictates of their own *conscience* – regardless of where that may lead them.

The question, and therefore the referenced chapter, is supposed to prove there is life after death, but of course it doesn't; nor could it, as it is one of the completely unanswerable questions, along with 'does God really exist? On such issues, people can only have *opinion* coupled with personal belief or faith; they are impossible to quantify or answer, regardless of what people, especially Mormons, claim they think they 'know' through ethereal means alone.

What is the purpose of life? (Alma 34).

The big, and quite obvious, question here which no Mormon seems ever to contemplate is simply, why does there have to *be* a purpose? Life is what it is, we live and we die, as with all species. We have learned to *think* and to *reason*; two so-called 'attributes' which will probably be our ultimate downfall as a species, but that doesn't make us special when compared to other life forms.

Nevertheless, humankind reaches out with hope, as no one wants to die and never wake up again. The fact that we did not exist for billions of years before we were born and we didn't seem to mind doesn't even occur to Mormons because Smith cleverly invented the concept that we lived as spirits before we arrived here and before that we always existed as 'intelligences'; we have always been around and we always will be. It's a nice thought, but it is scientifically unsustainable by any measure we know of – that is, until someone like Joseph Smith claims to represent an unquantifiable form of deity and tells us otherwise – and we believe him and enter a delusional state of acceptance.

# WHAT IS THE ROLE OF THE BOOK OF MORMON?

The reference for this is *Alma 34* which contains fictitious prophets Zenos and Zenock who have never been heard of before or since. In *Alma 34*, the two are 'quoted' as if they wrote material in the early Old Testament time frame. They didn't – as they never existed. Once again 'Christ' is going to come. This was supposedly 74 BCE, many hundreds of years before the title was invented.

The whole purpose of life according to *Alma 34* is to submit to the Mormon God and do all He says – or else. There is no shortage of vengeful retribution.

Following the idea in v.15, that "thus he shall bring salvation to all those who shall believe on his name; this being the intent of this last sacrifice..." which is the carrot, naturally the chapter can't end without bringing out the big stick – yet again.

> **Alma 34:28.** And now behold, my beloved brethren, I say unto you, do not suppose that this is all; for after ye have done all these things, if ye turn away the needy, and the naked, and visit not the sick and afflicted, and impart of your substance, if ye have, to those who stand in need—I say unto you, *if ye do not any of these things, behold, your prayer is vain, and availeth you nothing, and ye are as hypocrites who do deny the faith.* (Emphasis added).

> **35.** For behold, *if ye have procrastinated* the day of your repentance even until death, behold, *ye have become subjected to the spirit of the devil, and he doth seal you his*; therefore, the Spirit of the Lord hath withdrawn from you, and hath no place in you, and *the devil hath all power over you; and this is the final state of the wicked.* (Emphasis added).

Why can't the Mormon God, just for once, be *nice – **ever?***

> Why does God allow evil and suffering to occur? (2 Nephi 2; Alma 14:9–11; 60:13).

The *2 Nephi 2* and *Alma 60:13* references cover the idea that people who do evil deeds and seem to get away with them in this life, will be condemned and ultimately pay for them in the next. There, they will get their just deserts for their evil deeds.

> **Alma 60:13.** For the Lord suffereth the righteous to be slain that his justice and judgment may come upon the wicked; therefore ye need not suppose that the righteous are lost because they are slain; but behold, they do enter into the rest of the Lord their God.

But what if there is no next life? In part, do some people cling to their faith in a life beyond death because they simply cannot cope with the alternative concept that really bad people who have done terrible things may actually never be brought to account – ever? It is not a good justification for clinging to the concept of life after death. There must be more to it than that.

The story of Alma and Amulek in Alma 14 sounds suspiciously familiar. Compare the story of Shadrach, Meshach, and Abed-nego in the Book of Dan.

In that story, of course the three do *not* burn, yet in Smith's story the people who get cast into the furnace *do* burn. This apparently Alma and Amulek could have stopped through their faith in God but they 'allow' in order for it to be a testimony against the evil doers. Not to waste a good plot line or miss out on plagiarising the rest of the story, Smith does indeed tell a tale elsewhere in the *Book of Mormon* in which people surrounded by fire do *not* burn, just as with Shadrach, Meshach, and Abed-nego:

> **Helaman 5:23.** And it came to pass that Nephi and Lehi were encircled about as if by fire, even insomuch that they durst not lay their hands upon them for fear lest they should be burned. Nevertheless, Nephi and Lehi were not burned; and they were as standing in the midst of fire and were not burned.

Does my infant need to be baptized? (Moroni 8).

Whilst some religions do baptise babies, the *purpose* in many instances is not that dissimilar to Mormons blessing babies, and actual church *membership* comes much later when a form of confirmation takes place. In Mormonism, once a child is 'blessed', as young as a few days old, they are then statistically counted and included as members, and they have been for the last two or three decades since overall annual increase in numbers started to slow significantly.

**A question that investigators should ask** is if the Mormon Church does not believe children should be baptised and therefore become 'members' of the Church, why do they cheat in their failing statistics and pretend that babies who are 'blessed' are indeed *members* of the Mormon Church?

In the Eastern churches, the Holy Spirit is conferred on infants straight after baptism. In the West, most denominations insist that participants should be old enough to understand the significance of promises. In Catholicism, partaking of the sacrament starts at the age of 'discernment', usually at about age seven. In Mormonism, children start to take the sacrament as soon as they can manage to do so. In Catholicism, actual *confirmation*, which involves a series of *classes*, is usually at age thirteen or fourteen, although there is no set age. Mormon children are baptised *and* confirmed at age eight, with no specified learning or personal understanding – parents simply request it. The child is 'interviewed' and may have to learn some Articles of Faith, parrot fashion, but what does an eight year old child know other than what his or her parents teach him or her?

# WHAT IS THE ROLE OF THE BOOK OF MORMON?

Serious consideration of the term 'pots and kettles' is more than required when reviewing the Mormon argument against other churches.

In Judaism, boys are thirteen and girls twelve when they formally commit to live by Jewish laws. This is known as becoming a 'bar mitzvah' (son of the commandment), after which they become obligated to observe all of the commandments. Confirmation is a somewhat less widespread 'coming of age' ritual that occurs when a child is sixteen or eighteen.

Baptism at age eight is *not* biblical. No age for baptism is specified in the Bible at all. In *Luke 2:41-50*, Jesus was twelve when he was found in the temple talking with the 'doctors' and he was thirty before he became a preacher for three short years. When Jesus was baptised he was in fact already preaching and was about thirty years old. He never did define a suitable baptismal age.

The Mormon Church derived the concept that eight is the appropriate age for baptism from Joseph Smith:

> **D&C 68:25.** And again, inasmuch as parents have children in Zion, or in any of her stakes which are organized, that teach them not to understand the doctrine of repentance, faith in Christ the Son of the living God, and of baptism and the gift of the Holy Ghost by the laying on of the hands, when eight years old, the sin be upon the heads of the parents.
>
> **68:27.** And their children shall be baptized for the remission of their sins when eight years old, and receive the laying on of the hands.

The fact is that an eight-year-old knows absolutely *nothing* upon which he or she could ever base such a personal decision as being baptised and just does what his or her parents arrange. A child born into Mormonism is groomed for the event almost from birth and accepts it as normal. It is a perfect age to manipulate a child ready for their Mormon future, and a terrible age at which to suggest that any child actually knows what they are doing. As a member, of course I was totally blind to this additional method of early indoctrination and I accepted it as a blessing for my very *lucky* children. Now, of course, I would suggest a *minimum* age of eighteen, or even twenty-one, along with mandatory education regarding many other aspects before someone would ever be allowed to make such a decision.

There are even more questions in the list which the lesson manual claims are answered in even more *Book of Mormon* references but really they don't do any more than confirm what Smith vaguely wrote about such things in his fictional book. They really are not worth the effort of repeating, just for the reader to be completely bored and possibly even put to sleep by the lacklustre references. If you have the time, energy and inclination, these are the remaining questions and references.

Does God know me? (Alma 5:38, 58).
Does God answer prayers? (Enos 1).
How can I find peace and joy? (Mosiah 2, 4).
How can my family be happier and more united? (Mosiah 2).
How can I balance my family and career? (3 Nephi 13).
How can I strengthen my relationship with my spouse? (3 Nephi 14).
How can I avoid the evils that threaten my family? (Alma 39).
How can I avoid sin? (Helaman 5).

The manual claims "As we read the Book of Mormon with the guidance of the spirit, it helps us to answer personal questions. It teaches that prayer and revelation are the keys to solving particular problems. It helps us have faith that God will answer our prayers". *(Manual p.107).* As a member, you tend to believe and accept that, but in my experience you do have to stretch the limits in *finding*, or believing you have found real answers. As an ex-member, it is perfectly clear that what is really required to experience such things is a deeply deluded state of mind, whereupon we will of course see what we want to see in almost anything.

### The Book of Mormon Draws People Nearer to God

Regarding the Book of Mormon, the Prophet Joseph Smith said that "a man would get nearer to God by abiding by its precepts, than by any other book" (introduction to the Book of Mormon). The Book of Mormon is a springboard to testimony and personal revelation. Use the Book of Mormon to help people have spiritual experiences especially a witness from the Holy Ghost that the book itself is true. By consistently inviting people to live the principles found in the Book of Mormon, you help them develop faith in Jesus Christ and draw nearer to God. President Gordon B. Hinckley declared: "Those who have read [the Book of Mormon] prayerfully, be they rich or poor, learned or unlearned, have grown under its power. ... Without reservation I promise you that if you will prayerfully read the Book of Mormon, regardless of how many times you previously have read it, there will come into your hearts ... the Spirit of the Lord. There will come a strengthened resolution to walk in obedience to his commandments, and there will come a stronger testimony of the living reality of the Son of God" ("The Power of the Book of Mormon," *Ensign,* June 1988, 6). *(Page 108).*

I will let the above paragraph speak for itself. As a faithful member, wanting to believe such things, of course you do and manage to 'see' everything from a positive perspective. As an ex-member, looking at the *Book of Mormon* for

# WHAT IS THE ROLE OF THE BOOK OF MORMON?

what it really is in the cold light of day, even with a sympathetic hat on, there is little of anything that is convincing.

If someone *is* to get "nearer to God by abiding by its precepts, than by any other book" then they also have to accommodate all the lies it contains; the many thousands of alterations to the original text, grammar and punctuation; fictitious ancient prophets cited as if they were from the Old Testament time period; Jesus Christ being known and quoted BCE; fictitious animals; crops; currency; metallurgy; industry; agriculture; weapons; transport; cities; and the concept that God is a spirit; along with many other equally impossible claims.

It doesn't take faith; it takes the deepest delusional thinking one could ever imagine. It is only after the event and a long and painful extraction from such a delusional state that someone can truly appreciate what the brain allowed them to 'shelve' that just did not 'compute'.

## Use the Book of Mormon to Respond to Objections

This is an incredible stand to take. Using the *Book of Mormon* to overcome objections to the very things the book talks about and stands for… still, most investigators will hopefully see through the psychology, as it is very weak and absolutely pointless.

> Many people will not believe everything you teach. President Ezra Taft Benson taught how the Book of Mormon can be the central resource in responding to such situations: "We are to **use the Book of Mormon in handling objections** to the Church. … All objections, whether they be on **abortion, plural marriage, seventh-day worship,** etc., basically hinge on whether Joseph Smith and his successors were and are prophets of God receiving divine revelation. … The ***only problem the objector has to resolve for himself is whether the Book of Mormon is true***. For if the Book of Mormon is true, then Jesus is the Christ, Joseph Smith was his prophet, The Church of Jesus Christ of Latter-day Saints is true, and it is being **led today by a prophet receiving revelation.**" (Emphasis added). *(Pages 108-109).*

It is staggering that the one and *only* mention of polygamy in the entire manual is couched in the term "plural marriage" in the above statement. The answer, it claims, is in the *Book of Mormon* – and if it is true, then Smith was a prophet and the rest is academic. The problem is that the *Book of Mormon* affirms in no uncertain terms plural marriage is and always was an *abomination* to God. We discussed this in Chapter 14 *(see: pp 301-2)*. The sixth prophet, Joseph F. Smith, confirmed that as a *fact* in the Reed Smoot Senate Hearings. *(See TMD Vol.1:220-1).*

# THE MORMON DELUSION

If the only thing an investigator has to do is decide whether or not the *Book of Mormon* is true, they should be in no doubt whatsoever that it is in fact a crude nineteenth-century work of fiction. It is so full of lies and impossibilities that the whole thing is entirely impossible for any sane and rational person to even begin to accept or believe. It is only those who, like me at age fourteen, consider just the very limited, extensively falsified, information Mormon missionaries are taught to convey, who ultimately become members. Like me, they will pray *wanting* to know that it is true and somehow manage to convince themselves that it could be – and then that it is. The rest somehow manage to see through the hoax and escape their brief brush with Mormonism relatively unscathed.

Note also above that Ezra Taft Benson claims the Church is "led today by a prophet receiving revelation", yet Gordon B. Hinckley publicly admitted he never had any and led the Church by feelings alone. *(See p.304)*. The manual continues to assert that:

> The way to know that Joseph Smith is a prophet of God is to read and pray about the Book of Mormon." ***Investigators must resolve for themselves their concerns and objections.*** You can help as you focus them on what will strengthen their faith in Jesus Christ—***reading and praying about the Book of Mormon. When they strengthen their testimony of the Restoration, they will have the strength to overcome their objections and concerns.*** As you answer concerns, remember that our understanding comes from modern prophets—Joseph Smith and his successors—who receive direct revelation from God. Therefore, ***the first question for an investigator to answer is whether Joseph Smith was a prophet, and he or she can answer this question by reading and praying about the Book of Mormon.*** *(Page 108-109)*.
>
> ***One way to know that Joseph Smith is a prophet of God is to read and pray about the Book of Mormon.*** *(Page 109)*.

The middle section of the above statement from the lesson manual means as the delusion is accepted and deepens, it will become easier to accept absolutely *anything* they are told and 'objections' which were actually valid and *real*, and which never did get satisfactorily answered, are simply forgotten, amid the euphoria of newfound faith in an entirely false and fraudulent religion which all started as a hoax.

If missionaries can get their investigators to become hooked on the concept that the *Book of Mormon* really is true history concerning real people, then such investigators can, and obviously occasionally do, come to believe that it *is* true. Invariably, at that stage they will have no knowledge whatsoever of about 99% of what is actually *in* the book. The Church grows by two-hundred-and-some-

# WHAT IS THE ROLE OF THE BOOK OF MORMON?

thousand new members each year, after allowing for about a hundred thousand babies born into the Church.

After that, the brain will filter everything out that just doesn't fit with the newfound 'reality' and the deluded convert will assume that there must be an answer somewhere, someday, if not in this life then perhaps the next. Whatever the problem, it won't affect their eternal salvation – plus all the other nonsense the Church teaches people to rely on in order to overcome any subsequent cognitive dissonance.

## How Should You Use the Book of Mormon?

The experience that all missionaries face is that most people do not read the *Book of Mormon* when they are left a copy. They don't usually even read the marked passages. The Church realises this happens and instructs missionaries to read it *with* their investigators. It is the only way it will usually happen at all.

> Many investigators either do not read the Book of Mormon or do not understand what they read. Those who do not read or understand the Book of Mormon will have difficulty receiving a witness that it is true.
>
> Read the Book of Mormon with your investigators…
>
> As you read together, pray that the Holy Ghost will testify to the investigators that the Book of Mormon is true. *(Page 110).*

There was never a more obvious statement than "Those who do not read or understand the Book of Mormon will have difficulty receiving a witness that it is true". Note the instructions given to missionaries in order to 'get through' to investigators. The manipulation of missionaries and then their investigators is revealed in these instructions where they are to concentrate on specifics which may just convince someone who actually wants to be convinced. Direct and explicit exposure to most of the rest of the book, coupled with modern-day scientific evidence, would invariably convince almost any investigator *against* the Church without the need for prayer or other devices. That should tell them something.

Despite the fact that missionaries are encouraged to have investigators read from the beginning, experience suggests that if ever anyone actually does, they rarely get beyond *2 Nephi 6*, where several chapters of Isaiah are inserted. The first part of the *Book of Mormon* is manageable enough, although people have to absorb the storyline without understanding the real origins of most of it, which were impossible or plagiarised; e.g: no Native Americans migrated from the Holy Land to the Americas and Lehi's dream was identical to a dream that Smith's own father had.

> You can help investigators by reading the Book of Mormon with them. Pray for help as you select passages that address their concerns and problems. You may read with them as part of a teaching appointment or during a follow-up visit. You can also arrange for members to read with investigators. Some particularly **important passages include the title page,** (Emphasis added).

As discussed elsewhere, the title page includes confirmation that Jesus Christ is in fact *God*, as Smith was monotheistic when he wrote it.

> ...and also to the convincing of the Jew and Gentile that ***JESUS is the CHRIST, the ETERNAL GOD, manifesting himself*** unto all nations... (Capitals in original. Emphasis added).

The manual then tells missionaries to encourage their investigators to read the 'Introduction' and *Moroni 10:3-5* which suggests asking God if it is true and he will tell you that it is – but note that you have to *want* it to be true first.

> **Moroni 10:4.** And when ye shall receive these things, I would exhort you that ye would ask God, the Eternal Father, in the name of Christ, if these things are not true; and if ye shall **ask with a sincere heart, with real intent, having faith** in Christ, he will manifest the truth of it unto you, by the power of the Holy Ghost. (Emphasis added).

My own downfall, at age fourteen, was to do just as the missionaries asked. I had never prayed before in my life. I had never considered a God to exist before that. They taught me the selected passages and suggested that I prayed, on the *assumption* that God *was* there and that He *would* answer my prayers if I believed enough, but that I had to ask with *real intent, wanting* to know it was true. I did want it to be true; it sounded quite wonderful. Before I knew it, that 'desire' turned into probability which in turn the following day turned into a delusional reality which I clung to for the next forty-three years. Achieving a continuing belief is accomplished by faithfully observing the 'rule' that anything outside Church authorised and published material could contain lies and cost someone their testimony – so you never dare look.

Naturally, if investigators do read the introduction to the *Book of Mormon*, they won't really understand or take in the reality. The introduction is currently located here: http://lds.org/scriptures/bofm/introduction?lang=eng. Notes from the introduction are reviewed below, interspersed with my own comments...

# WHAT IS THE ROLE OF THE BOOK OF MORMON?

> The Book of Mormon is a volume of holy scripture comparable to the Bible.

No, it is *not*. It is *provably* fiction. It is neither 'holy' nor is it remotely 'scripture'. I am not elaborating on that here, as it should already be perfectly clear from all the evidence already covered in this volume and in *TMD Vol. 2*.

> It is a record of God's dealings with the ancient inhabitants of the Americas and contains, as does the Bible, the fulness of the everlasting gospel.

No it is *not* – and no it does *not*. No Native Americans *ever* left Jerusalem and ultimately populated the Americas – in their millions. Extensive MtDNA research conclusively proves that this was *not* the case. As discussed in earlier chapters, what the Mormon Church declares is now the 'fullness of the gospel' certainly does *not* appear in the book at all. Indeed, the entire *Book of Mormon* completely contradicts modern-day Mormon Church theology – particularly the nature of God, who, in the book, is not only a spirit with no body, but also one and the same being as Jesus. God Himself came to earth in the form of a man.

> The book was written by many ancient prophets by the spirit of prophecy and revelation. Their words, written on gold plates, were quoted and abridged by a prophet-historian named Mormon.

The book was written by Joseph Smith and his cohorts who used a variety of sources from which storylines and plots were plagiarised to create a saleable book. There were no gold plates and no one ever saw any gold plates despite Mormon Church claims about entirely discredited witnesses.

> The record gives an account of two great civilizations. One came from Jerusalem in 600 B.C., and afterward separated into two nations, known as the Nephites and the Lamanites. The other came much earlier when **the Lord confounded the tongues at the Tower of Babel**. This group is known as the Jaredites. After thousands of years, all were destroyed except the Lamanites, and **they are among the ancestors of the American Indians.** (Emphasis added).

No civilisation *anywhere* in the Americas has myths, legends, language, customs, culture, currency system, crops, industry, metallurgy, cities, vehicles, agricultural equipment, weapons, wheels, chariots, animals or cereals, claimed to have been used in the *Book of Mormon*. The entire plot fails on *every* level.

Anyone with any knowledge of world migration and population knows that the 'confounding of tongues' and 'scattering' story was just that – a fable of the day. The Church is stuck with it, as Smith included it in his *Book of Mormon*, but they must know it is pure fiction and *provably* so. The simple truth is that the recorded history of languages around the world proves that to be the case beyond any possible dispute – even if such a *place* as Babel did exist, which is somewhat uncertain.

Even the above paragraph in the introduction has been watered down *very* recently. Until lately, it read that the Lamanites were **"the *principle* ancestors of the American Indians."** The *Book of Mormon* claims when Lehi and his family arrived in the Americas that they had the entire continent to themselves and that is what *all* Mormons and their leaders, from the very beginning have *always* understood to be the case.

> **2 Nephi 1:5.** …we have obtained a land of promise, a land which is choice above all other lands; a land which ***the Lord God hath covenanted with me should be a land for the inheritance of my seed. Yea, the Lord hath covenanted this land unto me, and to my children forever***, and also all those who should be led out of other countries by the hand of the Lord.

> **2 Nephi 1:9.** Wherefore, I, Lehi, have ***obtained a promise***, that inasmuch as those whom the Lord God shall bring out of the land of Jerusalem shall keep his commandments, they shall prosper upon the face of this land; and ***they shall be kept from all other nations, that they may possess this land unto themselves.*** And if it so be that they shall keep his commandments they shall be blessed upon the face of this land, and ***there shall be none to molest them, nor to take away the land of their inheritance***; and they shall dwell safely forever. (Emphasis added).

Since evidence has proven there never were any such crossings to America from Israel, where those arriving eventually filled the entire continent and the islands of the sea as well, the Church has started watering down the previously unassailable concept that this *was* indeed the case.

> **Mormon 1:7.** The whole face of the land had become covered with buildings, and the people were as numerous almost, as it were the sand of the sea.

Now, having to accommodate the fact that Native Americans existed in the Americas for thousands of years *before* Smith's pretended Jaredites, and later Lehi and his family arrived, they have suddenly been reduced to a population that may have *integrated* instead, making the *Book of Mormon* itself *lie* about it, and now they are only "among the ancestors" instead; proving yet again, the duplicity of the Mormon Church leaders, their lack of integrity, and perhaps

# WHAT IS THE ROLE OF THE BOOK OF MORMON?

*faith* to stand by *original* claims. God is supposed to be the same yesterday, today and forever. Unfortunately, Mormon claims shift with the wind and new evidence – and also at times with changing public opinion – such as in the case of the priesthood being given to *all* men in 1978, despite earlier doctrine that this would not occur until the millennium. *(See TMD Vol 2:250-60).*

> The crowning event recorded in the Book of Mormon is the personal ministry of the Lord Jesus Christ among the Nephites soon after his resurrection. It puts forth the doctrines of the gospel, outlines the plan of salvation, and tells men what they must do to gain peace in this life and eternal salvation in the life to come.

This was not so much a 'crowning event' as *proof* of the hoax. Smith has Jesus appear to the Nephites and repeat almost *exactly* the same words that were recorded in the *KJV*, as if they were Christ's original *spoken* words in the Holy Land… the only problem is that Christ's words, as recorded in the New Testament, were written decades to centuries *after* he lived, by people who never actually heard first hand what he *really* may have said. Thus the New Testament record we have is at best an *idea* of what the Saviour *may* have said, or perhaps concepts that he spoke *about*. The one thing that is absolutely *certain* is that he did not *literally* say, word for word, what is recorded in the Bible. No one ever wrote down what Christ said at the time he spoke and the gospels contain at best, second or third hand perceptions of what he may have spoken *about.* Yet, time after time, Smith has Christ not only speaking the exact words that are recorded in the New Testament, he also uses much of the same *punctuation* as the *KJV*. The word 'impossible' just isn't enough. *(See: Appendix E, for a classic example of Smith's plagiarism from the KJV where he impossibly has Jesus Christ recite the Beatitudes – almost verbatim).*

> After Mormon completed his writings, he delivered the account to his son Moroni, who added a few words of his own and hid up the plates in the hill Cumorah. On September 21, 1823, the same Moroni, then a glorified, resurrected being, appeared to the Prophet Joseph Smith and instructed him relative to the ancient record and its destined translation into the English language.

In point of fact, Smith couldn't make up his mind what to call the angel and finally seemed to settle on the name of 'Nephi'. Later, the Church *falsified* the accounts which read 'Nephi', changing them to 'Moroni'. The claim was that Smith mostly called the angel Moroni and the 'Nephi' falsifications were to standardise the references – simply for 'clarification'. An angel's name should be clear enough in the first place, should it not? By the time I researched this area *(See: TMD Vol. 2, Chs.4&5)* I had learned not to trust what the Mormon

Church claims to be the case and discovered that in fact they had made a huge mistake.

I located twenty-five accounts regarding the visiting angel which appear to be generally accepted as reliable. Of these, eight refer specifically to dreams rather than a vision.

> 1 refers to a dream about treasure.
> 1 refers to an unidentified ghost in a dream.
> 3 refer to an unidentified spirit or spirit of the almighty in a dream.
> 3 refer to an unidentified angel (or angel of light or of God) in a dream.
> 1 refers to an unidentified spirit in a vision.
> 7 refer to an unidentified angel. (*One tells Smith Moroni is someone *else*).
> 1 refers to an unidentified personage or messenger.
> 2 refer to the angel Moroni. (Cowdery in 1835 and Smith in 1838).
> **6 refer to angel Nephi.** (1838 on, 4 Smith, 1 quoting him and 1 Lucy Mack).

No account, other than Lucy Mack's and one by Cowdery, identifies *any* name, apart from Smith who uses 'Moroni' only ***once***; 'Nephi' appearing the rest of the time in all of his accounts where a name appears at all. Lucy Mack Smith, who would have been aware of any name her son used, follows suit, using the name of 'Nephi' in her writing. *(See: TMD Vol 2:77-8 for full details and references).*

> Certainly Smith appears to have wanted to ultimately name his visiting angel *Nephi*. He was, after all, Smith's first main character in his *Book of Mormon*. As time passed and *Moroni* became a more natural, appropriate and logical candidate for the role, as he had supposedly been the one to bury the fictitious gold plates, the angel 'became' Moroni. All things considered, it appears that it was a tidying up process after Smith's death, to make the sequence of events into a more logical, effective and believable overall story.
>
> Had the story actually been true, given the number of times Smith claims he was visited, Moroni's name should most certainly have been given from the start in most, if not all accounts, especially Smith's own records. In the event, Smith's first record of the event in 1832 (nine and five years after the 1823 and 1827 visitations respectively) describes the visitor as "an angel of the Lord" who told him that the plates were "engraven by Maroni" [later Moroni] with the *visiting* angel not giving his own name at all.
>
> This clearly indicates that when Smith first considered his experience, the angel had certainly not introduced himself as Moroni (or Nephi) as the angel spoke *of* Maroni [Moroni] in the third person, and did not give his own name. Had the name of Moroni been given as

# WHAT IS THE ROLE OF THE BOOK OF MORMON?

the name of the angel, Smith's initial writings would have had to read differently and the name of Nephi would never have appeared in the first place.

As with the First Vision, the fabricated story of Moroni's visits evolved over many years. It all started with the idea of finding gold plates, using his money digging seer stone that he found in a well; it developed through to spirits and angels with no name; finally becoming a divinely instructed occurrence involving an angel who Smith ultimately decided to call Nephi, who is now known as Moroni. *(See Faulring 1989:56-7)*. An effigy of the angel Moroni now appears, clad in gold leaf, atop Mormon Temples, with Smith's choice of angel (Nephi) relegated to the pages of the *Book of Mormon. (TMD Vol. 2:73)*.

Back to the Introduction to the *Book of Mormon* which goes on to say:

> In due course the plates were delivered to Joseph Smith, who translated them by the gift and power of God. The record is now published in many languages as a new and additional witness that Jesus Christ is the Son of the living God and that all who will come unto him and obey the laws and ordinances of his gospel may be saved.

The missionaries are not taught to explain to investigators exactly *how* Smith managed the translation. I doubt many of them even know. Following the loss of the first one-hundred-and-sixteen pages, the imaginary Urim and Thummim were supposedly 'confiscated' by an angel and Smith was left to his own devices. That took the form of his old money-digging seer stone that he previously put in his hat in order to pretend he could locate hidden treasure; not that he ever found any. Now he used the same technique, and the very same pebble in his hat where the words of the *Book of Mormon* would apparently 'appear'. Meanwhile, the precious gold plates were either tied up in a cloth or buried elsewhere and never actually even looked at during the so-called translation process.

Investigators are of course not taught that prior to this 1828-9 translation 'process', Smith had used the same stone and a hat as a con artist, from about 1819-1828, in his treasure seeking exploits, or that he was taken to court in 1826 and convicted of that crime. *(See TMD Vol. 2:51-2)*. This begs two questions. Firstly, why on earth did the Nephites bother with gold plates when they were not needed or used? Secondly, why is the Church so secretive about the translation process with investigators, when the Church fully accepts the method, as previously mentioned, according to Apostle Nelson? *(See: Russell M. Nelson, A Treasured Testament, Ensign, Jul 1993:61)*.

# THE MORMON DELUSION

> In addition to Joseph Smith, the Lord provided for eleven others to see the gold plates for themselves and to be special witnesses of the truth and divinity of the Book of Mormon. Their written testimonies are included herewith as "The Testimony of Three Witnesses" and "The Testimony of Eight Witnesses."

The Church still cites the 'three' and 'eight' so-called *witnesses* to the *Book of Mormon* despite all of them, along with all the other Smith witnesses, being completely discredited. The 'three' only 'saw' the plates in their imagination. They were all later excommunicated. The 'eight' were mainly from two close families, some of whom were very reluctant about signing anything.

Smith's claim to any *credible* witnesses fell apart completely when he persuaded twelve men and nineteen women to sign an affidavit confirming that polygamy did *not* exist and that monogamy was the *only* approved form of marriage. They all knew very well this was *not* the case and that Smith had already taken sixteen plural wives. *(Times and Seasons 1 Oct 1842. Vol 3. No. 23:939).* No witness who ever signed *anything* for Smith is reliable or credible.

This was a legal document signed in front of, and witnessed by, a Justice of the Peace and would stand up in court. Two of the signatories were apostles John Taylor and Wilford Woodruff and whilst Taylor didn't take his first plural wife until the following year and Woodruff didn't take his for another three years or so, both were aware of and complicit in the cover up of Joseph Smith's practice. Two of the other signatories were Bishop Newel K. Whitney and his wife Elizabeth. We know they were lying, as the couple had given their own seventeen-year-old daughter, Sarah, to Smith as a plural wife just over two months earlier, and Elizabeth was at the ceremony. Two other signatures came from Sarah M. Cleveland and Eliza R. Snow, both of whom were already Smith wives. These people all lied outright in a legal document for Smith.

Ergo: *no* document ever signed by anyone for Joseph Smith can be trusted. His credibility, if ever there was any in the first instance, is completely washed away in his fully evidenced conspiracy to deceive.

> The Book of Mormon is a powerful resource in conversion. Use it as your main source for teaching restored truth. *(Page 111).*

Missionaries are instructed to use the *Book of Mormon* as their main resource when teaching investigators. We have covered The *Book of Mormon* quite extensively, one way and another in this volume, and it should now be quite clear that it is anything *but* a reliable witness of anything other than Smith's elaborate hoax. However, someone who takes what the missionaries are taught to teach at face value may well become seduced by the concepts and deluded into considering that it really is a true account of a real people.

## WHAT IS THE ROLE OF THE BOOK OF MORMON?

I certainly did, and several hundreds of thousands of people still seem to manage to do so every year. After researching and writing four volumes, I am still no nearer understanding how you can ever get through to a faithful believer and break down their wall of faith in the fiction that Joseph Smith taught.

I have become convinced that each individual Mormon must have his or her own personal epiphany which comes from uncertainty and questioning that arises along the way. Until something triggers the *desire* to 'seek', a member will never 'find' the ultimate truth.

If you try to face a believer with the truth, that person invariably rejects the messenger and the message. Something may get through sometimes, but generally members will not thank you for trying to 'destroy' their testimony. The messenger is under the influence of Satan, the message is fraught with lies, and members already 'know' and cling to the truth – just as they were taught to. That is called faith.

**As long as people *want* the Mormon Church to be true,
more than they are willing to face the possibility that it is not,
they will not entertain evidence or reason.
Delusion becomes a *choice*.**
*Jim Whitefield*

# CONCLUSION

Whilst the title of this book includes the words "A Conspiracy to Deceive", I do not mean to suggest modern Mormon leaders themselves deliberately set out to deceive the public and convert them to a known hoax for personal gain. The deception was Joseph Smith's – and inevitably Brigham Young's as well. The most senior modern leaders were born into the cult, raised with the deception, taught and trained by parents and leaders who themselves suffered the same fate simply through the coincidence of when, where and to whom they were born. Had the same people been born in a different time and place, they would no doubt have believed fervently in entirely different concepts regarding God. For them, Mormonism is entirely related to circumstance rather than choice.

Some senior leaders in the Seventies Quorums are converts, but whatever the case, so far as I am aware, they all fervently believe in what is taught and would not dream of deliberately deceiving anyone. They are however certainly aware there are things that are very wrong in many areas but seem to be content to ignore them in favour of their faith. When something *is* substantiated, they just dismiss it; such as was the case when I proved to one General Authority that polyandry was practiced, something he was completely unaware of and equally disinterested in, when he said that it didn't matter; his 'assurances' were enough and Joseph Smith still saw God and Jesus and still translated the *Book of Mormon*. I don't doubt their sincerity. However, they do accommodate many known lies, such as *D&C 101*, the *1890 Manifesto*, and the modern-day student manuals which also contain known lies, so I *do* question their *integrity*.

The four volumes that now constitute 'The Mormon Delusion' were not written in order to force-feed the faithful and convince them that they are wrong. Risk warnings at the start of each volume and on my web site should keep faithful members, who wish to retain their testimonies, away from the truth. My work is firstly for my still Mormon children and grandchildren who I hope may one day have the courage to read my books and discover the truth behind things I taught them, in all innocence, that I once considered the truth. They are also for others who are questioning or have already had their own epiphany and discovered that the Mormon Church simply cannot be true. My work should help establish in almost every respect exactly *why* no God could ever have been involved with the Mormon Church. I have tried to put all of the evidence at their fingertips. This fourth volume is also for those investigating the Mormon Church so they can discover the truth rather than enter a lifetime of delusion.

# THE MORMON DELUSION

In the four TMD volumes, we have considered each aspect that an investigator would ultimately need to verify in their own minds as true – through prayer.

It has been conclusively shown that:
All the claimed events surrounding Smith's First Vision were impossible.
The First Vision idea itself was a late and evolving idea, not based on reality.
The claimed subsequent persecution was a fabrication and the Church admits it.
There was no angel named Nephi or Moroni and there were no gold plates.
The Book of Mormon was a nineteenth-century work of pure fiction.
The Inspired Revision of the Bible was neither inspired nor correct in any way.
The Book of Abraham was a complete hoax and characters' exploits - fictional.
The Doctrine and Covenants is full of nonsense and of no merit whatsoever.
Polygamy was lied about to early converts by apostles using false scripture.
Polyandry was practiced when it was completely contrary to Mormon doctrine.
The Manifesto is canonised yet admitted as entirely a lie rather than from God.
Blood atonement was a real doctrine in practice and yet today it is denied.
Adam-God was a real and *enforced* doctrine which today is completely denied.
The endowment did not originate with Adam or Solomon; it was Masonic.
The true history of the Church has been entirely falsified to obfuscate the truth.
Modern-day leaders do *nothing* to correct the lies and deceptions of the past.
Modern-day leaders thus perpetuate the conspiracy to deceive members today.
Therefore Mormon missionaries are also trained in this deception.

Obviously, some of the aspects that are listed above will never be spoken of to an investigator, but of those that are taught, *none* are left which have any basis of reality. Ergo; there is nothing left to take to the Lord in prayer. You can determine the truth for yourself. Do not bother Him with such matters.

I am truly sorry that Mormonism is not just '*not* true', but that it is provably an entire *hoax* from beginning to end. It is not a happy or comfortable destination to reach after such a long journey through the facts and evidence. Nevertheless it is the ultimate, inevitable and *only* destination for the earnest enquirer who seeks after truth through evidence. What matters, above all else in life, is truth and integrity; the Mormon Church as an institution has *neither*. There is not one single thing about the Mormon Church that is *not* tainted with lies and deception – *not one*. We have reviewed everything and the conclusions reached are not based on opinion or supposition; they are based on *facts* and *evidence* alone. **That is the ultimate test; the evidence is in; case proven; case closed.**

**The question, at every stage throughout this work was: could or would any *God* ever have been involved with such things? The answer is now clear.**

# Appendix A

## Apologists Dispute the Existence of Nephite Coins

Referenced from Chapter 6, page 139.

Unlike such as the 'white and delightsome' issue, where apologists tried to defend their leaders' recent change to the text of the *Book of Mormon*, FAIR (Foundation for Apologetic Information and Research) has produced a video that actually attacks an 'inspired' header to the *Book of Mormon* and claims a text regarding *coinage* does not mean what it has clearly been perceived as by millions of Mormons and their leaders for one-hundred-and-eighty years.

With no apparent mandate from the First Presidency and *no* change of *Book of Mormon* text or header, apologists claim, through historical Old World data, common sense and reason, that the Nephites did *not* have coinage as declared *by* the book and the chapter heading. Without a First Presidency mandate, this act undermines and discredits not just the Church and its current leaders but many previous leaders and their 'inspired' writings.

They seem to be agreeing with detractors through sheer logic – a refreshing change, but of significant damage to their leaders' credibility.

The following notes were posted to 'Exmormon Forums' and also appeared on the 'Recovery from Mormonism' bulletin board in March of 2010. They are updated here and followed by notes on foreign language versions and a short section which is from *TMD Vol 2* covering Nephite coins in more detail.

## FAIR concedes Nephites did NOT have coins, dig themselves a hole and jump right in!

I came across this video clip from FAIR which was new to me, but it may well have been available for some time. As I have written on this subject myself, I felt it worth relaying this absurd claim made by FAIR.

Until the 2005 film "The Bible v. The Book of Mormon" was released, no one ever seemed to question the concept of Nephite 'coins' in the Book of Mormon. Everyone knew and accepted that the Nephites developed and used their own currency system.

Subsequent to the film, in a remarkable turn-around concerning all that Mormons previously understood about coins from simply reading the *Book of Mormon*, FAIR claims the heading to Alma 11 is "almost certainly wrong" and that the Nephites did *not* have coins after all.

It is notable that as ever there has been no official response from the First Presidency or Quorum of Twelve Apostles who are the ones, rather than mere apologists, who are supposed to actually represent God. Apologists just stir up a hornets nest and the 'big fifteen' just seem to keep quiet.

In a three minute clip, entitled "The Book of Mormon and Coins", John Welch, founder of FARMS (Foundation for Ancient Research and Mormon Studies) introduces what is news (to them, but not the rest of the world) that:

> Sometimes people criticise the *Book of Mormon* saying that it talks about coins, and coinage wasn't really invented until after Lehi has left Jerusalem.

Daniel C. Peterson, PhD – Middle Eastern Studies, makes this astounding confession:

> There have been no coins found in Ancient America because they didn't exist – and they don't exist in the Book of Mormon.

He adds:

> The header note to Alma 11 which describes Nephite coinage is almost certainly *wrong*.

Brant Gardner, Scholar, Mesoamerican Studies then claims:

> The header is a modern addition. It has nothing to do with the text. It certainly isn't unusual that people will read that section of the *Book of Mormon* and assume that it's coins but we do that with the Bible too.

# APPENDIX A – NEPHITE COINS

> We will read ourselves back into it and make assumptions about the early culture based on what we believe, so we read these things and say it must have been coins.

Kerry Shirts, Contributing Researcher, Foundation for Apologetic Information and Research then says:

> But those headings were not on the plates. From our understanding, some of the modern brethren put those headings to try to give us kind of a guide but the actual text itself describes different *weights*.

Peterson then confirms this view:

> It describes pieces of metal; it says nothing about them being stamped or minted which is what makes a piece of metal a coin. There is no reason to expect to find Nephite coins because I don't think they ever existed and the *Book of Mormon* doesn't claim they do.

Kerry Shirts:

> The actual idea of the differing weights being used as a weight system in the monetary system is actually in the Mesopotamian, the Arcadian – and the old Babylonian, come to think of it. This is how they used their money was through weight.

John Tvedtnes, Senior Scholar chimes in:

> In fact even the Israelites used weights initially. The Bible mentions some. The most common was called the shekel which comes from the verb 'to weigh' – actually it is the verb meaning to weigh.

Back to Peterson:

> We know that coinage first appeared apparently in Libya, in modern Turkey or Anatolia and you see in some burials clearly the transition that occurs after Lehi's departure by about a century or so from the new world. You see mixed hoards of stamped minted coins and also specific weights of metal that are not shaped, minted or stamped. So, there was an evolution there in a sense. People went from fixed weights of metal to actual coins. Lehi left just before that change took place.

John Welch concludes:

> And that's what we have in this *weights* and *measures* section of chapter eleven. It's part of a big picture of the legal reforms that explains why those weights and measures were initiated at that time and they conform with what one would have expected from the ancient world.

Peterson:

> We always have the problem of trying to impose on the text our own imagination of things. If you read the text very carefully and try to filter out your own cultural presupposition the ancient people didn't necessarily live, think or act exactly the same way we do.

The three minute clip from which the above text is drawn is available here: http://www.youtube.com/watch?v=_TC-JJhVL3U

The question is, after a long succession of Mormon 'prophets' who have been aware of the header, if it *is* wrong, then when the headers were first introduced, somewhere around 1920 it seems, why did the prophet of the day (Heber J. Grant) allow such an *error* to be included in the heading and why hasn't the Mormon God revealed the supposed error to a later prophet and had him 'clarify' it. Clearly, Church authorities have no idea what the truth is and do not appear to venture an explanation – or even an *opinion*. It is left to apologists to make such statements, presumably in some kind of attempt to escape the inevitable alternative conclusion that Nephite 'coinage' is yet another evidence of the Joseph Smith hoax.

Until late 2010, the heading to the internet version of Alma 11 included the words: "*Nephite coinage set forth...*" http://scriptures.lds.org/en/alma/11 now redirects to the new.lds.org version which has changed to "***monetary system***".

Verse 4 confirms they had actual **coins** (stamped or imprinted or not) and such manufactured 'pieces' just do *not* decompose over time. If they existed in *any* form, some should (and would) have been found decades ago. The word 'pieces' used in this context in Joseph Smith's day, *meant* coins – that's a given fundamental, and previous to an apologetic need for such fanciful conjecture, completely accepted *fact*.

Regarding the use of the word 'pieces' in this context in Joseph Smith's day, it was in common use in reference to such earlier coinage as 'pieces of eight', and 'pieces of gold' would have been readily understood to represent *coins* rather than ingots as such by early Mormons. Smith was also obsessed with the idea of finding Captain Kidd's treasure in some of his money digging exploits, which was considered to contain many 'pieces' – meaning ***coins***.

# APPENDIX A – NEPHITE COINS

Alma 11:4. Now these are the names of the different *pieces* of their gold, and of their silver, according to their *value*. (Emphasis added).

This verse is not just a header to be discarded, it *is* the actual *text* and clearly states that the *pieces* each had an individual *value* – and were not just part of a *weights* system. The word *value* does not mean, nor is it equal to, the word *weight*. Each named *piece* had a *value*. Coins would indeed be of equal weight but the text uses the words "according to their value" which is indicative of the purchasing power of actual coins (or pieces) that would not need to first be weighed.

FAIR completely ignores this obvious textual problem. If they claim that it needs 'clarification', thus completely altering the entire meaning from what **everyone** previously clearly understood to be the case, then once again they make their God look foolish and incompetent when it comes to an initial plain and simple explanation of the actual case. God would know this and *avoid* it.

Knowing such confusion would one day exist, why did the Mormon God **not** dictate the words "according to their **weights**" into Joseph Smith's hat?

FAIR claims that the word 'pieces' of gold or silver doesn't mean they were imprinted – which would only then make them 'coins'. The notion that they would need imprinting to qualify as currency is absurd when you consider the many different early forms of currency, metallic and otherwise, that have existed around the world without imprinting.

Amazingly, they also seem to think that such *pieces* would only be *found* if they *were* imprinted. Since when did refined pieces gold or silver decompose, whether stamped or imprinted or *not*? They would still **exist** and be **found.**

Peterson says that later burials contained "mixed hoards of stamped minted coins and also specific weights of metal that are not shaped, minted or stamped." So, in the Americas, let's *not* expect to ever find *imprinted* coins and just settle for "hoards" of "specific weights of metal that are not shaped, minted or stamped" instead; that seems reasonable for the sceptic to concede.

Where in all the Americas have any of the *millions* of these *pieces* of any size, shape or weight *ever* been discovered? The Americas have seen more archaeological research than anywhere else on the planet and yet there is not a single Nephite *'piece'* to be seen from *any* digs anywhere whatsoever.

References to weights and measures of the Old World do no more than verify the fact that Smith made up the idea of Nephite coinage in the first place as they would have had no knowledge of such things – just as detractors have long argued. Now, apologists play their usual mind games, meant to capture the faithful before they lose faith, and exploit their delusion further by explaining away the inexplicable in a new idea that the 'header' was wrong all along, misleading everyone, and only they as academics can 'clarify' matters and now explain everything away satisfactorily. The problem is they can't and don't.

These *pieces* can hardly be considered *just* measures of 'weight' by any stretch of the imagination. Joseph Smith clearly recorded what God supposedly told him via his seer stone in his hat. No alternative pieces have been found, any more than any coins have, and no other gold or silver usage in any such complex refined form has *ever* been used or discovered in the Americas.

Gold dust was used in quills by the Aztecs and Maya who also used measures of 24,000 cocoa beans as a form of 'currency'. Despite the FAIR claim that some civilisation *somewhere* used *weights*, most used no form of currency at all, and using 24,000 cocoa beans has nothing to do with weight and everything to do with simple numbers.

The Nephite 'pieces' of precious metal were equal to, or multiples of, other specific *values*. Therefore each 'piece' also had to be of equal *specific* weight.

Such *pieces* are therefore effectively coins – minted and/or stamped or not; each piece would have weighed the *same* and perhaps, if they were real, could have been shaped in order to easily recognise the differences.

The apologists 'shekel' reference does not mention the fact shekels were definitely NOT 'pieces' that each weighed the same. A shekel was indeed a measurement of the weight of any number of sizes from dust to ingots, making up an appropriate *weight*. This has always been perfectly clear and understood by anyone who has studied it.

The Nephite system, whatever you conceive it to be, must be admitted as being 'pieces' of precious metal and therefore should still be locatable and dateable – with or without any imprints. Gold and silver doesn't miraculously deteriorate just because it has no imprint. They had to have had *millions* of these so-called 'pieces' and *none* have ever been found at all. Also, in the case of Biblical shekels, which are mentioned in the video clip, archaeological digs have not only located evidence of such in the form of gold, silver and bronze ingots, but also evidence of the methods of weighing them, naturally, dating to long *before* the time Lehi supposedly left Jerusalem, just as apologists (only now) admit. If similar things existed anywhere in the Americas – they would ultimately have been found by now.

So, where in all of the Americas is the archaeological evidence for methods of weighing these millions of missing Nephite 'pieces' of metal – or at least ingots of gold and silver – which were manufactured *later* than those found in the Holy Land, to substantiate the apologetic claim?

The apologists don't bother to mention the measures of barley (Alma 11:7 & 15) that could *not* have been used against the value of the Nephite coins (or pieces) as claimed, even as *weights*, as there never was any domesticated barley in the Americas. Pathetically, some apologists cling to the idea that a few grains of a type of small barley of some description may have been found in one or two minor locations dating to the *Book of Mormon* time period. Unfortunately for them, Arizona does not help the problematic geography

## APPENDIX A – NEPHITE COINS

associated with the *Book of Mormon*, so one problem always leads to another.

Additionally, it is completely different to the species of *domesticated* barley claimed to have been introduced to America from the Near East by *Book of Mormon* characters. The evidence is that no such crop existed in the Americas.

Remember, Smith claimed they brought barley with them and that it was a *staple* that had to feed *millions* of people. It is a conclusive fact that this was *not* the case. Of course, devious apologists may next claim that 'barley' may have meant some other type of grain of convenience; just as tapirs were once claimed to possibly have been meant instead of horses, in order to at least have *something* to pull fictitious *Book of Mormon* chariots; another fanciful and ludicrous apologetic notion, which has hopefully (and sensibly) now faded out of apologetic fashion. There were *no* animals in the Americas to pull *anything*.

The reality is that the Spanish introduced barley to South America in the 16th century. British and Dutch settlers introduced it to the United States in the 17th century. Soil core samples from across the continent show *nothing* prior to that and according to the *Book of Mormon* it was a staple and used against the coinage (or now suddenly the 'weights') system that the Nephites employed.

Barley is a pollen producing crop and *no* soil core sample has ever located domesticated barley in America prior to the much later colonisation. Whether coins or weights – it makes no difference; the whole concept is outrageous and a study of all Native American tribes and civilisations proves beyond doubt that no such system as described in the *Book of Mormon* (whether coins *or* weights) was ever employed by *any* of them.

Following this article, I have included a section on Nephite currency from *The Mormon Delusion Volume 2*, so anyone who cares to revue the absurdity of Smith's Nephite currency ideas can do so. If you want to substitute the word 'coin' with the word 'weight' regarding Nephite currency, everywhere in my work – which is quite a stretch for FAIR to now claim – nevertheless, *all* the problems still *remain*. It solves *nothing* and questions everything – including this:

FAIR claims the chapter heading (which mentions *coinage* system) was "a modern addition" and "it has nothing to do with the text". They claim "some of the modern brethren put those headings" with the "wrong" *assumption* that it relates to coins. The apologists didn't bother to consider two things.

**Firstly**, the headings appear to have been introduced in 1920. They were approved by the First Presidency or they would never have appeared. The header today remains the *same*. It clearly states "COINAGE" which was *always* accepted as the case by *everyone*. There have been dozens of members of the 'big fifteen' since that time. Each one of them is sustained as a prophet, seer and revelator. Additionally, new footnotes and headings were added to the 1981 edition by a committee which included Apostle Bruce R. McKonkie and yet the header to Alma 11 *still* remained the same. How is it that the Mormon

God has not once seen fit to 'inspire', let alone 'reveal', the truth regarding this matter to any of those leaders (including **ten** actual prophets) in all those years – and still chooses not to do so – to avoid such a problematic situation arising?

Recognising that actual coinage *is* an impossibility in supposed Nephite times, but accepting the *Book of Mormon* must still be shown to be true at *any* cost – what authority from that God do mere apologists claim in order to decry their own leaders (and their God) who permitted such an error (obvious only to them) in the first instance?

Do the Mormon leaders and their God now rely on academics to explain what is really meant in the "most correct book ever written" – which to most of us is really the most 'fictitious book ever corrected' – with its thousands of subsequent alterations?

If the First Presidency are still happy with the header, then, as they reign supreme in the Church, apologists should accept that it does mean *coins*, unless and until the First Presidency concede otherwise and declare it on behalf of their God. The fact that it is still there affirms as of today, either they accept the Nephites supposedly *had* coins or, the only alternative (thanks to the apologists who pointed it out) is they accept the fact that the apologists are correct and yet are quite content for the headers not to be 'corrected' and thus perpetuate yet another lie? Which is it? Either apologists are wrong and they should say so, or Church leaders persist in publishing yet another conceded *deception*.

**Secondly**, B.H. Roberts seemed quite satisfied to believe they had coins, not just weights, when he wrote, "we have also a number of names of Nephite *coins* and the names of fractional values of *coins*..." B. H. Roberts 'explains' the coinage system and their relative values and then states "there is stated a system of relative *values* in these *coins* that bears evidence of its being genuine". *(A New Witness for God. 3:145. Italics added).*

So, apologists are now also disrespecting Roberts' explanation which was clearly accepted by the entire Mormon Church, leaders and members alike, until this very day. No one I know locally has any more doubt about the 'coin' system than they have any idea that apologists now decry it.

If Church leaders do one day alter the header to read that it was purely a system of measurement by weights, *none* of the surrounding problems then disappear. It would just add even more complications for the Church, as it would show a reliance on academic postulations based on delusional reasoning rather than revelation from God. What a way to run a railroad that would be.

Looking deeper into what the Church considers to be the real case, there are some clues to be found in various headers and also indexes.

As mentioned above *(p.466)*, the http://scriptures.lds.org/en/alma/11 link previously showed the header as: *Nephite* **coinage** *set forth –*

# APPENDIX A – NEPHITE COINS

The link at: http://new.lds.org/scriptures/bofm/alma/11.20?lang=eng#19 for the New LDS Scriptures has the header: *"The Nephite **monetary system** is set forth –"* Verse 20 includes "…that they might get **money**…"

In the Index to the above, under the word 'coin' we find the following: "*See also* Amnor; Ezrom; Limnah; Money; Onti; Senine; Senum; Seon; Shiblon; Shiblum; Shum. Alma 11: 1-9. Nephite coins and measures explained."

The index to the online Triple Combination has the same list – with the added word '**coin**' after both 'Amnor' and 'Shiblon'.

Back to the scriptures.lds.org web site, where we find under "Study helps", the following information confirming the current *official* Church position which is crystal clear.

| | |
|---|---|
| IN Amnor | *Nephite **coin*** |

**Amnor** was also the name of a Nephite spy in 87 BCE. (Alma 2:22). Clearly, someone named their son after a coin…

| | |
|---|---|
| IN Antion | *Nephite **coin*** |
| IN Ezrom | *Silver **coin*** |
| IN Onti | *Silver **coin*** |
| IN Senine | *Nephite **coin*** |
| IN Senum | *Nephite **coin*** |
| IN Seon | *Nephite **coin*** |
| IN Shiblon | *Nephite **coin*** |

**Shiblon** was also a name – of the second son of Alma – also apparently named after a coin…

| | |
|---|---|
| IN Shiblum | *Nephite **coin*** |
| IN Shum | *Nephite **coin*** |

**Shum** was the name of a *people* in Moses 7:5; Enoch beholds the valley of 'Shum'; and in Moses 7:7 the people of Canaan are to destroy the people of Shum. Perhaps their consolation was to later have a coin named after them…

Footnote 'b' for 'senine' in *Alma 11:3* refers to *Alma 30:33* where the term "one senine" is used – "I have never received so much as even one senine for my labor;" The context *cannot* refer to *weight* and "one senine" can *only* mean a **coin**. For *weight* it would have to read "one senine of gold" to be correct. See also the Saviour's use of 'senine', replacing 'farthing' in the Nephite version of the Beatitudes. *(See Apx E. Pp.510-11 re 3 Nephi 12:26 & Matthew 5:26).*

The apologists may have been better advised to leave well alone. They look increasingly foolish trying to be clever about things which are already complete nonsense and they just make matters worse. Why would God dictate the most 'correct' book into Smith's hat leaving such ambiguity about what has become, due to meddling apologists wanting to look the part and appear clever enough to explain the inexplicable, yet another monumental problem for the Church?

I can't help but wonder how such delusion still prevails in people who can see the truth and yet instead of facing it, spend their lives searching for and publishing supposed plausible but entirely unfounded alternative postulations in response to evidence against this – and *all* other claims made by the Church.

After the millions of words that apologists have been obliged to write in order to fabricate supposed explanations to the numerous problems surrounding Mormon so-called scriptures, isn't it time that at least some of them had their own epiphany and realised the real answer to it all is extremely obvious and very simple. It is ALL impossible and Smith made it up.

**Facts do not cease to exist because they are ignored.** *(Aldous Huxley).*

## Afterthoughts.

Suppose the First Presidency are still quite happy that the Nephites did indeed develop a currency system of actual coins, just as explained in the *Book of Mormon*, and suppose they always were and still are comfortable with the header, and suppose they still agree with B. H. Roberts that it was indeed used by the Nephites?

Does it matter, theologically, that coinage as such had *not* been invented prior to Lehi leaving Jerusalem? Why could they not have developed their coins simultaneously to some other cultures, just as all Mormons previously assumed and accepted? After all, the *Book of Mormon* also claims that the Jaredites developed submersible vessels and and were told they could not use glass windows, many centuries before either concept ever existed. The question is; has the First Presidency ever questioned coins? Do they even care about it?

What gives mere apologists the authority to question what all others in the Church, including their own leaders accept as factual? Surely this represents, not a required explanation, for it is already clearly explained and accepted – no, surely this represents a lack of faith to believe what has been published for years by those in authority who should know far better than apologists who are just academics and not prophets or seers (let alone revelators) with no 'God given' authority whatsoever.

Surely, unless they can confirm the First Presidency have their own doubts and have asked apologists to make up an alternative theory – and they also now change the header to read 'weights' system, this claim is actually the equivalent of the 'philosophies of men, mingled with scripture' as Satan would say during the temple endowment, and they are on the road to apostasy. If they have been given no such mandate, then shame on them for their lack of faith and such an egotistical attitude as to decry the work and view of their God given leaders as incorrect.

# APPENDIX A – NEPHITE COINS

Apologists have no right – and they have no case.
Apologists now have three choices.

1. Produce a mandate from the First Presidency authorising their work.
2. Renounce it and retract it, as, if they have no mandate, then it is a heresy.
3. Go one step further and apply the same logic, common sense and reason to hundreds of other *Book of Mormon* problems and come to the only possible conclusion. Not only did coins not exist, neither did the Nephites. The book is demonstrably no more than fiction.

The following is an interesting note, posted to my thread on RfM by my friend 'Cricket' from the Salamander Society. If there is any truth to such a claim, perhaps the First Presidency would care to enlighten the world by producing said coins and submitting them for independent analysis and dating – oh, and at the same time, perhaps slap the wrists of the apologists who have disrespected the clear Mormon Church position as stated in the *Book of Mormon* header.

Cricket posted:

> The following post I got years ago from Sandra Tanner's Messenger Magazine:
>
> "I did have the opportunity of taking the testimony of two persons from my home town, a man and his wife, Brother and Sister Robinson, who brought what was reported to be a Nephite coin to the offices of the First Presidency around the turn of the century.
>
> He had served in the Southern States as a missionary. He came back from the Southern States with what he believed to be a Nephite coin. His mission president, Ben E. Rich, had so identified it.
>
> I do not know the means by which the mission president made the identification. But Brother Robinson was told that it was a Nephite coin. He was told also by his mission president to take it to the First Presidency when he returned home.
> He did so. I took the testimony from him and from his wife, had it recorded and then read it to them and had them sign it. They testify that such a coin was delivered to the Church. I was also told in that interview that they were shown a bag of coins of similar nature, by members of the First Presidency. This, as I say, happened around the turn of the century, around 1890". (James R. Clark, Book of Mormon Institute, BYU, December 5,1959, p.55).
>
> Posted at the Salamander Society here:
> http://www.salamandersociety.com/museum/vault/

# THE MORMON DELUSION

## Foreign Languages.

A friend recently interested me in foreign language translations of the *Book of Mormon* regarding Alma. Did Mormon Church leaders have these *pieces* represented as *coins* or *weights*, in foreign language editions? He pointed out the text of the German version he had used while on his mission in 1961 and also a couple of Spanish versions. This led me to check what Church appointed and approved translators made of the Alma 11 header and verse 4 in other languages. The following are from official Mormon Church internet versions (and hard copy where shown) of the *Book of Mormon.* Each translation is by machine so they are a guide rather than definitive. But the resulting machine translations appear to support the idea that the denominations listed relate to coins and values rather than to weights. I will leave readers to make up their own minds. Translations appear *below* the foreign language text in each case.

This once again, for reference, is the English version:

### Alma 11:4.

**English** online header until late 2010: Alma 11. Nephite *coinage* set forth. **New.lds.org** header from late 2010: The Nephite *monetary system* is set forth.

v.4: Now these are the names of the different *pieces* of their gold, and of their silver, according to their *value.*

*******************

### Danish.

No header.

v.4: Her er navnene på de forskellige guld-og sølvmønter efter værdi.

Here are the names of the various gold and silver *coins* by *value.*

*******************

### Chinese.

Header: 說明尼腓人的幣制
Translates *'currency'*.

v.4: 以下是他們按照不同價值的金幣、銀幣

The following is their different *values* in accordance with gold and silver *coins.*

# APPENDIX A – NEPHITE COINS

### Dutch.

No header.

v.4: Dit nu zijn de waarden van de verschillende goud- en zilverstukken volgens hun waarde.

And these are the values of the various gold and silver *coins* according to their *value.*

*******************

### Finnish.

No header.

v.4: Nyt nämä ovat heidän erilaisten kulta- ja hopearahojensa nimet, niiden arvojen mukaisesti.

Now these are their various gold and silver *monies* and the names of their *values*.

*******************

### French.

No header.

v.4: Or, voici les noms des différentes pièces de leur or et de leur argent, selon leur valeur.

Now, here are the names of different parts of their gold and *money*, according to their *value*.

*******************

### German.

No header.

v.4: Das folgende nun sind die Namen ihrer verschiedenen Stücke Gold und Silber, gemäß ihrem Wert.

The following are now the names of their various *pieces* of gold and silver, according to their *Value.*

# THE MORMON DELUSION

Added German edition information from my friend, John Bleazard.

**From a 1961 German copy of the *Book of Mormon*.**

Header: Nephitische Münzen und Mäße
Translates: Nephite *Coins* and Measures.

v.4: Dies sind die Namen ihrer verschiedenen Gold- und Silbermünzen nach ihrem Wert.

These are the names of their various gold and silver *coins* according to their ***value.***

JB explains: "In German there is no ambiguity over the German word for "piece" or "coin." The German word for "piece" is "Stück" and its plural "Stücke." While the totally unambiguous word for coin is "Münze," plural "Münzen." That word can only mean *coin.*"

Note the significant difference between the wording in the 1961 German *Book of Mormon* and the 2010 internet versions above *(p.474).*

*********************
**Hungarian.**

Header: *A nefita pénzrendszer leírása*

The description of the ***monetary*** system nefita (Nephite).

v.4: Most, ezek aranyuk és ezüstjük különböző darabjainak a nevei, azok értéke szerint.

Now, their gold and silver ***pieces*** of different names, according to their ***value.***

*********************
**Italian.**

No header.

v.4: Ora, questi sono i nomi dei loro vari pezzi d'oro e d'argento, secondo il loro valore.

Now, those are the names of their ***pieces*** of gold and silver, according to their ***value.***

# APPENDIX A – NEPHITE COINS

## Korean.

Header: 니파이인의 화폐 체계가 설명됨

Nephite *monetary* system explained…

v.4: 이제 이는 그 값어치를 따라 그들의 금과 그들의 은의 각기 다른 조각의 명칭이니,

Now, according to which the *worth* of their different *pieces* of gold and silver in their name are you,

\*\*\*\*\*\*\*\*\*\*\*\*\*\*\*\*\*\*\*

## Portuguese.

No header.

v.4: Ora, estes são os nomes das diversas moedas de ouro e de prata, segundo seu valor.

Now these are the names of several gold and silver, according to its *value*.

\*\*\*\*\*\*\*\*\*\*\*\*\*\*\*\*\*\*\*

## Norwegian.

No header.

v.4: Nå, dette er navnene på deres forskjellige gull og sølvmynter etter den verdi de hadde.

Now, these are the names of their various gold and silver *coins* for the *value* they had…

\*\*\*\*\*\*\*\*\*\*\*\*\*\*\*\*\*\*\*

## Spanish.

No header.

v.4: Y éstos son los nombres de las diferentes monedas de su oro y de su plata según su valor…

And these are the names of the *currencies* of its gold and its silver by *value*…
Added Spanish edition information from John Bleazard:

### From a 1980 Spanish edition.

Heading: Los jueces y su compensación. *Monedas y medidas de los nefitas.*
The judges and their compensation. *Coins and measures of the Nephites.*

v.4: Reads the same as the internet version above. *(Page 477).*

*********************

### From a 1992 Spanish edition.

Heading: Se describe el sistema monetario de los nefitas
The monetary system of the Nephites described

v.4: Reads the same as the internet version above.

*********************

### Swedish.

Header: *Nephiternas myntsystem förklaras*

Nephite *coin* system explained

v.4: 4 Och detta är namnen på deras olika guldstycken och deras silverstycken efter deras värde.

And these are the names of their various *pieces* of gold and their silver *pieces* for their *value.*

*********************

### Tagalog (Filipino).

No header.

v.4: Ngayon, ito ang mga katawagan ng iba't ibang piraso ng kanilang ginto, at ng kanilang pilak, alinsunod sa halaga nito.

Now, these are the names of different *pieces* of their gold and their silver, according to its *value.*

# APPENDIX A – NEPHITE COINS

Despite many translations into various languages no one, leaders or translators, has yet been 'inspired' to read anything other than **coins** into Alma 11:4. To date, everyone seems to be quite happy with descriptions of *pieces, coins* and *values*. The concept of *weights* is still conspicuous by its absence.

On the one hand, apologists are perfectly correct, the Nephites did *not* have coins – as the Nephites never existed. On the other hand, the *Book of Mormon* definitely claims that they *did* have coins, not just in English but also in many 'inspired' translations into other languages.

---

**Note:** The www.scriptures.lds.org web site was the 'current' site as of the time the original article was written in March 2010. www.new.lds.org/scriptures was the 'beta' site which eventually replaced the original site. In this work, the article has been updated to accommodate the recent change in web sites.

As noted *(on p.466)*, there has been at least *one* change to one chapter heading on the new web site.

Pp: 470-1: As mentioned above *(p.466)*, the http://scriptures.lds.org/en/alma/11 link previously showed the header as: *Nephite **coinage** set forth –*

The link at: http://new.lds.org/scriptures/bofm/alma/11.20?lang=eng#19 for the New LDS Scriptures has: *The Nephite **monetary system** is set forth –*

No doubt there are more changes and no doubt someone will locate them.

The following seven pages comprise
an extract from *TMD Volume 2*
regarding Nephite coins.

There is a note regarding the first paragraph, at the end of this appendix.

## THE MORMON DELUSION. VOLUME 2. CHAPTER 12.

### Joseph Smith's Flights of Fantasy

### Anachronisms - Impossible Book of Mormon Claims

### Extract: Pp. 232-238.

**Currency**

A complete monetary system, consisting of silver and gold coinage, is described in detail in the *Book of Mormon*. (Alma 11:3-20). Note that cleverly, Smith has Alma declare they did not copy the system used in Jerusalem (or by any Jews), but they made up their own system and adjusted it, generation by generation, to suit their needs. Smith clearly had no idea about any monetary system (which then *did* only consist of weights, as currency in the form of coins was yet to be invented) that was in use in Jerusalem when Lehi and his family supposedly left there around 600 BCE. With no knowledge of Judean currency, Smith decided to invent his own very complex (and completely unnecessary) monetary system instead. He didn't even glean and use the words: *shekel*; (tribute) *penny*; (widows) *mite*; *talent* of silver etc., from the Bible. That may have landed him in trouble, had he got some of the multiples or usage dates wrong. *(See Volume 4 added note at the end of this appendix).*

Had Smith known the system, the three most important *weights* in the Bible were the talent, shekel and gerah. According to the *Jewish Virtual Library; Weights, Measures and Coins (available at* www.jewishvirtuallibrary.org), the talent (kikkar) was the largest unit of weight in the Bible. A talent was 3000 shekels (3,600 in Mesopotamia). '1000 silver' means 1000 *shekels* (of silver) in *Genesis 20:16,* but the *name* of the weight is omitted as it is self explanatory. The shekel was bartering material, *not* a minted coin. It was weighed out. *(Jer. 32:9).* A 'beka' was a half shekel *(Gen. 24:22; Ex. 38:26)* and the 'gerah' a $20^{th}$ of the shekel. *(Ex. 30:13).* In turn, the shekel was a $50^{th}$ part of the 'maneh' and the maneh was the $60^{th}$ part of the talent. The maneh and the talent were only units of *account* and remained so during the Second Temple period when the shekel became a coin denomination.

# APPENDIX A – NEPHITE COINS

In short, this highly workable system consisted of:

| | |
|---|---|
| Talent | = 60 maneh or 3,000 shekels. |
| Maneh | = 50 shekels or 100 beka or 1,000 gerahs. |

Note the differential between the talent and gerah. (60,000-1). Scales and weights of the shekel unit have been found in excavations, as have gold, silver and bronze ingots, predating *BOM* claims for currency in the Americas (seventh to sixth centuries BCE). One would therefore expect *BOM* gold and silver coins, which are claimed to have been minted in abundance, over many generations, to likewise, have been discovered –*somewhere.*

This is the substance of the value system which Smith claims to have been in existence in America in 82 BCE. Strangely, sets of four silver and four gold coins are *equal* in value, meaning eight coins with four values. In a real setting, this bizarre coinage would have to be very carefully manufactured to ensure the correct silver and gold content was maintained for each corresponding value.

### Silver Coins

| | |
|---|---|
| Senum | = a Senine of gold and for a measure of barley or any other grain. |
| Amnor | = 2 Senums (therefore also equal to a Seon of gold). |
| Ezrom | = 4 Senums (therefore also equal to 2 Amnors; also a Shum of gold. |
| Onti | = as great as them all (presumably worth 7 Senums)? |

### Gold Coins

| | |
|---|---|
| Senine | = to a Senum of silver and for a measure of barley or any other grain. |
| Seon | = 2 Senines (and also equal to an Amnor of silver). |
| Shum | = 2 Seons (and also equal to an Ezrom of silver). |
| Limnah | = the value of them all (presumably worth 7 Senines)? |

### Lesser Coins (no mention of the metal used in manufacture).

| | |
|---|---|
| Shiblon | = half a Senum and for half a measure of barley. |
| Shiblum | = half a Shiblon. |
| Leah | = half a Shiblum |
| Antion (of gold) | = 3 Shiblons. |

That is more or less how the currency is listed in the *Book of Mormon*. As a member of the Church, when you read it as written, you quickly get confused and just gloss over it, accepting that it was their currency, giving it no further thought, as it is unimportant. It is only when you stop to question it and decide to look more closely, that once again the truth shines through like a torch in the darkness. It may be easier to rank the coins in value to show how confusingly useless such a 'doubling up' and gold and silver 'equal value' coinage system would be in practice:

| | |
|---|---|
| Leah | = lowest denomination. |
| Shiblum | = 2 Leahs. |
| Shiblon | = 2 Shiblums (4 Leahs) or half a measure of barley). |
| Senum or Senine | = 2 Shiblons (4 Shiblums or 8 Leahs). |
| Antion | = 3 Shiblons (6 Shiblums or 12 Leah). |
| Amnor or Seon | = 2 Senum/Senine (4 Shiblons, 8 Shiblums, or 16 Leah). |
| Ezrom or Shum | = 2 Amnor/Seon (4 Senum/Senine, 8 Shiblons, 16 Shiblums, or 32 Leah). |
| Onti or Limnah | = "as great as them all" or "the value of them all". |

The four silver and four gold coins, being *identical* in value, make the point of the system silly, as the only difference in eight gold and silver coins of four equal values would have to have been in size, weight and percentage purity, rather than *purpose*. There is *no* logic to it and the refining and manufacturing requirements far too complex to undertake in such a society. The lesser coins also all double in value, with the exception of the strange *Antion* coin. Smith's problem with his currency is that it is a ludicrous system which would not work at all well in a real setting, but he also has other, far more difficult problems that we will come back to. There has never been a system that doubles five or six times, sufficing for everything, for one very good reason, it is completely impractical. No one would invent such a system as it simply would not work in everyday use. That's ignoring the fact that Native Americans didn't actually need or use any currency at all, all those years ago.

The old British (Imperial) system of twelve pence to a shilling and twenty shillings to the pound (£), which survived until 1971, probably seems as complicated as any real currency to those only familiar with a decimal system. Early English coinage would break down a penny to a half-penny (pronounced HAYP-nee), a farthing (quarter-penny) and even a half-farthing. (In some British colonies, third and quarter farthings were circulated). There was once a 'groat' which was four-pence and also a half-groat. There was a three-penny piece (pronounced thruppence) and a sixpence. The shilling was also minted in multiples, the florin (a two-shilling piece), half-crown (two shillings and six-pence), and a crown (five-shillings). Ten-shillings and upwards became *notes* when paper money was invented. An odd one out, the *term* 'guinea' (£1 and 1 shilling), was invented and used around the 1800s-1900s as a more gentlemanly term. Traders were paid in pounds but gentlemen paid in guineas. My own first suit was bought in guineas when I was fifteen, in 1961. However, larger values over £1, as with most currency, were and are still, multiplied in fives or tens. There is much more to this fascinating currency with which I was

# APPENDIX A – NEPHITE COINS

raised, but in the interests of not straying too far from the point, we must leave it there.

Whilst the idea of 240 pence to £1 may seem strange, in reality it served for greater division than decimal currency which can only be divided into halves, quarters, fifths, tenths, twentieths, twenty-fifths and fiftieths. The English pre-decimal system could be exactly divided into halves, thirds, quarters, fifths, sixths, eighths, tenths, twelfths, fifteenths, sixteenths, twentieths, twenty-fourths, thirtieths, fortieths, forty-eighths, sixtieths, eightieths and one-hundred-and-twentieths. It was extremely versatile.

Smith's currency system does not measure up to either standard. No one would invent and use a system that doubles five times, with an intermediate 3x coin and a top value equal to *all* the others, let alone one where the four sets of silver and gold coins were of *equal* value. It is completely absurd and far too narrow in value differentials.

If we look then at Smith's system and equate a measure of barley (although there was no such cereal as barley in the Americas, thus the 'measure of barley' idea is yet another anachronism) to a penny (for the sake of example), then we get the following. The silver Senum (or gold Senine) would be our 'penny', the Shiblon would be a half-penny, the Shiblum, a farthing and the Leah a half-farthing. That's the base line and works so far, in line with the imperial system. However, we then have a problem - not just in the absurdity of four coins of gold and silver being *identical* in value - but that (in our comparison) they are only worth one penny (Senum or Senine), a penny-ha'penny (Antion), tuppence (Amnor or Seon), fourpece (Ezrom or Shum) and (seemingly) the highest value is just seven-pence (Onti or Limnah).

There is no shilling or pound equivalent. There is nothing of at least ten times value, let alone a hundred times value, which is essential in any currency.

If you increase the values, then there is *no* lower currency available to purchase what would have been very low value items. If we ignore that problem and assume people had to purchase things in multiples, needed or not (which in reality would never be the case), as there was no 'small change', you still only get up to fourteen pence or twenty-eight pence at best for the highest denomination. All currencies allow for coinage with a value low enough to be able to individually purchase the smallest of items available.

A larger item, such as a (*BOM* claimed) chariot, in Smith's currency terms would take thousands upon thousands of these coins to even begin to buy one. Add a couple of (again, *BOM* claimed) horses to go with the new chariot and the figures become so astronomical as to be incredulous. I am sure apologists would quickly argue that there must have been some further unmentioned denominations, despite Smith's seemingly complete coverage of the topic, but whatever they may say (or assume), to cover the lack of believability, not a single one of these *millions* of coins ever has been, nor I venture to suggest (with extreme confidence), ever will be - *located*.

A Senine of gold was a days pay for a judge. Smith has the character Zeezrom try to persuade Amulek to deny the existence of a Supreme Being for six Onties of silver. That equates to just fourteen days pay for a judge and is therefore hardly a *real* temptation. *(BOM Alma 11:22)*. Yet v.25 states that six Onties were 'of great worth'. Smith did not think it through. The real problem lies within the multiples. Despite the imperial system being so versatile, there were only *three* denominations, the pound, the shilling and the penny. The ratios were 12-1, 20-1 and 240-1. The differential between the early low value coin (half-farthing) and £1 is a massive 1920-1. Today, British currency is decimal (a half-penny was used at first but demonitised due to inflation in 1984), with just the penny and the pound and a ratio of 100-1. Sensibly, intermediate coins are (2p, 5p, 10p, 20p, and 50p) and thus of course have differentials of 2, 5, 10, 20 and 50 respectively. Most currencies are now established this way with just *two* denominations and an overall ratio of 100-1.

Smith has a total of *twelve* denominations, although, as four are identical, there are really just *eight*. The differential between the lowest and the highest of these is only 56-1 with a pointless *six denominations* in between them. The highest valued coin was just fifty-six times the value of the cheapest thing that could be purchased. No one would create a system of twelve denominations containing an overall differential of just 56-1. It simply would not happen. It gets worse, as the smallest denomination of gold and silver coins (Senum and Senine) were worth only eight times the Leah, which purchased the cheapest of items. It is not feasible that manufactured gold or silver coins could be worth so little and lesser metals would be used in a society that really could mint such a currency.

The Imperial system had a 'silver' thruppenny piece (it actually had a low silver content) and that was worth twelve times the farthing of its day. Smith's system needed coins valued to at least ten, fifty or a hundred times the value of some lower denomination to work satisfactorily. Of course there could have been coins valued at higher numbers of Onti or Limnah but it would still leave a gaping hole in the workability of the system below that. There are no listed multiples of the highest denominations which would provide a workable monetary system, but if they existed, they appear to work in multiples of seven (the value of them all), making the whole idea preposterous and completely incompatible with reality or common sense.

Smith's bizarre currency has two major flaws, quite apart from considering the ability for early Native Americans to actually manufacture all the different coins, sizes and weights, each needing the correct percentage of purity (as they had to *equally* match each of four silver and gold values). There are two other complete impossibilities regarding his ideas.

# APPENDIX A – NEPHITE COINS

Firstly, it was set against (undetermined) 'measures' of *barley*. What Smith did not know was that domesticated barley was not in existence there at the time and was not a part of the diet at all. Whilst barley has been cultivated for over 10,000 years elsewhere, it was only introduced to South America by the Spanish in the 16th century and to the United States, by English and Dutch settlers in the 17th century. *(See TMD Vol. 2:239-241).*

Secondly, currency, in the form of minted coins was never used within *any* Native American Indian tribe prior to them having the idea introduced to them by colonists. The earliest form of 'currency' used, which replaced bartering or trading, was 'wampum', first introduced many centuries after *BOM* times.

It is accepted that the evolution of a species does not reverse, at least not unless there is a very good reason to seemingly do so for a specific underlying purpose – such as in blind cave fish, but even this can be concluded to be an evolutionary, rather than regressive, condition, as the sacrifice of eyes allows further sensitive development of more useful attributes and organs, and the same is true of the evolution of inventions and ideas. They do *not* reverse. In other words, when something that helps a species (such as ours) evolve in any way (through invention or discovery), once well established, an invention or idea is not usually reversed unless a population is overrun or wiped out. It continues to be used until something *better* supercedes it. In terms of the invention of currency, it also *evolves*; it is unheard of to abandon the use of it completely once it has been successfully introduced. Smith claims his system of gold and silver currency was used for several *centuries* by his *Book of Mormon* characters. If that was the case, where is the cultural evidence of it?

Smith ignores the fact that up until shortly before his own time, Wampum (beads) and shell pendants had been used for generations as gifts and currency; the only *money* used was minted by the United States. Apart from adorning themselves with jewelry, the wearing or presenting of it also had many social, political and religious implications in addition to sometimes signifying belonging to a particular group. This was the system of Native Americans when they were first discovered in the 1600s.

Wampum (some originally from a particular type of clam shell) quickly evolved into a formal currency with which some European traders then exploited Native Americans. Metal coins were scarce, so wampum became the currency for colonists as well as Native Americans. The Dutch even mass produced wampum (a fathom of white beads was worth ten shillings and purple beads £1). Wampum remained in use right through until the American Revolution, which was not that long before Joseph Smith was born.

The notion Native Americans somehow *reverted* from a comprehensive currency system of gold and silver coins, to *no* currency at all and then *later* to wampum (beads of shell, glass and metal), seventeen centuries after such an advance in culture, is unthinkable. I have researched every known Native

American tribe for the use of coins and there is *no* Native American tribe with a history of the manufacture of metallic coins or even the early use of money in *any* form before the use of wampum.

The Incas (Peru) reached their high level of civilization without *any* form of money whatsoever and the Aztecs and Maya (Mexico) used gold dust (kept in transparent quills) and also cocoa beans (in sacks of 24,000) as their 'money'.

Smith's coins fit no known civilization, yet he claimed Native Americans are descendants of his *BOM* characters. (For a comprehensive study of the history of money, see *Davies: 2002).*

Notwithstanding there being no record of any coins used historically by any Native American tribe or any cultures of Central or South America, Smith claims they were used extensively. The population he describes existing as Nephites and Lamanites, consisted of hundreds of thousands if not millions of people over the centuries between 600 BCE and 425 CE. With the exception of a few old *Spanish* coins, lost *after* the Spanish arrived in the 1600s, not a single coin (or anything else related to the *BOM* for that matter) of any description has ever been located anywhere in the Americas.

I have not touched on the idea presented that as the judges handled law suits for a Senine a day, they stirred up riots and disturbances so people would sue and they would then get more employment. An early form of 'ambulance chasing' boldly appears in the Book of Mormon.

The following does not even deserve comment as it is so ludicrous.

> **Alma 11:20.** Now, it was for the sole purpose to get gain, because they received their wages according to their employ, therefore, they did stir up the people to riotings, and all manner of disturbances and wickedness, that they might have more employ, that they might get money according to the suits which were brought before them; therefore they did stir up the people…

The reality is, the metallurgy that would have been required in order to manufacture many items described in the Book of Mormon, did not commence in the region until long after *BOM* times, somewhere around the 9th century CE. Even then, it was not used for the purposes that Smith described. Archeological evidence confirms the true history and it is not remotely as claimed by Joseph Smith. There never was such a monetary system as he describes, anywhere in the world, let alone in the Americas. It existed only in Smith's imagination.

**Vol. 4 note** regarding the first paragraph *(see p.480)*: As my good friend and editor, Jean Bodie, pointed out when she read this: If the Nephites were actually Jews, why wouldn't they continue their old world, monetary system and Jewish names of such? If you moved to an uninhabited country and actually needed some form of currency, would you not use something familiar? Why invent a whole new system of names when you already possess them?

# Appendix B

## Mosiah 12 & 13

Referenced from Chapter 14, page 309.

In the following verses, plagiarised material from the *King James Version* is shown in ***bold italics*** for reference.

Deletions from the *KJV* text are in parenthesis (round brackets). Additions by Smith appear in [square brackets]. These are provided to show some minor meaningless word changes Smith made. The text of short statements, which are identical to both the *KJV* and the *Torah* should of course be identical in Smith's text. Such cases are still emphasised to identify the continuity in his plagiarism.

It is clear that the *KJV* was Smith's source for all the commandments. See the chart in Chapter 14 *(pp.310-12)* comparing them with an Early Modern English version of the *Tanakh*. The objective here is to show how Smith incorporated his plagiarised text into his *Book of Mormon* storyline. Although it is dealt with in-chapter, Smith's evidenced monotheism is also <u>underlined</u> for reference.

> **Mosiah 12:33.** But now Abinadi said unto them: I know if ye keep the commandments of <u>God</u> ye shall be saved; yea, if ye keep the commandments which the Lord delivered unto Moses in the mount of Sinai, saying:
> **34.** ***I am the Lord thy God***, (which have) [who hath] ***brought thee out of the land of Egypt, out of the house of bondage.***
> **35.** ***Thou shalt have no other God before me.***
> **36.** ***Thou shalt not make unto thee any graven image, or any likeness of any thing*** (that is) ***in heaven above***, or (that is) [things which are] ***in the earth beneath*** (, or that is in the water under the earth:).
> **37.** Now Abinadi said unto them, Have ye done all this? I say unto you, Nay, ye have not. And have ye taught this people that they should do all these things? I say unto you, Nay, ye have not.

**Mosiah 13:1.** And now when the king had heard these words, he said unto his priests: Away with this fellow, and slay him; for what have we to do with him, for he is mad.

**2.** And they stood forth and attempted to lay their hands on him; but he withstood them, and said unto them:

**3.** Touch me not, for God shall smite you if ye lay your hands upon me, for I have not delivered the message which the Lord sent me to deliver; neither have I told you that which ye requested that I should tell; therefore, God will not suffer that I shall be destroyed at this time.

**4.** But I must fulfil the commandments wherewith God has commanded me; and because I have told you the truth ye are angry with me. And again, because I have spoken the word of God ye have judged me that I am mad.

**5.** Now it came to pass after Abinadi had spoken these words that the people of king Noah durst not lay their hands on him, for the Spirit of the Lord was upon him; and his face shone with exceeding luster, even as Moses' did while in the mount of Sinai, while speaking with the Lord.

**6.** And he spake with power and authority from God; and he continued his words, saying:

**7.** Ye see that ye have not power to slay me, therefore I finish my message. Yea, and I perceive that it cuts you to your hearts because I tell you the truth concerning your iniquities.

**8.** Yea, and my words fill you with wonder and amazement, and with anger.

**9.** But I finish my message; and then it matters not whither I go, if it so be that I am saved.

**10.** But this much I tell you, what you do with me, after this, shall be as a type and a shadow of things which are to come.

**11.** And now I read unto you the remainder of the commandments of God, for I perceive that they are not written in your hearts; I perceive that ye have studied and taught iniquity the most part of your lives.

**12.** And now, ye remember that I said unto you: *Thou shalt not make unto thee any graven image, or any likeness* of (any thing that is) [things which are] *in heaven above, or* (that is) [which are] *in the earth beneath, or* (that is) [which are] *in the water under the earth.*

**13.** And again: *Thou shalt not bow down thyself* (to) [unto] *them, nor serve them; for I the Lord thy God am a jealous God, visiting the* (iniquity) [iniquities] *of the fathers upon the children, unto the third and fourth generations of them that hate me;*

**14.** *And* (shewing) [showing] *mercy unto thousands of them that love me and keep my commandments.*

**15.** *Thou shalt not take the name of the Lord thy God in vain; for the Lord will not hold him guiltless that taketh his name in vain.*

**16.** *Remember the sabbath day, to keep it holy.*

**17.** *Six days shalt thou labor, and do all thy work;*

# APPENDIX B – MOSIAH 12 & 13

**18.** *But the seventh day,* (is) *the sabbath of the Lord thy God,* (in it) *thou shalt not do any work, thou, nor thy son, nor thy daughter, thy man-servant, nor thy maid-servant, nor thy cattle, nor thy stranger that is within thy gates;*

**19.** *For in six days the Lord made heaven and earth,* [and] *the sea, and all that in them is;* (and rested the seventh day) *wherefore the Lord blessed the sabbath day, and hallowed it.*

**20.** *Honor thy father and thy mother, that thy days may be long upon the land which the Lord thy God giveth thee.*

**21.** *Thou shalt not kill.*

**22.** *Thou shalt not commit adultery. Thou shalt not steal.*

**23.** *Thou shalt not bear false witness against thy neighbor.*

**24.** *Thou shalt not covet thy neighbor's house, thou shalt not covet thy neighbor's wife, nor his man-servant, nor his maid-servant, nor his ox, nor his ass, nor anything that is thy neighbor's.*

**25.** And it came to pass that after Abinadi had made an end of these sayings that he said unto them: Have ye taught this people that they should observe to do all these things for to keep these commandments?

**26.** I say unto you, Nay; for if ye had, the Lord would not have caused me to come forth and to prophesy evil concerning this people.

**27.** And now ye have said that salvation cometh by the law of Moses. I say unto you that it is expedient that ye should keep the law of Moses as yet; but I say unto you, that the time shall come when it shall no more be expedient to keep the law of Moses.

**28.** And moreover, I say unto you, that salvation doth not come by the law alone; and **were it not for the atonement, which God himself shall make for the sins and iniquities of his people,** that they must unavoidably perish, notwithstanding the law of Moses.

**29.** And now I say unto you that it was expedient that there should be a law given to the children of Israel, yea, even a very strict law; for they were a stiffnecked people, quick to do iniquity, and slow to remember the Lord their God;

**30.** Therefore there was a law given them, yea, a law of performances and of ordinances, a law which they were to observe strictly from day to day, to keep them in remembrance of God and their duty towards him.

**31.** But behold, I say unto you, that all these things were types of things to come.

**32.** And now, did they understand the law? I say unto you, Nay, they did not all understand the law; and this because of the hardness of their hearts; for they understood not that **there could not any man be saved except it were through the redemption of God.**

**33.** For behold, did not Moses prophesy unto them concerning **the coming of the Messiah, and that God should redeem his people?** Yea, and even all the prophets who have prophesied ever since the world began—have they not spoken more or less concerning these things?

**34.** Have they not said that **God himself should come down among the children of men, and take upon him the form of man, and go forth in mighty power upon the face of the earth?**

**35.** Yea, and have they not said also that **he should bring to pass the resurrection of the dead, and that he, himself, should be oppressed and afflicted?**

Apart from the abundance of monotheistic statements, and notwithstanding Smith's plagiarism, Abinadi is supposedly *reading* the commandments. Look at the changes in Smith's *own* text between Mosiah 12:36 and 13:12 where Abinadi stops reading them and then starts again. Abinadi's 'recapped' words should of course be *identical*… he was **reading** them…

> **12:36.** Thou shalt not make unto thee any graven image, or any likeness of *any thing* in heaven above, or *things* which are in the earth beneath.

> **13:12.** Thou shalt not make unto thee any graven image, or any likeness of *things which are* in heaven above, or which are in the earth beneath, *or which are in the water under the earth.*

Abinadi's 'reading' is somewhat different the second time. This should not be the case at all if he was reading from an original Hebrew text. It should be word for word the *same*. Equally, God should have had it read the same when He dictated it into Smith's hat. He did *not*.

Note that in v.19 Smith has Abinadi completely leave out the words "and rested the seventh day" which appear, not just in the *KJV*, as "and rested the seventh day" but also in the Hebrew version where the *Tanakh* translates as "and rested on the seventh day". The modern-day Tanakh reads "and **He** rested on the seventh day". These are obviously very close translations and clearly representative of original words from early Hebrew text. If Abinadi *had* been reading these out, he would invariably have included those words which would be *impossible* to miss. He did *not*. Again, neither did God when dictating words into Smith hat. If the *Book of Mormon* were true, this could *not* happen.

Not that this matters in context of the missionary lessons and investigators agreeing to live by the commandments, but as for Abinadi, he was supposedly teaching rebels in the BCE period about Mosaic laws and what king Noah and his people should be doing about them. Why then, did Abinadi not *continue* and provide the rest of the Law of Moses regarding other gods, instructions on altar building, and details of God's required sacrifices, descriptions of which follow in both the *KJV* and the *Torah*?

# APPENDIX B – MOSIAH 12 & 13

> **Exodus 20:22.** And the Lord said unto Moses, Thus thou shalt say unto the children of Israel, Ye have seen that I have talked with you from heaven.
> **23.** Ye shall not make with me gods of silver, neither shall ye make unto you gods of gold.
> **24.** An altar of earth thou shalt make unto me, and shalt sacrifice thereon thy burnt offerings, and thy peace offerings, thy *sheep*, and thine *oxen*: in all places where I record my name I will come unto thee, and I will bless thee.
> **25.** And if thou wilt make me an altar of stone, thou shalt not build it of hewn stone: for if thou lift up thy tool upon it, thou hast polluted it.
> **26.** Neither shalt thou go up by steps unto mine altar, that thy nakedness be not discovered thereon. (Emphasis added).

Of course, there were no sheep or oxen in the Americas, so it would have made no more sense to king Noah than would the earlier verses that mention them.

Nevertheless, apparently 'burnt offerings' of some description continued in the Americas as part of the Law of Moses, according to a few *Book of Mormon* references; although such mentions are scant, as Smith had little of any idea about such things, but they *do* get mentioned in the *Book of Mormon* and certainly should have appeared here as part of Abinadi's explanation to king Noah concerning God's requirements. They do *not*.

# Appendix C

## Note differences between an Early Modern English *Tanakh* and 3 Nephi 24 – which almost *exactly* matches *Malachi 3* in the *KJV*.

Referenced from Chapter 14, page 344.

| 3 Nephi 24 | Tanakh – Malachi 3 |
|---|---|
| 1. Behold, I *will* send my messenger, and he shall *prepare* the way before *me*, and the Lord whom ye seek *shall* suddenly come to *his* temple, *even* the messenger of the covenant, whom ye delight in; behold, he *shall come*, saith the Lord of Hosts. | 1. Behold, I send My messenger, and he shall *clear* the way before *Me*; and the Lord, whom ye seek, *will* suddenly come to *His* temple, *and* the messenger of the covenant, whom ye delight in, behold, he *cometh*, saith the LORD of hosts. |
| 2. But who may abide the day of his coming, *and* who shall stand when he appeareth? For he is like a refiner's fire, and like *fuller's* soap. | 2. But who may abide the day of his coming? *And* who shall stand when he appeareth? For he is like a refiner's fire, and like *fullers'* soap; |
| 3. And he shall sit as a refiner and purifier of silver; and he shall purify the sons of Levi, and purge them as gold and silver, *that they may* offer unto the Lord *an offering* in righteousness. | 3. And he shall sit as a refiner and purifier of silver; and he shall purify the sons of Levi, and purge them as gold and silver; *and there shall be they that shall* offer unto the LORD *offerings* in righteousness. |
| 4. Then shall the offering of Judah and Jerusalem be pleasant unto the Lord, as in the days of old, and as in *former* years. | 4. Then shall the offering of Judah and Jerusalem be pleasant unto the LORD, as in the days of old, and as in *ancient* years. |
| 5. And I will come near to you to judgment; and I will be a swift witness against the sorcerers, and against the adulterers, and against false swearers, and against those that oppress the hireling in his wages, the widow and the fatherless, and that turn aside the stranger, and fear not *me*, saith the Lord of Hosts. | 5. And I will come near to you to judgment; and I will be a swift witness against the sorcerers, and against the adulterers, and against false swearers; and against those that oppress the hireling in his wages, the widow, and the fatherless, and that turn aside the stranger *from his right*, and fear not *Me*, saith the LORD of hosts. |

| | |
|---|---|
| 6. *For* I *am* the Lord, *I* change not; *therefore* ye    sons of Jacob are not consumed. | 6.    I    the LORD    change not; *and* ye, *O* sons of Jacob, are not consumed. |
| 7. *Even* from the days of your fathers ye *are gone away* from *mine* ordinances, and have not kept them. Return unto *me* and I will return unto you, saith the Lord of Hosts. But ye say: Wherein shall we return? | 7.    From the days of your fathers ye *have turned aside* from *Mine* ordinances, and have not kept them. Return unto *Me*, and I will return unto you, saith the LORD of hosts. But ye say: 'Wherein shall we return?' |
| 8. Will a man rob God? Yet ye *have robbed* me. But ye say: Wherein have we robbed thee? In tithes and offerings. | 8. Will a man rob God? Yet ye *rob*    *Me*. But ye say: 'Wherein have we robbed Thee?' In tithes and *heave-* offerings. |
| 9. Ye are cursed with *a* curse, *for ye have robbed* me, even this whole nation. | 9. Ye are cursed with *the* curse,    *yet ye rob*    *Me*, even this whole nation. |
| 10. Bring ye *all the tithes* into the storehouse, that there may be *meat* in *mine* house; and *prove me* now herewith, saith the Lord of Hosts, if I will not open you the windows of heaven, and pour you out a blessing that there shall *not be room enough to receive it.* | 10. Bring ye the    *whole tithe*    into the store-house, that there may be *food* in *My* house, and *try Me* now herewith, saith the LORD of hosts, if I will not open you the windows of heaven, and pour you out a blessing, that there shall *be more than sufficiency.* |
| 11. And I will rebuke the devourer for your *sakes*, and he shall not destroy the fruits of your *ground*; neither shall your vine cast *her* fruit before the time in the *fields*, saith the Lord of Hosts. | 11. And I will rebuke the devourer for your *good*, and he shall not destroy the fruits of your *land*; neither shall your vine cast *its* fruit before the time in the *field*, saith the LORD of hosts. |
| 12. And all nations shall call you *blessed*, for ye shall be a delightsome land, saith the Lord of Hosts. | 12. And all nations shall call you *happy*; for ye shall be a delightsome land, saith the LORD of hosts. |
| 13. Your words have been    *stout* against *me*, saith the Lord. Yet ye say: *What*    have we spoken against thee? | 13. Your words have been *all too strong* against *Me*, saith the LORD. Yet ye say: '*Wherein* have we spoken against thee?' |
| 14. Ye have said: It is vain to serve God, and what *doth it* profit that we have kept his *ordinances* and that we have walked mournfully *before*    the Lord of Hosts? | 14. Ye have said: 'It is vain to serve God; and what    profit *is it* that we have kept His *charge*,    and that we have walked mournfully *because of* the LORD of hosts? |
| 15. And now we call the proud happy; yea, they that work wickedness are *set* up; yea, they *that tempt* God *are even* delivered. | 15. And now we call the proud happy; yea, they that work wickedness are *built* up; yea, they    *try*    God, *and are* delivered. |
| 16. Then they that feared the Lord spake *often* one *to* another, and the Lord hearkened and heard; | 16. Then they that feared the LORD spoke    one *with* another; and the LORD hearkened, and heard, |

# APPENDIX C

| | |
|---|---|
| and a book of remembrance was written before *him* for them that feared the Lord, and that thought upon *his* name. | and a book of remembrance was written before ***Him***, for them that feared the LORD, and that thought upon ***His*** name. |
| **17.** And they shall be ***mine***, saith the Lord of Hosts, in ***that*** day ***when*** I make ***up my jewels***;    and I will spare them as a man spareth his own son that serveth him. | **17.** And they shall be ***Mine***, saith the LORD of hosts, in ***the*** day ***that*** I ***do*** make, ***even Mine own treasure***; and I will spare them, as a man spareth his own son that serveth him. |
| **18.** Then shall ye ,***return and*** discern between the righteous and the wicked, between him that serveth God and him that serveth ***him*** not. | **18.** Then shall ye ***again*** discern between the righteous and the wicked, between him that serveth God and him that serveth ***Him*** not. |

The above is not to suggest that Smith's God should have ***exactly*** matched an Early Modern Translation of the Hebrew text, any more than it should ***not*** match the *KJV*. Logically however, it should be much *closer* to the Tanakh, when it is *not*, and yet it *does* closely match the *KJV*, which it should not.

Note also that the Jews *always* capitalise any reference to God, including words such as Me and Mine etc., whereas Christian versions, including the *KJV*, generally do not extend capitalisation to such words. Smith's Nephites were of course Jews, so should have followed the same tradition of capitalisation in the *Book of Mormon*; at least, until God taught them Christianity – in the BCE period no less.

# Appendix D

## Extract from TMD Volume 2:99-108

Referenced from Chapter 17, p.431.

### The Professor Charles Anthon Fable

One 'evidence' of the true church, which is a favourite among Mormons, is the Charles Anthon story. It is purported to be in fulfilment of a prophecy from Isaiah 29:11-12.

> 11. And the vision of all is become unto you as the words of a book that is sealed, which men deliver to one that is learned, saying, Read this I pray thee: and he saith, I cannot: for it is sealed:
> 12. And the book is delivered to him that is not learned, saying, Read this I pray thee: and he saith, I am not learned.

Joseph Smith claimed fulfilment of this prophecy when the gullible Martin Harris took copies of some of the supposed characters from the gold plates to Professor Charles Anthon for verification.

The belief is that the copied characters were taken to one who was 'learned' and he then made the prophecy fulfilling statement that he could not read a sealed book. Then the one 'not learned' (Joseph Smith) translated it by the gift and power of God. The fact that the Isaiah scripture was taken out of context and meant something else entirely is completely missed by Mormons today.

A reading of *Isaiah 29:11-14* reveals that it meant that the whole vision, related in verses 1-10, was *treated* like a sealed scroll by them, so if given to someone who could read, they would say they couldn't as it was sealed, and if given to someone who could not read, they would simply say they didn't know how to read. The Lord takes these as excuses, saying they draw near to Him with their mouth (made up of rules of men) but their hearts are far from him. He will therefore deal 'marvellously' with them and their wisdom will perish.

This is significantly different from the claim of Mormons that it is a prophecy ultimately fulfilled by Harris, Anthon and Smith.

# THE MORMON DELUSION

To establish the claim Smith made, it is best to let him tell his own version of events. *(Smith and Harris version: PoGP; Joseph Smith-History 1:63-65).*

> 63. Sometime in this month of February, the aforementioned Mr. Martin Harris came to our place, got the characters which I had drawn off the plates, and started with them to the city of New York. For what took place relative to him and the characters, I refer to his own account of the circumstances, as he related them to me after his return, which was as follows:
>
> 64. "I went to the city of New York, and presented the characters which had been translated, with the translation thereof, to Professor Charles Anthon, a gentleman celebrated for his literary attainments. Professor Anthon stated that the translation was correct, more so than any he had before seen translated from the Egyptian. I then showed him those which were not yet translated, and he said that they were Egyptian, Chaldaic, Assyriac, and Arabic; and he said they were true characters. He gave me a certificate, certifying to the people of Palmyra that they were true characters, and that the translation of such of them as had been translated was also correct. I took the certificate and put it into my pocket, and was just leaving the house, when Mr. Anthon called me back, and asked me how the young man found out that there were gold plates in the place where he found them. I answered that an angel of God had revealed it unto him."
>
> 65. He then said to me, 'Let me see that certificate.' I accordingly took it out of my pocket and gave it to him, when he took it and tore it to pieces, saying that there was no such thing now as ministering of angels, and that if I would bring the plates to him he would translate them. I informed him that part of the plates were sealed, and that I was forbidden to bring them. He replied, 'I cannot read a sealed book.' I left him and went to Dr. Mitchell, who sanctioned what Professor Anthon had said respecting both the characters and the translation."

If this really was a fulfilment of ancient prophecy, it was an astonishing occurrence, unprecedented in history and a powerful witness of spiritual truth. The Church confirms its belief in this very strongly, in its student manual, *Church History in the Fullness of Times 341-343:46.*

> ...Martin went to Harmony to obtain a copy of some of the characters from the plates to show several noted linguists of the time, which fulfilled the prophecy of Isaiah 29:11–12 to help convince an unbelieving world. Martin visited at least three men with reputations as able linguists. In Albany, New York, he talked with Luther Bradish, a diplomat, statesman, world traveler, and student of languages. In New York City he visited Dr. Samuel Mitchill, vice president of Rutgers Medical College. He also visited a man who knew several languages

# APPENDIX D

> including Hebrew and Babylonian. This was Professor Charles Anthon of Columbia College in New York City, who was perhaps the most qualified of Martin's contacts to judge the characters on the document. He was among the leading classical scholars of his day. At the time of Martin Harris's visit, Charles Anthon was adjunct professor of Greek and Latin. He knew French, German, Greek, and Latin, and was familiar, if books in his library are evidence, with the latest discoveries pertaining to the Egyptian language including the early work of Champollion. According to Martin Harris, Professor Anthon examined the characters and their translation and willingly gave him a certificate stating to the citizens of Palmyra that the writings were authentic. Anthon further told Martin the characters resembled Egyptian, Chaldean, Assyrian, and Arabic, and expressed his opinion that the translation was correct. Martin put the certificate in his pocket and was about to leave when Anthon called him back and asked how Joseph Smith found the gold plates in the hill. Martin explained that an angel of God revealed the location to Joseph, whereupon Charles Anthon asked for the certificate, which Martin gave to him. "He took it and tore it to pieces, saying, that there was no such thing now as ministering of angels, and that if I [Martin] would bring the plates to him, he would translate them. I informed him that part of the plates were sealed, and that I was forbidden to bring them. He replied, 'I cannot read a sealed book.'" Martin Harris's trip was significant for several reasons. First, it showed that scholars had an interest in the characters and were willing to give them serious consideration as long as an angel was not part of their story. Second, it was, in the view of Martin and Joseph, the direct fulfillment of prophecy relative to the Book of Mormon. Third, it was a demonstration that translating the record would require the assistance of God; intellect alone was insufficient (see Isaiah 29:11–12; 2 Nephi 27:15–20). Finally, it built up Martin's own faith. He returned home confident that he had evidence to convince his neighbors of Joseph Smith's work. He was now ready to wholeheartedly commit himself and his means to the bringing forth of the Book of Mormon.

Despite the fact that Harris actually had *no* "evidence to convince" anyone, most Mormons (as with most teachings) simply take all of the above at face value, accept it as another reinforcement of their testimony of Joseph Smith and mentally file it along with everything else. Details will only resurface when and if it is taught in a Church class of some description. No one would usually consider checking the validity of it from historical sources. It is inconceivable that it would even be necessary. *The brethren* have already verified the truth of the matter and they would never deceive us. Such is the total submission of Mormons to the will of those believed to represent the Lord. Such is the absolute trust in the Church and its leaders that the *faithful* will *never* question.

However, once the *honesty* ice melts in one area, one feels impelled to look a little more closely at others. As always, the reality is somewhat different to the myth. Harris certainly did take copies of some characters to New York and the results of his visits are available from the very people he approached.

Although they are no longer alive for us to ask personally, others of the era, fortunately, did question the validity of Harris's assertions and they were answered at the time, in *writing*. Thus we do have *first hand* responses.

Martin Harris asserts that he went first to see Professor Charles Anthon and then Dr. Samuel L. Mitchell. The nineteenth-century author, Eber D. Howe, in his book *Mormonism Unvailed* [sic] includes a letter from Professor Anthon which he received in response to his enquiry about the very matter. Anthon immediately states that the claim made by Harris is "perfectly false" and also says that Harris brought a note from Dr. Mitchell, thus showing that Harris went to see Dr. Mitchell *before* rather than after Anthon as he claimed. Original spelling has been retained throughout the following complete letter.

Howe introduces the response from Anthon by saying:

> It is asserted in the Mormon Bible, that the engravings upon the plates, were in the "Reformed Egyptian." In conformity to this, the Mormonite preachers, and others of the sect, have frequently declared that the engravings upon the plates were, by some of our learned men, who had a specimen shown them, pronounced to be "reformed Egyptian hieroglyphics," or "ancient short hand Egyptian." -- Among others, Professor Anthon, of New York, was frequently mentioned as giving such an opinion. This act of deception and falsehood is only one among hundreds of others, equally gross, which are resorted to by these impostors to gain prosseytes. It being calculated to have considerable weight, when fully believed, we took the liberty to inform Mr. Anthon of the vile use that was made of his name, in this country; and to request of him a statement of the facts respecting it. The following is his reply:

*New York, Feb. 17, 1834.*

Dear Sir -- I received this morning your favor of the 9th instant, and lose no time in making a reply. The whole story about my having pronounced the Mormonite inscription to be "reformed Egyptian hieroglyphics" is *perfectly false.* Some years ago, a plain, and apparently simple-hearted farmer, called upon me with a note from Dr. Mitchell of our city, now deceased, requesting me to decypher, if possible, a paper, which the farmer would hand me, and which Dr. M. confessed he had been unable to understand. Upon examining the paper in question, I soon came to the conclusion that it was all a trick, perhaps a *hoax.*

# APPENDIX D

When I asked the person, who brought it, how he obtained the writing, he gave me, as far as I can now recollect, the following account: A "gold book," consisting of a number of plates of gold, fastened together in the shape of a book by wires of the same metal, had been dug up in the northern part of the state of New York, and along with the book an enormous pair of *"gold spectacles"!* These spectacles were so large, that, if a person attempted to look through them, his two eyes would have to be turned towards one of the glasses merely, the spectacles in question being altogether too large for the breadth of the human face. Whoever examined the plates through the spectacles, was enabled not only to *read* them, but fully to *understand* their meaning. All this knowledge, however, was confined at that time to a young man, who had the trunk containing the book and spectacles in his sole possession.

This young man was placed behind a curtain, in the garret of a farm house, and being thus concealed from view, put on the spectacles occasionally, or rather, looked through one of the glasses, decyphered the characters in the book, and, having committed some of them to paper, handed copies from behind the curtain, to those who stood on the outside. Not a word, however, was said about the plates having been decyphered "by the gift of God." Everything, in this way, was effected by the large pair of spectacles. The farmer added, that he had been requested to contribute a sum of money towards the publication of the "golden book," the contents of which would, as he had been assured, produce an entire change in the world and save it from ruin. So urgent had been these solicitations, that he intended selling his farm and handing over the amount received to those who wished to publish the plates. As a last precautionary step, however, he had resolved to come to New York, and obtain the opinion of the learned about the meaning of the paper which he brought with him, and which had been given him as a part of the contents of the book, although no translation had been furnished at the time by the young man with the spectacles.

On hearing this odd story, I changed my opinion about the paper, and, instead of viewing it any longer as a hoax upon the learned, I began to regard it as part of a scheme to cheat the farmer of his money, and I communicated my suspicions to him, warning him to beware of rogues. He requested an opinion from me in writing, which of course I declined giving, and he then took his leave carrying the paper with him. This paper was in fact a singular scrawl. It consisted of all kinds of crooked characters disposed in columns, and had evidently been prepared by some person who had before him at the time a book containing various alphabets. Greek and Hebrew letters, crosses and flourishes, Roman letters inverted or placed sideways, were arranged in perpendicular columns, and the whole ended in a rude delineation of a circle divided into various compartments, decked with various strange marks, and evidently copied after the Mexican Calender given by Humboldt, but copied in such a way as not to betray the source whence it was derived. I am thus particular as to the contents of the paper, inasmuch as I have frequently conversed with my friends of the subject, since the Mormonite excitement began, and well remember that the paper contained any thing else but *"Egyptian Hieroglyphics."*

Some time after, the same farmer paid me a second visit. He brought with him the golden book in print, and offered it to me for sale. I declined purchasing. He then asked permission to leave the book with me for examination. I declined receiving it, although his manner was strangely urgent. I adverted once more to the roguery which had been in my opinion practised upon him, and asked him what had become of the gold plates. He informed me that they were in a trunk with the large pair of spectacles. I advised him to go to a magistrate and have the trunk examined. He said the "curse of God" would come upon him should he do this. On my pressing him, however, to pursue the course which I had recommended, he told me that he would open the trunk, if I would take the "curse of God" upon myself. I replied that I would do so with the greatest willingness, and would incur every risk of that nature, provided I could only extricate him from the grasp of rogues. He then left me.

I have thus given you a full statement of all that I know respecting the origin of Mormonism, and must beg you, as a personal favor, to publish this letter immediately, should you find my name mentioned again by these wretched fanatics.

Yours respectfully, CHAS.ANTHON. *(Howe 1834:Ch.18:269-272).*

Professor Anthon immediately states that the idea of him confirming the validity of Joseph Smith's claim is "perfectly false" and that he had concluded it a trick or a hoax. He then relates accurate details that Harris had imparted to him concerning the plates and method of translation and of his being asked to finance publication. Despite Harris asserting that Anthon confirmed the correct translation of some of the transposed characters, Anthon comments "although no translation had been furnished at the time by the young man with the spectacles". Anthon then concludes that Harris's visit was not so much an attempted hoax on the learned, such as Mitchell and himself, but rather it was to convince Harris and thus cheat him out of his money. Anthon warns Harris of this, advising him not to get involved.

Refusing to verify the characters, Anthon says the paper contained anything *but* "Egyptian Hieroglyphics". Harris later returned to Anthon with a copy of the published *Book of Mormon* which Anthon refused to purchase or borrow. The opinion and actions of Anthon could not be clearer. It is interesting, in Harris's account, that he claims Anthon confirmed some of the scribbles to be true Chaldean, Assyrian and Arabic characters. This is strange, as Smith never claimed they were anything other than "reformed Egyptian" and never referred

# APPENDIX D

to *anything* Chaldean, Assyrian or Arabic. Why would characters be in four different languages, from one single section (or even different sections) of the plates? As with some of Smith's other imaginings, it appears Harris reported what he would have liked to have happen rather than what actually did happen. *If* the *BOM* was *remotely* real and true, it would have been written in *Hebrew.*

A few years later, another letter was sent by Professor Anthon in response to an enquiry by the Rev. Dr. T. W. Coit which is recorded in the Rev. John A. Clark's book:

New York, April 3d, 1841.

Rev. and Dear Sir:

I have often heard that the Mormons claimed me for an auxiliary, but, as no one, until the present time, has even requested from me a statement in writing, I have not deemed it worth while to say anything publicly on the subject. What I do know of the sect relates to some of the early movements; and as the facts may amuse you, while they will furnish a satisfactory answer to the charge of my being a Mormon proselyte, I proceed to lay them before you in detail.

Many years ago, the precise date I do not now recollect, a plain looking countryman called upon me with a letter from Dr. Samuel L. Mitchell requesting me to examine, and give my opinion upon, a certain paper, marked with various characters, which the Doctor confessed he could not decypher, and which the bearer of the note was very anxious to have explained. A very brief examination of the paper convinced me that it was a mere hoax, and a very clumsy one too. The characters were arranged in columns, like the Chinese mode of writing, and presented the most singular medley that I ever beheld. Greek, Hebrew and all sorts of letters, more or less distorted, either through unskilfulness or from actual design, were intermingled with sundry delineations of half moons, stars, and other natural objects, and the whole ended in a rude representation of the Mexican zodiac. The conclusion was irresistible, that some cunning fellow had prepared the paper in question for the purpose of imposing upon the countryman who brought it, and I told the man so without any hesitation. He then proceeded to give me the history of the whole affair, which convinced me that he had fallen into the hands of some sharper, while it left me in great astonishment at his simplicity.

The countryman told me that a *gold book* had been recently dug up in the western or northern part (I forget which), of our state, and he described this book as consisting of many *gold plates,* like leaves, secured by a gold wire passing through the edges of each, just as the leaves of a book are sewed together, and presented in this way the appearance of a volume. Each plate, according to him, was inscribed with unknown characters, and the paper which he handed me, a transcript of one of these pages. On my asking him by whom the copy was made, he gravely stated, that along with the golden book there had

## THE MORMON DELUSION

been dug up a very large *pair of spectacles!* so large in fact that if a man were to hold them in front of his face, his two eyes would merely look through one of the glasses, and the remaining part of the spectacles would project a considerable distance sideways! These spectacles possessed, it seems a very valuable property, of enabling any one who looked through them, (or rather through one of the lenses,) not only to decypher the characters on the plates, but also to comprehend their exact meaning, and be able to translate them!! My informant assured me that this curious property of the spectacles had been actually tested, and found to be true. A young man, it seems, had been placed in the garret of a farm-house, with a curtain before him, and having fastened the spectacles to his head, had read several pages in the golden book, and communicated their contents in writing to certain persons stationed on the outside of the curtain. He had also copied off one page of the book in the original character, which he had in like manner handed over to those who were separated from him by the curtain, and this copy was the paper which the countryman had brought with him. As the golden book was said to contain very great truths, and most important revelations of a religious nature, a strong desire had been expressed by several persons in the countryman's neighbourhood, to have the whole work translated and published. A proposition had accordingly been made to my informant, to sell his farm, and apply the proceeds to the printing of the golden book, and the golden plates were to be left with him as security until he should be reimbursed by the sale of the work. To convince him more clearly that there was no risk whatever in the matter, and that the work was actually what it claimed to be, he was told to take the paper, which purported to be a copy of one of the pages of the book, to the city of New York, and submit it to the learned in that quarter, who would soon dispel all his doubts, and satisfy him as to the perfect safety of the investment. As Dr. Mitchell was our "Magnus Apollo" in those days, the man called first upon him; but the Doctor, evidently suspecting some trick, declined giving any opinion about the matter, and sent the countryman down to the college, to see, in all probability what the "learned pundits" in that place would make of the affair. On my telling the bearer of the paper that an attempt had been made to impose on him and defraud him of his property, he requested me to give him my opinion in writing about the paper which he had shown to me. I did so without hesitation, partly for the man's sake, and partly to let the individual "behind the curtain" see that his trick was discovered. The import of what I wrote was, as far as I can now recollect, simply this, that the marks in the paper appeared to be merely an imitation of various alphabetical characters, and had, in my opinion, no meaning at all connected with them. The countryman then took his leave, with many thanks, and with the express declaration that he would in no shape part with his farm, or embark in the speculation of printing the golden book.

# APPENDIX D

The matter rested here for a considerable time, until one day, when I had ceased entirely to think of the countryman and his paper, this same individual, to my great surprise, paid me a second visit. He now brought with him a duodecimo volume, which he said was a translation into English of the "Golden Bible." He also stated, that notwithstanding his original determination not to sell his farm, he had been induced evidently to do so, and apply the money to the publication of the book, and had received the golden plates as a security for payment. He begged my acceptance of the volume, assuring me that it would be found extremely interesting, and that it was already "making great noise" in the upper part of the state. Suspecting now that some serious trick was on foot, and that my plain looking visitor might be in fact a very cunning fellow I declined his present, and merely contented myself with a slight examination of the volume while he stood by. The more I declined receiving it, however, the more urgent the man became in offering the book, until at last I told him plainly, that if he left the volume, as he said he intended to do, I should most assuredly throw it after him as he departed. I then asked him how he could be so foolish as to sell his farm and engage in this affair; and requested him to tell me if the plates were really of gold. In answer to this latter inquiry, he said, that he had never seen the plates themselves, which were carefully locked up in a trunk, but that he had the trunk in his possession. I advised him by all means to open the trunk and examine its contents, and if the plates proved to be of gold, which I did not believe at all, to sell them immediately. His reply was, that. if he opened the trunk, the *"curse of heaven would descend upon him and his children."* "However," added he, "I will agree to open it, provided you take the 'curse of Heaven' upon yourself, for having advised me to the step." I told him I was perfectly willing to do so, and begged he would hasten home and examine the trunk, for he would find that he had been cheated. He promised to do as I recommended, and left me, taking his book with him. I have never seen him since.

Such is a plain statement of all I know respecting the Mormons. My impression now is, that the plain looking countryman was none other than the prophet Smith himself, who assumed an appearance of great simplicity in order to entrap me, if possible, into some recommendation of his book. That the prophet aided me by his inspiration, in interpreting the volume, is only one of the many amusing falsehoods which the Mormonites utter relative to my participation in their doctrines. Of these doctrines I know nothing whatever, nor have I ever heard a single discourse from any of their preachers, although I have often felt a strong curiosity to become an auditor, since my friends tell me that they frequently name me in their sermons, and even go so far as to say that I am alluded to in the prophecies of Scripture!

If what I have here written shall prove of any service in opening the eyes of some of their deluded followers to the real designs of those who profess to be the apostles of Mormonism, it will afford me satisfaction equalled, I have no doubt, only by that which you yourself will feel on this subject.

I remain, very respectfully and truly, your friend,
                    CHAS. ANTHON. *(Clark 1842:233-238).*

Again Anthon immediately describes the paper that Harris presented as a clumsy hoax. This time, he adds that he did write down an opinion for Harris (but not one of the characters themselves) which was that the characters had *no* meaning at all "partly for the man's sake, and partly to let the individual 'behind the curtain' see that his trick was discovered." The gullible Harris, eager to make a profit from the sale of the *Book of Mormon* and equally keen for it to be true, leaves out this detail and in fact it was probably Harris himself who tore up any such negative statement, relaying to Smith a more positive and 'prophecy fulfilling' version of events, thus adding credence to the story. The whole episode, as reported by Harris, later found its way into *Book of Mormon* prophecy which at that time had not yet been 'translated' and was actually 'borrowed' from Isaiah.

Anthon included similar details as were provided in his earlier letter to Howe. The Mormon Church criticises Anthon for saying "the Mormons claimed me for an auxiliary, but, as no one, until the present time, has even requested from me a statement in writing, I have not deemed it worth while to say anything publicly on the subject", quoting (and thus acknowledging) him as having written his earlier letter to Eber D. Howe. It is perfectly obvious Anthon was saying that it was *Mormons* who had not asked him for anything in writing since Harris's visits to date, and *that* is why he hadn't said anything publicly on the matter. He had felt no need to. The only two people to ask about it were from outside the Church and they both got an immediate, clear and definitive response, along with permission, and even persuasion, to publish his responses.

Anthon had concluded his earlier personal reply to Howe, feeling to "beg you, as a personal favor, to publish this letter immediately, should you find my name mentioned again by these wretched fanatics." Clearly, although this was not a *public* statement, Howe had Anthon's permission to publish it as one.

Anthon retells what happened when Harris visited him and then in light of this second request from outside the Church, Anthon says: "If what I have here written shall prove of any service in opening the eyes of some of their deluded followers to the real designs of those who profess to be the apostles of Mormonism, it will afford me satisfaction equalled, I have no doubt, only by that which you yourself will feel on this subject." This statement qualifies his opening remark that he meant it was the Mormons who had never asked him to confirm in writing what had actually happened when Harris visited him.

# APPENDIX D

Perhaps they were afraid to ask, as after Howe published in 1834, Smith and his cronies already knew the answer which would not help their cause in the least. The unconfirmed myth was far more enticing than confirming the embarrassing reality. If not, why did the Church never go back and ask Anthon for a definitive statement that they could publish? Smith and his cohorts would have read Howe and left Anthon well alone.

# Appendix E

Referenced from Chapter 17, p.455.

## The Beatitudes

Investigators may wish to ask Mormon missionaries why it was that in the *Book of Mormon*, Christ decided to repeat almost the exact same words that He *supposedly* spoke in the Holy Land, which would not be recorded for several more decades on the other side of the world, which after several translations and updates ended up expressed that way in Early Modern English in the *KJV*.

How did the words (which Christ did *not* actually speak this way in the first place) get spoken this way *by* Christ to the Nephites, converted from Hebrew into Reformed Egyptian, and then dictated into Smith's hat, then come to be written down almost *exactly* as they appear in the *KJV*, including much of the punctuation? If ever there was claim to a 'miracle' of such an impossible series of coincidences, then surely this is the most outrageous one ever.

The New Testament gives a picture or an idea of what people, who handed down the stories, *thought* Christ included in his preaching. Joseph Smith just copied the *KJV* into his *Book of Mormon*. Presumably Smith thought it was a first hand account written down as Christ was speaking? Who knows? Had the Nephites been a real people and had the Christ visited them, we would have a beautiful first hand rendering of His words which would be entirely different to the *KJV*. The one thing that it could and would *not* be – is almost the ***same***.

Smith did seem to like Jesus to use the word 'and' quite a lot at the start of his sentences. Interestingly, Jesus does not use 'and' in the same way at all in Matthew. It is as if someone else entirely is speaking...

Words that Smith or *changed* or *added* to the text in *3 Nephi 12*.

Words that Smith *changed* or *deleted* when copying from *Matthew*.

| 3 Nephi 12 | Matthew 5 |
|---|---|
| 3. *Yea*, blessed are the poor in spirit *who come unto me*, for theirs is the kingdom of heaven. | 3. Blessed *are* the poor in spirit: for theirs is the kingdom of heaven. |
| 4. *And again*, blessed are all they that mourn, for they shall be comforted. | 4. Blessed *are* they that mourn: for they shall be comforted. |
| 5. *And* blessed are the meek, for they shall inherit the earth. | 5. Blessed *are* the meek: for they shall inherit the earth. |
| 6. *And* blessed are all they *who* do hunger and thirst after righteousness, for they shall be filled *with the Holy Ghost*. | 6. Blessed *are* they *which* do hunger and thirst after righteousness: for they shall be filled. |
| 7 *And* blessed are the merciful, for they shall obtain mercy. | 7. Blessed *are* the merciful: for they shall obtain mercy. |
| 8. *And* blessed are all the pure in heart, for they shall see God. | 8. Blessed *are* the pure in heart: for they shall see God. |
| 9. *And* blessed are all the peacemakers, for they shall be called the children of God. | 9. Blessed *are* the peacemakers: for they shall be called the children of God. |
| 10. *And* blessed are all they *who* are persecuted for *my name's* sake, for theirs is the kingdom of heaven. | 10. Blessed *are* they *which* are persecuted for *righteousness'* sake: for theirs is the kingdom of heaven. |
| 11. *And* blessed are ye when men shall revile you and persecute, and shall say all manner of evil against you falsely, for my sake; | 11. Blessed are ye, when men shall revile you, and persecute *you*, and shall say all manner of evil against you falsely, for my sake. |
| 12. *For ye shall have great joy* and be exceeding**ly** glad, for great *shall be* your reward in heaven; for so persecuted they the prophets who were before you. | 12. *Rejoice*, and be exceeding glad: for great *is* your reward in heaven: for so persecuted they the prophets which were before you. |
| 13. *Verily, verily, I say unto you, I give unto you to be* the salt of the earth; but if the salt *shall lose its* savor wherewith shall *the earth* be salted? *The salt shall be* thenceforth good for nothing, but to be cast out and to be trodden under foot of men. | 13. Ye are the salt of the earth: but if the salt *have lost his* savour, wherewith shall *it* be salted? *it is* thenceforth good for nothing, but to be cast out, and to be trodden under foot of men. |
| 14. *Verily, verily, I say unto you, I give unto you to be* the light of *this people*. A city that is set on a hill cannot be hid. | 14. Ye are the light of *the world*. A city that is set on an hill cannot be hid. |

# APPENDIX E – THE BEATITUDES

| | |
|---|---|
| **15.** *Behold*, do men light a candle and put it under a bushel*? Nay,* but on a candlestick, and it giveth light *to* all that are in the house; | **15.** *Neither* do men light a candle, and put it under a bushel, but on a candlestick; and it giveth light *unto* all that are in the house. |
| **16.** *Therefore* let your light so shine before *this people*, that they may see your good works and glorify your Father who is in heaven. | **16.** Let your light so shine before *men*, that they may see your good works, and glorify your Father which is in heaven. |
| **17.** Think not that I am come to destroy the law or the prophets. I am not come to destroy but to fulfil; | **17.** Think not that I am come to destroy the law to, or the prophets: I am not come to destroy, but to fulfil. |
| **18.** For verily I say unto you, one jot nor one tittle *hath not passed away* from the law, *but in me it hath* all be*en* fulfilled. | **18.** For verily I say unto you, *Till heaven and earth pass*, one jot or one tittle *shall in no wise pass* from the law, *till* all be fulfilled. |
| **19.** *And behold, I have given you the law and the commandments of my Father, that ye shall believe in me, and that ye shall repent of your sins, and come unto me with a broken heart and a contrite spirit. Behold, ye have the commandments before you, and the law is fulfilled.* | **19.** Whosoever therefore shall break one of these least commandments, and shall teach men so, he shall be called the least in the kingdom of heaven: but whosoever shall do and teach them, the same shall be called great in the kingdom of heaven. |
| [Smith changes v.19 to say they have been given the commandments and should repent and come to Jesus. Why would Jesus, if He was really speaking, use almost identical words to the *KJV* and then alter this verse for no reason?] | [The *KJV* has Jesus admonishing people not to break the commandments or teach others to but to live them and teach them – they will be called great in the kingdom. Smith alters this well written verse and the result is Jesus makes less of a statement.] |
| **20.** *Therefore come unto me and be ye saved; for verily I say unto you, that except ye shall keep my commandments, which I have commanded you at this time, ye shall in no case enter into the kingdom of heaven.* | **20.** *For I say unto you, That except your righteousness shall exceed the righteousness of the scribes and Pharisees, ye shall in no case enter into the kingdom of heaven.* |
| [Because Smith can't use 'scribes and Pharisees' in his text (as they didn't have any), instead he has Jesus repeat what he has just said in v.19.] | [Smith cannot use v.20, as the Nephites didn't have scribes or Pharisees and he obviously couldn't think of alternative people to have righteousness 'exceed'. He has Jesus repeat what He said already and then slips back into the *KJV* text in v.21.] |

| | |
|---|---|
| **21.** Ye have heard that it ***hath been*** said by them of old time, ***and it is also written before you, that*** thou shalt not kill, and whosoever shall kill shall be in danger of the judgment ***of God;***<br>**22.** But I say unto you, that whosoever is angry with his brother shall be in danger of ***his*** judgment. And whosoever shall say to his brother, Raca, shall be in danger of the council; ***and*** whosoever shall say, Thou fool, shall be in danger of hell fire.<br><br>[v.22: Smith leaves out Christ's caveat "without just cause" and also has judgement coming from the *brother* which is impossible. Human judgement cannot be associated with hell fire.]<br><br>**23.** Therefore, if *ye shall come unto me, or shall desire to come unto me,* and rememberest that thy brother hath aught against thee—<br>**24.** Go thy way ***unto thy brother, and*** first be reconciled to thy brother, and then come ***unto me with full purpose of heart, and I will receive you.***<br><br>[Perhaps Smith remembered what he had Jesus say in *3 Nephi 9:19* about burnt offerings being done away with. The question is why would Christ use the same words, just altering a few, if the original scenario didn't apply?]<br><br>**25.** Agree with thine adversary quickly *while* thou art in the way with him, lest at any time ***he shall get thee,*** and thou shalt be cast into prison.<br><br>**26.** ***Verily,*** verily, I say unto thee, thou shalt by no means come out thence ***until*** thou hast paid the uttermost ***senine.*** | **21.** Ye have heard that it ***was*** said by them of old time, Thou shalt not kill; and whosoever shall kill shall be in danger of the judgment:<br>**22.** But I say unto you, That whosoever is angry with his brother ***without a cause*** shall be in danger of ***the*** judgment: and whosoever shall say to his brother, Raca, shall be in danger of the council: ***but*** whosoever shall say, Thou fool, shall be in danger of hell fire.<br><br>[The judgement, which follows on from the use of the phrase in v.21, is firmly established as *divine* judgement, as it places someone in danger of hell fire yet in 3 Nephi Smith has Christ *change* this.]<br><br>**23.** Therefore if ***thou bring thy gift to the altar,*** and ***there*** rememberest that thy brother hath ought against thee;<br>**24.** ***Leave there thy gift before the altar, and*** go thy way; first be reconciled to thy brother, and then come ***and offer thy gift.***<br><br>[Matthew is emphasising reconciliation should take place before a person is worthy to offer gifts at the altar. In Smith's version in *3 Nephi 12*, he has Christ use the same text but alters a few words to change the statement entirely.]<br><br>**25.** Agree with thine adversary quickly, *whiles* thou art in the way with him; lest at any time ***the adversary deliver thee to the judge, and the judge deliver thee to the officer,*** and thou be cast into prison.<br><br>**26.** Verily I say unto thee, Thou shalt by no means come out thence, ***till*** thou hast paid the uttermost ***farthing.*** |

# APPENDIX E – THE BEATITUDES

*And while ye are in prison can ye pay even one senine? Verily, verily, I say unto you, Nay.*
[A **senine**, a *silver* Nephite coin, was worth *8 Leahs*, missing the point of Christ's claimed statement entirely. For this to be real, Christ would have used the lowest known coin of the day. In Nephite terms that was the **Leah**.] [See also Apx. A, and in particular page 469 for further details of Nephite coins.]

**27.** *Behold, it is written* by them of old time, **that** thou shalt not commit adultery;
**28.** But I say unto you, that whosoever looketh on a woman, to lust after her, hath committed adultery already in his heart.

**29.** *Behold, I give unto you a commandment, that ye suffer none of these things to enter into your heart;*

**30.** *For it is better that ye should deny yourselves of these things, wherein ye will take up your cross, than that ye should be cast into hell.*

[Smith completely ignores v.29-30 from Matthew and replaces them with yet another 'follow me or go to hell' statement. Perhaps Smith didn't understand Matthew 5:29-30?]

**31.** It hath been **written, that** whosoever shall put away his wife, let him give her a writing of divorcement.
**32.** *Verily, verily*, I say unto you, that whosoever shall put away his wife, saving for the cause of fornication, causeth her to commit adultery; and

[A **farthing** was the lowest denomination. A **senine**, according the *Book of Mormon*, was a *silver* coin. (See Alma 11). There were several lower denominations and had this been a true comparison by Christ, He would surely have used the lowest: **Leah**.] [See Apx. A, where apologists try to claim these were not coins, but rather *weights*.]

**27.** *Ye have heard that it was said* by them of old time, Thou shalt not commit adultery:
**28.** But I say unto you, That whosoever looketh on a woman to lust after her hath committed adultery **with her** already in his heart.

**29.** *And if thy right eye offend thee, pluck it out, and cast it from thee: for it is profitable for thee that one of thy members should perish, and not that thy whole body should be cast into hell.*

**30.** *And if thy right hand offend thee, cut it off, and cast it from thee: for it is profitable for thee that one of thy members should perish, and not that thy whole body should be cast into hell.*

[The real question is that if Christ really was (somewhat miraculously) speaking identically to Matthew 5 text, why would He deviate for two verses and then jump right back in where He had left off?]

**31.** It hath been **said**, Whosoever shall put away his wife, let him give her a writing of divorcement:
**32. But** I say unto you, That whosoever shall put away his wife, saving for the cause of fornication, causeth her to commit adultery: and

| | |
|---|---|
| whoso shall marry her who is divorced committeth adultery.<br>**33**. *And* again *it is written*,<br><br>thou shalt not forswear thyself, but shalt perform unto the Lord thine oaths;<br>**34**. But *verily, verily*, I say unto you, swear not at all; neither by heaven, for it is God's throne;<br>**35**. Nor by the earth, for it is his footstool;<br>[Smith is obliged to leave out the *city* as it would not be known to Nephites].<br>**36**. Neither shalt thou swear by thy head, because thou canst not make one hair **black or white**;<br><br>[Note reversed wording: Christ's bad memory – or evidence of a hoax?]<br><br>**37**. But let your communication be Yea, yea; Nay, nay; for whatsoever **cometh of** more than these *is* evil.<br>**38**. *And behold, it is written*,<br>an eye for an eye, and a tooth for a tooth;<br>**39**. But I say unto you, that ye **shall not resist** evil, but whosoever shall smite thee on thy right cheek , turn to him the other also;<br>**40**. And if any man will sue thee at the law and take away thy coat, let him have thy *cloak* also;<br>**41**. And whosoever shall compel thee to go a mile, go with him twain.<br>**42**. Give to him that asketh thee, and from him that would borrow of thee turn thou not away.<br>**43**. *And behold it is written also, that* thou shalt love thy neighbor and hate thine enemy;<br>**44**. But *behold* I say unto you, love your enemies, bless them that curse you, do good to them that hate you, and pray for them who despitefully use you and persecute you; | whosoever shall marry her that is divorced committeth adultery.<br>**33**.     Again, *ye have heard that it hath been said by them of old time*,<br>Thou shalt not forswear thyself, but shalt perform unto the Lord thine oaths:<br>**34**. But           I say unto you, Swear not at all; neither by heaven; for it is God's throne:<br>**35**. Nor by the earth; for it is his footstool:<br>*neither by Jerusalem; for it is the city of the great King.*<br>**36**. Neither shalt thou swear by thy head, because thou canst not make one hair **white or black.**<br><br>[If Christ really had been repeating this *verbatim*, he would *not* have reversed it].<br><br>**37**. But let your communication be, Yea, yea; Nay, nay: for whatsoever     *is* more than these **cometh** of evil.<br>**38**. *Ye have heard that it hath been said,* An eye for an eye, and a tooth for a tooth:<br>**39**. But I say unto you, That ye   *resist not*    evil: but whosoever shall smite thee on thy right cheek, turn to him the other also.<br>**40**. And if any man will sue thee at the law, and take away thy coat, let him have thy *cloke* also.<br>**41**. And whosoever shall compel thee to go a mile, go with him twain.<br>**42**. Give to him that asketh thee, and from him that would borrow of thee turn not thou away.<br>**43**. *Ye have heard that it hath been said,* Thou shalt love thy neighbour, and hate thine enemy.<br>**44**. But         I say unto you, Love your enemies, bless them that curse you, do good to them that hate you, and pray for them which despitefully use you, and persecute you; |

# APPENDIX E – THE BEATITUDES

| | |
|---|---|
| **45.** That ye may be the children of your Father *who* is in heaven; for he maketh his sun to rise on the evil and on the good. | **45.** That ye may be the children of your Father *which* is in heaven: for he maketh his sun to rise on the evil and on the good, *and sendeth rain on the just and on the unjust.* |
| **46.** *Therefore those things which were of old time, which were under the law, in me are all fulfilled.* | **46.** *For if ye love them which love you, what reward have ye? do not even the publicans the same?* |
| **47.** *Old things are done away, and all things have become new.* | **47.** *And if ye salute your brethren only, what do ye more than others? do not even the publicans so?* |
| [A further meaningless Smith deviation in v.46-47 before finally ending more or less in line with Matthew 5:48]. | |
| **48.** *Therefore I would that ye should* be perfect even as *I, or* your Father *who* is in heaven is perfect. | **48.** Be     *ye therefore* perfect, even as your Father *which* is in heaven is perfect. |

Note in v.25, Matthew's text reads "lest at any time *the adversary deliver thee to the judge, and the judge deliver thee to the officer*, and thou be cast into prison. Smith changes Christ's words in the Americas to read "lest at any time *he shall get thee*, and thou shalt be cast into prison." The phraseology is neither Christ-like nor is it a viable expression of the day – it is nineteenth century nonsense, presumably altered as Smith couldn't remember whether he had included 'judges' and 'officers' in that context in his *Book of Mormon*. In point of fact he actually had, so he could have left the verse just as it was in the *KJV*. It begs the question, if we accept Christ actually was there and that He did say these things, why did he change the text in this way? "Lest any time *he shall get thee*" is just evidence of a hoax, along with some very bad language.

> **Alma 11:2.** Now if a man owed another, and he would not pay that which he did owe, he was complained of to *the judge; and the judge* executed authority, and sent forth *officers* that the man should be brought before him; and he judged the man according to the law... (Emphasis added).

Smith altered the word 'which' to the word 'who' several times for no valid reason other than to show his ignorance of the style of Early Modern English. *(See verses 6, 10, 45 and 46).*

Whereas in Matthew, Jesus often says something like – ye have heard that 'it hath been *said*', Smith changes the text in each case in *3 Nephi 12* to read 'it hath been *written*' or something similar. In the Holy Land, most people could not read, and in any event, they certainly did not have their own 'scriptures' to read. Scrolls of scripture were hand copied, kept and read to the people by a Rabbi. Therefore, most people would only have *heard* what was *said*. Although Lehi and his family were Jews and supposedly had the Brass Plates on which were written many of the scriptures, Smith never considers ongoing Jewish traditions or ceremonies in his *Book of Mormon*. Six hundred years of history had passed without the mention of any readings or Jewish religious observance at all. (Scant references to 'sacrifices' or 'burnt offerings' are all that will be found and can be counted on one hand). They would not have *heard* anything much at all, as Smith didn't include the idea. That left him with just the written word – and only one copy of it at that. Whatever Smith's reason, he changed the words in each case. The question is: Would Jesus have done that if He really had been speaking – on top of repeating almost the same words as found in *Matthew*? *(See verses 21, 27, 31, 33, 38 and 43).* Why would he say 'heard' in the first instance and then change it to 'written' half a dozen times when speaking to the Nephites? Clearly, he wouldn't.

The bigger problem for the Mormon Church is the fact that the gospels were recorded decades to centuries after Christ lived and they were written by people who did not hear Christ speak in the first person. They are at best second or third hand accounts of things Christ *may* have said or ideas of what he spoke *about*. Despite some Christian claims that *Matthew* was penned by the apostle Matthew, it almost certainly was not. It is the near-universal position of scholarship that the *Gospel of Matthew* is dependent upon the *Gospel of Mark*. It is also the consensus position that the evangelist was *not* the apostle Matthew. A worthwhile summary of this area is available at the following link: http://www.earlychristianwritings.com/matthew.html

The fact is that *Matthew* was written around 80 CE and possibly as late as 100 CE. It would be utterly impossible for it to contain the exact spoken words of Christ – which He then reiterated in the Americas almost word for word.

# Appendix F

**Gordon B. Hinckley denies knowing that God was once a man.**

Referenced from Chapters: 3, p.58; 4, p.66; 5, p.103.

*San Francisco Chronicle*, 13 Apr 1997:3/Z1 Don Lattin, religion editor, interview with Gordon B. Hinckley.

**Q:** There are some significant differences in your beliefs [and other Christian churches]. For instance, don't Mormons believe that God was once a man?

**Hinckley:** I wouldn't say that. There was a little couplet coined, "As man is, God once was. As God is, man may become." Now that's more of a couplet than anything else. That gets into some pretty deep theology that we don't know very much about.

———————

*Time Magazine*, 4 Aug 1997, quoting Gordon B. Hinckley:

On whether his church still holds that God the Father was once a man, [Hinckley] sounded uncertain,

"I don't know that we teach it. I don't know that we emphasize it... I understand the philosophical background behind it, but I don't know a lot about it, and I don't think others know a lot about it."

The Church claimed Hinckley had been taken out of context and misquoted in the *Time Magazine* article. However, the *Time* reporter's transcript of the interview with Hinckley was then made public:

> **Q:** Just another related question that comes up is the statements in the King Follett discourse by the Prophet.
>
> **Hinckley:** Yeah.
>
> **Q:** ... about that, God the Father was once a man as we were. This is something that Christian writers are always addressing. *Is this the teaching of the church today, that God the Father was once a man like we are?* (Emphasis added).
>
> **Hinckley:** *I don't know that we teach it. I don't know that we emphasize it. I haven't heard it discussed for a long time in public discourse. I don't know.* I don't know all the circumstances under which that statement was made. I understand the philosophical background behind it. But I don't know a lot about it and I don't know that others know a lot about it. (Emphasis added).
>
> *(See: San Francisco Chronicle, 13 Apr 1997:3/Z1 Don Lattin, religion editor, interview with Gordon B. Hinckley; also Time Magazine, 4 Aug 1997).*

The question is that if a modern day prophet doesn't know what every Mormon knows for an absolute fact, that God was indeed once a man, then what hope is there of anything *any* supposed prophet says being reliable?

# Appendix G

## Adam-God and Blood Atonement

Referenced from Chapter 1, page 23; Chapter 9, page 174.

The above two topics are more fully covered in *TMD Vol. 3*. Originally, I was not going to write about them at all, accepting the Church claim that neither one was 'real'. Once I researched and discovered the basis of each established 'doctrine', the topics resulted in some sixty-thousand words in *Volume 3*. As it turned out, I could have written an entire book regarding the evidence on each of the two subjects. In respect of the fact that some readers may not own a copy of *Volume 3*, the following details, many of which appear in it, should suffice to provide an outline of the truth behind modern-day claims.

### Adam-God

In 1938, Apostle John A. Widtsoe claimed the whole idea was a *myth* and not even so much as a theory, stating that anyone who read Brigham Young's remarks concerning it could be confused if they were read superficially "but very clear if read with their context." He goes on to say, regarding Young's first recorded mention of Adam-God in his 1852 sermon:

An honest reading of this sermon and of other reported discourses of President Brigham Young proves that the great second President of the Church held no such views as have been put into his mouth in the form of the Adam-God myth. *(Improvement Era Nov 1938:652&690; Also cited in Widtsoe 1960:67-71).*

Prophet, Spencer W. Kimball, decried the idea as "false doctrine" in 1976.

We warn you against the dissemination of doctrines which are not according to the scriptures and which are alleged to have been taught by some of the General Authorities of past generations. Such, for instance, is the Adam-God theory. We denounce that theory and hope that everyone will be cautioned against this and other kinds of false doctrine. *(Spencer W. Kimball. Ensign. Nov 1976:77).*

Whatever it was, it was certainly *not* a myth put into the unwitting mouth of Brigham Young to discredit him. It was certainly no 'theory' either.

On 8 Oct 1854, at a Church Conference, Brigham Young gave a further sermon that was not finally published until the 1970s, well over a hundred years later. It included the following remarks:

***The God and Father [of] our Lord Jesus Christ is the Father of our spirits.***

***…Adam is the Father of our spirits.*** He lived upon an earth; he did abide his creation, and did honor to his calling and Priesthood; and obeyed his Master or Lord, and probably many of his wives did the same, and ***they lived, and died upon an earth, and then were resurrected again*** to Immortality and Eternal Life.

Our spirits and ***the spirits of all the human family were begotten by Adam, and born of Eve.***

Adam planted the Garden of Eden, and he with his wife Eve partook of the fruit of this Earth, until their systems were charged with the nature of Earth, and then they could beget bodies, for their spiritual children.

***I tell you, when you see your Father in the Heavens, you will see Adam; when you see your Mother that bear your spirit, you will see Mother Eve.*** *(Campbell 1992:86-103).* (Emphasis added).

I can only assume that in 1938, Apostle John A. Widtsoe was not aware of this discourse when he said the whole idea was just a myth. However, I have to agree that the words are indeed "very clear if read with their context" as the context of the above could in fact not be clearer. Unfortunately for Widtsoe, that clarity is entirely the opposite of his own argument.

# APPENDIX G – ADAM-GOD & BLOOD ATONEMENT

Some of the most powerful evidence that Adam-God was doctrine stems from the fact that *two* Apostles just could not accept it and their membership became threatened if they would not capitulate and accept it. Amasa M. Lyman had problems with this doctrine and other teachings. Lyman did not 'confess' (as Orson Pratt finally did in 1868) and he was dropped from the Quorum of Twelve Apostles on 6 Oct 1867 and later excommunicated, on 12 May 1870. *(Church Almanac. 2006:60).* Orson Pratt obviously knew he would go the way of Lyman if he did not 'confess' and agree with Young's Adam-God doctrine.

Pratt agonised over his dissention with Young and the other apostles but was certainly still bold in his approach to the subject. On 4 April 1860, he outlined his 'grievances' thus:

> I would like to ennumerate [those] items. First preached and publish[ed] that Adam is the fa[ther] of our spirits, & father of Spirit and father of our bodies. When I read the Rev given to Joseph I read directly the opposite. Lord spake to Adam, which Man eventually became Adam's[.] [1]

Faced with Pratt quoting Joseph Smith as an ally, Young now (and for the first time ever) introduces a very powerful basis for his own teachings, which he later repeated more than once. He countered that they actually originated with none other than Joseph Smith himself. There was no better way to shoot Pratt down in flames. No one however, has ever found any conclusive evidence that Smith did go that far in his own teachings which would support Young's claim, other than in him saying that Adam was the "Ancient of Days" in a few of his *D&C* revelations. Here Young calls on none other than founding prophet, Joseph Smith, as the source of his Adam-God doctrine.

> Your statements to night, you come out to night & place them as charges, & have as many against me as I have [against] you. One thing I have thought that I might still have omitted. ***It was Joseph's doctrine that Adam was God*** &c When in Luke Johnson's at O Hydes the power came upon us, or shock that alarmed the neighbourhood. God comes to earth & eats & partakes of fruit. Joseph could not reveal what was revealed to him, & if Joseph had it revealed, he was told not to reveal it… [2] (Emphasis added).

The debate continued the following day, between Orson Pratt and the other Apostles. Almost all the other apostles accepted the Adam-God doctrine.

> President Young said Adam was Michael the Ark angel & he was the Father of Jesus Christ & was our God and that ***Joseph taught this principle***. *(Journal of Wilford Woodruff. V.6:381, 16 Dec 1867).* (Emphasis added).

...the period will come when the people will be willing to *adopt Joseph Smith as their* Prophet, Seer and Revelator and *God!* But *not the father of their spirits*, for *that was* our father *Adam. (Journal of Wilford Woodruff, V.5:361, 11 Dec 1869. Brigham Young Addresses 1865-1869. Elden J. Watson, Feb. 1982).* (Emphasis added).

Orson Pratt finally confessed that he had been wrong and accepted Adam was indeed God. He was obliged to write a confession *(Copy in TMD Vol. 3. Apx. G).* The doctrine was presented by Young in the temple, as recorded by Wilford Woodruff "...President [Brigham Young] was present and delivered a lecture at the veil some 30 attndg" in his own journal, thus confirming that it was indeed given at the veil by Young himself on 1 February 1877. That evening, Young amended it and he gave the lecture again on Wednesday 7 February.

This is a little of what Young's 'Lecture at the Veil' included, as recorded in L. John Nuttall's journal. *(The full text appears in TMD Vol. 3:60-70).*

*Adam was an immortal being when he came. on this earth* he had lived on an earth similar to ours he had received the priesthood and the Keys thereof. and had been faithful in all things and *gained his resurrection and his exaltation and was crowned with glory immortality* and eternal lives and *was numbered with the Gods* for such he became through his faithfulness. and *had begotten all the spirit that was to come to this earth. and Eve our common mother who is the mother of all living bore those spirits in the celestial world.*

And when this earth was organized by Elohim. Jehovah and *Michael who is Adam our common father.* Adam and Eve had the privilege to continue the work of Progression. consequently *came to this earth and commenced the great work* of forming tabernacles for those spirits to dwell in. and when Adam and those that assisted him had completed this kingdom our earth he came to it. and slept and forgot all and became like an Infant child...

*Father Adam's oldest son (Jesus the Saviour) who is the heir of the family is father Adams first begotten in the spirit world. who according to the flesh is the only begotten as it is written.* (In his divinity he having gone back into the spirit world. and came in the spirit [glory] to Mary and she conceived for when Adam and Eve got through with their work in this earth. they did not lay their bodies down in the dust, but returned to the spirit World from whence they came.

# APPENDIX G – ADAM-GOD & BLOOD ATONEMENT

Young is fully evidenced as teaching that Adam *was* God. He claimed Joseph Smith taught him the doctrine. Most of the apostles gained a personal witness from God that it was true. Later Prophets, namely Taylor, Woodruff and Snow are also confirmed as having taught it, with both Taylor and Woodruff enforcing it through disciplinary councils as doctrine. *(TMD Vol. 3).*

On 12 October 1897, at a meeting of the Quorum of Twelve, the President of the Apostles, Lorenzo Snow…

> led out on Adam being our father and God. How beautiful the thought it brot. God nearer to us. *(Quinn 1997:799).*

Snow became the next prophet. His understanding was very clear.

The next prophet was Joseph Fielding Smith, who had been an apostle throughout the time Adam-God had been an accepted doctrine. The fact is that Smith knew very well what the doctrine was and he recorded his understanding in his journal. As an apostle and Counsellor in the First Presidency to Young (as well as the next three prophets) before he himself became the Prophet, he knew *exactly* what was taught and believed. Joseph Fielding Smith himself had recorded what Brigham Young taught, during the School of the Prophets in June 1871:

> Elohim, Yahova & Michael, were father, Son and grandson. They made this Earth & Michael became Adam. *(Joseph F. Smith Journal. 17 Jun 1871, LDS archives).*

Smith seems to have made no comment either way for over thirty years but once he became President, everything changed. He simply ignored the past and the doctrine got shelved and ultimately forgotten. Now it is completely *denied.*

---

Notes.

1. The following references contain more details of the difficult position that Pratt was placed in:
*The Adam-God Doctrine.* David John Buerger. Dialogue. V.15. No1. Spring 1982:14-58. (See pp. 24-25).
*The Orson Pratt - Brigham Young Controversies: Conflicts Within the Quorums, 1853 to 1868* by Gary James Bergera. Dialogue. V.13. No.2. Summer 1980:7-49. (See p. 26) citing: Minutes of meeting at Historians Office, 4 Apr 1860.
Bergera is also cited in Tanner 1987:178c.

2. *Minutes of meeting at Historian's Office.* Great Salt Lake City. 7 p.m. 4 Apr 1860. Cited in Item # 87 in *Adam-God* http://www.xmission.com/~plporter/lds/ag.htm

## Blood Atonement

When I asked about blood atonement, the stock answer I got from Church leaders was always that the concept applied (only) to the atonement of Jesus Christ, who shed his blood for all people. There is *no* other application and the Church has *never* taught or believed in individual blood atonement for sins the Saviour's blood could *not* accommodate. However, I now discover that earlier leaders *did* teach the 'Law of Blood Atonement' and that it *was* practiced.

> 27 July 1902. *Deseret News* editorial, "Blood Atonement," affirms: "We take the ground that the **only atonement a murderer can make for his guilt is the shedding of his blood** according to the divine mandate."
>
> Under the new and everlasting covenant, as well as under the Mosaic law and the patriarchal law which preceded it, **an adulterer who is under a sacred vow not to commit that crime is also worthy of death.** But this is not sanctioned by modern civil law; therefore, the penalty cannot be executed. For the church is commanded of God to obey the laws of the land. *(Quinn 1997:805)*. (Emphasis added).

Perhaps the law would not allow for that in the twentieth century, but did it in the nineteenth century? There was no established law in Utah which could stop the Church from preaching it or from practicing it, as the Church under Young was effectively a law unto itself. However, there were a number of people who *recorded* what happened. Additionally, once the law could be effectively enforced, the resulting trials confirm accusations, names and deeds.

> Utah incorporated in the laws of the Territory provisions for the capital punishment of those who willfully shed the blood of their fellow men. This law, which is now the law of the State, granted unto the condemned murderer the privilege of choosing for himself whether he die by hanging, or whether he be shot, and thus **have his blood shed in harmony with the law of god; and thus atone, so far as it is in his power to atone**, for the death of his victim. *(Smith, Joseph Fielding 1954: V.1:136)* (Emphasis added).
>
> As a mode of capital punishment, hanging or execution on a gallows does not comply with the **law of blood atonement**, for the blood is not shed. *(McConkie 1958:314)*. (Emphasis added).

The above are all twentieth century statements. We learn from Smith, then President of the Quorum of Twelve Apostles and later to become the Prophet, that shedding blood is the "law of God". McConkie, then a member of the First Council of Seventy and later apostle, admits to the "law of blood atonement".

# APPENDIX G – ADAM-GOD & BLOOD ATONEMENT

Historical records and documented deeds agree; they do *not* support the claim blood atonement did not exist; rather, they provide more than sufficient evidence that it most certainly did. Mormon murders were well documented from the very beginning.

> A number of Mormons lost their lives during these early years. Unfortunately, however, many Mormon historians have overlooked the other side of the story. During the early years of Mormonism it was frequently alleged that the leaders of the church sanctioned the practice of putting both Gentiles and Mormon apostates to death. *(Salt Lake City Messenger, Issue No. 92, April, 1997, available at* www.utlm.org*)*.

Many accounts of ecclesiastical judgements, leading to barbaric and cruel behaviour which included whipping, castration, murder and massacre, due to the 'Law of God' and 'blood atonement' are contained in journals, diaries, newspaper articles, court proceedings and a number of published books. *(See: TMD 3, Section 4 for several examples and further recommended reading)*.

There are far too many clearly authenticated accounts to claim Young's teachings were purely rhetorical. The killings went on for so many years, that had Young really objected, had he considered that members were taking his sermons too literally, he had more than ample time and opportunity to say so.

There is not a single reference where Young is recorded as telling the Saints *not* to take his words literally and to *stop* the castrations, *stop* slitting throats of adulterers and *stop* killing apostates and gentiles; **not one.**

Following Joseph Smith's death, an *Oath of Vengeance* was incorporated into the endowment ceremony, which obligated members to take retribution on the State and the Country, given *any* such opportunity. *(See also: TMD Vol.3, Section 3: under 'The Law (or Oath) of Vengeance' Pp.167-168)*.

> You and each of you do solemnly promise and vow that you will pray, and never cease to pray, and never cease to importune high heaven to avenge the blood of the prophets on this nation, and that you will teach this to your children and your children's children unto the third and fourth generation. *(Reed Smoot Case 1907 V.4:495-96)*.

These are quotes from Brigham Young, Heber C. Kimball and J. M. Grant:

> I say, rather than that apostates should flourish here, I will unsheathe my bowie knife, and conquer or die. (Great commotion in the congregation and a simultaneous burst of feeling, assenting to the declaration). Now, **you nasty apostates, clear out, or judgement will be put to the line and righteousness to the plummet**. (Voices generally, 'Go it, go it.') If you say it is all right, raise your hands (all hands up). **Let us call upon the Lord to assist us in this and every good work…** *(JD V.1:83. Brigham Young. 27 March 1853)*.

> This is loving our neighbour as ourselves; if he needs help, help him; and if he wants salvation and *it is necessary to spill his blood upon the ground in order that he may be saved, spill it.* *(JD V.4:220; Deseret News V.6:397).*
>
> ...for *we wipe all unclean ones out of our midst; we not only wipe them from the streets, but we wipe them out of existence*. And if the world wants to practice uncleanness, and bring their prostitutes here, if they do not repent and forsake their sins, *we will wipe the evil out*. We will not have them in this valley unless they repent, for so help me God, while I live *I will lend my hand to wipe such persons out*, and I know this people will. *(Deseret News, 16 August 1854; Millennial Star, V.16:738-9. President Heber C. Kimball 19 July 1854).*
>
> I say there are men and women here that I would advise to go to the president immediately, and ask him to appoint a committee to attend to their case, and then *let a place be selected, and let that committee shed their blood*. *(Deseret News V.6:235. Pres. J. M. Grant. 21 September 21, 1856).* (Emphasis added in above statements).

If Brigham Young never preached blood atonement with the intent that it should be carried out on apostates and outsiders, why then did he make specific reference to having people 'used up' and why were murders that were carried out *by* Mormons so prolific in Utah?

> ...as it is said in the Report of these officers, *if I had crooked my little finger, he would have been used up, but I did not bend it.* If I had, the sisters alone felt indignant enough to have chopped him in pieces. I did not, however, do it, but suffered him to fill up the measure of his shame and iniquity until his cup is running over. He was not hurt in the least...
> ...*Every man that comes to impose upon this people, no matter by whom they are sent, or who they are that are sent, lay the axe at the root of the tree to kill themselves.* I will do as I said I would, last Conference. *Apostates, or men who never made any profession of religion, had better be careful how they come here, lest I should bend my little finger.* (Brigham Young, Tabernacle, 19 Jun 1853. JD V.1:185-190). (Emphasis added).

It would be impossible to cover all the available evidence in a short note on the subject so I will just cover a legal case which typifies the way the concept was implemented and accepted. It concerns Apostle George A. Smith when he used the following argument in his defense of Howard Egan, who had murdered James Monroe, who had seduced one of Egan's wives. She was a willing partner and had a baby by Monroe while Egan was absent.

# APPENDIX G – ADAM-GOD & BLOOD ATONEMENT

> The principle, the only one that beats and throbs through the heart of the entire inhabitants of this Territory, is simply this: ***The man who seduces his neighbors wife must die, and her nearest relative must kill him!*** *(Apostle George A. Smith. First Judicial District Court of the United States for the Territory of Utah. Great Salt Lake City, October Term, 1851. JD V.1:97)*

The case was simple enough. Howard Egan had murdered Monroe in a premeditated act of revenge. He did not deny it. He was guilty of a capital crime and the law was clear regarding his punishment. There was no possibility (in law) that a 'not-guilty' verdict could ever be accommodated. But, it was a Mormon apostle who was defending the case, a Mormon judge presiding and an all Mormon jury deciding it. They all believed that blood atonement was the *only* course of action that would save an adulterer, so Egan was *theologically* correct when he 'saved' Monroe by shedding his blood. A Mormon jury would never go against anything that an apostle directed in civil court any more than in theological matters. The Mormon judge, whose summation should have remained completely impartial of course, included theocratic direction to the jury. This is a little of what Smith had to say:

> I argue that in this territory it is a principle of mountain common law, that no man can seduce the wife of another without endangering his own life…

Smith openly acknowledged the fact that Egan had killed Monroe in cold blood, stating "…After Mr. Egan had killed Monroe…" within his argument.

> Mr. Horner [a witness] knew the common law of this Territory: he was acquainted with the genius and spirit of this people: he knew that Monroe's life was forfeited, and the executor was after him…

> I will refer to the case of "New Jersey v. Mercer," for killing Hibberton, the seducer of his sister. The circumstance took place upon a public ferry-boat, where Hibberton was shot in a close carriage in the most public manner. After repeated jury sittings upon his case, the decision was NOT GUILTY. ***We will allow this to be set down as a precedent, and, if you please, call it American common law.*** I will refer to another case: that of "Louisiana v. Horton," for the killing of the seducer of his sister. The jury in this case also found the prisoner NOT GUILTY. This is the common practice in the United States, that a man who kills the seducer of his relative is set free…

> ***…If Howard Egan did kill James Monroe, it was in accordance with the established principles of justice known in these mountains. That the people of this Territory would have regarded him as accessory to the crimes of that creature, had he not done it, is also a plain case.***

> Every man knew the style of old Israel, that the nearest relation would be at his heels to fulfil the requirements of justice. Now I wish you, gentlemen of the jury, to consider that the United States have not got the jurisdiction to hang that man for this offence: the laws are not applicable to it; they have ceded away the power to do that thing: it belongs to the people of this territory; and, as a matter of course, we deny the right of this court to hang this defendant, on principles that have been ceded away to somebody else to act upon.
>
> ...we are called upon to hang a man according to the customs of a nation ten thousand miles from here, whose principles, organization, spirit, ideas of right and wrong, of crime and justice, are quite different from those which prevail in this young and flourishing territory... **This act of killing has been committed within the Territory of Utah, and is not therefore under the exclusive jurisdiction of the United States...**
>
> I make this appeal to you, that you may give unto us a righteous verdict, which will acquit Mr. Egan, that it may be known that the man who shall insinuate himself into the community, and seduce his neighbor's wife, or seduce or prostitute any female, may expect to find no more protection than the wolf would find, or the dog that the shepherd finds killing the sheep: that he may be made aware that he cannot escape for a moment. (Emphasis added).

Smith did not use any legal argument other than to reference a couple of cases where acquittal had been achieved, but he did not indicate whether the accused were acquitted through *justification* of the act, or a *lack of evidence* with which to convict them. As there was nothing else to argue, he then simply used the logic that 'mountain law' or common, *unwritten* law, which was effectively *Church law*, allowed for (and even *required*) that Egan kill Monroe as a *duty* and that he would have been 'guilty' had he *not* committed the act.

When Mormon Judge, Snow, supposedly without bias, summed up, he used a series of statements to lead the jury to only one possible conclusion. The fact that Judge, jury and counsel all believed in a higher law that required the next of kin to murder the perpetrator of such a crime, would supersede any verdict any other court may have legally imposed. In his preamble, Snow commented that: "The safety of ourselves individually, and of society, depends on the correct and faithful administration of good and wholesome laws." After that it went downhill with the wind regarding any possible chance of a conviction for the crime.

> No one ought to be punished unless he be guilty of an act worthy of punishment ... In this case, there is no pretence but that the defendant, at the time of the alleged killing of James Monroe, was of sound mind and discretion... If you find the defendant gave him the mortal wound, you will then inquire whether the killing was lawful or unlawful... The

# APPENDIX G – ADAM-GOD & BLOOD ATONEMENT

> law does not permit a person to take the redress of grievances into his own hands. Though the deceased may have seduced the defendant's wife, as he now alleges, still he had no right to take the remedy into his own hands... If, for seduction, the law inflicted the punishment of death, it would not justify nor excuse the injured party from guilt, if he inflicted death without a judgment of the law to that effect, nor even with such a judgment, unless he be the officer of the law appointed for that purpose... If, as it is contended by the defendant's attorney, he killed Monroe in the name of the Lord, it does not change the law of the case.

Thus far, Snow is saying all the right words and he is not seen as being in any way biased, but then:

> Should you be of the opinion in all these things, that the defendant is guilty, then the place in which the act was committed becomes material. This would not in most cases affect the general result, provided the crime be committed within the jurisdiction of the court trying the accused.
>
> The jurisdiction of the United States courts is separate and distinct from the jurisdiction of the State courts. But in the Territories, the same judges sit in matters arising out of the constitution and laws of the United States, as well as the laws of their respective Territories...
>
> ...the crime must be committed within the places over which the United States have the sole and exclusive jurisdiction. You will look to the evidence given you in court for the facts of the case; if you find the crime, if any has been committed, was committed within that extent of country between this and the Missouri river, over which the United States have the sole and exclusive jurisdiction, your verdict must be guilty. If you do not find the crime to have been committed there, but ***in the Territory of Utah, the defendant, for that reason, is entitled to a verdict of, not guilty.*** (Emphasis added).

Snow did not explain *why* the verdict must be not guilty; it was still murder, wherever it took place. He was of course referring (as did Smith) to 'mountain law' or the 'law of God'. If it was true that "in the Territory of Utah, the defendant, for that reason, is entitled to a verdict of, not guilty", then the case need never have gone to trial in the first place. Clearly it was too public an offence *not* to deal with it and therefore a trial had to be seen to have taken place and a jury decision registered. The all Mormon jury, who were hardly likely to go against their religious teachings, let alone an apostle (not and survive anyway), deliberated for all of fifteen minutes, during which time they also had to write up their verdict, which was unanimous – not guilty. The

Church considered Smith's defence summary and Judge Snow's summation to be significant enough in detail to publish them both in the *Deseret News*, print two pamphlets, and include them both in the *Journal of Discourses. (See: TMD Vol. 3, Apx: K & L for full transcripts; also at:* http://journalofdiscourses.org).

The Egan case *was* blood atonement. Notwithstanding denials from modern Church leaders in twentieth century writings, there is abundant evidence of Church sanctioned, approved and even *ordered* murder, castration, beating, whipping, and threats to commit such acts against people for 'sins' of adultery or stealing and even for wanting to marry someone that a local leader desired.

> Murder after murder has been committed with impunity within the precincts of Great Salt Lake City, still such occurrences do not seemingly attract much attention, particularly when the murdered have had the reputation of being thieves and murderers or of associating with such characters from day to day… *(23 May 1860. Deseret News editorial).*

One example of such an action, which included the presence of an apostle and the first hand confirmation of a reliable witness, is the murder of an excommunicated lawyer.

> 3 May 1853. Month after Brigham Young publicly condemns and excommunicates lawyer Jesse T. Hartley, he starts for eastern states, apparently without Young's safe conduct pass. William A. Hickman murders him during trip with apostle Orson Hyde and Hosea Stout in canyon. Stout's diary verifies Hickman's later account of this. *(Quinn 1997:751).*

The fact that people even *needed* such a thing as a "safe conduct pass" from Young is evidence in itself that murder was *authorised,* if not *required* in the ***absence*** of one. Many atrocities occurred in Utah under Church leaders' direction at various levels, from local leaders authorising the castration or murder of those considered to have sinned sufficiently enough to require it (or who were thwarting their own carnal desires) or who became apostate, to Young's voiced approval of 'using up' or taking 'over the rim of the basin' many gentiles who were passing through. Gentiles were viewed with suspicion and considered possible spies for the army. People were accused of crimes for which there was often no actual evidence and even if there was some evidence, there was absolutely no legal authority to take such retribution as was meted out by ecclesiastical leaders. The concept was that the 'law of God' superseded the 'law of the land'. As Utah territory was controlled by Brigham Young, he determined what was correct regarding procedure. If anyone did not agree with the leaders, then they were not likely to survive in the valley and were equally unlikely to succeed in leaving it – not and remain alive.

# Bibliography, Recommended Books & Web Sites
(The following relate to Volumes 1, 2, 3 & 4 of this work).

Anderson, Lavina F. (ed.). 2001. *Lucy's Book. A Critical Edition of Lucy Mack Smith's Family Memoir.* Salt Lake City, UT: Signature Books.
Anderson, Rodger I. 1990. *Joseph Smith's New York Reputation Re-examined.* Salt Lake City, UT: Signature Books.
Andrus, Hyrum Leslie. 1968. *God, Man, and the Universe.* Salt Lake City, UT: Bookcraft.
Baer, Dick & Robertson, Jim. (Comp.). 2002. *False Prophecies of Joseph Smith.* Mesa, AZ: Concerned Christians.
Bagley, Will. 2004. *Blood of the Prophets: Brigham Young and the Massacre at Mountain Meadows.* Oklahoma, OK: University of Oklahoma Press.
Bancroft, Hubert Howe. 1889. *History of Utah.* San Francisco, CA: The History Company. †
Barrett, David B; Kurian, George Thomas; Johnson, Todd M. 2001. *World Christian Encyclopaedia.* New York, NY: Oxford University Press.
Baskin. R.N. 1914. *Reminiscences of Early Utah.* Salt Lake City, UT: Tribune. †
Bauder, Peter. 1834. *The Kingdom and the Gospel of Jesus Christ: Contrasted with That of Anti-Christ. A Brief Review of Some of the Most Interesting Circumstances, Which Have Transpired Since the Institution of the Gospel of Christ, from the Days of the Apostles.* Canajoharie, New York, NY: A. H. Calhoun.
Beadle, J. H. 1872. See: Hickman, Bill.
Bennett, John C. 1842. *Mormonism Exposed - History of the Saints.* Boston, MA: Leland & Whiting. †
Bergera, Gary James. (ed.). 1989. *Line upon Line. Essays on Mormon Doctrine.* Salt Lake City, UT: Signature Books.
— 2002. *Conflict in the Quorum.* Salt Lake City, UT: Signature Books.
*A Book of Commandments, for the Government of the Church of Christ, organised According to Law, on the 6$^{th}$ April, 1830.* 1833. Reprinted 1972. Independence, MO: Herald House. †
*The Book of Mormon*, (BOM) 1830. Joseph Smith Jr. New York, NY: Egbert B. Grandin. †
— 1981 Edition. Joseph Smith Jr. Salt Lake City, UT: LDS Church. †
Brodie, Fawn M. 1963. *No Man Knows My History: The Life of Joseph Smith, the Mormon Prophet.* Great Britain 1$^{st}$ Edition. London: Eyre & Spottiswoode. (First U.S. Edition 1945. New York, NY: Alfred A. Knopf). §
Brooks, Juanita. 2003. *The Mountain Meadows Massacre.* Oklahoma, OK: University of Oklahoma Press.
Brown, Hugh B. 1965. *The Abundant Life.* Salt Lake City, UT: Bookcraft.
Budge, E.A. Wallis. 1989. (First published 1893). *The Mummy, A Handbook of Egyptian Funerary Archaeology.* New York, NY: Dover Publications Inc.
Buerger, David John. 2002. *The Mysteries of Godliness: A History of Mormon Temple Worship.* Salt Lake City, UT: Signature Books.

Campbell, Alexander. 1832. *Delusions: An Analysis of The Book of Mormon.* Boston, MA: Benjamin H. Greene. †

Campbell, Eugene E. 1988. *Establishing Zion.* Salt Lake City, UT: Signature Books. †

— (ed.). 1992. *The Essential Brigham Young.* Salt Lake City, UT: Signature. †

Cannon, Frank J. & Harvey J. 1911. *Under the Prophet in Utah; the National Menace of a Political Priestcraft.* Boston, MA: C.M. Clark Publishing. †

Cannon, George Q. 1907. *The Life of Joseph Smith, the Prophet.* Salt Lake City, UT: Deseret News.

*The Catholic Encyclopedia.* 1907-1912. New York, NY: Appleton. † Online version of original print publication: 2003. Kevin Knight. Located at: www.newadvent.org

Christensen, Culley K. 1981. *The Adam-God Maze.* Independent Publishers.

*Church Almanac.* (Published annually as *Deseret Morning News Church Almanac*). 2006 & 2007 editions cited. Salt Lake City, UT: Deseret Morning News.

Clark, Rev. John Alonzo. 1842. *Gleanings by the Way.* Philadelphia, PA: W.J. & J.K. Simon; New York, NY: Robert Carter.*

Collier, Fred C. & Harwell, William S. (eds.). 2002. *Kirtland Council Minute Book.* Salt Lake City, UT: Collier's Publishing Co.

Collier, Fred C. 1979. *Unpublished Revelations of the Prophets and Presidents of The Church of Jesus Christ of Latter-Day Saints.* 3 Vols. Salt Lake City, UT: Collier's Publishing Co.

— 2005. (ed.). *Nauvoo High Council Minute Books of The Church of Jesus Christ of Latter Day Saints.* Salt Lake City, UT: Collier's Publishing Co.

*Comprehensive History of the Church.* See: Roberts, B. H. 1978.

Compton, Todd. 1997. *In Sacred Loneliness: The Plural Wives of Joseph Smith.* Salt Lake City, UT: Signature Books. §

Cowan, Marvin W. 1997. *Mormon Claims Answered.* Salt Lake City, UT: UTLM. †

Cowley, Matthias F. 1964. *Wilford Woodruff: History of his Life and Labors.* Salt Lake City, UT: Bookcraft.

Davies, Glynn. 2002. *A History of Money from Ancient Times to the Present Day.* Cardiff: University of Wales.

Dawkins, Richard. 2003. *The Devil's Chaplain.* London: Weidenfeld & Nicolson.

— 2006. *The God Delusion.* London: Bantam Press. (Transworld). §

— 2009. *The Greatest Show on Earth: The Evidence for Evolution.* London: Bantam Press. §

Daynes, Kathryn M. 2001. *More Wives than One, Transformation of the Mormon Marriage System 1840 - 1910.* Urbana & Chicago, IL: University of Illinois Press. †

*Dialogue, A Journal of Mormon Thought.* An ongoing series of articles concerning the Church, available online www.dialoguejournal.com or www.lib.utah.edu/digital

*A Dictionary of the Bible.* (10 Vols). 1900. Hastings, James (1852-1922). New York, NY: C. Scribner's sons. (Referenced: Vol 2: Part 1. 2004. Hastings, James. (ed.). University Press of the Pacific).

*Doctrine and Covenants* (D&C). 1981. Salt Lake City, UT: LDS Church. †

Duncan, Malcolm A. 1866. *Duncan's Masonic Ritual and Monitor. (Duncan's Ritual of Freemasonry:* 2007). New York, NY: Dover Publications. Complete 1866 original work available online at: www.sacred-texts.com/mas/dun/

# BIBLIOGRAPHY, RECOMMENDED BOOKS & WEB SITES

*The Elders' Journal of The Church of Jesus Christ of Latter Day Saints.* (Elders' Journal). 4 Issues. (Vol.1:1-4): Oct & Nov 1837 (Kirtland, OH), Jul & Aug 1838 (Far West, MO).

*Encyclopædia Britannica.* 2007. Online version also available at www.britannica.com

*Encyclopedia of Mormonism.* (EM) 1992. Online Version. New York, NY: Macmillan. Available at: www.lib.byu.rdu/Macmillan/

Evans, Arza. 2003. *The Keystone of Mormonism.* St. George, UT: Keystone Books. §

Evans, Richard C. 1920. *Forty Years in the Mormon Church: Why I Left It!* Toronto, Canada: Bishop R. C. Evans (Self Published). †

FAIR — *The Foundation for Apologetic Information and Research.* (Mormon Apologetics). Available online at: www.fairlds.org/

FARMS — *The Foundation for Ancient Research and Mormon Studies.* Now renamed: *The Neal A. Maxwell Institute for Religious Scholarship.* (Mormon Apologetics). Available online at: http://farms.byu.edu/

Faulring, Scott H. (ed.). 1989. *An American Prophet's Record: The Diaries and Journals of Joseph Smith.* Salt Lake City, UT: Signature Books.

Fielding, Robert Kent. 1992. *The Unsolicited Chronicler.* New Mexico: Paradigm.

Froiseth, Jennie Anderson. (ed.). 1881. *The Women of Mormonism: Or The Story of Polygamy as Told by the Victims Themselves.* Detroit, MI: C.G.G. Paine. † §

Gibbs, Josiah F. 1910. *Mountain Meadows Massacre.* Salt Lake City, UT: Salt Lake Tribune. †

Hall, William. 1852. *The Abominations of Mormonism Exposed.* Cincinnati, OH: I. Hart & Co.

Hardy, B. Carmon. 1992. *Solemn Covenant, the Mormon Polygamous Passage.* Illinois: University of Illinois Press.

Hickman, Bill. (The Danite Chief of Utah). 1872. *Brigham's Destroying Angel.* Salt Lake City, UT: Shepard Publishing Co. 1904 edition online at UTLM. †

Hill, Donna. 1977. *Joseph Smith: The First Mormon.* New York, NY: Doubleday.

*History of the RLDS Church.* 1951. RLDS Church. Independence, MO: Herald House.

*History of the Church of Jesus Christ of Latter-day Saints.* (HC) 1902 on. 7 Vols. Salt Lake City, UT: LDS Church.

*History of the (Reorganised) Church of Jesus Christ of Latter-day Saints.* 1897-1908. 4 Vols. Smith, Joseph III & Smith, Heman Conoman. (Vol 2:1897 cited). Lamoni, IA: RLDS. Herald Publishing House.

Hoth, Hans Peter Emanuel. 1853-1857. *Hoth Diary.* Translation from original German. Berkeley, CA: University of California, Berkeley: The Bancroft Library. († UTLM).

Howe, E.D. 1834. *Mormonism Unvailed. [sic]* Painesville, OH: Howe. †

Hyde, John Jr. 1857. *Mormonism, Its Leaders and Designs.* New York, NY: W. P. Fetridge & Co.†

Hyde, Orson. 1842. *Ein Ruf aus der Wüste, eine Stimme aus dem Erhoofe der Erbe.* Frankfurt. (A Cry from the Wilderness, a Voice from the Dust of the Earth). Translated in 1962 and available in English via an internet search on 'Orson Hyde First Vision'.

*An Inspired Revision of the Authorised Version.* (IR). *(The Holy Scriptures: Inspired Version),* Joseph Smith. 1980. Independence, MO: Herald House. RLDS. †

*The International Standard Bible Encyclopedia.* 1995. (4 Vols. Fully Revised) by Geoffrey W. Bromiley. Grand Rapids, MI: William B. Eerdman Publishing.
Jenson, Andrew. (comp.). 1887. *The Historical Record.* 9 Vols. Salt Lake City, UT: Jenson.
— 1899. *Church Chronology.* Salt Lake City, UT: Deseret News.
Jessee, Dean. (comp.). 1984. *The Personal Writings of Joseph Smith.* Salt Lake City, UT: Deseret Book.
*Journal of Discourses* (JD) 1854-1884 by Brigham young, President of the Church of Jesus Christ of Latter Day Saints, His Two Counsellors, The Twelve Apostles and Others. 26 Volumes. Liverpool: R. James. †
Kenney, Scott. (ed.). 1984. *Wilford Woodruff's Journal 1833-1898.* Salt Lake City, UT: Signature Books.
Kimball, Spencer W. 1976. *Marriage and Divorce.* Salt Lake City, UT: Deseret Book.
Kirkham, Francis W. 1942. *A New Witness for Christ in America.* Independence, MO: Zion Printing & Publishing Co.
— 1951. *A New Witness for Christ in America.* Vol. 2. Independence, MO: Zion Printing & Publishing Co.
*Kirtland Elder's Quorum Record 1836-1841.* 1985. Cook, Lyndon W. & Backman, Milton V. Jr., (eds.). RLDS Church Archives. Provo, UT: Grandin Book Co. †
*Kirtland Revelation Book.* 1831-1839. Salt Lake City, UT: LDS Church Archives.
Lamb, Rev. M. T. 1887. *The Golden Bible.* (Reprint of Original). Salt Lake City, UT: UTLM.
Larsen, Charles M. 1992. *By His Own Hand Upon Papyrus: A New Look at the Joseph Smith Papyri.* Grand Rapids, MI: Institute for Religious Research. † (Part).
Larson, Stan. (ed.). 1993. *A Ministry of Meetings: The Apostolic Diaries of Rudger Clawson.* Salt Lake City, UT: Signature Books, in association with Smith Research Associates.
— 1997. *Quest for the Gold Plates: Thomas Stuart Ferguson's Archaeological Search for the Book of Mormon.* Salt Lake City, UT: Freethinker Press, in association with Smith Research Associates.
Lee, John D. 1877. *Mormonism Unveiled.* 2001. Albuquerque, NM: Fierra Blanca Publications, facsimile 1891 reprint, St. Louis, MO: D.M. Vanderwalker & Co.
Lewis, Catherine. 1848. *Narrative of Some of the Proceedings of the Mormons.* Lynn, MA: C. Lewis.
Linn, Alexander. 2001. *The Story of the Mormons.* Seattle, WA: The World Wide School. †
Lyman, Edward Leo. 1986. *Political Deliverance: The Quest for Utah Statehood.* Chicago, IL: University of Illinois Press.
Marquardt, H. Michael. 2005 *The Rise of Mormonism: 1816-1844. Fairfax, VA:* Xulon Press.
Marquardt, H. Michael & Walters, Wesley P. 1994. *Inventing Mormonism.* Salt Lake City, UT: Signature Books.
McConkie, Bruce R. 1958. *Mormon Doctrine.* Salt Lake City, UT: Bookcraft.
Morgan, Dale. 1986. *Early Mormonism: Correspondence and A New History*, Salt Lake City, UT: Signature Books.

# BIBLIOGRAPHY, RECOMMENDED BOOKS & WEB SITES

Morgan, William. 1827. *Illustrations of Masonry by One of the Fraternity Who has Devoted Thirty Years to the Subject.* Batavia, NY: David C. Miller. †

Naifeh, Steven & Smith, Gregory White. 1988. *The Mormon Murders - A True Story of Greed, Forgery, Deceit and Death.* New York, NY: New America Library, division of Penguin.

*The Neal A. Maxwell Institute for Religious Scholarship.* See FARMS.

Nelson, Leland R. (comp.). 1979. *The Journal of Joseph Smith.* Provo, UT: Council Press.

Newell, Linda King & Avery, Valeen Tippetts. 1994. 2nd Edition. *Mormon Enigma: Emma Hale Smith.* Chicago, IL: University of Illinois Press.

Nibley, Hugh W. 1957. *An Approach to the Book of Mormon.* Salt Lake City, UT: Deseret Book & FARMS.

O'Bryan, Aileen. 1956. *The Dîné: Origin Myths of the Navaho Indians.* Washington, D.C: Bulletin 163 of the Bureau of American Ethnology of the Smithsonian Institution.

*The Pearl of Great Price.* (PoGP). A selection from the revelations, translations, and narrations of Joseph Smith. 1981. Salt Lake City, UT: LDS Church. †

Pratt, Orson. 1840. *An Interesting Account of Several Remarkable Visions, and of the Late Discovery of Ancient American Records.* Edinburgh: Ballantyne & Hughes. †

— 1850. *Divine Authenticity of the Book of Mormon.* Liverpool. †

Pratt, Parley P. 1837. *A Voice of Warning.* New York, NY: W Sanford. †

Quinn, D. Michael (ed.). 1992. *The New Mormon History.* Salt Lake City, UT: Signature Books.

— 1994. *The Mormon Hierarchy: Origins of Power.* Salt Lake City, UT: Signature Books.

— 1997. *The Mormon Hierarchy: Extensions of Power.* Salt Lake City, UT: Signature Books.

— 1998. *Early Mormonism and the Magic World View.* Salt Lake City, UT: Signature Books.

*Reed Smoot Case.* 1907. *Proceedings Before the Committee on Privileges and Elections of the United States Senate in the Matter of the Protests Against the Right of Hon. Reed Smoot, a Senator from the State of Utah, to Hold his Seat.* 4 Volumes covering the 1904-1906 hearings. Washington, D.C: Govt. Printing Office.

Reimherr, Otto. (ed.). 1987. *Quest for Faith, Quest for Freedom.* Susquehanna, PA: Susquehanna University Press.

*The Revised Laws of Illinois.* 1833. Vandalia, IL: Greiner & Sherman.

Roberts, B.H. 1895. *New Witnesses for God.* (V.3 cited) Salt Lake City, UT: George Q. Cannon & Sons Co.

— 1978. *Comprehensive History of the Church.* (CHC) Salt Lake City, UT: Brigham Young University.

Robinson, John J. 1993. *A Pilgrim's Path: Freemasonry and the Religious Right.* New York, NY: M. Evans & Co.

Robinson, Stephen E. 1993. *Are Mormons Christians?* Salt Lake City, UT: Deseret Book.

Rupp, I. Daniel. (ed.). 1844. *An Original History of the Religious Denominations at Present Existing in the United States*. Philadelphia, PA: J. Y. Humphreys.*

Schele, Linda & Freidel, David. 1990. *A Forest of Kings: The Untold Story of the Ancient Maya*. NY: Quill. William Morrow.

Schindler, Harold. 1993. *Orrin Porter Rockwell: Man of God/Son of Thunder.* Salt Lake City, UT: University of Utah Press.

Schwartz, Marion. 1998. *A History of Dogs in the Early Americas.* New Haven, CT. & London: Yale University Press.

*Senate Document 189.* (Danite Treason Trial). 1841. 26th Congress, 2nd session. Available as a photo Reprint: Salt Lake City, UT: UTLM.

*Senate Hearings* - See: Reed Smoot Case 1907.

SHIELDS — *Scholarly & Historical Information Exchange for Latter-Day Saints.* (Mormon Apologetics). Available online at: www.shields-research.org

Smith, Lucy Mack. 1853. *Biographical Sketches of Joseph Smith the Prophet, and his progenitors for many generations.* Liverpool: S. W. Richards. (Photo reprint of the original 1853 edition: Tanner. *Joseph Smith's History by his Mother.* Salt Lake City, UT: UTLM).

Smith, Ethan. 1825. *View of the Hebrews*. Poultney, VT: Smith & Shute. Available as a Photo reproduction (including *The Parallels Between the Book of Mormon and the View of the Hebrews,* by the Mormon Historian B. H. Roberts): Salt Lake City, UT: UTLM.

Smith, Joseph Fielding (Jr). 1905. *Blood Atonement and the Origin of Plural Marriage.* Salt Lake City, UT: Deseret News Press.

— 1938. (Comp). *Teachings of the Prophet Joseph Smith by Joseph Smith.* Salt Lake City, UT: Deseret News Press.

— 1954. *Doctrines of Salvation.* 3 Vols. Salt Lake City, UT: Bookcraft.

— 1972. *Essentials in Church History.* Salt Lake City, UT: Deseret Book.

Smith, William B. 1883. *William Smith on Mormonism.* Lamoni, Iowa: RLDS. †

*Smoot, Reed. Senate Hearings.* See: Reed Smoot Case 1907.

Sorenson, John L. 1985. *An Ancient American Setting for the Book of Mormon.* Salt Lake City, UT: Deseret Book & FARMS.

Southerton, Simon G. 2004. *Losing a Lost Tribe: Native Americans, DNA and the Mormon Church.* Salt Lake City, UT: Signature Books.

Sperry, Sidney B. 1964. *The Problems of the Book of Mormon.* Salt Lake City, UT: Bookcraft.

Staker, Susan. (Ed.). 1993. *Waiting for World's End.* Salt Lake City, UT: Signature Books.

Stenhouse, Fanny. (Mrs. T.B.H). 1874. *Tell It All, the Story of a Life's Experience in Mormonism.* Hartford, CT: A. D. Worthington. † §

Stenhouse, T.B.H. 1873. *The Rocky Mountain Saints - A Full and Complete History of The Mormons.* New York, NY: D. Appleton & Co. Available as a Photo reproduction: UTLM. §

Stewart, John J. 1966. *Joseph Smith: The Mormon Prophet.* Salt Lake City, UT: Mercury.

Stout, Hosea. 1844-1869 Diary. Available at: http://robandsusanpages.com (Histories page).

# BIBLIOGRAPHY, RECOMMENDED BOOKS & WEB SITES

Tanner, Jerald. 1988. *Tracking the White Salamander.* Salt Lake City, UT: UTLM. †

Tanner, Jerald & Sandra. 1968 The Case Against Mormonism. (Vol 2 referenced). There are 3 Volumes, published 1967, 1968 & 1971. Salt Lake City, UT: UTLM. §

— 1970a. *Mormon Scriptures and the Bible.* Salt Lake City, UT: UTLM.

— 1970b. *Joseph Smith and Money Digging.* Salt Lake City, UT: UTLM.

— 1971. *Falsification of Joseph Smith's History.* Salt Lake City, UT: UTLM.

— 1980a. *Following the Brethren (Benson & McConkie)* Salt Lake City, UT: UTLM. †

— 1980b. *The Changing World of Mormonism.* Chicago, IL: Moody Press. †

— 1982. *Clayton's Secret Writings Uncovered: Extracts from the Diaries of Joseph Smith's Secretary William Clayton.* Salt Lake City, UT: Modern Microfilm.

— 1987. *Mormonism - Shadow or Reality?* 5th Edition. Salt Lake City, UT: UTLM §

— 1991. Flaws in the Pearl of Great Price. Salt Lake City, UT: UTLM. §

— 1996. *3,913 Changes in The Book of Mormon.* Salt Lake City, UT: UTLM. §

Taylor, Samuel Woolley. 1974. *Family Kingdom.* Salt Lake City, UT: Zion Book.

*The Temple Lot Case.* 1893. The RLDS Church, complainant, vs. the LDS Church at Independence, Missouri. Complainant's abstract of pleading and evidence. United States Circuit Court. (8th Circuit). Lamoni, IA: Herald Publishing. Available as a Photo reproduction: Salt Lake City, UT: UTLM.

Tullige, Edward Wheelock. 1877. *The Women of Mormondom.* New York, NY: Tullige & Crandall.

Van Waggoner, Richard S. 1989. *Mormon Polygamy: A History.* Salt Lake City, UT: Signature Books. §

— 1994. *Sidney Rigdon: A Portrait of Religious Excess.* Salt Lake City, UT: Signature Books.

Vlachos, Chris A. 1979. *Adam is God???* Salt Lake City, UT: UTLM.

Vogel, Dan. 1986. *Indian Origins and the Book of Mormon.* Salt Lake City, UT: Signature. †

— (ed.). 1996-2003. *Early Mormon Documents.* 5 Vols. Salt Lake City, UT: Signature.

Wallace, Irving. 1961. *The Twenty Seventh Wife.* New York, NY: Simon & Schuster.

Walters, Wesley P. 1990. *The Use of the Old Testament in the Book of Mormon.* Salt Lake City, UT: UTLM.

Werner, M.R. 1925. *Brigham Young.* New York, NY: Harcourt, Brace & Co. Available as a photo reproduction: Salt Lake City, UT: UTLM.

Whitefield, Jim. 2009a. *The Mormon Delusion. (TMD) Volume 1. The Truth Behind Polygamy and Secret Polyandry.* Raleigh, NC: Lulu Press Inc.

— 2009b. *The Mormon Delusion. (TMD) Volume 2. The Secret Truth Withheld From 13 Million Mormons.* Raleigh, NC: Lulu Press Inc.

— 2009c. *The Mormon Delusion. (TMD) Volume 3. Discarded Doctrines and Nonsense Revelations.* Raleigh, NC: Lulu Press Inc.

Whitmer, David. 1887. *An Address to All Believer's In Christ.* Richmond, MO: D. Whitmer. † §

Whitney, Orson F. 1888. 2nd ed. 1945. *Life of Heber C. Kimball*. Salt Lake City, UT: Stevens & Wallace Inc.

Widtsoe, John A. 1960. *Evidences and Reconciliations*. Salt Lake City, UT: Bookcraft.

*The World Christian Encyclopaedia*. 2001. Barrett, David B; Kurian, George T; Johnson, Todd M. Oxford: Oxford University Press.

Wyl, Wilhelm. (Wilhelm Ritter von Wymetal). 1886. *Joseph Smith the Prophet, His Family and Friends*. Salt Lake City, UT: Tribune Printing & Publishing Co.

Young, Ann Eliza. 1876. *Wife No. 19, Or the Story of a Life in Bondage, being a Complete Exposé of Mormonism and Revealing the Sorrows, Sacrifices and Sufferings of Women in Polygamy*. Hartford, CT: Dustin, Gilman & Co.†

Bibliography Notes.

§ A dozen or so selected books, recommended initial reading.

\* Complete book available to read online at *Google Book Search*.

† Fully downloadable, readable (or excerpts available) online via an internet search on the title. Sometimes, a search on an author's name brings up locations where you can read part, if not all of a book which may not show as available to read via *Google Book Search*.

Many books are available to read online at *The Anti-Mormon Preservation Society*, located at http://antimormon.8m.com and also at the *Utah Lighthouse Ministry* (UTLM) at www.utlm.org. Books notated above with † *and* UTLM, are currently available there.

Mormon (LDS) Scriptures, including the *King James Version Bible*, *Book of Mormon, Doctrine and Covenants*, and *Pearl of Great Price* are all available to research at: http://scriptures.lds.org

Various versions of complete Bible texts are available for comparison and research, including *Young's Literal Translation* (which I have referenced in these volumes) at: www.biblegateway.com

Many of the early newspapers cited in my work, such as *Messenger and Advocate, Times & Seasons* and others, are now available to read online via a search on the name and year of the publication.

Various Church manuals and magazines (such as the *Ensign*) can be researched via the online library at: www.lds.org/gospellibrary

# BIBLIOGRAPHY, RECOMMENDED BOOKS & WEB SITES

If I had to recommend *one* book in which to locate clinically written evidence (as a reference book) against the Mormon Church, it would resoundingly be *Mormonism - Shadow or Reality?* by Jerald & Sandra Tanner, whose research and findings are painstakingly detailed and highly accurate, not to mention easily readable and well indexed. It is a veritable encyclopaedia of the real truth. A beautifully written favourite account of the truth in more flowing book form is by Fawn Brodie (niece of David O. McKay), *No Man Knows My History. (Brodie 1945). (Brodie 1963 for the U.K.).*

Likewise, if I had to choose *one* book that eloquently relates the experience of the British (and European) Saints concerning early lies about polygamy, emigration to Salt Lake and the real underlying and heartbreaking polygamy story, blood atonement and more, *Tell It All* by Fanny Stenhouse is heartfelt and revealing, enthralling and yet devastating. It will break your heart. You can feel her torment, anguish and confusion. You simply *cannot* put it down. It places period drama into an entirely new dimension. And yet it is unfortunately a true and accurate account of what actually happened.

There are many Mormon and ex-Mormon websites. A good starting point for anyone who is questioning Mormonism and its beliefs, or needs help in their recovery from Mormonism is www.exmormon.org which provides hundreds of stories, articles and a debating forum, plus links to several other sites at the bottom of the home page. I would also recommend Richard Packham's web site for succinct and accurate answers to questions. His home page and many other useful links can be located by searching his name, directly from the *exmormon* link or at: http://home.teleport.com/~packham/ or www.salamandersociety.com/links/ which is another very useful web site.

There are dozens of links available to various web sites (many Christian), and some excellent source material on Mormonism, further resources, scriptures, documents, information, books, newspapers and periodicals through UTLM. The direct link to the page for these resources is: www.utlm.org/navotherwebsites.htm

Mountain Meadows Massacre - movie: *September Dawn* (released 2008). This film weaves a fictional love story into the history of the massacre. Whilst it is not entirely accurate according to historical evidence, it is close and depicts the general details well.

A documentary one hour video evidencing the *Book of Abraham* fraud is available online, courtesy of The *Institute for Religious Research -* www.irr.org. This excellent and highly recommended programme can be purchased as a video or DVD or viewed free online. The detail is accurate and the evidence is conclusive. *The Lost Book of Abraham: Investigating a Remarkable Mormon Claim* can be viewed free of charge at the following direct link: www.irr.org/mit/lboa-video.html

Similarly, a documentary film regarding DNA and the *Book of Mormon* can be viewed free, courtesy of Living Hope Ministries: www.lvhm.org/vid_dna_med.htm

The Mormon Church manipulated votes, financially and organisationally, against gay rights during the 'Proposition 8' campaign in California in 2008. A DVD of the documentary movie '8: The Mormon Proposition' is available from Amazon et al.

# INDEX

Aaron, identified descendants automatically ordained Bishops; 356.
Aaron (Nephite missionary); 66-68, 74.
Aaronic Priesthood, claimed conferred; 112.
Abel; 203.
Abinadi; 307.
abortion a sin; 315.
Abraham; 203, 205.
Adam (and Eve); 151, 200, 203.
- fall of; 283.
- knew of Christ; 159.
- named all the birds and animals; 199
Adam-God; 22, 58, Apx G.
Adam's altar; 257, 282.
adultery; 316.
age of the Earth; 257.
agency; 151, 263.
alcohol; 50.
Alger, Fanny; 116, 176, 317, 370, 372.
all things bear record of God; 149-150.
Alma & Amulek; 25, 74, 446.
- story similar to Shadrach, Meshach & Abed-nego in Dan; 446.
Alternatives to Marriage Project; 43-44.
Ammon; 66-68.
An Interesting Account of Several Remarkable Visions (booklet), O. Pratt; 12-13, 106.
Apache are Lamanites; 436.
Apollos; 218.
apostasy; 51, 86.
Apostle (office); 360.
Apostles (Christ's) will be killed; 87.
Articles of Faith; 12, 13, 72, 349, 378.
atonement; 42, 51, 171, 176.
Augustine (St.); 31, 40.
babies born into polygamy, post manifesto; 14.
baptism:
- altered in early church; 77.
- child's right on eighth birthday; 301.
- rebaptism for health or repentance; 196.
- required; 172, 299.
- symbolism; 247.
- third principle of the Gospel; 246-251.
Baptist 'revival' conversions (1824); 96.
barley:
- for all useful animals; 330.
- for mild drinks; 330.
BCE references of Jesus Christ; 233.
beer, Danish not against WoW in 1904; 324.
Benson, Ezra Taft; 34, 406, 441, 450.
Bible references used or mentioned:
- 1 Corinthians 3:22; 218.
- 1 Corinthians 15:43-49; 174-175.
- 1 John 2:1; 231.
- 1 John 1:7; 176.
- 1 Peter 3:19-20; 192.
- 1 Peter 4:6; 192.
- 2 Corinthians 5:6; 150.
- 2 Corinthians 12:4; 188.
- 2 Peter 1:19; 41.
- 2 Peter 1:20-21; 279.
- 2 Peter 2:11; 214.
- Acts 2:30; 428.
- Acts 2:38; 368.
- Acts 9; 443.
- Acts 10:43; 440.
- Acts 17:9; 143.
- Amos 3:7; 305.
- Ecclesiastes 12:7; 189.
- Ephesians; 4:11-14; 378.
- Exodus 20; 306.
- Exodus 31:14; 295.
- Exodus 40:12-13; 80-81.
- Ezekiel 2:9; 428.
- Ezekiel 37:15-17; 426.
- Ezekiel 37: 18-22; 426-427.
- Galatians 1:6; 82.
- Genesis 1:1; 147.
- Genesis 1:26;155.
- Genesis 2:15-17; 156.
- Genesis 14:16-20; 333.
- Genesis 38:1-10; 277.
- Hebrews 7:4; 333.
- Hebrews 12:9; 143.
- Isaiah 3:18-23; 235-236.
- Isaiah 14:12; 40, 41.
- Isaiah 29:4-18; 431.
- Isaiah 30:15; 228.
- Isaiah 55:1, 8-9; 274-275.
- Jeremiah 1:5; 145.
- Job 11:17; 41.
- John 1:23; 204.
- John 3:16-17; 176, 219, 229.
- John 5:22; 211.
- John 5:29; 216.
- John 5:39; 280.
- John 7:17; 239.
- John 10:16; 430.
- John 17:1-3; 219.
- John 20:31; 440.
- Jude 1:8; 214.

- Judges 19:16-30; 278-279.
- Luke 3:4; 204.
- Luke 10:22; 102.
- Mark 13:13; 221.
- Mark 16:16; 182.
- Matthew 10:14.
- Matthew 22:36-40; 377.
- Matthew 24:9; 87.
- Matthew 24:13; 221.
- Matthew 25:40.
- Psalm 34:18; 234.
- Psalm 51:17; 234.
- Psalm 89:14; 237.
- Revelation 1:6; 103.
- Romans 5:12; 31.
- Romans 11:16-26; 365-366.
- Song of Solomon 4, 5, 7; 276-277.

Bible, contradictions; 275.
Bible, manufactured English word; 421.
biblical minimalists; 69.
births: 39.7% to unmarried women; 43.
Bishop; 379.
Blood Atonement; 22, 58, Apx G.
Book of Abraham hoax; 144-145, 199.
- Gods in the plural, contradicting Book of Moses; 148.

Book of Commandments 1833; 97, 104, 120.
Book of Mormon:
- 3 Nephi 24 *is* Malachi 3; 340-344.
- A Bible, we have got a Bible; 420.
- all nations will write records; 439.
- and Bible support each other; 425.
- animals that did not exist in the Americas; 136.
- animals that existed in the Americas; 136; 312.
- Bible, word appears in; 133-134.
- Bishops not in book; 408.
- butter – impossible inclusion; 137.
- Celestial kingdom not mentioned; 265.
- citing minds forward; 332.
- condemns polygamy; 302.
- convincing evidence; 51.
- Cowdery not to help translate; 60.
- crops – impossible claims; 137-138.
- currency system; 138, Apx A.
- David and Solomon contradictions; 302.
- Deacons not in book; 408.
- devil has children; 143.
- exaltation not mentioned; 265.
- falsified, post publication; 88, 98.
- fruit of thy loins; 429.
- fullness of doctrine; 408-412.
- fullness of gospel 'boxes': see **Fullness**.
- geography; 126-127.
- glass windows; 135.
- grammar is entirely incorrect; 88.
- horses, an impossible claim; 128.
- impossible names and events; 87.
- 'in other words' references; 287.
- Introduction; 124, 452, 453-459.
- Jesus born in Jerusalem mistake; 410.
- Jesus mentioned BCE; 429.
- keystone of our religion; 406.
- Law of Moses lived; 134.
- linguistic problems; 128.
- Lord alone will be exalted; 265.
- milk – impossible inclusion; 137.
- monotheistic verses; 60, 88.
- Moroni's promise; 124.
- New Testament wording in; 134-135.
- Patriarchs not in book; 408.
- polygamy, an abomination; 302.
- priority for investigators; 426.
- published 1830; 97, 104.
- refined metals included; 138.
- role of for missionaries; 403
- sacrifice and burnt offerings; 312.
- scimitars in pre-Moslem era; 128.
- seven day week problem; 410-411.
- Seventies not in book; 408.
- silk mentioned when impossible; 128.
- steel bow in pre-steel era; 128.
- stick of Joseph; 425-428.
- stick of Judah; 425-428.
- Telestial kingdom not mentioned; 264.
- Terrestrial kingdom not mentioned. 264.
- testifies of Christ; 413-425, 429.
- thousands of later alterations; 88.
- title page; 452.
- voice from heaven declared it correct; 88.
- wheel; 135.
- witness of Christ; 406-407.

Book of Mormon chapters referenced:
- Introduction; 124, 452, 453-459.
- Title Page; 452.
- 1 Nephi 3:7; 240.
- 1 Nephi 4:13; 307.
- 1 Nephi 8; 35
- 1 Nephi 9:5; 415.
- 1 Nephi 11; 35, 87.
- 1 Nephi 12; 37.
- 1 Nephi 13:20-25; 432.
- 1 Nephi 13:26-29; 433.

# INDEX

- 1 Nephi 13:40, 41; 434.
- 1 Nephi 14; 37.
- 1 Nephi 15; 37.
- 1 Nephi 17; 146.
- 1 Nephi 19; 205, 206.
- 1 Nephi 19:10; 362.
- 2 Nephi 1:5; 454.
- 2 Nephi 1:9; 455.
- 2 Nephi 2:6; 233.
- 2 Nephi 2:7-10; 158.
- 2 Nephi 2:13; 160, 163.
- 2 Nephi 2:25-30; 164-165.
- 2 Nephi 2; 34, 446.
- 2 Nephi 3:3-6, 9-14; 438-439.
- 2 Nephi 3:12; 429.
- 2 Nephi 4; 69.
- 2 Nephi 9:1-24; 179, 188, 210, 226, 442-443.
- 2 Nephi 9:27; 169.
- 2 Nephi 12:11, 17, 31; 265.
- 2 Nephi 13:18-23; 236.
- 2 Nephi 25:23-29; 415-416.
- 2 Nephi 26:15-16; 417.
- 2 Nephi 28:23; 212.
- 2 Nephi 29:6-8; 420.
- 2 Nephi 29:8; 440.
- 2 Nephi 29:11-14; 418.
- 2 Nephi 31; 180-181, 220-221.
- 2 Nephi 33:13-15; 414.
- 3 Nephi 9:13; 226, 227.
- 3 Nephi 9:20; 234-235.
- 3 Nephi 10:16; 207.
- 3 Nephi 11:25, 27; 355, 409.
- 3 Nephi 11:33-34; 182.
- 3 Nephi 18:32; 226.
- 3 Nephi 23:1; 435,
- 3 Nephi 23:6; 339.
- 3 Nephi 24:1; 340.
- 3 Nephi 27; 32, 49, 226.
- 3 Nephi 28:10; 216.
- 4 Nephi 1; 188.
- Alma 5:15-21; 212.
- Alma 6:3, 6, 8; 348.
- Alma 7:10; 411.
- Alma 7:11-13; 178.
- Alma 11:38-40; 180.
- Alma 11; 99-100, 175.
- Alma 12:12-14; 212.
- Alma 12:32; 260.
- Alma 13:1, 15; 332.
- Alma 13:3-13; 357-358.
- Alma 14; 446.
- Alma 18; 27, 66-68, 70, 100-101, 153.
- Alma 22; 27-28, 66-68, 70, 72-72, 101, 153, 441.
- Alma 30; 146.
- Alma 33:3,13,15,17; 206-207, 208.
- Alma 34; 445.
- Alma 34:7; 207.
- Alma 34:8-10; 178, 189, 235.
- Alma 34:28, 35; 445-446.
- Alma 34:31-35; 169.
- Alma 36; 190, 443.
- Alma 37:2; 415.
- Alma 40; 188, 190, 443-444.
- Alma 42:4,10; 169.
- Alma 42:13-15, 22-23; 210.
- Alma 42:17; 163.
- Alma 42:22-25; 237.
- Alma 60:13; 446.
- Enos 1:13; 422-423.
- Helaman 5:23; 447.
- Helaman 8:19-20; 207.
- Helaman 14:15-18; 226.
- Helaman 15:11; 207.
- Jacob 1:15; 302.
- Jacob 2:23-24; 302.
- Jacob 4:1-6; 421-422.
- Jacob 5:1; 207, 362.
- Jacob 5:47; 363.
- Jacob 5:70-75; 364-365.
- Jacob 6:1; 207.
- Jacob 6:8-9; 210.
- Mormon 1:7; 455.
- Mormon 7:8-9; 435-436.
- Moroni 3:1-4; 379.
- Moroni 6:5, 7; 348.
- Moroni 8; 447.
- Moroni 10; 188.
- Moroni 10:3-5; 452.
- Mosiah 2:3; 312.
- Mosiah 3:19; 170.
- Mosiah 13:18-19; 410.
- Mosiah 13:28-35; 313.
- Mosiah 15:9; 137.
- Mosiah 15; 100.
- Mosiah 18:13-15; 355.
- Mosiah 18:18; 356.
- Mosiah 18:17; 354.
- Mosiah 18:26; 337.
- Mosiah 18:27-28; 344.
- Mosiah 28:3; 367.
- Omni 1:25-26; 423.
- Omni 1:26; 347.

**Book of Mormon tests for investigators;**
   126, 127, 128-130, 132, 135, 135, 136, 137-138, 138.
Book of Moses – God in the singular, contradicting Book of Abraham; 148.
born again; 300.
brainwashing, self-induced; 241.
Brass Plates of Laban; 68, 69, 74.
bread, eaten by sweat of face; 157.
burden of guilt and shame; 172.
burka; 266.
BYU Religious Studies Centre admits Smith lied in his 1838 First Vision story; 107.
Caleb; 203, 205.
callings and releases; 375.
Campbell, Alexander; 104.
Cannon, George Q; 268.
captivity and death; 165.
Catholic Encyclopaedia referenced; 75-76.
celestial – meaning; 173.
Celestial kingdom; 22, 53, 173, 174, 213, 264, 373.
Cephas; 218.
chastity, law of; 313.
Cherokee are Lamanites; 437.
cholera; 289-290.
Christ – as a title, CE invention; 70, 75, 235.
   - Greek origin; 75.
   - no formal church organisation; 77.
   - use of title in Book of Mormon BCE; 74.
Christian denominations – 34,000 plus; 71.
Church growth; 390-391.
Church named:
   - Church of Christ (1829-1830); 120.
   - Church of the Latter Day Saints (1834); 120.
   - The Church of Jesus Christ (after 1834); 120.
   - The Church of Jesus Christ of Latter Day Saints (1838); 120.
Church of God or Church of Christ; 354-355.
Church pension scheme shortfall; 305.
coffee; 50.
Cola drinks; 331.
commandments; 259.
confession and discipline; 353-354.
corn for the Ox; 328.
Cowdery, Oliver; 13, 60.
   - Letter about Fanny Alger; 116.
   - Priesthood restoration story conflicts; 111-113, 114, 117.
   - resigned, also excommunicated; 61, 116.

creation; 146-150.
Cry from the Wilderness, A (booklet), O. Hyde; 13, 106.
Cult believed they would never die; 71.
David and Solomon contradiction; 302.
Dawkins, Richard; 283.
Deacon (office); 360.
death and hell; 212, 227.
Doctrine and Covenants, 1835; 97, 104.
D&C Sections referenced;
   - 3:16-20; 424.
   - 7; 119.
   - 8:2-3; 273.
   - 9; 59-60.
   - 10:46-48; 425.
   - 13; 111-112.
   - 14:7; 219.
   - 19; 177.
   - 20:5-10; 250.
   - 20:27-28; 250.
   - 20:37; 249.
   - 20:38-65; 358-359.
   - 20; 64, 132, 141.
   - 27:5-7; 248.
   - 27; 117, 201.
   - 29:43-44; 220.
   - 33:8-11; 368.
   - 42:22-26; 317, 370.
   - 45:3-5; 230.
   - 45:8; 220.
   - 45:72-75; 232.
   - 49:15-16; 372-373.
   - 50:14; 32.
   - 56:18; 234.
   - 59:9-24; 295-297.
   - 59:23; 32.
   - 61; 283-291.
   - 63:16; 317.
   - 68:9; 183.
   - 68:25, 27; 447.
   - 76:36-37, 98-99; 217-218.
   - 76:100; 204.
   - 77: 201.
   - 84; 61, 111, 203, 204, 366-367.
   - 88; 147.
   - 88:77-79; 378.
   - 88:81; 361.
   - 89; 320, 325, 326.
   - 93:19; 220.
   - 101 (original, discarded 1876); 15, 58.
   - 107:39; 379.
   - 107:69-76; 356.

# INDEX

- 107:99-100; 377.
- 119:1-7; 345.
- 122-123; 90.
- 123:12; 32.
- 124:91-92; 381.
- 130:20-21; 266.
- 130:22; 26-27.
- 131:1-4; 372.
- 132:7; 372.
- 132:1, 38-39; 302.
- 132:60; 318.
- 132:61-66; 318-319.
- 132:65; 260.
- 137; 216, 226.
- 138; 192-195, 202.

daily missionary schedule; 23.
damned, condemned or punished; 183-184.
Delusions, An Analysis of the Book of Mormon. Campbell. 1832; 104.
depression in Mormonism; 267.
Deseret News:
   - Utah divorces outstrip nation; 47.
Devil; 41.
dignities, also glorious, heavenly, celestial, angelic majesties and supernatural beings; 215.
disappointment; 54-55.
DNA research, ten lost tribes; 419.
Do not spread disease germs; 12.
dust from feet, washing or shaking; 367.
earrings; 50.
Earth – to become Celestial; 174.
   - to last 7,000 years; 281.
earthy; 174
Egyptus; 199.
Elder (office); 360.
Elias and Elijah; 200, 201, 218, 248.
Elihu; 203, 205.
endless torment; 180.
endure to the end; 254-257.
Enoch; 203.
endowment; 77.
enduring to the end; 172, 384-385.
Esaias and Isaiah; 201, 205, 218.
eternal life; 176, 209, 218, 219, 222, 229, 275.
eternal marriage; 369-374.
ets, Hebrew word meaning; 428.
Evangelist; 378-379.
   - is a Patriarch in Mormonism; 379.
Eve, joy in her redemption; 157.
Evening and Morning Star, 1832-4; 104.
everlasting fire; 180.

everlasting life; 229.
evolution not addressed in Mormonism; 152, 282.
exaltation; 173, 218.
exalted; 53.
eye worm; see: loa loa.
faith; 172.
fall (the); 42, 164-166, 167.
   - man is not responsible for; 172.
families – teach as a priority; 43, 401.
family history; 50, 374-375.
Family Home Evening; 50.
fast, law of the; 346-348.
fathers preside over families; 370.
feelings can't be trusted; 125.
Ferguson, Thomas Stuart; 412.
fire and brimstone; 179, 212, 217, 227-228, 264.
First Estate; 168.
First Law of the Gospel, obedience; 260-264.
First Principle of the Gospel, faith; 229, 237.
First Vision; 50, 58, 250.
   - 1832 version; 93.
   - 1835 versions; 93-94.
   - 1838 official version; 95-97.
flocks; 136, 312.
flood; 195-199, 281.
Follow the prophet; 301.
food chain; 149.
Fourth Principle of Gospel – Holy Ghost; 251-253.
Fruit of thy loins; 429-430.
**Fullness of the Gospel 'boxes';** 133, 143, 146, 152, 191, 213, 222, 409(4), 410(2).
Gad; 203, 205.
gambling; 50.
Garden of Eden; 156.
garment used in temples; 79.
gays; 43, 161-162, 314-315.
Gifts of the Spirit; 394-395.
Gift of tongues; 394-395, 397-399.
glossolalia; 398-399.
God:
   - flesh and bones; 27.
   - great spirit; 27, 71-72.
   - Heavenly Father; 66.
   - Holy One of Israel; 180.
   - influences us to do good; 167.
   - Mormon version ever-changing; 188.
   - nature of; 28.
   - not involved with Mormonism; 31.
   - omnipresent spirit; 27, 102, 104.

- our literal Father; 50-51.
- repeating Himself; 287.
- show Himself in Jerusalem as Jesus; 179.
- unchangeable; 188.

gods, invention of; 160.
gold plates; 51.
Gospel:
- preached to the dead; 192.
- what is it; 24.
- why preach it; 24.
- why teach with power and authority; 24.

Gospel Principles Manual (Honesty); 15, 350.
Gospels; not written by apostles; 84, 89.
Great Spirit; 27, 71-72, 74, 75, 100-101.
Guatemalans are Lamanites; 436.
guilt (and shame, or remorse); 172, 175, 212, 227, 228.
Harris, Martin; 106.
Haun's Mill; 33.
HaSaTan; 31, 40.
heaven; 53, 264.
heleyl ben shachar; 41.
Hell; 174, 180, 187, 264.
heterosexuals; 43.
Hinckley, Gordon B;
- confesses never received any revelations; 120-121, 304, 450.
- didn't know God once a man; 58, Apx F.
- polygamy, "It's behind us"; 14, 21-22.

Holy Ghost; 39, 59, 251-253, 392-393.
- CE concept; 64, 68.
- denying; 174, 212.
- gift of; 172, 300.

Holy One of Israel; 227, 228.
Holy Spirit:
- God's energy; 68, 158.
- mind of God; 158.
- of promise; 393-394.

Holland, Jeff; 52-53.
homosexuality; 48.
Honesty and Integrity; 15, 350.
households:
- 55% approve unmarried cohabitation; 43.
- 90% value all types of family; 43.
- almost 40% unmarried incl. children; 43.
- cohabiting is up by 88%; 43.
- headed by unmarried; 43.
- majority consider unmarried household of no effect on children; 43.
- majority cohabit before marriage; 43.
- non-married couples on increase; 43.
- one person households equal 27%; 43.

- only a quarter are traditional family; 44.
Howe, E. D; 104.
Humanitarian Aid; 270.
Huntington, Zina Diantha; 16.
Huxley, Aldous; 302.
Hyde, Orson; 13, 106, 107.
- drank whisky; 323.

Hyrcanus, John; 414.
Idumeans; 414.
immortality; 209, 210, 218, 219, 222, 229, 275.
Information Boxes; 24-26.
- Box type 1: Consider this; 24.
- Box type 2: Remember this; 24.
- Box type 3: Scripture study; 25.
- Box type 4: Activity; 26.
- Box type 5: Red Boxes; 26.

Initiatory temple ordinances altered; 78.
inspiration; 388-389.
Inspired Revision of the Bible; 89, 97, 103.
Isaiah and Esaias; 201.
Isaiah in Book of Mormon, same as KJV; 68, 69, 74, 273, 274-275.
Jacobs, Henry B; 16.
Jehovah's Witness growth; 391.
Jeramias and Jeramiah; 201.
Jeremy; 203, 205.
Jeremy and Jeremiah; 205.
Jericho; 280.
Jerome's Vulgate; 41.
Jethro; 203, 205.
Jesus Christ:
- born in Jerusalem mistake; 411.
- created the Earth; 146.
- is God; 101.
- known by prophets since beginning; 171
- morning star; 42.
- not His real name; 153, 158, 338.
- origin of name and title; 338-339.

Jesus the Christ (book); 57.
John the Apostle, claimed still living; 118.
John the Baptist; 112-113, 116.
Joseph Smith–History; 91, 108, 125.
Judaism; 31.
judgement; 211-212.
justice and mercy; 210-211, 237.
Kimball, Heber. C; 78.
Kimball, Helen Mar; 242.
Kimball, Spencer W:
- 130,000 Lamanites are Mormons; 437.
- identifies Lamanites; 424-425, 436-437.
- temple marriage divorce rate; 46-47.

# INDEX

King, Larry: Hinckley interview; 22.
kingdoms of glory; 212.
knowing that the Church is true; 352.
Laban; 307.
lake of fire and brimstone; 180, 212.
Lamanites:
    - number 60 million (1971); 425.
    - number 130 million (1975); 437.
Lamoni; 27-28, 66, 74.
Lane, Elder George; 96.
language of prayer; 395.
Latter Day Saints Messenger & Advocate, 1834-36; 13, 104.
Lattin, Don: Hinckley interview; 120-121, 2.
law and punishment; 210.
law of chastity; 313.
law of Sarah; 260, 373.
Law of the fast; 346-348.
laws and ordinances; 351-352.
Lectures of Faith; 102, 104.
Lehi; 68, 70, 307.
Lehi's dream; 35-39.
liberty and life; 165.
life on Earth; 167-170.
Light of Christ; 392.
Loa loa (eye) worm; 149, 271.
Lord alone to be exalted; 265.
Lucifer; 40-41.
Lyon, Windsor; 78.
man:
    - can become like God; 146.
    - in image of only begotten son; 155-156.
Manifesto (1890); 13, 14, 58.
marriage, history and types; 45.
Maya are Lamanites; 437.
Maya calendar; 411.
McIlwain's Bend, Missouri River; 283-291.
McKay, David O; 301.
Melchizedek; 203.
mercy and justice: See: justice and mercy.
message of the restoration: what is it; 24.
    - why is it so important; 24.
Messiah (or Messias); 70, 75, 233-234.
Methodist 'revival' conversions (1824); 96.
Millennial Star, 1840-1970; 105.
Mind of God – energy; 64.
misery comes through circumstance, not sin; 160.
missionary:
    - accountability; 399.
    - daily schedule; 23.
    - disappointment; 55.
    - discouragement; 55.
    - how is success measured; 24.
    - improving teaching skills; 402.
    - performance evaluation; 62.
    - personal study; 23.
    - power and authority; 24, 29, 71.
    - purpose; 24.
    - recommended reading material; 57.
    - responsibility to convert; 24.
    - results reducing over the years; 390-391.
    - work; 361-369.
missions; 50.
Missouri River; 285.
    - ferry disaster of 1976; 286.
    - flood of 1927; 286.
Mohawk are Lamanites; 436.
money digging; 51.
    - syndicate; 109, 114.
monotheism of Joseph Smith; 27, 64, 88, 205-206, 211, 216, 222.
Mohicans are Lamanites; 437.
Mormonism in all Ages, 1842; 105.
Mormonism – Shadow or Reality; 97.
Mormonism Unvailed [sic] 1834. Howe; 104.
morning star; 42.
Moroni; 58.
    - angel, originally called Nephi; 456.
Moses; 203, 205, 272.
mothers to nurture children, not preside; 370.
Mountford, Lydia; 13.
Naming of the Church; 120.
Native African destiny; 34.
    - intermarriage; 34, 35.
natural disasters; 149, 162.
Navajo are Lamanites; 436, 437.
'Negro and the Priesthood' doctrine; 30, 45, 161.
Nelson, Russell. M: A Treasured Testament; 52, 99, 364, 458.
Nemetchek, Helmut – Hinckley interview; 335.
Nephi; 307, 456.
Neum; 206.
Noah; 203.
Noah and the flood; 195-199.
non-married households on increase; 43.
Oaks, Dallin H; 53.
oats for the horse; 329.
Obedience, first law of the gospel; 260-264, 266.
obey and honour the law; 349.
Observer newspaper, London; 419.

Official Declaration 1; 13.
Old Testament – when written; 69.
olive oil used in temple anointing; 78.
olives in vineyard error; 362-366.
ordinances should not be altered; 77, 81.
original sin; 31, 40.
Our Heritage (book); 57.
Our Search for Happiness (book); 57.
Outer darkness; 174, 191, 212, 264, 443.
Packer, Boyd K; 12.
Palmyra Reflector; 105.
Paradise; 188.
Pastors; 378-379.
   - are teachers, not Bishops; 379.
Patriarch; 379.
Patriarchal blessing; 380.
Patriarchs to the Church; 382-384.
Pentecostal groups; 300.
percentage of scriptures used from where; 26.
persecution; 95, 96.
personal revelation; 388-391.
Peruvians are Lamanites; 436.
Peter, James and John; 116.
Petersen, La Mar; 118.
Pima are Lamanites; 437.
Piutes are Lamanites; 437.
Plan of Redemption; 71.
plural marriage; 450.
polyandry; 16-17.
polygamy; 450.
   - became a requirement; 22.
   - illegal; 13, 58, 85.
   - not mentioned in lesson manual; 85.
Polynesians are Lamanites; 436.
poor mental health in Utah; 267.
Pope, accepts evolution; 283.
Pope Damasus I; 41.
power and authority for missionaries; 21, 71.
   - why teach with; 24.
Pratt, Orson; 12, 105, 106.
Pratt, Parley P; 104.
   - drank whisky; 323.
prayer; 50, 267.
Pre-mortal intelligences; 144.
Pre-mortal life; 142-145.
   - loss of memory of; 146.
Preach My Gospel, Lesson Pages referenced:
   - Cover; 32.
   - p.v; 19,20.
   - p.vii; 21.
   - p.viii; 23.
   - p.1; 24, 32.

- p.1-2; 33.
- p.2; 34, 35.
- p.3; 39, 42-3, 46.
- p.5; 49.
- p.6; 49, 50.
- p.7; 51.
- p.8; 53.
- p.9; 53, 54.
- p.10; 54.
- p 10-11; 55.
- p.17; 57.
- p.18; 59.
- p.19; 61.
- p.31; 64, 65, 66.
- p.32; 66.
- p.35; 76.
- p.36; 84, 85, 86, 87, 90.
- p.37; 111, 119, 120.
- p.39; 131.
- p.43; 131.
- p.47; 142.
- p.48; 142-143.
- p.49; 146, 151.
- p.50; 66, 152, 164, 167.
- p.51; 170 172, 173.
- p.52; 185, 186.
- p.54; 223.
- p.60; 226, 227.
- p.61; 228, 229, 230, 232.
- p.61-62; 237.
- p.62; 238, 239, 243, 245.
- p.63; 245-246.
- p.64; 246, 247.
- p.65; 251, 253.
- p.66; 254.
- p.71; 259.
- p.72; 262.
- p.73; 267, 269, 273.
- p.74; 291, 297.
- p.75; 299, 301, 304.
- p.76; 306.
- p.77; 314, 315.
- p.78; 320, 332.
- p.79; 334, 346.
- p.82; 351, 352.
- p.83; 353.
- p.84; 354, 361.
- p.85; 369-70, 371.
- p.86; 374.
- p.87; 376.
- p.88; 377.
- p.89; 388, 389.

# INDEX

- p.90; 391, 392.
- p.91; 393, 394.
- p.93-95; 395.
- p.95; 275.
- p.96; 396.
- p.99; 396-7.
- p.103; 404, 405.
- p.104; 405, 406.
- p.105; 423.
- p.106; 426, 438.
- p.107; 439, 446.
- p.108-9; 449.
- p.109; 449.
- p.110; 450.
- p.111; 457.
- p.133; 397.
- p.150-51; 399-400.
- p.159-60; 401, 401-2.
- p.188-90; 320.
- p.190; 402.

Priest (office); 360.
Priesthood authority; 51.
Presbyterians:
- Lucy Mack joined in 1824; 96.
- 'revival' conversions (1824); 96.

Probation on Earth; 168.
Problems of the Book of Mormon: Sperry; 99.
promptings of the spirit; 396-397.
Proposition 8 (California); 45.
purpose of a missionary; 24.
**Questions that investigators should ask;**
125, 127-128, 133, 133-134, 134, 134-135, 137, 138-139, 148, 151, 161, 181, 182, 188, 196, 264, 265, 273, 417, 447.
Quinn, D. Michael cited; 118-119, 337.
racism; 30.
Realms of deity chart; 189.
Redeemer known since world began; 171.
redemption; 34, 42, 70-71.
referrals; 361.
Reformed Egyptian; 74.
Religions, numerical breakdown; 444.
repentance; 53, 164, 172, 243-246.
resurrection, a gift for everyone; 172, 173, 176.
Restoration of the Gospel; 51, 83.
Revelation, book of; 85.
revelation, personal; 388-391.
Revival in 1824, not in 1820; 95, 96.
Richards, LeGrand; 302.
Rigdon, Sidney; 115.
Roman Catholic Church growth; 391.

rye for birds and pigs; 329.
Sabbath day; 291.
sacrament; 247.
Salt Lake Tribune:
- Utah divorce rate outstrips nation; 47.
Salvation through Christ; 232.
Satan:
- attacking families; 39, 46, 370.
- choosing to follow; 174.
- misrepresented as Lucifer; 41.
- mythical creature; 46.
- tempts us to sin; 167, 253.
Saviour, need for; 167.
Scripture study; 272.
Second Estate; 168.
Second Principle of Gospel – Repentance; 243.
seer stone; 51.
service; 375-377.
seven day week problem; 409-410.
Seventy (office); 360.
sexual orientation hardwired; 46.
sin; 31, 33, 49, 142, 160, 244.
Sins:
- and sinners; 29
- cause guilt and shame; 167.
- concept created by humans; 142.
- lead to unhappiness; 167.
- means of control; 160.
- of commission; 50, 167.
- of omission; 50, 167.
Sioux are Lamanites; 436.
slaves; 30, 34.
Smith, Joseph, Jr; 42, 51.
- contradictions, David and Solomon; 302.
- drank wine; 322-323.
- head in hat translating; 60, 69, 131.
- joins Methodist Sunday School; 109.
- lies about Inspired Revision; 103-104.
- lies about persecution; 107-108.
- married Zina D. Huntington; 16.
- money-digging seer stone; 60.
- monotheistic years; 27, 64, 88, 205-206, 211, 216, 222, 423.
- ordinances should not be altered; 77.
- plagiarism; 456, Apx E.
- smoked cigars; 322.
- wives; 58.
Smith, Joseph F. (Fielding) Sr:
- arrested and fined for cohabitation; 14.
- published official declaration (1904); 14.
- vision – Section 138; 193.

Smith, Joseph. Snr:
- his dream the origin of Lehi's dream; 38.
- move to Manchester; 95, 96.
Smith, Lucy, born in Palmyra; 96.
Smith, Lucy Mack:
- had no idea about a First Vision; 105.
smoking; 50.
Son of God is the Father; 100, 180.
soul is the spirit; 144.
Sperry, Sidney B; 99.
Spirit children of God before this life; 142-143.
spirit is the soul; 190.
Spirit of Christ; 39.
Spirit of God; 64.
Spirit Prison; 187-188, 192.
- spirits in prison; 193.
- two states in, Paradise and Hell; 187.
Spirit World; 185-191, 192.
- previously the Spirit Prison; 187-188.
Spirit World has two states:
- happiness and unhappiness; 186-188.
- Paradise and Spirit Prison; 186-188.
spiritual death; 151, 227.
Sticks of Joseph and Judah; 425-428.
suicide; 267.
swearing; 50.
Tanakh; 40, 64, 68, 306, 308-311.
Tanner, (Jerald &) Sandra; 13, 97, 127.
tattoos; 50.
Taylor, John; 58, 268.
- drank whisky; 323.
tea; 50.
Teacher (office); 360.
teaching and learning; 377-384.
Telestial kingdom; 173, 174, 212, 213, 264.
telestial – no such word; 173.
temple ceremony, evolution; 79-80.
temple marriage:
- annulment and remarriage; 380-381.
- or nothing; 369.
temples and family history; 374-375.
Ten Commandments; 306.
terrestrial – meaning; 173.
Terrestrial kingdom; 173, 174, 213, 264.
Thatcher, Margaret; 30.
Third principle of Gospel – Baptism; 246-251.
three degrees of glory; 173, 213.
Tiffany's – Martin Harris interview; 106.
tithing; 50, 238, 275, 332-346.
- 10% of assets for early Mormons: 345.
- paid local leaders' salaries; 337.

Times and Seasons. 1839-46; 13, 105.
tongues, gift of; 394-395, 397-399.
Tower of Babel; 454.
Treasured Testament, A. Nelson; 52, 99.
Tree of Life; 35-39.
True to the Faith (book); 57.
turkeys, domesticated; 312.
Turner, J. B; 105.
universal apostasy; 81.
Urim & Thummim; 52.
Utah divorce statistics; 47.
vineyards containing olives error; 362-366.
Voice of Warning, A, Parley P. Pratt; 104.
Walters, Wesley P; 96.
washing and anointing:
- ceremony in temples; 79-80.
- only symbolic these days; 81.
washing, or shaking dust from feet; 367.
Wentworth Letter; 13.
wheat for man; 328-329.
witness of the spirit; 412.
Women:
- and the Priesthood; 45, 161-162.
- have no authority or say at all; 354.
- ministers; 30.
- to raise children, not work; 370.
Woodruff, Wilford; 13.
- drank brandy and coffee; 325.
Word of Wisdom; 238, 320-331.
Young, Brigham;
- married Zina D. Huntington; 16.
- penalty for interracial marriage; 34.
Young, Joseph; 13.
Young's Literal (Bible) Translation; 183.
Zeezrom; 99-100.
Zenock; 205-207.
Zenos; 205-207.